T0190361

Communications
in Computer and Information Science   1676

More information about this series at https://link.springer.com/bookseries/7899

Teresa Guarda · Filipe Portela ·
Maria Fernanda Augusto (Eds.)

Advanced Research in Technologies, Information, Innovation and Sustainability

Second International Conference, ARTIIS 2022
Santiago de Compostela, Spain, September 12–15, 2022
Revised Selected Papers, Part II

Editors
Teresa Guarda ⓘ
Universidad Estatal Península de Santa
La Libertad, Ecuador

Filipe Portela ⓘ
University of Minho
Guimarães, Portugal

Maria Fernanda Augusto ⓘ
BITrum Research Group
Leon, Spain

ISSN 1865-0929   ISSN 1865-0937 (electronic)
Communications in Computer and Information Science
ISBN 978-3-031-20315-2   ISBN 978-3-031-20316-9 (eBook)
https://doi.org/10.1007/978-3-031-20316-9

This Springer imprint is published by the registered company Springer Nature Switzerland AG
The registered company address is: Gewerbestrasse 11, 6330 Cham, Switzerland

Preface

The need for a greener and more digital world leads academia, governments, industry, and citizens to look for emerging, sustainable, intelligent solutions and trends.

These new solutions and ideas must promote communication and ubiquitous computing between society agents, i.e., citizens, industry, organizations, networked machines and physical objects, and provide a promising vision of the future, integrating the real world of knowledge agents and things with the virtual world of information. The emerging approaches under study or development can address several dimensions with a technological focus like information, innovation, and sustainability and topics such as computing solutions, data intelligence, ethics, security, privacy, and sustainability.

The change observed in society modifies the landscape of human activity, particularly regarding knowledge acquisition and production, offering new possibilities and challenges that need to be explored, assessed, and disseminated.

To expose and disseminate such information, ARTIIS arose. ARTIIS is an international forum for researchers and practitioners to present and discuss the most recent innovations, trends, results, experiences, and concerns from the varying perspectives of technology, information, innovation, and sustainability. This book is split into two volumes and contains a selection of papers accepted for presentation and discussion at the second International Conference on Advanced Research in Technologies, Information, Innovation and Sustainability (ARTIIS 2022) and its workshops. ARTIIS 2022 received 191 contributions from authors in 37 countries worldwide. The acceptance rate was 37.69%, with the program comprising 72 regular papers.

The first volume of the book contains all the papers on the topics of Computing Solutions and Data Intelligence:

- Computing Solutions addresses the development of applications and platforms involving computing and related to some area of knowledge or society. It includes papers on networks, pervasive computing, gamification, and software engineering.
- Data Intelligence focuses on data (e.g., text, images) acquisition and processing using smart techniques or tools. It includes papers on computing intelligence, artificial intelligence, data science, and computer vision.

The second volume collates all papers relating to Sustainability or Ethics, Security, and Privacy:

- Ethics, Security, and Privacy focuses on a more strict and secure area of information systems where the end-user is the main concern. Vulnerabilities, data privacy, and cybersecurity are the main subjects of this topic.
- Sustainability explores a new type of computing which is more, green, connected, efficient, and sustainable. Subjects like immersive technology, smart cities, and sustainable infrastructure are part of this topic.

ARTIIS 2022 had the support of the CIST Research and Innovation Center of the Universidad Estatal Peninsula de Santa Elena, Ecuador, and the Algoritmi Research Center of Minho University, Portugal. It was realized in a hybrid format, taking place both face-to-face and virtually at Xunta Cultura y Educación Secretaría Xeral de Política Lingüística, Santiago de Compostela, Spain, during September 12–15, 2022.

The Program Committee was composed of a multidisciplinary group of more than 175 experts from 29 countries, with the responsibility for evaluating, in a double-blind review process, the papers received for each of the main themes proposed for the conference and special sessions. Each paper was reviewed by at least 3 Program Committee members and final acceptance decisions were made by the Program Committee chairs.

The papers accepted to ARTIIS 2022 are published in this volume in Springer's Communications in Computer and Information Science (CCIS) series. It is indexed in DBLP, Google Scholar, EI-Compendex, SCImago, and Scopus. CCIS volumes are also submitted for inclusion in ISI Proceedings.

Besides the main conference, ARTIIS 2022 hosted 12 special sessions:

– ACMaSDA 2022 - Applications of Computational Mathematics to Simulation and Data Analysis
– CICITE 2022 - Challenges and the Impact of Communication and Information Technologies on Education
– CICT 2022 - Cybersecurity in Information and Communication Technologies
– ET-AI 2022 - Emergent Technologies and Artificial Intelligence
– GAT 2022 - 2nd Workshop on Gamification Application and Technologies
– IHEDIE 2022 - Inclusive Higher Education and Disruptive Innovation in Education International Workshop
– ISHMC 2022 - Intelligent Systems for Health and Medical Care
– IWEBTM 2022 - International Workshop on Economics, Business and Technology Management
– IWET 2022 - International Workshop on Electronic and Telecommunications
– RTNT 2022 - Emerging Technologies to Revitalize Tourism
– SMARTTIS 2022 - Smart Tourism and Information Systems
– TechDiComM 2022 - Technological Strategies on Digital Communication and Marketing

We acknowledge those who contributed to this book: authors, organizing chairs, steering committee members, Program Committee members, and special sessions chairs. We sincerely appreciate their involvement and support that were crucial for the success of the ARTIIS 2022.

The success of this second edition gives us a lot of confidence to continue the work. So, we hope to see you at the third edition in 2023.

September 2022   Teresa Guarda
                                                       Filipe Portela
                                              Maria Fernanda Augusto

Organization

Honorary Chair

Brij Bhooshan Gupta   NIT Kurukshetra, India

General Chairs

Teresa Guarda   Universidad Estatal Peninsula de Santa Elena,
                               Ecuador
Filipe Portela   University of Minho, Portugal

Program Committee Chairs

Teresa Guarda   Universidad Estatal Peninsula de Santa Elena,
                               Ecuador
Filipe Portela   University of Minho, Portugal
Maria Fernanda Augusto   BITrum Research Group, Leon, Spain

Organizing Chairs

Maria Fernanda Augusto   BITrum Research Group, Spain
José Manuel Neira   Federación de Asociaciones para la Movilidad
                               Europea, Spain
Jorge Oliveira e Sá   Universidade do Minho, Portugal
José Maria Diaz   Universidad a Distancia de Madrid, Spain

Steering Committee

Andrei Tchernykh   CICESE Research Center, Mexico
Beatriz De La Iglesia   University of East Anglia, UK
Bruno Sousa   University of Coimbra, Portugal
Enrique Carrera   Universidad de las Fuerzas Armadas ESPE,
                               Ecuador
Ricardo Vardasca   ISLA Santarem, Portugal
Wolfgang Hofkirchner   Technische Universität Wien, Austria

Workshops Chairs

Abrar Ullah	Heriot-Watt University Dubai, UAE
Teresa Guarda	Universidad Estatal Peninsula de Santa Elena, Ecuador

Special Sessions Chairs

Alanis, Arnulfo	Tijuana Institute of Technology, Mexico
Almeida, Sofia	European University of Lisbon, Portugal
Augusto, Maria Fernanda	Universidad Estatal Peninsula de Santa Elena, Ecuador
Balsa, Carlos	Polytechnic Institute of Bragança, Portugal
Baltazar Flores, Rosario	Technological Institute of León, Mexico
Calderón Pineda, Fausto	Universidad Estatal Península de Santa Elena, Ecuador
Chuquimarca, Luis	Universidad Estatal Península de Santa Elena, Ecuador
Gama, Sílvio	University of Porto, Portugal
Garzozi-Pincay, René Faruk	Universidad Estatal Península de Santa Elena, Ecuador
Guarda, Teresa	Universidad Estatal Península de Santa Elena, Ecuador
Guivarch, Ronan	University of Toulouse, France
Lopes, Isabel	Polytechnic Institute of Bragança, Portugal
Mota Pinto, Filipe	Polytechnic Institute of Leiria, Portugal
Ninahualpa, Geovanni	Armed Forces University, Ecuador
Pinto, Mario	Polytechnic Institute of Porto, Portugal
Pombo, Nuno	University of Beira Interior, Portugal
Portela, Filipe	University of Minho, Portugal
Queirós, Ricardo	Polytechnic Institute of Porto, Portugal
Ribeiro, Isabel	Polytechnic Institute of Bragança, Portugal
Rivero Pino, Ramon	Universidad Estatal Península de Santa Elena, Ecuador
Silva, Bruno	University of Beira Interior, Portugal
Sousa, Bruno	University of Coimbra, Portugal

ARTIIS Program Committee

Abreu, Maria José	University of Minho, Portugal
Alanis, Arnulfo	Tijuana Institute of Technology, Mexico
Aljuboori, Abbas	Al Zahra College for Women, Oman
Almeida, Sofia	European University of Lisbon, Portugal

Álvarez Rodríguez, Francisco	Autonomous University of Aguascalientes, Mexico
Andrade, António	Universidade Católica Portuguesa, Portugal
Araújo, Silvia	University of Minho, Portugal
Augusto, Maria Fernanda	Universidad Estatal Peninsula de Santa Elena, Ecuador
Azevedo, Ana	Polytechnic Institute of Porto, Portugal
Bacca Acosta, Jorge Luis	University of Girona, Spain
Baczynski, Michal	University of Silesia in Katowice, Poland
Balsa, Carlos	Polytechnic Institute of Bragança, Portugal
Baras, Karolina	University of Madeira, Portugal
Biloborodova, Tetiana	Volodymyr Dahl East Ukrainian National University, Ukraine
Braghin, Chiara	University of Milan, Italy
Bravo-Agapito, Javier	Complutense University of Madrid, Spain
Cano-Olivos, Patricia	Universidad Popular Autónoma del Estado de Puebla, Mexico
Carrera, Enrique V.	Armed Forces University, Ecuador
Casillas Martín, Sonia	University of Salamanca, Spain
Castro Silva, Daniel	University of Porto, Portugal
Ciumasu, Ioan	University of Versailles Saint-Quentin-en-Yvelines, France
Costa, Ângelo	University of Minho, Portugal
Dourado, Antonio	University of Coimbra, Portugal
Dutta, Kamlesh	National Institute of Technology Hamirpur, India
Falkman, Göran	University of Skövde, Sweden
Fatahi Valilai, Omid	Jacobs University Bremen, Germany
Fernandes, António	Polytechnic Institute of Bragança, Portugal
Gago, Pedro	Polytechnic Institute of Leiria, Portugal
Garcia Clemente, Felix	University of Murcia, Spain
Gatica, Gustavo	Andrés Bello National University, Chile
Gohar, Neelam	Shaheed Benazir Bhutto Women University, Pakistan
Gomes de Oliveira, Gabriel	State University of Campinas, Brazil
Gomes, Luis	University of the Azores, Portugal
Gomes, Raphael	Federal University of Goiás, Brazil
González Briones, Alfonso	University of Salamanca, Spain
Guarda, Teresa	Universidad Estatal Península de Santa Elena, Ecuador
Guerra, Helia	University of the Azores, Portugal
Gupta, Nishu	Chandigarh University, India
Härer, Felix	University of Fribourg, Switzerland
Hornink, Gabriel	Federal University of Alfenas, Brazil

Hossian, Alejandro	National Technological University, Argentina
Ilarri, Sergio	University of Zaragoza, Spain
Kirsch-Pinheiro, Manuele	Pantheon-Sorbonne University, France
Latorre-Biel, Juan-Ignacio	Public University of Navarre, Spain
Laurent, Anne	University of Montpellier, France
León, Marcelo	Guayaquil Business Technological University, Ecuador
Lopes, Frederico	Federal University of Rio Grande do Norte , Brazil
Lopes, Isabel	Polytechnic Institute of Bragança, Portugal
Lopez, Josue	CETYS University, Mexico
Lopezosa, Carlos	University of Barcelona, Spain
Lucena Jr., Vicente	Federal University of Amazonas, Brazil
Machado, José	University of Minho, Portugal
Marques, Bertil P.	Polytechnic Institute of Porto, Portugal
Maskeliunas, Rytis	Kaunas University of Technology, Lithuania
Matos, Luis	University of Minho, Portugal
Mazon, Luis	Universidad Estatal Península de Santa Elena, Ecuador
Méndez Reboredo, José Ramón	University of Vigo, Spain
Messina, Fabrizio	University of Catania, Italy
Mishra, Pankaj	Pantnagar University, India
Mota Pinto, Filipe	Polytechnic Institute of Leiria, Portugal
Mura, Ivan	Duke Kunshan University, China
Oliveira e Sá, Jorge	University of Minho, Portugal
Oliveira, Pedro	Polytechnic Institute of Bragança, Portugal
Panagiotakis, Spyros	Hellenic Mediterranean University, Greece
Peixoto, Hugo	University of Minho, Portugal
Pinto, Mario	Polytechnic Institute of Porto, Portugal
Pombo, Nuno	University of Beira Interior, Portugal
Portela, Filipe	University of Minho, Portugal
Queirós, Ricardo	Polytechnic Institute of Porto, Portugal
Quintela, Helder	Polytechnic Institute of Cávado and Ave, Portugal
Ribeiro, Isabel	Polytechnic Institute of Bragança, Portugal
Rodriguez, Alejandro	Polytechnic University of Madrid, Spain
Rufino, José	Polytechnic Institute of Braganca, Portugal
Rusu, Eugen	"Dunarea de Jos" University of Galati, Romania
Scherer, Rafal	Częstochowa University of Technology, Poland
Schütz, Christoph	Johannes Kepler University Linz, Austria
Semaan, Felipe	Fluminense Federal University, Brazil
Simões, Alberto	Polytechnic Institute of Cávado and Ave, Portugal
Sousa, Bruno	University of Coimbra, Portugal

Stalidis, George	Alexander Technological Educational Institute of Thessaloniki, Greece
Stavrakis, Modestos	University of the Aegean, Greece
Swacha, Jakub	University of Szczecin, Poland
Tchernykh, Andrei	Ensenada Center for Scientific Research and Higher Education, Mexico
Utz, Wilfrid	OMiLAB, Germany
Van Der Haar, Dustin	University of Johannesburg, South Africa
Vardasca, Ricardo	ISLA Santarem, Portugal
Vicente, Henrique	University of Évora, Portugal
Villao, Datzania	Universidad Estatal Península de Santa Elena, Ecuador
Vito, Domenico	Polytechnic University of Milan, Italy
Winter, Johannes	National Academy of Science and Engineering, Germany
Younas, Muhammad	Oxford Brookes University, UK

Special Sessions Program Committee

Aguiar, Jose	Polytechnic Institute of Bragança, Portugal
Aguirre, Luis Eduardo	Ecuadorian Air Force, Ecuador
Alanis, Arnulfo	Tijuana Institute of Technology, Mexico
Almeida, Sofia	European University of Lisbon, Portugal
Alves, Carlos	Federal Center for Technological Education of Rio Janeiro, Brazil
Andrade, Roberto	National Polytechnic School, Ecuador
Balsa, Carlos	Polytechnic Institute of Bragança, Portugal
Baltazar Flores, Rosario	Leon Institute of Technology, Mexico
Barriga Andrade, Jhonattan Javier	National Polytechnic School, Ecuador
Borovac Zekan, Senka	University of Split, Croatia
Branco, Frederico	University of Trás-os-Montes and Alto Douro, Portugal
Calderón Pineda, Fausto	Universidad Estatal Península de Santa Elena, Ecuador
Campos, Ana Cláudia	University of Algarve, Portugal
Castellanos, Omar	Universidad Estatal Península de Santa Elena, Ecuador
Chertovskih, Roman	University of Porto, Portugal
Chuquimarca, Luis	Universidad Estatal Península de Santa Elena, Ecuador
Cobos Alvarado, Edgar Fabián	Universidad Estatal Península de Santa Elena, Ecuador
Contreras, Sergio Octavio	Universidad De La Salle Bajío, Mexico

Correia, Ricardo	Polytechnic Institute of Bragança, Portugal
Cunha, Carlos R.	Polytechnic Institute of Bragança, Portugal
Diaz, Estrella	University of Castilla-La Mancha, Spain
Diaz, Paul	Armed Forces University, Ecuador
Fajardo, Marcelo	Escuela Superior Politecnica del Litoral, Ecuador
Felizardo, Virginie	University of Beira Interior, Portugal
Fernandes, António	Polytechnic Institute of Bragança, Portugal
Fernandes, Paula Odete	Polytechnic Institute of Bragança, Portugal
Fonseca, Xavier	Polytechnic Institute of Porto, Portugal
Gama, Sílvio	University of Porto, Portugal
Garzozi Pincay, Yamel Sofia	Universidad Tecnológica Equinoccial, Ecuador
Garzozi-Pincay, René Faruk	Universidad Estatal Península de Santa Elena, Ecuador
Gaxiola Vega, Luis	Autonomous University of Baja California, Mexico
González, Nelia	Universidad de Especialidades Espíritu Santo, Ecuador
González, Nelia Josefina	Milagro State University, Ecuador
Grinberga-Zalite, Gunta	Latvia University of Life Sciences and Technologies, Latvia
Groma, Linda	Latvia University of Life Sciences and Technologies, Latvia
Guarda, Teresa	Universidad Estatal Península de Santa Elena, Ecuador
Guivarch, Ronan	University of Toulouse, France
Hernandez Leal, Fabiola	Tijuana Institute of Technology, Mexico
Hernández, Patricia	Technical University of Cotopaxi, Ecuador
Jurado Reyes, Pedro Omar	Universidad Católica de Santiago de Guayaquil, Ecuador
Lopes, Isabel	Polytechnic Institute of Bragança, Portugal
Magdaleno Palencia, Jose Sergio	Tijuana Institute of Technology, Mexico
Magnere, Milton	Alas3 Ingeniería Limitada, Chile
Maridueña Arroyave, Milton	University of Guayaquil, Ecuador
Marques, Bertil P.	Polytechnic Institute of Porto, Portugal
Márquez, Bogart Yail	Tijuana Institute of Technology, Mexico
Martinez, Rosa Maria	University of Almería, Spain
Mazon, Luis	Universidad Estatal Península de Santa Elena, Ecuador
Mesquita, Susana	Aveiro University, Portugal
Messina Scolaro, María del Carmen	University of the Republic, Uruguay
Montella, Raffaele	University of Chicago, USA
Moreno Brieva, Fernando Javier	King Juan Carlos University, Spain

Moreno, David	Polytechnic School of Chimborazo, Ecuador
Muyulema-Allaica, Carina Alexandra	CAAPTES Asesorías Y Consultoria En Proyectos, Ecuador
Muyulema-Allaica, Juan Carlos	Universidad Estatal Península de Santa Elena, Ecuador
Ninahualpa, Geovanni	Armed Forces University, Ecuador
Orrala, Néstor	Universidad Estatal Península de Santa Elena, Ecuador
Palacios, Marcela	Instituto Tecnológico Superior de Purísima del Rincón, Mexico
Paparella, Francesco	New York University Abu Dhabi, UAE
Pedrosa, Isabel	University of Coimbra, Portugal
Peñafiel, Carlos	Universidad Nacional de Chimborazo, Ecuador
Piloto, Paulo	Polytechnic Institute of Braganca, Portugal
Pirela, Alonso	Universidad Estatal Península de Santa Elena, Ecuador
Pombo, Nuno	University of Beira Interior, Portugal
Pucha-Medina, Paola Martina	University of Cantabria, Ecuador
Quezada Cisnero, Maria	Tijuana Institute of Technology, Mexico
R. Souza Pereira, Leonice	University of Beira Interior, Portugal
Ramires, Ana	European University of Lisbon, Portugal
Ramirez, Margarita Ramirez	Autonomous University of Baja California, Mexico
Ramos, Celia	University of the Algarve, Portugal
Reis, Rosa	Polytechnic Institute of Porto, Portugal
Renteria, Leonardo	Universidad Autónoma de Chiapas, Ecuador
Ribeiro, Isabel	Polytechnic Institute of Bragança, Portugal
Rivera, Oscar	National Autonomous University of Mexico, Mexico
Rocha, Cristian Javier	University of Seville, Spain
Rodriguez, Rosalba	Armed Forces University, Ecuador
Romero Rodríguez, Wendoly	Instituto Tecnológico Superior de Guanajuato, Mexico
Rubio, Yoshio	Center for Research and Development of Digital Technology, Mexico
Rufino, José	Polytechnic Institute of Braganca, Portugal
Ruiz, Ulises	National Institute of Astrophysics, Optics and Electronics, Mexico
San Andrés Laz, Esthela	Technical University of Manabi, Ecuador
Sangurima, Miguel	Universidad Católica Andrés Bello, Ecuador
Seabra, Claudia	University of Coimbra, Portugal
Silva Sánchez, Marianella	Universidad Estatal Península de Santa Elena, Ecuador

Silva Sprock, Antonio	Central University of Venezuela, Venezuela
Silva, Bruno	University of Beira Interior, Portugal
Swacha, Jakub	University of Szczecin, Poland
Temperini, Marco	Sapienza University of Rome, Italy
Tomalá, José Xavier	Universidad Estatal Península de Santa Elena, Ecuador
Tutivén, Christian	Escuela Superior Politecnica del Litoral, Ecuador
Vaca-Cardenas, Leticia	Technical University of Manabi, Ecuador
Vasconcelos, Paulo	University of Porto, Portugal
Vieira, Luís	University of Porto, Portugal
Vrellis, Ioannis	University of Ioannina, Greece
Wembe, Boris	University of Toulouse, France
Yoo, Sang Guun	National Polytechnic School, Ecuador
Zacarias, Henriques	University of Beira Interior, Portugal
Zambrano, Marcelo	Universidad Técnica del Norte, Ecuador

Sponsors

Universidad Estatal Peninsula de Santa Elena, Ecuador
Universidade do Minho, Portugal
Universidad a Distancia de Madrid, Spain
Xunta de Galicia, Spain
Compostela Group of Universities

Contents – Part II

Ethics, Security, and Privacy

Contents – Part I

Data Intelligence

Sustainability

Housing with Energy Self-sufficiency and Zero Co2 Emissions

Ismael Costa[1] (iD) and Teresa Guarda[2,3,4(✉)] (iD)

[1] ISLA Santarém, Santarém, Portugal
[2] Universidad Estatal Península de Santa Elena, La Libertad, Ecuador
`tguarda@gmail.com`
[3] CIST – Centro de Investigación en Sistemas y Telecomunicaciones, Universidad Estatal Península de Santa Elena, La Libertad, Ecuador
[4] Algoritmi Centre, Minho University, Guimarães, Portugal

Abstract. One of the sectors with the greatest contribution to energy consumption and global CO2 emissions is construction. The typology of buildings and the technologies used to increase energy efficiency in use are becoming increasingly important. Global energy consumption is estimated to increase significantly. According the International Energy Agency (IEA) in 2018 the housing\residential consumption sector alone accounted 20% of global energy consumption in IEA Countries in 2018 [1].

In 2018, the Directorate-General for Energy and Geology (DGEG) reported that 27% of the need for primary energy consumption was met by Renewable Energy Sources. In 2020, the target set by a community directive is 31% for primary energy from Renewable Energy Sources [2]. It is therefore extremely important to create a strategy to boost construction with zero emissions, making an important contribution to the overall reduction of energy consumption and to the reduction of CO2 emissions. This work intends to identify the main concepts of construction with zero emission and present a case study of a multifamily housing following this concept. The case study presented demonstrated that the success of a zero-emission construction depends in large part on the elaboration of an energy budget based on consumption habits, on the energy production capacity of the house and on the energy performance that is intended to be achieved during use, as well as the effectiveness of how this budget is presented to the owners, demonstrating the cost vs benefit of the energy efficiency solutions presented. It is concluded that using the current technology combined with construction elements, it is possible to guarantee a Zero CO2 Emission in a self-sufficient housing in terms of energy. Given the current needs for energy savings and increased environmental sustainability, the future of civil engineering may be in zero-emission homes.

Keywords: House with self-sufficiency energy · Zero emission construction · ZEB · Sustainable construction

T. Guarda et al. (Eds.): ARTIIS 2022, CCIS 1676, pp. 3–14, 2022.
https://doi.org/10.1007/978-3-031-20316-9_1

1 Introduction

The construction sector is one of the sectors with the greatest contribution to energy consumption as well as to global CO_2 emissions. Between 2010 and 2030 world marketed global energy consumption is estimated to increase by 33% [3, 4]. IAE published a report suggesting that the housing consumption sector represented 14% of global energy consumption in 2017 (see Fig. 1) [5].

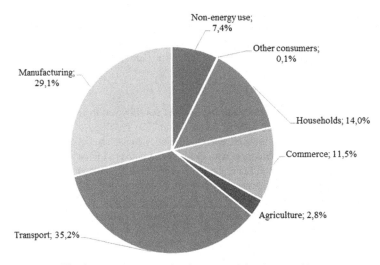

Fig. 1. Final consumption in Portugal for the year 2017

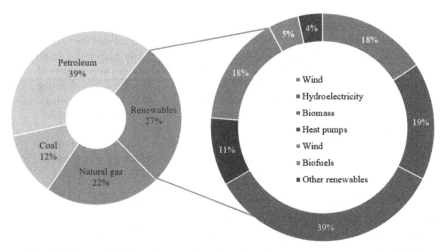

Fig. 2. The contribution of renewable energy to primary energy consumption 2018

The Directorate General of Energy and Geology (DGEG) states in the latest report issued that Renewable Energy Sources (RES) contributed 27% to primary energy consumption. Biomass represents a contribution of 43%, water 19%, wind 18%, heat pumps 11% and 5% biofuels (see Fig. 2) [6].

In relation to final energy consumption, RES accounted for 30% of the total need. Of these 41% it originates in biomass, 19% in hydroelectricity and 18% in wind power. At 13% and 5% respectively, heat pumps and biofuels are located [6] (see Fig. 3).

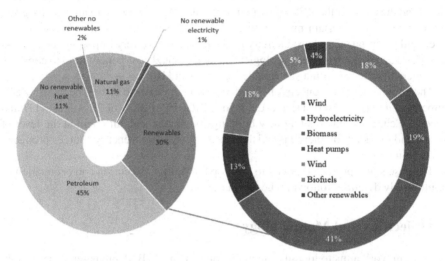

Fig. 3. The contribution of renewable energy to final energy consumption 2018

By 2020 the target of 31% of the contribution of RES to final energy consumption (Community Directive 2009/28/EC) should be reached [6] (see Fig. 4). In 2018, heat pumps used for heating were also considered AS FER.

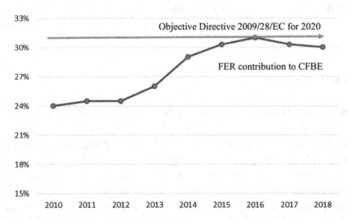

Fig. 4. Objective for the incorporation of RES in gross final energy consumption by 2020.

Zero emission building (ZEB) will be one of the most effective strategies for reducing global energy consumption and reducing CO_2 emissions. However, it is often reported that the increased costs of a ZEB construction will be a significant barrier to the implementation of this strategy [7, 8]. Total construction costs include direct costs and indirect costs. Building materials, labor, construction equipment, energy, water will be the main direct costs. Indirect costs include costs related to the construction project, commissures, licensing fees, documentation, and other legal fees [9]. The normally higher construction cost of a ZEB construction will be something of a direct perception for the owner, on the other hand the gains of the ZEB construction are of low perception and are usually given only estimative to a certain number of years, and these estimates include the energy, water, and potential energy productivity gains. It is therefore very important to carry out an analysis and demonstrate the ecological advantages and cost-benefit ratio to convince the owners to proceed with a sustainable ZEB project [10].

The definition of the concept of "buildings with almost zero energy needs" (NZEB) deliberated in Article 16 of Decree-Law No. 118/2013 of 2013 of 20 August [11] and successive changes requires that new buildings be almost self-sufficient at the level of energy, and the need for energy is satisfied through renewable energy sources produced on site or nearby.

The case study presented aimed to develop the design, execution and occupation of a multifamily dwelling following the ZEB concept.

2 Objectives and Methodology

The present work aims to identify the main concepts of ZEB, demonstrate a case study of a Zeb multifamily dwelling, and answer the question, Is a habitation with energy self-sufficiency and zero CO_2 emission possible with current technology?

The search for the literature review was done on the website of Elsevier publisher, ScienceDirect, Google Scholar and Google search engine. In the document search process, key words related to the theme of energy efficiency in construction were used, such as, "energy efficiency in construction"; " sustainable construction"; "energy efficiency"; "Zero Energy Building"; "low-energy buildings"; "Green buildings". The most relevant documents and most recent date between the periods 1950 and 2020 were considered in the selection.

3 Literature Review

Self-contained energy buildings (ZEBs) may be completely independent of an energetic external network. All the energy needed for own consumption originates from its own energy systems, usually solar energy systems and energy storage systems sized to ensure a continuous supply of energy [12]. The first attempts at zero energy constructions emerged in North America [13], reaching the concept in Europe in the late 1970s [14].

Energy Use Intensity (EUI) represents the energy use of a building depending on its size or number of users. The EUI is expressed as energy per square meter and per year (kWh/m^2 per year or $kBTU/m^2$ per year) or as per capita energy per year (see Fig. 5) [15].

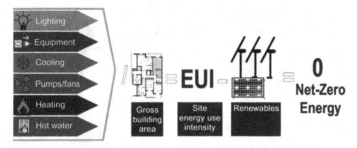

Fig. 5. Calculation of zero energy balance.

In the ZEB concept there are some fundamentals (see Fig. 6) and 4 basic principles to consider in the design phase.

Fig. 6. The fundamentals of the ZEB project.

Figure 7 shows a series of measures applicable to the 4 basic principles of this concept [15]. The project phase should include the four principles for identifying the most appropriate measures that respect these foundations or principles [15].

According to the information contained in the (DGEG) Member States have been encouraging the improvement of energy performance and comfort conditions of buildings through various initiatives in line with Directive 2002/91/EC of 16 December and its recast, Directive 2010/31/EU of 19 May, both European Parliament and of the Council, energy performance of buildings.

These Directives set out the general framework for a methodology for calculating the integrated energy performance of buildings, as well as the application of minimum requirements for the energy performance of new buildings and existing buildings that are undergoing renovation works.

Among all the legislation related to the energy efficiency of buildings available in DGEG, the most relevant for the theme of this work stands out.

Decrees-Law No 78/2006, 79/2006 and 80/2006, all of 4 April and successive amendments related to the Energy Certification of buildings, were revised considering an approach already oriented to the new European Energy Performance of Buildings Directive (EPBD). The Directive was published on 19 May 2010 by the Official Journal of the European Union as Directive 2010/31/EU and successive amendments by the European

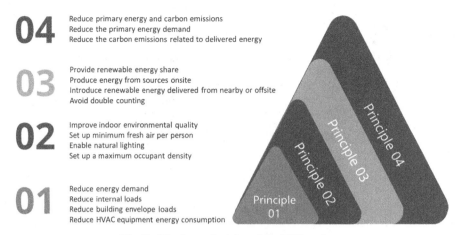

Fig. 7. The four principles of the ZEB project.

Parliament and the Council and reinforces minimum requirements for buildings in the context of energy efficiency. In Portugal, this new Directive presents aspects with great impact, such as the introduction of the concept of cost/benefit from an extended life-cycle cost perspective in buildings. The energy benefits will have to be thought of in the long run and not just considering the immediate cost of construction.

The concept of "buildings with near zero emission buildings" (NZEB) also emerges, requiring that, "by 31 December 2020 at the latest, all new buildings have very high energy performance", and that their energy needs should be covered by renewable energy sources.

Decree-Law No. 118/2013 of 20 August and successive amendments ensures the transposition into national law of Directive 2010/31/EU and successive amendments and the revision of the national legislation on the Energy Certification System (SCE) of Buildings, in force since 2006. For the citizen to be informed about the thermal quality of the buildings, when building, selling leases or leasing thereof, there is a legal obligation to implement an energy certification system.

In existing buildings with the aim of reducing energy expenditure and improving the energy efficiency of the property, the energy certificate demonstrates the possible measures to implement energy performance improvement and indoor air quality. In new buildings, energy certification proves the application of thermal regulation and indoor air quality, among other obligations, is the implementation of renewable energy systems.

The actual energy performance situation of a property is demonstrated through the SCE (EC) Certificate, which is a document issued by a qualified expert under the SCE. The property is classified according to its energy performance on a scale of 8 classes (from A+ to F), obtained by calculating the annual energy consumption scans and indoor air quality.

Directive 2010/31/EU and successive amendments by the European Parliament and the Council of 19 May 2010 relate to the energy performance of buildings. This Directive clarifies some of the principles of the text of the previous Directive 2002/91/EC of 16 December 2002 and successive amendments, introducing new guidelines strengthening measures to promote energy performance in buildings in accordance with the targets agreed by Member States for 2020.

Decree-Law No. 118/2013 of 20 August and successive amendments approves the Energy Certification System for Buildings, the Regulation on energy performance of residential buildings and the Energy Performance Regulation of Trade and Service Buildings, and transposes Directive 2010/31/EU and successive amendments, of the European Parliament and of the Council of 19 May 2010 on the energy performance of buildings. Among the various objectives of the Decree, it can be mentioned that it aims to ensure the regulatory application of energy efficiency conditions and the use of renewable energy systems, certify energy performance in buildings and identify corrective measures and/or improve energy performance.

The Regulation of Energy Performance of Housing Buildings (REH) promotes the improvement of thermal behavior, efficiency of technical systems and the minimization of the risk of occurrence of surface condensations in the elements of the surrounding.

The technical behavior and efficiency requirements of the technical systems of the buildings, as well as the methodology for determining the energy performance class of the pre-certificates and certificates of the SCE is defined by Ordinance No. 349-B/2013 of November 29 and successive amendments.

Ordinance No. 349-C/2013 of December 2 and successive amendments establishes the elements to be included in the licensing or prior reporting procedures of urban building operations and their authorization for use.

Order 15793-D/2013 of December 3 and successive amendments presents the conversion factors between useful energy and primary energy to be used in determining the annual nominal primary energy needs.

Order 15793-H/2013 of 3 December and successive amendments publish the rules for quantifying and accounting for the contribution of systems to the use of renewable energy sources. The calculation methodologies for determining the nominal needs of useful energy to produce sanitary hot water (AQS), the annual nominal requirements of useful energy for heating and cooling environment and the global nominal global primary energy needs are presented in Order 15793-I/2013 of 3 December and successive amendments.

Order 15793-J/2013 of 3 December and successive amendments publish the rules for determining the energy class.

Order 15793-K/2013 of December 3 and successive changes publish the thermal parameters for the calculation of the values of Global Heat Transfer Coefficient, Surface Thermal Transmission Coefficient, Solar Radiation Absorption Coefficient, Solar Factor of Glazed Spans, Air Renewal Rate, among others. Under the energy rationalization plan, in Order 15793-L/2013 of 3 December and successive amendments, the methodology for clearance the economic viability of the use or adoption of a certain energy efficiency measure was published.

Decree-Law No. 28/2016 of June 23 and successive amendments make the fourth amendment to Decree-Law No. 118/2013 of 20 August and successive amendments, which approved the Energy Certification System of Buildings, the Regulation of Energy

Performance of Housing Buildings and the Regulation of Energy Performance of Buildings of Commerce and Services, and transposed Directive 2010/31/EU of the European Parliament and the Council of 19 May 2010 on the energy performance of buildings.

The methodology for determining the energy performance class for the typology of pre-certificates and SCE certificates, as well as the requirements of thermal behavior and efficiency of technical systems of new buildings and subject to intervention was published in Ordinance No. 319/2016 of December 15 and successive amendments to the second amendment of Ordinance No. 349-B/2013, 29, amended by Ordinance No. 379-A/2015 of October 22.

4   Case Study

First self-contained multi-family building located in Switzerland (see Fig. 8).

Fig. 8. Self-contained multi-family construction project (ZEB) https://www.umweltarena.ch/

It was considered the first multifamily housing construction in the world 100% self-sufficient without the need for external supply of any type of energy. The Umwelt Arena Schweiz combined with its partners built the first housing with nine apartments fully supported in solar energy. This energy project was inaugurated on June 6, 2016, receiving its first residents, selected by casting process to identify the ideal profiles to test the project in real environment.

After the first winter the housing demonstrated a high energy efficiency without any electricity failure and guaranteed all the necessary thermal comfort. It was thus proved that the simulations in the development phase of the project carried out for the values of energy production and consumption corresponded to reality. Residents needed only half the energy (2,200 kWh) instead of 4,400 kWh per apartment/year, a figure considered normal for Switzerland. Only the fuel cell responsible for generating electricity and heat using hydrogen generated in the summer through solar energy was insufficient at the beginning of the cold season. However, this inefficiency can be easily addressed only with a review of the energy management system. At the end of the first winter the results showed a small difference of 10% of electricity below the estimated value, but that can be addressed by improving the efficiency of hydrogen production during the summer. Already in the summer of 2018 there was a surplus of energy produced. Hydrogen storage was at full capacity in August, the following year (2019) was even earlier, validating improvements to the energy management system.

In order not to waste the excess electricity produced and thus increase the efficiency of the system, the housing was connected to the electricity grid on 1 September 2019 thus becoming an energy producer.

In May 2016 the Dössegger family after being selected in the casting process went to live in the model dwelling. Benjamin Dössegger does not know exactly what were the characteristics that allowed the selection of his family, not least because he is not an environmental fanatic, however living in the unique model housing in the world has undoubtedly come to pay more attention to the use of energy efficiency equipment and energy consumption. Each apartment has a tablet installed on the wall (see Fig. 9), showing the percentage of compliance with the daily, and weekly and monthly energy consumption plan. At the time of the interview, energy consumption was 50 to 60% of what was planned.

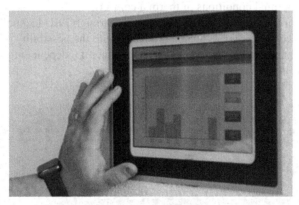

Fig. 9. Tablet with control of energy consumption (https://www.umweltarena.ch/).

In housing (see Fig. 10) all equipment and systems are of high energy efficiency. One of the examples is the elevator, whenever you make a descent is creating electricity to power the system. As there is a great ease of access to energy consumption, being always available at all times and divisions of housing, residents start to pay special attention to their consumption, almost as if they were in a family game, where there is some competition to see who makes the least consumption.

As for performance, with 25 occupants the total consumption of housing is equal to 35 kWh/m^2 per year. Of this consumption, 14% goes to heating needs, 57% for varied equipment, 14% for mechanical ventilation and 15% for lighting.

Part of the energy efficiency concept includes thermal insulation of high-yield housing. Thermal insulation is responsible for reducing the energy requirement for thermal comfort by 50%. This thermal comfort was guaranteed through low temperature heating of the optimized distribution system by the housing, being this system powered by the energy generated by the Water Heat Pump with Geothermal probe. To reduce heat pump energy consumption, a exchanger system was also used to generate heat from the outside air and injecting it controlled into the ventilation circuit. There are two types of storage, the medium and short-term, 13 days of storage per battery, and the long-term one with 25 days of storage by gaseous medium in the form of hydrogen cells.

On the façade there are non-reflective photovoltaic energy modules, and these elements are integral in the aesthetics of the housing. The entire roof is covered with photovoltaic modules. Solar energy is converted into an electric current by solar cells and stored in batteries for short- or medium-term use. For long-term storage, up to 25 days, the electric current generated by solar modules undergoes a process of conversion into hydrogen thus leaving energy stored in the gaseous state. When necessary, usually in the winter months with less sun exposure, stored hydrogen is converted back into electrical and thermal energy. During hydrogen production there is a use of the heat generated by this process, which is used for heating domestic water.

Two water tanks with 250,000 L store hot water for use all year round. The management system adapts the storage temperature and the circulation flow through the housing according to the optimal conditions of thermal comfort.

The lighting of the housing is done exclusively through LED technology.

System management controls all smart devices with the possibility of connecting to PC, smartphone, or tablet. The lighting is turned on and off independently by the system, which also controls heating systems and blinds.

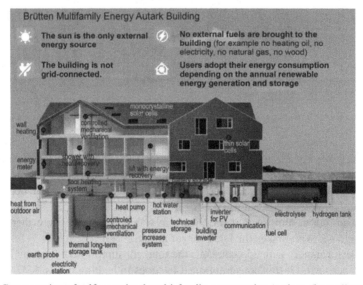

Fig. 10. Cross-section of self-contained multi-family construction project. (https://www.umwelt arena.ch/)

5 Conclusions

The housing model design presented in the case study is considered a state-of-the-art ZEB construction. In this model project, it is possible to confirm the importance of permanent access of residents to information on system consumption, electricity, and water, to ensure their commitment to achieve or even exceed the objective of energy performance.

For the success of a ZEB construction, it is of great importance to draw up an energy budget based on consumption habits, the energy production capacity of the housing and the energy performance that is intended to be achieved. This budget will make residents rethink their style of energy consumption, thus ensuring a 100% clean power supply without interruptions or the need to obtain power by external supply network.

On the other hand, there was a greater concern of residents to acquire equipment of high energy efficiency, as well as all lighting by LED system. These residents became more aware of their environmental footprint and changed some attitudes towards developing a sustainable lifestyle for all.

To make ZEB construction sustainable and attractive to new owners, an assertive cost vs. benefit approach of this type of construction is needed, just in the initial phase of the construction project development process.

Today's architecture and technology make it possible to build ZEB by applying a variety of energy-efficient solutions, such as orientation of housing and openings for maximum use of sunlight and natural ventilation, thermal insulation of walls, automated blinds for the use of natural lighting and thermal optimization, generation of electricity by photovoltaic cells (solar energy) placed on facades and roofs, storage by hydrogen cells, etc.

A ZEB construction brings benefits such as reducing electricity consumption, possibility of selling surplus energy to the grid, contributing to the sustainability of the environment, housing with sustainable use, possibility of amortization of the initial extra cost in a few years.

With the model design shown in Sect. 4 of this work, it was possible to confirm that it is effectively possible to build a self-sufficient housing in energy terms, also ensuring zero CO_2 emission only using current technology. Due to the characteristics of energy saving and sustainability, ZEB housing could be the future of civil engineering.

Using the ZEB concept of model housing presented in the case study of this work, new investigations may be considered using another type of buildings, other geographical areas with different environmental characteristics and other residents with different behaviors and concerns about the environment.

References

1. Abdelaziz, E., Saidur, R., Mekhilef, S.: A review on energy saving strategies in industrial sector. Renew. Sustain. Energy Rev. **15**(1), 150–168 (2011). https://doi.org/10.1016/j.rser.2010.09.003
2. Attia, S.: Towards regenerative and positive impact architecture: a comparison of two net zero energy buildings. Sustain. Cities Soc. **26**, 393–406 (2016). https://doi.org/10.1016/j.scs.2016.04.017

3. Attia, S.: Evolution of definitions and approaches. In: Net Zero Energy Buildings (NZEB), pp. 21–51. Elsevier (2018). https://doi.org/10.1016/b978-0-12-812461-1.00002-2

4. Cornago, E.: The Potential of Behavioural Interventions for Optimising Energy Use at Home. IEA, Paris (2021). https://www.iea.org/articles/the-potential-of-behavioural-intervent ions-for-optimising-energy-use-at-home

5. Decree-Law No. 118/2013 of 20th August. 2013. Diário da República, 1.a série, No. 159. Ministry of Economy and Employment Portugal (n.d.)

6. DGED: DGEG - General Directorate of energy and geology (2020). http://www.dgeg.gov.pt/

7. IEA.: Portugal 2021: Energy Policy Review. IEA (2021). https://doi.org/10.1787/3b485e 25-en

8. IEA: Portugal 2021: Energy Policy Review. IEA, Paris (2021). https://www.iea.org/reports/ portugal-2021

9. Khoshbakht, M., Gou, Z., Dupre, K.: Cost-benefit prediction of green buildings: SWOT analysis of research methods and recent applications. Procedia Eng. **180**, 167–178 (2017)

10. Kim, J.L., Greene, M., Kim, S.: Cost comparative analysis of a new green building code for residential project development. J. Constr. Eng. Manag. **140**(5) (2014). https://doi.org/10. 1061/(ASCE)CO.1943-7862.0000833

11. Pless, S., Torcellini, P.: Controlling capital costs in high performance office buildings: a review of best practices for overcoming cost barriers. ACEEE Summer Study on Energy. NRL, California (2012)

12. Steinmüller, B., Bruno, R.: The energy requirements of buildings. Energy Build. **2**(3), 225–235 (1979). https://doi.org/10.1016/0378-7788(79)90008-2

13. Torcellini, P., Pless, S., Leach, M.: A pathway for net-zero energy buildings: creating a case for zero cost increase. Build. Res. Inf. **43**(1), 25–33 (2015). https://doi.org/10.1080/09613218. 2014.960783

14. Voss, K., Goetzberger, A., Bopp, G., Häberle, A., Heinzel, A., Lehmberg, H.: The self-sufficient solar house in Freiburg—results of 3 years of operation. Sol. Energy **58**(1–3), 17–23 (1996). https://doi.org/10.1016/0038-092X(96)00046-1

15. Yudelson, J.: The Green Building Revolution. Island Press (2010)

HiMLEdge – Energy-Aware Optimization for Hierarchical Machine Learning

Julio Wissing[1](✉)(iD), Stephan Scheele[1](iD), Aliya Mohammed[1](iD), Dorothea Kolossa[2](iD), and Ute Schmid[1,3](iD)

[1] Fraunhofer IIS, Fraunhofer Institute for Integrated Circuits IIS, Erlangen, Germany
`{julio.wissing,stephan.scheele}@iis.fraunhofer.de`
[2] TU-Berlin, Berlin, Germany
`dorothea.kolossa@tu-berlin.de`
[3] University of Bamberg, Bamberg, Germany
`ute.schmid@uni-bamberg.de`

Abstract. Smart sensor systems are a key factor to ensure sustainable compute by enabling machine learning algorithms to be executed at the data source. This is particularly helpful when working with moving parts or in remote areas, where no tethered deployment is possible. However, including computations directly at the measurement device places an increased load on the power budget. Therefore, we introduce the Hierarchical Machine Learning framework "HiMLEdge" which enables highly specialized models that are tuned using an energy-aware multi-criteria optimization. We evaluate our framework with prognostic health management in a three-part feasibility study: First, we apply an exhaustive search to find hierarchical taxonomies, which we benchmark against hand-tuned flat classifiers. This test shows a decrease in power consumption of up to 47.63% for the hierarchical approach. Second, the search strategy is improved with Reinforcement Learning. As a novel contribution, we include real measurements in the reward function, instead of using a surrogate metric. This inclusion leads to a different optimal policy in comparison to the literature, which shows the error that may be introduced by an approximation. Third, we conduct tests on the system level, including communication and system-off power draw. In this scenario, the optimized hierarchical model can perform four times as many readings per hour as a flat classifier while achieving the same five years of battery life with similar accuracy. In turn, this also means that the battery life can be increased by the same amount if the readings per hour are kept constant.

Keywords: Edge AI · Energy efficiency · Hierarchical machine learning

1 Introduction

The advancement of artificial intelligence (AI) might be one of the biggest impact factors when it comes to achieving the United Nations' Sustainable Development

T. Guarda et al. (Eds.): ARTIIS 2022, CCIS 1676, pp. 15–29, 2022.
https://doi.org/10.1007/978-3-031-20316-9_2

Goals (SDGs) [17]. Monitoring and managing natural disasters or explainable AI for health care [5], there are many possible applications for machine learning (ML) or AI to accelerate progress on the SDGs.

Previously, the dominant data processing method followed a centralized architecture, in which sensor data is transferred to cloud resources and processed remotely. However, this approach has the downside of a high energy consumption overhead due to the excessive communication of unfiltered sensor data. Particularly, considering that many applications include an event or anomaly detection, there is a waste of energy due to avoidable data transmissions. In recent years, the widespread adoption of machine learning in edge computing under the term "tinyML" enabled intelligent applications on resource-constrained IoT devices. Thereby, the on-device execution of machine learning models is becoming a considerable alternative to the centralized approach of data processing [12]. Nonetheless, a key requirement of such wireless systems is energy efficiency, a mandatory factor to ensure long-lasting battery life of months or even years for tiny embedded sensor systems. Achieving this goal is a challenge demanding highly efficient ML-Models, which are optimized with respect to energy consumption and accuracy. In current studies, hierarchical machine learning (HIML) has been explored as method to save energy. In its simplest form, it is already present in everyday devices like, e.g., keyword spotting based natural language processing pipeline. However, scaling this idea to multiple hierarchy levels and applying it to arbitrary problems is challenging.

Hence, we introduce our framework HiMLEdge that makes use of *automatically optimized* HiML models, which represent the decision task as a classification hierarchy. This allows for lazily triggered computations that only consume the energy needed. We see this technology as an enabling factor for many applications that are currently not practically solvable. Especially in remote areas with no connection to direct power (e.g., undeveloped areas, rain forests, or the sea), on device computing can be very beneficial [13]. Increasing the battery life or duty cycle of such system is therefore the ultimate goal and enables more TinyML devices to achieve progress on the SDGs.

1.1   Synopsis

This paper discusses the impact of HiML for energy efficient inference with the help of the newly introduced framework HiMLEdge. To do so, Sect. 2 introduces the works related to the topic. Next, Sect. 3 describes the structure, background, and general functionalities of HiMLEdge, which we test in a feasibility study in Sect. 4. We structure the study in four steps. First, we describe the measurement setup. Second, we conduct an initial experiment on optimization with an exhaustive search strategy, which we improve with reinforcement learning as a third step. Fourth, we take a system-wide view of energy consumption with HiML, including communication and leakage power. Finally, we conclude our findings and discuss possible future directions in Sect. 5.

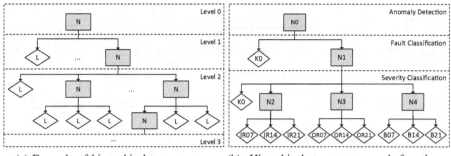

(a) Example of hierarchical taxonomy

(b) Hierachical taxonomy used for the CWRU dataset

Fig. 1. Description of hierarchical taxonomies in a general example and applied to the CWRU dataset. For the applied case the labels no fault (K0), Inner Race fault (IR07-IR21), Outer Race fault (OR07-OR21) and Ball fault (B07-B21) are shown as leafs.

2 Related Works

Hierarchical classification has already been applied in several application scenarios [11,18], often with the motivation to improve the quality of the classification results rather than to reduce energy consumption. However, previous work has shown that hierarchical classification can also be used as a partitioning method to increase the energy efficiency of a ML-model by using cascaded processing [7], modularizing its classification taxonomy [2] or by distributing its subcomponents and workload across multiple edge devices [15].

While the algorithm selection problem (ASP) for a non-hierarchical (flat) classifier is already a research field on its own [4], it becomes a more complex task when switching to a multi-model approach. The authors in [1] solve the ASP for hierarchical taxonomies with reinforcement learning by interpreting the selection of each classifier in the hierarchy as actions. The agent then collects a reward based on accuracy *and* theoretical computational complexity. Building up on this idea, we include energy measurements during the search to verify Adams et al. surrogate energy metric.

In contrast to previous works we also include the feature extraction in the search space to only compute necessary features at every step in the hierarchy. HiMLEdge allows us to streamline the process of training, optimizing and deploying HIML models towards embedded devices.

3 The HiMLEdge Framework

The HiMLEdge framework makes use of hierarchical machine learning to find an energy efficient pipeline. Based on a class hierarchy, the classification task is partitioned into a class taxonomy of decisions. The class taxonomy can be represented as a directed acyclic graph (DAG) or similarly a poset $(N, \prec)$, where

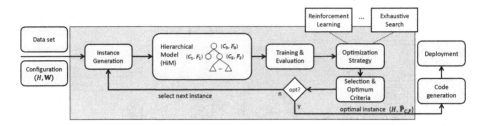

Fig. 2. Visualization of the HiMLEdge-Framework.

N is a finite set of nodes and a partial order $\prec$ over N that is asymmetric, anti-reflexive and transitive. This structure can be simplified to a tree known from a classical hierarchy scheme, e.g., as shown in Fig. 1a, where levels or even single nodes can be represented by a unique classifier instance consisting of a feature extraction and a model solving stage. We will denote such hierarchical classifiers by *Hierarchical Model* (HiM) in the following.

Contrarily, a flat classification approach is represented by a single complex multilabel classifier, responsible for classifying all labels. The authors in [14] introduce an abstract description of such hierarchical structures, describing multiple approaches of which we use the *local classifier per parent node* variant to build a HiM for energy-efficient execution. In this approach, each parent node inside the HiM is modularised and can be represented by a different classifier instance to achieve the highest degree of flexibility. The modularity of hierarchical models has the advantages that (i) similarly to a divide-and-conquer algorithm, a complex multilabel classification problem is partitioned into simpler sub-problems that can be solved more efficiently; (ii) for each node we can select the best suitable and problem-specific classification algorithm; (iii) the node-wise modularization makes it possible to optimize individual parts of a hierarchical model, to adapt them more efficiently to changes and to scale the model to a distributed system architecture. This enables the combination of a broad variety of target platforms starting from specialized custom circuits such as neuromorphic hardware, embedded microcontrollers, or multi device networks. The HiMLEdge framework[1] as shown in Fig. 2 is able to handle the complete process of generating, training, selecting and transpiling to C-code of a HiM for an embedded platform. In the optimization process, the framework generates a HiM in a JSON-like representation out of a possible permutation of given feature and classifier sets for a specific class taxonomy. Any HiM formulated in this representation can then be read in, trained and evaluated by the framework, building the basis for the optimization process. Training and testing of a HiM is made possible with a DAG based recursive algorithm, following the taxonomy from top to bottom. Each node is modeled to have access to its own classifier as well as feature extraction and holds references to its following node(s). In that way, each node can call the train/predict function of the next node(s)

---

or terminate the recursion if a leaf node has been reached. For the ASP the user can choose an optimization strategy, which is able to include direct feed-back of the energy consumption with real measurements of the HiM model in question, or use an approximation for the energy consumption to find an HiM without measurement hardware. Currently, the framework is able to utilize an exhaustive search approach or a reinforcement learning based optimization like shown in [1], but will be extended with further techniques like e.g. Evolutionary Algorithms [3] in the future.

3.1 Optimization Problem

We use a local classifier per parent node approach, because each classifier and feature extraction in every node of the HiM can be chosen independently. Let $\mathcal{C} = \{c_1, ..., c_j\}$ and $\mathcal{F} = \{F_1, ..., F_k\}$ be finite sets of classifier and feature labels, respectively. The ASP can be described by the optimization problem to maximize the reward function

$$R(\hat{\mathbb{P}}_{C,F}) = \lambda \mathcal{A}(\hat{\mathbb{P}}_{C,F}) + \frac{1}{\lambda}\hat{E}(\hat{\mathbb{P}}_{C,F}), \tag{1}$$

where $\hat{\mathbb{P}}_{C,F}$ is a finite set indexed by N that contains for each node $n \in N$ a possibly optimal classifier-feature pair $(\hat{C}_n, \hat{F}_n)$, which combines a single classifier $\hat{C}_n \in \mathcal{C}$ with a set of feature labels $\hat{F}_n \in \mathcal{P}(\mathcal{F})$. The reward consists of a weighted sum of the accuracy $\mathcal{A}$ and the approximated energy consumption score $\hat{E}$, which may be replaced by a real measurement. The weighting factor λ is a hyperparameter that can be used to shift the optimization towards energy consumption or classification performance. In our tests, $\lambda = 2$ showed a good trade-off between both criteria. A smaller value led to trivial classifiers and an increased λ to inefficient models. This is because for more extreme values of λ the optimization solely focuses on either accuracy or energy consumption. The optimization procedure picks from a configuration set

$$\mathbb{W} = \{(\mathbb{c}_0, \mathbb{f}_0), (\mathbb{c}_1, \mathbb{f}_1), \dots (\mathbb{c}_N, \mathbb{f}_N)\}, \tag{2}$$

where each $\mathbb{c}_n \in \mathcal{P}(\mathcal{C}) \setminus \emptyset$ and $\mathbb{f}_n \subseteq \mathcal{P}(\mathcal{F})$.

3.2 Reinforcement Learning

As an alternative approach to the exhaustive search, we also test Reinforcement Learning (RL) to solve the ASP for a HiM. RL is a machine learning method that aims to learn the optimal sequence of actions called *policy* required to reach a specific goal. It consists of an *environment*, and an *agent* that exists in certain *states*. The agent is the main actor, that interacts with the environment by performing actions. The agent gets the feedback from the environment as a *reward* and a new *state*. The agent's goal is to maximize its reward over time. In [1], the authors propose a RL method for the ASP of hierarchical classification

---

Algorithm 1: Reinforcement Learning Algorithm for Hierarchical Classification

---

    Input   : ε, α, γ, λ, X, Y
    Output: The optimal policy π*
1 Initialize Q-table, **for** $episode = 0...Episodes$ **do**
2 | **for** $i = 0...I$ **do**
3 | | Select X_k and Y_k for hierarchy level k
4 | | Select testing instance x_i, y_i
5 | | Build training set: $X_k \setminus x_i$, $Y_i \setminus y_n$
6 | | Select an action type $a \in A$
7 | | Train classifier of type a using training set
8 | | Predict label for x_i using trained classifier
9 | | Move to next state s' based on the prediction
10 | | Update Q(s,a)
11 | | **if** s' *is a leaf node* **then**
12 | | | Break;
13 | | **else**
14 | | | Return to line 3;
15 | | **end**
16 | | **for** $s \in S$ **do**
17 | | | π*(s) = $\underset{a}{\operatorname{argmax}}$ Q(s,a)
18 | | **end**
19 | **end**
20 **end**

---

problems. We extend this method by testing it on an embedded device and performing real-life measurements. In this context, the set of states are considered
to be the different levels in the hierarchy. The set of actions are the different
classification algorithms. In every episode, the agent selects a classifier type and
trains it, then conducts inference on a random test instance of the dataset. Based
on the generated prediction, the agent moves to the new state in the next level
and collects a reward. An episode is complete when the agent reaches a terminal
state. The reward function is similarly defined as in Eq. 1, with $\hat{E}(\hat{\mathbb{P}}_{C,F})$ being
replaced by the measurement

$$R(\hat{\mathbb{P}}_{C,F}) = \lambda \mathcal{A}(\hat{\mathbb{P}}_{C,F}) - (1 - \lambda)\hat{E}(\hat{\mathbb{P}}_{C,F}).$$

Here we use a different weighting method, where λ is between 0 and 1 to keep
comparability with [1]. The complete process of training the RL-Agent to select
a classifier for each node can be seen in Algorithm 1. As shown in the literature, we apply the Monte-Carlo on-policy strategy, where the Q-table is updated
after every episode. X and Y are the sets of data samples and their corresponding labels, respectively. The parameter ϵ balances exploitation and exploration
in RL algorithms. The learning rate is denoted with α, and γ is the reduction
factor. We implement an interface to handle communication from the host to
the embedded device. The interface is able to obtain direct feedback from a

source measurement unit (SMU) about energy consumption and current inference results from the micro controller. First, the host conducts the action selection and the classifier training. It then sends the trained classifier's parameters and a test instance to the embedded device that uses the sent parameters to perform inference. Simultaneously, the embedded device triggers a measurement of the energy consumption while inference is performed. Lastly, the Host receives the prediction from the embedded device and the energy consumption from the SMU. This information is used to update its Q-table and continues to perform a new episode with a new test instance. After several episodes the agent learns an optimal policy, which is a sequence of classifier types for every level in the hierarchy.

4 Feasibility Study

To show the real-world benefits of applying automated HiML, we conduct a feasibility study using the HiMLEdge framework with three experiments. We start by applying an exhaustive search algorithm, followed by reproducing the reinforcement learning based algorithm selection introduced by [1]. As a third step we conduct tests on a system level view of energy consumption by simulating an application scenario including communication, data retrieval and classification.

4.1 Dataset

For evaluation we chose condition monitoring as a target application, which is part of the SDG Goal 9 working towards sustainable industrialization. Therefore, we are using the well-studied CWRU-Bearing dataset [9], which was recorded using a 2HP motor connected to a dynamometer via a torque transducer/encoder. This also gives us the opportunity to see the applicability of a different dataset to hierachical machine learning in comparison to [1]. The bearings used in this test are supporting the motor shaft and have been artificially damaged at different locations with fault depths ranging from 0.007" to 0.021". The vibration data included in the dataset was collected using single-axis accelerometers with a sampling rate of 12 kS/s (fan-end). The data is separated into windows of 512 samples, with a split of 60% training, 20% validation, and 20% test data.

4.2 Measurement Setup

All classifiers used by the HiMLEdge framework are trained with the Scikit-Learn module in python. Before any data is evaluated, the input features are scaled to have zero mean and unit variance. For the features in the frequency space, a Fast fourier transform is used with an FFT size equal to the number of samples in a window. To describe the classifier and feature selection steps we will use the following abbreviations: DT = Decision Tree, LR = Logistic Regression, SVM = Support Vector Machine, RF = Random Forest, MLP =

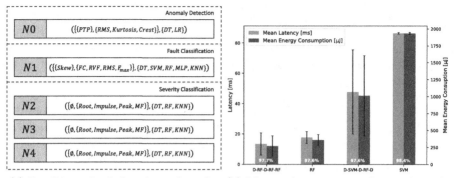

(a) Possible tuple choices for each node.   (b) Measured energy per inference from the exhaustive search results

Fig. 3. Possible tuple choices for each note during exhaustive search (left) and search results with energy consumption (right).

Mulit-Layer-Perceptron, KNN = k-Nearest Neighbours, PTP = Peak-To-Peak, RMS = Root Mean Square, FC = Frequency Centroid, RVF=Root Variance Frequency, F_{max}= Maximum Frequency, and MF = Mean Frequency. The calculation of the statistical features in both time and frequency domain can be found in [8]. The hyperparameters of each classifier are tuned by a grid search based approach on a validation set. After training, the selected classifiers are ported to plain C using the micromlgen[2] module and compiled using gcc with optimization (-O3) enabled. The ported classifiers are tested on an Arduino Nano 33 BLE Sense by using a subset of windows from the test-set. The energy consumption is measured with a source measurement unit (PXIe-4145). To reduce the influence of background systems and sensors, we first measure the base power consumption of the microcontroller during idle. This base power is subtracted from the power consumption measured during inference, resulting in the energy consumption in Joule per inference.

4.3   Exhaustive Search

In the first experiment, we use an exhaustive search algorithm to obtain a complete overview of the search space. In this way, we are able to construct a knowledge base, which can later be used to form heuristics for future search algorithms. We separate the classification task in three levels: Anomaly detection (i = 0), fault classification (i = 1) and severity detection (i = 1, 2, 3) (cf. Figure 1b). Due to the large search space we chose to approximate the energy consumption with the mean latency per inference τ measured on the host PC, which is normalized with respect to the highest measured latency during the search.

$$\hat{E}(\hat{\mathbb{P}}_{C,F}) = (1 - \frac{\tau(\hat{\mathbb{P}}_{C,F})}{\tau_{max}}). \tag{3}$$

---

[2] https://github.com/eloquentarduino/micromlgen.

The two best performing HiMs are transpiled (source-to-source compiled) to plain C and deployed to the embedded device. As baseline models, two flat classifiers (SVM and RF) are compared to the optimized HiMs in terms of energy consumption and accuracy. For the hierarchy in Fig. 1b, we let the optimization pick out of the sets shown in Fig. 3a, which use the following configuration $\mathbb{W} = \{(\mathbb{c}_0, \mathbb{f}_0), (\mathbb{c}_1, \mathbb{f}_1), \ldots, (\mathbb{c}_4, \mathbb{f}_4)\}$ with

$$\mathbb{c}_0 = \{DT, LR\},$$
$$\mathbb{f}_0 = \{\{PTP\}, \{RMS, Kurtosis, Crest\}\},$$
$$\mathbb{c}_1 = \{DT, SVM, RF, MLP, KNN\},$$
$$\mathbb{f}_1 = \{\{Skew\}, \{FC, RVF, RMS, F_{max}\}\},$$
$$\mathbb{c}_2 = \mathbb{c}_3 = \mathbb{c}_4 = \{DT, RF, KNN\},$$
$$\mathbb{f}_2 = \mathbb{f}_3 = \mathbb{f}_4 = \{\emptyset, \{Root, Impulse, Peak, MF\}\},$$

leading to a total of 12964 permutations.

The results shows improvements in energy consumption for both HiMs over the baseline (cf. Figure 3b). A significantly influencing factor for the hierarchical model is the fault-detection, which is presumably responsible for most of the computations in the model. This is because of the inclusion of an FFT in the feature extraction process and the more complicated classification task. Therefore, we will continue comparing the hierarchical model with a RF at its core with the RF baseline and the SVM core with the SVM baseline.

Comparing the RF-based models, a decrease in both mean energy consumption and latency of 24.96% can be achieved using the hierarchical approach while obtaining a slight increase in accuracy of 0.1%. This improvement is most likely connected to the distribution of the dataset, where 25% of the cases are non-faulty. Here, the use of a DT with only time-domain features is enough for the decision to stop the computation. The additional overhead introduced by the hierarchical structure might be compensated by the severity detection, where in the case of the found model for some fault classes no additional features are needed.

When comparing the two SVM-based approaches, the gap between the flat classifier and the hierarchical model increases further with a decrease of 47.63% in energy consumption, but with a slightly worse accuracy of 97.6% (SVM-baseline 98.4%). This increase in energy efficiency for the hierarchical model can be explained with the complexity of a SVM, which in the worst case can be $O(n^3)$ [10]. With the higher number of input features as well as possible classes, the cubic complexity becomes a problem in this scenario. The decrease in accuracy can be explained by error propagation through the model. If a classification error is made in any node, it is forwarded through the complete hierarchy and therefore influences the final decision.

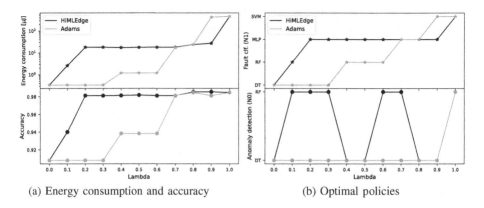

(a) Energy consumption and accuracy   (b) Optimal policies

Fig. 4. Influence of λ on energy consumption, Accuracy and model selection.

4.4 Reinforcement Learning

To test the capabilities of the RL-based selection approach, we narrow down the search space to stay comparable to [1] by only optimizing the classifiers. For all nodes ($n \in \{0, 1, \ldots, 4\}$) the agent can pick out of the set $c_n = \{DT, RF, MLP, SVM\}$. Logistic regression and KNN classifiers were left out in this experiment, as they did not show adequate results during the exhaustive search. Additionally, the RFs have been limited to a maximum of ten estimators due to higher memory constraints introduced by the runtime in the background. The same feature sets found in Sect. 4.3 are used.

With feedback from measurements the experiment resulted in the optimal policy {DT, MLP, RF, MLP, RF }, which differs compared to the policy found when using adams et al.'s approximation ({DT, RF, DT, DT, DT }). During testing we explored that even though an MLP had a much higher complexity measure in comparison to a RF, the measurement resulted only in a slight increase in energy consumption. Because of the higher accuracy of the MLP, the agent probably decided to lean towards picking the MLP over the RF. Additionally, the training process converged after only a few hours of training on a single desktop PC, while the exhaustive search was run in the course of multiple days. This shows the importance of a suitable algorithm selection techniques that does not only save energy for the inference, but also needs less power during optimization and training. Without a proper approach, the ASP becomes unsolvable for hierarchical classification with an exhaustive search in increasing search spaces and the positive impact on sustainability becomes questionable.

Influence of Trade-off Parameter λ. The model selection process is highly influenced by the trade-off parameter λ, which shifts the selection from maximum energy awareness ($\lambda = 0$) to maximum accuracy ($\lambda = 1$). While both Adams et al.'s surrogate metric and our framework behave as expected with an increase in energy consumption and accuracy for rising values of λ (cf. Figure 4a), the two approaches differ at the point this increase starts. Our approach reaches near

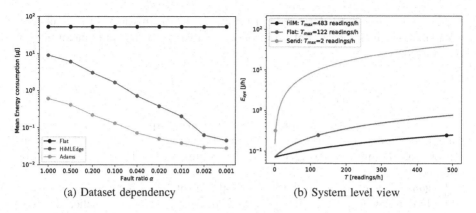

(a) Dataset dependency   (b) System level view

Fig. 5. Dataset dependency for different ratios between faulty and normal cases (left) and system level view (right). The maximum possible duty cycle for 5 years of run time are marked

peak accuracy much earlier ($\lambda = 0.2$) than Adams et al.'s approach, but the energy draw only reaches a modest value of 18.28 µJ/Inference. This behavior is also reflected in the classifier choice of both approaches shown in Fig. 4b. The optimal policies for fault detection (N1) seem to be highly correlated with the energy consumption. This verifies the assumption made in Sect. 4.3 that the fault classification is most influential for the energy consumption of the complete HiM. In general, our approach seems to favor an MLP outside of extreme values for λ, while the agent collecting the reward from a surrogate metric sticks to tree-based algorithms (RF, DT) most of the time. This difference can be explained with a not optimal approximation of the energy for an MLP. While in theory, the MLP should be much more computational intensive in comparison to e.g. RF, the regular matrix computations used in a Neural Network are easier to optimize for a compiler. This leads to only a modest increase in energy consumption, but with the benefit of a much more precise model. Additionally, the Cortex M4 can utilize DSP functionalities for the optimal execution of matrix operations. Therefore, the search process should not only include theoretical compute complexity, but also measurements or hardware-aware surrogate models.

Dataset Dependency. Due to the nature of hierarchical classification, the energy consumption is inherently dataset dependent. This is especially the case if the hierarchy includes a lightweight anomaly detection like in our case. Here, the ratio between faulty and non faulty events

$$\alpha = \frac{\#FaultyEvents}{\#NormalEvents} = \frac{\alpha_f}{\alpha_n},$$

has the highest impact on the energy needed. As discussed before, with λ set to 0.5, our approach needs more energy compared to Adams et al.'s approach. However, it benefits from a higher classification performance. While this view is true for the standard dataset distribution ($\alpha \approx 4$), in the field α is usually much smaller. In this case, both approaches converge to the same mean energy consumption

$$\overline{E} = \frac{\alpha_n E_{N0} + \alpha_f \overline{E_f}}{\alpha_n + \alpha_f} = \frac{\alpha_n E_{N0} + \alpha \alpha_n \overline{E_f}}{\alpha_n + \alpha \alpha_n} = \frac{E_{N0} + \alpha \overline{E_f}}{1 + \alpha} \underset{\alpha \to 0}{=} E_{N0}$$

if the energy draw of the anomaly detection E_{N0} is equal for both approaches (same policy for N0 cf. Figure 4b). For α nearing zero, the mean energy consumption of the remaining nodes (N1-N4) $\overline{E_f}$ becomes negligible, which can also be observed in Fig. 5a.

In general, this shows that the applicability of HiML for energy efficiency is highly dataset-dependent. If a problem can be solved by a classifier that can be partitioned into multiple stages with increasing degrees of complexity, and if the low-complexity nodes are executed more often, the hierarchical approach works well. However, in scenarios where complex computations are needed at every point in time, a HiM might even consume more energy due to the added overhead.

In conclusion, the tests conducted with RL show not only the dataset dependency and the influence of λ on the selection process. They also highlight the importance of an applicable search strategy. The exhaustive search discussed in Sect. 4.3 took multiple days on a cluster of CPUs to find a solution, while the RL agent was trained in hours on a single machine including measurement feedback. This training time decreases further with Adams et al.'s surrogate metric. In general, a combination of heuristics, search strategy, and hardware-aware surrogate models should be used to build a precise AutoML tool for HiML.

4.5 System Level Energy Consumption

As a last test we want to evaluate a system view to get insight in the power consumption in an application scenario. Before, we always focused on optimizing the energy consumption of the machine learning pipeline isolated from the total power draw of other components and communication. Therefore, in the following we will calculate a system level energy score per hour

$$E_{sys} = T[\alpha \overline{E_f} + (1 - \alpha)E_{N0}] + E_{off}, \tag{4}$$

where T denotes the readings per hour and E_{off} the system-off power consumption per hour. To simulate a real-life application scenario, we changed the dataset distribution to $\alpha_f = 1$ and $\alpha_n = 20$. Thus, a fault only occurs in 5% of the measurements. With this setting, we compare three cases: A flat classifier (RF), the best performing HiM from Sect. 4.3 and sending data only. In the case of classification, the result is sent via BLE if a fault has been detected, while in the sending data case the complete window holding 512 values is always sent to the host. The power-off energy is taken from the datasheet of the NRF58240 (71.28 mJ/h). The goal of this test is to find the maximum possible duty cycle T to achieve 5 years of battery life with a single CR2477 coin cell battery holding

1000 mAh (10800 J @ 3 V) of charge in the respective scenarios and thereby see the impact on energy consumption of hierarchical classification in an application scenario.

It is clearly visible in Fig. 5b that the automatically found HiM is able to achieve the best duty cycle and perform 3.95 times more classifications per hour in comparison to the flat model, coming very close to real-time monitoring of the machine in question. Additionally, the gap between the two classification scenarios and the wireless sending mode shows that filtering and classifying the sensor data should always be the preferred method if applicable. Considering that in other more extreme cases BLE might not be available due to its low range, different communication methods might draw even more energy. Therefore, an efficient filtering method should be especially useful in remote areas. Additionally, when looking at this test from a battery-life point of view, the more efficient algorithms could also be used to increase battery life, or decrease the battery capacity instead of applying a higher duty cycle. This perspective helps to improve sustainability in an industry 4.0 scenario and to enable further, new applications.

5   Conclusion

With the HiMLEdge framework, we were able to evaluate 12,964 hierarchical model architectures to find the best performing one w.r.t. accuracy *and* energy usage. The optimized HiMs achieve a reduction in energy consumption of up to 47.63% over the baseline in the standard distribution of the CWRU dataset (25% no-faults). These improvements are mainly linked to (i) the anomaly-detection as the first stage of evaluation and (ii) the modularized selection of features and classifiers. We explored RL as a selection method for HiMs, showing the potential behind more efficient optimization algorithms. We have demonstrated that the viability of an energy approximation measure needs to be validated before applying it to the optimization process. In our case, the unrealistic approximation lead to a different optimal policy in comparison to the optimal policy obtained by including real energy measurements. The system-level view on hierarchical classification exhibits the strength of efficient processing at the edge. It lead to a near real time execution of the monitoring while using only a coin cell battery for five years of run time. In a more realistic dataset distribution (95% no-fault), the HiM was able to perform 3.95 more readings per hour than a flat classifier. On the flip side this advantage in energy efficiency could also be transferred to longer battery life.

However, there are additional points that need to be investigated in future works. Further optimization techniques should be explored, e.g., evolutionary algorithms [3]. Even though RL showed promising results, it is unclear how it would handle an increased search space. The optimization process might also be positively influenced by a surrogate model that precisely estimates the energy consumption of a pipeline [6]. Additionally, further modularization of features could improve the energy consumption by, e.g., utilizing a Multirate Filterbank [16] to decompose the input signals. Furthermore, the hierarchy is constructed with expert knowledge, so an automatic approach to learn hierarchical structures should be investigated as an alternative. Currently it is unclear how beneficial the approach would be in other scenarios. Even though we were able to show that in the case of condition monitoring, HiML can be very beneficial, other application areas might not benefit as much. Therefore, a study comparing the impact of HiML on energy efficiency in a broad range of contexts should be conducted in future work.

Acknowledgement. This work was supported by the Bavarian Ministry of Economic Affairs, Regional Development and Energy through the Center for Analytics - Data - Applications (ADACenter) within the framework of "BAYERN DIGITAL II" (20–3410-2-9-8).'

References

1. Adams, S., et al.: Hierarchical fault classification for resource constrained systems. Mech. Syst. Signal Process. **134**, 106266 (2019) https://doi.org/10.1016/j.ymssp.2019.106266 https://linkinghub.elsevier.com/retrieve/pii/S0888327019304819
2. Akbari, A., Wu, J., Grimsley, R., Jafari, R.: Hierarchical Signal Segmentation and Classification for Accurate Activity Recognition. In: Proceedings of the 2018 ACM International Joint Conference and 2018 International Symposium on Pervasive and Ubiquitous Computing and Wearable Computers. pp. 1596–1605. UbiComp '18, Association for Computing Machinery, New York, NY, USA (2018). https://doi.org/10.1145/3267305.3267528
3. Aquino-Brítez, D., Ortiz, A., Ortega, J., León, J., Formoso, M., Gan, J.Q., Escobar, J.J.: Optimization of Deep Architectures for EEG Signal Classification: An AutoML Approach Using Evolutionary Algorithms. Sensors **21**(6), 2096 (2021) DOI: https://doi.org/10.3390/s21062096,https://www.mdpi.com/1424-8220/21/6/2096, number: 6 Publisher: Multidisciplinary Digital Publishing Institute
4. Bischl, B., Mersmann, O., Trautmann, H., Preuß, M.: Algorithm selection based on exploratory landscape analysis and cost-sensitive learning. In: Proceedings of the 14th annual conference on Genetic and evolutionary computation. pp. 313–320. GECCO '12, Association for Computing Machinery, New York, NY, USA (2012). https://doi.org/10.1145/2330163.2330209
5. Bruckert, S., Finzel, B., Schmid, U.: The Next Generation of Medical Decision Support: A Roadmap Toward Transparent Expert Companions. Front. Artif. Intell. **3** (2020) https://www.frontiersin.org/article/10.3389/frai.2020.507973
6. García-Martín, E., Rodrigues, C.F., Riley, G., Grahn, H.: Estimation of energy consumption in machine learning. Journal of Parallel and Distributed Computing **134**, 75–88 (2019) https://doi.org/10.1016/j.jpdc.2019.07.007,https://www.sciencedirect.com/science/article/pii/S0743731518308773
7. Goetschalckx, K., Moons, B., Lauwereins, S., Andraud, M., Verhelst, M.: Optimized Hierarchical Cascaded Processing. IEEE Journal on Emerging and Selected Topics in Circuits and Systems **8**(4), 884–894 (2018). https://doi.org/10.1109/JETCAS.2018.2839347

8. Lei, Y.: 2 - Signal processing and feature extraction. In: Lei, Y. (ed.) Intelligent Fault Diagnosis and Remaining Useful Life Prediction of Rotating Machinery, pp. 17–66. Butterworth-Heinemann (Jan 2017). https://doi.org/10.1016/B978-0-12-811534-3.00002-0,https://www.sciencedirect.com/science/article/pii/B9780128115343000020

9. Neupane, D., Seok, J.: Bearing Fault Detection and Diagnosis Using Case Western Reserve University Dataset With Deep Learning Approaches: A Review. IEEE Access 8 (2020). https://doi.org/10.1109/ACCESS.2020.2990528

10. Ns, A.: Time complexity analysis of support vector machines (SVM) in Lib-SVM. Int. J. Comput. Appl. **128**(3), 957–8887 (2015). https://doi.org/10.5120/ijca2015906480

11. Pech, M., Vrchota, J., Bednář, J.: Predictive maintenance and intelligent sensors in smart factory: Review. Sensors 21(4) (2021). https://doi.org/10.3390/s21041470,https://www.mdpi.com/1424-8220/21/4/1470

12. Ren, H., Anicic, D., Runkler, T.A.: The synergy of complex event processing and tiny machine learning in industrial IoT. In: Proceedings of the 15th ACM International Conference on Distributed and Event-based Systems, pp. 126–135. DEBS '21, Association for Computing Machinery, New York, NY, USA (Jun 2021). https://doi.org/10.1145/3465480.3466928

13. Schwartz, D., Selman, J.M.G., Wrege, P., Paepcke, A.: Deployment of Embedded Edge-AI for Wildlife Monitoring in Remote Regions. In: 2021 20th IEEE International Conference on Machine Learning and Applications (ICMLA), pp. 1035–1042 (Dec 2021). https://doi.org/10.1109/ICMLA52953.2021.00170

14. Silla, C.N., Freitas, A.A.: A survey of hierarchical classification across different application domains. Data Mining and Knowledge Discovery **22**(1), 31–72 (2011). https://doi.org/10.1007/s10618-010-0175-9

15. Thomas, A., Guo, Y., Kim, Y., Aksanli, B., Kumar, A., Rosing, T.S.: Hierarchical and distributed machine learning inference beyond the edge. In: 2019 IEEE 16th International Conference on Networking, Sensing and Control (ICNSC), pp. 18–23 (2019). https://doi.org/10.1109/ICNSC.2019.8743164

16. Vaidyanathan, P.: Multirate digital filters, filter banks, polyphase networks, and applications: a tutorial. In: Proceedings of the IEEE **78**(1), 56–93 (1990). https://doi.org/10.1109/5.52200

17. Vinuesa, R., et al.: The role of artificial intelligence in achieving the Sustainable Development Goals. Nature Commun. **11**(1), 233 (2020). https://doi.org/10.1038/s41467-019-14108-y

18. Zhou, F., Gao, Y., Wen, C.: A Novel Multimode Fault Classification Method Based on Deep Learning. J. Control Sci. Eng. 2017 (2017). https://doi.org/10.1155/2017/3583610,https://www.hindawi.com/journals/jcse/2017/3583610/

A Strategic-Operational Contribution to the One-Dimensional Multi-period Cutting Stock Problem for Sawmills

Oscar Saldías[1]([🖂]) [iD], Carla Guerrero[1] [iD], Rodrigo Olivares[1] [iD],
Daniel Morillo-Torres[2] [iD], and Gustavo Gatica[1] [iD]

[1] Facultad de Ingeniería - CIS, Universidad Andres Bello, Antonio Varas 880,
Providencia, Santiago de Chile, Chile
{o.saldasmerino,cguerreroavila1,r.olivaresreyes1}@uandresbello.edu,
ggatica@unab.cl
[2] Pontificia Universidad Javeriana de Cali, Calle 18 No. 118-250, Cali, Colombia
daniel.morillo@javerianacali.edu.co

Abstract. This paper presents a model aimed at solving a Multi-period Cutting Stock Problem (MPCSP) for a sawmill at a strategic-operational level. The study seeks to minimize raw material and storage costs to manufacture square wood planks for packing batches of wood boards and panels. For these purposes, the study used real data from an actual Chilean sawmill. The resolution of the Gurobi model allows a 20.4% cost reduction when comparing the empirical method with the model implemented in the sawmill.

Keywords: Multi-period · One-dimensional cutting stock problem · Sawmill · Industrial application

1 Introduction

The Cutting Stock Problem (CSP) is a classic mathematical programming problem with several industrial applications, and it is categorized as an NP-Hard problem [23,24]. It is considered one of the most studied operations research problems due to its high applicability in the industry of various raw materials such as paper, wood, steel, leather, among others [3,11,21,24]. The CSP presents a group of objects (raw material) that must be cut in different smaller dimensions and in the quantities specified by a requirement set. The objective is to minimize raw material waste.

A strategic-operational problem is presented, motivated by a real problem identified at a Chilean sawmill company with a large production capacity. The final product corresponds to square wood planks produced by the same sawmill and used to pack lumber and wood boards. Its manufacturing cost implies a significant impact on the financial statements of the companies. Hence, this paper outlines a contribution from a Multi-period Cutting Stock Problem (MPCSP)

T. Guarda et al. (Eds.): ARTIIS 2022, CCIS 1676, pp. 30–41, 2022.
https://doi.org/10.1007/978-3-031-20316-9_3

applied to the sawmill industry. The costs incurred in raw materials and storage of square wood planks are minimized by solving a model implemented in Gurobi 9.5.0 ©.

The following section provide an overview of the MPCSP applied at the afore-mentioned sawmill. Subsequently, Sect. 3 reviews the existing literature and discusses how the problem has been applied in several industries. Section 4 describes the case study; meanwhile Sect. 5 presents the model developed for the MPCSP, and its results are exposed in Sect. 6.2. Finally, Sect. 7 discusses the conclusions of this research study conducted at the sawmill.

2   Problem Description

The One-Dimensional CSP is an NP-HARD problem and can be modeled by integer programming [5]. This model seeks to minimize waste generated by cutting raw materials, from a standard dimension, to generate products with smaller dimensions according to customer requirements.

[19] abbreviates this problem as a 1D-CSP (One-Dimensional Cutting Stock Problem). Here two sets are defined: one for the materials that will be cut ($N = \{1, ..., i, ..., n\}$) and another for the smaller products that will be produced ($M = \{1, ..., j, ..., m\}$), which must respect dimensional limitations specified and meet the required demand.

As a result of this problem, there is also the possibility of overproduction at a given moment, which means that finished products must be stored to fulfill later demands. Although this may lower input costs, it increases storage costs. According to [15], this extension can be identified as the MPCSP and a set $T = \{1, ..., t, ..., f\}$ associated with the planning periods is included therein.

3   Literature Review

For decades, cutting and packing problems have been addressed in the operations research literature and encompass recurrent combinatorial optimization problems at the industrial level [8]. [13] proposes the first formulations through a variable cutoff assignment model. Later, [6,7] provide the classic model that introduces the concept of cutting patterns by restricting the model to a set of feasible cutting combinations.

Subsequently, [3] proposed a single cut model for variable length materials. Furthermore, [2] suggested a graph theory model for solving a standard cutting problem. In the following years, research on shear problems increased significantly, to the point where an updated typology was needed. Within this context, [24] compiled 445 publications to organize and classify cutting and packing problems into new categories. These problems are defined as 'pure' if they only involve cutting or 'extended' if they include additional aspects. In addition, they are classified as 'standard' problems if they only seek optimization and as 'variant' if the problem addresses multiple objectives problem, such as the problem reviewed by [25].

The cutting problem is deemed as strategic-operative because, as it is routine problem in industries [4], applications have been generated to contribute to production processes. [21] implements a CSP solution at an aluminum factory, specifically to produce window frames, to reduce the standard length required to satisfy production orders by 2.2%. In turn, [22] discuss a procedure for solving the problem of cutting paper rolls with different quality grades. Later, [12] added a process for joining smaller rolls to generate other longer patterns. [16] apply a solution to a Brazilian furniture company, which is subsequently adapted by [10] to increase profits by 28%. Recently, [17] solve the problem at a metallurgical company to minimize waste when cutting steel bars, thereby considering inventory constraints, and re-using shards to reduce 80% of the resulting waste. [18] extend the formulation of the problem for manufacturing off-road trucks. In addition, they propose specialized heuristics for its resolution.

Further, [1] worked with the multi-period model in a beam production, which was executed using the CPLEX solver. Then, [14] propose two mathematical models, as an extension of the cutting pattern model from [6] and the graph model proposed by [2] respectively, which are solved using the Column Generation-based Heuristic (CGH) and an Indirect Dynamic Programming-based Heuristic (IDPH). [20] extend the formulation in the planning of the concrete structures production, specifically for manufacturing hollow-core slabs. The formulation proposed by [13] is adapted for solving by a Mixed Integer and Linear Programming (MILP) model, and it is compared against an adaptation from [6].

The literature has generally focused on the development of solutions to generate final products. Therefore, a model for cutting, producing and stacking wood planks requires transporting, storing and collecting raw materials and final products. The foregoing is a contribution to the MPSCP.

4   Case Study

The case study takes place in a sawmill located in the south-central zone of Chile. This sawmill reports a monthly sawn and planed wood production capacity of 30 000 m^3. The company generates, in one of its subprocesses, packaging materials for finished wood products, specifically square wood planks (Fig. 1).

The wood planks are used to raise plywood board packages from the floor, thus they can be taken and moved by forklifts Wood plank lengths range from 800 to 1 200 mm, with a maximum tolerance of up to −10 mm. For security and package stability reasons, these planks must be proportional to the width of each package. The method used by the company, before our intervention in their production process, consisted of cutting several plank units with a package crosscut saw, wherein the operator cut 4 060 mm long planks in three cuts of 1 200 mm each (Fig. 2) for storage. Then, the other sawmill production processes take these plank packages and cut them to the exact size they require, depending on the product that the production line is processing.

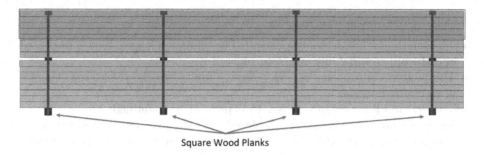

Square Wood Planks

Fig. 1. Plywood board packages diagram.

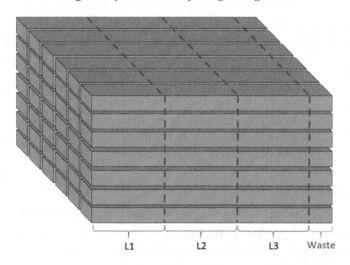

L1   L2   L3   Waste

Fig. 2. Plank cutting diagram.

The waste generated in the first cutting process has a length of 430 mm +30 mm of kerf losses, 11.3% of the raw material. An additional 12.6% waste is estimated during the subsequent final cuts. Hence, approximately 23.9% of the total raw material is wasted.

5   Proposed Mathematical Model

To solve this CSP problem, this study proposes a mathematical model based on the formulation presented by [13]. Proposed model includes a multiple time period component (MPCSP). In this sense, the company generates a strategic planning for the following four consecutive weeks, thus reducing storage costs. In addition, a parameter associated with kerf losses generated by cutting is included. In this case, a chainsaw with a 10 mm kerf was considered.

The assumptions considered in the model are as follows:

- The length of all packages is identical. The minimum length 4060 is respected and the upper variability is not considered.
- The production capacity of each period is limited to the processing capacity of incoming packets.
- The demand for each specific length is previously quantified.
- There are no additional costs associated with the production sequence.
- The production sequence has no impact on the operation of the other processes.
- There can be no surplus production outside the evaluation period.

The proposed integer linear programming model is described below. First, the sets, parameters and variables are defined, and then the mathematical model is presented.

Sets:

- $T = \{1, \ldots, f\}$ set of planning periods, with an index of t.
- $N = \{1, \ldots, n\}$ set of cutting packages, with an index of i.
- $M = \{1, \ldots, m\}$ set of products, with an index of j.

Parameters:

- C_t: raw material costs for the t period [USD].
- H_t: storage costs for the t period [USD].
- $D_{j,t}$: demand for product j in the t period [um].
- Q_t: production capacity for the t period [um].
- P: standard package length (raw material) [mm].
- L_j: Product j lenght [mm].
- K: Kerf losses [mm].

Variables:

- $x_{i,j,t}$: Number of products at a length of j in package i for the t period.
- $y_{i,t}$: Use of package i in the t period.
- $z_{j,t}$: Excess amount of product j in the t period.

Integer Programming Model Proposed:

$$\text{minimize } z = \sum_{t=1}^{f} \left(\sum_{i=1}^{n} C_t * y_{i,t} + \sum_{j=1}^{m} H_t * z_{j,t} \right) \quad (1)$$

s.t:

$$z_{j,t-1} + \sum_{i=1}^{n} x_{i,j,t} = D_{j,t} + z_{j,t}, \quad \forall j \in M, \forall t \in T \tag{2}$$

$$\sum_{j=1}^{m} ((L_j + K) * x_{i,j,t}) \leq P * y_{i,t}, \quad \forall i \in N, \forall t \in T \tag{3}$$

$$\sum_{i=1}^{n} y_{i,t} \leq Q_t, \quad \forall t \in \tag{4}$$

$$z_{j,0} = 0, \quad \forall j \in M \tag{5}$$

$$x_{i,j,t} \in [z^+ \cup 0], \quad \forall i \in N, \forall j \in M, \forall t \in T \tag{6}$$

$$y_{i,t} \in \{0,1\}, \quad \forall i \in N, \forall t \in T \tag{7}$$

$$z_{j,t} \in [z^+ \cup 0], \quad \forall j \in M, \forall t \in T \tag{8}$$

The target function (1) corresponds to the need to minimize the raw materials cost together with storage costs. However, constraint (2) indicates the need to satisfy the planned demand $D_{j,t}$, while establishing that any surplus production will be used in the following period.

Constraint (3) corresponds to the cutting feasibility for each package, wherein the sum of the lengths of each product cannot exceed the total length of the package. Given the variability in the physical lengths of the wood, considering a minimum length of 4 060 mm, a last cut must always be made to match the final product, so that, for example, to obtain 4 products from a single package, a 4th cut must be considered even if no waste cut is generated (Fig. 3). Constraint 4 conditions planning to respect the production capacity for each period. Constraint (6) indicates that there is no beginning inventory. Finally, constraints (6) to (8) describe the domain of the variables.

6   Results

The model is implemented in Gurobi 9.5.0 for Python 3.10.1. Hardware specifications included a computer with an AMD Ryzen 5 1600 Six-Core Processor with 3.20 GHz and 16 Gb RAM.

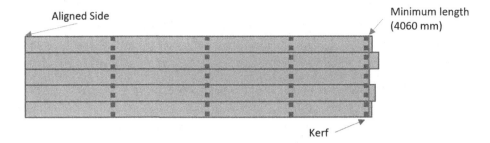

Fig. 3. Alignment cutting diagram.

Four planning periods are considered, with 13 products and a constant production capacity of 30 packages per period. Overall, 1 732 variables and 176 constraints are generated. The demand used to plan production is denoted in Table 1. Furthermore, raw material costs correspond to $C_t = \{500, 515, 500, 515\}$ USD considered to determine the importance of the model in cases where estimated costs vary over time. In addition, a constant storage cost is used $H = \$5$ USD per period.

Table 1. Planned demand.

Length (j)	Demand (t)			
	$t = 1$	$t = 2$	$t = 3$	$t = 4$
800	2	3	4	3
850	3	2	2	3
870	1	3	3	1
900	3	2	5	1
920	4	5	7	4
980	13	10	7	13
1 000	5	3	4	7
1 030	4	8	3	6
1 050	6	4	5	3
1 070	4	3	6	4
1 100	4	8	5	6
1 150	7	5	5	5
1 200	10	10	10	10

Two scenarios are presented in which demand is varied for each period in order to visualize differences between results.

6.1 First Case

On average, after running the algorithm for 49 s, the best solution found corresponds to a total of 70 cut packages, as shown in the Table 2, reaching a cost of 35 530 USD. As iterations of over 8 h failed to find better solutions, a 3.41% gap is generated for a possible improvement in the target value with respect to the associated linear programming problem.

Table 2. Used material.

Periods	Cut Packages	Linear Packages (mm)	Produced Length (mm)	Trimm Losses (mm)
$t = 1$	20	81,200	76,640	4,100
$t = 2$	15	60,900	59,300	1,600
$t = 3$	21	85,260	80,100	5,160
$t = 4$	14	56,840	55,320	1,520

The result obtained reflects the generation of surplus inventory in periods $t = 1$ and $t = 3$, which have lower production costs, as detailed in the Table 3 below. On the other hand, the loss of material generated corresponds to 4.36% of the material consumed, while it is estimated that the empirical method incurs a loss of 23.92% and a use of 18 additional packages as shown in the Table 7 below.

In addition, a second instance of the model is assessed by modifying the 10-mm kerf value to identify savings from changing the cutting element and

Table 3. Surplus production (inventory).

Length (j)	Period (t)				
	$t = 0$	$t = 1$	$t = 2$	$t = 3$	$t = 4$
800	0	0	0	0	0
850	0	0	0	0	0
870	0	0	0	0	0
900	0	0	0	0	0
920	0	0	0	0	0
980	0	0	0	0	0
1 000	0	1	0	1	0
1 030	0	2	0	1	0
1 050	0	0	0	0	0
1 070	0	0	0	0	0
1 100	0	1	0	0	0
1 150	0	3	0	1	0
1 200	0	1	0	8	0

reducing material losses to 5 mm. In this case, we obtained a target value of $35,520 USD through $10 USD savings for the period under evaluation.

6.2   Second Case

On average, the algorithm takes 48 s to find the best solution corresponding to $36,035 USD with a gap of 4.95% (Table 4).

Table 4. Planned demand.

Length (j)	Demand (t)			
	$t = 1$	$t = 2$	$t = 3$	$t = 4$
800	8	2	7	0
850	3	2	2	3
870	2	2	5	2
900	3	3	3	5
920	4	5	7	4
980	8	9	4	11
1 000	5	3	4	7
1 030	3	8	3	6
1 050	4	4	4	3
1 070	3	3	6	4
1 100	4	8	4	6
1 150	7	5	5	5
1 200	12	12	12	10

In total, 70 packages are cut, as described in Table 5 thus, 11 overproduction cuts are generated, where nine correspond to the first period and two in the third period (Table 6). As a consequence of these results, the % of lost material corresponds to 5.9%, as shown in Table 7.

Table 5. Used material. (Second case)

Periods	Cut	Linear	Produced	Trimm
	Packages	Packages (mm)	Length (mm)	Losses (mm)
t = 1	21	85,260	78,060	7,200
t = 2	15	60,900	57,960	2,940
t = 3	18	73,080	69,370	3,710
t = 4	17	69,020	65,810	3,210

Table 6. Surplus production (inventory) (Second case).

Length (j)	Period (t)				
	$t = 0$	$t = 1$	$t = 2$	$t = 3$	$t = 4$
800	0	0	0	0	0
850	0	0	0	0	0
870	0	0	0	0	0
900	0	0	0	0	0
920	0	0	0	0	0
980	0	0	0	0	0
1 000	0	0	0	0	0
1 030	0	0	0	0	0
1 050	0	0	0	0	0
1 070	0	0	0	0	0
1 100	0	0	0	0	0
1 150	0	0	0	0	0
1 200	0	9	0	2	0

An instance is also evaluated for this scenario where the kerf is modified from 10 mm to 5 mm, obtaining a result of \$35,035 USD (by saving the use of 2 packages equivalent to $1,000$ USD) and the reduction of wasted material to $\%1.6USD$.

Table 7. Comparison between models and scenarios.

	Proposed model (1)	Proposed model (2)	Empirical method
Cut packages	70	71	88
Linear length (mm)	284,200	288,260	357,280
Produced Length (mm)	271,820	271,200	316,800
Useful length (mm)	271,820	271,200	271,820
Trimm losses (mm)	12,380	17,060	85,460
% loss	4.36%	5.92%	23.92%
Cost (USD)	\$35,530	\$36,035	\$44,660

7   Conclusions

This study reveals the results from applying a MPCSP model within the sawmill industry. An estimated solution to the empirical method used by the company represents a cost of 44 660 USD compared with the target solution found of

35 530 USD. However, an instance of this model where the savings generated by reducing the cutting kerf by 5 mm are simulated. This simulation reveals a $1,000 USD recovery during the evaluation period when considering a different demand, which can be important to economically evaluate the feasibility of acquiring and using a technology with a lower kerf.

Hence, the application of a model generates 20.4% savings during the evaluation period. Nevertheless, the software was not able to determine optimum savings in a reasonable time period for the company's operations. As future work, the objective would be to implement metaheuristics to reduce this gap, as25 seen in [9] where a combination between sequential heuristic procedure and branch-and-bound is tested to obtain almost optimal solutions, while keeping low time complexity.

Other opportunities for future work could arise when studying a model variant that includes using cutting patterns to compare target value results.

References

1. de Athayde Prata, B., Pitombeira-Neto, A.R., de Moraes Sales, C.J.: An integer linear programming model for the multiperiod production planning of precast concrete beams. J. Constr. Eng. Manag. **141**(10), 04015029 (2015)
2. de Carvalho, J.V.: Exact solution of cutting stock problems using column generation and branch-and-bound. Int. Trans. Oper. Res. **5**(1), 35–44 (1998)
3. Dyckhoff, H.: A new linear programming approach to the cutting stock problem. Oper. Res. **29**(6), 1092–1104 (1981)
4. Foerster, H., Wäscher, G.: Pattern reduction in one-dimensional cutting stock problems. Int. J. Prod. Res. **38**, 1657–1676 (2000). https://doi.org/10.1080/002075400188780
5. Garey, M.R., Johnson, D.S.: Computers and Intractability, vol. 174. Freeman San Francisco (1979)
6. Gilmore, P.C., Gomory, R.E.: A linear programming approach to the cutting-stock problem. Oper. Res. **9**(6), 849–859 (1961)
7. Gilmore, P.C., Gomory, R.E.: A linear programming approach to the cutting stock problem-Part II. Oper. Res. **11**(6), 863–888 (1963)
8. Goulimis, C.: Optimal solutions for the cutting stock problem. Eur. J. Oper. Re. **44**, 197–208 (1990)
9. Gradisar, M., Trkman, P.: A combined approach to the solution to the general one-dimensional cutting stock problem. Comput. Oper. Res. **32**, 1793–1807 (2005). https://doi.org/10.1016/j.cor.2003.11.028
10. Gramani, M.C.N., França, P.M.: The combined cutting stock and lot-sizing problem in industrial processes. Eur. J. Oper. Res. **174**(1), 509–521 (2006)
11. Hinxman, A.I.: The trim:loss and a survey assortment problems'. Eur. J. Oper. Res. **5**, 8–18 (1980)
12. Johnson, M., Rennick, C., Zak, E.: Case studies from industry: skiving addition to the cutting stock problem in the paper industry. Siam Rev. **39**(3), 472–483 (1997)
13. Kantorovich, L.V.: Mathematical methods of organizing and planning production. Manag. Sci. **6**(4), 366–422 (1960)
14. Liu, B., Long, R., Zhu, C.: Withdrawn: development of regional logistics economy based on FPGA and embedded system. Microprocess. Microsyst., 103517 (2020). https://doi.org/10.1016/j.micpro.2020.103517

15. Melega, G.M., de Araujo, S.A., Jans, R.: Classification and literature review of integrated lot-sizing and cutting stock problems. Eur. J. Oper. Res. **271**(1), 1–19 (2018)
16. Morabito, R., Arenales, M.: Optimizing the cutting of stock plates in a furniture company. Int. J. Prod. Res. **38**(12), 2725–2742 (2000)
17. Morillo-Torres, D., Baena, M.T., Escobar, J.W., Romero-Conrado, A.R., Coronado-Hernández, J.R., Gatica, G.: A mixed-integer linear programming model for the cutting stock problem in the steel industry. In: Figueroa-García, J.C., Díaz-Gutierrez, Y., Gaona-García, E.E., Orjuela-Cañón, A.D. (eds.) WEA 2021. CCIS, vol. 1431, pp. 315–326. Springer, Cham (2021). https://doi.org/10.1007/978-3-030-86702-7_27
18. Nonås, S.L., Thorstenson, A.: A combined cutting-stock and lot-sizing problem. Eur. J. Oper. Res. **120**(2), 327–342 (2000)
19. Scheithauer, G.: On the MAXGAP problem for cutting stock problems. Elektronische Informationsverarbeitung und Kybernetik **30**(2), 111–117 (1994)
20. Signorini, C.d.A., de Araujo, S.A., Melega, G.M.: One-dimensional multi-period cutting stock problems in the concrete industry. Int. J. Prod. Res., 1–18 (2021)
21. Stadtler, H.: A one-dimensional cutting stock problem in the aluminium industry and its solution. Eur. J. Oper. Res. **44**(2), 209–223 (1990)
22. Sweeney, P.E.: One-dimensional cutting stock decisions for rolls with multiple quality grades (1988)
23. Vidal, G.H., Hernández, J.R.C., Minnaard, C., Gatica, G., Schwarzenberg, P.: Statistical analysis of manufacturing system complexity. Int. J. Adv. Manuf. Technol. **120**, 3427–3436 (2022). https://doi.org/10.1007/s00170-022-08981-z
24. Wäscher, G., Haußner, H., Schumann, H.: An improved typology of cutting and packing problems. Eur. J. Oper. Res. **183**(3), 1109–1130 (2007)
25. Yang, C.T., Sung, T.C., Weng, W.C.: An improved tabu search approach with mixed objective function for one-dimensional cutting stock problems. Adv. Eng. Softw. **37**(8), 502–513 (2006)

A New Approach for Air Quality Monitoring: A Case Study of Recife, Brazil

Ryan Gomes Paiva$^{(\boxtimes)}$ ⓘ, Rômulo César Carvalho de Araújo$^{(\boxtimes)}$ ⓘ,
Juliana de Albuquerque Souza Costa ⓘ, Paulo Vitor Barbosa Santana ⓘ,
Silvanio da Silva Assunção ⓘ, Welton Pereira da Luz Felix ⓘ,
Henrique Correia Torres Santos$^{(\boxtimes)}$ ⓘ, Izavan dos Santos Correia ⓘ,
and Steffano Xavier Pereira ⓘ

Instituto Federal de Educação, Ciência e Tecnologia de Pernambuco (IFPE), Campus
Recife, Recife, PE, Brazil
{rgp,jasc,pvbs,ssa,wplf,isc1,sxp}@discente.ifpe.edu.br,
{romuloaraujo,henrique.santos}@recife.ifpe.edu.br
https://www.ifpe.edu.br/

Abstract. The association of quality of life and air quality are intrinsic to the factors of analysis of the development of urban spaces and their sustainable assessment. Inserted in urban expansion and population growth, factors such as air pollution are commonly related to the understanding of the dynamics of the city and therefore, this factor constitutes a fundamental study for solution and planning. Thus, every year, new guidelines are formulated for the understanding of air pollution and its monitoring, however, contexts such as those of Brazil present the growth of urban spaces and therefore the increase of air pollution but still without the presence of appropriate plans for the management of air quality, which leaves cities helpless as to the level of pollutants in the air. In 2021, IEMA [9] showed that 16 Brazilian state capitals did not have air quality monitoring, one of them being Recife, capital of Pernambuco, therefore, this work gathers methods already used in the state of the art and proposes a new approach as to the development method for monitoring networks in places that present monitoring deficiency, being addressed the case study of Recife. The results of this work a modifiable methodology for the implementation of monitoring networks evaluating essential collection points and proposing a device model to meet the urban contexts in order to assess urban pollutants and collaborate with the urban dynamics and for the city management through the improvement of data collection and air quality management.

Keywords: Air-quality · Pollutants · WSN · Low-cost sensors ·
Sustainability

1 Introduction

The concern for climate change and its impacts on the way of life in the city brings up the debate about air quality [19], so every year new studies arise

T. Guarda et al. (Eds.): ARTIIS 2022, CCIS 1676, pp. 42–56, 2022.
https://doi.org/10.1007/978-3-031-20316-9_4

regarding the topic and it is important an effective participation of technological innovations in the process of air monitoring. To develop this point of sustainability, that is, the control of air pollution, researchers around the world have been applying solutions in remote monitoring network hardware [13].

Such technological advent, according to [13], has come to promote a revolutionary change for the advancement in air quality assessment and monitoring. Through low-cost sensors increasingly popularized in the last decade, it has been possible to develop new monitoring programs designed by foreign research groups and government organizations, this is the case of the Environmental Protection Agency of the United States of America (USA) as well as being worked on by the European Union for its new air quality directive [2]; thus moving from monitoring based on the single system of governments to a monitoring network coming from decentralized and sometimes collaborative groups with government data, something made official in Europe and the USA.

In the resolution of CONAMA (National Council of Environment) in 1989, Brazil presented its first action in air quality monitoring, establishing the basic monitoring instruments aimed at the welfare and development of the population through an environmentally safe management, adopting strategies for national air quality standards and monitoring. Still, the Air Quality platform, created by the Institute of Energy and Environment (IEMA) [9] shows that 16 of the 26 Brazilian states do not monitor air pollution, and among those that currently monitor, not all have autonomous stations, presenting only averages of daily measurements. Therefore, these stations are not always monitored with the aforementioned hardware and also do not provide real-time information. Data from the World Air Quality Index, a non-profit project that promotes a database prepared by environmental protection agencies around the world, shows that only in São Paulo are air quality data available in real time [20], a necessary reality for accurate data and better-grounded measures, but still uncommon in Brazil.

The paradigm shift addressed by [17] is definitely established in Brazil through the release of the Technical Guide for Monitoring and Assessment of Air Quality prepared and presented by the Ministry of Environment in 2019 [10]. In the guide, new objectives and instructions for monitoring are presented, with the implementation of standardized monitoring networks now planned for the entire national territory. The new instructions date new priorities regarding the types of pollutants and new types of sensors are already included, such as those cited by [13], thus establishing the new need to modernize the ways of supervising the quality of life in Brazilian cities using new electronic artifices along with a friendly environmental management.

Within these parameters, the RailBee® Telemetric System uses its structure to develop a module for monitoring pollutants, autonomously and in real time, with a system of modular technology and low cost. The RailBee® Telemetric System is an innovative system for monitoring and automation of road and rail networks that uses the transmission of signals via radio frequency, according to the ZigBee communication protocol, which is in accordance with the international standard Institute of Electrical and Electronic Engineers (IEEE) IEEE

802.15.4 and is composed of embedded systems, sensors and microcontrollers. This system allows a constant evaluation of factors that influence the performance of the trains and currently monitors the South Line of the Companhia Brasileira de Trens Urbanos/Metrô do Recife (CBTU - Recife), located covering the Metropolitan Region of Recife (RMR), and connecting the center of the city of Recife to its outskirts and neighboring cities.

Thus, it is proposed the development of the Air Quality Monitoring Module applied to the RailBee® Telemetric System, to be applied as a system for monitoring the air quality, in real time, inside the trains (passenger lounge), in the public areas of the passenger stations and on the traffic lane where the metro-rail vehicles circulate, analyzing the air quality index in the transportation on rails and on the permanent way of the South Line of the RMR subway system and enabling a database that contributes to the improvement of sustainable environmental management in RMR and Recife subway system. Applying the system method to the city's subway system as a small case study that contributes to the construction of new methods of monitoring network air quality for similar study regions.

2   Objectives

The goal is to develop an innovative and sustainable low-cost technology to improve management and sound decision making for the reduction of air pollutant emissions. As also, the advancement of the research, extension and innovation group contributing to the growth of services for transportation users as a form of clean transportation. Even more specifically, it is intended to:

- Develop the Air Quality Monitoring Module for application in the RailBee® Telemetric System;
- Monitor in real time the levels of atmospheric pollutants through the RailBee® Telemetric System;
- To provide an inventory of air pollutants present inside (passenger hall) trains circulating in the South Line of the Metro Rail System of the Metropolitan Region of Recife;
- Analyze results of the application process and report difficulties and necessary improvements to the regulations;
- To provide an inventory of the atmospheric pollutants present on the track where the trains of the Southern Line of Recife's Metropolitan Area Subway System circulate;
- Analyze the data collected by the Modules and enable improvements in data collection for the new meters that contribute to the improvement of CBTU-Recife's Management and Utility.

3   Methods

3.1   The Study Site: The RailBee® Telemetric System

The RailBee® System is composed of four subsystems differentiated by the functions of their devices in the Wireless Sensor Network (WSN) and by the direction of the information, the subsystems are named as follows: Mobile Stations (MS), Router Stations (ER), Base Stations (EB) and the Central Station (EC).

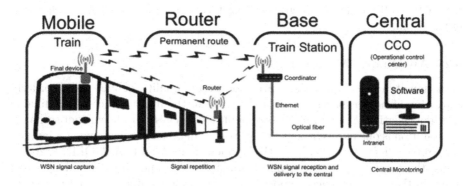

Fig. 1. RailBee® telemetry system overview

The Mobile Station (see Fig. 1) is an embedded electronic device that is located inside the command cabin of the Train Electric Unit (TUE), acting as an end node of the network, obtaining data from the sensors by the onboard computer in the cabin [14]. Also, according to [14], the basic composition of a ME is formed by sensors, a microcontroller, and a radio frequency (RF) XBee transmitter. The sensors are the devices that capture the electrical signals from the monitored variables. The microcontroller is responsible for receiving the electrical signals from the sensors and performs its encoding, such as data packaging, while the transmitter is responsible for transmitting these signals via radio signal to other parts of the system with the Base Stations as the final destination.

The Routing Station is a device located along the track, more specifically between the passenger stations throughout the CBTU-Recife South Line, and has the function of system communication. The ER acts as a router in the network, it receives information and amplifies the signal to another device in the network through its XBee Module responsible for receiving the Radio Frequency signals coming from the MS and sending these signals to the Base Station, in case direct contact between Base Station and Mobile Station is not possible.

The Base Stations are located in the passenger stations and their purpose is to receive the radio frequency signals coming from the ER and EM, so that the information from these signals are now sent back to the Central Station through a CBTU-Recife intranet. This station is composed of an XBee Module configured as network coordinator, receiving the signals, and a microcontroller, which will perform the network gateway function, encoding the data for the Ethernet/IP (Internet Protocol) protocol, which assigns an IP Address for each passenger station and is interconnected to CBTU-Recife's operational intranet, sending the data to the CE through an operational fiber optic network.

The Central Station is a desktop that has the RailBee® monitoring software installed and is located in the Operational Control Center (CCO). The CE receives the data coming from all the EBs through the CBTU-Recife intranet, processes this data, stores it in a hard drive, and finally displays it in real time to the CCO Traffic Controllers, giving them the same vision as the train operator in the cabin.

3.2   Air Quality Monitoring

Although it has as cause the search for better quality of life, the disorderly expansion of urban spaces can be a challenge to the maintenance of sustainable relations in cities. Among the types of pollution discussed in the current scenario, air pollution is one more concern because of the degradation of ecosystems and its widespread effect on the health of their populations (MOLINA; MOLINA, 2004). Thus, the association between better quality of life and cities is undone when living in these urban spaces exposes the population to higher concentrations of pollutants.

Based on guidelines from the World Health Organization (WHO), CONAMA Resolution No. 491 of 19/11/2018 [6] defines that air pollutants are: "Any form of matter in quantity, concentration, time or other characteristics, which make or may make the air unfit or harmful to health, inconvenient to the public welfare, harmful to materials, flora and fauna, or harmful to the safety, use and enjoyment of property or to the normal activities of the community".

As for the formation of these gases, the WHO, in its guidelines, establishes that a pollutant can be defined in 2 ways, emitted or formed. Primary pollutants are those emitted into the atmosphere directly from a source, such as car exhaust or a chimney. Secondary pollutants, on the other hand, are those formed in the atmosphere from chemical or photochemical reactions between primary pollutants and natural components of the atmosphere, such as water or oxygen.

Large cities like Beijing, Los Angeles, Mexico City and São Paulo often have high concentrations of the main atmospheric pollutants, these are: Particulate Matter (PM), Ozone (O3), Sulfur Dioxide (SO2), Carbon Monoxide (CO), Nitrogen Oxides (NOX) and Greenhouse Gases such as Carbon Dioxide (CO2) and Methane (CH4), responsible for environmental changes on a global scale (MOLINA; MOLINA, 2004). The emission of these pollutants has origins already known as the burning of fossil fuels coming from non-modernized transport and industrial chimneys, which in turn are representatives of essential urban activities, whether the work or their daily transport.

Although the relationship between environmental effects and population growth is already a concept that justifies the increased concentration of pollutants in urban centers, populations do not stop growing. In a United Nations

[18] report on estimates for the urban world, the urban population will increase from 4.22 to 6.68 billion by 2050, more than $\frac{2}{3}$ of the projected population for the year. However, according to [12], based on UN Reports, they argue that even with a large population concentration, it is still possible to build sustainable cities by following 3 criteria:

- Appropriate plans for air quality management that include the establishment of adequate monitoring capabilities for the supervision of environmental quality and health status of populations;
- Adequate access to clean technologies, including the provision of a training and development of international information networks;
- Improved data collection and assistance so that national and international decisions can be based on sound information.

Thus, air quality monitoring plays a key role in the sustainability of cities. The city of São Paulo besides [12] report, was already cited in reports by the UN and the World Health Organization (WHO); due to its importance as a Megacity and since 1985, the State of São Paulo issues reports on air quality based on WHO guidelines. The Environmental Company of the State of São Paulo (CETESB) is responsible for the publication of data and reports, which presents some of its methodologies, of which served as reference for the Technical Guide for Monitoring and Evaluation of Air Quality of the Ministry of Environment, and publishes them each year in its Air Quality report [4].

3.3   Low-Cost Sensors for Air Quality Monitoring

Low-cost sensors have become popular with the promotion of advances in electronics and electrical engineering. From the advances in microfabrication techniques and the development of MEMS, it was possible a strong presence of these sensors in applications using WSN and Internet of Things (IoT) due to its easy acquisition and advances in computing, which promoted a user-friendly data visualization [17]. As an example, these sensors can be used in different segments of Air Quality management, such as deploying sensors in order to complete a monitoring network, expand data that can be used by the community, monitor compliance by pollution sources, and monitor personal emissions.

Also, according to [17], the measurement principle used in these devices can be divided into two: sensors that interact with the sensing material by means of reactions, and sensors that perform their measurements by measuring the absorption of visible light. As for its hardware composition, as seen in Fig. 2, the sensor can be comprised of a sensor element, responsible for detection; a transducer, capable of transforming the responses into electrical signals; data storage or connection with a communication device (radio transmitter); and a power source (battery, power supply by wire, or photovoltaic panels). For [13] and [17], these devices fulfill a paradigm-shifting role in air quality monitoring because of their usefulness for monitoring by communities and researchers. For [17], as citizens are exposed to more information about air quality, it is possible to familiarize them with the topic and then develop strategies to reduce air pollution based on community decisions.

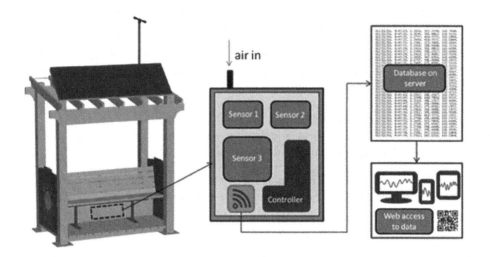

Fig. 2. New monitoring models based on WSN [17]

3.4   State of the Art of Implementations in Use

For the analysis and air quality, first we need to understand which materials can be harmful to human health, according to The NATIONAL COUNCIL OF THE ENVIRONMENT - CONAMA, in the form of RESOLUTION No. 491, OF NOVEMBER 19, 2018, the following materials, from specific and individual concentrations, determined in the resolution, can generate health risks: Particulate Matter - MP10, Particulate Matter - MP2.5, Sulfur Dioxide - SO2, Nitrogen Dioxide - NO2, Ozone - O3 and Carbon Monoxide - CO. However, it is good to make it clear that it is not necessary, in cases of studies that aim to determine their analysis from the standpoint of a specific pollutant, that this analysis be extended to the others, as we can see in [11], which focuses its study on PM2.5.

Moreover, as exposed in [8], a complete understanding of the dynamics and meteorological parameters in the planetary boundary layer is necessary, since this is the medium of propagation, over long distances, of the pollutants present in the air. One of the factors that can influence the fidelity of the data collected through the analysis and monitoring of air quality is the dispersion of pollutants, according to [5] the dispersion is influenced directly by the turbulence found in the planetary boundary layer, but with the natural randomness of turbulence, this cannot be determined precisely, except an approximation through statistical methods, which will result in the impossibility of having a monitoring method that accurately portrays reality, since there will always be a minimum value of dispersion that cannot be eliminated.

With the popularization of means that allow the democratization of the analysis and air quality, this has been gaining space, a fact that increasingly encourages the development of new methods for this purpose, consequently improving the measurements, from the reduction of distortions caused by interference, since such new methods seek an advance in the state of the art.

3.5   The Recife's Context and Structure on Air Quality Monitoring

According to data from the Brazilian Institute of Geography and Statistics [7], the Metropolitan Region of Recife, present in the State of Pernambuco, has an estimated population of over 4 million inhabitants, being the 6th most populous in Brazil. Given the large population of the RMR, public transportation is of fundamental importance for locomotion in the urban region, highlighting the Recife Metro, which connects important points of the city, transporting about 400,000 passengers per day, according to the Brazilian Company of Urban Trains (CBTU, 2022) [1].

According to [11], the Metropolitan Region of Recife (RMR) presents air quality problems related to the emissions of pollutant gases from land vehicles, thus requiring the adoption of policies aimed at improving air quality. If not properly treated, these problems can lead to serious health risks for the inhabitants of the metropolis.

The monitoring and adoption of policies to control the emission of pollutants in the São Paulo Metropolitan Region, as verified by [3], resulted in a tendency to reduce the concentration of pollutants in the atmosphere, with the Vehicle Emission Control Program being responsible for reducing about 90.

Thus, following the guidelines as to the objectives of the Technical Guide for Monitoring and Evaluation of Air Quality, the monitoring in strategic regions of the Recife Metro will bring an unprecedented survey of the air quality in population concentrations, allowing an evaluation of the impacts of emissions, due to the proximity between the railroads and these spaces, thus being an essential landmark as a case study for the development of air quality monitoring networks, since it is a large urban center that is not yet listed in the Air Quality Platform of IEMA [9] or other databases. Furthermore, a study of emissions from combustion vehicles can contribute to solutions and a monitoring of the means of transportation for the cities, as well as evaluate the pollution from the traffic routes and the impact on the environment of the terminals of the Integrated Structural System (SEI), the current bus transportation system in the city of Recife. This contributes to sustainable decision making and technological innovation by organizations that use the data.

The RailBee® Telemetric System was chosen as a site study due to its current structure already installed on the South Line of the Recife Subway. This line is a key strategic location for the reading of data on pollutants emitted in Recife, since it passes through points of high population density, large circulation of motor vehicles, and transition zones between road and subway transport. In addition, it is the line that circulates more people in the city of Recife, counting with 12 stations, where these stations are located among the municipalities with the highest population concentration.

4   Results

4.1   Most Indicated Variables to Be Considered

The Recife Metro is an important tool in the urban life of the Metropolitan Region of Recife, connecting important points of the city, from the center of Recife to 3 neighboring municipalities, while the RMR is composed of 15 municipalities in the State of Pernambuco, with an estimated population of over 4 million inhabitants [15]. Following the guidelines as to the objectives of the Guide, the monitoring in strategic regions of the Recife Metro will bring a survey on Recife's air quality in population concentrations, allowing an evaluation and comparison with the variation in the emission matrix of pollutants, such as peak hours, holidays, vehicle fleets and etc. This contributes to sustainable decision making, allied to technological innovation, by the organizations that will use the data.

The parameters used are being chosen due to their concentrated presence in urban environments, which will enable the study in urban transition environments, from an external environment with a high concentration of pollutants from the burning of fossil fuels, to the routes between passenger stations, an environment without burning fuels. Currently, the project is studying four pollutants to be detected: Carbonic Gas (CO_2), Carbon Monoxide (CO) and Nitrogen Dioxide (NO_2), and Particulate Matter up to $2.5\,\mu m$ (PM2.5).

Although carbon dioxide is essential for the most varied activities of living beings, such as breathing, its high concentration in the atmosphere, enhanced by human action, makes it one of the main atmospheric pollutants and participant gases in the Greenhouse Effect. This pollutant has a difficult detection and a high life span in the atmosphere, and because of this, this gas can move between hemispheres or even globally, causing impacts on a much larger scale than other urban pollutants. According to the WHO, carbon dioxide, because of its nature, is not found in concentrations much higher than the environment, and it is possible to detect large differences in environments that have one source emitting large amounts. This makes it possible to evaluate how much carbon dioxide needs to be reduced near the stations. In addition, processes such as burning of fossil fuels, wildfires, and deforestation are related to the release of carbon dioxide, so with CO2 monitoring it is also possible to monitor possible outbreaks of such phenomena.

Carbon monoxide is one of the pollutants released in the incomplete combustion of coal-based fuels. This pollutant is invisible to the human senses, but its effects are serious to health, and can even cause poisoning when exposed to high concentrations [22]. Based on a region close to sources such as cars and other vehicles, it will be possible to understand the concentrations in real time based on the dynamics of the city throughout the day, which will contribute to measures aimed at reducing the emission of the pollutant.

NO2 - Nitrogen Dioxide, like the other two pollutants, is formed from combustion, however, in 2005 the WHO already warned about the danger of this specific pollutant. Nitrogen Dioxide is one of the primary pollutants responsible for the formation of harmful pollutants, such as tropospheric ozone. Besides its role in forming other pollutants, it can also lead to other environmental impacts, such as photochemical smog. Based on the alert issued by the WHO in 2005 and the CONAMA resolution issued in 2018, by monitoring the Nitrogen Dioxide levels it will be possible to observe what measures have been taken to reduce its emission and contribute to new standards to be proposed. Particulate Matter or PM can be classified into two categories:

- PM10 are particles with size between 2.5 and 10 μm usually found in industrial regions, which require specific analysis and escape the focus addressed in the present work.
- PM2.5 are particles up to 2.5 μm in size found in urban regions, which is the region of interest in this work.

PM2.5 is present in some types of aerosols and emitted when organic materials and fossil fuels are burned. Because of its microscopic size, when present in the atmosphere it can easily be responsible for cases of respiratory and cardiovascular diseases, being a relevant pollutant in determining the air quality.

According to [16], particulate matter up to 2.5 μm is considered the main pollutant in European and Asian countries that perform monitoring, but in Brazil, besides monitoring being limited to only 10 states plus the Federal District, PM2.5 monitoring is only performed in 5 of them and all with considerable parcels of insufficient monitoring [9], thus PM2.5 is generally not considered in the calculation of the air quality index, resulting in a falsely favorable index due to the lack of one of the most relevant pollutants.

4.2   Model for an Air Quality Monitor Device

Based on the visualization needs at different urban points, 3 essential collection points are characterized: mobile points, fixed points for monitoring large concentrations of pollutants (background concentrations) and fixed points for monitoring large movements of people. For this, a monitoring device must have in its structure, the possibility of modularization that adapts it to such collection points.

The proposed model plans to integrate air pollution sensors to the RailBee® Telemetric System, so that downtown and peripheral regions are monitored in real time. There is an urgent need for real-time monitoring, both for alerts and immediate decision making for the gases that pose the greatest risk to human health, and so that the data can be used and analyzed at any time, without the dependence on waiting for the data to be released every certain time interval.

The proposed module has in its composition a set of sensors for pollutant gases, where each module has the ability to monitor up to 4 types of pollutants, being under study the following gases: Carbon Dioxide (CO_2), Nitrogen Dioxide

(NO2), Carbon Monoxide (CO) and Particulate Matter 2.5; furthermore, its communication is given by a sensor network in star mesh, so the communication can be done continuously, even if one of the sensors falls and for this a ZigBee network is used (IEEE 802. 15.4), this is a basic structure for the construction of the Air Quality Monitoring Modules, this means that more sensors can be inserted or removed, depending on the choice of the object under study, so, as an example, sensors of other pollutants can be added, as well as the addition of GPS, accelerometer, pressure sensors, humidity and wind.

These sensors will be implemented in the RailBee® Telemetric System, installed in the Mobile Stations, where it is possible to use the device portably throughout the city, an installation in the Routing Station gives access to fixed points in the city, where pollutants near housing areas can be visualized, and the capture of background concentration pollutants, by being able to install in higher locations where these gases can circulate and analyze their effects considering climatic factors, and by installing at Base Stations, the pollutants circulating in areas where there is foot traffic are analyzed and data capture at combustion vehicle stations, as Base Stations are located between train and bus stations, location. Thus, a facility configuration like this will offer a strategic position and monitored at the Operational Control Center (CCO) of CBTU-Recife through management software, storage, processing and real-time display of data, which may in the future generate specific reports, which will be essential for an adequate and standardized monitoring following the norms of the Technical Guide for Monitoring and Evaluation of Air Quality or other international standards for monitoring.

For the local context of Recife, following the guidelines of the Guide, it was analyzed the viability through this model the disposal of reports of the impacts of the concentration of pollutants on vulnerable populations, the levels of background concentration or other impacts on the environment, being made the availability of these data for CBTU-Recife, in its sustainable management or any other environmental agency. It is also possible to analyze impacts of emissions near population dwellings, due to the proximity between the tracks and these study spaces. It is also feasible to study the emission of pollutants by means of transportation on tires, using the strategic position. A study of emissions from combustion vehicles can contribute to solutions and a monitoring of the means of transport for the cities, as well as evaluating the impact on the integration environment of the bus terminals, and also evaluating and monitoring the pollution coming from the transit roads, since stations like the Tancredo Neves Bus Station, present on the South Line, is at a distance from the carriageway of only 60 m, approximately (see Fig. 3). As such modules can be arranged at different points on the permanent way by the RailBee® System, depending only on the object of study targeted for supervision and monitoring.

Other collection points are spread around the city that already have the stations of the RailBee® System, one of them is the Central Station of Recife, located in the center of the city and located at a point where there is a large circulation of people, as well as being close to poor communities in the Metropoli-

Fig. 3. Tancredo Neves Train Station next to the Tancredo Neves Bus Station and the avenue of great flow near the stations

tan Region of Recife (see Fig. 4), where through mobile and fixed points, it is possible to understand the pollutants of the social study object and the urban pollutants study object.

Therefore, the feasibility of a conscious planning and management of environmental footprints in the RMR is concluded, using the criteria recommended by the UN [21] through the monitoring network. Based on these recommendations, the Air Quality Monitoring Module will be able to monitor the main emission sources in urban space and will contribute to a good planning of urban spaces, which consequently will reduce the environmental impacts caused by air pollution, as well as reduce ecological footprints, a fundamental and urgent step to improve the quality of life in cities [12,21].

4.3   Methodology for Implementation

According to the Technical Guide for Air Quality Monitoring and Assessment, some factors should be taken into account when planning the implementation of air quality monitoring in urban regions, such as, for example, location of the monitoring stations, collection height, ground cover around the station and proximity to obstacles. For the measurement of pollution emitted by mobile sources, the distance from roads with high traffic is of particular importance, since the vehicles that are the source of the emission are in circulation and also emit pollutants in the residential area. For continuous monitors, in order

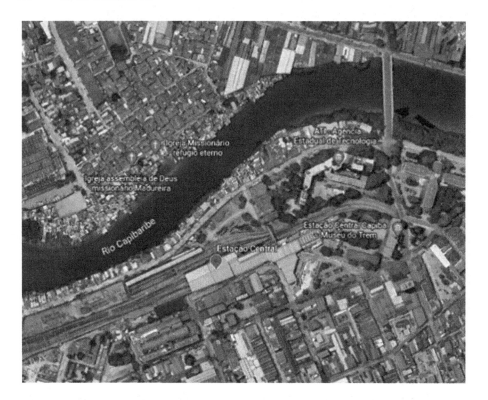

Fig. 4. Recife Central Station near the city center and housing communities

to ensure continuous generation and representation of the monitoring data, the collection of consecutive hourly averages is recommended.

For regions where the focus of the study is the analysis of air pollutants near communities for the study of general effects to the population and for observation of high concentration monitoring objects, according to the Guide, it is appropriate to use a neighborhood or urban scale, thus the distance between the monitoring station and traffic routes should vary between 15 and 140 m for when pollutants are observed on a neighborhood scale and between 80 and 140 when pollutants are observed on an urban scale.

Therefore, for the construction of the Monitoring Modules, the approximate radius of detection of the sensors is taken into consideration, which is on average close to 20 m. For the data collection methodology, in cases of studies on general effects on the population it is important to monitor by hourly averages, since this can contribute to the understanding of emissions along the hours of greatest peak urban activity, the same procedure is understood for the analysis of mobile sources. These data can also be separated and used simultaneously hourly averages for the cases presented and daily averages for the study of city background pollution, as these present more subtle changes and vary according to periods of the year, together the data can also be presented in monthly averages and in this way a macro view can be presented of the dynamics of urban pollutants throughout the year.

5 Discussion

The research presented brings as its results a methodology and development of monitoring networks for air quality in environments where these are currently non-existent. Through the review of the current rules and regulations for monitoring in Brazil, as well as evaluating which recommendations would be appropriate for the contexts found, being the 3 essential collection points: mobile points, fixed points for monitoring of large concentrations of pollutants (background concentrations) and fixed points for monitoring of large circulation of people. Through this the proposed device construction model comprises wide-range techniques see the necessity of using low-cost sensors for urban pollutants that can work in wireless sensor networks and the availability of data in real time, thus outlining the plan for the Recife site of study, where the necessary means and materials are presented, as well as the importance and how these methods can evaluate urban pollutants in order to collaborate with the urban dynamics and for the management of the city.

The importance of the study in gathering theoretical and technical information about air quality monitoring and in presenting a plan for the construction of a monitoring network, even in areas of null development in the sector through an adjustable device for the case studies, is believed. In this way, space is opened for the evaluation of this model when compared to other development and monitoring methods, since the approach presented in the model uses strategies focused on a local or urban scope, still without the knowledge of the functionality of this application in different quantitative contexts for the effective use of data for air quality assessment purposes.

References

1. CBTU homepage (2022). https://www.cbtu.gov.br
2. Borrego, C., et al.: Challenges for a new air quality directive: the role of monitoring and modelling techniques. Urban Clim. **14**, 328–341 (2015)
3. Carvalho, V.S.B., et al.: Air quality status and trends over the metropolitan area of São Paulo, Brazil as a result of emission control policies. Environ. Sci. Policy **47**, 68–79 (2015)
4. CETESB: Qualidade do ar no estado de São paulo 2019 (2020)
5. Chang, J.C., Hanna, S.R.: Air quality model performance evaluation. Meteorol. Atmos. Phys. **87**(1), 167–196 (2004)
6. CONAMA, Diário Oficial [da] República Federativa do Brasil: Resolução conama no 491, de 19 de novembro de 2018. dis-põe sobre qualidade do ar (2018). https://www.in.gov.br/web/guest/materia/-/asset_publisher/Kujrw0TZC2Mb/content/id/51058895/do1-2018-11-21-resolucao-n-491-de-19-de-novembro-de-2018-51058603
7. IBGE: Ibge population estimations (2022). https://www.ibge.gov.br/estatisticas

8. Jayamurugan, R., Kumaravel, B., Palanivelraja, S., Chockalingam, M.P.: Influence of temperature, relative humidity and seasonal variability on ambient air quality in a coastal urban area. Int. J. Atmos. Sci. **2013**, 264046 (2013). https://doi.org/10.1155/2013/264046

9. Instituto de Energia e Meio Ambiente: Plataforma da qualidade do ar (2021). https://energiaeambiente.org.br/qualidadedoar

10. Ministry of Environment - Ministério do Meio Ambiente: Technical guide for air quality monitoring and assessment (2019). https://www.gov.br/mma/pt-br/centrais-de-conteudo/mma-guia-tecnico-qualidade-do-ar-pdf

11. de Miranda, R.M., de Fatima Andrade, M., Fornaro, A., Astolfo, R., de Andre, P.A., Saldiva, P.: Urban air pollution: a representative survey of pm2. 5 mass concentrations in six Brazilian cities. Air Qual. Atmos. Health **5**(1), 63–77 (2012)

12. Molina, M.J., Molina, L.T.: Megacities and atmospheric pollution. J. Air Waste Manag. Assoc. **54**(6), 644–680 (2004)

13. Morawska, L., et al.: Applications of low-cost sensing technologies for air quality monitoring and exposure assessment: how far have they gone? Environ. Int. **116**, 286–299 (2018)

14. Pereira, S.X., de Araújo, R.C.C.: Desenvolvimento de módulos das Estações móveis para Aplicação ao Sistema Telemétrico RailBee. In: Engenharia Elétrica e de Computação: Atividades Relacionadas com o Setor Científico e Tecnológico 3, pp. 49–62. Atena Editora, October 2020. https://doi.org/10.22533/at.ed.6032006105

15. Governo Do Estado De Pernambuco: Região metropolitana do recife (2022). https://www.pdui-rmr.pe.gov.br/RMR

16. Siciliano, B., Dantas, G., Silva, C.M.d., Arbilla, G.: The updated Brazilian national air quality standards: a critical review. J. Brazilian Chem. Soc. **31**, 523–535 (2020)

17. Snyder, E.G., et al.: The changing paradigm of air pollution monitoring. Environ. Sci. Technol. **47**(20), 11369–11377 (2013)

18. UN-DESA: World urbanization prospects: the 2018 revision (st/esa/ser.a/420) (2019)

19. Völgyesi, P., Nádas, A., Koutsoukos, X., Lédeczi, Á.: Air quality monitoring with SensorMap. In: 2008 International Conference on Information Processing in Sensor Networks (IPSN 2008), pp. 529–530. IEEE (2008)

20. WAQI: World's air pollution: real-time air quality index (2021). https://waqi.info/

21. WHO: Urban air pollution in megacities of the world (1992)

22. WHO: Who air quality guidelines global update 2005. Report on a working group meeting, Bonn (2005)

Factors that Influence the Perceptions of the Obstacles to Innovation in the Context of a Developing Country, Case of Ecuador

Gustavo Hermosa-Vega[(✉)] [ID], Astrid Aguilar-Vega[ID], Marianela Reina-Cherrez[ID], and Myriam Moreno-Achig[ID]

Universidad Central del Ecuador UCE, Quito, Ecuador
gghermosa@uce.edu.ec

Abstract. Currently, innovation has become a key factor for the development of a country and for each of the companies that comprise it, and it is essential to mention the individual development of the human beings themselves, who constantly seek to generate changes and adapt to the current context as a requirement of globalization. Nowadays, we can find a large number of goods and services that adapt to our needs in any part of the world without having to move from our home; and despite being a great advantage, this situation is a direct threat to business competitiveness. (Madero and Barboza 2015). This research aims to analyze the factors that influence the perception of obstacles to innovation, why some companies perceive more, or fewer obstacles and which sectors of economic activity have more difficulties in innovating.

The research findings reveal the main characteristics that influence the perception of obstacles to innovation as it is; age of the company, business cooperation, size and sector to which the industry belongs.

Keywords: Innovation · Developing · Companies · Probit · Ecuador · Obstacles

1 Introduction

According to the neo-Shumpeterian theory, the analysis of innovation is considered a variable of vital importance at the business level; if a study is carried out over time, it can be considered that, in the 1980s, there was no emphasis on this aspect; but in market and economic efficiency, while, in the neoclassical analysis, the decisions made by companies to invest in research and development are prioritized, taking into account their individual capacities and how these will allow the generation of new products or services for society (Fernández 2015).

Now, companies face great challenges, one of the greatest is the existing competition, according to Armijos, the competition will no longer be really defined according to the size of the company, but according to the speed with which these respond to the business macro environment and adapt to seize opportunities and mitigate threats, but this process will only be possible if it goes hand in hand with adequate public policies that encourage

© The Author(s), under exclusive license to Springer Nature Switzerland AG 2022
T. Guarda et al. (Eds.): ARTIIS 2022, CCIS 1676, pp. 57–71, 2022.
https://doi.org/10.1007/978-3-031-20316-9_5

and allow adequate development for the benefit of society and the defense of equity (Guaipatin and Schwartz 2014).

Despite being a broad and necessary subject of study due to the great economic and development benefits that business innovation implies, there is very little research that analyzes the barriers that hinder business innovation and the existing variations according to size and the limitations that companies face in order to implement an efficient development that generates broad benefits (Hölzl and Janger 2011). Enterprises that excel in innovation face a pressing need to overcome barriers that limit their growth and expansion; among these we can mention the cultural barriers that limit the development of goods or services to be able to cover a specific market segment that demands according to their desires and needs. (Zhao 2006).

This research aims to analyze the business, sectoral and regional factors that influence the perception of barriers to innovation broken down into cost, knowledge and market factors, in the context of a developing country such as Ecuador; In order to evaluate the hypothesis, it can be stated that there are empirical studies that have been developed in countries such as France and Italy that choose some factors mentioned in this study, and this examination is based on the studies by Madeira et al. (2017), Castro et al. (2017) and Hölzl and Janger (2011).

The document is structured as follows: Sect. 2 summarizes the literature on obstacles to innovation, Sect. 2.3 studies the factors that affect the perception of barriers to innovation, Sect. 3 details the data source and models used for econometric estimation, Sect. 4 analyzes the results of the econometric tests and finally Sect. 5 indicates the general conclusions found in the study.

2 Review of the Literature on Barriers to Innovation

2.1 External and Internal Barriers to Innovation

Innovation is crucial to determine business growth and competitiveness (Mohnen and Rosa 2002); The level of innovation varies from one company to another and is determined by several complex factors, which can facilitate and motivate the start of innovation, or generate barriers (D'Este et al. 2012). These barriers can be classified as external when companies acquire external resources or knowledge (Hadjimanolis 1999), according to Hölzl and Janger (2011) these barriers arise when the company interacts with other companies, agents or institutions in the innovation procedure. The internal barriers, associated with difficulties in implementing internal changes in their organizational processes, according to Saatçioglu and Ozmen (2010) and (Hadjimanolis 1999) the main ones are: lack of qualified personnel, lack of R&D, difficulty in controlling the costs of innovation and financing innovation. D'Este et al. (2012) includes lack of funds, high costs of innovation, lack of information about markets, and effective interactions between innovation cooperation partners.

Innovative companies need to face these obstacles, to a greater or lesser degree depending on their environment; however, there are companies that discourage participation in innovation due to certain barriers involved, for this reason it is important to distinguish the different types of innovation barriers for policy formulation and timely action by management, according to Baldwin and Ozmen (2002) the perception of the importance of such barriers show that the greater the participation of the company in R&D and other innovation activities, the greater the importance attributed to impediments to innovation. Certain barriers are not effectively perceived until the companies face them and depending on the degree of innovation, the problem will increase (Galia and Legros 2004).

According to the National Survey of Innovation Activities (NSIA) 2015, the barriers to innovation are grouped into 3 types of factors (Factor costs, knowledge and market), detailed in Table 2. Galia and Legros (2004), explore the factors that explain the perception of obstacles to innovation faced by French manufacturing companies, distinguishing between obstacles to innovation in proposed projects and obstacles in abandoned projects. According to Iammarino et al. (2009), the perception of obstacles to innovation plays a key role in shaping the characteristics of the local technological environment; the factors they analyze are: type of company, location of the company and sectors of economic activity.

2.2 Factors that Hinder Innovation Activities

According to the NSIA (2015), within the cost factors, the following variables are considered: the lack of funds within the company, lack of external financing and the high costs of innovation, the high costs of innovation, research and development activities are considered to be the most important barriers to implement innovation in the company, preventing SMEs from financing activities related to innovation (Larsen and Lewis 2007). Public support through credits has contributed to the increase of R&D in investing companies and others that wish to do so as well; having different sources of financing can exert positive effects on innovation behavior.

In the Knowledge Factor, the following variables are considered: lack of qualified personnel in the company, lack of qualified personnel in the country, lack of information on technology, lack of information on markets, and difficulty in finding cooperation partners. The lack of qualified personnel is related to the condition of the employee when adopting innovation in the company due to the aversion to change (Rora and Nabila 2020), generating internal resistance and endangering the competitiveness of a company. According to Zwick (2002), a high level of employee resistance can be caused by the perceived risk of job loss after the changes generated, which can be mitigated by providing guarantees or compensation to employees. The lack of information on technology and the market is a barrier to the development of innovative corporate processes, the pressure that demanding and sophisticated clients currently exert on companies encourage them to compete and innovate (Amara et al. 2016); however, companies must know their market and adapt to its current demands (Madeira et al. 2017). Establishing contact with internal or external partners has an important influence on the innovative capacity of companies to generate greater probabilities of introducing new products in the market (Fukugawa 2006). Innovation cooperation with other companies can improve shock absorption capacity and benefit from additional resources for R&D; but the difficulty to find cooperative partners for innovation is a major barrier; however, there are companies that successfully innovate without resorting to cooperation partners, which shows that innovation strategies based on their capabilities are more significant (Freel and Harrison 2011).

Finally, the market factor according to NSIA (2015) considers as elements: the dominant markets for established companies and the uncertainty for the demand for goods and services. The links between innovation and market dominance are more complex and multifaceted than cross-sectional studies typically convey (Cohen 2010) and economists have put forward a number of theoretical arguments giving different and contradictory results about the effects of market structure on the innovation; Some economists support Schumpeter who mentions that companies in concentrated markets have a stronger incentive to invest in innovation because they seek to prevent other competitors from entering. Porter (1980) mentions that the active pressure of rivals stimulates innovation due to the fear of being left behind and the incentive to capture a greater market share.

2.3 Factors that Affect the Perception of Obstacles to Innovation

Firm-level characteristics play a crucial role in shaping innovation activity across technology areas and industries (Archibugi et al. 2013). In this study, the following characteristics are considered: size of the company, regional factors, sectors of economic activity, export status, how old the company is, state of internationalization of the firms, business cooperation and type of innovative company. Regarding the size of the company, according to Hadjimanolis (1999), small and medium-sized companies, even in industrialized countries, face more barriers to innovation than large ones due to the lack of internal resources, experience, technological infrastructure and inadequate policy; SMEs in particular tend to use networking to overcome these barriers; The Schumpeterian hypothesis establishes that large companies are in a better position to be innovative by taking advantage of market imperfections and can distribute the costs of innovation in the production units (Castro et al. 2017).

In relation to regional factors, location plays an important role. The grouping of certain regions can help companies improve their specific advantages as mentioned by Suarez and Rama. The support in carrying out subcontracting processes, and the specialization of certain regions allows companies to save resources that can later be channeled into R&D. Depending on the sectors of economic activity, according to the OECD (2018), companies are classified as follows: depending on their activity; depending on the sectors of high, medium, or low technological intensity, the capacity for innovation does not depend only on the company per se, but also depends on the characteristics of the sector in which it operates; market needs and other external factors. For Madeira et al (2017), industrial companies perceive cost obstacles and lack of financing to a greater degree and, according to Segarra et al. (2017), manufacturing companies tend to be more sensitive to access to financing.

Regarding export status, according to Hölzl and Janger (2011), exporting firms perceive higher barriers to innovation than non-exporting firms, indicating that international markets face severer innovation competition. Latin American exporters are less likely to abandon R&D projects during a crisis (Castro, and others 2017). In relation to the age of the companies, younger companies tend to seek new investment opportunities and innovations, and challenging existing corporations (Archibugi et al. 2013). However, these companies tend to perceive more financial barriers (Segarra et al. 2017).

Regarding the state of internationalization of firms, for Iammarino et al. (2009), multinational companies have high levels of accumulated competition, which makes them more intensive in research. Being part of a multinational group reduces the perception of barriers associated with the lack of technological and market knowledge (Hölzl and Janger 2011), while companies that are part of a business group (national or foreign) perceive lower barriers to innovation related to costs, financing, and market (Fuentes et al. 2018). The Schumpeterian approach emphasizes the bidirectional relationship between multinational expansion and innovation. Business cooperation to innovate with other companies and with institutions allows them to benefit from additional resources that can be allocated to R&D (Castro et al. 2017); Ahuja (2000) mentions that cooperation activities with other companies are opportunities to access complementary technological resources that can contribute to the faster development of innovations, better access to the market, economies of scale and scope, shared costs, and distribution of risks.

3 Methodology

3.1 Design and Sample

This research uses data from the National Survey of Innovation Activities for the period 2012–2014 (NSIA), which contains information on 6,275 companies in Ecuador. Of these companies, 43.26% have perceived obstacles to innovation linked to factors: costs, knowledge and/or market. These factors are classified into 10 variables; companies value these variables as an obstacle according to their importance on a scale of high, medium, low, and not experienced. From this scale, a dichotomous variable is constructed for each obstacle based on the work of Holzl and Jünger (2011), the variable takes the value of one if the company considers the importance of the obstacle as high or medium and the value of zero for low or non-experienced.

3.2 Procedure

To analyze the problem, dichotomous variables were created for each obstacle to innovation activities and the model was run with the independent variables of interest that hinder innovation activities included in the factors: company characteristics (company size, age of the company, nationality, business cooperation, exporting companies, types of innovative companies), sectors of economic activity (Extended Classification of Economic Activities "ISIC") and region (provinces of Ecuador).

In the methodology applied in the study, probit models were used. Each of the factors that are perceived as obstacles to innovation constitute the dependent variables and the independent ones are expressed in the following variables: characteristics of the company, sectors of economic activity and region (provinces), the model expressed as follows:

Barriers = (Company Size, age, Domestic Company, Foreign Company, Export, Cooperate, Innovator, Sector, act, econ, Regions (Provinces)).

4 Results

In the Ecuadorian context, a descriptive review of relevant data is carried out regarding the barriers to innovation according to ENAI (2015), in relation to the importance of the factors to innovation, the following factors are (Table 1):

Table 1. Obstacles to innovation

	FACTOR	High	Medium	Low	n/a.
Costs	Lack of funds	20,85%	24,49%	13,41%	41,25%
	Lack of financing	16,57%	14,66%	13,24%	55,32%
	High Innovation Costs	29,69%	21,58%	11,71%	37,02%
Knowledge	Lack of qualified personnel	10,79%	24,05%	19,67%	45,49%
	Lack of qualified personnel in the country	8,77%	16,94%	19,48%	54,81%
	Lack of information about technology	11,16%	23,09%	19,48%	46,26%
	Lack of information on the markets	10,09%	21,84%	19,19%	48,88%
	Difficulty finding cooperation partners for innovation	12,27%	12,41%	11,27%	64,05%
Market	Market dominated by companies	18,90%	22,21%	14,14%	44,75%
	Uncertainty in the demand for goods and services	18,01%	24,60%	15,06%	42,32%

n/a (not applicable).

The factor that most hinders innovation activities for Ecuadorian companies is the cost factor, 67.11% consider it high. Within this factor, companies consider the high costs of innovation to be the most important: 29.69%. In the knowledge factor, the difficulty in finding cooperation partners is considered to have a high impact at 12.27%; the lack of qualified personnel, 10.79%; and in the market factor, 18.90% of companies consider that a market dominated by companies has a high impact on innovation.

Subsequent, the probit regression models are applied to the cost, knowledge, and market factors, perceived as obstacles to innovation.

V1 (Lack of funds), V2 (lack of financing), V3 (high costs), V4 (lack of company qualified personnel), V5 (lack of qualified country personnel), V6 (lack of technological infrastructure), V7 (lack of market infrastructure), V8 (partner cooperation), V9 (market dominating companies), V10 (demand uncertainty). D1 (Small business), D2 (Big company), D3 (company age), D4 (Domestic company), D5 (foreign company), D6 (Business cooperation), D7 (Cooperation institutions), D8 (Cooperation companies institutions), D9 (Exporter), D10 (non-innovative investor), D11 (Non-investor innovator), D12 (Manufacturers_BIT), D13 (Manufacturing_MBIT), D14 (Manufacturers_MAIT), D15 (Manufacturers_AIT), D16 (Knowledge intensive service), D17 (Service provider), D18 (extractive sector), D19 (Building), D20 (Azuay), D21 (Bolívar), D22 (Cañar), D23 (Carchi), D24 (Cotopaxi), D25 (Chimborazo), D26 (Oro), D27 (Esmeraldas), D28

Table 2. Results of applied models for cost, knowledge, and market factors

	Independent variables									
	V1	V2	V3	V4	V5	V6	V7	V8	V9	V10
D1	.12287531	.15333061	.20662065*	-.12691057	-.10427345	-.07558789	.05988586	.02582412	.09085677	.15333061
	(.0906857)	(.0933642)	(.0916537)	(.0899952)	(.095892)	(.0916202)	(.0948091)	(.0980616)	(.0906485)	(.0933642)
D2	.2317211*	-.1978752*	-.05749256	-.290858**	-.16300259	-.09094563	-.04680036	-.02562516	-.08160101	-.1973752*
	(.0930546)	(.0968171)	(.0934196)	(.0923527)	(.0977497)	(.0936973)	(.0969766)	(.1008053)	(.0923516)	(.0968171)
D3	-.0040316*	-.00390273*	-.00137783	-.00114197	-.00403608*	-.00187299	-.00186878	-.00332353	-.00360176*	-.00390273*
	(.0017792)	(.0019312)	(.0017357)	(.0017611)	(.0018672)	(.0017894)	(.0018408)	(.001902)	(.0018201)	(.0019354)
D4	.221778**	-.2011284*	-.07717348	.02519123	-.03055275	-.09386243	-.02918339	-.09883997	.00962748	-.2019284*
	(.0797564)	(.0852275)	(.078505)	(.0806289)	(.0852221)	(.0806492)	(.0821788)	(.0872312)	(.0792651)	(.0122434)
D5	.50006***	.71786***	-.38979***	-.40875***	-.2725479*	-.325874**	-.311162**	-.20242893	-.309919**	-.71786***
	(.1089694)	(.1325065)	(.102812)	(.1158816)	(.1159288)	(.1129222)	(.1130433)	(.1181554)	(.1057494)	(.1325065)
D6	.18481751*	.11841619	.297668***	.399113***	.298633***	.288856***	.359642***	.2617043**	.432123***	.11841619
	(.072796)	(.0780003)	(.0725039)	(.0769004)	(.0808065)	(.0751435)	(.0778468)	(.081694)	(.0745274)	(.0780003)
D7	.24404224	.17550418	.39681713	.67573203*	.32506651	.61921644*	.4285524	.52433285	.1393279	.17550418
	(.2921058)	(.3213549)	(.2976956)	(.3025611)	(.3371296)	(.3047993)	(.3171242)	(.3287473)	(.3228972)	(.3213549)
D8	.335338***	.364519***	.505501***	-.27269538	.511258***	.416724***	.504236***	.485501***	.635354***	.364519***
	(.0913487)	(.0958295)	(.0921551)	(.3006193)	(.098312)	(.094083)	(.0962451)	(.0995657)	(.0922382)	(.0958295)
D9	-.00818663	.09291478	-.04680595	-.04352649	.11512762	-.14954828	-.09559279	-.15745642	-.15443316	.09291478
	(.081462)	(.0862545)	(.0793148)	(.0827207)	(.084728)	(.0832237)	(.0843545)	(.0886217)	(.0806925)	(.0862545)
D10	-.608858***	-.565595***	-.71266***	-.3810657**	-.27576728*	-.433568***	-.452089***	-.3634809**	-.434141***	-.565599***
	(.1140187)	(.1317485)	(.1132998)	(.1199122)	(.124574)	(.1175054)	(.1241347)	(.1258695)	(.1160146)	(.1317485)

(continued)

Table 2. (continued)

	Independent variables									
	V1	V2	V3	V4	V5	V6	V7	V8	V9	V10
D11	-.22314798	-.2762886	-.416788**	-.610884***	-.31441904*	-.15975491	-.03146175	-.21467467	.00924064	-.2762886
	(.136959)	(.1474952)	(.1338111)	(.1548167)	(.1542894)	(.1407574)	(.1400185)	(.1517399)	(.1374739)	(.1474952)
D12	.2878926***	.3270951***	.282003***	.12961344	.1822046*	.11584953	.03445452	.10994213	.2128201**	.3270391***
	(.0714552)	(.074087)	(.0711481)	(.0719836)	(.0748789)	(.0722114)	(.0727683)	(.0766813)	(.0710251)	(.074087)
D13	.23921577*	.12886157	.12815427	.09506802	.19931194	.12880426	.23642112*	.03962612	.02396297	.12886157
	(.1112252)	(.1170404)	(.1121633)	(.1142955)	(.1183897)	(.1138788)	(.1134251)	(.1223558)	(.1132393)	(.1170404)
D14	.23202619*	.3787378***	.14796245	.09813194	.22184599*	.14665467	-.01429334	.102257	.12594921	.3787368***
	(.1038916)	(.1081585)	(.1036968)	(.1069921)	(.1101971)	(.1083278)	(.1088018)	(.1145089)	(.1050417)	(.1081585)
D15	.02799145	-.06041151	.12086642	.07376599	.25354584	.21923397	-.01226871	.37231016	.02077598	-.06041151
	(.2364396)	(.2433639)	(.2248297)	(.2332815)	(.2271993)	(.2265078)	(.238852)	(.23335)	(.2196858)	(.2433639)
D16	-.0004126	-.08332192	.02127765	-.01491386	-.08144702	-.18044557*	-.1402625	.10856629	.07127011	-.08332192
	(.0728779)	(.0782911)	(.0720703)	(.0744771)	(.078461)	(.0750063)	(.0754367)	(.0770514)	(.0719533)	(.0782911)
D17	-.06004318	.27259353	-.30955678	.01361894	.00668854	-.20170327	-.47295724*	-.10249082	-.48537229*	.27259353
	(.2050238)	(.2174221)	(.2021504)	(.1970032)	(.2116091)	(.2041524)	(.2301827)	(.2266996)	(.2061841)	(.2174221)
D18	.62819025**	.47197321*	.64020398*	.18780047	.3251616	.28639801	.1177653	.44590603	.10298736	.47197321*
	(.2404978)	(.2215671)	(.262888)	(.2310642)	(.2319605)	(.2342761)	(.2420753)	(.2323869)	(.2362897)	(.2215671)
D19	.02156517	.15311548	-.10300705	-.07030732	-.07265584	-.022188	-.02396988	.05682796	.10618718	.15311548
	(.1042113)	(.1089222)	(.1057077)	(.1104411)	(.1164888)	(.1079715)	(.1105854)	(.1139043)	(.1043986)	(.1089222)
D20	.15734123	-.0744743	.18938169	.22152125*	.16199669	.2835302**	.18181984	-.18450477	.04303593	-.0744743
	(.1025373)	(.1067089)	(.1023302)	(.1043368)	(.1080091)	(.1032857)	(.1053511)	(.1150679)	(.1029511)	(.1067089)

(continued)

Table 2. (*continued*)

	Independent variables									
	V1	V2	V3	V4	V5	V6	V7	V8	V9	V10
D21	-.21076223	.31889428	-.37757411	-.10296896	-.40337775	.00076692	-.89417658	-.87861051	-.0657921	.31889428
	(.3994917)	(.4029731)	(.385276)	(.3882322)	(.4387728)	(.386923)	(.533792)	(.5076178)	(.381518)	(.4029731)
D22	.31117613	.05838648	-.02088213	-.3030529	-.50856911	-.18512274	-.38431048	-.92353828	-.78468468*	.05838648
	(.310422)	(.3164583)	(.317614)	(.3485055)	(.4127424)	(.3459504)	(.3716143)	(.5117659)	(.3578416)	(.3164583)
D23	-.12706795	-.41716035	-.02921616	.10127788	-.42967307	.34973164	.29814271	-.15346518	.16843677	-.41716035
	(.2634514)	(.2976145)	(.2842613)	(.2687551)	(.3406096)	(.2705381)	(.2720838)	(.2973541)	(.2656258)	(.2976145)
D24	.23699606	.16056455	.31421955*	.43129688**	.29055928*	.5295362***	.26124573	.30681421*	-.05220137	.16056455
	(.1438389)	(.1416722)	(.1462333)	(.1421171)	(.1452614)	(.1430098)	(.1423144)	(.1437392)	(.1403378)	(.1416722)
D25	-.07221612	-.01382934	.04450119	.25840434	.06191975	.46426532**	.10909375	-.10757796	-.06412019	-.01382934
	(.1580478)	(.1610429)	(.160707)	(.1580736)	(.1655394)	(.1582286)	(.1599569)	(.1670084)	(.1575931)	(.1610429)
D26	.175624	.21536881	.4391266**	.2787077	.27484062	.3853988*	-.10439704	-.04986483	-.09404917	.21536881
	(.1643489)	(.1615273)	(.1691726)	(.1647805)	(.1677262)	(.1659121)	(.176425)	(.1742909)	(.1686403)	(.1615273)
D27	.48933601**	.6323248***	.32331083	.35711565*	.08999336	.6611272***	.6304734***	.2224861	.28973414	.6323283***
	(.1855882)	(.1817837)	(.1833557)	(.1779625)	(.1873187)	(.1762714)	(.1765143)	(.18648)	(.1823834)	(.1817837)
D28	-.2969979***	-.405685***	-.26531***	-.20025931*	-.2426236**	-.20226303*	-.2549666**	-.307948***	-.18738803*	-.405685***
	(.0768342)	(.0841796)	(.0755642)	(.0789522)	(.0837721)	(.0797337)	(.0807317)	(.0857522)	(.0758124)	(.0841796)
D29	-.14944019	-.22710954	-.05023331	-.02762813	-.24914457	-.00330128	-.02825758	.0919558	-.03614266	-.22710954
	(.13731839)	(.1479751)	(.1377697)	(.1380563)	(.1547812)	(.1397501)	(.1404508)	(.1425913)	(.1352865)	(.1479751)
D30	.61158996**	-.00777589	.42011292*	.14806125	.25459924	.24588077	.0381491	.08421855	-.16524911	-.00777589
	(.2000029)	(.1959218)	(.2061129)	(.1872095)	(.1973961)	(.1948396)	(.1916515)	(.2028004)	(.19736)	(.1959218)

(*continued*)

Table 2. (continued)

Independent variables

	V1	V2	V3	V4	V5	V6	V7	V8	V9	V10
D31	-.47929276*	-.8132994**	-.4773299*	-.34353515	-.51968095	-.55802482*	-.28265117	-.21378854	-.46429305*	-.8132994**
	(.2277018)	(.2731614)	(.2165316)	(.2258193)	(.2658166)	(.2494803)	(.2279769)	(.229668)	(.2185298)	(.2731614)
D32	-.19980652	-.20492607	-.25272795	-.05153808	-.13064955	-.06334543	-.29575064*	-.31247849*	-.32591118*	-.20492607
	(.1366877)	(.1402331)	(.1343277)	(.1387022)	(.1463879)	(.1396041)	(.1456095)	(.1575573)	(.1370967)	(.1402331)
D33	1.1751559*	.77607101	1.3170398*	11.471.055	.17966324	.68088882	.74268471	1.2147059*	-.19003955	.77607101
	(.5960768)	(.5006616)	(.6070459)	(.606791)	(.6293524)	(.594825)	(.5384426)	(.5738513)	(.6261787)	(.5006616)
D34	.44915071	.46906637	.69055422	.88216519*	.85193889*	.19988381	.94885605*	.36647987	-.41859942	.46906637
	(.403244)	(.3844413)	(.4166495)	(.408798)	(.3906312)	(.3823288)	(.3954984)	(.380528)	(.3955581)	(.3844413)
D35	-.05882871	-.64281086	.04341421	.69420548*	-.32609625	.17811718	.54034541	-.09991636	-.92022225*	-.64281086
	(.3441615)	(.4220483)	(.3422199)	(.3492739)	(.4223701)	(.3506048)	(.3388488)	(.3852784)	(.4219107)	(.4220483)
D36	.01430599	-.00499488	-.0286718	.24473364*	.2021078*	.2248269*	.25241263*	.13206933	.03864088	-.00499488
	(.0983045)	(.1011102)	(.0985102)	(.0985098)	(.1014379)	(.0992126)	(.0990193)	(.1015043)	(.0981241)	(.1011102)
D37	-.01217716	-.53404239	-.0149112	.79026064	.97538907	.75432712	.81485088	.80898906	.49226133	-.53404239
	(.6526922)	(.7386407)	(.620966)	(.6705892)	(.6649747)	(.6794282)	(.6952747)	(.6720057)	(.7051537)	(.7386407)
D38	-	-	-	.22951126	.50419261	-	-	-	.24866782	-
	(omitted)	(omitted)	(omitted)	(.8623336)	(.8216799)	(omitted)	(omitted)	(omitted)	(.9608468)	(omitted)
D39	.03113574	.02877864	.30406725	.15164544	.06456516	.37539006	-.00091849	.24614696	.25980967	.02877864
	(.219199)	(.22116)	(.2233685)	(.2211813)	(.2310469)	(.2183064)	(.2205433)	(.2244131)	(.2180568)	(.22116)

(continued)

Table 2. (continued)

	Independent variables									
	V1	V2	V3	V4	V5	V6	V7	V8	V9	V10
D40	.02747875	.09685608	.02661109	.44016412*	−.06994417	.43411388*	.47019453*	.08980273	.24054238	.09685608
	(.2157763)	(.217958)	(.2185151)	(.2173873)	(.2304186)	(.2164675)	(.2167999)	(.228902)	(.2189263)	(.217958)
D41	−.07193948	−.11727294	−.07780204	−.35941052*	−.35254405	−.13527766	−.34043045	−.28197362	−.4933155**	−.11727294
	(.1654432)	(.1710073)	(.1657358)	(.1777381)	(.1936184)	(.1697434)	(.1787794)	(.1872376)	(.1777396)	(.1710073)
D42	.27719994	−.08423844	.05950347	.56953875	−.00189487	.10743339	−.03955736	.25350922	−.12136696	−.08423844
	(.2897465)	(.3052225)	(.3199275)	(.2943541)	(.328594)	(.3041812)	(.3034912)	(.2876624)	(.3033318)	(.3052225)
_cons	−.15693557	−.506531***	−.2666163*	−.547005***	−.767519***	−.57399***	−.711697***	−.836057***	−.502309***	−.506532***
	(.1174857)	(.1251914)	(.1176786)	(.1208742)	(.1275714)	(.1200127)	(.1251948)	(.1303417)	(.1173352)	(.1251914)
Ob	2713	2713	2713	2715	2715	2713	2713	2713	2715	2713
R	0.0767	0.0842	0.0693	0,0583	0,045	0.0513	0.0537	0.0430	0.0514	0.0848
log	−1.725,14	−1.541,81	−1.749,41	−1.652,84	−1.477,92	−1.653,33	−1.607,05	−1.449,07	−1.744,16	−1.540,73

* $p < 0.05$; ** $p < 0.01$; *** $p < 0$.

(Guayas), D29 (Imbabura), D30 (Loja), D31 (Ríos), D32 (Manabí), D33 (Morona Santiago), D34 (Napo), D35 (Pastaza), D36 (Tungurahua), D37 (Zamora Chinchipe), D38 (Galapagos), D39 (Sucumbíos), D40 (Orellana), D41 (Santo Domingo de los Tsáchilas), D42 (Santa Elena), Ob (Observations), R (pseudo R2), Log pseudolikelihood (log).

Depending on the size of the companies, large companies perceive fewer obstacles to innovation due to lack of funds, lack of financing, lack of qualified personnel and uncertainty in demand; and small-sized companies mostly perceive the high costs of innovation as an obstacle. The age of the company has a negative influence on the perception of lack of funds, lack of financing, lack of qualified personnel in the country and markets dominated by established companies. Younger companies are more likely to perceive obstacles to innovation compared to companies with more years of experience in the market, older companies have opportunities to access financing, with personnel who have managed to accumulate experience in the market. However, it is the younger companies that are more likely to innovate.

Foreign companies perceive fewer obstacles to innovation. On the other hand, domestic companies tend to perceive less the obstacles related to: lack of funds within the company or group, lack of financing from sources outside the company and uncertainty of the demand for innovative goods and services. Companies that are part of a business group have fewer obstacles. Exporting companies are more likely to perceive obstacles to innovation due to lack of financing from foreign sources, lack of qualified personnel in the country, and uncertainty regarding the demand for innovative goods and services. However, the results in the study are not significant. Future research should extend this study. Regarding cooperation, companies that cooperate with other companies (clients and consumers, competitors, suppliers and consultants) are more affected by: lack of funds, high costs for innovation, knowledge factors, difficulty in finding cooperation partners for innovation and markets dominated by established companies. Although cooperation can create a competitive advantage for companies and institutions by participating in cooperation networks, it works as long as selfish behavior is eliminated and trust between partners is fostered.

Finally, companies that cooperate both with companies and with institutions tend to perceive more strongly all the obstacles to innovation related to: costs, knowledge and market. Since these companies cooperate with all possible partners, they will encounter more obstacles, and the more cooperating partners intervene, the more complex innovation becomes.

Investing non-innovative firms and non-investing innovative firms are less likely to perceive obstacles to innovation than R&D innovating firms. By not developing their own R&D, these companies do not experience the high costs that these activities generate. Regarding the sector of economic activity, manufacturing companies with low technological intensity, manufacturers with medium-low technological intensity, manufacturers with medium-high technological intensity and the extractive sectors are more likely to perceive obstacles to their innovation activities related to cost factors. In addition to these factors, manufacturers of low technological intensity and manufacturers of medium-high technological intensity tend to perceive more strongly the obstacle of lack of qualified personnel in the country. The results contrast with the literature reviewed, where companies operating in the manufacturing sector are characterized by having a more technological nature, which leads to demanding economic resources, human resources, and other specific materials. A greater evaluation of the obstacles is more frequent in companies that belong to the most innovative sectors, or in those that have greater adoption of R&D and technology.

Companies that belong to knowledge-intensive services and service providers tend to perceive less the obstacles of lack of market information and markets dominated by other companies compared to non-knowledge-intensive service companies. This is because these companies develop innovations of a non-technological nature that are oriented towards the market, so their innovations do not require significant resources. Regarding the results of the province, the provinces that perceive the most obstacles to innovation associated with lack of funds, high costs of innovation activities, lack of financing, lack of qualified personnel, lack of information on technology, lack of information on markets, difficulties in finding partners for cooperation and uncertainty in demand are the provinces of Azuay, Cotopaxi, Chimborazo, El Oro, Esmeraldas, Loja, Morona Santiago, Napo, Tungurahua, Orellana, taking the province of Pichincha as a reference. On the other hand, the provinces that least perceive these obstacles are the provinces of Guayas, Los Ríos, Manabí, Pastaza and Santo Domingo de los Tsachilas. Talented workers are attracted to regions with a good quality of life. Therefore, many companies in certain geographical areas will perceive greater obstacles to innovation due to a lack of qualified personnel. Provinces with more concentrated industries will tend to have concentrated innovation. This concentration can occur in the following ways: natural resources, scale, transport costs, intensive in R&D, intensive in skilled labor and intensive in scientific knowledge.

5   Conclusions

The factors that influence the perception of barriers to innovation differ depending on the types of barriers of cost, knowledge, and market. Large companies are the ones that perceive the obstacles to innovation the least compared to medium-sized companies, especially the factor that they perceive the least is the lack of qualified personnel linked to theory. Large companies with their experience and know-how in the market tend to know their labor market, which means that they perceive it to a lesser degree. These companies have easier access to credit and capital, which justifies that they perceive these factors less intensely. In relation to small companies, they perceive the high costs of innovation more intensely. In relation to age, it is important to mention that as companies grow old, they perceive fewer obstacles to innovation in relation to lack of funds, financing, lack of qualified personnel, market dominated by established companies and uncertainty, contributing especially to their experience.

Regarding cooperation, this is a factor that allows companies to benefit from additional resources that they can allocate to innovation activities, and, in the case of Ecuadorian companies, it is important to note that companies that cooperate with institutions and other companies, they perceive more obstacles to innovation. Other important considerations are that, in relation to non-innovative investment companies, they perceive the cost, knowledge and market factor to a lesser degree, which is justified by the theory that states that companies that do not participate in innovation processes tend to underestimate their obstacles. In relation to the sector to which a company belongs, the theory repeatedly mentioned that manufacturing companies perceive more obstacles related to the cost factor. In Ecuador, this result is reiterative, but significantly in manufacturers of low technological intensity. The justification is due to the fact that these companies, in order to survive in the market, constantly need to invest in innovation, which entails a demand for greater financing and investment.

Finally, it is important to consider that these analyzes, and contributions are for a developing economy and provide an action guide for possible public policies that can focus their efforts and actions to encourage and develop innovative activity in the country. Future research should consider deepening the study of the barriers to innovation, taking into account current market trends resulting from globalization and the technological change itself that is affecting due to the constant updates and challenges faced by companies in different sectors but that must be taken into account due to their importance in business competitiveness. The limitations of the present study are related to the database (ACTI), a survey that was applied for the last time in 2014 and there is no current data available that allows for an in-depth investigation to obtain relevant information applicable to companies.

References

Ahuja, G.: Collaboration networks, structural holes, and innovation: a longitudinal study. Adm. Sci. Q. **45**(3), 425–455 (2000)

Albis, N.: Determinantes de la innovación y la productividad en las subsidiarias extranjeras y las empresas exportadoras en la industria en Colombia. Revista de Estudios Empresariales **2**(2), 49–73 (2015)

Amara, N., D'Este, P., Landry, R., Doloreux, D.: Impacts of obstacles on innovation patterns in KIBS firms. J. Bus. Res. **69**(10), 4065–4073 (2016)

Archibugi, D., Filippetti, A., Frenz, M.: Economic crisis and innovation: is destruction prevailing over accumulation? Res. Policy **42**(2), 303–314 (2013)

Baldwin, J., Ozmen, O.T.: Impediments to advanced technology adoption for Canadian manufacturers. Res. Policy **31**(1), 1–18 (2002)

Calvo, C., Beltrán, F., Martínez, C.: Ministerio de Economía, Fomento y Turismo. Obstáculos para la innovación en Chile. https://ctci.minciencia.gob.cl/wp-content/uploads/2018/01/Obst%C3%A1culos-para-la-innovaci%C3%B3n.pdf. Accessed 03 June 2022

Castro, L., Adelheid, H., Ruth, R., Luis, M.: Economic crisis and company R&D in Spain: do regional and policy factors matter?. Ind. Innov. **25**(8), 729–751 (2017)

Cohen, W.M.: Fifty years of empirical studies of innovative activity and performance. In: Handbook of the Economics of Innovation, vol. 1 no. 1, pp. 129–213 (2010)

D'Este, P., Iammarino, S., Savona, M., Von Tunzelmann, N.: ¿Qué frena la innovación? Barreras reveladas versus barreras disuasorias. Política de Investigación **41**(2), 482–488 (2012)

Fernández, J.: Economía neo-shumpeteriana, innovación y política tecnológica. Cuadernos de Economía **38**(107), 79–89 (2015)

Freel, M., Harrison, R.: Innovation and cooperation in the small firm sector: evidence from Northern Britain. Reg. Stud. **40**(4), 289–305 (2011)

De Fuentes, C., Santiago, F., Temel, S.: Perception of innovation barriers by successful and unsuccessful innovators in emerging economies. J. Technol. Transf. **45**(4), 1283–1307 (2018). https://doi.org/10.1007/s10961-018-9706-0

Fukugawa, N.: Determining factors in innovation of small firm networks: a case of cross industry groups in Japan. Small Bus. Econ. **27**(1), 181–193 (2006)

Galia, F., Legros, D.: Complementarities between obstacles to innovation: evidence from France. Res. Policy **33**(8), 1185–1199 (2004)

García, F., Avella, C.: Intensidad exportadora y percepción de las barreras a la exportación. Investigaciones Europeas de Dirección y Economía de la Empresa **13**(3), 93–106 (2007)

Guaipatin, C., Schwartz, L.: Escuela Politécnica Nacional. Ecuador, Análisis del Sistema Nacional de Innovación. https://www.epn.edu.ec/wp-content/uploads/2017/03/CTI-MON-Ecu ador-An%C3%A1lisis-del-Sistema-Nacional-de-Innovaci%C3%B3n.pdf. Accessed 03 June 2022

Hadjimanolis, A.: Barriers to innovation for SMEs in a small less developed country (cyprus). Technovation **19**(9), 561–570 (1999)

Hölzl, W., Janger, J.: Barreras a la innovación entre tipos de empresas y países. Österreichisches Institutoutahfür Wirtschaftsforschung **6**(426), 1–29 (2011)

La misma de arriba

Iammarino, S., Sanna Randaccio, F., Savona, M.: The perception of obstacles to innovation. Foreign multinationals and domestic firms in Italy. Revue d'économie Industrielle **4**(125), 75–104 (2009)

Larsen, P., Lewis, A.: How award-winning SMEs manage the barriers to innovation. Creat. Innov. Manag. **16**(2), 142–151 (2007)

Madeira, M., Carvalho, J., Moreira, J., Duarte, F.: Barriers to innovation and the innovative performance of Portuguese firms. J. Bus. **9**(1), 2–22 (2017)

Madero, S., Barboza, G.: Interrelación de la cultura, flexibilidad laboral, alineación estratégica, innovación y rendimiento empresarial. Scielo **60**(4), 735–756 (2015)

Coronado, A., Echeverría, A., Arias, J.: Aproximación a la cooperación en innovación en empresas del programa de asociatividad y desarrollo empresarial sectorial –pades– en Antioquia (Colombia). Revista Facultad Ciencias Económicas **22**(2), 185–205 (2014)

Mohnen, P., Rosa, J.: Barriers to innovation in service industries in Canada. Inst. Syst. Geogr. Innov. **25**(1), 231–250 (2002)

OECD. Manual de Frascati 2015: Guía para la recopilación y presentación de información sobre la investigación y el desarrollo experimenta, pp. 1–147 (2015)

Porter, M.: Competitive Strategy: Techniques for Analyzing A Business, Industry and Competitors. Free Press, New York (1980)

De Propis, L.: How are creative industries weathering the crisis? Camb. J. Reg. Econ. Soc. **6**(1), 23–35 (2013)

Rora, P., Nabila, A.: Barrier in design innovation of fashion business: evidence from indonesian moslem fashion SME. J. Dinamika Manajemen **9**(1), 1–11 (2020)

Saatçioglu, Ö.Y., Ozmen, O.T.: Analyzing the barriers encountered in innovation process through interpretive structural modelling: evidence from Turkey. Yönetim ve Ekonomi **17**(2), 207–225 (2010)

Segarra, A., García, J., Teruel, M.: Financial constraints and the failure of innovation projects. Technol. Forecast. Soc. Change **10**(1016), 2–61 (2017)

Zhao, F.: Technological and organizational innovations: case study of siemens. Int. J. Innov. Learn. **1**(1), 95–109 (2006)

Zwick, T.: Employee resistance against innovations. J. Manpow. **23**(6), 542–552 (2002)

Sustainable and Social Energy on Smart Cities: Systematic Review

Regina Sousa[ID], Diogo Lopes[ID], António Silva[ID], Dalila Durães[(✉)][ID],
Hugo Peixoto[ID], José Machado[ID], and Paulo Novais[ID]

ALGORITMI Research Center, School of Engineering, University of Minho,
Gualtar Campus, 4710-057 Braga, Portugal
`regina.sousa@algoritmi.uminho.pt`, `pg42823@alunos.uminho.pt`,
`{antonio.silva,dalila.duraes}@algoritmi.uminho.pt`,
`{jmac,pjon}@di.uminho.pt`
`https://algoritmi.uminho.pt`

Abstract. Sustainability and social energy are two concepts associated with smart cities. They aim to combat and contain the alarming environmental and socio-economic repercussions that urbanization has been causing on our planet. Smart sustainable cities drive to improve the life quality of citizens while ensuring that they meet the needs of the current and future generations. Sustainability is essential for urban transformation to achieve more resource-efficient, resilient and smart cities. The main objective of sustainable cities is to guide decisions for interventions in the city. Monitoring systems are examples of measures that aspire to ensure greater sustainability and energy efficiency, such as the application of air quality meters or smart water and light meters. Throughout the analysis of the collected data, it's possible to develop alert systems and optimization models considering various metrics based on artificial intelligence. Therefore, allowing users to make better decisions to positively affect the course of actions in their cities and make it possible to apply sustainability and social energy measures. Thus, it is possible to reduce and improve the consumption of natural resources. Industry 5.0 is crucial in the evolution of smart cities. The complementarity role that this industry has been demonstrating is related to the technologies being developed, in which artificial intelligence plays an important role. This industry places its technology at the service of human beings, society and the environment.

Keywords: Sustainability · Social energy · Smart cities · Smart sustainable cities · Energy efficiency · Monitoring systems

1 Introduction

Cities have been transformed into hubs to meet the needs of modern civilizations. Due to this continuous transformation, a great impact on the use of natural

T. Guarda et al. (Eds.): ARTIIS 2022, CCIS 1676, pp. 72–84, 2022.
https://doi.org/10.1007/978-3-031-20316-9_6

resources has been caused by these cities as they seek to provide better conditions for their citizens. Data from the United Nations Department of Economic and Social Affairs, DESAP, predict that around 68% of the world's population will live in urban areas by 2050. This population growth brings countless new challenges for governments beyond the impact on natural resources, such as pollution, displacement problems due to traffic and congestion, high costs of living and security problems [5]. Related to sustainability and the fact that natural resources are not unlimited, there is a huge concern to make cities sustainable, connected and optimized thanks to the influence and evolution that technology has had [8].

The study and development of the concept of smart cities have been a topic of great interest for several years. The first steps were made by focusing on the study of some general aspects. Forced by the fact that cities are constantly evolving, over the years, the scientific community has started to implement different approaches and new technologies to develop more sustainable measures. They are seeking better solutions to improve the life quality of citizens in crowded areas like cities, to make them more efficient and optimize their resources [5]. Today there is a great diversity of methods focused on sustainability estimation. However, the complexity and multidimensionality of these concepts usually become barriers and difficulties [8].

As stated, cities, regardless of their size, are constantly developing in search of solutions that improve life quality and efficiency. These cities are called smart sustainable cities. With the use of information technologies (ICTs), they ensure that they meet the needs of present and future generations concerning economic, environmental and cultural aspects. Industry 5.0 plays an important role in the evolution of information and communication technologies. An increasing number of projects have been launched to create information management systems [5], with a vast potential to contribute to cities' needs, such as systems to improve the energy consumption of schools or houses. Energy efficiency is one of the most relevant issues for the scientific community and society since greater energy consumption will contribute to better global sustainability. It is important to note that buildings, on average, are responsible for 40% of the total energy consumed [2]. However, in all of these developments, it is important to take into account some aspects that are closely related to citizens and their respective environments as smart city models must be useful and evolve alongside their population. These developments must be efficient yet flexible and easy to implement with other existing smart city tools. ICTs play an important role in this, as they are a key element in the infrastructure that provides a city with intelligence and sustainable devices [5].

Environmental sustainability requires the minimization of the human impact activities in the area where they take place. With the population growth, the energy demand is higher as the population demands more comfort. Smart sustainable buildings play an essential role in the future generation of smart cities. The main goal of these buildings is to reduce the impact of energy consumption [2]. Ensuring higher energy efficiencies will contribute to worldwide sustainability.

The area of sustainability is highly diversified and has been witnessing an enormous evolution, since sustainability range from environmental to socio-economic measures. Sustainable socio-economic development depends on, among other factors, the availability and accessibility of natural resources such as energy and water [9]. Water management and energy recovery systems, are examples of sustainable and efficient cost-effective solutions, as they can improve the resource use efficiency, where the waste of water and energy can be minimized, which allows the cities to become more efficient and sustainable. Implementation of sustainable and social energy measures and systems, incorporated with the citizen's help throughout intelligent systems, such as a web application, are key factors for the constant development of smart cities.

Bearing in mind that the goal of a systematic review is to look for the most recent scientific publications to give us an overview of the current state of the art. This helps because we obtain a better perspective on the state of the development of different approaches and technologies related to the theme of sustainability and social energy applied and developed in favour of a Smart City and what has been and is being done in this domain. That said, this research was conducted based on the principles of a systematic review. The following Research Questions have been proposed:

- **RQ1:** What strategies and tools have already been developed and used to implement and integrate sustainable and social energy measures in smart cities?
- **RQ2:** How can sustainability measures improve citizens' lives in a smart city, and how to make them active contributions?

This paper is structured as follows: Sect. 2 describes the methodology carried out to do the research and review process, taking into account its main steps, i.e., the selection of data sources, the search strategy, and the selection criteria and the respective results. Section 3 provides the results obtained throughout the relevant literature search and review described in the previous section. Next, Sect. 4 presents a discussion of the results obtained and the relevant articles and documents are presented. Finally, Sect. 5 summarises and compiles the set of conclusions, lessons learned and contributions obtained through the review. In addition, proposals for future work are presented.

2   Methodology

This review was conducted based on PRISMA[1] (*Preferred Reporting Items for Systematic Reviews and Meta-Analyses*) statement and respective checklist [7]. This choice was mainly due to PRISMA being widely accepted by the scientific community. Therefore, the following steps were taken into consideration:

---

[1] http://www.prisma-statement.org.

1. Identification of the study's research questions and relevant keywords;
2. Creation of the research query;
3. Definition of the eligibility criteria to filter and reduce the articles sample;
4. Analysis of the resultant set of studies and papers;
5. Presentation and discussion of the results.

The preliminary research was conducted on 21 April 2022 and the used data source was SCOPUS[2], due to its size, quality assurance and wide coverage in terms of publication subjects.

To carry out the relevant literature and documentation research, some keywords were defined as a starting point. These keywords were applied in the following fields: title, abstract and keywords. To organize the search resources, the keywords were organized into two groups, which are combined in conjunction. Keywords in each group are combined with disjunctions. This choice fulfils the purpose of each group selecting all documents that include at least one of its keywords and then ensuring that only documents that contain at least one term from each of the groups are selected. The first group is related to the areas and technical subjects directly related to the research topic ("*Social Energy*", "*Sustainable Energy*", "*Smart Cities*", "*Smart Sustainable Cities*" and "*Energy Efficiency*"). The second group aims to filter by broader areas of the technological scope ("*Monitoring Systems*", "*Information Systems*", "*Data Management Systems*" and "*Decision Support Systems*"), in order to focus the results in the context of information systems and agents. Therefore, by applying the strategy described above, the following research query arose:

```
1  ( TITLE-ABS-KEY ( social  AND energy )
2  OR  TITLE-ABS-KEY ( social  AND energy )
3  OR  TITLE-ABS-KEY ( sustainable  AND energy )
4  OR  TITLE-ABS-KEY ( smart  AND cities )
5  OR  TITLE-ABS-KEY ( smart  AND sustainable  AND cities )
6  OR  TITLE-ABS-KEY ( energy  AND efficiency )
7  AND
8  ( TITLE-ABS-KEY ( monitoring  AND systems )
9  OR  TITLE-ABS-KEY ( indicators )
10 OR  TITLE-ABS-KEY ( information  AND systems )
11 OR  TITLE-ABS-KEY ( data  AND management  AND systems )
12 OR  TITLE-ABS-KEY ( decision  AND support  AND systems ) ))
```

To screen the articles and studies collected, some eligibility criteria (in the form of exclusion criteria) were defined. As such, all documents that matched any of the following criteria were excluded:

EC1 : Not accessible in *OPEN ACCESS* mode.
EC2 : Were not produced in the last 3 years or have not yet been fully published.
EC3 : Do not come from the field of *Computer Science* or *Engineering*.

---

[2] https://www.scopus.com.

EC4 : Are not an Article or a Review/Survey
EC5 : Article or a Review/Survey are not written in English.
EC6 : Article or a Review/Survey are not with the accordance with the area of investigation.
EC7 : Were not produced inside the European Union (due to similar policies regarding extraction, manipulation and exploitation of data for the production of knowledge, as well as data protection).
EC8 : Do not focus on the variables studied or are out of context.

3   Results

The initial database resulting from the previously described search returned more than 87 800 documents and the document selection process is summarized in the Fig. 1.

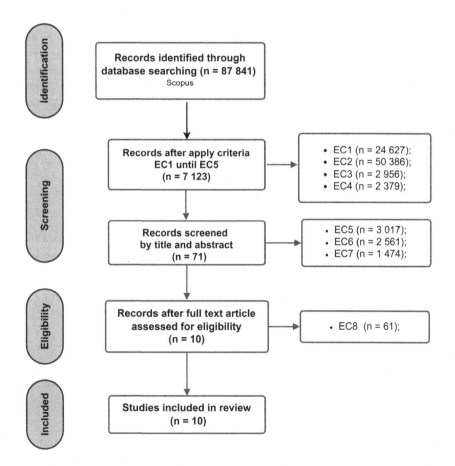

Fig. 1. Adaptation of the PRISMA Flowchart applied in this study.

The first two criteria (EC1 and EC2) were applied using the SCOPUS direct filtering system, resulting in a subset of documents that are freely accessible and written no more than three years ago. Of the obtained 12 828 studies, the third and fourth criteria (EC3 and EC4) were applied. The results were a subset of engineering and computer science documents written in English. In the 7 123 studies, the following three criteria (EC5 to EC7) were applied, again using the SCOPUS direct filtering system, resulting in articles or reviews that are in line and area of investigation and produced in countries inside the European Union. As a result, 71 studies were left for full reading, which resulted in a final set of 10 that were considered relevant and reviewed in detail. The other 61 documents were excluded due to not focusing on sustainability and social energy (EC8).

Considering the final set of suitable studies, Quijano et al. [8] developed a framework with the aim of covering multiple pillars of smart and sustainable cities. Related to the mySMARTLife project, this framework concerned the main pillars of smart and sustainable cities, such as environment and energy. This framework was validated in real case studies implemented in the cities of Nantes, Hamburg and Helsinki. The insights obtained from the evaluation performed, lead to measures to boost the scaleup of the sustainable solutions in the cities.

Hernández et al. [6] benefiting from the use of ICTs, started developing a monitor and control tool. This tool is yet to reach its final version. Making use of artificial intelligence for the automated decision-making process in buildings, they seek to produce optimal comfort measures for their occupants to achieve energy efficiency. The state-of-the-art building control systems are based on simple decision-making processes, which does not help to obtain the most suitable comfort measures and energy efficiency. This tool is being validated in a real case study implemented in a school in Turkey. Nevertheless, being currently under development, the marks obtained so far with their tool show promising results in applying artificial intelligence to buildings. Therefore, the integration of prediction techniques such as those found in the project BRESAER (BREakthrough Solutions for Adaptable Envelopes in building Refurbishment), a building energy management system (BEMS), has shown several advantages in making more efficient use of the energy.

Garcia-Retuerta et al. [5] also benefited from the use of ICTs, and as networks and services are more flexible and effective, they were able to develop a platform to improve the cities operations for the benefit of its citizens. The presented platform has as its main objective analyzing and creating dashboards, to be used in alert systems. Nowadays, cities have data acquisition types of equipment to collect data for their own systems. This information is used to optimise resource consumption. Addressing a gap found, this research team developed this platform with optimization models for the decision-making process, which have proven to be more effective when compared to the systems that don't make use of these models. Their platform is also the cornerstone of smart territory development. To estimate pedestrian traffic, the platform was validated in a real case study implemented in Melbourne (Australia). To sum up, it is important to state that Deepint.net made the creation of an advanced crowd detection dashboard possible through advanced machine learning algorithms.

García-Fuentes et al. [4] implemented a multi-criteria decision methodology based on relevant district sustainability indicators, that allow individuals to make effective decision-making about energy efficiency improvements. This methodology can evaluate the district complexity in terms of the specific features associated (buildings, urban areas, energy systems) providing solutions to implement the best combination of energy efficiency according to buildings' typology, standards and regulations.

CRISTEA et al. [3] conclude that in the current state-of-the-art there is a lack of intelligent transportation platforms/systems. Therefore, began to study and develop a platform that assists in the mobility of citizens. This intelligent mobility assistant is a data platform developed for public authorities, businesses and casual users. The goal is to enhance citizens' level of comfort, safety and environmental awareness. The current state of the application leads to an innovative portable solution, easily deployable and configurable. The key feature of this platform is that it is able to integrate data provided by third-party systems. The prototyped device can be used to determine, store and provide useful notifications through the visualization and management tools that offer.

Ramos et al. [9] study renewable energy sources used in the water sector in order to improve the system's efficiency. Developed a water and energy nexus model, in a real case study, to improve the system's efficiency and sustainability. In terms of social impacts, this study has shown that renewable energy can contribute to better air quality and promote the idea of eco-friendly and more sustainable life in the local communities.

Benavente-Peceset al. [2] study the information and communication technologies, ICTs, their respective techniques, their key characteristics and their contribution in order to obtain higher energy efficiencies in smart buildings. It presents the most suitable and new emerging technologies and their applications in smart buildings. Energy efficiency and the technologies make it possible to increase this improvement in energy efficiency and energy savings. As stated, information and communications technologies play a relevant role. Until now, as a result of the study developed, smart devices such as thermostats, temperature sensors, and light intensity meters have been applied to buildings, demonstrating the ability to provide and obtain better consumption, improving energy savings.

Salom et al. [10] present an evaluation framework which defines key performance indicators to evaluate the energy sustainability of neighbourhoods which are distributed in five categories: energy and power performance, GHG emissions, indoor environmental quality, life cycle costs and social sustainability. The authors conclude that future work is still needed in regard to testing and validating the proposed assessment framework as well as further research regarding the selected performance indicators.

Akande et al. [1] report on an evaluation and raking of 28 European capital cities based on their current state of transition towards fully smart and sustainable cities. The authors were able to conclude that Berlin and the other Nordic capitals lead the ranking. On the other hand, Sofia and Bucharest obtained the lowest scores and therefore concluded that they are not yet on the path to becoming smarter and more sustainable cities. The authors also stated that there is a positive correlation with the cities' GDP per inhabitant, which is an indicator of wealth and its progress in the transition.

Finally, Sánchez et al. [11] proposes a control and monitoring system for irrigation systems based on a new irrigation algorithm that uses rainfall probability data to regulate the irrigation of the installation. This algorithm has the particularity of being complemented by the verification of sending and receiving information in the LoRa network. In this way, it is possible to reduce the loss of information packets.

4   Discussion

This section explores and discusses the findings of the review against the research questions. The Subsect. 4.1 presents different strategies, tools and developments that have already been developed and used to implement and integrate mechanisms and measures of sustainability in smart cities. Next, Subsect. 4.2, is related to how sustainable and social energy measures can improve citizens' lives in a smart city, and how it's possible to make them active contributors.

4.1   Strategies and Tools that Have Already Been Developed and Used to Implement in Smart Cities

The work developed by the scientific community, in terms of strategies and tools, to implement and integrate sustainable and social energy measures in smart cities, is extremely relevant as it serves as a foundation for future developments and experiences. Table 1 presents the articles identified and analysed, those that

Table 1. Strategies and tools implemented for sustainable and social energy measures in smart cities.

Authors(s)/Article	Strategies/Tools
Quijano et al. [8]	Propose an evaluation framework developed with the aim of covering multiple pillars of smart and sustainable cities.
Hernández et al. [6]	Present a monitor and controlling tool to optimize the comfort of the people inside buildings in order to improve its energy efficiency.
Garcia-Retuerta et al. [5]	Introduce a platform that captures, integrates, analyses, and creates dashboards, alert systems, and optimisation models, to make services more flexible, effective, and sustainable.
García-Fuentes et al. [4]	Multi-criteria decision methodology based on relevant district sustainability indicators.
CRISTEA et al. [3]	A smart assistant platform for smart mobility to enhance the level of comfort, safety and environmental awareness of the transportation users

are considered to be the most relevant for the application of sustainability and social energy.

The solution presented by Quijano et al. [8] is a framework that contains more than 150 actions, such as environment and energy, aiming to help in the smart and sustainable transformation of cities. Related to the mySMARTLife project, their framework was validated in real case studies implemented in the cities of Nantes, Hamburg and Helsinki. On energy and the environment, this solution seeks sustainable ways to ensure energy efficiency, implying a reduction in energy consumption, through measures such as smart lighting. The insights obtained, lead to measures to boost the scaleup of the sustainable solutions in the cities.

Following the same principle, the approach proposed by Hernández et al. [6] emerges as a solution for the energy efficiency problem. However, the tool base is a little different. Benefiting from the use of ICTs, started developing a monitor and control tool that uses artificial intelligence for the automated decision-making process to achieve energy efficiency in buildings. Making use of artificial intelligence for the automated decision-making process in buildings has proven to produce optimal comfort measures for their occupants to achieve energy efficiency. In Turkey, as part of the H2020 BREASER project, this tool was validated in a real case study implemented in a school. Through the implementation of fuzzy logic techniques, this system has allowed the best possible management of the energy resources of a school.

The big problem for cities lies in the way in which data can be processed and analysed. With the possibility of complementing the previous approaches, the work presented by Garcia-Retuerta et al. [5] addresses the problem by presenting the deepint.net platform. This platform includes several data analysis algorithms developed through artificial intelligence techniques and aims to collect, integrate, analyse, and create dashboards, alert systems and optimization models. This use case is a clear example of the applicability of an efficient system, implemented through a platform that offers multiple possibilities for managing the collected data and thus making it possible to apply various sustainability measures since we can monitor and manage resource consumption, such as water and electricity in buildings or cities.

To have better platforms for creating and analysing dashboards, and generating alerts, it is necessary to have a good decision system. A comprehensive approach is a key factor for an effective decision-making system aiming for, i.e., energy efficiency improvement. Therefore, the multi-criteria decision system presented by García-Fuentes et al. [4] addresses interventions on a wider scale. The necessity of developing new methodologies to address projects for improving the energy efficiency in buildings has become one of the main concerns in recent years. This proposed approach is based on a set of indicators, ranging from the diagnosis to the final assessment.

To maintain sustainability in urban areas, maintaining population mobility sustainably and securely is another very important factor. The platform presented by CRISTEA et al. [3] consists of a smart assistant platform for smart mobility inside smart cities. Based on a prototype of a portable device, this tool was developed to assist public authorities, business and casual users, in various transportation/mobility scenarios. So, it manages to guarantee greater sustainability in a large city and guarantee a better quality of life for its citizens.

All approaches evidence slightly different strategies but they are all related to the implementation of sustainable and social energy measures in smart cities. In all of them, it's proven that through their application citizens' life quality in crowded areas was improved. These tools also helped in the optimization of resources and costs associated with them.

4.2 Improvement of Citizens' Sustainability and Strategies to Make Citizens Active Contributors

In smart cities, citizens can not only interact and engage with the services provided to make their lives easier and more sustainable in urban centres but also can be active contributors through some of these services. Concerning the strategies to make citizens active contributors, those considered most relevant are presented in Table 2.

Table 2. Strategies and tools implemented to make citizens' active contributors in smart cities.

Authors(s)/Article	Strategies/Tools
Ramos et al. [9]	Presents a water and energy nexus model, in a real case study, to improve the system's efficiency and sustainability
Benavente-Peces [2]	Describes the most suitable and the new emerging technologies and their applications in smart buildings

The work presented by Benavente-Peces [2] concerning the study of information and communication technologies, ICTs, their respective techniques and their contribution in order to obtain higher energy efficiencies in smart buildings also can make citizens contribute to more sustainable measures. The study presented focuses on the evolution of information and communication technologies and the respective role that they have been playing in the development of smart cities, namely in the fact that they can improve the energy performance of buildings by making them into smart sustainable buildings. Energy efficiency is one of the most relevant issues for the entire scientific community and society in general since greater energy efficiencies will contribute to better global sustainability. One way to ensure greater global sustainability in terms of energy consumed by buildings, since these are responsible for about 40% of the total energy consumed, they use renewable energy emerges. This is where the common citizen can come in. Throughout the presented study, various forms of renewable energy are studied, such as solar panels and wind generators, all of which show positive results and undoubtedly contribute to better energy efficiency in buildings. That said, citizens can contribute to the cause of sustainability by using renewable energies.

Another case where the citizens were active contributors was in the water and energy nexus model developed by Ramos et al. [9]. With the help of the population of Mozambique, and once the water system supply of Nampula showed promising potential for energy recovery, a case study was conducted there. With the help of the population and with the application of a pump-as-turbine (PAT), thanks to the development of ICTs, was possible to reduce the system costs and lower the environmental impacts while making it more sustainable and increasing the system's efficiency.

Both approaches evidence improvements in sustainability in cities, through the contribution of their citizens'. In both cases, the authors concluded that is fundamental to make citizens active contributors to obtain better results in the application of sustainable and social energy measures.

5   Conclusion

A Smart City is an environment that uses technology to make networks and services more flexible, effective and sustainable, thus bringing greater benefit to its citizens. Therefore, these cities represent a solution that aims to combat and contain the alarming environmental and socio-economic repercussions. So, to improve the quality of life in these urban centres and preserve natural resources, the involvement of citizens in the mechanisms of transition to smarter cities is indispensable and essential for the implementation of sustainable and social energy measures.

In this paper, a systematic review was conducted to analyse all the relevant literature and documentation related to the fields of sustainability and social energy measures and applications in a smart city. The review was based on the PRISMA model using the SCOPUS database as the source. In total 87 800 studies were identified. After the application of the PRISMA methodology, a set of 71 documents were selected, however, only 10 of those were considered relevant and found within the intended scope and are relevant to answering the previously defined research questions.

From the proposed research questions, the state of the art was assessed regarding the role and purpose of sustainability and social energy in smart cities. The collected studies suggest that sustainability and social energy measures applied to urban centres or cities can combat and contain the alarming environmental and socio-economic repercussions that urbanization has been causing on our planet. Furthermore, using ICT and other means that aim to improve the quality of life and efficiency, are helpful to the development of sustainable measures such as sensors on lampposts to measure air quality, monitoring systems associated with smart water and light meters, to optimize the consumption of this resources, are some examples of developments being carried out and adopted by the scientific, in this case, to reduce the consumption of these natural resources, while ensuring that they meet the main needs of the current and future generations. Energy efficiency is also one of the most relevant issues to ensure a better sustainable world. Knowing that buildings are responsible for a high percentage of the energy consumed in the world, smart buildings have been playing a very important role to make cities more sustainable. Through sensors, technologies and communication standards, techniques and algorithms of artificial intelligence, these buildings seek to reduce the impact of energy consumption. Finally, in most of the analysed case studies, all authors agreed that socio-economic sustainability is a key factor to maintain sustainable and social energy measures in smart cities.

This work was developed as part of a research project whose goal is to study the application of sustainable and social energy measures in smart cities' infrastructure and framework. As such, and given all the compiled information, future work includes the study and development of a platform to integrate all these concepts into a viable and helpful information system that can bring value to the smart city paradigm and the citizens' lives where it is applied.

Acknowledgements. This work has been supported by FCT-Fundação para a Ciência e Tecnologia within the R&D Units Project Scope: UIDB/00319/2020 and the project "Integrated and Innovative Solutions for the well-being of people in complex urban centers" within the Project Scope NORTE-01-0145-FEDER-000086.

References

1. Akande, A., Cabral, P., Gomes, P., Casteleyn, S.: The lisbon ranking for smart sustainable cities in europe. Sustain. Cities Soc. **44**, 475–487 (2019). https://doi.org/10.1016/J.SCS.2018.10.009
2. Benavente-Peces, C.: On the energy efficiency in the next generation of smart buildings-supporting technologies and techniques. Energies **12**, 4399 (2019). https://doi.org/10.3390/en12224399
3. CRISTEA, D.S., et al.: An IoT environmental and motion assistance system for the smart mobility context. Stud. Inf. Control **29**, 433-443 (2020). https://doi.org/10.24846/v29i4y202005
4. García-Fuentes, M.A., García-Pajares, R., Sanz, C., Meiss, A.: Novel design support methodology based on a multi-criteria decision analysis approach for energy efficient district retrofitting projects. Energies **11**, 2368 (2018). https://doi.org/10.3390/en11092368
5. Garcia-Retuerta, D., Chamoso, P., Hernández, G., Guzmán, A.S.R., Yigitcanlar, T., Corchado, J.M.: An efficient management platform for developing smart cities: Solution for real-time and future crowd detection. Electronics **10**, 765 (2021). https://doi.org/10.3390/electronics10070765
6. Hernández, J.L., Sanz, R., Corredera, A., Palomar, R., Lacave, I.: A fuzzy-based building energy management system for energy efficiency. Buildings **8**, 14 (2018). https://doi.org/10.3390/buildings8020014
7. Page, M.J., et al.: The prisma 2020 statement: an updated guideline for reporting systematic reviews. BMJ **372**, (2021). https://doi.org/10.1136/bmj.n71
8. Quijano, A., et al.: Towards sustainable and smart cities: Replicable and KPI-driven evaluation framework. Buildings **12**, 233 (2022). https://doi.org/10.3390/buildings12020233

9. Ramos, H.M., Morillo, J.G., Diaz, J.A.R., Carravetta, A., McNabola, A.: Sustainable water-energy nexus towards developing countries' water sector efficiency. Energies **14**, 3525 (2021). https://doi.org/10.3390/en14123525

10. Salom, J., et al.: An evaluation framework for sustainable plus energy neighbourhoods: Moving beyond the traditional building energy assessment. Energies **14**, 4314 (2021). https://doi.org/10.3390/EN14144314

11. Sánchez-Sutil, F., Cano-Ortega, A.: Smart control and energy efficiency in irrigation systems using LoRaWAN. Sensors **21**, 7041 (2021). https://doi.org/10.3390/S21217041

A Dispersed Park as a Tool for Realizing the Concept of Ecosystem Services

T. A. Churiakova[✉], M. E. Mishsina, and S. A. Mityagin

Saint-Petersburg National Research University of Information Technologies, Mechanics and Optics (ITMO University), 197101 Saint-Petersburg, Russia
churyakovat@itmo.ru

Abstract. This paper about sustainable urban development from an ecological perspective. With increasing urbanization and the degradation of green infrastructure, the concept of ecosystem services helps to assess the services people receive from their interaction with nature. Cultural ecosystem services refer to intangible goods that play an important role in improving quality of life and environmental sustainability. There are major efforts around the world to incorporate ecosystem services and their value into policy, finance, and governance. This paper considers the concept of using dispersed parks as a tool for the implementation of cultural ecosystem services in the existing urban planning context and analyzes its effectiveness. The management system of a dispersed park makes it possible to realize a sustainable UGI facility at the neighborhood scale under current urban planning conditions. The paper contains a representation of the potential dispersed park.

Keywords: Urban green infrastructure · Cultural ecosystem services · Dispersed park · Connected green network

1 Introduction

The United Nations' New Urban Agenda recognizes the importance of public green spaces and nature in cities and the need to safeguard and enhance the ecosystem services they provide [1]. In the conditions of growing urbanization, the issue of development and maintenance of urban green spaces is of particular importance. However, the already existing dense buildings and demarcated lands limit the possibilities for the development of green spaces and often exclude the possibility of creating new green areas. On the other hand, the diversity of social groups represented in the city requires a variety of leisure activities, and urban landscaping, represented mainly by parks, gardens and squares, performs a recreational function, which in conditions of a large anthropogenic load hinders the fulfillment of their original ecological function. The traditional method of urban greening in these conditions is the approaches associated with the formation of green frameworks and the renovation of certain areas of the city for recreational functions. But these approaches do not solve environmental problems in the current dense urban environment. It should be noted that the degradation of urban green infrastructure (UGI) leads to the impossibility of providing ecosystem services, and ecosystem services are a

T. Guarda et al. (Eds.): ARTIIS 2022, CCIS 1676, pp. 85–96, 2022.
https://doi.org/10.1007/978-3-031-20316-9_7

link between man and nature and are of great importance for human well-being, then the protection and sustainable use of ecosystems are a key component of global sustainable development [2].

One of the approaches to solve these problems is the creation of dispersed parks. The paper considers the concept of using dispersed parks as a tool for the implementation of cultural ecosystem services in the existing urban planning context and analyzes its effectiveness. The dispersed park takes as a basis the existing green networks in the city to strengthen the existing connections and to manage the area in the most efficient way. The main purpose of creating dispersed parks is to create opportunities to meet the needs of different population groups in different leisure activities [3]. The management system of a dispersed park includes criteria that are highlighted in cultural ecosystem services according to Millennium ecosystem assessment (MEA) 2005 [4]. This makes it possible to realize a sustainable UGI facility at the neighborhood scale under current urban planning conditions.

This article reviews the literature on assessing the cultural ecosystem services of urban green infrastructure. The study is limited to the existing urban planning context, without considering the creation of new green spaces. Opportunities for implementing cultural ecosystem services (CES) in areas are identified according to the existing classification of urban green spaces. Paragraph 3 describes what dispersed park is and how it can be useful in implementing CES. An illustration of the definition of dispersed parks and their potential is provided in paragraph 3.2 using Saint-Peterburg, Russia as an example.

2 Literature Review

Understanding ecosystem services in megacities undergoing dynamic change is essential to achieving sustainability goals in urban policy and planning [5]. The ecosystem services framework is useful for planning because it provides a general approach to valuation to better understand the impacts of land use and management decisions on a range of stakeholders [6, 7]. Valuation of ecosystem services in certain landscapes includes non-monetary and monetary methods [6, 8]. The functions of the same sites and their inclusion in green infrastructure may vary across different spatial scales [9]. The work uses the following classification of urban green areas [10, 11] (Table 1).

Urban greenery, through its use by and interaction with people, produces vital cultural ecosystem services that can contribute to social and environmental sustainability. However, cultural ecosystem services refer to intangible goods that make them difficult to quantify and monetize, compared to other tangible services [12].

The authors of a review of valuation of cultural ecosystem services [13] found that methods for valuing cultural ecosystem services mainly focused on recreation and ecotourism valuation, which may be due to a lack of clear definitions of other categories. Ambiguous categories such as inspiration or sense of place, which do not have a consistent classification system, are an obstacle to assessing cultural ecosystem services. There is also the difficulty of categorizing cultural ecosystem services, as some services can be classified under more than one category. Therefore [14] suggested that cultural ecosystem services cannot be clearly grouped into a category. Paper [15] wrote if the

Table 1. Classification of urban green areas.

Object	Planning role	Area, ha	Activities	Availability, min
Square	Space for short-term rest and transit	0,1–1	Short breaks, walks, meeting point, pedestrian transit, decoration	2
Local park	The main recreational space of the micro district	1–10	Playground, meeting point, passive rest, sports activities, possible concert venue	5
District park	The main recreational space of the district	10–15	Picnics, pitch, playgrounds, dog walking areas	15
City park	The main recreational space of the city	>15	Public service, walks, passive rest, active rest, certain types of entertainment	15

impacts of land-use changes on ecosystem services are not assessed beforehand, there may be considerable costs involved in the loss or restoration of these services. Due to the lack of space at high population densities, technologies that provide compact municipal services are often more cost-effective than maintaining or restoring extensive natural systems. It is important to find a balance because this risks degradation and loss of urban green infrastructure, resulting in the inability to perform natural functions, which in turn affect other ecosystem services [16]. Paper [17] note that the loss of green infrastructure may lead to a loss of resilience, increasing a city's vulnerability to shocks, such as heat waves, flooding, hurricanes. Further negative impacts are associated with loss of social and cultural values, including loss of sense of place, loss of identity, and reduced social engagement.

New green space planning is often based on simple quantitative standards that record the recommended amount of green space per person [18] or calculating minimum accessibility times from residential buildings. The minimum functional content of recreational areas is also regulated in normative documents. Regulatory documents of the Russian Federation provide for the placement of a variety of public playgrounds in the residential areas of neighborhoods (blocks): playgrounds for children, recreation areas for adults, for sports, for walking dogs [19]. Due to the limited space available, playgrounds infrastructure for citizens with children is implemented in the projected free areas. However, the article [20] demonstrates that children are attracted to parks with particular facilities, and parents/guardians may be willing to travel further if necessary. A better understanding of the features that drive park usage will help inform park planning and design.

Based on all the above, to ensure a high quality of life and to protect urban green infrastructure, urban resources need to be allocated efficiently.

3   Conception of Dispersed Park

The main purpose of creating disperse parks is to create opportunities to meet the needs of different population groups in different types of leisure activities [3]. A dispersed park is a type of local park in which the main functions of a universal park are distributed between small and medium-sized green public spaces (parks and squares) located within walking distance of each other. Since the territories under study are in a dense modern development and are intended for recreation of the nearby population, the problem is formulated as a lack of functional diversity of leisure, with a deficit of green areas and communication with nature for city residents. The dispersed park structure makes it possible to ensure the presence and diversity of park functions in the absence of a large natural area in the context of folded development.

Existing methods suggesting the design of dispersed parks are based on research methods associated with sociological surveys, field surveys, and other methods of the humanities, these methods are not universal, expensive, and time-consuming, as a result, a need arose for a universal, quickly working software-implemented method using tools spatial analysis, and which would allow the use of open data from the Internet.

The method proposes to combine these territories according to the indicated characteristics into clusters, where each small territory will be assigned its function, which this territory does not perform or can effectively perform as a node of a dispersed park. Thus, the efficiency of the use of territories will increase and there will be opportunities for functional diversity that will attract new users. Index of dispersed park presented in Table 2.

Table 2. Dispersed park criteria.

Criteria	Meaning
Connectivity	How closely green areas are located within the research area, their ability to be perceived as a single object of the urban environment, despite their fragmentation. Even a small green area must be connected and involved in the overall green structure, only in this way it is possible to create and maintain a system beneficial to the environment and society
Provision	How many people will have access to a new park without having access to a large city park. Large parks already provide the needs of different social groups
Functionality	How the current parks perform recreational functions based on what objects they are filled with; this index is calculated by spatial join by location methods and is based on available data from OpenStreetMap

A dispersed park has an "anchor" park, to which the included public greenery areas are transferred for the management of these areas to manage these areas effectively. As a potential anchor object of the future dispersed park, we consider green areas with the status of urban significance, with an area of 1–10 hectares, typical for local parks, as the object should become a potential point of attraction for citizens and the presence of a larger area, and the status of urban significance satisfy these conditions.

A 15-min pedestrian accessibility isochron is established from the potential anchor site. For each pair of parks in the isochron, the optimum distance is calculated. Using the selected data, we construct a non-directional graph where the vertices are numbers of the parks and the edges are the links between them, the weight of an edge is the travel time between the parks.

In the collected graphs we extracted subgraphs with the highest density and number of vertices. Using random sampling method, the subgraphs are extracted from the graph. The density for undirected graphs is:

$$d = \frac{2m}{n(n-1)'} \tag{2}$$

where n – is number of nodes and m – is the number of edges in graph.

3.1 Dispersed Park to Realization Cultural Ecosystem Services

Since valuing cultural ecosystem services involves most criteria that are difficult to measure, a backward approach is proposed. The concept of dispersed parks is based on assessing the presence of functional diversity, and established communities which suggest social and cultural values in an area. According to the concept of ecosystem services, defines the area under investigation as a sustainable system at the neighborhood scale [21].

In a study [22], the authors highlight the fact that linking ecosystem services to multi-criteria analysis can facilitate green space planning. Linking environmental quality to functionality can act as a conceptual framework to demonstrate the relative values of cultural ecosystem services. In concept of dispersed park, functionality is a criterion showing how the parks perform recreational functions based on what objects they are filled with. There are three types of activities: passive recreation, active recreation, and public services (Table 3). Each type of activity is represented by leisure, for each of which there are infrastructure objects, information about the location is obtained from the OpenStreetMap open data. The presence or prevalence of a certain type of leisure can then set the theme of the park.

Table 3. Kinds of objects.

Passive recreation	Active recreation	Public services
Resting place	Playground	Community center
Water	Pitch	Unique object
Memorable place	Dog park	Education
Cultural heritage	Winter attraction	

Based on the MEA 2005 classification, cultural ecosystem services include: spiritual and religious values, inspiration, aesthetic values, learning, sense of place, recreation and ecotourism, cultural heritage values [4].

Consider how the values described in the concept of cultural ecosystem services are expressed in a dispersed park.

Spiritual and religious values. In an urban context, these functions may be represented by memorial sites, religious sites, such as temple parks or historic cemeteries. The activities in such places are predominantly quiet rest, contemplation.

Recreation and ecotourism. Places that people choose to spend their leisure time. At the level of an urban neighborhood, these are places, within walking distance, capable of meeting the needs of nearby residents. The problem is that urban areas most often have limited scale, and when placing a function, preference is given to the most popular and easiest to implement function - playground and horizontal bars. Every vacant lot has a playground of medium quality, and often there is not enough space for a quiet rest. Not to mention dog lovers who must walk their dogs on every lawn. This all creates conflict between the different social groups who are trying to adapt the existing environment to their needs.

Aesthetics, which should ensure aesthetically pleasing landscapes. The main problem is that typical solutions are usually used for urban landscaping. Planning each site individually can result in dull and monotonous views. An integrated approach to landscaping can give you a variety of species and a more conscious choice of sites.

Sense of place. In the context of neighborhoods, there is a particular focus on a sense of place. Participatory methods are used all over the world to understand what people want and to help them improve the area. It is about creating neighborhood communities. Having already established neighborhoods facilitates the search for identity and strengthens the sense of belonging to a place through participation in the development of that place.

Inspiration. The search for identity can be inspired by characteristics of a place that make it special or unique, evoking a sense of belonging and attachment. The presence of unique objects that are points of attraction in an urban or local context can also be sources of inspiration.

Cultural heritage. The presence of cultural heritage sites in the study area imposes several peculiarities. Depending on the function of the site, the identity of the area and the theme of the park itself may be constructed. Cultural heritage represented by a temple, or a historical cemetery disposes to quiet contemplation. Architectural heritage adds to the aesthetics of a site.

Learning. The presence of educational features in the study area helps to increase the number of people interested in the area and make the threshold for entry easier, communities of common interest are formed on this basis.

To summarize, despite the abstract wording, it is possible to apply them at the neighborhood level. Table 4 identifies, for each value, the sites that can realize it.

Table 4. Comparison.

Value. CES	Object. dispersed park
Spiritual and religious	Memorable place
Recreation and ecotourism	Playground, pitch, dog park, winter attraction
Aesthetic	Resting place, water
Inspirational	Unique object
Sense of place	Community center
Cultural heritage	Cultural heritage
Learning	Education

3.2 Application

The context of the study is Saint-Peterburg, Russia. In Saint-Petersburg there are 2072 urban greenery and 4924 municipality greenery, including 95 large parks with area more than 10 ga (Fig. 1). Data on public green spaces are presented as a layer in geojson format, data source - platform RGIS Saint-Petersburg, February 2020.

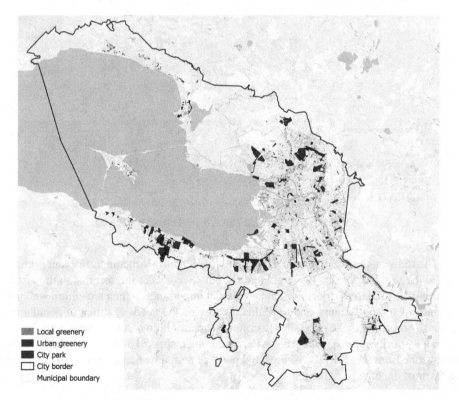

Fig. 1. Public green spaces, Sant-Peterburg, Russia

At the time of the research there are many scattered landscaped areas that either did not perform the leisure function, or in a limited area there were park leisure facilities, which, due to the limited area, were not able to fully meet the needs of each social group. We assess the availability of potential dispersed parks to provide cultural ecosystem services. Potential dispersed parks include public green spaces with appropriate legal status. According to the connectivity criterion, the boundaries of potential dispersed parks are defined according to a method based on graph theory. Figure 2 shows 66 potential dispersed parks in Saint-Petersburg.

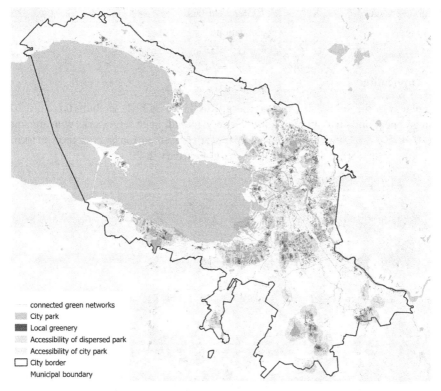

connected green networks
City park
Local greenery
Accessibility of dispersed park
Accessibility of city park
City border
Municipal boundary

Fig. 2. Potential dispersed parks, Saint-Petersburg, Russia

The study on the improvement of the district green infra-structure is relevant primarily for the residents of the potential location, but we consider the fact that in the urban environment are large parks of urban and district importance, which are within walking distance of some residents, and thus already provide the needs of different population groups. According to the accessibility criterion, areas within accessibility to large parks are not a priority for dispersed park. After excluding dispersed parks within the accessibility zone from the analysis, 14 potential parks remain. Duplicates were also excluded in favor of the highest ranked.

According to the functionality criterion, we determine the number of kinds of objects represented in the area. Only the presence of a particular type is considered, but not the number of objects of that type, as the criterion involves determining the diversity of functions. Calculations for each of the 14 potential parks are presented in Table 5.

Table 5. The results of the calculations.

Id park	Count function	Description
634	2	Water, memorable place
690	2	Playground, pitch
618	3	Playground, pitch, memorable place
625 (Fig. 3, right)	3	Resting place, playground, water
636	3	Resting place, playground, memorable place
765	3	Playground, pitch, memorable place
1249	4	Resting place, playground, pitch, water
413	4	Playground, pitch, memorable place, water
982	4	Resting place, playground, pitch, memorable place
1518	4	Resting place, playground, pitch, unique object
621	5	Resting place, playground, pitch, memorable place, water
1354	5	Resting place, playground, pitch, memorable place, unique object
1365	5	Resting place, playground, pitch, memorable place, unique object
541 (Fig. 3, left)	5	Resting place, playground, pitch, memorable place, unique object

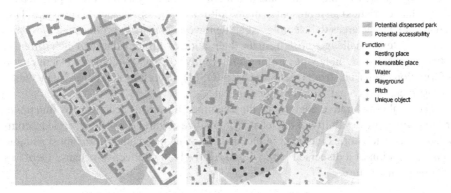

Fig. 3. Examples of dispersed parks

Two examples characteristic of urban development. The left example on Fig. 3 the residential area is dominated by playgrounds, pitch. However, there is an object of attraction in the area - the Unique object. It's a good basis around which to develop a theme of identity of place, to create communities. There is also a memorable place, around which there is already a resting place. In case a right example there is only a minimal recreation set. In this case, the area does not have an established identity.

With increasing urbanization and the degradation of green infrastructure, it is especially important to preserve and enhance green spaces. If an area has conditions that foster cultural ecosystem services, attention should be paid to these areas, development can take place at the lowest possible cost.

4   Discussion

The study considered the dispersed park as a green space planning approach within the existing urban context. The definition of a potential dispersed park according to the criterion of connectivity highlights existing connected areas. These areas already form part of the green frame and are a more sustainable ecological system. The criterion of availability will show to what extent the area can be demanded by residents. The criterion of functionality shows how people can interact with nature, according to a representation of cultural ecosystem services.

The proposed dispersed park approach has several disadvantages and limitations to its application. The main limitation is the need to allocate space for anchor objects that simultaneously act as service centers of the dispersed park. Even though they do not require significant space like traditional parks, sometimes this can be a problem. The concept of a green park should be considered in conjunction with the city's transport system, since the conditions for creating green corridors change the requirements for the use of parts of the road network.

5   Conclusion

As we explore the existing urban context, our aim is to identify a potential dispersed park whose characteristics can represent as many cultural ecosystem services as possible. This will allow suitable areas to be combined at the lowest cost and to produce the most sustainable system. Challenges arise from the integration of different data and their different data qualities, for example when mixing authoritative data and Volunteered Geographic Information (VGI) data from OpenStreetMap (OSM). Therefore, sophisticated metadata management plays a particularly important role.

The final comparative analysis of the examined territories according to functional criteria will show the ability of the territory to realize cultural ecosystem services, compared to other territories included in the analysis. This means that in the most suitable area the creation of a dispersed park will be relatively cost-effective because there is a suitable infrastructure.

Acknowledgements. This research is financially supported by The Russian Science Foundation, Agreement №22-21-20081.

References

1. UN: New Urban Agenda. United Nations (2017)
2. Van der Jagt, A.P.N., et al.: Co-creating urban green infrastructure connecting people and nature: a guiding framework and approach. J. Environ. Manag. **233**, 757–767 (2019). https://doi.org/10.1016/J.JENVMAN.2018.09.083
3. Lozhkin, A., Smirnova, M., Razzhivina, D., Golodyaev, K., Gizhitskaya, S.: Green Novosibirsk: the concept of development of green public spaces of citywide significance (2017)
4. MAE: Millennium ecosystem assessment ecosystems and human well-being: synthesis (2005)
5. Haase, D., et al.: A quantitative review of urban ecosystem service assessments: concepts, models, and implementation. Ambio **43**, 413–433 (2014). https://doi.org/10.1007/S13280-014-0504-0/FIGURES/7
6. Hasan, S.S., Zhen, L., Miah, M.G., Ahamed, T., Samie, A.: Impact of land use change on ecosystem services: a review. Environ. Dev. **34**, 100527 (2020). https://doi.org/10.1016/J.ENVDEV.2020.100527
7. Ahern, J., Cilliers, S., Niemelä, J.: The concept of ecosystem services in adaptive urban planning and design: a framework for supporting innovation. Landsc. Urban Plan. **125**, 254–259 (2014). https://doi.org/10.1016/J.LANDURBPLAN.2014.01.020
8. Cheng, X., van Damme, S., Li, L., Uyttenhove, P.: Evaluation of cultural ecosystem services: a review of methods. Ecosyst. Serv. **37**, 100925 (2019). https://doi.org/10.1016/J.ECOSER.2019.100925
9. Adem Esmail, B., Cortinovis, C., Suleiman, L., Albert, C., Geneletti, D., Mörtberg, U.: Greening cities through urban planning: a literature review on the uptake of concepts and methods in Stockholm. Urban For. Urban Green. **72**, 127584 (2022). https://doi.org/10.1016/J.UFUG.2022.127584
10. DOM RF, STRELKA CB: Part 3. The standard of development of free territories, Moskow (2019)
11. Gorokhov, V.A.: Urban Green Building: A Textbook for Universities (1991)
12. Pauleit, S., et al.: Advancing urban green infrastructure in Europe: Outcomes and reflections from the GREEN SURGE project. Urban For. Urban Green. **40**, 4–16 (2019). https://doi.org/10.1016/J.UFUG.2018.10.006
13. Cheng, X., van Damme, S., Uyttenhove, P.: A review of empirical studies of cultural ecosystem services in urban green infrastructure. J. Environ. Manag. **293**, 112895 (2021). https://doi.org/10.1016/J.JENVMAN.2021.112895
14. Chan: Cultural services and non-use values (2011)
15. Niemelä, J., et al.: Using the ecosystem services approach for better planning and conservation of urban green spaces: a Finland case study. Biodivers. Conserv. **19**, 3225–3243 (2010). https://doi.org/10.1007/S10531-010-9888-8/TABLES/3
16. Hansen, R., Olafsson, A.S., van der Jagt, A.P.N., Rall, E., Pauleit, S.: Planning multifunctional green infrastructure for compact cities: what is the state of practice? Ecol. Ind. **96**, 99–110 (2019). https://doi.org/10.1016/J.ECOLIND.2017.09.042
17. Gómez-Baggethun, E., Barton, D.N.: Classifying and valuing ecosystem services for urban planning. Ecol. Econ. **86**, 235–245 (2013). https://doi.org/10.1016/J.ECOLECON.2012.08.019
18. Moseley, D., Marzano, M., Chetcuti, J., Watts, K.: Green networks for people: application of a functional approach to support the planning and management of greenspace. Landsc. Urban Plan. **116**, 1–12 (2013). https://doi.org/10.1016/J.LANDURBPLAN.2013.04.004
19. Urban development. Urban and rural planning and development. https://docs.cntd.ru/document/456054209. Accessed 15 Apr 2022

20. Flowers, E.P., Timperio, A., Hesketh, K.D., Veitch, J.: Comparing the features of parks that children usually visit with those that are closest to home: a brief report. Urban For. Urban Green. **48**, 126560 (2020). https://doi.org/10.1016/J.UFUG.2019.126560
21. Liu, Y., Huang, T.T., Zheng, X.: A method of linking functional and structural connectivity analysis in urban green infrastructure network construction. Urban Ecosyst. **1**, 1–17 (2022). https://doi.org/10.1007/S11252-022-01201-2/FIGURES/10
22. Krellenberg, K., Artmann, M., Stanley, C., Hecht, R.: What to do in, and what to expect from, urban green spaces – indicator-based approach to assess cultural ecosystem services. Urban For. Urban Green. **59**, 126986 (2021). https://doi.org/10.1016/J.UFUG.2021.126986

Smart Hospitality: Opportunities and Challenges from Stakeholder Perspective in Santa Elena Province

Datzania Villao[1]([✉]) [iD], Andres Padilla[1,2] [iD], Soraya Linzan[2] [iD], and Luis Mazón[1,2] [iD]

[1] Universidad Estatal Península de Santa Elena, La Libertad, Ecuador
datzaniavillao@gmail.com
[2] BITrum Research Group, Leon, Spain

Abstract. Currently, staying in a hotel is very different from how it was in the past, this happens thanks to technology that advances faster and brings many updates and tools that can be used to make the guest's stay more comfortable and pleasant. However, the decision and the way to apply technology to a hotel comes from owner, investors and managers who are important operational stakeholders. That is why, the purpose of the paper is to explore the opportunities and challenges for smart hospitality in Santa Elena Province from the perspective of stakeholders. In depth interviews were conducted with five hotel stakeholders in Santa Elena Province such as managers and owners of hotels. The opportunities identified are current technology available, new guest preferences and potential of Santa Elena Tourist places. The challenges identified are finance barriers, nonclear public policy and lack of human resources specialized.

The findings also shows that smart hospitality is just starting in Santa Elena province and few four- and five-stars hotels have some tools to consider smart. In addition, there is a big gap in the opportunities and challenges identified in the literature compared with a specific context like Ecuador in Santa Elena province.

Keywords: Smart hospitality · Challenges · Stakeholder

1 Introduction

Currently, staying in a hotel is very different from how it was in the past, this happens thanks to technology that advances faster and brings many updates and tools that can be used to make the guest's stay more comfortable and pleasant, with faster processes and fewer errors when extracting data, which has become a key component in the hotel industry. Proof of this is that almost 65% of tourists from all over the world book their hotel through the Internet and around 75% use the Internet to get inspired, choose a destination and look for leisure and professional activities during their stay [1].

Although there is no exact definition of what a smart hotel is, it can be said that a smart hotel makes use of devices connected to the Internet and these devices can communicate or interact with each other [2]. This sometimes becomes the Internet of Things (IoT), which means that even ordinary devices and appliances can send and

T. Guarda et al. (Eds.): ARTIIS 2022, CCIS 1676, pp. 97–111, 2022.
https://doi.org/10.1007/978-3-031-20316-9_8

receive data, making them smart. The ability of these devices to communicate with each other allows users to control multiple devices from a single point of control (remote control, smartphone, tablet or smart speaker). This means that the devices can send or receive data that mostly facilitates administrative management, giving great added value to the final service received by the client [3].

Hotel stakeholders invest in technology due to three essential reasons such as: process automation, to avoid human errors and increase employee productivity, operational efficiency and cost reduction [4]. In this sense, according to the management model of relationships with stakeholders in the hospitality industry, there are four types of relationships that identify the relationships of stakeholders with an organization. These are: 1) supportive or enabling; 2) functional; 3) normative, and 4) diffuse [5]. Within which those stakeholders of support and functional are those that are directly related to the operational part of the hotel such as shareholders, investors, financial institutions, government, managers, employees, suppliers, travel agencies, services of tourism and tourists. Given the importance that investors or owners have in the decision making of invest in technology to strengthen their operational and human resources and meet the new demand, is critical to study this type of stakeholders in the hotel industry.

In Ecuador, tourism sector represents 2.2% of GDP of the country [6]. Despite the hard blow that the tourism sector has experienced due to the Covid-19 pandemic, investors consider that there are still business opportunities in the hotel industry. For instance in the big cities such Guayaquil and Quito there are some hotels that are using current technology to be considered smart. In Quito for example there are hotels that work with state-of-the-art technology, they are smart buildings in many areas such as energy and water savings. For example, the hot water comes from the Heat Pump heat transfer system, which consists of modern equipment that consumes less than half the electricity required by traditional water heating systems. The electrical system of these smart hotels is also innovative and consistent with the intention of avoiding, as much as possible, environmental pollution. They have LED lighting to save energy in percentages from 60% to 80%. They also have an energy saving system in each room through a control card so that, in the event that the guest forgets to turn off the lights, they will turn off automatically [7].

Ministry of Tourism has pointed out that this year $95 million of private investment will enter Ecuador's tourism sector, it would be 11 contracts for lodging, food and beverages and tourism operations, which will mean new 580 jobs specially in Guayaquil and Quito [8]. In addition, there are 10 investment projects in the country related to the hotel industry. One of the projects is precisely in the Province of Santa Elena, which is one of the most touristic provinces in the country, which has unique beaches and natural tourist places that make the Province an attractive place for national and foreign tourists [9].

That is why, to stay open and build the seeds of resurgence by the time the coronavirus has receded, owners and investors are realizing that their hotels must become more tightly managed businesses intelligent. They need to become managed hotels in the most efficient and effective way possible; it means that they need to become smart hotels. Therefore, it is necessary to think about which strategies will help the business to grow in a scalable way, focusing on a differentiating component from the competition and fitting it into the demands of the new generation of travelers. However, current literature on smart hotels has presented the benefits for the tourist about smart hotels [10] and there are very few studies focused on the point of view of the stakeholders of the operational part such as investors, owners, managers and employees, who are the decision makers about the adoption and application of technology in the hotel industry [11]. For this reason, it is essential to know their point of view about the current knowledge they have about smart hotels. For this reason, the objective of the research is to explore what are the opportunities and challenges of smart hospitality in this specific context such as the Province of Santa Elena in Ecuador from the point of view of stakeholders such us investors, owner and managers. To achieve this, two research questions have been stated: What are the opportunities for smart hospitality? and What are the challenges for smart hospitality?

The paper is organized as followed: in the next section, literature about the opportunities and challenges is presented. The section of methodology presents the details about the methods used to collect the information needed to answer the research questions, and the findings of the research. Last section presents the conclusion of the study.

2   Literature Review

2.1   Opportunities in Smart Hospitality

Operational Opportunities

More Sustainable Hotel Rooms.
One of the biggest advantages of a smart hotel room, from a hotel owner's perspective, is the enhanced sustainability available. This is mainly related to the possibilities of saving energy inside the rooms, which can be favored by the automation offered by the Internet of things. For example, light bulbs can be set to automatically increase or decrease wattage, based on the light levels in the room at the time. Similarly, the heating can be set to automatically maintain a certain temperature, with the radiators turning off once that temperature is reached. All this leads to a reduction in energy bills [12].

Sustainability, is a current trend and characteristic of the hotel sector, it has become essential in 2022. This translates into broader ethical and environmental considerations, especially in the decisions made at the hotel management level, including the reduction of the use of disposable plastics, the elimination of superfluous paper thanks to opt-in receipts and the reduction of food waste. Decisions about things as simple as which towel rails to install in renovations have far-reaching implications when implemented on a large scale. Simple green gestures include replacing miniature toiletries with larger dispensers and using local produce, choosing ethical bedding made from organic materials, and reducing energy use with smart light bulbs [13].

In this sense, smart sensors can detect and respond to fluctuations in occupancy. In addition, smart energy management systems use complex machines to analyze historical movements to optimize energy consumption. This also reduces costs in a significant way in a 20% approximately. They can also significantly increase the resale value of a hotel [12]. For instance, thank to sensors, hotels chains like Hilton have reduce lighting and heating bills and in 2017 in partnership with World wildlife fund this hotel chain launched a water stewardship strategy in order to address water usage in their hotels [14]. On the other hand, Body area sensors also detect occupancy and reset thermostats, automatically turning lights off to reduce energy use. In addition, sensors can activate bathroom path lights when a guest gets out of bed.

Preventive Maintenance and Repairs

Hotel owners can benefit from the ability of a smart hotel for preventative maintenance and repairs. In simple terms, this can be achieved because IoT enables hotel staff to view performance information and operational data for specific devices, in real time. This allows hotel staff to detect problems quickly, or even before they happen, allowing repairs to be made sooner. As a result, fewer guests will encounter interruptions, earlier repairs can save hotel owners money on replacement devices, and far less money will be lost due to rooms being out of service [15].

On the other hands there are also robots that make some things that employees can do. For example, the American company Savioke, created the Relay robot who delivers food, toothpaste, towels and other items to hotel guests' rooms. Relay's work begins when a customer calls the front desk for room service. At that moment, the receptionist opens the compartment located in the front part of the robot, introduces the objects that the client has requested and types the room number. Relay, who activates the elevator button remotely, calls the room phone when he arrives at his destination. The back cover opens immediately when the customer opens the door for them to remove the objects. Once the job is done, Relay asks the customer if they are happy with their service via a message on the rear screen and opens and closes its eyes and performs a little dance with electronic sounds when the guest presses the five stars button to express their satisfaction [16].

Personalization

Today, customers have developed new expectations in terms of personalization. Establishments are already making a special effort to offer a personalized welcome to their customers, thanks to mail tools that allow customization on a large scale, ensuring very specific communications adapted to the chosen audience [17]. Far beyond simply adding a guest's name to a welcome message, data provides insights into past buying habits, allowing hotels to personalize their offers and promotions, and automatically offer services inspired by previous stays. Technological tools use big data to create individual interactions between the client and their host. Chatbots have proven to be a boon to customer service, both during the booking process and to answer recurring questions [18]. Hotel operations are increasingly driven by the use of management systems to analyze and optimize revenue, guest relations, real estate, networks and reputation. Not to mention the growing importance of integrated messaging, predictive analytics, customer profiling, and middleware, all of which aim to connect any disparate system. For example, in 2021 The hotel chain Accor in England announced the opening in London of the first completely digital hotel, the ibis Styles London Gloucester Road was classified as the first totally digital hotel of the Accor chain, whose contactless solutions presented guests and collaborators with an experience according to the needs and expectations of the guests. The initiative is part of a pilot plan for technological integration, aimed at implementing a series of applications for customers to quickly, easily and safely access the services and common spaces of the building [19].

Guest's Experience

Enhanced Levels of Customization
A smart hotel offers good opportunities for fulfilling customization. For instance, TVs can be remotely configured to refer to guests by name, while guests can use a central control point to set conditions within the room. Through IoT technology, some devices can automatically create those conditions. In addition, smart TVs and smart speakers can give guests the ability to access their own accounts on services like Netflix and Spotify.

A Brilliant Booking Engine
Booking software solution offers exactly what hotel owners require. Offering exceptional tools and features, it can be customized to fit the needs of a hotel brand. A fully functional booking engine like this should also be quick and easy to use; designed to provide a consistent experience across hotel websites that puts guests at ease and makes them much more likely to book directly rather than through an OTA. It is about retaining guests and, therefore, maximizing conversions [20].

Work Spaces Within Hotels
Today, remote work has become commonplace for many employees and this trend is not going away any time soon. An unprecedented number of large companies, led by web giants like Twitter, Facebook and Amazon, have announced that they will take a hybrid or flexible approach to work for the long term. In 2021, the global percentage of employees working remotely full-time was doubled. This means that hotel establishments are and will be used as a workplace by travelers, as well as by local inhabitants seeking a temporary change of workplace. This trend represents, for hotel and restaurant establishments, an excellent capitalization opportunity that allows them to adapt their offer to the needs and desires of this new type of clientele, such as numerous power outlets, free high-debit WIFI and excellent coffee [21].

Digitized Customer Experience
Mobile applications are becoming an increasingly important part of investors manage the services they provide to their guests, as well as the analysis of the experience they provide. Traditional services, in direct contact with customers, have been transformed thanks to the more frequent use of options supported by technologies, such as mobile check-in, contactless payments, voice control and biometrics. Consumers who have grown accustomed to unlocking their smartphones and laptops through facial recognition and fingerprints will soon expect the same service to access their hotel rooms [22]. For example, in W Paris hotel, staff use WhatsApp to answer guest questions, and at Virgin Hotel Chicago in U.S.A, guests already use their mobile phones to check room temperature or room service [23].

Virtual and Augmented Reality
To offer visually appealing content, companies in the hospitality industry are looking

to take advantage of certain features, such as virtual tours. The latter offer consumers, in a fun and immersive way, the opportunity to virtually immerse themselves in what could be a vacation spot. Once there, visitors should be able to whip out their trusted companion, their smartphone, and point it at real-world artifacts for additional information. Augmented reality uses graphic or informational overlays to enhance on-site environments. After downloading the corresponding app, customers can also use this tool to access restaurant opening hours, reviews or interactive tourist information maps and potentially create content as a user [24].

Management in Hotel Industry

Data-Driven Decision Making
It is essential that stakeholders in the hospitality industry take care with smart hotel systems, especially when it comes to protecting customer privacy. As long as hotels are transparent and comply with data protection legislation, some of the customer information obtained from smart hotel solutions can be useful. While it will be necessary to securely delete client voice commands and other data from devices like the Amazon Echo, some information, including basic usage data, may be collected. This can allow hotels to find out what the most popular TV channels or radio stations are, allowing them to make data-driven decisions about what to set as default options [25].

A Great Guest Management Platform
Smartly managed hotel would be making use of a management system that is really GMS (guest management system); being able to leverage its functionality to not only collect guest data, but also analyze details of guest social attributes, stay behavior, and historical spend. In turn, this would provide the investors with invaluable insight into their core clients, ensuring that the platform can help smart ads reach these customers with relevant and personalized content and offers, thus converting them into bookers precisely when and when needed. In addition, from its single central panel, such an intelligent GMS would take control of messaging. It would manage marketing emails and social media messages to all hotel supporters, as well as analyze these supporters [26].

Smart Advertisement
In fact, investors need to look to high-end smart ads software to complement and enhance their PPC activity. Such a solution would be designed to exploit valuable hotel information to drive and improve Google Ads performance by targeting the most likely bookers and thus, in turn, maximizing room reservations and increasing additional spending on hotel rooms services and amenities. Smart ad software solutions like this are at the sharp end of in-room advertising, ensuring investors and owners can reap the rewards of the latest integrated marketing techniques and digital technology. They seek to increase revenue at a time when the industry is facing great instability [27].

2.2 Challenges

Reluctance to Digitalization Investment
One of the main challenges in smart hospitality is the lack of predisposition or lack of

interest in investing in digital technology in hotels. This lack of interest occurs due to little knowledge of the usefulness of technologies both in the operative part, administration and in the experience of the guests. In addition, there are many investors who prefer to continue providing comfort to their hotel guests and therefore prefer to do business in the normal and traditional way. However, not considering the current technology that can be applied in hotels would be to waste the great benefits of smart hospitality, especially in terms of savings [28].

The Right Tech Partner
Owners and investors are overwhelmed by several technology suppliers which sometimes can be an impediment to the different process. This can affect directly in an positive or negative way. That is why is very important that investors can be sure about the responsibility and commitment of technological suppliers in order they can improve their investments. If owners invest in technology, they must make sure that it is new enough to attract attention and that they do not make an expense that in the end will not benefit them [29].

Fast- Paced Technology
Currently technology is changing so fast, which means hotel businesses need to pay attention to last technology in this area to become competitive in this market. As the technology change constantly, hotel investors and owner need to invest in technology to keep up with client´s needs and expectations. The hotel industry faces a great modernization challenge, growing and innovating, but not all hotels in all destinations have the same needs. Little by little modernization is reaching this sector, for example, today in many hotels it is possible to check-in through an App or special modules in the lobby, which is beneficial because it speeds up the process and saves time. Another example is the television screens in the rooms. Years ago, few hotels had screens, and those that did represented a certain luxury. Today, with the analog blackout, it became a necessity and obligation for all hotels to migrate to this technology [30].

In many cases, starting to innovate may seem like a crazy process for hotel companies, since they may have an idea of the steps to follow, but not how to order and apply them correctly. It is highlighted that the application of an innovation roadmap is essential, which allows hotels to follow and maintain a specific plan, which not only includes immediate measures, but also long-term, to ensure that improvement is maintained in the future [31]. In addition, the route must propose to manage change, adapt and collaborate openly. In this sense, companies must be aware that adaptation is constant, and that of course it is impossible to advance without cooperation and teamwork.

On the other hand, customers are increasingly demanding immediate response, even within an hour when using digital channels. Providing a quick response through traditional channels is very costly, time-consuming, and inefficient, especially for travelers who occasionally book a last-minute reservation and need immediate answers about their potential room.

To avoid high costs, to improve response time and customer satisfaction, every hotel or hospitality business must implement a technology solution that can provide automated customer service from the get-go. For instance, according to McKinsey, the majority of travel bookings are made through digital channels: around 60% of bookings in Europe and the US are digital [32]. Customers feel comfortable making a reservation across multiple platforms and apps, uploading photos, and inserting credit card details, all because they trust brands to keep their information safe and secure. However, a small breach in a large hotel group's system can leave information open to hackers who can steal it, use it to cause tremendous damage and ruin years of brand reputation. In general, according to a study, which has been carried out in collaboration with the Cotec Foundation for Innovation analyzed the relationship between innovation and the sector with the statistical information available between 2003 and 2018 in Spain and identified a set of barriers to innovation, among which are included: Access to finance, the shortage of own funds and public subsidies, difficulties in finding partners to cooperate in their activities, market dominance by established companies, difficulties in recruiting qualified personnel [33].

3 Methodology

Qualitative research through in-depth interviews were conducted with five hotel stakeholders in Santa Elena Province such as managers and owners. These five hotels are considered in the category 4 and 5 stars for the Ministry of Tourism in Ecuador. Each interviewee was asked about the two research questions, followed by questions for clarification. First, it was scheduled a day to interview stakeholders according to their availability. The interview for owner representative was through zoom application and for managers the interview was face to face. The interviews were recorded and the transcript was validated by a professor specialized in hotel management from Universidad Estatal Península de Santa Elena.

The two research questions were:

What are the opportunities for smart hospitality?

What are the challenges for smart hospitality?

The background of the interviewees are presented in Table 1.

4 Findings

4.1 Opportunities for Smart Hospitality

New Guest Preferences

Interviewees agreed in general that hospitality business models need to understand the new preferences and behaviors of consumers. Each time, different preferences are seen especially in young adults who are looking for new experiences but also need comfort. In this sense Owner representative, A pointed out *"We are in a time of great challenges for tourism, and especially for the hotel industry, which must learn to adapt to the forms of communication and interaction demanded by millennials, where technology plays a fundamental role"*. In the same way, Owner representative B said *"The growing use of digital devices by consumers has created new standards for customer service and communication. Customers expect hotels to provide a digital service"*.

The Technology Available for Smart Hospitality

Interviewees mentioned that today science has developed system management software

Table 1. Interviewees' background in Santa Elena Province

Stakeholder	Company background
Owner representative A	His company owns a local hotel chain with four hotels around Ecuador. One hotel is in Santa Elena. The number of hotel rooms is between 40 to 60
Owner representative B	His company owns an international hotel chain with three hotels around Ecuador. One hotel is in Santa Elena. The number of hotel rooms is between 80 to 100
Manager A	He is the general manager of a four stars hotel in Santa Elena Province. He has experience of 15 years as a manager
Manager B	He is the general manager of a five stars hotel in Santa Elena Province. He has experience of 6 years as a manager in hotel industry
Manager C	He is the general manager of a four stars hotel in Santa Elena Province. He has experience of 8 years as a hotel manager

packages that offer hoteliers unprecedented in-room management and control throughout the property. But they highlighted that the most important technology is the one that is focused in save energy and basic resources like water as well. In this sense. Manager A said *"I have realized that sensors are a great tool to detect occupancy and reset thermostats, automatically turning lights off to reduce energy use"*.

Furthermore, Manager B established *"The Internet is big and a driver of digital strategies in the hospitality industry, with the potential to provide an almost infinite limit to the reach of the audience. This allows your hotel to reach the eyes and ears of people who, a few years ago, did not know it existed"*.

Manager C also pointed out *"Travelers have an endless variety of accommodation possibilities and can easily choose another hotel if it offers a better price, location, or special benefits. That is why, in a world full of hotel websites, a brand must be unique to attract more customers, especially with the digital alternatives it offers therefore this is an opportunity to grow"*.

Owner A and B agreed that technology brings a good opportunity to compete in in an increasingly globalized world.

The Tourist Places in Santa Elena for New Markets in Tourism Industry
Interviewees also pointed out that one of the opportunities in hospitality industry in that Santa Elena is one of the most privileges provinces in Ecuador, because it has beautiful beaches and natural places that are highly demanded by tourists, especially foreigners. Owner A pointed out *"There is a specially reasons to invest in the country in the field of tourism, especially because the country can become a 'High End' or exclusive destination, a segment that represents millions of tourists a year in the world, given its natural beautiful landscapes specially in Santa Elena Province"*.

On the other hand, Owner B said *"There is still space and there are new markets to looking for but we believe that the public and private sector need to work together to grow in this sector"*.

Given the years of experience of three managers interviewed, they agreed that Santa Elena is a province with a big potential to invest in the hospitality industry, especially for its natural attractive, gastronomy and local people.

4.2 Challenges for Smart Hospitality

All interviewees agreed that although there are several opportunities in hotel operations, management and experience client as was explained above, there are also four challenges to pay attention to continue moving forward in smart hospitality.

Financial Challenges

Interviewees, said that although the implementation of smart technologies is a good opportunity to grow, it also is expensive specially with the high tariff values that represent their acquisition and It implies specialized technical equipment for its assembly and installation, as well as access to an after-sales service that in most cases increases the value of the investment and reduces profitability. Owner representative A pointed out *"The situation is very complicated. There is no enough backing from the government that offered hotel investors a 15-year loan, with three grace periods. There is no such line of credit and that even some tourism investors are not subject to credit, because the banks consider it a risky sector"*.

In the same way, Owner representative B said *"In 2020, the hotels had operating losses due to the pandemic. That is, revenues were not sufficient to cover operating costs and expenses. This generated the consumption of liquidity, and the servicing of the public and private debt was compromised. Given the cost of new technologies, at this time it becomes difficult to invest"*.

Public Policy Support Challenges

Interviewees pointed out that there are not enough public policies that encourage the incorporation of smart hotel technology aimed specially at reducing energy consumption and therefore aimed at reducing the carbon footprint on the atmosphere by the hotel industry, which discourages the investors to invest in technological structure for saving energy. However, few owners have invested in Ecuador in hotels with technology to save energy and water. In this sense, Owner representative A established *"Constantly changes in government regulations represent new restructuring and fiscal considerations for hotel companies"*.

On the other hand, Owner B said *"although, there is needed specific public policy to invest in technology, I think Ecuador is a developing country where there are still opportunities, but it is important to create public policy where public and private sector can work together in order to strengthen tourism sector"*.

While Manager A, B and C agreed that although government make effort to motivate private investment in tourism sector, there is still a lack specific and clear public policy to improve investment specially in smart technologies.

Technological Challenges

In order to decide and implement smart technologies, investors need to invest in specific infrastructure and make some changes in operation processes. Owner representative A pointed out that although they have already investment in changes in operation processes, it is still necessary to invest in infrastructure specially for energy management which is more expensive compared with operation procedures such us payment procedures, automatic check in, social networks among others. He pointed out *"In the province of Santa Elena we see that the greatest investment in elements that lead to a Smart Hotel lies in the acquisition of technological elements that reduce energy consumption and in the provision of free internet points for hotel guests. There is a lack of investment in elements such as the use of hotel management software, channel manager, security, maintenance, augmented reality, artificial intelligent and robots".*

In the same way Representative B said *"Hotels have had to adapt their physical infrastructure, but also their digital strategy, to avoid physical contact. This implies that, when the guest is already in the facilities, they move in a more digital way".*

However, all managers agreed that technical procedures need also human resources that have a specific knowledge about new technologies. For instance, Manager A said *"Definitely at this point, hotel industry has had to reinterpret technology to ensure a safe return for their traditional guests, new guests and a new generation of guests. The objective is that the lodging and the experience of the guest be safe, However, the assembly, maintenance and use of these technologies requires specific knowledge in information technologies, networks, and systems, which increases the demand for multitasking personnel who are capable of functioning in totally technological environments, which in the country are very scarce".*

On the other hand, manager B pointed out *"navigating in the rooms and common spaces through virtual reality allow the guest can have certain security, even before the reservation, that they will be going to a safe place but for this is necessary to hire more specialized human resources".* In the same way manager C said that hotels have benefited from new technological tools and have changed the rules of the game, manager pointed out *"In the tourism sector, operating or travel agencies no longer work through an office, all reservations must be made digitally, trying to position yourself in social networks and in search engines and metasearch engines today is essential for business development, however in Santa Elena Province only few hotels can considered smart, the majority still uses operational processes and infrastructure in a traditional way".*

The Right Tech Partner Challenge

All interviewees agreed that suppliers of technological infrastructure for smart hotel in the country are intermediaries of the international companies that are the developers of these technologies because no technological component for Smart Hotels is manufactured in the country. All this means that the incorporation of technological elements capable of turning hotels into smart is minimal due to all the barriers that exist for its implementation and especially the costs and taxes that are involved in the acquisition of these technologies. Owner representative A pointed out *"If hotels invest in technology, we must make sure that it is new enough to attract attention and that they do not make an expense that in the end will not benefit us, but in the country is very difficult to find suppliers of technology, we need to look for foreigner companies which implies time and money".*

Owner B established that *"we know the importance of technology in our hotels, but this es very expensive, because in the country there is not enough human resources with the knowledge to implement some technology. However, we have implemented in one of our hotels magnetic cards for the rooms which was expensive, because We had to pay all travel expenses for the human resources that were foreigners".*

Once that it was collected the answers about the opportunities and challenges that investors and managers think exists for smart hospitality, they also were asked about the technology that currently they have implemented in their hotels and Table 2 was the results of the available technology that they have in their hotels.

Table 2. Technology implemented in hotels of Santa Elena Province

Area	Technology	Hotel A	Hotel B	Hotel C	Hotel D	Hotel E
Infrastructure	Automatic doors	√				
	Light sensors	√		√		√
	Technological equipment for events	√	√			√
	Speakers with Bluetooth connection	√	√	√		√
	Touch free	√				
	Smart thermostat	√				
	Stream from mobile device to TV	√	√			
	Air purifier	√	√			
	Magnetic Card	√	√			
	LCD displaying with signaling	√	√	√	√	√
Systems	Hotel management system	√	√	√		√
	Web page	√	√	√	√	√
	Wi-Fi	√	√	√	√	√
	Social networks	√	√	√	√	√
	Electronic ways of payment	√	√	√	√	√
	Web check in	√	√	√		
	Electronic menu	√	√			√

5 Conclusion

Currently, technology is in the heart of the hotel experience, before or after the trip, in the room or in the common areas of a hotel. This trend will lead to the development of new concepts and more innovation in the sector, while contributing to the emergence of an increasingly individualized offer. Nowadays, everyone involved in hotel industry should prioritize turning their hotel into a smart hotel, as it can significantly improve the customer experience, make life easier for staff, and save owners money. Although some customers are still reliant on human interactions, the investors need to remember that digitalization is the only way to survive in the market for a long time. Indeed, the challenges are numerous and very hard to overcome, needing extensive research, training and investments, but once they have been reduced, the investors will enjoy great success and profit. The new technologies linked to digitization in the tourism sector in Ecuador are still in their first steps, but they are expected to completely revolutionize the industry soon. Even though there is a great variety of technologies developed for different fields and with important applications in the sector tourism, especially in the biggest cities such as Guayaquil and Quito, but its use in Ecuador has not been documented in empirical studies. This studied was focused specially in the opinion of stakeholders such as owners and managers of hotel industry, who have a big responsibility to make a decision to invest and apply technology in their hotel to become them in smart. As a result of the research the main opportunities identified are; current technology available, new guests preferences and the natural and beautiful tourist places that the Province have to open new markets. On the contrary, the challenges identified are; financial problems, human resources specialized in technology, lack of public policy and difficulties to find a tech partner in the country. It is important to point out that comparing with the big opportunities that the literature offer in terms of technological innovation for smart hotels, in Santa Elena Province few hotels have some basic tools to consider smart. These tools are focused specially in saving energy and the use of social networks. In addition, literature said that one challenge for smart hospitality is Reluctance to digitalization investment, however in Ecuador investors want to invest in technology, but there are some barriers to avoid invest on technology. The research have a big limitation, it was used only 5 stakeholders of hotels in the Province which means that the findings cannot be generalized for the whole hotel industry in Ecuador.

References

1. Accor (2022). https://all.accor.com/hotel/B1C5/index.es.shtml
2. Amatulli, C., De Angelis, M.: Analyzing online reviews in hospitality: data-driven opportunities for predicting the sharing of negative emotional content. Curr. Issue Tour. **22**(15), 1904–1917 (2019)
3. Atlata, J.: Hotel Management (2019). https://www.hotelmanagement.net/tech/10-ways-smart-technology-reshaping-hotel-industry
4. Avila, Y.: Odd (2021). https://www.oddarchitects.com/post/odd-la-firma-de-arquitectos-en-quito-dise%C3%B1a-hoteles-con-certificaci%C3%B3n-de-ecoeficiencia
5. Buhalis, D., Leung, R.: Smart hospitality—Interconnectivity and interoperability towards an ecosystem. Int. J. Hosp. Manag. **71**, 41–50 (2018)

6. Car, T., Stifanich, L.: Internet of things in tourism and hospitality: opportunities and challenges. Tourism in South East Europe **5**(163), 163–175 (2019). https://d1wqtxts1xzle7.clo udfront.net/66894304/293-internet-of-things-iot-in-tourism-and-hospitality-opportunities-and-challenges-with-cover-page-v2.pdf?Expires=1657577761&Signature=CDZIUaDfRrf5 PAlxULGje0jY-yzI-i2aGxg9mCmmTvIegLxY60i9jp5RwLBQWw69HpU9trg0X

7. Castillejo, E.:. In: Proceedings of The Sixth International Conference on Mobile Ubiquitous Computing, Systems, Services and Technol (2012). https://d1wqtxts1xzle7.cloudf ront.net/30795457/ubicomm_2012_3_10_10055-with-cover-page-v2.pdf?Expires=165758 4321&Signature=NztbeudpAQIrjhPlKNu-v0XIycBiYLcZGdZYn3KirAHrB5aElg~04UAij xucfmb-MxRSKauvXukZTyFwLxUpwsw9xz0gdx6oND2u38fPg8vha~yn-JUDRh3toqQq7 HfTsK7J

8. Commbox. Commbox (2020). https://www.commbox.io/es/overcoming-customer-commun ication-challenges-in-hospitality-and-tourism/

9. control, G.E. Global Expertise in Pest Control (2020). https://www.rentokil-pestcontrolindia. com/hospitality/challenges/

10. COTEC Foundation. (s.f.). COTEC Foundation. https://cotec.es/proyectos

11. Dash, M., Bakshi, S.: An exploratory study of customer perceptions of usage of chatbots in the hospitality industry. Int. J. Customer Relations **7**(2), 27–33 (2019)

12. Digital Society. Digital Society (2022). https://medium.com/digital-society/opportunity-and-challenges-of-the-hospitality-sector-6f98fe16e4e1

13. El Universo. (2022). https://www.eluniverso.com/noticias/ecuador/ministro-niels-olsen-anu ncia-inversion-de-475-millones-para-la-promocion-turistica-de-ecuador-nota/

14. Eysenck, G.: Sensor-based big data applications and computationally networked urbanism in smart energy management systems. Geopolitics, History, Int. Relations **12**(1), 52–58 (2020)

15. Flore, D.: Ecuador Chequea Fundamedios (2021). http://www.ecuadorchequea.com/el-tur ismo-lucha-por-superar-el-desastre-economico-de-la-pandemia/

16. Hsu, M., Ting, H., Lui, T., Chen, S.: Guest editorial: challenges and prospects of AIoT application in hospitality and tourism marketing. J. Hosp. Tour. Technol. **13**(3), 349–355 (2022)

17. Instituto Valenciano de Tecnologías Turísticas. Instituto Valenciano de Tecnologías Turísticas (2014). https://www.thinktur.org/media/Big-Data.-Retos-y-oportunidades-para-el-tur ismo.pdf

18. Kansakar, P., Munir, A.: Technology in the hospitality industry: Prospects and challenges. Consumer Electronics Magazine **8**(3), 60–65 (2019)

19. Leung, R.: Smart hospitality: Taiwan hotel stakeholder perspectives. Tourism Review **74**(1), 50–62 (2019). https://doi.org/10.1108/TR-09-2017-0149

20. Líderes, R.: (2016). https://www.revistalideres.ec/lideres/intel-inversion-empresas-robots-tec nologia.html

21. Lim, C., Maglio, P.: Data-driven understanding of smart service systems through text mining. Serv. Sci. **10**(2), 154–180 (2018)

22. Luo, X., Pan, Y.: A Study on the customer experience design through analyzing smart hotels in China. J. Korea Convergence Society **12**(3), 115–124 (2021)

23. Mercan, S., Cain, L., Akkaya, K., Cebe, M., Uluagac, S., Alonso, M.:. Improving the service industry with hyper-connectivity: IoT in hospitality. International Journal of Contemporary Hospitality Management, XII(V), pp. 23–40 (2020). http://www.ijaema.com/gallery/4-ijaema-may-3869.pdf

24. Neuhofer, B., Buhalis, D.: Smart technologies for personalized experiences: a case study in the hospitality domain. Electron. Mark. **25**(3), 243–254 (2015)

25. Ojino, R.: Proceedings of ENTER2018 PhD Workshop (2018). https://enter-conference.org/ wp-content/uploads/2020/10/ENTER2018_PhD.pdf#page=54

26. Ortiz, Y., Varga, E., Nava, R.: Los stakeholders de la industria hotelera: una clasificación a partir de sus intereses ambientales. Universidad & Empresa **18**(30), 97–120 (2016). https://doi.org/10.12804/rev.univ.empresa.30.2016.05
27. Salazar, A.: Hospitality trends: opportunities and challenges. Worldwide Hospitality Tourism Themes **5**(6), 592–602 (2018)
28. Shabani, N., Munir, A.: E-Marketing via augmented reality: a case study in the tourism and hospitality industry. Potentials **38**(1), 43–47 (2018)
29. SKIFT. SKIFT (2016). https://skift.com/2016/08/26/how-smart-hotels-use-messaging-to-connect-with-guests/
30. Adamo Software: Adamo Software (2021). https://adamosoft.com/blog/challenges-for-the-hospitality-industry/
31. Tourism, I.E.: Invest Ecuador Tourism (2022). https://investecuadortourism.com/wp-content/uploads/2021/11/Santa-Elena_RADISSON-BLUE-PUNTA-CENTINELA-OCT-2021.pdf
32. Verma, M.: Implementation of blockchain-based technique to a hostel room booking system: practical aspects. Int. J. Res. Applied Science Eng. Technol. **9**(5), 1–4 (2021)
33. Wise, N.: Developing smart tourism destinations with the Internet of Things. Big data and innovation in tourism, travel, and hospitality, pp. 21–29 (2019)

Land Systems, Natural Hazards, and Risks. How a Unique Geospatial Model Integrates Multi-natural Hazard Risks into the Land Administration System

Rodolfo Salazar[1,2]($\boxtimes$), Dennis Ushiña[3], and Yomaira Quinga[4]

[1] Universidad de las Fuerzas Armadas ESPE, Av. Gral. Rumiñahui s/n,
P.O. BOX 171-5-231B, Sangolquí, Ecuador
rjsalazar@espe.edu.ec
[2] Departamento de Desarrollo Regional e Integración Económica, Universidad de Santiago de Compostela, Campus Santiago, Santiago de Compostela, Spain
[3] Faculty ITC, University of Twente, Hengelosestraat 99, 7514 AE Enschede, The Netherlands
[4] Departamento de Geografía y Ordenación del Territorio, Universidad de Zaragoza, Pedro Cerbuna 12, 50.009 Zaragoza, Spain

Abstract. The frequency and magnitude of natural disasters, increased by anthropic factors such as the intensification of agricultural activities, population growth, pressure on natural resources, and climate change, cause economic losses and negatively impacts the economy, health and security. One of the most effective solutions to deal with the risks associated with these events is prevention through proper land use planning, in which land administration systems provide land-related data for better decision-making, policy frameworks, and information infrastructures. The Land Administration Domain Model (LADM), ISO 19152:2012, allows each plot's rights, restrictions, and responsibilities, among others, to be considered at the municipal level, in accordance with adequate risk management. In this work, 1) the LADM, 2) the AS/NZS ISO 31000:2009 risk management system developed for New Zealand, and 3) the criteria used in Ecuador for the spatial planning of municipalities are combined in a single process. Next, applying the business management model to define the stakeholders and the main integrated processes in a single system was considered. Finally, the conceptual model for using land administration tools in managing natural hazards is presented, relating in a single system, the cadaster, tenure, value, planning, and use of the land.

Keywords: Natural hazard · Risk · Land administration system

1 Introduction

Vulnerable communities fail to create a complete land use planning (LUP) process to prevent or avoid natural multi-hazard losses increased by the characteristics and location of the communities and the lack of mitigation subjects in their local plans and development ordinances [1]. The significance of spatial planning for disaster prevention and mitigation is a better approach than the emphasis given to the preparedness and response processes usually resulting in more severe disasters [2]. Many case studies show that poorly planned land development, as well as urbanization and chaotic population growth on impermeable soil, increase the risk of disaster, and human and physical high damage.

"Natural disaster management has more to do with people than with land" [3] is a true statement related to poor land administration in less developed countries, where local governments have little incentive to develop strong hazard mitigation planning programs on their own [1].

Planning organizations are spread, resistant to change, not critical of their limitations, and usually have inadequate human, technical, and economic resources, reducing the research capacity to create scenarios for their local problems; therefore, collaborative synergies between planning institutions and research organizations can be a first positive step. At the national level, universities and research institutions can identify impacts and risks, and scientists can help in understanding the results of those models, encouraging the discussion to reduce their uncertainty [4], to finding the needs for new local specific research.

The LUP paradox is established when local governments fail to adopt mitigation practices even though disaster losses are primarily local because of the lack of mitigation measures that are not always visible in the short term of elected authorities. Local land use planners think that hazard mitigation planning is not under their profile but is under the control of emergency planners nationally that opposite have limited experience in LUP. On the other hand, local administrators believe that the government will meet their needs to minimize risk and recover from disaster and have less incentive to spend limited resources on mitigation [1]. Therefore, an integration process to develop risk disaster information in a unique distributed system is needed.

1.1 Overview of Concepts

In this part of the paper, among others, the United Nations International Strategy for Disaster Risk Reduction, UNISDR (2009) main concepts regarding to land governance (LG) and risk governance (RG) are considered, analyzed, and adapted within the land administration (LA) domain.

Land Use Planning (LUP). LUP is a public state responsibility process proposed to predict future land developments and to transform them into programs, plans, and activities including the practice of zoning for the best location of areas for different residential, commercial, industrial, and recreational uses, as well as to identify risky zones, using a multi-hazard risks reduction approach. It is a practical community empowered based process to provide people awareness of natural disasters, improve emergency plans for evacuation, relocation, and resettlement, and share information to reduce natural hazards´ losses making communities be resilient [1].

Land Governance (LG). LG is a political process considered the basis for human development and the creation of a sustainable living environment [5]. Related to natural disaster management, it is concerned to predict, prevent, and mitigate potential risks by integrating LUP processes with developing master and local plans, legal zoning, regulated standards, participative land policies, and the legal rights, restrictions, and responsibilities of all land uses [6]. It can be applied when urban communities have skilled planning offices to build consensus among stakeholders, integrating complementary planning within the social, economic, cultural, and biophysical dimensions to create multidimensional perspectives. Together with national and state institutions, as well as private experiences, local governments can develop LG instruments to increase financial and technical resources to support the study, design, and implementation of actions to reduce their vulnerability and enhance their adaptation [4] to the risk of disasters.

Land Administration (LA). Efforts to reducing poverty and social inequity can contribute to reduce social vulnerability by providing opportunities for sustainable development in rural and urban areas. One of these efforts is the use of LA to secure land tenure (LT) and reduce the vulnerability of people to natural disasters through improving the capacity on decision making to developing land policies using, among others: 1) the lessons learned from previous disasters, 2) real land valuation, and 3) the integration of risky areas and resettlement options in LUP in consultation with the community [7].

Poor people frequently have informal tenure, and usually are the most vulnerable to natural disasters when their houses are in risky and unplanned areas. LT including ownership and residential rights is usually considered within the traditional cadastre while restrictions and responsibilities may be additionally considered according to the new concepts of the Land Administration Domain Model (LADM) [8]. The LADM describes each parcel (object) with its proper characteristics like area, boundaries, and type of rights (rights, restrictions, and responsibilities) associated and identified by the name, legal title, address of the owner/holder (subject), as well as the knowledge about the land physical features like topography, soil, natural resources, infrastructures and networks, natural hazards, and roads.

Integrating the whole land information (LI) provided by a multi-purpose cadastre, it becomes easy to identify every parcel affected by multi-hazards and its landowner. If comprehensive LT and land valuation (LV) processes are additionally included, the local authority may have enough information to implement the legal issues related to land use (LU) rights, restrictions, and responsibilities in potential disaster areas, describing how resources and benefits need to be allocated into the management of land [9]. LA is the support of sustainable development that include institutional arrangements, legal frameworks, processes, standards, land information management and dissemination systems, spatial data infrastructures (SDI), and technologies required to support allocation, land markets, valuation, control of use, and development of interests in land (Bennet et al., 2013).

Risk. Risk has different meanings, and the most common concept refers to the probability of some potentially damaging event or a combination of likelihood and consequence. The well-known definition is Risk = Vulnerability x Hazard [2], or as stated by van Westen & Damen (2013), Risk = Hazard x Vulnerability x Quantity (of elements exposed). Risk results from the combination of hazards, conditions of vulnerability and insufficient capacity of measures to reduce the potential negative consequences. The risk of disaster is usually considered as the combination of the exposure to a hazard, the conditions of vulnerability and the lack of capacity to cope with the potential negative consequences, sometimes considered as the social or economic value of losses [10]. When the hazard becomes a reality, it is a disaster, whose impacts may include loss of life, injury, disease, and other negative effects on human and social well-being, damage to property, destruction of assets, loss of services, social and economic disruption and environmental degradation.

Risk Management (RM). "Risk management is a formal planning process used to identify risk, estimate its potential impact, develop strategies to manage it, and monitor it over time.", and "mitigation is part of a larger risk management process and specifically refers to a-priori structural and non-structural actions or measures taken to reduce the potential impact of disasters."; the concept of prevention is related to the actions taken to avoid totally the damage from hazards [2].

Risk Governance (RG). "Risk governance applies the principles of good governance to the identification, assessment, management and communication of risks" [11].

2 Methodology

2.1 Processes and Interactions Among LUP and LA

LUP is a political process to legalize what is administrative and reasonably suitable for a space of land and, among others, what is restricted or under responsibility in a vulnerable area. It synchronizes different land uses (LU) according to national, regional, and local land policies, considering all tenure rights, providing regulations, and creating standards [1] to regulate the intensity of uses by formulating legal and administrative instruments to support the process. LUP tools, including zoning (ZO), subdivision regulations, building codes, and public financing of capital improvements to limit the level of exposure to hazards before an event occurs, should be applied by practicing mediation, negotiation, facilitation, and policy dialogue with all stakeholders involved [1].

The complexity of LUP increases due to continuously changing conditions such as the relation of land components and uses (residential, forest, water, agricultural soil, natural hazards), and the national, regional, local, or specific jurisdictions shared by multiple authorities that can promote different patterns of LU according to changing circumstances [12]. These ZO and land allocation processes divide a delimited territory into zones specifying permitted or prohibited uses and construction regulations to reduce potential conflicts between different land uses and disaster risk areas. Zoning maps, policies, regulations, and standards are created to enforce legal restrictions and responsibilities in sensible locations.

Improving LT in LUP processes also provides security to protect access to land, reducing the risk of future disasters to those holders of rights including owners, renters, as well as squatters considered the most vulnerable groups [13]. Creating restrictions and responsibilities in conjunction with recording all existing land rights, may contribute to each phase of disaster risk reduction (DRR): preparedness, recovery, risk identification and assessment, and prevention and mitigation; these also allow standards to be developed for areas vulnerable to natural disasters. In Fig. 1, letters A, B, C, D, E, F, G, and H describe the interactions between processes and represent the information provided and received from each other, which are specified later in Fig. 2.

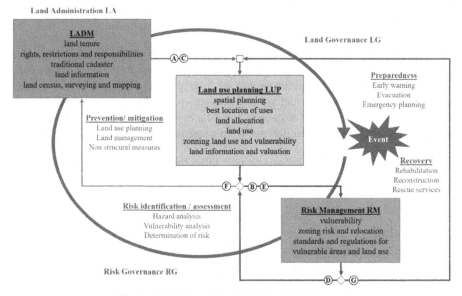

Fig. 1. RG, LG and LA within the DRR phases.

Before an event occurs, decisions and actions must have been planned in order to lead the recovery phase, considering: the affected population by displacement, relocation or resettlement, the demolition and reconstruction of damaged immoveable, the sites for disposal of waste and potentially recycling of these materials, the energy, the water and service lines for supply and transportation, and the farmland. Poor coordination between authorities could increase the magnitude and severity of natural disaster emergencies. In this context, one of the LUP's most essential tasks is coordinating the institutions and actors of RM representing specific interests. In most emerging countries, the LUP department and those responsible for RM operate in separate organizations; this brings little coordination among them due to specific mandates, orientations, and budgets. There is a mutual competition or ignorance with regarding land allocations such as transportation, environment, agriculture, residential, commercial, military, and parks, and little agreement on land and infrastructures development priorities [6].

In a good RG, the preparedness must have institutional, legal, and financial support to develop knowledge and capacities at all social and governmental levels. Given the bases to create well-organized response and recovery organizations that encourage resilient communities and individuals to anticipate, respond, and recover from the impacts of predicted multiple hazards. The prevention process deals with avoiding adverse impacts of natural hazards through actions taken in advance like the construction of dams or embankments to eliminate flood risks, the creation of land use regulations to restrict settlements in high-risk zones, and the improvement of seismic engineering standards for building in any predicted scale of earthquake. When the anticipation of losses is not entirely possible, prevention shifts into a mitigation process considered a sequence of structural and non-structural processes to reduce future damages, minimizing the impacts of natural hazards and disasters. It is divided into four categories: public information (hazard, exposition, mapping, and education), structural property protection (building and infrastructure strengthening, standards for construction), natural resource protection (preservation of ecosystems like dunes wetlands, and forests) and hazard avoidance (limited development, and relocation) [1].

3 Results and Discussion

Laws and ordinances regulate the development by dividing the community into zones and setting development criteria for each zone. ZO can keep inappropriate development out of areas located in hazardous zones and can improve LUP by placing certain areas for conservation, public use, or agriculture. A comprehensive LUP provides a mechanism to prevent development in hazardous areas and allows some developments in a manner that minimizes damage from hazards.

The levels of LUP depend on national, regional, and local public institutions and including RM in the planning process defines the ZO, nature and level of risks. Conformity among national, regional, and local planning is compulsory. First, by clarifying the national LUP at the regional level by locating and delimiting a risky zone more precisely and, secondly, by creating local legal standards to ensure control on LUP (providing restrictions and responsibilities), LT (providing formal property or possession rights) and LV (providing parcel value used primarily for taxation and conveyance). ZO can be used for DRR by prohibiting certain uses and constructions within risky flooding, landslides, erosion, volcanic or tsunami zones, and is a way to translate the concept of vulnerability in terms of restrictions and responsibilities to the spatial location of vulnerability and hazards.

Incorporating legal considerations, the ZO should enforce restrictions and responsibilities to land and property proper use. It does not mean that a state takes into custody a private land or property that must remain in the hands of the legal owner, who is obliged to respect the restrictions and responsibilities related to LU. It might be a prohibition to do something (restriction), like construct a residence in a flooding zone, or an obligation to act in a certain way (responsibility) like relocation after a certain period of time [14]. Therefore, within LA, risk assessment process, ZO may represent the spatial extension of risky zones associated with a set of regulations and standards concerning land use, land sub-division, and building.

Non-agriculture and risky land usually do not have formal LT, have limited infrastructure with poor LG support, and the parties occupying these areas have settled there because they do not have other means of access to land. These landholders need to find ways to live with the threat of the disaster, respond when the disaster occurs, and to rebuild their homes and livelihoods after the event [7]. This is the case of annual flooding in lowlands of the river basins in Ecuador. Therefore, security of tenure is an essential factor in the reconstruction and restitution after a natural disaster and should be considered as an element of the vulnerability of communities to natural disasters in a good LG approach.

Using property data overlapped with multi hazard data is crucial to identify vulnerable structures and assess vulnerability and loss estimation. A good RG process reinforces the creation of websites to access and download hazard information. It should encourage the development of a community-based risk spatial data infrastructures (SDI) to continue promoting comprehensive and cost-effective analyses to be used in local land use plans and ordinances that reduce losses due to natural hazards. An example of the importance of creating SDI that includes not only land data, but also environmental and natural hazards information is the case of Portoviejo, Ecuador. The city was most affected by the 2016 earthquake; after the casualties and losses caused by natural phenomena, the municipality has implemented an SDI containing all municipal spatial data. It has emphasized planning and natural hazard information; nevertheless, the information is not yet adequately linked to parcels in the form of restrictions and responsibilities.

3.1 A Conceptual Business Process Approach to Integrate Multi Hazard Risk Analysis in RG, LUP and LA

LA process needs to consider standards such as ISO 19152 LADM [8], to continuously improve the requirements related to a variety of spatial registers of land like topography or buildings, and administrative information like names of persons, companies and their addresses [9]. It is important to define the contents of these data to avoid overlaps and to allow the re-use of information. However, there must be a constant updating of these independent/related registers to maintain consistency within and among databases. Spatial data support decision-making, spatial planning, and land and risk governance processes when integrated into an SDI to provide easy access and databases distribution.

Integrated inter-organizational business process management reduces administrative efforts based on good cooperation; solving territorial problems require information from many stakeholders with the complexity that it is stored at different locations and in specific data models [8]. The business process provides a clear methodology to visualize and organize the main processes and data produced by RM, LUP, and LA, where the ISO 19152 LADM can be the standard to shift into a parcel-based analysis. The first level of interactions is presented in Fig. 2, where the Disaster Risk Analysis is considered an external process (EDRA), provided by institutional processes outside the local (municipal) RM, which is the case in Ecuador. Each process at the same time is composed of sub-processes interacting through receiving, processing, providing, and sharing information. They are represented in the second level of processes and interactions.

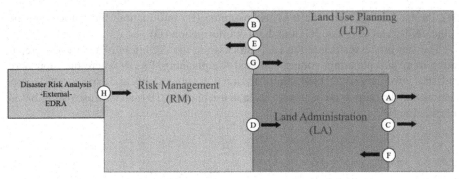

A. Cadastral Information (Traditional multi-purpose)
B. Land Use Planning Information
C. Land Administration Information in LADM
D. Risk Information
E. Land Use Information
F. Parcel Based Land Use Information
G. Vulnerability and Exposure Information
H. Disaster Risk Analysis Information

Fig. 2. Main interactions among LUP, RM and LA

The RM uses disaster risk analysis information provided by external organizations and transforms it into vulnerability, exposure and risk information by combining it with land use planning and land use information, which is produced using cadastral and land information.

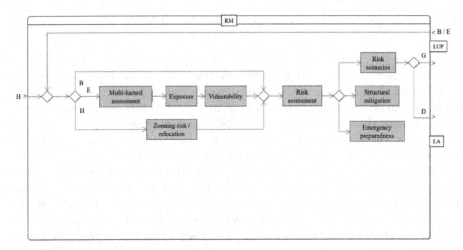

Fig. 3. Second level processes of RM related to LUP (B/E, G), LA (D) and EDRA (H).

The sub-processes considered in RM, at the second level, Fig. 3, are multi-hazard risk analysis, exposure and vulnerability definition, zoning risk and relocation, risk assessment, the definition of risk scenarios, preparation of issues for structural mitigation and emergency preparedness. The inputs for this process are the disaster risk analysis

(H), the land use (E) and the land use planning (B) information; the outputs are the vulnerability and exposure (G) and the risk information (D).

The sub-processes inside the LUP process are the definition of land uses, preparation of spatial planning, zoning and land use planning, Fig. 4, where the inputs are cadastral information (A), land administration (C), vulnerability and exposure (G) information; and the outputs are land use (E), land use planning (B) and land use parcel-based information (F).

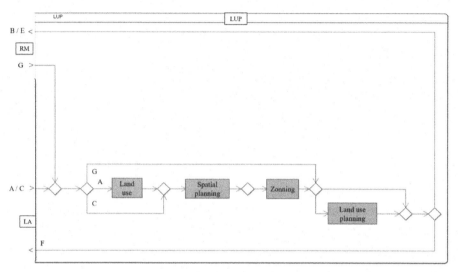

Fig. 4. Sub processes of LUP in second level and relations to LA (A/C, F) and RM (B/E, G).

Finally, in Fig. 5, the integrating process LA comprises the ongoing sub-processes of the land census, traditional cadastre, land information and valuation. These sub-processes produce land allocation, the definition of standards and land tenure policies, and the restructuration of cadastral information in terms of LADM ISO 19152, incorporating the tenure rights, risk restrictions and responsibilities which will be used in a parcel-based LUP process. The inputs are risk information (D) and parcel-based land use information (F); the outputs are cadastral (A) and land administration (C) information.

The restrictions and responsibilities are introduced (c) in Fig. 5, not just considering parcel and rights information from the traditional cadastre but complemented with the restrictions and responsibilities defined by the LUP process and risk analysis. At this point, the LA, the RM, and LUP processes are integrated into a unique parcel (Object/Spatial Unit) based information process. The parcel-based information process provides the rights, restrictions, and responsibilities (Rights/RRR) acquired from the risk and land use analysis, together with the parties involved (Subjects/Parties). This schema fits the new cadastre conceptual framework of Cadastre 2014, Objects - Rights - Subjects [15].

To provide a first approach to the classes used in the new integrated LADM model, the restrictions and responsibilities established in an external Basic Administrative Unit, such in this case as the river basin, are incorporated, Fig. 6.

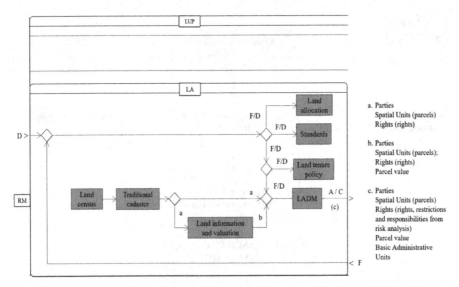

Fig. 5. Integrating LA using LADM as the link between RG (D) and LUP (A/C)

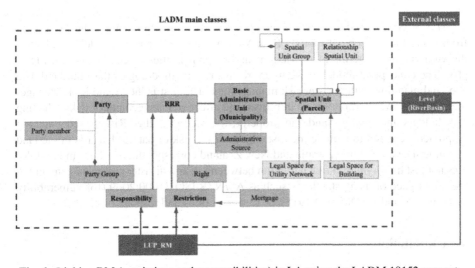

Fig. 6. Linking RM (restrictions and responsibilities) in LA using the LADM 19152 concept

The process of managing this risk results are LUP and RM which interactions correspond to the outputs B (Land Use Planning Information), E (Land Use Information), G (Vulnerability and Exposure Information), and D (Risk Information) as it is presented in Fig. 3 and Fig. 4.

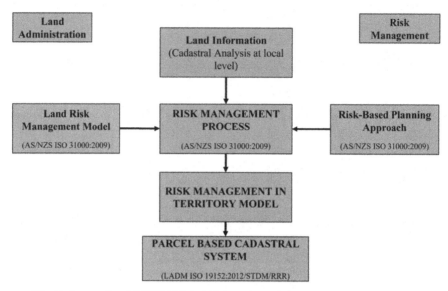

Fig. 7. Integrating AS/NZS ISO 31000:2009 in LADM 19152, adapted from [16]

This external-based approach named Level (River Basin) to manage the risk comes from using the conceptual model "Risk Management in Territory Model" to identify the vulnerability in terms of restrictions and responsibilities as can be seen in Fig. 7 [16]. The conceptual model in the figure relates two methodologies that link land data and land planning with disaster risk management. The first is the "Land Risk Management Model", which proposes an improved and effective management of risks affecting stakeholders and treating land and property; the second is the "Risk-Based Planning Approach", created to include the assessment of the risk of natural hazards in the land planning. Developed in Australia and New Zealand correspondingly, these methodologies not just highlight the stretch relation between LA and disaster risk management but the importance of using standards such as AS/NZS ISO 31000:2009 (for vulnerability assessment), and LADM ISO 19152:2012 (restrictions and responsibilities).

4 Conclusions

Innovation within the use of the LADM may benefit jurisdictions without sufficient standardization and integration for RG, LG, and LA processes. This issue mainly affects countries with no tradition in including risk analysis in planning processes, no proper registration of tenure rights in the cadastre, and where different organizations are in charge of executing these processes at different levels of government decision-making.

The main idea is to use LADM in LA to link RM and LUP in a parcel-based model to provide information on the vulnerable parcels considering restrictions and responsibilities in an LUP process including RM. Working in terms of processes allows managing the isolated input/output information in a single system, although they are executed by different organizations and in different places; that is one of the goals of SDIs.

As it was considered, in Ecuador, the DRA is an external process executed by state organizations together with universities and research institutions. However, LA is a typical municipal process developed mainly for taxation; meanwhile, land tenure rights are under the property registry autonomous process. Land administration has the concept of territorial order and is considered a product following the LUP. Another critical issue is that there is no standard or model for the core cadastre system at the time of this research, driving the municipalities to have different cadastral systems and regulations. Therefore, the main idea is to standardize a group of municipalities in a unique methodology, process, and information management for DRR, including LUP, RM, and LA, using the LADM ISO 19152 standard to integrate them.

In the same way, it is important to consider the vulnerabilities, hazards and risks within the proposed model for the planning of new areas to be urbanized, leaving aside the traditional cadastre that consists of determining the relationship of geometric, economic, and legal data of the parcels with their owners, as in the case study developed in the municipalities of Aloag, Aloasí and Machachi, where a support tool is incorporated to design a land administration model with biophysical, socio-environmental, and risk criteria in areas of urban expansion.

References

1. Berke, P., Smith, G.: Hazard Mitigation, Planning, and Disaster Resiliency: Challenges and Strategic Choices for the 21st Century. de Building Safer Communities. Risk Governance, Spatial Planning, and Responses to Natural Hazards, Amsterdam, IOS Press BV, pp. 1–20 (2009)
2. Etkin, D.: Patterns of Risk: Spatial Planning as a Strategy for the Mitigation of Risk from Natural Hazards. de Building Safer Communities. Risk Governance, Spatial Planning, and Responses to Natural Hazards, Amsterdam, IOS Press BV, pp. 44–60 (2009)
3. Roy, F., Ferland, Y., Lakrikba, E.M.: Land use planning for reducing natural disaster risk and damages. de TS07A - Land Administration, Natural Disaster and Climate Change - 6693, Abuja, Nigeria (2013)
4. Sánchez, R.: Vulnerability and Adaptation to Climate Change in Urban Areas. A Role for Urban Planning. de Building Safer Communities. Risk Governance, Spatial Planning, and Response to Natural Hazards, Amsterdam, IOS Press BV, pp. 105–124 (2009)
5. Economic and Social Council for Europe. Social and Economic Benefits of Good Land Administration, UN (1998)
6. FAO, «Voluntary Guidelines on the Responsible Governance of Tenure of Land, Fisheries and Forests in the Context of National Food Security,» UN, Roma (2012)
7. Mitchell, D.: «Reducing Vulnerability to Natural Disasters in the Asia Pacific through Improved Land Administration and Management,» de Surveyors Key Role in Accelerated Development, Eilat, Israel (2009)
8. Lemmen, C.: A Domain Model for Land Administration, Delft: Sieca Repro BV (2012)
9. Ali, Z.: Developing a Framework to Apply Total Quality Management Concepts to Land Administration (The case of Islamic Republic of Pakistan), Enschede: ITC Printing Department (2013)
10. van Westen, C., Damen, M.: National Scale Multi-Hazard Risk Assessment with an example of Georgia, F. o. G. S. a. E. O. (. University Twente, Ed., Enschede: UNU-DRM Centre for Spatial Analysis and Disaster Risk Management (2013)

11. International Risk Governance Council, «International Risk Governance Council,» 14 01 (2019). https://irgc.org/risk-governance/what-is-risk-governance/

12. UN-Habitat, FAO, «Land and Natural Disasters: Guidance for practitioners,» UN, Nairobi (2010)

13. I. E. R. C. G. T. N. UN-Habitat, «Land Tenure and Natural Disasters. Assessing Land Tenure in Countries Prone to Natural Disaster,» UN, Rome (2011)

14. United Nations International Strategy for Disaster Risk Reduction, UNISDR, Terminology on Disaster Risk Reduction, Geneve: UNISDR (2009)

15. J. Kaufmann y D. Steudler, «Cadastre 2014. A vision for a future cadastral system,» FIG-Commision 7, Brighton (2009)

16. Ushiña, D., Salazar, R.: Aplicación de herramientas de administración territorial en la gestión de riesgos naturales. caso, valle de los chillos – ecuador. Geoespacial **16**(2), 33–52 (2019)

The Tourism Experience: A Smart Tourism Ecosystem Perspective

Pedro Vaz Serra[1](✉) , Cláudia Seabra[1,2] , and Ana Caldeira[1,2]

[1] University of Coimbra, Coimbra, Portugal
pedrovazserra@hotmail.com
[2] CEGOT - Geography and Spatial Planning Research Centre, Coimbra, Portugal

Abstract. With the tourist experience at the heart of tourism and considering that it is shaped and influenced by the interaction between supply and demand, the nature of this interaction is a fundamental concept, namely for its design, communication, and facilitation. The smart tourism ecosystem integrates (i) systems, which include actors, who exchange skills, experiences, and knowledge; (ii) institutions, which promote the integration of resources, based on a common set of social arrangements; (iii) technology, which generates and renews social arrangements. It is a reality with multiple impacts, susceptible to change in various elements of the market, such as the exchange object, actors, structure, institutions, and practices. Also in business models, it is possible to admit significant changes, at the levels of customer segments and relationships, value propositions, channels, revenue streams, resources, activities, partnerships, and cost structure. Given the above, a conceptual approach is proposed, highlighting the importance of a positively differentiating tourism experience from the perspective of a smart tourism ecosystem, considering its multi-participant structure. This will be the first stage of a broader work, where we hope to obtain far-reaching results, highlighting the importance of interaction between stakeholders, mediated by technology, capable of providing a positively differentiating tourist experience. The suggested approach has relevant implications at the management level, given the need to obtain differentiating factors, with the incorporation of added value for the parties involved, capable of achieving and renewing balances between supply and demand, using technology, which is now unavoidable.

Keywords: Tourism experience · Smart tourism ecosystem · Value co-creation

1 Introduction

The growth and development of tourism — which, in the face of challenging global scenarios, imply rigorous and committed responses, in the face of climate change, the impact of the COVID-19 pandemic (Seabra et al. 2021), the need to contribute to economic efficiency and social justice, in addition to the opportunities generated by the new horizons induced by technology (Xiang et al. 2021) — enhance the reinterpretation of its planning, essential for the balance between supply and demand, by integrating tangible

T. Guarda et al. (Eds.): ARTIIS 2022, CCIS 1676, pp. 125–136, 2022.
https://doi.org/10.1007/978-3-031-20316-9_10

and intangible elements, and by the ability to read, interpret and anticipate market needs, expectations and trends (Beritelli et al. 2020).

The multidisciplinary nature of the tourist experience, as well as its role in the evolution of tourism, namely in favor of the competitiveness and sustainability of accommodation units (Henrique de Souza et al. 2020) and destinations (Rasoolimanesh et al. 2021), has taken on increasing importance in the literature (Kim and Fesenmaier 2017).

These developments – theoretical, methodological, and empirical – gave rise, among others, to the concept of a smart tourism ecosystem (Gretzel et al. 2015), which, in addition to integrating various components, processes, and actions in the design of a place, advocates certain results through the virtuous convergence of technological resources, business environments and value-inducing experiences (Xiang et al. 2021).

From the perspective of a smart tourism ecosystem, the production and consumption of tourist value – which, hopefully, should be socially, culturally, environmentally, and economically sustainable (Phi and Dredge 2019) –, is shared, and generate distinctive experiences (Buhalis and Amaranggana 2015), and the corresponding interactions are promoted by technology, through the collection, processing, and communication of data (Guo et al. 2014).

This will be the first stage of a broader work, where we hope to obtain far-reaching results, highlighting the importance of interaction between stakeholders, mediated by technology, capable of providing a positively differentiating tourist experience.

This conceptual paper should result in theoretical contributions regarding the specificity of the tourist experience within the framework of a smart tourism ecosystem, with a view to the competitiveness and sustainability of accommodation and destinations.

2 The Tourist Experience

Conceptually, a tourist experience corresponds to a past event, related to a trip, sufficiently remarkable to integrate the long-term memory (Larsen 2007), showing its ascendancy in consumers, even to the detriment of the products or services themselves, or diluting them in the whole (Jensen 2012). In the same direction, neuroscience suggests that consumers are driven less by functional arguments than by internal sensory and emotional elements (Zaltman 2003).

As the experiences are personal, i.e., they occur in the individual's body and mind, the outcome depends on how the consumer, contextualized by a specific situation and mood, reacts to the enacted encounter (Walls et al. 2011).

The seminal work of Hirschman and Holbrook (1982) emphasizes that, compared with information processing models, based on the utilitarian dimension, the experiential view focuses on the symbolic, hedonic, and aesthetic nature of consumption, where the search for feelings and stimuli positive is a reality, supported by psychophysical relationships (Voigt et al. 2010).

As for the dimensions of the tourist experience, investigations are usually structured in their phases, influences, and outcomes (Cutler and Carmichael 2010).

In this sense, the model developed by Clawson and Knetsch (1966) and applied to tourism (Cohen 1979; Graburn and Barthel-Bouchier 2001) constitutes an important reference, which includes five distinct but related phases: anticipation, travel to the destination, activity at the destination, return trip and remembrance, bearing in mind that reading and the effect of experiences change over time (Borrie and Roggenbuck 2001) and, therefore, must be approached from a multiphase perspective (Agapito 2020).

However, in addition to the multiphase nature, personal influences and outcomes must be considered, as the traveler arrives at a destination with ideas about the types of experiences that can occur, arising from the social construction of an individual and that can include information or perceptions taken from communication networks and digital channels, product images, expectations, knowledge and previous travel experiences, in addition to activities in which it participates and the types of interaction, with various environments and social dynamics, even informal, that occur (Nickerson 2006; Vaz Serra and Seabra 2021). Thus, the most relevant influences are the physical environment, the staff, other tourists, and the products available (Nickerson 2006; Mossberg 2007), from which the complex nature of tourist experiences can be inferred.

As for the outcomes, there are multiple approaches. Larsen (2007) presents an idea of the tourist experience based on expectations and events, which are built through memory, forming new expectations. Hayllar and Griffin (2005) suggest that there are several essential characteristics of the tourist experience, namely authenticity and the notion of place. Rojas and Camarero (2008) argue that visitors look for results identified with leisure, education, and social interaction. McIntosh and Prentice (1999) conclude that both affective and cognitive and personal dimensions must be considered. The study by Vogt (1976) indicates that the search for experiences that provide personal growth is the main reason for travelers, and thus may arise from (i) the experience of different environments, i.e., physical configurations; (ii) the ability to learn about oneself, i.e., self-identity; (iii) the knowledge; (iv) the ability to develop intense relationships, even if transitory, i.e., with social aspects.

Thus, Cutler and Carmichael (2010) propose a conceptual model of influences and outcomes of the tourist experience (see Fig. 1), considering that this corresponds to what happens during a tourist event, which comprises the trip to the destination, the activity, and the return trip, but which also considers the anticipation and recollection phases, taking

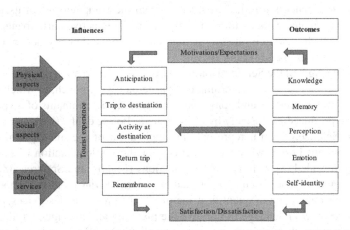

Fig. 1. Influences and outcomes of the tourist experience. Source: (Cutler and Carmichael 2010) – adapted.

into account that the experience is planned before a trip takes place and remembered long after it has ended, with the assumption that, during the outward trip, the tourists can still be involved in the process of developing expectations, in the same way, that, when returning, they can reflect on what they experienced (Cutler and Carmichael 2010).

Taking into account the aforementioned models and theoretical foundations, a conceptual framework emerges that includes personal and internal factors, but also influencing and external factors, which interact at various stages and influence the perception of the global tourist experience, i.e., the process in which the stimuli related to experience are processed, organized and interpreted, and knowledge of internal factors is considered fundamental to effectively manage external factors (Larsen 2007).

Therefore, the tourist experience – which constitutes the core of most products and services offered by hospitality and tourism companies (Miao et al. 2014) and creates a competitive advantage that is difficult to imitate and replace (Manthiou et al. 2014) – can encompass cognitive, sensory, affective, and social dimensions, likely to be pleasant, exciting, satisfying and meaningful (Tung and Ritchie 2011; Kim and Perdue 2013).

3   From a Product-Oriented View to a Service-Oriented One

The transition from a product/producer-oriented view to a service-oriented one, led to the development of various theories of service, with the aim of redefining services and value exchanges, according to the new dogma (Lovelock and Gummesson 2004).

In this context, the Service-Dominant Logic (Vargo and Akaka 2012) and the General Theory of Science, Management, and Service Engineering, originally called Service Science, conceived by the multinational IBM (Maglio and Spohrer 2007) are of particular importance, both having identified the main elements involved in the exchange of services from different angles and with an impact on organizational configurations.

In the Service-Dominant Logic (Vargo and Akaka 2012) three concepts are presented, through a service-for-service view (i) service and the relationship between goods and services; (ii) the customer-supplier relationship; (iii) the value. The exchange of services, which generates benefits for all actors, stems from the competencies of users, if each stakeholder co-creates value, with users being considered active participants, actor-to-actor, and, as such, resource integrators that shape service delivery depending on the specific context (Vargo and Akaka 2012).

Thus, in the light of the Service-Dominant Logic, the co-creation of value is the result of the exchange of resources, according to a participatory approach, in which users are, at the same time, producers and consumers and become determinants of a value that is no longer be produced exclusively by the suppliers (Polese et al. 2018).

Service Science, in turn, represents an application of the main premises of the Service-Dominant Logic, where the practices for the implementation of new service systems are revealed, as well as their implications (Maglio and Spohrer 2007). Thus, Service Science, an interdisciplinary research stream, advances in the elaboration of models for the application of scientific principles to the provision of services, promoting the creation of new knowledge to improve the planning and management the delivery, to the evaluation of the services. in terms of productivity, effectiveness, and efficiency (Maglio and Spohrer 2007).

Thus, service systems emerge, later renamed smart service systems, given the widespread impact of information and communication technologies (ICT) on the provision of services and the exchange of resources, which emphasize the role of technology (Polese et al. 2018). And there are also smart service ecosystems (see Fig. 2), which define the social bonds underlying co-creation, that is, the system focuses on technology and the ecosystem focuses on the social (Polese et al. 2018).

In this context, systems allow a micro analysis of service-for-service exchanges, and interactions between users who share information through technology (Polese et al. 2018). In turn, ecosystems have a macro perspective, of the global interactions of the network between the different social systems, expanding the field of vision, with the aim of including social prerequisites, i.e., the promoters of the exchange of synergistic resources that, in the long term, they can generate value co-creation and new knowledge (Polese et al. 2018).

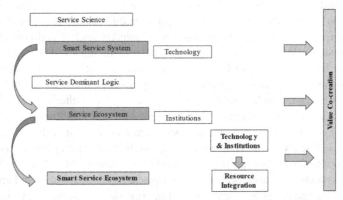

Fig. 2. Integrated framework for a smart service ecosystem. Source: (Polese et al. 2018) – adapted.

Smart service systems are conceived as organizational models that benefit from the application of modern technologies to the design and delivery of services, to promote real-time interactions, accelerate co-creation processes and induce systematic innovation, based on renewal, continuous improvement, and the exchange of knowledge (Barile et al. 2017), and they optimize and manage their goals through self-configuration, to enable lasting behavior, capable of satisfying all the members involved (Barile et al. 2017).

The vision of ecosystems, in turn, adopts two perspectives (i) reductionist, which identifies the vectors of value co-creation; (ii) holistic, which considers the emergence of innovation at a broader level and considers the importance of social norms in the formation of exchanges and in the generation of new value (Vargo and Akaka 2012).

In summary, smart tourism ecosystems are systems of actors that aim to (i) use preexisting technology and institutions for the co-creation of value, in the short term; (ii) create modern technologies, through innovation, or new institutions, praxis, social rules, values, in the long term (Polese et al. 2018).

4 The Smart Tourism Ecosystem Perspective

Based on the aforementioned fundamentals and models, the transposition to tourism is carried out, with four key dimensions of a smart tourism ecosystem − human, technological, social, and interactive − which is made up of (i) actors, who exchange skills, experiences, and knowledge; (ii) institutions, which promote the integration of resources, based on a common set of social arrangements; (iii) technology, which generates and renews social arrangements (Gretzel et al. 2015).

We are therefore faced with a scenario of smart tourism (see Fig. 3) − defined as innovative, supported by a technological infrastructure, which enhances the sustainable development of tourist areas, making them accessible and participatory, insofar as it facilitates interaction and integration with the surroundings (Gretzel et al. 2015) − improving the tourist experience and the well-being of resident communities, advocating solutions for mobility, availability, and allocation of resources aimed at promoting satisfaction and quality of life, with sustainability criteria (López de Avila 2015).

For this to occur, data assume special importance (i) by collecting and supporting information; (ii) through the exchange, supporting interconnectivity; (iii) by processing, supporting visualization, analysis, integration, and user-facing a wide range of technologies (Tu and Liu 2014), from the decision to the recommendation, from context to source search, from the environment to augmented reality, among others (Lamsfus et al. 2015).

Thus is, therefore, a reality of multiple impacts, capable of altering various elements of the market, such as the exchange object, actors, structure, institutions, and practices (Sigala 2015), so also in business models, significant changes are allowed at the levels of customer segments, value propositions, channels, customer relationships, revenue streams, resources, activities, partnerships, and cost structure (Morabito 2015).

It is a perspective focused on tourist businesses, multi-stakeholder, where are consumers, visitors, and residents; suppliers and intermediaries; support services; communication platforms and social networks; regulatory bodies and the public sector; carriers; technology companies; consulting services; tourist and residential infrastructure; as well as other companies from different sectors (Guo et al. 2014).

The resulting experiences (see Fig. 4) − which, in the work we are developing, focus on accommodation units in properties with heritage value − mediated by technology (Buhalis and Amaranggana 2015), are optimized through personalization, context awareness, and real-time monitoring, with information aggregation, ubiquitous connectivity, and synchronization being essential (Neuhofer et al. 2015). Here, the role of national governments is also praised, as they are more open to technology and emerge as providers of infrastructure and data (Buhalis and Amaranggana 2015).

Although the smart tourism ecosystem corresponds to a fluid and heterogeneous set of connections and interactions, tourists have a crucial role, as co-creators, yes, but also as users, highlighting the main objectives to be achieved in relation to them (i) anticipation of their needs, with the ability to make suggestions for activities, specific to the context; (ii) improving experiences by providing information, personalized and location-based interactive services; (iii) allow and encourage the sharing of their experiences, interfering in the decision-making process of third parties, namely family and friends, but also reliving and reinforcing experiences, as well as building their own image on social networks (Sigala 2015; Yoo et al. 2015).

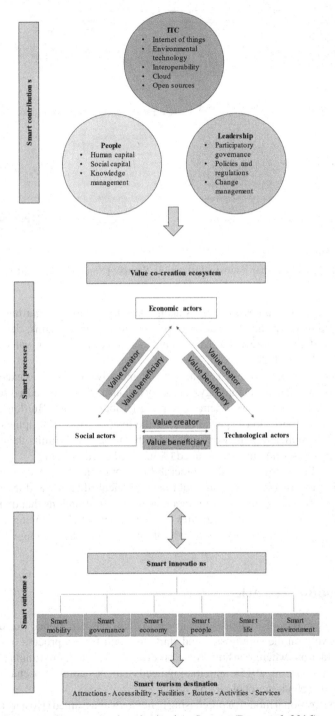

Fig. 3. Structure of a smart tourism destination. Source: (Boes et al. 2016) – adapted.

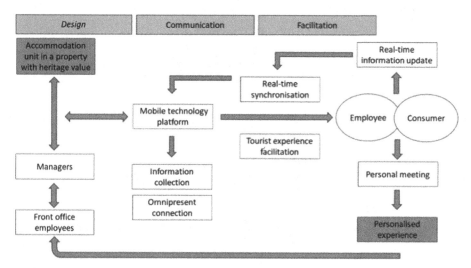

Fig. 4. Structure of a smart tourism destination. Source: (Neuhofer et al. 2015) – adapted.

On the side of companies and other stakeholders, expectations regarding the benefits of the ecosystem lie in the automation of processes, efficiency gains, development of new products, demand forecast, crisis management, and, in general, value co-creation (Sigala 2015; Yoo et al. 2015).

Other important issues are related to security and privacy as well as excessive exposure to and dependence on technology, primarily because of location-based services that, very useful for travelers, make them vulnerable (Andrejevic and Burdon 2015), even though privacy in tourism is a special case, as the interaction with suppliers and, therefore, with their applications is usually of short duration, which limits the construction of a trusted process, often underestimated (Anuar and Gretzel 2011).

Being a reality exposed to risks, vulnerabilities, or even conducive to segmentation – Minghetti and Buhalis (2010) highlight technological illiteracy and the difficulty in accessing state-of-the-art mobile equipment, as well as destinations that do not have, or cannot have smart tourism infrastructures – we are, nevertheless, facing a stimulating environment in the identification and study of new models and paradigms (Boes et al. 2016).

5 Concluding Remarks

From the perspective of a smart tourism ecosystem, the experience no longer originates exclusively on the supply side and starts to result from a process of co-creation, through interaction, where consumers are predisposed, invited, or stimulated, to be co-producers (Gretzel et al. 2015), anticipating needs and exceeding expectations, through personalization (Neuhofer et al. 2015).

For years, a rational model of purchasing behavior was assumed (Hosany and Whitam 2009), but more recently, cognitive models alone have been considered inadequate to explain consumption, which includes rational and emotional dimensions (Kuppelwieser and Klaus 2021).

We are, hopefully, facing a scenario of smart tourism (Boes et al. 2016), which results in more convenient, safe, and sustainable spaces (Williams et al. 2020), more personalized experiences, more opportunities for new services, models of business and emerging markets, with more flexible structures and different perspectives of value creation (Koens et al. 2021), where the appeal to ICT is unavoidable (Buhalis and Amaranggana 2015).

The smart tourism ecosystem assumes, in this context, a decisive role, with no predefined labels and roles assigned to the various stakeholders, as far as any of the integral elements can become a consumer, producer, or intermediary, depending, for such, resources, experiences and connections (Gretzel et al. 2015).

This means that relationships between stakeholders must be redefined, emerging innovative approaches to cooperation (Anttiroiko et al. 2014), as the ecosystem translates into an open environment, with participants from other origins, able to explore resources or establish relationships (Gretzel et al. 2015).

In the next stages of our work, we will develop a research project, through a multi-case study and considering the multi-phase approach of the experience, with data collection from managers and front-office employees of accommodation units with heritage value, focusing on the pre-visit, visit and post-visit phases; as well as the online consultation of potential tourists, in the pre-visit phase, and to on-site guests of these units, in the visit phase, complete with netnography, to study post-visit impressions.

Qualitative data, collected from the offer and the analysis of comments on social networks, will be analyzed by the appropriate content analysis. The quantitative data, collected by questionnaire, will be the object of statistical analysis.

We intend to extract implications and formulate useful recommendations, based on empirical results, for the design, communication, and facilitation of the tourist experience, within the framework of the smart tourism ecosystem, with a view to the competitiveness and sustainability of accommodation and destinations.

Acknowledgments. This research received support from the Centre of Studies in Geography and Spatial Planning (CEGOT), funded by national funds through the Foundation for Science and Technology (FCT) under the reference UIDB/04084/2020.

References

Agapito, D.: The senses in tourism design: a bibliometric review. Ann. Tour. Res. **83**, 102934 (2020). https://doi.org/10.1016/j.annals.2020.102934

Andrejevic, M., Burdon, M.: Defining the sensor society. Television New Media **16**(1), 19–36 (2015). https://doi.org/10.1177/1527476414541552

Anttiroiko, A.-V., Valkama, P., Bailey, S.J.: Smart cities in the new service economy: building platforms for smart services. AI & Soc. **29**(3), 323–334 (2014). https://doi.org/10.1007/s00146-013-0464-0

Anuar, F., Gretzel, U.: Privacy Concerns in the Context of Location-Based Services for Tourism (2011)

Barile, S., Ciasullo, M.V., Troisi, O., Sarno, D.: The role of technology and institutions in tourism service ecosystems: findings from a case study. The TQM Journal **29**(6), 811–833 (2017). https://doi.org/10.1108/TQM-06-2017-0068

Beritelli, P., Reinhold, S., Laesser, C.: Visitor flows, trajectories and corridors: Planning and designing places from the traveler's point of view. Ann. Tour. Res. **82**, 102936 (2020). https://doi.org/10.1016/j.annals.2020.102936

Boes, K., Buhalis, D., Inversini, A.: Smart tourism destinations: ecosystems for tourism destination competitiveness. Int. J. Tourism Cities **2**(2), 108–124 (2016). https://doi.org/10.1108/IJTC-12-2015-0032

Borrie, B., Roggenbuck, J.: The dynamic, emergent, and multi-phasic nature of on-site wilderness experiences. J. Leis. Res. **33**, 202–228 (2001). https://doi.org/10.1080/00222216.2001.11949938

Buhalis, D., Amaranggana, A.: Smart tourism destinations enhancing tourism experience through personalisation of services. In: Tussyadiah, I., Inversini, A. (eds.) Information and Communication Technologies in Tourism 2015, pp. 377–389. Springer, Cham (2015). https://doi.org/10.1007/978-3-319-14343-9_28

Clawson, M., Knetsch, J.: Economics of Outdoor Recreation. John Hopkins University Press (1966)

Cohen, E.: A phenomenology of tourist experiences. Sociology **13**(2), 179–201 (1979). https://doi.org/10.1177/003803857901300203

Cutler, S., Carmichael, B.: The dimensions of the tourist experience. In: The Tourism and Leisure Experience, pp. 3–26. Channel View Publications (2010). https://doi.org/10.21832/9781845411503-004

Graburn, N.H.H., Barthel-Bouchier, D.: Relocating the tourist. Int. Sociol. **16**(2), 147–158 (2001). https://doi.org/10.1177/0268580901016002001

Gretzel, U., Sigala, M., Xiang, Z., Koo, C.: Smart tourism: foundations and developments. Electron. Mark. **25**(3), 179–188 (2015). https://doi.org/10.1007/s12525-015-0196-8

Gretzel, U., Werthner, H., Koo, C., Lamsfus, C.: Conceptual foundations for understanding smart tourism ecosystems. Computers in Human Behavior **50**(C), 558–563 (2015). https://doi.org/10.1016/j.chb.2015.03.043

Guo, Y., Liu, H., Chai, Y.: The embedding convergence of smart cities and tourism internet of things in China: an advance perspective. Advances in Hospitality and Tourism Res. **2**, 54–69 (2014)

Hayllar, B., Griffin, T.: The precinct experience: a phenomenological approach. Tour. Manage. **26**, 517–528 (2005). https://doi.org/10.1016/j.tourman.2004.03.011

Henrique de Souza, L., Kastenholz, E., Barbosa, M.A.: Relevant dimensions of tourist experiences in unique, alternative person-to-person accommodation—sharing castles, treehouses, windmills, houseboats or house-buses. Int. J. Hospitality Tourism Admin. **21**(4), 390–421 (2020). https://doi.org/10.1080/15256480.2018.1511495

Hirschman, E.C., Holbrook, M.B.: Hedonic consumption: emerging concepts, methods and propositions. J. Mark. **46**(3), 92–101 (1982). https://doi.org/10.2307/1251707

Hosany, S., Witham, M.: Dimensions of cruisers' experiences, satisfaction, and intention to recommend. J. Travel Res. **49**, 351–364 (2009). https://doi.org/10.1177/0047287509346859

Jensen, J.M.: Shopping orientation and online travel shopping: the role of travel experience. Int. J. Tour. Res. **14**(1), 56–70 (2012). https://doi.org/10.1002/jtr.835

Kim, J., Fesenmaier, D.R.: Tourism experience and tourism design. In: Fesenmaier, D.R., Xiang, Z. (eds.) Design Science in Tourism. TV, pp. 17–29. Springer, Cham (2017). https://doi.org/10.1007/978-3-319-42773-7_2

Kim, D., Perdue, R.R.: The effects of cognitive, affective, and sensory attributes on hotel choice. Int. J. Hosp. Manag. **35**, 246–257 (2013). https://doi.org/10.1016/j.ijhm.2013.05.012

Koens, K., Smit, B., Melissen, F.: Designing destinations for good: using design roadmapping to support pro-active destination development. Ann. Tour. Res. **89**, 103233 (2021). https://doi.org/10.1016/j.annals.2021.103233

Kuppelwieser, V.G., Klaus, P.: Measuring customer experience quality: the EXQ scale revisited. J. Bus. Res. **126**, 624–633 (2021). https://doi.org/10.1016/j.jbusres.2020.01.042

Lamsfus, C., Martín, D., Alzua-Sorzabal, A., Torres-Manzanera, E.: Smart tourism destinations: an extended conception of smart cities focusing on human mobility. In: Tussyadiah, I., Inversini, A. (eds.) Information and Communication Technologies in Tourism 2015, pp. 363–375. Springer, Cham (2015). https://doi.org/10.1007/978-3-319-14343-9_27

Larsen, S.: Aspects of a psychology of the tourist experience. Scand. J. Hosp. Tour. **7**, 7–18 (2007). https://doi.org/10.1080/15022250701226014

López de Avila, A.: Smart destinations: XXI century tourism. In: Journal of Destination Marketing & Management. ENTER2015 Conference on information and communication technologies in tourism, Lugano, Switzerland (2015)

Lovelock, C., Gummesson, E.: Whither services marketing? in search of a new paradigm and fresh perspectives. J. Services Research **7**, 20–41 (2004). https://doi.org/10.1177/1094670504266131

Maglio, P., Spohrer, J.: Fundamentals of service science. J. Acad. Mark. Sci. **36**, 18–20 (2007). https://doi.org/10.1007/s11747-007-0058-9

Manthiou, A., Lee, S.(Ally), Tang, L., Chiang, L.: The experience economy approach to festival marketing: vivid memory and attendee loyalty. J. Services Marketing **28**, 22–35 (2014). https://doi.org/10.1108/JSM-06-2012-0105

McIntosh, A.J., Prentice, R.: Affirming authenticity: consuming cultural heritage. Annals of Tourism Research **26**(3), 589–612 (1999). https://doi.org/10.1016/S0160-7383(99)00010-9

Miao, L., Lehto, X., Wei, W.: The Hedonic value of hospitality consumption: evidence from spring break experiences. J. Hosp. Market. Manag. **23**, 99–121 (2014). https://doi.org/10.1080/19368623.2013.766582

Minghetti, V., Buhalis, D.: Digital divide in tourism. J. Travel Res. **49**(3), 267–281 (2010). https://doi.org/10.1177/0047287509346843

Morabito, V.: Big Data and Analytics: Strategic and Organizational Impacts (2015)

Mossberg, L.: A marketing approach to the tourist experience. Scand. J. Hosp. Tour. **7**(1), 59–74 (2007). https://doi.org/10.1080/15022250701231915

Neuhofer, B., Buhalis, D., Ladkin, A.: Technology as a catalyst of change: enablers and barriers of the tourist experience and their consequences. In: Tussyadiah, I., Inversini, A. (eds.) Information and Communication Technologies in Tourism 2015, pp. 789–802. Springer, Cham (2015). https://doi.org/10.1007/978-3-319-14343-9_57

Nickerson, N.: Some Reflections on Quality Tourism Experiences, pp. 227–235 (2006). https://doi.org/10.1016/B978-0-7506-7811-7.50023-7

Phi, G., Dredge, D.: Critical issues in tourism co-creation. Tour. Recreat. Res. **44**, 281–283 (2019). https://doi.org/10.1080/02508281.2019.1640492

Polese, F., Botti, A., Grimaldi, M., Monda, A., Vesci, M.: Social innovation in smart tourism ecosystems: how technology and institutions shape sustainable value co-creation. Sustainability **10**(1), 140 (2018). https://doi.org/10.3390/su10010140

Rasoolimanesh, S.M., Seyfi, S., Hall, C.M., Hatamifar, P.: Understanding memorable tourism experiences and behavioural intentions of heritage tourists. J. Destin. Mark. Manag. **21**, 100621 (2021). https://doi.org/10.1016/j.jdmm.2021.100621

Rojas, C., Camarero, C.: Visitors' experience, mood and satisfaction in a heritage context: evidence from an interpretation center. Tour. Manage. **29**, 525–537 (2008). https://doi.org/10.1016/j.tourman.2007.06.004

Seabra, C., Cravidão, F., Gomes, G.: Tourism industry after the COVID-19 crisis in Portugal - Now what?. In: "Over Tourism" and "Tourism Over" Recovery from COVID19 Tourism Crisis in Regions with Over and Under Tourism. Eds. Anna, T., Tomasz, D., Jurgen, S.: World Scientific Publisher, London (2021)

Sigala, M.: Gamification for crowdsourcing marketing practices: applications and benefits in tourism. In: Garrigos-Simon, F.J., Gil-Pechuán, I., Estelles-Miguel, S. (eds.) Advances in Crowdsourcing, pp. 129–145. Springer, Cham (2015). https://doi.org/10.1007/978-3-319-18341-1_11

Tu, K., Liu, A.: Framework of Smart Tourism Research and Related Progress in China. pp. 140–146 (2014)

Tung, V., Ritchie, J.R.: Exploring the essence of memorable tourism experiences. Annals of Tourism Research - Ann Tourism Res **38**, 1367–1386 (2011). https://doi.org/10.1016/j.annals.2011.03.009

Vargo, S., Akaka, M.: Value cocreation and service systems (re)formation: a service ecosystems view. Serv. Sci. **4**, 207–217 (2012). https://doi.org/10.1287/serv.1120.0019

Vaz Serra, P., Seabra, C.: Digital influencers and tourist destinations: cristiano ronaldo and madeira island, from promotion to impact. In: Guarda, T., Portela, F., Santos, M.F. (eds.) ARTIIS 2021. CCIS, vol. 1485, pp. 302–317. Springer, Cham (2021). https://doi.org/10.1007/978-3-030-90241-4_24

Vogt, J.W.: Wandering: youth and travel behavior. Ann. Tour. Res. **4**(1), 25–41 (1976). https://doi.org/10.1016/0160-7383(76)90051-7

Voigt, C., Howat, G., Brown, G.: Hedonic and eudaimonic experiences among wellness tourists: an exploratory enquiry. Annals of Leisure Research **13**(3), 541–562 (2010). https://doi.org/10.1080/11745398.2010.9686862

Walls, A., Okumus, F., Kwun, D.: An epistemological view of consumer experiences. Int. J. Hospitality Manage. – Int. J. Hosp. Manag. **30**, 10–21 (2011). https://doi.org/10.1016/j.ijhm.2010.03.008

Williams, A., Rodríguez Sánchez, I., Makkonen, T.: Innovation and smart destinations: critical insights. Annals of Tourism Res. **83**, 102930 (2020). https://doi.org/10.1016/j.annals.2020.102930

Xiang, Z., Stienmetz, J., Fesenmaier, D.R.: Smart tourism design: launching the annals of tourism research curated collection on designing tourism places. Ann. Tour. Res. **86**, 103154 (2021). https://doi.org/10.1016/j.annals.2021.103154

Yoo, K.-H., Sigala, M., Gretzel, U.: Exploring TripAdvisor. In: Egger, R., Gula, I., Walcher, D. (Eds.): Open Tourism – Open Innovation, Crowdsourcing and Collaborative Consumption challenging the tourism industry (2015)

Zaltman, G.: How Customers Think: Essential Insights into the Mind of the Market (1st edition). Harvard Business School Press (2003)

Exploring COVID-19 Technological Impacts on Portuguese Hotel Chains– CEO´s Perspective

Susana Mesquita[1]([⊠]) [iD], Sofia Almeida[2] [iD], and Maria José Sousa[3] [iD]

[1] Research Unit On Governance, Competitiveness and Public Policies (GOVCOPP),
Universidade de Aveiro, Aveiro, Portugal
smvm@ua.pt

[2] Universidade Europeia, CEG-Territur Universidade de Lisboa, Lisbon, Portugal

[3] Instituto Universitário de Lisboa (ISCTE-IUL), Business Research Unit (BRU-IUL),
Lisbon, Portugal

Abstract. This paper is about the perspectives of Portuguese big players, such as hotel companies between the two lockdowns. This research intends to capt the reaction of the CEOs of the biggest hotel chains in Portugal. The aims of this research are: 1) to identify different types of impacts in the hotel sector; 2) to ascertain different solutions which help to take managing decisions mainly related with technologies; 3) to help creating a strategy that will leverage the economy now that this pandemic is no longer an unknown subject but still to be considered one of the biggest crises that affected the tourism sector. To assure the achievement of the referred aims a qualitative method is applied to this research. Two semi-structured interviews were applied to the most ranking hotel chains´ decision-makers in Portugal. The script was based on the Literature Review about COVID-19 and crisis impacts. The paper highlights some of the most important economic, financial impacts, technological, organizational and operational impacts that were experienced by Portuguese hotel chains during those hard times. As limitations authors identified the small sample. An extension of the sample to other hotel companies will make the results more representative.Conclusions and implications drawn are critical to improve the experience in the tourism sector after covid-19 crisis.

Keywords: Hotel chains · COVID-19 · Impacts · Economic crisis · Portugal

1 Introduction

Tourism is an umbrella industry with an amalgam of sub sectors, and it is, nowadays, considered one of the most economically important industries in the world [1], as well as one of the most vulnerable to crises [2, 3]. In this sense, it is important to understand the impacts that the present situation of pandemic due to COVID-19 brought to one of the most important tourism sub sectors - hospitality, and the way that two of the biggest hotel chains in Portugal deal with the crisis. The COVID-19 led to financial concerns and therefore businesses asked governments and lending institutions for financial aids

T. Guarda et al. (Eds.): ARTIIS 2022, CCIS 1676, pp. 137–149, 2022.
https://doi.org/10.1007/978-3-031-20316-9_11

packages, tax break considerations and interest waivers on loans [4]. Tourism investments provided immediate benefits to the local economy through exports promotion,
employment creation, and transfer of new technologies and ideas. However, one of the
risks was the economic dependence and the environmental damage [5]. To date, numerous econometric studies, since the early 2000s, have empirically highlighted the link
between tourism and long-run growth. The results of these studies suggest that it is
difficult to find a robust relationship between international tourism and growth [6]. In
addition, some researchers have attempted to identify a relationship between investment,
tourism and economic growth [7, 8], with divergent results.

Although the literature has already abundantly studied the direct interaction between
investments and economic growth and tourism, there is a notable gap in empirical studies
evaluating the effects of COVID-19 Pandemic in the hospitality sector [9]. Most of the
studies are mainly literature-review or qualitative research [9]. Thus, this study intents to
analyse the economic, financial, organizational, operational and technological impacts
of the pandemic crises in the investments in hospitality industry, based in two case studies
of two of the biggest hotel chains in Portugal.

Following this context, and driving from theory, one research question arises: What
are the main impacts of the pandemic crises of COVID-19 in hotel companies? To answer
this question two objectives were designed: i) to examine the economic, financial, organizational, operational, and technologic impacts of the pandemic crises in the investments
in hospitality industry; ii) to create a strategy for hotel chains that will leverage the
economy after this pandemic.

This paper is structured as follows: first, a literature review about tourism and
COVID-19 and economic, financial, organizational, operational and technological
impacts is present. Subsequently, the methodology is described. Next, there is an analysis
and discussion of results, followed by the presentation of conclusion and implications for
hotel chains' managers to promote strategies to overcome the losses experienced during
this period. This section also provides theoretical, practical, and policy implications. It
also presents the limitations and future research under study related to this topic.

2   COVID-19 and Tourism

Tourism is a highly exposed industry that is affected by external factors and can have
environmental, political and socio-economic impacts [11]. This means that over time
tourism has become resilient in overcoming different crisis/disasters (e.g., terrorism,
earthquakes, Ebola, tsunami…) [10, 12]. Despite this, the global pandemic of the novel
coronavirus (COVID 19) has proved to be different [9, 11]. The outbreak caused by
the pandemic challenged the normal operations of enterprises [9, 13]. Still, there was
a unanimous opinion to see this pandemic as an opportunity to improve the tourism
sector. In 2020 a new issue was raised by the World Health Organisation (WHO), when
declaring on the 30[th of] January a global health emergency that, in approximately two
months (March 2020), was named a pandemic [14]. COVID -19 caused big impacts on
the global economic, political and socio-cultural systems [11].

An organization's functioning and survival can be largely affected by natural disasters, industrial accidents, terrorism, and this is a fact, especially in the case of hospitality

and tourism industry [15, 16]. The history of tourism is marked by countless disaster situations (e.g., the 11th of September 2001 terrorist attack in New York, the tsunami in Thailand in 2004, the hurricane disaster in New Orleans in 2005, the November 2008 terrorist attack in Mumbai in India) [17] but none with such a dimension as the one of COVID-19. Comparable patterns on smaller scales can be taken from previous studies on other disasters, such as the bird-flu [18], Ebola [19] or influenza A (H5N1), known as Avian Flu, originally a bird-specific flu [20].

Both public and private sectors were affected and to minimize the negative impacts of COVID-19 several measures have been undertaken by governments worldwide [4]. These measures include social distancing, travel and mobility restrictions, community lockdowns, stay at home campaigns, self or mandatory quarantine, curbs on crowding, closing some sectors of the service industries considered less essential [11, 14]. Quickly, the sector, sought to adapt to this new reality with new policies, such as flexi-cancellation policies, flexi-rates for all services and strict hygiene policies [13].

Concerning the private sector, crises always required high levels of focus, resources, managerial accountability, and innovation. There are some researchers who have analysed crisis management actions and strategies to the hospitality and tourism sectors [16, 17, 21–24]. However, the dimension of consequences of this crisis imposes much more studies due to its amalgam complexity. Changes are needed on the demand and supply sides. According to Zenker and Kock [25] this pandemic can create deep marks in the way tourist's think and act during their trips. As a result, it is expected for tourists to increase the selection of domestic destinations in the aim of supporting the national economy, which may constitute a barrier in tourist behaviour on far distant destination choices [25]. Another aspect to have in consideration is the trend to avoid crowdedness and mass-tourism destinations, giving place to less populated destinations [25, 26].

As the effect of pandemics is crucial for tourism on the business side changes are also expected as some aspects of our behaviour will also shift [4].

2.1 Economic and Financial Impacts Post Lockdown

In times of crises, the positive and negative impacts in tourism related to investments are numerous and in several key areas, namely capital, technology and organizational structures and practices. In a potentially volatile and fragile economy [27] resultant of the COVID-19 pandemic hotel chains can be more robust and stable than local firms and thus help to ensure the stability (and confidence in) of the economy [28].

The diversification of the products and services is leading to innovative responses with impact on human resources, as new rules for safety at work are needed, and in addition new development skills to follow all the safety and security standards [29].

Hotel chains continue to find new services for the tourists with new loyalty programs, and the development of new Apps to help the clients in all the situations and to maintain a close relationship with their customers [30]. The impact on local firms is very high as tourism related hotel chain traditionally try to establish linkages with local suppliers and distributors, which generate economic activity and business opportunities. However, the pandemic crises imposed a focus on the government requests and actions, and the hotel chains assumed a very important role in helping the healthcare professionals – which means that they continue to support the suppliers and distributers but at a lower level of dynamism.

This context of crisis has negative impacts in the Balance-of-payments as hotel chains traditionally repatriate profits [31], but at the same time they boost tourist arrivals and hence foreign exchange earnings considerably [28]. With the lockdown of the countries and the safety measures the sector was even more volatile and vulnerable. However, the governments defined new policies to overcome the difficult economic situation, and to maintain and increase foreign involvement in tourism and hospitality industry [31]. The policy framework was focused in encouraging the firm's capability to continue their business and to recover the losses of the past months. To take full advantage of Foreign Direct Investment (FDI) as a catalyst and a complement to domestic investment, a coherent and integrated policy framework was essential.

The economic uncertainty derived by the global pandemic lead the multinational enterprises (MNEs) to restrict capital expenditures, which impacts negatively the investments flows. The decrease of MNEs profits lead to less profits for reinvesting. According to Unctad reports [32] the reinvested earnings were 40% of the total investments inflows, resulting from the economies hardest impact of COVID-19. The main global impacts in hospitality regarding the factors that condition the FDI in the sector were of several nature. They included organizational impacts, with new practices, mainly regarding health and safety at the workplace, but also concerning the infrastructures used by the customers, as a faster movement regarding technological transformations, with the creation of new digital services [31], to facilitate the relationship with costumers, regarding the booking process, the check in and the check-out processes (with automatized systems, without human contact).

Regarding hospitality management, new leadership models are needed to lead remote workers that perform back-office activities. It is a challenge, and it requires new skills regarding management by goals, motivation, coaching, and also about new ways of improving the efficiency and efficacy of work. Also, a new management models is required to focus on health issues at first, to ensure that the health and safety principles are defined, implemented, and followed in order to preserve the lives of the workers and of the customers. The management processes are being influenced, and also the relationships between the hospitality sector and the customers, which requires the development of new skills, strengthening the capacity of hospitality from professionals regarding their relationships with the customers. These transformations require the development of new skills from the hospitality professionals All those impacts required investment and the hotel companies needed not only the financial support from governments [29], but also a structured plan of investment in terms of the future of the hotel chains in order to guarantee the sustainability of the business, and also the future economic growth [31].

2.2 Organizational and Operational Impacts Post Lockdown

As one of the major employment providers, in a short time tourism industry had to deal with an unusual situation that led to a huge layoff of workforce both in different sectors, due to the direct and indirect effects of COVID -19 virus. Known for its "high seasonality", those who were as temporary employees saw their jobs cut due to the new coronavirus. Since the announcement of the pandemic by World Health Organization

(WHO) in March 2020, human resources had to deal with the fear concerning their health and uncertainties about their jobs. With the help of companies' employee self-efficacy, hope, resilience, and optimism were maintained [34]. An estimated number of millions of workers found themselves unemployed [4]. The business accountability laws CSR (Corporate social responsibility) and the responsibility of businesses towards their employees were essential for the "credibility" of businesses [4].

2.3 Technological Impacts Post Lockdown

It is widely recognized that technology has become intrinsically connected with the travel and tourism industry [35]. Some of the main strategies referred by researchers to minimize the impacts of COVID-19 on the tourism sector involve technologies [11].

Currently, The *World Wide Web* is one indispensable channel for information searching [36] and for the hotel industry is the web-effectiveness [37]. The physical distance imposed by the circumstance prevented people from accessing information using traditional means. Thus, internet became the most common way to search for information. With permission, this is an effective way to obtain more information about the buying profile of the customers. This allows hotel suppliers the chance to communicate adequately with their target audience, refining their message and service delivery [37]. The solutions are in giving accurate information in order to reach potential customers [38]. A hotel website is a mean of communication and an important electronic platform which increases sales volume and improves the hotel notoriety [38]. In the literature Pre COVID, findings indicated a poor effectiveness of hotel-web [39, 40]. Contactless technology is important for building customer confidence. Eliminating guests' touchpoint is one of the biggest concerns of hotel managers. This can be achieved by digital platforms, QR codes, apps minimizing the staff interaction. Self-service kiosks and customers mobile devices allow customers to complete check-in and check-out automatically without involving contact with employers [41, 42].

In a crisis like COVID-19 it was important for hotel companies to adopt strategies to actively try to minimize economic and social impacts. Other changes were implemented by hospitality managements as it will be stated in the present study.

3   Methodology

One of the most important concerns of qualitative methods is rigor. Bearing this is mind, authors were looking for explaining their strategy with detail [43]. Qualitative data tend to be rich [44] and collected on an ongoing basis in order not to lose its relevance [45] or deriving from participants or data sources with differing perspectives [46]. To collect information, authors used in-depth interviews. According to Veal [47] this instrument is appropriate when there is a small number of subjects. The Interviewer guided the answers. After being transcribed, the results were categorized according to the themes of the literature review.

Nevertheless, categorization is the heart of qualitative analysis. Van Maanen [48, p.541] mentioned "categorizing" as a step to move from data to more general findings. It is important to actively construct categories based on the existing knowledge and the categorization process [49, 50]. In this research it was used the *Active Categorization Framework* [51] to create different categories in order to analyze the content. "Approaching the data with specific questions that researchers want answers to" [51, p. 42] is the basis of research. Categories of this research were created through the literature review and tourism reports about the impacts of COVID-19 and the answers given by two CEOS. Both are references in the hotel management sector having experience in crisis management in difficult economic periods.

3.1 Sample

The population of this research was identified through the *Atlas da Hotelaria* [52], an annual ranking of the biggest 20 hotel chains in Portugal. In 2020, the first five hotel chains were: 1st Pestana Group; 2nd Vila Galé; 3rd Accor Hotels; 4th Minor Hotels and 5th Hoti Hotels/Melia Resorts. For this research the first two were chosen to deeply analyze different impacts on the hotel operation after the appearance of COVID-19.

The Pestana Hotel Group opened its first hotel in 1974 at Funchal, Madeira: The Pestana Carlton. In 1998 the Group started its international process to Mozambique. The Expansion for Europe, started in 2010 with the first hotel in London. A process of rebranding took place in 2015 and five years later the Group opened its 100th hotel. Nowadays, Pestana Group has the following sub-brands: Pestana Hotels and Resorts; Pestana Pousadas de Portugal; Pestana Collection Hotels and Pestana CR7 Lifestyle Hotels.

Vila Galé is the second largest Portuguese hotel group, and it is among the 200 largest hotel companies in the world. The Vila Galé Group was founded in 1986. The first hotel of the group was Vila Galé Atlântico at Praia da Galé, founded in 1988. In 2001, the Group started operations in Brazil, in Fortaleza. Different service standards allow Vila Galé to have different concepts which illustrates the Group's demanding standards: Inevitable (restaurants), Satsang (spa and health club), Clube NEP (space dedicated to children) and Santa Vitória (wines and olive oils) (Table 1).

Table 1. Sample characterization (2020)

	Pestana hotel group	Vila Galé group
- Year / place of foundation	Funchal, Madeira	Praia da Galé, Algarve
- CEO	Dionisio Pestana	Jorge Rebelo de Almeida
- Total number of hotels around the world	Total: 100 hotels Portugal = 80; Europe = 5; North America = 2; South America = 5 and Africa = 8	Total: 37 hotels Portugal = 27; South America = 10
- Total number of bedrooms	8.137	4.463
- Total number of beds	16.596	9.237
- Total number of employees	+ 7.000 employees	3. 200 employees

Source: authors

3.2 Data Collection Procedure

Concerning the data collection procedures, both interviews took place in Lisbon after the first lockdown, in July. The duration varied between one to two hours. The conditions under which the interviews were conducted considered the following procedures: i) each of the interviews was recorded with the authorization of the interviewees; ii) the interviews were transcribed and analysed.

The interviews were composed of 10 open questions, constructed from the literature review on the impacts of Covid'19 and from industry reports. The respondents are hotel chains administrators, working for more than 10 years in their hotel companies. Regarding the data analysis methods, the authors used content analyses to this research. The interview has three different sections. In the first section, the respondents shared their point of view about general impacts on this incomparable situation, being more focused on the different dimensions of the impacts, such as: economic, financial; technological; organizational and operational. In the second section, it was explaining how Portuguese hotel chains adapted to this crisis giving few operational examples. In the third section it was explained how hotel companies turned the current crisis into an opportunity. Pestana Administrator will be the Respondent 1 (R1) and Vila Galé Administrator will be the Respondent 2 (R2).

4   Results

Confronted with different points of view about the impacts of this virus on the tourism sector, both interviewers agreed that the bigger impact was to cease all the operation. In case of R2 the operation in all the hotels was closed. According to the respondent: *"The main impact was to close all operations and to take some important decisions concerning some projects: 1st new hotels; 2nd hotels that had been closed in the low season were now starting to open and 3rd hotels that would reopen after renovations"*. R1 said that: *"most of the portfolio ceased activity with the exception of a few hotels that kept operating in cooperation with local governments (Cape Verde or S. Tomé) or with Portuguese Government Health programs"*. Meanwhile R2 highlighted the lack of data and of some counter-information as one of the main problems: *"the group had to reflect on what was coming out in terms of legislation, recommendations"*.

Concerning the economic impacts such as the employment, R1 referred that during the confinement, their employment strategy was reinforced in some specific areas: well-being, education, communication and social responsibility. A Contingency Plan with preventive measures was swiftly implemented, protective individual equipment was handed out and telework was encouraged. The company invested in digital education and offered external access to a learning platform with over 6000 videos on broad areas such as management, leadership, digital marketing or soft skills. The group maintained its commitment with Social Responsibility, within Pestana Planet Guest program, both internally and externally. Pestana volunteers donated their skills, offering online legal advice or private lessons to their coworkers' children, and the company provided computers for workers households for tele schooling purposes. R2 explained that the group integrated 85% of people on layoff, and four people per shift in each of the hotels. In the central offices, employers went home and worked from there. Both interviewers agreed that the best option was to incentive the telework, even before the Emergency State decreed.

Relative to the financial impacts, R2 mentioned that despite everything, this pandemic did not change the timetable for the acquisition of new units and the renewal of the existing ones, once that the budget was already fully awarded. The respondent said that *'The Alter and Serra da Estrela hotels were in the final stages of construction. The pipeline already included an extension to the Douro hotel and another renovation in São Paulo, Brazil. We did not stop any of these projects because they were all nearing completion'*. R1 denoted as financial impacts the changing of objectives. After the lockdown, the group objective was to work to avoid registering a negative EBITDA, which is clearly a very different scenario from the last three years, where results had been consecutively very good. *"Despite this, Pestana Hotel Group is financially solid"* said the responsible.

Regarding the technological impacts, the same respondent, R1 pointed out the improvement of the website by creating a specific COVID-19 area. Permanently updated with the group's news related to COVID-19. It has been one of the most visited areas of our site'. The Reservations and Call Center has been rendering constant support to guests due to the changes and cancellations of reservations that had to be dealt, offering alternatives, better deals, specifically targeted packages and penalty free cancelations when needed. A social media campaign has been up running since the beginning of the crisis, under the motto #BeSafe #BePositive #BeInspired. Another technological impact is about the Business Intelligence area, which has been critical in providing thorough analysis on the markets', competition, and opportunities, informing all areas, and namely Revenue Management, and allowing for swift informed decisions in response to demands and trends, helping to detect opportunities for reopening. The last impact mentioned by the R1 was about the Pestana App, which was redesigned and improved for easy reservation, digital check in and check out, digital door opening, ordering new services such as food and beverage, reserving restaurants and other services, access to information and media, among others, improving the guests' experience, while contributing to social distancing. R2 responds to the same challenge, describing technological impacts as the acceleration of the IT department - accelerated tech projects that involve digitalization of services and different forms of interaction with the customer. 'My Vila Galé is the new App, and the group is considering new digital platforms in purchases'. Both respondents were already working in a new app to help customers during their journey in the hotels and boost their experience. This crisis only accelerated its use in the market.

According to R1, the organizational impacts are described as the telework model brought by the crisis and it will be integrated in the new management model – even if at a different level – and in particular for their shared services. According to R1 *'Acceleration of digital competencies is a priority for all companies who wish to maintain attractiveness. Business models will necessarily integrate innovation, such as the Pestana App, for instance'*. About this same theme, R2 stated that another big transformation is changing the logic of promotional campaigns. Until now the campaigns were multimarket and multisegmented. With this virus and the borders closed, the group had to concentrate everything in Portugal. The responsible mentioned that *'The group is waiting for the opening of the borders with Spain to carry out test-campaigns with this market. The second step will be to test the German market because the UK market is still very confused. The Group's focus is on Portugal, on families and on indirect discount and add on in all types of rooms*, as additional offer for those who book with dinner; additional discounts for large families additional incentives for those staying more than seven nights. The logic is not promoting the direct discount but making indirect promotions. Another impact is the transformation of buffets. A new buffet model appears, the prior mandatory appointment for all types of services and this will bring changes in the organization of the company. 'Some of these measures will be transitory, others will remain', referred R2.

In the optic of R1 the operational impacts in the hotel companies caused by this virus are the implementation of new measures including strategically planned out and well-marked ways which allow to move around the properties to control traffic flow and ensure social distancing. Also new services and features on the Pestana App allow guests to have less in-person contact with team members, along with acrylic protective barriers at check-in areas. Another operational impact is the frequency and procedures of the cleaning regimens, which have been reinforced in both public spaces and guestrooms. Team members are always wearing protective gear (masks, gloves, shoe protection) and guests will be reminded of the recommendations from the health authorities about social distancing. In the perspective of R2, this virus will require some changes at operational level, namely the imposition of social distance between employers and guests. Vila Galé must adopt new measures to guarantee the implementation of these rules. Human contact continues to exist always, but the group will try to overlook the bureaucratic and administrative part of check ins and guests' reception.

Once that lockdown forced people to change their social habits, hotel companies also had to rethink the business in order to develop new practices launched to attract tourists. Accordingly, R2 defends that one of the actions launched to get new customers is to invest in digital platforms to streamline, for example, the purchase process to help with cost analysis. This will be an internal tool for hotel managers to control the areas of shopping and hotel management. This tool permits to help in the purchase of quantities; compare prices of different suppliers; provide better suggestions, quantity recommendations based on a history and business intelligence. R2 said that '*My Vila Galé app allows customers to check in and check out online, filling out online questionnaires, checking their account, seeing news, and giving feedback. It's almost ready*'. R1 mentioned that the group launched a special campaign exclusive to healthcare workers for all their hard work and commitment in managing the effects of the pandemic in Portugal. Until the end of the year, these professionals can enjoy a 50% discount in their stays at the Pousadas de Portugal. The goal is to target the internal market – as borders and restrictions remain in place – the purpose is to remind our Portuguese guests of the group's diversity and safety. Its portfolio covers the whole territory and caters to all. All these advantages and campaigns are also available via the Pestana App. R1 referred that the Group has redesigned its loyalty program.

With reference to new trends after COVID-19, R1 said that '*Telework for back-office services*' is one of the trends, another is the reinforcement of the safety and hygiene regulations and standards. The third trend is the diversification and specialization of specific services and niches – eco-tourism, cultural tourism. '*I think this has reinforced the use of digital media, both in research and in reservations and purchases'* said R2. The Respondents added that many restaurants use this tool to present their menus. This pandemic accelerated some trends, as exclusive experiences in less crowded areas.

5 Conclusion

The present research allows an understanding of how COVID-19 and the lockdown brought several damages for society and for the economy. Since that Tourism is one of the most harmed sectors, the accommodation is going through one of the biggest crises ever. Kibrom, Kibrom and Woldemichael [53] mentioned that people are still look for solutions with reduced personal interactions and information and communications technology (ICT) are providing solutions. Beside this, Governments around the world are helping hotel companies with specific measures, special layoff help and support for more investment. The ultimate objective is gaining knowledge to help creating a strategy that will leverage the economy after this pandemic. Administrators believe that investment is part of a longtime strategy, once that they already had plan to new hotels abroad. Hopefully, investments will help to create a smarter hospitality industry, which is in line with the literature review and the interviewees' answers.

The main contributions for policy are an analysis the impacts of COVID-19 in hospitality companies, which can provide information for the definition of new strategies regarding the technological aspects, the skills development and the organizational aspects related to health procedures. In this regard, this research is a call for action from policymakers to develop policies more focused on the crises challenges of hospitality industry. Policymakers can also work with the hospitality industry to help them to transform their services to contribute with essential services during the COVID-19 crises and support them to manage their increased operating risks [27]. The present article contributes to both theory and practice. As far as theoretical contributions are concerned, this paper contributes to the existing literature as a first attempt to empirically investigate the impacts of COVID-19 in hospitality industry and provides theoretical insights considering different types of impacts in the tourism sector. First, it adds value regarding the economic, financial, organizational, operational and the technological impacts post lockdown. Related to managerial contributes this research intends to be an insightful approach for hotel companies, once that they can follow the examples of the big leaders of the industry. Research results also provide some highlights about the future of the hotel sector after the COVID-19, helping industry professionals to take more informed decisions. In an increasingly, complex, uncertain and fast-moving world, hopefully these results will help to decode the future.

As limitations the authors identified the small sample. An extension of the sample to other hotel companies will make the results more representative. Instead of using an interview, a survey would allow to extract more information and send it to more decision makers. Another important limitation was concerned with the geographical scope of the study. It would be desirable to extend the study to a larger sample of countries.

This approach would enable to have the opinion of a wide variety of cultural environments and hotel contexts, which would contribute to allow to extrapolate this reality to other hotel players in a more reliable way. It would be interesting in the future to analyse other sub-sectors, namely, travel agencies and tour operators, the transport sector, in particular aviation companies, tourist entertainment companies, events and restaurants.

A comparative analysis would be useful to find out what are the common points of tourism operation and to identify divergences of a sector with so much influence on the GDP of the receptive countries. As for further research authors recommended cross-validation with other active methods. Comparing the obtained results with the point of view of experts for each type of impacts, through a focus group or a survey. From this comparison and data extrapolation, the application of Delphi methodology would help to identify future trends for different expertise areas and look for new impacts.

References

1. UNWTO Guidelines for Institutional Strengthening of Destination Management Organizations (DMOs) – Preparing DMOs for new challenges (2019). https://www.e-unwto.org/doi/pdf/https://doi.org/10.18111/9789284420841
2. Constantoglou, M., Prinitis, M.: Tourism destination crisis management: the case study of Lesvos Island. J. Tourism Sustainability 3(2), 14–31 (2020)
3. Pforr, C., Hosie, P.J.: Crisis management in tourism: preparing for recovery. J. Travel Tour. Mark. 23(2–4), 249–264 (2008). https://doi.org/10.1300/J073v23n02_19
4. Khan, S.: COVID-19: Tourism at crossroads. Where next? Journal on Tourism and Sustainability, 3, (2), 32- 40 (2020)
5. Kumar, N.: Financial inclusion and its determinants: evidence from India. J. Financial Economic Policy 5(1), 4–19 (2013). https://doi.org/10.1108/17576381311317754
6. Sintes-Inchausti, F.: Tourism: economic growth, employment and dutch disease. Annals of Tourism Research, Elsevier 54(C), 172–189 (2015) https://doi.org/10.1016/j.annals.2015.07.007
7. Fauzel, S., Seetanah, B., Sannassee, R.V.: A dynamic investigation of foreign direct investment and poverty reduction in Mauritiu. Theoretical Economics Letters 6(2), 289–303 (2016)
8. Yu-Chi, S., Lin, H.P.: Causality relationship between tourism, foreign direct investment and economic growth in Taiwan. Asian J. Econ. Model. 6(3), 287–293 (2018)
9. Chen, C.C., Zou, S.S., Chen, M.H.: The fear of being infected and fired: examining the dual job stressors of hospitality employees during COVID-19. Int. J. Hosp. Manag. 102, 103131 (2022)
10. Park, E., Woo-Hyuk, K., Sung-Bum, K.: How does COVID-19 differ from previous crises? a comparative study of health-related crisis research in the tourism and hospitality context. Int. J. Hospitality Manage. 103199 (2022)
11. Sigala, M.: Tourism and COVID-19: impacts and implications for advancing and resetting industry and research. J. Bus. Res. 117, 312–321 (2020)
12. Novelli, M., Burgess, L.G., Jones, A., Ritchie, B.W.: "No Ebola … still doomed" – the Ebola-induced tourism crisis. Ann. Tour. Res. 70, 76–87 (2018). https://doi.org/10.1016/j.annals
13. Ranasinghe, R., et al.: Tourism after Corona: impacts of Covid 19 pandemic and way forward for tourism, hotel and mice industry in Sri Lanka. Hotel and Mice Industry in Sri Lanka (2020)
14. Williams, C.C., Kayaoglu, A.: COVID-19 and undeclared work: impacts and policy responses in Europe. The Service Industries J. 40(1314), 914–931 (2020)
15. Caponigro, J.R.: The Crisis Counselor: A Step-by-Step Guide to Managing a Business Crisis. Contemporary Books, Chicago (2000)
16. Faulkner, B.: Towards a framework for tourism disaster management. Tour. Manage. 22(2), 135–147 (2001)

17. Racherla, P., Hu, C.: A framework for knowledge-based crisis management in the hospitality and tourism industry. Cornell Hospitality Quarterly **50**(4), 561–577 (2009)
18. Rittichainuwat, B.N., Chakraborty, G.: Perceived travel risks regarding terrorism and disease: the case of Thailand. Tour. Manage. **30**(3), 410–418 (2009)
19. Cahyanto, I., Wiblishauser, M., Pennington-Gray, L., Schroeder, A.: The dynamics of travel avoidance: the case of Ebola in the US. Tourism Manage. Perspectives **20**, 195–203 (2016)
20. Page, S., Yeoman, I., Munro, C., Connell, J., Walker, L.: A case study of best practice—visit Scotland's prepared response to an influenza pandemic. Tour. Manage. **27**(3), 361–393 (2006)
21. Blake, A., Sinclair, M.T.: Tourism crisis management: US response to September 11. Ann. Tour. Res. **30**(4), 813–832 (2003)
22. Faulkner, B., Vikulov, S.: Katherine, washed out one day, back on track the next: a postmortem of a tourism disaster. Tour. Manage. **22**, 331–344 (2001)
23. Ritchie, B.W.: Chaos, crises and disasters: a strategic approach to crisis management in the tourism industry. Tour. Manage. **25**(6), 669–683 (2004)
24. Taylor, M.S., Enz, C.A.: GMs' responses to the events of September 11, 2001: voices from the field. Cornell Hotel and Restaurant Administration Quarterly **43**(1), 7–20 (2002)
25. Zenker, S., Kock, F.: The coronavirus pandemic—a critical discussion of a tourism research agenda. Tour. Manage. **81**, 104–164 (2020)
26. Wang, I.M., Ackerman, J.M.: The infectiousness of crowds: crowding experiences are amplified by pathogen threats. Pers. Soc. Psychol. Bull. **45**(1), 120–132 (2019)
27. World Bank: World Development Indicators (database), (2020). https://datacatalog.worldb ank.org/dataset/world-development-indicators
28. Niewiadomski, P.: COVID-19: from temporary de-globalisation to a re-discovery of tourism? Tour. Geogr. **22**(3), 651–656 (2020). https://doi.org/10.1080/14616688.2020.1757749
29. Ketteni, E., Kottaridi, C.: The impact of regulations on the FDI-growth nexus within the institution-based view: a nonlinear specification with varying coefficients. Int. Bus. Rev. **28**, 415–427 (2019)
30. Lucke, N., Eichler, S.: Foreign direct investment: the role of institutional and cultural determinants. Appl. Econ. **48**(11), 935–956 (2016)
31. Sumner, A., Hoy, C., Ortiz-Juarez, E.: Estimates of the impact of COVID-19 on global poverty. UNU-WIDER, pp. 800–809 (2020)
32. UNCTAD (2020), Global Investment Trend Monitor, n°.33, https://unctad.org/system/files/ official-document/diaeiainf2020d1_en.pdf
33. Castellani, D., Meliciani, V., Mirra, L.: The determinants of inward foreign direct investment in business services across European regions. Reg. Stud. **50**(4), 671–691 (2016)
34. Mao, Y., He, J., Morrison, A.M., Andres Coca-Stefaniak, J.: Effects of tourism CSR on employee psychological capital in the COVID-19 crisis: from the perspective of conservation of resources theory. Current Issues in Tourism, pp. 1–19 (2020)
35. Chan, A.P.H., Tung, V.W.S.: Examining the effects of robotic service on brand experience: the moderating role of hotel segment. J. Travel Tour. Mark. **36**(4), 458–468 (2019)
36. Ho, C.I., Lin, M.H., Chen, H.M.: Web users' behavioral patterns of tourism information search: from online to offline. Tour. Manage. **33**(6), 1468–1482 (2012)
37. Maier, T.A.: International hotel revenue management: web-performance effectiveness modelling- research comparative. J. Hosp. Tour. Technol. **3**(2), 121–137 (2012)
38. Aplar, O., Algur, S., Cengiz, F.: Content Analysis of Accommodation Establishment websites in Alanya Region, Hosteur **19**(2), 2532 (2010)
39. Sigala, M.: The information and communication technologies productivity impact on the UK hotel sector. Int. J. Oper. Prod. Manag. **23**(10), 1224–1245 (2003). https://doi.org/10.1108/ 01443570310496643
40. Zafiropoulos, C., Vrana, V.: An evaluation of the performance of hotel web sites: the case of Greece. Information Technol. Tourism J. **8**, 239–254 (2006)

41. Ivanov, S., Webster, C.: Adoption of robots, artificial intelligence and service automation by travel, tourism and hospitality companies – a cost-benefit analysis. In: International Scientific Conference "Contemporary tourism – traditions and innovations", pp. 19–21. Sofia University (2017)
42. Kim, M., Qu, H.: Travelers' behavioral intention toward hotel self-service kiosks usage. Int. J. Contemp. Hosp. Manag. **26**(2), 225–245 (2014)
43. Glaser, B.G., Strauss, A.L.: The Discovery of Grounded Theory: Strategies for Qualitative Research. Aldine, Chicago (1967)
44. Langley, A.: Strategies for theorizing from process data. Acad. Manag. Rev. **24**(4), 691–710 (1999)
45. Lopez, S.H., Phillips, L.A.: Unemployed: white-collar job searching after the great recession. Work. Occup. **46**(4), 470–510 (2019)
46. Lofland, J., Snow, D., Anderson, L., Lofland, L.H.: Analyzing Social Settings: A Guide to Qualitative Observation and Analysis. 4th edition. Wadsworth/Thomson Learning, Belmont, CA (1971)
47. Veal, A.J.: Research methods for leisure and tourism. Pearson UK (2017)
48. Van Maanen, J.: The fact of fiction in organizational ethnography. Adm. Sci. Q. **24**(4), 539–550 (1979)
49. Berger,P.L., Luckmann,T.: Aspects sociologiques du pluralism. Archives de sociologie des religions, 117–127 (1967)
50. Searle, J.R., Willis, Y.S.: The Construction of Social Reality. Simon and Schuster (1995)
51. Grodal, S., Anteby, M., Holm, A.L.: Achieving rigor in qualitative analysis: the role of active categorization in theory building. Acad. Manag. Rev. **46**(3), 591–612 (2021)
52. ATLAS da Hotelaria: Delloite consulting, 15ª edition (2020). https://www2.deloitte.com/pt/pt/pages/real-estate/articles/atlas-hotelaria-2020.html
53. Kibrom, A., Kibrom, T., Andinet, M.: Winners and Losers from COVID-19: Global Evidence from Google Search. Policy Research Working Paper; No. 9268. World Bank, Washington, DC. © World Bank (2020). https://openknowledge.worldbank.org/handle/10986/33852 License: CC BY 3.0 IGO"

Managing Emotions in the Purchasing Process

Carolina Ribeiro[1](✉) and Sofia Almeida[2] (iD)

[1] Universidade Europeia, Lisbon, Portugal
`carolina.ribeiro12345678910@gmail.com`
[2] Universidade Europeia, CEG-Territur Universidade de Lisboa, Lisbon, Portugal

Abstract. Emotions influence individuals' behaviour, so companies need to manage and assess them in their relationship with their customers in order to ensure their profitability. On the one hand, today's society incorporates the digital world more and more intensely, and people are increasingly using social networks to share their experiences and emotions. On the other hand, there is a great development of the tourism offer, appealing to the positive experiences and emotions, in order to influence the purchasing process, so it is important, after the use, to evaluate the emotions expressed by customers. The rationale of this research is the analysis of the emotions expressed by the guests of the five main 5-star hotels in Lisbon, according to the Booking classification, regarding the 3rd quarter of 2021, which corresponds to a period of high season. For the development of the work, a literature review was carried out in terms of emotions, marketing management, purchasing process and social media to assess the current state of the art, using as work methodology, netnography, since it is a suitable method for the investigation of consumer behavior in virtual communities. The study was carried out through the comments left by customers at Booking which is a site of great credibility and notoriety. It is also observed, in the post purchase process, that companies carry out a very detailed analysis of the negative comments and respond to customers either to provide clarifications or to inform them of the rectification of any anomalies presented in order to maintain a positive relationship and loyalty. The analysis and research carried out allowed us to identify some topics for future research that, if developed, will be useful for business management and will enrich the knowledge in this area.

Keywords: Emotions · Management · Consumer · Buying process · Hotel business

1 Introduction

Management as well as emotions are something inherent in the daily lives of all human beings, and the purpose of this paper is to understand how to manage emotions in the buying process and to understand how they can be managed by marketing professionals in order to improve sales. The consumer is constantly exposed to emotions, which can be intrinsic, or a response to an external stimulus that can be elicited [1]. The academia will add further value by investigating how emotion management can influence the buying process, more specifically in the post-purchase, broadening the spectrums of the study and alerting to its importance with the customer and its influence in the commercial terms of consumer behavior, the problem will allow understanding how emotion management can be optimized in order to provide a better experience to consumers, ensuring maximum satisfaction. Social media is today an extremely relevant tool to take into account in the study of emotions expressed by consumers. In this paper we will have the opportunity to see the practical application of one of the social media for the study as is the case of Booking.com. The research question of this paper is "How to manage and evaluate emotions in the post-purchase period?" applied specifically to the tourism sector. In order to answer the research question and for that the following objectives were defined: (i)identify the emotions in the post-use of five-star hotels in Lisbon; and (ii) identify how hotels manage their guests' emotions perceived in the post-purchase. In this sense, the study developed identified the emotions in the post-purchase period of 5-star hotels in Lisbon and how hotels manage their guests' emotions in the post-purchase period. This research is relevant because it allowed to verify that the evaluation of emotions of a stay in luxury hotels has a global character, interconnecting emotions with the post-purchase, within the luxury hotel sector in Lisbon. It also allows a detailed analysis of the negative emotions expressed through negative reviews and rectification of the situations that gave rise to them. It is also important to highlight the importance of reviews on Booking.com for an effective post-purchase follow-up that became essential for the development and respective conclusions drawn from the work developed. The present study is structured in six sections. In the first, a literature review is carried out.

The second section presents the methodology applied in the study. After a brief presentation on qualitative methods, the use of netnography is specified, the identification of the population, the 5 star hotels in Lisbon, as well as the characterization of the sample analyzed, the top 5 five five star hotels in Lisbon according to the Booking.com ranking. In the next section, the results obtained with each one of the five hotels are analyzed. Section five discusses the results obtained along with a comparative analysis of previous studies with the one now discovered in this study. The final section exposes the conclusions allusive to this study, as well as the limitations that existed during the writing of the study, also presenting possible paths for future research.

2 Literature Review

According to [2], Management can be defined as a set of activities that addresses the resources of an organization in order to achieve the organizational objectives in a more efficient and effective way. Also, according to Griffin [2], management involves four basic planning functions, namely decision-making, organization, command, and control. In addition to the competences already presented, there are also varied definitions of management that should be observed as complementary. Fayol [3] adds to this definition of management, a process of prediction, planning, organization, command, coordination, and control [4].

2.1 Buying Process

At the time of purchase, the first decisions that the consumer is faced with are what, how much, when where and how to buy, however, the decision-making process involves four stages, these being problem recognition, information search and evaluation, purchase processes and post-purchase behavior [5]. The buying process always involves decision making, which varies in terms of the involvement of the consumer, who may be involved in the purchase [4].

The purchase process is formed by a continuum in which the consumer identifies several types of decisions that merge, ranging from the identification or perception of the need, through the search and analysis of various alternatives to culminate in the purchase [4]. Engel [6], considers that decision making related to the buying process takes place in initial purchases and in purchases by repetition, and the consumer's behavior and involvement varies considering these two situations. It is within this continuum that most of the decisions related to the buying process are made, however it must be considered that there are still two special categories, which are the impulse buying and the variety buying [4]. The initial purchases include in themselves extended, medium range and limited decision-making processes [4, 7].

According to Pettinger [4], the extended decision making presents a great involve-ment in the purchase, whereby the buyer conducts previous research concerning the prod-uct to be purchased, followed by an evaluation of the alternatives, is usually observed in products that involve high monetary risk [4]. The author [4] considers that the extended decision-making process can also occur without the need to measure and/or evaluate what the product may eventually provide, simply using emotions as a decision criterion. Engel [6] pin-pointed the extended decision-making process as a time when evaluation and thinking precede the purchase act due to the importance of making the right choice. Regarding the medium-term decision making and according to Engel [6], it lies between the extended decision-making process and the limited decision-making process. In this way the consumer evaluates his alternatives already within a predefined spectrum and chooses the option that best fits his needs. Regarding the process of limited decision-making, the consumer does not have the time, resources, or motivation to get too involved in the purchase, thus acts in accordance with the situation presented and tries as much as possible to simplify the decision-making process where it is, reducing the number and variety of alternatives previously available, as well as the criteria they use to evaluate [6]. McMellon [7] also believe that with regard to limited decision-making, consumers establish in advance which criteria to use to evaluate the brand and the product in ques-tion, establishing "rules" for themselves, since the product does not have a high level of relevance. Regarding decision-making in repeat purchases, it is carried out in a repeated and habitual manner or by brand loyalty. The repeat purchase process is always based on inertia [7]. Engel [6] identify two special categories previously mentioned, impulse buying and variety buying. The authors [6] state that impulse buying is characterised as a moment of triggered by exposure to a product or promotion at the point of sale. Accord-ing to Engel [6] and Mowen [8]the main characteristics that define an impulse buying are summarized in the urgency aggregated to a high emotional involvement adding the absence of a careful reasoning, leading to a disregard of the consequences that the even-tual decision making in the purchase may reflect. The search for variety occurs when the consumer presents "fatigue" in relation to a particular product and perceives several alternatives similar to the product category he seeks, even if the current choice provides satisfaction [6, 8].

2.2 Post Purchase

Post purchase is designated as the period of time after a customer has experienced a product or service [9]. It is the last phase of the buying process. The post-purchase phase that concerns consumer behaviour as well as loyalty towards the service. It is a relevant phase for the customer, but also for the company that provided it, because it is decisive to ensure the extended satisfaction and future repetition of service purchase [9]. In addition to this fact, it is also a phase of the buying process crucial to the purchase of products or services, "it is the final phase in which customers evaluate their satisfaction with the purchase and will consider whether or not to buy the product/service in the future" [9]. According to the author [9] the ways of determining the level of consumer satisfaction should also be considered, as they will more accurately mirror all the reactions present post purchase, of the product or service. The intention to revisit is also dependent on the performance that the product or service presented and is something that is defined in the post-purchase, as well as the intention to recommend it [10, 11]. The process of evaluating the consumer experience is a crucial part of customer satisfaction and of utmost importance in their post-purchase behavior [12]. Customer loyalty is dependent on customer satisfaction and is a decisive factor in the profit growth and performance of a given company [13, 14]. Churchill and Surprenant [15] designate customer satisfaction as an outcome of the purchase taking also into account the response to the evaluation of a given service. With the increasing evolution of the online, one should also consider the reviews made there as a possible and strong influencer on post-purchase behavior and decisions. According [16], in online media, satisfaction was found to have a significant impact on the customer's propensity to post reviews. Post-purchase behavior is seen as a series of steps in which consumers compare their expectations with perceived reality, experience satisfaction and its opposite and act influenced by that satisfaction or dissatisfaction [17]. If the result of the comparison of expectations leads to dissatisfaction, the consumer may complain [17]. The response of the company will be evaluated according to the expectations, also resulting in a degree of satisfaction or dissatisfaction with the response to the complaint [17]. Ensuring the existence of means capable of managing consumers' post-purchase expectations, namely toll-free numbers, warranties, and other post-purchase services, are a determining factor when it comes to customer satisfaction, especially when it comes to goods of high economic involvement [18]. Post-purchase support is considered necessary to gauge a company's intentions towards its customers [18]. In the face of positive consumption performance, product image raises favorable perceptions in the evaluation and purchase phases, but also increases consumer satisfaction in the post-purchase phase [19].

2.3 Emotional Marketing

Emotions can be positive or negative, intense and frequent and are extremely motivating [20]. They derive from a circumstance or relationship with a third party and constitute a determining factor with regard to action, interest and curiosity lead to a strong desire for knowledge [20]. Although intrinsic to human beings, emotions are intentional and are present in actions, events, thoughts and feelings, being sensitive to personal and professional factors and contexts [21].

In relation to organizations, more specifically the workplace it should be noted that the key piece that people bring to organizations is emotion [22]. Emotion serves as organizational unity and brings together the different people who form part of an organization, be they employees, managers, customers or consultants favoring individual performance as well as the lived environment [22]. Behaviors, thoughts and actions have emotions present, these being a determining factor, so it is necessary to develop a deeper relationship between emotion and organization [22]. In the health sector, several studies have found that the management of emotions and the emotional work of health professionals has a very important impact on the quality of care and patients' health outcomes; however, this emotional work can also be exhausting, resulting in experiences of extreme stress and burnout [23]. When faced with these types of situations emotion management and positive emotions can help with personal and interpersonal issues [23].

In education leadership behaviors with associated emotional implications are repeatedly recommended, such as giving support, demonstrating moral integrity and safety, fostering collaboration, contributing to intellectual stimulation, encouraging learning and practicing individual and shared decision making [24].Emotional knowledge encourages an assessment and management of emotions in stressful situations at individual and group level, and this fact is quite relevant in sport [25]. A sports organization sensitive to emotional control will have more tools for conflict resolution [25]. Emotions can also be perceived as positive or negative depending on their variation [1]. Positive emotions are generated by pleasant experiences, which can vary in terms of cognitive and physiological activation [26] states that pleasure, enthusiasm, hope and pride activate positive emotions and that carelessness and indifference are responsible for deactivating them. As opposed to positive emotions, negative emotions are experienced as unpleasant, however these can also vary in terms of physiological and cognitive activation. According Prinz [26] anxiety and shame activate negative emotions, whereas doubt and boredom deactivate them. Some consensuses can be found regarding the study of basic emotions, counted as six and being specifically joy, sadness, fear, surprise, anger and disgust [26, 27]. They are considered innate and basic emotions in a psychological and biological way [26, 27]. Table 1 shows the synthesis of identification of a part of the mentioned areas, as well as the concept and main results observed.

Table 1. Management of emotions in various areas (Source based on [20, 22, 23, 25, 28]).

Authors	Areas	Application	Method and technique	Main Results
Ashkanasy (2002)	Organizations (workplace)	Managing emotions contributes to better conflict management and a more favorable working environment	Conferences	Twenty-one tools were identified that enable the management of emotions in the workplace

(continued)

Table 1. (*continued*)

Authors	Areas	Application	Method and technique	Main Results
Beatty (2010)	Education	The management of emotions in education is extremely relevant for both the professionals in the field and the beneficiaries of the field	Interviews	Understanding the role of emotions can be fundamental to a fuller appreciation of the intra- and intersubjective realities of life in schools in general and educational leadership in particular
Goodrum & Stafford (2012)	Criminal system	Difficulty in managing emotions for their benefit and for the benefit of the victims	Interviews	There is greater sensitivity depending on gender Professionalism is equated with emotional composure
Hsieh & Nicodemus (2015)	Health	Managing emotions is extremely necessary and has a huge impact on the individuals who work in it	Data bases and Google Academic	The management and performance of others' emotions, workers' own emotions, and the impacts of emotion work for health professionals were examined
Tur-Porcar & Ribeiro-Soriano (2020)	Sports	Emotions and behaviour play a crucial role in the world of sport	Analytic Hierarchy Process (AHP)	Motivation, and the management of emotions, are the most important criteria for generating commitment within sporting organizations

2.4 Social Media

Social media has been gaining a greater impact on society, and it has been possible to observe a huge growth regarding the number of users of the numerous platforms, with special emphasis on social media (Hootsuite 2022).

The term social media encompasses a wide functionality of mobile services that are internet driven and that allow their users to participate, create and share content in online communities [29]. There are numerous platforms and services associated with social media, including blogs, entertainment content, social networks, and the well-known websites, among others [29]. Technological and social factors, such as the greater development of electronic devices, a greater speed in what concerns the internet, a great adherence and acceptance of the younger age groups and also the growing commercial interest were at the basis of this social media growth [29]. Social media presents some characteristics such as search capability, quick and easy availability of content and accessibility that make them extremely versatile and that promote the participation of all its users, and may even enhance relationships among them [29]. It is also relevant to note that several companies from various sectors are increasingly investing in their online content, as well as in marketing strategies through social media [29]. They are a rich source of information and allow customers to express themselves regarding the product or service purchased [30]. They are also a means of expression and critical freedom, increasingly used for sharing opinions and experiences [30].

3 Methodology

The methodology of this research incorporates quantitative and qualitative aspects in a complementary way. The technique to be used is netnography applied to the hotel sector. Qualitative research or research methods were designed essentially by researchers and social scientists in order to study and understand the complexity of human beings [31]. The main advantage of using these types of methods is that they make the researcher delve more deeply into the complexity of the problem at hand, obtaining more specific and informative results [31].

They make it easier to answer questions that involve variables that are difficult to quantify, such as human characteristics, motivation, perception, experience, and they also answer the "why" of questions that might have previously been addressed by quantitative research [31]. The qualitative method focuses on particular individuals, events and contexts, is expressed in natural language, however no qualitative observation is immune to quantification [32]. It is an approach that allows us to examine people's experiences in detail, using a range of research methods, namely interviews, focus group, observation, content analysis, and biographies [33]. Qualitative research allows us to identify issues by taking into account participants' perspectives and understand the interpretations they give to behavior, events, or objects [33]. They observe people in their natural environment in order to identify how their experiences and behaviors are influenced by the social, economic, cultural, or physical context in which they live [33]. According to the authors, qualitative research also seeks to understand contextual influences on research questions. Quantitative research collects hard facts of statistical that or numerical nature, it is intended to analyze data to identify trends [34].

3.1 Netnography

The neologism "netnography" (netnography = net + ethnography) was originally coined by a group of North American researchers, Bishop, Star, Neumann, Ignacio, Sandusky and Schatz, in 1995, to describe a methodological challenge: to preserve the rich details of ethnographic field observation by using the electronic medium to follow the actors [35]. Netnography has also simplified the work of researchers by allowing them to reach certain groups of people they wish to study in a more accessible way.

To carry out this netnographic analysis, the comments made to each of the five-star hotels in Lisbon present in the top 5 of the Booking.com ranking were observed. The data observed and collected from the comments refer to the third quarter of 2021. After data selection, a quantitative analysis of the sample data was carried out, counting total comments, positive comments, negative comments, as well as the most repeated words in those comments, but also a qualitative analysis, with a netnographic approach, in order to determine which words could undoubtedly reflect emoticons [36].

3.2 Characterization of the Sample

The population is the 5-star hotels in the city of Lisbon. According to the Booking.com platform (2022), Lisbon and its surroundings account for a total of 51 five-star hotels, while in the city of Lisbon there are 42 five-star hotels (Booking.com 2022). The sample for this study consists of the selection of the five highest scoring five-star hotels existing in the city of Lisbon, in the third quarter of 2021, according to the Booking.com ranking on 02 February 2022. For our research we considered the first five hotels in the ranking, when selected the keywords: hotel + 5 stars + Lisbon. A characterisation of each of the hotels analysed is presented below, according to Table 2.

Table 2. Characterisation of the hotels analysed (Source based on Booking.com and the official websites of the respective hotels)

Hotels	Number bedrooms	Open Year	Ranking Evaluation Booking.com
Bairro Alto Hotel	87	2005	9.2
Corpo Santo Lisbon Historical Hotel	75	2017	9.5
Hotel Avenida Palace	82	1892	9.3
Memmo Principe Real	41	2013	9.2
Myriad by Sana	186	2012	9.3

3.3 Characterization of Booking.com

The digital ecosystem analyzed for this research was the Booking.com platform, founded in 1996 in Amsterdam (Booking.com). This platform uses a scale from 0 to 10 in order to evaluate the hotels. Its credibility lies in the fact that it has been in existence for several years, offering a wide and varied range of hotels all over the world, but also in Portugal and in Lisbon. It should be noted that only visitors who have actually stayed at a hotel on Booking.com's website have the opportunity to comment and/or report on their experience, as well as its positive and/or negative characteristics, thus giving credit to the website, as the comments belong to real guests who actually made the booking. The Facebook comments were not analyzed in this research because there were only 23 for the set of 5 hotels.

Regarding Youtube, the platform is fundamentally based on the publication of videos and, in the period under analysis, of the five hotels in presence, only the Avenida Palace published a video on 30 September 2021, which has 436 views and only 10 likes. Only Avenida Palace is present in the social network WhatsApp and none of the five hotels is present in WeChat, since these two platforms are fundamentally directed to the exchange of messages, so their use in the study is not relevant for the achievement of the objectives defined. In this study, the analysis of the comments made on Instagram was also not carried out since this social network is not adapted to the segment of the hotels under analysis.

4   Results Analysis

The results analysis observed the customer comments of the five main Lisbon 5-star hotels, according to the Booking platform classification on 02 February 2022: Avenida Palace, Bairro Alto Hotel, Corpo Santo, Memmo Príncipe Real and Myriad by Sana in the 3rd quarter of 2021, the period of greatest use of these hotel units. The 688 comments made at Booking.com were analysed in order to identify the emotions associated with them, based on the tables and graphs presented in order to respond to the objectives already defined. It can be seen that the comments made are adjusted to the offer presented to customers by the hotels and their feedback is mostly positive (99.1%), with negative comments representing 0.9% of the total. Of the selected hotels there are two without any negative comments, the Bairro Alto Hotel and the Hotel Avenida Palace.

The Corpo Santo Hotel and the Memmo Príncipe Real have less than 1% of unfavorable comments and only one of the hotels (Myriad by Sana) presents 1.5% of negative comments. The comments assess multiple criteria of the experience lived by the guests, namely the hotel location, cleanliness, ambiance, service, breakfast or the friendliness of the staff (Booking). Regarding the positive emotions shown, the ones that stand out the most in all five hotels are the words "Exceptional" with 37.7%, followed by "Superb" with 19.5% and "Fantastic" with 7.2%. The assessment "Great" appears in 6.4% of the comments and "Excellent" in 2.8% of the cases, with 26.4% of the positive comments referring to other types of expressions. It should be noted that the negative reviews, which represent only 0.9% of the comments, are analysed in detail by the hotels and, with the exception of one situation, are subject to a response from the hotel to the customers.

4.1   Post Purchase Reviews of Corpo Santo Lisbon Historical Hotel

In the analysis of the 127 comments made during the defined period, it was possible to identify some repetition with regard to various words. The words that are most repeated demonstrate satisfaction or express contentment on the part of the client with the service provided. Every time contentment or satisfaction is expressed, the emotion associated with these words is joy.

4.2   Post-purchase Comments on Myriad by Sana

In the analysis made of the two hundred comments, during the defined period, it was possible to notice some repetition regarding various terms. The words which are most repeated demonstrate satisfaction or express contentment on the part of the client with the service provided.

4.3   Post Purchase Reviews of Hotel Avenida Palace

The analysis made on the comments of this hotel allows to identify a satisfaction on the services provided. The words presented demonstrate satisfaction or express contentment on the part of the client with the service provided.

4.4   Post Purchase Reviews of Bairro Alto Hotel (9.2)

The analysis of the comments from this hotel shows a clear satisfaction with the services provided by the hotel. The words presented demonstrate satisfaction or express contentment on the part of the customer with the service provided.

4.5   Post Purchase Reviews of Memmo Principe Real (9.2)

The analysis of the comments from this hotel shows a clear satisfaction with the services provided by the hotel. The most repeated words demonstrate satisfaction or express contentment on the part of the customer with the service provided. We highlight the existence of two hotels that show 100% of positive emotions (Avenida Palace and Bairro Alto Hotel) and that only one hotel has less than 99% of comments related to positive emotions (Myriad by Sana with 98.5%).

The hotels Corpo Santo and Memmo Príncipe Real have 99,3% of the comments related to positive emotions. Table 3 shows the absolute number of comments made between 01 July and 30 September 2021 by guests of the five selected hotels, in a total of 688. The hotel that received the most comments was the Corpo Santo with 267, the Myriad by Sana in second position with 200 comments, followed by the Memmo Príncipe Real with 134, the Bairro Alto Hotel in fourth position with 73 comments and the Avenida Palace in fifth place.

Table 3. Total comments of positive emotions in absolute value (Source based on comments made at Booking.com)

Hotels	Avenida Palace Hotel	Bairro Alto Hotel	Corpo Santo Lisbon Historical Hotel	Memmo Principe Hotel	Myriad by Sana	Total
Total comments	14	73	267	134	200	688
Positive Emotions	14	73	265	133	196	682
Superb	0	15	37	31	50	133
Exceptional	1	27	93	41	95	257
Great	0	6	15	10	13	44
Excellent	0	0	8	4	7	19
Fantastic	6	1	42	0	0	49
Other positive	7	24	70	47	31	180
Negative emotions	0	0	2	1	4	6

5   Discussion of Results

A global analysis of the observed data, in addition to the results already described, also allows opening more global discussion lines. Nowadays, tourism organizations and destinations should be considered holistically given that their competitiveness is built by a multiplicity of factors [37], accommodation being only one component. The customer comments analyzed in this research assess multiple aspects of the guest experience, namely, the hotel location, cleanliness, environment, service, breakfast, or friendliness of the staff. Customer relationship management is a key objective in the hotel sector in order to ensure customer satisfaction and repeat purchases. There are several studies that analyze the issue of customer satisfaction in the hotel sector, particularly in five-star hotels, with the purpose of investigating the influence of service quality and satisfaction in customer behavior in luxury hotels [38]. The referred studies follow diverse methodologies in terms of data collection, ranging from paper surveys, interviews, online questionnaires and, more recently, resorting to the collection of comments in review platforms such as Booking.com, as is the case of the present study.

The sample size and period are also very variable, as is the methodology used to calculate results. The study of Pinto [39], on the determinants of customer satisfaction in 5-star hotels in Portugal, aimed to understand the customer perceptions in terms of service quality. The author studied, through the analysis of 155 answers to a survey obtained in eight 5-star hotels, the relationship between overall satisfaction and eight attributes considered relevant in the literature and obtained an average satisfaction of

6.23. The study of Silva [40] on the Hotel Industry market segment: Differentiation and Innovation Factors, analyzed the customer experiences with stays in four- and five-star hotels, assuming that these types of hotels are those that are able to provide their customers with a range of unique and distinctive experiences. For data collection, 5 interviews were carried out and 104 online surveys were processed, in a group of 6 hotels.

For the 5-star hotels, an average satisfaction score of 8.2 was obtained. In addition to assessing satisfaction, the study aimed to understand how innovation in the hotel sector would contribute to differentiation in the offer and to evaluate to what extent this strategy was perceived and valued by guests. In the case of the work regarding the Evaluation of Customer Satisfaction in Hotel Units [41] only one hotel unit was studied with the aim of identifying the factors that most impacted the customers' stay, in order to minimize future complaints. The work was carried out in 2019 through the collection of 975 comments in Booking.com and the analysis of 1095 surveys made to customers of the hotel, having been found an average satisfaction of 8.33. Although the objective in all previously conducted studies was to collect feedback about the customers' satisfaction level, none of them carried out a direct relationship between satisfaction assessment and emotion management, which was a key purpose in the present work. This research differs from the others since it intends to establish a relationship between satisfaction and emotions, given that the focus on emotional connections is mentioned [42] as a way to be used by hotel groups to promote repeat purchases, i.e. loyalty, since there is a relationship between guest experience, emotions and satisfaction [43].

According to Silva [40], the assessment of emotions resulting from a stay in luxury hotels has a holistic nature, which makes the management style to be adopted extremely relevant, which should pay attention to all the details inherent to the stay, thus confirming the relevance of the research question that it was possible to answer: "How to manage and assess emotions in the post-purchase period.". The analysis of the comments made reveals a total adjustment between the characteristics of the offer presented to customers by the hotel units and the feedback they externalize, given that almost all of their comments are positive (99.1%), with negative comments representing only 0.9% of the total. The global perspective incorporated by customers in their evaluation, which in most cases is summarized in a single word, expresses their experience in relation to all the stages experienced during their stay. The study made it evident that in order to respond to all the aspects encompassed in the evaluation of the emotions inherent to the totality of the experiences, it is decisive to have a detailed management of all the areas of the hotel units. The need to ensure the existence of communication channels and tools that allow customers to transmit their feedback in a simple but simultaneously relevant way for hotel management becomes absolutely clear within the scope of the work developed. The aspects mentioned confirm, therefore, the relevance and importance of the objective assumed and answered in the study in terms of "identifying emotions in the post-use of 5-star hotels in Lisbon". If it is important to perform a management that ensures an experience full of positive emotions in luxury hotels, given that this is the customers' expectation, the management of negative emotions that are evidenced in the evaluations is even more relevant. The analysis of this type of situations was the aim of the second objective also achieved with this study "to identify how hotels manage their guests' emotions perceived in the post-purchase period".

In the study carried out, this situation is mainly visible in what concerns negative comments, which are subject to detailed analysis by the management, and there is a concern to answer the customer to provide additional clarifications or inform about changes introduced in the operations. It should be noted that, nowadays, hotel management is concerned with building global experiences that present themselves as competitive advantages for customers [44]. The analysis of the results of the evaluation of Lisbon 5 star hotels by customers allows for the inference that, in this segment of luxury hospitality, special care should be taken in the introduction of any innovation or additional offer, given the holistic nature of the experience and the level of customer demand, given the need to maintain high levels of evaluation to ensure reputation and notoriety. The work carried out focused on the emotions expressed by customers regarding their experience, which incorporates a fairly wide range of variables, so it is clear that in order to guarantee the existence of positive evaluations, it is necessary to have a careful and detailed management of the different areas of the hotel unit, from the physical infrastructure, to the aesthetics, decoration, environment, or the extremely relevant area of human resources. Human resources management is also an absolutely critical area since their attitudes and behaviors have a huge impact on customer satisfaction [37]. The management of consumers' emotions is carried out by companies based on multiple factors such as communication, quality, the way products and services are presented or marketing.

6 Conclusion

In the hotel sector, the use of a five-star hotel by clients is considered not only as a simple stay, but rather as a global experience in which a multiplicity of experiences is integrated that should result in a set of positive emotions, thus influencing the purchase process. Therefore, it is relevant to analyses the underlying impact of this type of hotel offer on customer expectations, namely through the evaluation of their emotions in the post purchase phase. The developed research allowed answering the research question "How to manage and evaluate emotions in the post purchase phase" through the evaluation of comments associated with emotions inherent to the use of five star hotels in Lisbon, as well as the identification of how the hotel management manages the emotions perceived by customers. It is important to highlight that although in most cases the customers' evaluation is summarized in a single word, it nevertheless expresses a global experience relative to all the stages experienced during their stay, which confirms the importance of the objective assumed and answered in the study in terms of "to identify emotions in the post use of 5 star hotels in Lisbon". The present research analysed the comments made by customers regarding the use of the five main five-star hotels in Lisbon according to the Booking.com classification, namely: Corpo Santo Lisbon Historical Hotel, Myriad by Sana, Hotel Avenida Palace, Bairro Alto Hotel and Memmo Principe Real, in the third quarter of 2021. Of the 688 comments made in the 3rd quarter of 2021 by clients of the five hotels analysed, 99.1% show positive emotions which are, in their entirety, related to happiness. It is also important to note that, despite the positive experience that the hotels aim to provide, comments associated with negative emotions were also identified, although in a small percentage: 0.9%. To summarise the classification of the emotions expressed about the five hotels: "Excellent" characterise the Bairro Alto Hotel, the Corpo Santo, the Memmo Príncipe Real and the Myriad by Sana. The word "Fantastic" is the word that best describes the Avenida Palace. The analysis of the comments reveals an adjustment between the offer presented by the companies, reflected in the experience to be provided to the clients and the feedback obtained.

The positive feedback obtained from the customers is extremely relevant as it is a validation of the experience provided and indicates the continuation or even the increase of future purchases, thus forcing to maintain or even increase the level of efficiency of the operations. As far as negative comments are concerned, hotels manage the emotions perceived in the post-purchase period, giving feedback to the customer in the vast majority of cases. The concern shown by the management of the different hotels in the detailed analysis of the negative comments and the rectification of the situations that gave rise to them was evident. The evaluation of emotions resulting from a stay in luxury hotels has a holistic nature, which makes it relevant the management style to be adopted, which should pay attention to all the details inherent to the stay confirming, therefore, the relevance of the question of research "How to manage and evaluate emotions in the post purchase period", to which it was possible to respond. The work carried out reveals the need to guarantee the existence of communication channels and tools that allow customers to transmit their feedback in a simple but effective way in hotel management.

The study carried out makes it evident that in order to take into account all the aspects incorporated in the evaluation of emotions in relation to the totality of the experiences lived, it is decisive to have a detailed management of all the areas of the hotel units. The global perspective incorporated by guests in the evaluation, which in most cases is summarized in a single word, nevertheless expresses an experience relative to all the stages experienced during their stay. These aspects confirm the relevance and importance of the objective assumed for the study, which was achieved in terms of "identifying post-use emotions in 5-star hotels in Lisbon". If it is important to perform a management that ensures an experience full of positive emotions in luxury hotels, given that this is the customers' expectation, it is even more relevant to manage the negative emotions that are evidenced in the evaluations. The analysis of this kind of situations was the aim of the second objective of this study "to identify how hotels manage their guests' emotions perceived in the post-purchase", which was also possible to achieve. In the study carried out, this situation is mainly visible in what concerns negative comments, which are subject to detailed analysis by the management, and there is a concern to answer the customer to provide further clarifications or inform about changes introduced in the operations. This evaluation is crucial to understand the level of customer satisfaction, as well as the intentions after the purchase, in order to assess the adjustment between the expectations created and the emotions expressed, with a view to the introduction by the companies of possible alterations in the emotions management process or even in the operations themselves.

The work carried out is also a contribution, both for the hotel sector and for academia since it can be used as benchmarking for future work to be developed. In terms of academia, the literature review carried out intends to contribute to the body of literature in the area of emotions and the purchase process, facilitating future research. It should also be highlighted, in terms of academia, the contribution of this research, through a literature review that interconnects the thematic areas related to the buying process, marketing management and emotions management. In terms of manager contributes, the study is, in itself, a contribution to the hotel sector in terms of support for a more adequate definition of strategies with a view to maximizing customer satisfaction. The study also makes evident the need for and importance of the hospitality market to invest in the development and improvement of communication channels and tools with customers, in order to obtain feedback that can be operationalized in terms of implementing management measures that provide an increase in customer satisfaction and consequent loyalty.

References

1. Ben-Ze'ev, A.: The Subtlety of Emotions. MIT press v
2. Griffin, R.: Fundamentals of Management. Cengage Learning (2021)
3. Fayol, H., Gray, I.: General and Industrial Management (1984)
4. Pettinger, R.: Introduction to Management (2007)
5. Tyagi, C.L., Kumar, A.: Consumer behaviour. Atlantic Publishers & Dist (2004)
6. Engel, J.F., Blackwell, R.D., Miniard, P.W.: Consumer behavior, Chicago. J. Retail. **58**(1), 34–57 (1995)
7. McMellon, C.A., Schiffman, L.G., Sherman, E.: Consuming cyberseniors: Some personal and situational characteristics that influence their on-line behavior. ACR North American Advances (1997)
8. Mowen, J.C., Carlson, B.: Exploring the antecedents and consumer behavior consequences of the trait of superstition. Psychol. Mark. **20**(12), 1045–1065 (2003)
9. Dahl, M., Keitsch, M., Boks, C.: Post purchase experience-A multidisciplinary review.DS 85–1: Proceedings of NordDesign 2016, Volume 1, Trondheim, Norway, 10th-12th August, pp. 103–112 (2016)
10. Cronin, J.J., Jr., Taylor, S.A.: Measuring service quality: a reexamination and extension. J. Mark. **56**(3), 55–68 (1992)
11. Wang, X., Yu, C., Wei, Y.: Social media peer communication and impacts on purchase intentions: a consumer socialization framework. J. Interact. Mark. **26**(4), 198–208 (2012)
12. Han, H., Ryu, K.: The roles of the physical environment, price perception, and customer satisfaction in determining customer loyalty in the restaurant industry. J. Hospitality Tourism Res. **33**(4), 487–510 (2009)
13. Reichheld, F.F.: Loyalty-based management. Harv. Bus. Rev. **71**(2), 64–73 (1993)
14. Heskett, J.L., Sasser, W.E.: The service profit chain. In: Handbook of service science, pp. 19–29. Springer, Boston, MA (2010).
15. Churchill, G.A., Jr., Surprenant, C.: An investigation into the determinants of customer satisfaction. J. Mark. Res. **19**(4), 491–504 (1982)
16. Westbrook, R.A.: Sources of consumer satisfaction with retail outlets. J. Retailing (1981)
17. Gilly, M.C., Gelb, B.D.: Post-purchase consumer processes and the complaining consumer. J. Consumer Res. **9**(3), 323–328 (1982)
18. Halstead, D., Dröge, C., Cooper, M.B.: Product warranties and post-purchase service: a model of consumer satisfaction with complaint resolution. Journal of Services Marketing (1993)
19. Chen-Yu, H.J., Kincade, D.H.: Effects of product image at three stages of the consumer decision process for apparel products: alternative evaluation, purchase and post-purchase. J. Fashion Marketing Manage.: An Int. J. **5**(1), 2943 (2001)
20. Burkitt, I.: Emotions and Social Relations. Sage (2014)

21. Thompson: The Psychobiology of Emotions. Plenum Press (1988)
22. Ashkanasy, N.M., Zerbe, W.J., Härtel, C.E. (Eds.): The Effect of Affect in Organizational Settings. Ebrary (2007)
23. Hsieh, E., Nicodemus, B.: Conceptualizing emotion in healthcare interpreting: A normative eapproach to interpreters' emotion work (2015)
24. Beatty, K.: Teaching and Researching Computer-Assisted Language Learning, London Pearson Education (2010)
25. Porcar, T., Ribeiro-Soriano: The Role of Emotions and Motivations in Sport Organizations (2020)
26. Prinz, J.: Are emotions feelings? J. Conscious. Stud. **12**(8–9), 9–25 (2005)
27. Russell, J.A.: Measures of emotion. In: The Measurement of Emotions, pp. 83–111. Academic Press (1989)
28. Goodrum, S., Stafford, M.C.: The management of emotions in the criminal justice system. Sociol. Focus **36**(3), 179–196 (2003)
29. Dewing, M.: Social Media: An Introduction, vol. 1. Library of Parliament, Ottawa (2010)
30. Zeng, D., Chen, H., Lusch, R., Li, S.H.: Social media analytics and intelligence. IEEE Intell. Syst. **25**(6), 13–16 (2010)
31. Shull, F., Singer, J., Sjøberg, D.I. (Eds.): Guide to Advanced Empirical Software Engineering. Springer Science & Business Media (2007). https://doi.org/10.1007/978-1-84800-044-5
32. Gerring, J.: Qualitative methods. Annu. Rev. Polit. Sci. **20**, 15–36 (2017)
33. Hennink, M., Hutter, I., Bailey, A.: Qualitative Research Methods. Sage (2020)
34. Watson, R.: Nursing Standard (2014+); London Vol. 29, Ediç. 31, 44 (2015)
35. Braga, A.: Técnica etnográfica aplicaca à comunicação online: uma discussão metodológica. UNIrevista, vol. 1, julho 2001 (2001)
36. Kozinets, R.V.: Netnography: Redefined. Sage (2015)
37. Lourenço, H.M.S.P.: A gestão de recursos humanos no turismo: o caso da hotelaria na cidade de Lisboa (2021)
38. Oliveira, P.A.P.: Qualidade de serviço, satisfação e comportamento do cliente de hotéis de luxo (Doctoral dissertation, Universidade Tecnica de Lisboa (Portugal) (2011)
39. Pinto, J.C., Oliveira, A.P.: Determinantes na satisfação de clientes em hotéis de cinco estrelas em Portugal. Revista Portuguesa e Brasileira de Gestão **7**(2), 47–55 (2008)
40. Silva, I.G.D.: Estudo de segmento de mercado da indústria hoteleira: Fatores de diferenciação e inovação (Doctoral dissertation) (2013)
41. Matias, D.F.: Avaliação da Satisfação de Clientes em Unidades Hoteleiras: Estudo de Caso (Doctoral dissertation) (2021)
42. Instituto do Luxo. Caso de sucesso: o efeito da comunicação emocional na hotelaria (2020)
43. Alves, C.A., Marques, R.B., Stefanini, C.J., Nascimento, V.D.S.: Hospitalidade, experiências e emoções. Turismo: Visão e Ação, **21**, 373–398 (2020)
44. Fernandes, B.F.V.: O marketing de experiências na perspetiva da procura hoteleira: o caso do Grande Hotel (Doctoral dissertation) (2016)

Analysis of the Online Home Consumption Database Based on Data Mining

Javier Sotelo[1]($^{(\boxtimes)}$) ⓘ and Arnulfo Alanis[2] ⓘ

[1] Systems and Computer Department, National Technology of México, Campus Tijuana, Calzada del Tecnológico S/N, Fraccionamiento Tomas Aquino, 22414 Tijuana, Baja California, Mexico
`Javier.sotelo@tectijuana.edu.mx`
[2] Computer Systems Student, Department of Systems and Computing, National Technology of Mexico, Campus Tijuana, Calzada del Tecnológico S/N, Fraccionamiento Tomas Aquino, 22414 Tijuana, Baja California, Mexico
`alanis@tectijuana.edu.mx`

Abstract. In current times where there are smart devices for households, and that apart from having different functions that are helpful in daily household chores, such as being able to maintain a full pantry, and to generate errand lists, in the market these devices have a high cost for this reason is that it is proposed to create a low cost smart device, in this document an analysis is made using data mining, with tensor flow, of the purchases generated by the users, derived from the current situation by the pandemic of the COVID-19, generated an increase in online shopping, this analysis is intended to be a support for online errand shopping to visualize classification and prediction in the comparisons of users.

Keywords: Home automation · Internet of Things · Ambient intelligence · Internet of Things in homes · Data mining

1 Introduction

With the wide progress in mobile technologies, new devices are available that allow us to perform a wide variety of activities in our daily lives, in addition to this, we have advanced tools for the massive generation of data that require analysis to identify predictions. It is also possible to visualize growth in the volume and complexity of the data itself.

By conducting this research in some companies in the self-service sector, grouping purchases and sales in the area of retail, wholesale, they are already using data mining tools and techniques to leverage their historical data.

The evolution of the Internet has greatly supported the daily lives of users; this has given rise to the need to increase the reach of this technology. In this situation, companies and businesses have the opportunity to improve their services and their business in general.

Given the above there are no longer limitations on their geographic location, online communication supports and supports communication between buyers, which can be done from home, work or mobile devices.

T. Guarda et al. (Eds.): ARTIIS 2022, CCIS 1676, pp. 166–176, 2022.
https://doi.org/10.1007/978-3-031-20316-9_13

E-commerce "emphasizes financial and information transactions that are conducted electronically", and these are initiated between an organization and a user making a purchase [1]. Previously it was called traditional marketing. It should be noted that from the first instance in which the company adopts its web technology in its business mechanisms, this begins the process of evolution in its policies on how to do business, since its policies are modified in terms of costs and sales times. "In no context could it have been planned the great growth it would have based on information" [2].

The www generates and gives a transformation of marketing and business of companies in their business structures towards users. In current times many users enter and browse the Internet, regardless of geographical location; this gives guideline to the possibilities that their purchases to any company are very broad, and thus with them can meet their needs. Based on the above it could be said that companies must add tools that allow them to achieve their objectives.

The web can generate and grant one or several values to the activities, and these can be both to provide the purchase and the distribution, that is to say, the sale, not leaving aside that it allows the companies to have a wide margin to be able to commercialize their products in the world, and also to be able to look for suppliers.

A turning point and driver of globalization could be understood as the evolution and change in the technological field, starting from particular areas and interests to the impulse with technological advances. Transport and information processing.

2   Internet of Things

Internet of Things (IoC) is a global infrastructure for the information society, which enables advanced services through the interconnection of things (physical and virtual) based on existing and evolving information and communication technologies [4].

IOC architecture has the ability to intercommunicate between different nodes and objects in the network and exchange information and data specific to the world around them. Nowadays there are many intelligent devices that communicate with each other as well as with people. This concept is known as M2P (machine-to-person communications) [3].

The Internet of Things can be found almost anywhere there are smart devices that help in different tasks thanks to the communication capacity that exists between sensors, the cloud and devices, which we can find in homes, industries, schools, etc.,

The IOC, we can mention it as the space where computing tries to contemplate having classrooms, spaces, where technology supports the work with users, who can have and carry out one or more activities. Some characteristics that AmI systems have are the detection of the information in that environment, to be able to have a knowledge based on the data, to be able to take decisions for the actions to be taken in order to benefit its users [5].

When the term IoC is put into applications and developments in smart homes it started an evolution to context of use. This encompasses a broad coverage of how to control many devices. An example, as in the conventional home becomes a smart home for security management, energy management, thermostat temperature control, family entertainment and family business [6].

3 Data Mining

Any process of generating knowledge in today's times is a broad challenge, because of the data itself. The work with the so-called data mining results in an approach to find areas of solution to the large volumes of data [7].

In current times, the thought of managing and processing data is not so simple, and even more so when they can be associated and restricted to only 2 values, such as numbers or characters. The advances in the technological era for processes such as information management, i.e. databases, give an opening to be able to have integrated different types of data, such as images, videos, texts, in simple databases, which can facilitate the processing of a set of data.

The current processes in the web environment and its extensive development have led to the need for more advanced data mining-based technologies to interpret high volumes of information and knowledge of such data in a distributed manner.

The growth of demand will continue to be more and more extensive, and with it the access to large volumes of data, given that the development in the field of data mining will have a medium- and long-term growth, and as a consequence there will be an expectation to spend a lot of resources.

Starting "raw data is often not very supportive". It can be visualized with a value that is based on several points such as:

- The ability to extract information for decision making.
- Understanding the issue of the importance of the origin of the data.

Data analysis has been or has been traditionally performed manually. When the scale of data control manipulation, generalization and application and manipulation should be beyond human capacity, the help and support of information technologies for process automation is necessary.

4 Python

The Python programming language was created in 1991 [8]. Which is a high-level platform and in an interpreted scheme, this software emphasizes the readability of the code. It is based on dynamic typing processes and is multi-paradigm, i.e., it can support object-oriented, structured, functional, etc. programming.

n addition to the above, it is also used for neural network training [9].

As a result, Python has become the second most used language on GitHub [10, 11].

5 TensorFlow

The development of the so-called TensorFlow is a library created by Google [12] for developments such as neural networks. It has a predominance by Theano [13], and is used both for Google research [12].

Jupyter Notebook (or more commonly a plain "notebook"), is a document produced by the Jupyter Notebook App, containing both computer code (e.g. Python or R) and rich text elements (paragraphs, equations, figures, links, etc.). It is both a human-readable document, which may contain the description of a data analysis and its results (figures, tables, etc.), and a computer-executable document, which may contain code snippets that execute, for example, a data analysis.

Because of this ability to mix code and text elements, this type of document is ideal for placing the work of a data scientist, bringing analysis and results together in one place, while allowing it to be executed in real time [16].

A kernel is a computational "engine", which executes the code contained within the notebook. When a notebook is opened, the associated kernel is automatically executed. Then when a notebook is run (either cell-by-cell or from the Cell -> Run All menu, the kernel executes the computational calculations and produces the results.

By default, the application comes with a kernel for the Python language, but kernels for other programming languages such as R [16] can be added.

6   Proposal

The variety of data nowadays and of great diversity, of them, not only for who sells some product, but also for the users who acquire them contemplates the decision making to expand their decisions in the diversity of products, the trend of customers and the diversity of them.

In total, according to figures from the UN Food and Agriculture Fund (FAO) corresponding to October 2017, 1300 million tons of food produced for human consumption are lost, one third of the total world production. While in America and the Caribbean it is estimated that 6% of global food loss is wasted [7], in Mexico according to figures from SEDESOL 10, 431,000 tons of food is wasted 37% of the country's production [8].

For this article, the analysis is presented and developed in the classification and prediction of purchases made by users, in some online self-service stores, in time of the COVID-19 pandemic, through data mining, using the TensorFlow platform.

Nowadays, with the increase of online sales, analyses such as these can have a broader vision of growth, and visualize that with the advancement of time there will be greater acceptance by both users, both consumer users and service providers.

We have a number of sales provided by the mobile application EInt [16], which are randomly generated data through a simulation of sales by non-real people who purchase from 1 to 28 products already established with name and price by the program. This process was performed in this way given the restrictions that were had by the COVID-19 pandemic. And 6 scenarios are developed to demonstrate the prediction of the data.

An example of data generated in one simulation provided by the application EInt is shown in Table 1 and Table 2. First table data corresponds to a sales header, with information about the place and user and the second one corresponds to products purchased by the user. All sales are using the Mexican Peso currency (MXN). Note that all information is randomly generated and isn't based on any real data of any real person.

Table 1. Example of a sales simulation generated by the EInt application.

Date	2021-05-13 19:46:35
Store	Soriana
Branch	Downtown area
User Genre	Female
Age	31
Name	Silvia
Invoice	SoCe3268
Shipping cost	30.00 $ (MXN)
Total without shipping	142.00 $ (MXN)
Total	172.00 $ (MXN)

Table 2. Products of a sale generated by a simulation

Product ID	Name	Weight or amount	Weight unit	Price
1	Soda	2	Liter	60 $ (MXN)
14	Banana	500	Grams	14 $ (MXN)
15	Sugar	1	Kilogram	31 $ (MXN)
16	Cooking oil	1	Liter	33 $ (MXN)
27	Salt	250	Grams	4 $ (MXN)

The required information extracted from simulations is stored in a file with extension (.data) for each scenario. These files will be used in a Python application to get a prediction of the data that is evaluating the corresponding scenario. An example of a.data file containing nine total sales and, separated by a comma, the number of sales is shown in Fig. 1. Scenarios will extract different amount of data, depends on their requirements.

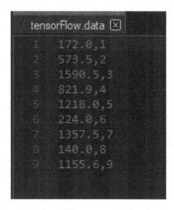

Fig. 1. Contents of a.data file generated by the EInt application.

For the upcoming scenarios, we can understand as a "Simulation" as the information obtained from the EInt application, that was shown above.

7 Results

7.1 Scenario 1

For the first scenario we are going to predict if the sales of the Soriana store, branch downtown, will go up or down. To achieve this, we have a simulation of 9 sales, each with a different total amount, these sales will be useful to be able to estimate what the future behavior of the store will be like.

The program written in Python is responsible for predicting future sales based on the data provided and then displaying them in a graph. The X axis represents the number of sales, Y axis the total cost of the sales, the dots indicate total cost per sale and the line shows the sales prediction, as shown in Fig. 2. The used currency is the mexican peso (MXN).

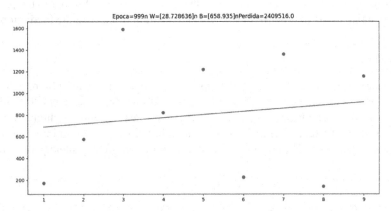

Fig. 2. Graph showing the total and number of sales obtained from simulation.

In summary, the graph has a slope towards the positive y-axis, showing that the sales of the store will have an increase. However, to achieve a more accurate prediction, it's recommended that the number of sales be higher. In this scenario, the number of sales used by the simulation was 9, this is because of hardware limitations.

7.2 Scenario 2

For scenario 2, we have a simulation of 200 people who bought in Calimax store, where we will take as a sample those who have made a purchase between 8:00 am. and 12:00 pm, as shown in Fig. 3. Note that the X axis represents the customer number and the Y axis represents the minutes, therefore 500 min is equivalent to 8:20 am. The dots represent money spent per customer.

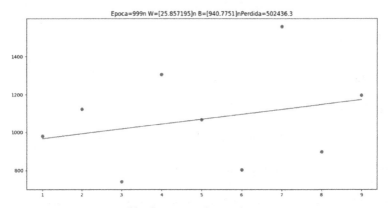

Fig. 3. Graph of scenario 2.

In this graph we can see that the customers of the store will decrease with the passage of the day. Note that the graph is evaluating if the store will increase or decrease the number of customers, also is showing only the first 9 customers. Similar to the previous scenario, a rise in the number of customers can result in more accurate prediction.

7.3 Scenario 3

This scenario takes as a reference 100 people who bought in a Walmart Store, where the sample consists of female customers and where total sales have exceeded 700 Mexican pesos. With these conditions, we can predict if the sales that took an high amount of money spent by the female users will go even higher or not, as shown in Fig. 4. X axis indicate the customers, Y axis money spent, dots represent money spent per customer.

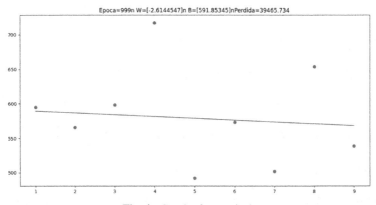

Fig. 4. Graph of scenario 3.

The result for this scenario tells us that future female customers who spent more than 700 mexican pesos, will spent even more money.

7.4   Scenario 4

For this scenario the simulation generates 100 sales made in random stores in the month of January. The sales made in Ley store will be taken as a sample. The graph shown in Fig. 5 shows that only 4 sales were found for the Ley branches out of the simulation. X axis represent the number of customers, Y the sales cost, and the dots the sale cost per customers.

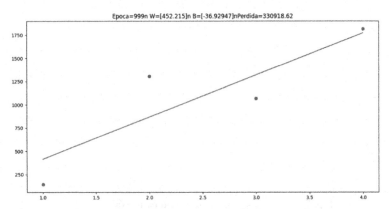

Fig. 5. Scenario 4 graph corresponding to Ley sales.

I theory, the graph shown a high increment of sales, however, due to the low amount of data provided by the simulation, we can understand this prediction as unreliable. Just adding a dot below 50 in Y (a sale), the graph can even turn negative. This result helps us to understand the importance of handling massive data when making predictions.

Now we are going to take Soriana's store sales as a sample using the same simulation of 100 random store sales. In this case, 12 sales are generated as shown in Fig. 6.

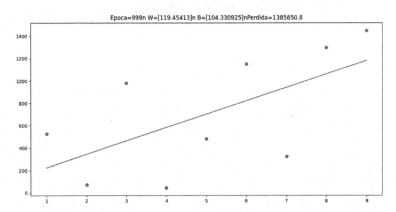

Fig. 6. Scenario 4 graph corresponding to Soriana's sales.

Although our number of sales is still too low to establish an accurate prediction, if a new sale was added to the last graph, the prediction would not change much, it would still show an increase in sales. The more data that is handled when generating a forecast, the lower the slope of the graph when a new data is presented. This can also be understood as: the greater the amount of data, the lower the margin of error.

To finish this scenario, we are going to show the sales of Walmart. There are 36 sales for the branches of this store, the graph is shown in Fig. 7.

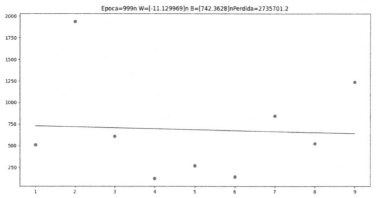

Fig. 7. Scenario 4 graph corresponding to Walmart sales.

In the case of Walmart, there is a higher number of sales, even so, and in the case of massive data, certain criteria must be used when dealing with predicted data, due to the fact that they are not real data and the estimation can fail. It can also be the case of a stochastic event, something out of our control that can change the course of our data.

7.5 Scenario 5

In this scenario, a simulation for 200 customers are generated. Our sample consists of sales made in Calimax branches, as shown in Fig. 8. X axis represent customers and Y axis the sales. The dots indicate the sales per customer.

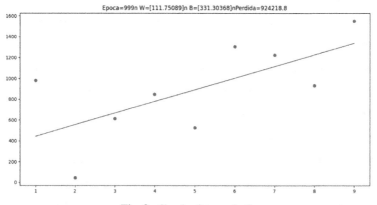

Fig. 8. Graph of scenario 5.

The result shown that the Calimax branches will have an increase in sales.

7.6   Scenario 6

In the last scenario of 50 customers, we have a sample of the number of products purchased for each sale in the Florido store, 5&10 branch. Figure 9 shows the graph of products purchased per sale. The X-axis represents the number of sales and the Y-axis the number of items sold, dots the number of items sold per sale.

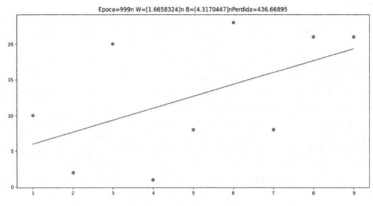

Fig. 9. Graph of scenario 6.

The graph shows an increase of the products sold per sale; this can also be interpreted as an increase of products sold in general.

8   Conclusions

There are times when a phenomenon does not behave as expected. This phenomenon can be the sales of a business, the shares of a company, the price of a raw material, etc. While we can't prevent that behavior, we can prepare for the unwanted behavior when it happens. This is where data prediction plays an important role. Using the data, we already know, we can discover, with a small margin of error, the behavior of said data in the future.

Tensorflow allows us to calculate data estimates that can be used to predict various situations such as: to know how much profit a company will have based on the predictions of the sales of its products, to know how many subscribers a web platform that provides multimedia services will have in the future, it can also be estimated in non-numerical data, such as photographs, if it contains a certain object whether it is a fruit, a plant or whatever is defined by the program.

Keep in mind that a prediction helps us to know the future behavior of a phenomenon, however, the fact of knowing it will not change its conduct. If it is necessary to change it, the events that provoke such behavior must be altered.

The article shows scenarios that present different results, such as increases in sales, which can also be understood as an increase in profits; losses in sales, as well as show what happens when predicting non-massive data, all this for the purpose of denote the operation of data prediction tools as well as exemplify the applications of this technology.

It is envisaged that in the future, the Tensorflow library could be used to support the prediction of data related to everyday life, like the food waste in households, electricity consumption in a house, how much a person sleeps a day, among other things.

References

1. Chaffey, D., Ellis-Chadwick, F.: Digital Marketing, Strategy, Implementation and Practice. Pearson Chaffey and Ellis-Chadwick, Mexico City (2014)
2. Ohmae, p. 72 (2005)
3. Salazar, J., Silvestre, Y.S.: Internet of Things
4. Gunturi, M., Kotha, H.D., Srinivasa Reddy, M.: An overview of internet of things. J. Adv. Res. Dyn. Control Syst. **10**(9), 659–665 (2018)
5. Cook, D.J., Augusto, J.C., Jakkula, V.R.: Ambient intelligence: technologies, applications, and opportunities. Pervasive Mob. Comput. **5**(4), 277–298 (2009)
6. Tania, L., Isabel, C.: Iot, El Internet De Las Cosas Y La Innovación De Sus Aplicaciones, UANL Sch. Business, FACPYA, Mexico, no. May, pp. 2313–2340 (2015)
7. Mitra, S., Acharya, T.: Data Mining: Multimedia, Soft Computing and Bioinformatics. Wiley (2003)
8. "Quora. https://www.quora.com/What-is-the-most-famous-software-written-inPython
9. GitHub. https://octoverse.github.com/
10. Stackify. https://stackify.com/popular-programming-languages-2018/
11. TensorFlow. https://www.tensorflow.org/
12. Wikipedia (TensorFLow). https://es.wikipedia.org/wiki/TensorFlow
13. Quora. https://www.quora.com/What-is-the-future-of-TensorFlow
14. [Online]. Available: https://www.tensorflow.org/guide/keras?hl=es-419
15. https://colab.research.google.com/github/efviodo/idatha-data-science-course/blob/master/notebooks/01%20-%20DS%20-%20Conceptos%20Basicos%20Jupyter%20Notebooks%20-%20R.ipynb#scrollTo=SWkPj_j40ye-
16. Guarda, T., Portela, F., Santos, M.F. (eds.): ARTIIS 2021. CCIS, vol. 1485. Springer, Cham (2021). https://doi.org/10.1007/978-3-030-90241-4

RULA (Rapid Upper Limb Assessment) Methodology for Ergonomics Using Inertial Sensors

Jenniffer D. Castillo[1]([✉]) [iD], Bogart Yail Marquez[2] [iD], Arturo Realyvazquez[1] [iD], and Arnulfo Alanis[1] [iD]

[1] Industrial Engineering Department, Technological Institute of Tijuana, Calzada Tecnologico S/N, 22414 Tijuana, Baja California, Mexico
{jenniffer.castillo,Arturo.realyvazquez, alanis}@tectijuana.edu.mx
[2] Chemistry and Engineering Faculty, Baja California Autonomous University, Calzada Universidad 14418, 22390 Tijuana, Baja California, Mexico
bogart@tectijuana.edu.mx

Abstract. Nowadays different studies have shown that workers in different areas such as the field of construction, manufacturing and others, can be affected by muscle and musculoskeletal problems caused by poor posture during working hours, which is why different methods have been developed for the prevention of this type of problems in the health of workers. One of these methods is RULA (Rapid Upper Limb Assessment) which allows us to quickly evaluate the posture and thus categorize the risk factors by means of a score with which a certain level of action is established and based on it indicate if the posture is acceptable or if it is necessary to make any changes. In this work, inertial sensors were used to obtain the values of the angles formed by the limbs and thus determine the score in each of them.

Keywords: Methodology · RULA · Ergonomics · Health · Posture · Disorder · Physical work · Sensors · Inertial

1 Introduction

The "Rapid Assessment of the Upper extremities" RULA method emerged in 1993 in a study to investigate the exposure of workers to risk factors caused by work posture that could cause musculoskeletal disorders (McAtamney and Corlett 1993).

This method consists of the evaluation of individual postures, sequences or sets of postures are not evaluated, so it must first be determined which posture will be evaluated by observing and studying the postures performed by the worker in several process cycles or postures that are repetitive. The measurements are made by obtaining the angles formed by the limbs with respect to certain references. The group is divided into two groups A for upper extremities (arms, forearms, wrists) and B for legs, trunk, and neck.

T. Guarda et al. (Eds.): ARTIIS 2022, CCIS 1676, pp. 177–190, 2022.
https://doi.org/10.1007/978-3-031-20316-9_14

1.1 Problem Statement

In this research it is proposed the use of the RULA methodology to obtain scores for different postures and evaluate the risk factor of suffering from any musculoskeletal disorder, to obtain a score it is first required to make the measurement of the angles of a given posture, this measurement can be obtained with different techniques some of them are through photographs or video, measure physically, and motion capture devices among others, this investigation plans to obtain these measurements with the help of inertial sensors, these sensors are integrated into the device "Perception Neuron 32 (LEGACY)" which consists of multiple sensors fixed in a wearable suit that allows the capture of movement in real time, which will be provided by the institution for the realization of measurements and analysis, which will help obtain the data through the software of this device. With this, the results could be obtained automatically, faster and more detailed measurement for later analysis. The methodology of this device and the advantages or disadvantages will compare to other methods to review the data acquisition.

1.1.1 The Problems of the Project

In the project, knowledge and understanding about the operation of the RULA methodology must be acquired, once the work team proposes research on the sensors and software to be used, the cost of materials and software, the state of the art must be evaluated. Other project restraint is that we do not have the necessary equipment with which the development is proposed, these sensors are of vital importance as well as the necessary software to obtain the measurements when carrying out the fieldwork, for this reason the work will consist of a documentary investigation that will help us prepare the bases for a future investigation where access to the device is available or that it can be replaced with some alternative of the market and thus be able to carry out our project making the necessary implementations to reach the expected results and meet our objectives, which are raised in Sect. 1.4 of the document.

1.2 Justification

The Rapid Assessment of the Upper Extremities (RULA) has had a lot of research, but it has never been possible to develop one that gives results on the exact benefits in the application of inertial sensors. A well-applied investigation can lead to the correct use of inertial sensors during the analysis of the RULA method, thus obtaining the correct methodology to apply it using sensors, so that all personnel using this method can use it correctly.

1.3 Questions

1.3.1 Central and Specific Questions

Does the RULA methodology represent a real help in ergonomics? How inertial sensors related to ergonomics using the RULA methodology? Is there a benefit to using these sensors?

1.4   Objectives

1.4.1   General Objectives

Explain how the RULA methodology works within ergonomics by using inertial sensors.

1.4.2   Specific Objectives

Define what the RULA methodology is and its advantages.
   Show how the RULA methodology applied in ergonomics.
   Explain how inertial sensors are used with the Perception Neuron 32 (LEGACY) device.

2   State of the Art

2.1   Background

In this research, different articles and studies have been compiled that tell us about the advances and results that have been achieved by applying the RULA methodology in different ways, for example, with sensors, with cameras or even with the Kinect device, these investigations help us to have a vision of the current state of this methodology and thus dimension the scope and limitations of our research. Below are some of the articles consulted in which the RULA method is applied.

   In the study "The Improvement Of Work Posture Using Rapid Upper Limb Assessment: Analysis To Decrease Subjective Disorders Of Strawberry Farmers In Bali" (Yusuf et al. 2016) is carried out on farmers in Indonesia, it seeks to improve the work system so that workers are healthier and productive, many of the tools used can cause uncomfortable postures and fatigue, as well as skeletal disorders. To counteract these problems, an analysis of the work posture was carried out, and tools were changed to improve work, one of these analyzes is the RULA (Rapid Upper Limb Assessment) method that allows us to evaluate the posture, style and movement of a work activity that demands the use of the upper extremities.

   Another study analyzing the fatigue of laboratory workers that will be measured using the RULA and REBA method to investigate workers' limb disorders entitled "Analysis Tingkat Ergonomi Postur Kerja Karyawan di Laboratorium KCP PT" (Imron 2020), the purpose of this research was to evaluate work postures that affect the achievement of productivity. It can be concluded that, according to the results of the analysis using the RULA method of posture at work in the laboratory, employees obtained a score of 6, that is, a moderate risk while based on the use of the REBA method, the results obtained a score of 7, that is, the action category 2, which is moderate risk, while the OWAS analysis method scored 1 in the not too risky category.

   An investigation has been carried out on the current use of wearable inertial sensors and their results regarding biomechanical exposure in physical works in the investigation: "A Narrative Review On Contemporary And Emerging Uses Of Inertial Sensing In Occupational Ergonomics" (Lim and D'Souza 2020), results of kinematics in the field of ergonomics have been deployed, this has been carried out in order to find information that can contribute to the emerging technology that seeks to help reduce musculoskeletal traumatic disorders that are related to the workplace. The use of observation methods to obtain this data is common even today, methods such as OWAS, RULA and REBA are a great example, however, with the portability and direct instrumentation.

The other research entitled "Study Of The Ergonomic Risk In Operators Of An Assembly Line Using The Rula Method In Real Working Conditions Through The Application Of A Commercial Sensor" (Villacís et al. 2022) used observation methods in working conditions, the most common of these is the use of RULA, however, the study tells us that these methods provide certain disadvantages, because the collection of data is subjective and is estimated in angles of photos and/or videos, which leaves the criteria to the evaluator. For these reasons, the use of the Kinect V2 commercial sensor is proposed as a tool for ergonomic evaluation in real working conditions. The implementation of the sensor in the RULA method is sought, in such a way that, the sensor will serve to obtain real data in addition to the estimation of the evaluator to obtain accurate information about the ergonomics of the work.

This article identifies the areas of sensitive and insensitive postures based on the sensitivity of RULA, which, together with the ordinal regression analysis, will take a closer look on the methodology used to evaluate postures. The work is called "Identification Of Indifferent Posture Zones In Rula By Sensitivity Analysis" (Joshi and Deshpande 2021). This analysis places great emphasis on postures, observing combinations of these that do not present discomfort and other negative aspects, considering the identification of the common body variable based on the RULA estimate.

Rapid Upper Extremity Assessment (RULA) has much research on its own use based on work-related musculoskeletal disorders (WRMDs) such as "Rapid Upper Limb Assessment (Rula) In Ergonomic Assessment: A Comprehensive Review" (Kumar and Kamath 2019). Despite this, at the time of creation of this article, there is no revised compilation on the uses of RULA in ergonomic evaluations. Therefore, the objective of this article is to collect articles related to the use of RULA of the evaluation of DSMT, taking as a reference different academic database.

In the research "Application of the Rula Technique in the Area of Packaging Using Kinect Technology" (Payán et al. 2015), we talk about how in Mexico, in the Federal Labor Law, in its table of occupational diseases and how this indicates the mechanical factors and variations of the elements of the environment. To which several questions lead to a study in the packaging area of a company in the food industry through the use of the RULA methodology, with which the body was divided into two groups, which would be group A the upper part (arms, forearms and wrists) and group B that would be the legs, trunk and neck. All this was done with the aim of measuring the degree of fatigue and disorders caused to the musculoskeletal system, in addition to all this, using kinect technology and inertial sensors.

2.2 Theoretical Perspectives

According to Lim and D'Souza (2020) wearable inertial sensors are those that represent a primary advance for the improvement of methodologies, leading to a smaller margin of error in the results of the data taken. This reduces the inherent risks of obtaining erroneous results or that the methodologies obtain similar results, they all should obtain the same conclusions.

The research of Imron (2020) helps us verify from another point of view the conclusion reached by Lim & D'Souza, since a data collection was maintained with three different methodologies, which were RULA, REBA and OWAS. The result of the 3 methods shows us 3 totally different conclusions. While the RULA methodology showed that the consequences of posture at work in laboratory employees obtained a score of 6, that is, moderate risk while based on the use of the REBA method, the results obtained a score of 7, that is, action category 2, which is moderate risk, while the OWAS analysis method scored 1 in the not too risky category.

Merbah's article (2020). Obtained information in the case of the RULA methodology in the use of mobile devices.

In the case of the research of Yong-Ku et al. (2018) provides information on the different types of tools for the evaluation of ergonomics that can be ALLA, REBA, OWAS and the main one RULA, within the area of farm work, and see how it helps us to be able to confirm data, being the center of our eye the RULA methodology. In addition to being able to see if the use of inertial sensors can help in the application of the RULA methodology.

Jara's article (2019) talks about the observations we have of the different methodologies for ergonomic risk factors.That their data collection is very subjective and that all of them are based on estimates of different angles projected in photos and videos. That is why we talk about the Kinect V12 sensor, about what it can do for ergonomic evaluations in real working conditions.

As Hernandez and Torres (2018) tells us, "A theory is a set of interrelated propositions capable of explaining why and how a phenomenon occurs", it constitutes a set of linked constructs (concepts), definitions and propositions that present a systematic view of phenomenon's by specifying the relationships between variables, with the purpose of explaining and predicting phenomena. This research is mainly based on the application of the existing RULA methodology so the fundamentals of this have been obtained to apply them to our project, the way to obtain the measurements of the angles of the extremities will be through inertial sensors. An approach will be given to our study based on what has already been studied and proven with this methodology, raising other questions oriented to our research and we will seek to deepen and expand elements of the theory and visualize new ways of applying it.

2.3 Conceptual Framework

The research of the RULA methodology covers three main sections, these being the inertial sensors, which will address the efficiency of the same through the scores that are collected in the field of research.

The historical framework of the project presents the stage of development in which the problem we are looking to develop is located, this is obtained based on the TRL (Technological Readiness Level) maturity levels created by NASA. Based on our theoretical framework and the information presented in the theoretical perspectives analyzed through the investigation of various processes and exercises generated in laboratories and field research in various sectors of the industry, we managed to define and reach an agreement among all the members of the team that the maximum level of maturity that is intended to be achieved in this research was 7:

TRL 1. Basic research: In this phase the necessary information would be collected to carry out the research, but still without any application.

TRL 2. Formulation of the technology: Here there would be speculations or assumptions of what the project could become.

TRL 3. Applied research - proof of concept: At this stage you can perform tests on the sensors on their own to learn how they work, and you will plan how to implement their use in the RULA methodology.

TRL 4. Small-scale laboratory development: Here we will try to reproduce the device in the laboratory as a prototype to perform the tests to know the power of the project and detect possible improvements.

TRL 5. Full-scale development: As this point indicates, the project is carried out on a real scale, but it continues to work only at the laboratory level.

TRL 6. Validated prototype in simulated environment: Here you can perform tests with a simulated environment or with characteristics like the real ones.

TRL 7. Prototype validated in real environment: In this phase you must have a functional prototype that works in real conditions, at this point you must already be able to make the necessary measurements in the test subjects.

The research variables that we can find in the databases investigated consist of various attributes that allude to movements of the parts of the body, as well as the positions generated for those movements. They are usually divided into two groups, which are divided into A and B. Group A is the parts of the body that usually perform the action, in which the forearms, arms and wrists are covered. Group B is the parts of the body that usually support movement, including the legs, trunk and neck. To make the measurements, the following variables were used:

Extension: Measures the extension of all the parts that make up the groups (Group A and Group B) which is defined in the position of the part at 20° or less.

Flexion: This variable defines the movement of the joints of the parts of the body that make up both groups (A and B) that is defined at more than 20°.

Position: Here the position in which the body part is located is defined, such as, for example, "On one side of the body", "Cross the midline", "Abducted arms".

Deviation: This defines the deviation that is in the parts that are being evaluated, such as in the wrist the radial deviation or the ulnar deviation.

Level of action: After evaluating all parts of groups A and B, the level of action defines the risks that these may have, which may become acceptable risks or also high risks that require an urgent change in tasks.

It was observed in the studies that the scores usually go in intervals from 0 to 4.

2.3.1 Ergonomics

Ergonomics is a science responsible for the study of how to adapt the relationship of the human being and his environment according to the Council of the International Ergonomics Association (IEA, for its acronym in English).

The OMS (World Health Organization) tell us that "it is the science that tries to obtain the maximum performance, reducing the risks of human error to a minimum, at the same time tries to reduce fatigue and eliminate as much as possible the dangers for the worker. Occupational risk: In the Federal Labor Law, article 473, defines the risk of work, as the diseases and accidents to which workers are being exposed in the exercise or on the occasion of work. Article 474 states that: "accident at work is any organic injury or functional disturbance, immediate or subsequent, or death, produced suddenly in exercise, or in connection with work, whatever the place and time in which it is provided". Also including accidents that occur when the worker moves from home to work and vice versa.

2.3.2 Ergonomic Occupational Risk

Analyzing the previous points, we can understand that the ergonomic occupational risk is one that poses a risk to workers who perform a physical activity derived from poor posture, depending on the activity that is performed, posture, frequency, etc. The level of risk can be calculated using different methods to anticipate or avoid the disorders that may be generated in workers.

2.3.3 Ergonomic Analysis of the Workplace

This consists of systematically and detailed inspection and description of the activity carried out by the worker in his workplace. To obtain the necessary information you can make use of observation, interviews, photographs, videos, etc. As well as the use of measuring instruments such as the luxmeter for lighting, the sound level meter for noise and the thermometer to measure the ambient temperature (Cuesta 2012).

2.3.4 Cognitive Ergonomics

It allows us to study the cognitive aspects of the interaction between people, the work system and the artifacts that we find in it, the objective is to design them so that the interaction is effective. These cognitive processes such as perception, problem solving or learning are very important in interaction and should be considered to explain cognitive activities, such as seeking information and interpreting it, decision making and problem solving (Cañas and Waerns 2001).

2.3.5 Geometric Ergonomics

Geometric ergonomics is characterized by adapting furniture, environments and work-stations to the essential needs of the employee. In the workplace, it is responsible for seeking the improvement of those aspects that influence the safety and productivity of the employees of an organization. This branch of ergonomics is based on the concept of anthropometry, which is responsible for studying the measurements and dimensions of the body. In this sense, in the work environment it is used to design customized workstations according to the needs of each employee (Ofiprix 2021).

2.3.6 Ergonomics Methodologies

The following are some of the most common ergonomic methodologies which are classified according to Diego-Mas (2022) in forces and biomechanics, repetitiveness, postural load, load handling, office posts, global evaluation, thermal environment, and utilities.

Forces and Biomechanics

Forces applied: Forces - EN1005-3. It assesses the risk of exerting forces based on the capacity of the workers following the calculation procedure established in the EN1005-3 standard.

Biomechanical Analysis: Bio - Mec. Performs biomechanical evaluations of coplanar static stresses based on posture adopted, load, and frequency and duration of efforts. It allows to know the risk of overload by joint, the maximum recommended load, and the stability of the posture.

Repeatability

OCRA Checklist. The Check-List version of the OCRA method allows rapid assessment of the risk associated with repetitive movements of the upper limbs.

JSI. JSI method. JSI assesses risks related to upper extremities. From semi-quantitative data offers a numerical result that grows with the risk associated with the task.

Postural Load

RULA. RULA method. This allows to evaluate the exposure of workers to risks due to the maintenance of inadequate postures that can cause disorders in the upper limbs of the body.

REBA. REBA method. It assesses workers' exposure to risk factors that can lead to cumulative traumatic disorders due to dynamic and static postural load.

OWAS. OWAS method. It is a simple method aimed at the ergonomic analysis of postural load. It bases its results on the observation of the different positions adopted by the worker.

EPR. EPR method. It allows to assess, in a global way, the postural load of the worker throughout the day. The method is intended as a preliminary examination indicating the need for a more thorough examination.

Work Load Handle

NIOSH. NIOSH equation. It allows to identify risks related to the tasks in which manual lifting of loads are carried out, intimately related to lumbar injuries.

GINSHT. GINSHT method. It evaluates risks related to the manual handling of loads developed by the National Institute of Safety and Hygiene at Work of Spain.

SNOOK and CIRIELLO. Tables of SNOOK and CIRIELLO allow to determine the maximum acceptable weights for different actions such as lifting, descent, pushing, dragging and transporting loads.

Office positions

ROSE. ROSA method. It is a Check List that allows quantifying the ergonomic risk associated with workstations in offices or with the use of data visualization screens.

Global Assessment

Check List LCE. It is a checklist (Check-List) of basic ergonomic principles applied to 128 items that proposes simple and low-cost ergonomic interventions, allowing practical improvements to be applied to existing working conditions.

LEST method. The LEST method. It evaluates working conditions, both in their physical aspect, and in that related to mental load and psychosocial aspects. It is a general method that contemplates in a global way many variables that influence the ergonomic quality of the workplace.

Thermal Environment

FANGER. FANGER method. It allows to estimate the global thermal sensation of those present in each thermal environment by calculating the Estimated Average Vote (PMV) and the Percentage of Dissatisfied People (PPD).

Utilities

FRI. Assessment of the physical load. Tool to estimate the hardship of a task through heart rate.

LSC. Length of body segments. Tool to estimate the length of body members from height.

MET. Estimation of metabolism. Tool to estimate metabolic rate using methods of estimating energy metabolism.

PSC. Weight of body segments. Tool to estimate the weight of body members from the weight of the individual.

AIS. Thermal insulation of clothes. Tool to stimulate the isolation of usual and work clothes.

RULER. Angles between body segments. Tool to measure angles between different members of the body on photographs.

2.3.7 Inertial Sensors

An inertial sensor is a type of sensor that measures acceleration and angular velocity, used in motion capture and analysis applications. It consists of accelerometers, gyroscopes and magnetometers. Accelerometers measure the linear acceleration with which the sensor moves, gyroscopes the angular velocity and magnetometers give information about magnetic north. With these three sensors it is possible to study the movement of the entire inertial sensor in plane or space.

2.4 Perception Neuron 32 (LEGACY)

It is a device that consists of 32 inertial sensors connected by cables in a harness that is placed throughout the body, including each finger of the hands, through the software of the device allows us to perform motion capture accurately which is implemented to obtain the measurements of the angles when using the RULA methodology (Noitom Motion Capture Systems 2022).

3 Research Methodology

3.1 Formulation of the Problem

The cases in which the part of this methodology is evaluated usually does not involve the use of these sensors, if it uses sensors or other devices such as the Kinect, which are used to obtain data on the positions of the bodies, mainly from the groups that are evaluated by the RULA methodology (Group A and B). The data obtained through these sensors such as the Kinect would obtain more accurate and real data evaluated.

This use of inertial sensors is implemented to see how it works within this methodology, to be able to define if there is a change for the better and how these can affect ergonomics and the RULA methodology. In addition looking for significant differences that can be found in the use of these tools in different people from different fields.

The sample size will be defined based on a small group of people taken as references for the use of the sensors, as well as documents taken as a reference. To carry out the research, the following intervention plan will be carried out:

Relevant research on the subject, with the aim of further expanding our knowledge.

Consideration of a wider range of resources to consider, in addition to those we already have contemplated.

Obtain the resources that are necessary for the realization of the case study.

3.2 Data Analysis and Collection

The measurements that will be obtained are scored according to the tables shown in Fig. 1, in paragraph a) Table A, the analysis of the arm, forearm and wrist, in paragraph

a)

ARM	FOREARM	1 TURN	1 WRIST	2 TURN	2 WRIST	3 TURN	3 WRIST	4 TURN	4 WRIST
		1	2	1	2	1	2	1	2
1	1	1	2	2	2	2	3	3	3
	2	2	2	2	2	3	3	3	3
	3	2	3	3	3	3	3	4	4
2	1	2	3	3	3	3	4	4	4
	2	3	3	3	3	3	4	4	4
	3	3	3	4	4	4	4	5	5
3	1	3	3	4	4	4	4	5	5
	2	3	4	4	4	4	4	5	5
	3	4	4	4	4	4	5	5	5
4	1	4	4	4	4	5	5	5	5
	2	4	4	4	5	5	5	5	5
	3	4	4	4	5	5	5	6	6
5	1	5	5	5	5	5	6	6	7
	2	5	6	6	6	6	7	7	7
	3	6	6	6	6	7	7	7	8
6	1	7	7	7	7	7	8	8	9
	2	8	8	8	8	8	9	9	9
	3	9	9	9	9	9	9	9	9

TABLE A — STEAM

b)

NECK	1 LEG		2 LEG		3 LEG		4 LEG		5 LEG		6 LEG	
	1	2	1	2	1	2	1	2	1	2	1	2
1	1	3	2	3	3	4	5	5	6	6	7	7
2	2	3	2	3	4	5	5	5	6	7	7	7
3	3	3	3	4	4	5	5	6	6	7	7	7
4	5	5	5	6	6	7	7	7	7	7	8	8
5	7	7	7	7	7	8	8	8	8	8	8	8
6	8	8	8	8	8	8	8	9	9	9	9	9

TABLE B — STEAM

c)

TABLE C	1	2	3	4	5	6	7+
1	1	2	3	3	4	5	5
2	2	2	3	4	4	5	5
3	3	3	3	4	4	5	6
4	3	3	3	4	5	6	6
5	4	4	4	5	6	7	7
6	4	4	5	6	6	7	7
7	5	5	6	6	7	7	7
8+	5	5	6	7	7	7	7

Fig. 1. Standard field sheet for determining physical working conditions in employees of a company

Note. Image obtained from docsity.com (Rodriguez 2021).

b) Table B, the analysis of neck, trunk and legs and with the table of subsection c) Table C, the score will be obtained with the sum of the score of Table A, muscle score and strength/load score. The general score of the RULA methodology is calculated based on the scores obtained by the groups as shown in Fig. 2, which are A (arm, forearm, and wrist), see Fig. 3 and B (neck, trunk, and leg) as seen in Fig. 4, which record their score based on the angles presented in different extremities when making an effort. After that, both scores will be recorded in a third table, from which the final score will be obtained.

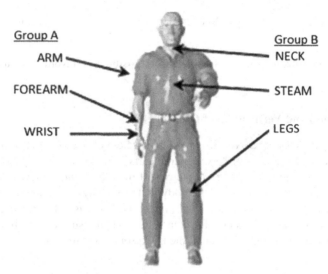

Fig. 2. Division of the RULA methodology groups
Note. Image obtained from uisek.edu.ec (uisek 2022).

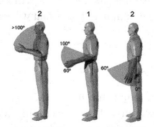

Fig. 3. Forearm movement Note. Image obtained from uisek.edu.ec (uisek 2022).

3.3 Model Development

The scores obtained using sensors yield numerical results that can be interpreted in multiple ways. Depending on the score obtained in each part of the body specified, these are analyzed to know if an extension of the study is necessary and help should be sought to try to obtain better results, or if everything is in optimal conditions and people do not

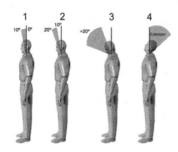

Fig. 4. Neck movement angles Note. Image obtained from uisek.edu.ec (uisek 2022).

require treatment or a modification of their work postures, so favorable results would be shown.

3.4 Validation and Verification of the Model

The model is verified from the results of various studies previously visualized, in general, it is appreciated that almost the same parameters are used among all the studies, in addition to being able to adjust to the metrics of the others, since they usually use the same metrics as well. The parts of the body that are always contemplated range from all the limbs to the head, spine and back in general. Likewise, the situations in which they are asked to make movements for data collection are usually very similar, making it possible to make an estimate from all the background and its results.

3.5 Experimentation and Optimization

Because we did not have access to the device and the software necessary to use it which will allow us to make the measurements, this work will only remain as a documentary investigation since the experimentation and tests that were planned to be carried out will not be carried out.

3.6 Interpretation of Results

As mentioned in the previous point due to the fact that the measurements and tests were not carried out, the research will remain unfinished for the moment since the implementation of the sensors will not be carried out.

3.7 Results and Analysis

This section is pending until the corresponding tests are performed and obtain results.

3.8 Conclusion

In conclusion, we can say that the RULA methodology is very important within ergonomics, this helps on our own central question, in which we asked ourselves if the

RULA methodology was useful within ergonomics. In addition to being able to identify many positive points of the inertial sensors that they have within this methodology.

We can compare different methodologies used for the evaluation of risk in ergonomics, this allows us to expand the panorama in terms of other techniques and methodologies to understand the advantages and benefits of each of them and which is the most convenient to implement in each situation. The state of the art was also addressed in which we can see the progress that has been made in this area, thanks to different studies and work carried out in the matter and support us for this research, we saw how different methodologies and different tools have been applied, in some cases inertial sensors are not used but other types of motion captures, such as photography, video or even manual measurement, and how it has evolved with new technologies.

3.9   Recommendations/Future Work

Although the project was not fully developed in this work, the foundations for subsequent work are laid, it is considered of great importance the documentation of the research so that it also serves as support for future research in which experimental research can be carried out with all the necessary tools.

References

Asensio Cuesta, S., Bastante Ceca, M.J., Diego Más, J.A.: Evaluación ergonómica de puestos de trabajo. Editorial paraninfo (2012)

Cañas, J.J., Waerns, Y.: Ergonomía cognitiva. Aspectos psicológicos de la interacción de las personas con la tecnología de la información. Madrid: Editorial Médica Panamericana, 46. Recuperado 22 de mayo de 2022 de (2001). https://www.researchgate.net/profile/Jose-Canas-2/publication/301358283_ERGONOMIA_COGNITIVA/links/57153b2708ae8ab56695a8d6/ERGONOMIA-COGNITIVA.pd

Chávez Cujilán, Y.T., Moran Olvera, B.M.: La ergonomía y los métodos de evaluación de carga postura. AlfaPublicaciones 4(1.1), 279–292 (2022). https://doi.org/10.33262/ap.v4i1.1.159

Diego-Mas, J.A.: Métodos para la evaluación ergonómica de puestos de trabajo. Universidad Politécnica de Valencia. Recuperado 20 de mayo de 2022 (2022). https://www.ergonautas.upv.es/metodos-evaluacion-ergonomica.html

Martha, G.F.: Ergonomía y la relación con los factores de riesgo en salud ocupacional. Revista Cubana de Enfermería, 22(4) Recuperado en 23 de mayo de 2022 (2006). http://scielo.sld.cu/scielo.php?script=sci_arttext&pid=S0864-03192006000400008&lng=es&tlng=es

Factores ambientales: INSST. Recuperado 18 de mayo de 2022 (2022). https://www.insst.es/riesgos-ergonomicos-factores-ambientales

Imron, M.: Analisis Tingkat Ergonomi Postur Kerja Karyawan di Laboratorium KCP PT. Steelindo Wahana Perkasa dengan Metode Rapid Upper Limb Assessment (RULA), Rapid Entire Body Assessment (REBA) dan Ovako Working Posture Analysis (OWAS). JITMI (Jurnal Ilmiah Teknik dan Manajemen Industri) 2(2), 147–153 (2020). Recuperado 28/02/22 de: http://openjournal.unpam.ac.id/index.php/JITM/article/view/3946

Jara, H.D.V., Orejuela, O.I.Z., Vizuete, D.E.A., Barragán, C.E.C.: Evaluación Ergonómica con el Método RULA en Condiciones Reales de Trabajo mediante Kinect V2. I+ T+ C-Investigación, Tecnología y Ciencia 1(13), 24–33 (2019)

Joshi, M., Deshpande, V.: Identification of indifferent posture zones in RULA by sensitivity analysis. Int. J. Ind. Ergon. 83, 103123 (2021). https://doi.org/10.1016/J.ERGON.2021.103123

Hernández-Sampieri, R., Torres, C.P.M.: Metodología de la investigación, vol. 4, pp. 310–386, 52–134. México. D.F. McGraw-Hill Interamericana (2018)

Kumar, A., Kamath, S.: Rapid upper limb assessment (RULA) in ergonomic assessment: a comprehensive review. Revista Pesquisa Em Fisioterapia 9(3), 429–437 (2019). https://doi.org/10. 17267/2238-2704rpf.v9i3.2465

Lim, S., D'Souza, C.: A narrative review on contemporary and emerging uses of inertial sensing in occupational ergonomics. Int. J. Ind. Ergon. 76, 102937 (2020). https://doi.org/10.1016/J. ERGON.2020.102937

McAtamney, L., Corlett, E.N.: RULA: a survey method for the investigation of work-related upper limb disorders. Appl. Ergon. 24(2), 91–99 (1993), ISSN 0003-6870. https://doi.org/10.1016/ 0003-6870(93)90080-S

Merbah, J., Jacquier-Bret, J., Gorce, P.: Effect of the presence or absence of upper limb support on posture when a smartphone user is in a seated position under ambient light conditions. Int. J. Ind. Ergon. 80, 103050 (2020). https://doi.org/10.1016/j.ergon.2020.103050

Organización Mundial de la Salud. OMS. Recuperado 17 de mayo de 2022. https://www.who. int/es

Payán, E.B., Rivera, V.J., Durán, R.R., Calderón, R.V., Martínez, G.L., Bazán, I.S.: Aplicación de la técnica RULA en el área de empaquetado mediante tecnología Kinect. RIDE Revista Iberoamericana para la Investigación y el Desarrollo Educativo 5(10) (2015)

Perception Neuron:. *Perception Neuron*. Perception Neuron Motion Capture. Recuperado 9 de mayo de 2022 (2021). https://neuronmocap.com/products/perception_neuron

Rodríguez, A.: Hoja de campo método RULA [Ilustración]. Docsity (2021). https://www.docsity. com/es/hoja-de-campo-metodo-rula/7712707/

Qué es la ergonomía geométrica: Ofiprix. Recuperado 20 de mayo de 2022 (2021). https://www. ofiprix.com/blog/que-es-la-ergonomia-geometrica/

RULA. (s. f.). Uisek. Recuperado 9 de mayo de 2022. https://repositorio.uisek.edu.ec/bitstream/ 123456789/3397/4/RULA.pdf

Sanabria, D., Vargas, A.R.: Método para la categorización postural en el puesto de liniero (2022). http://hdl.handle.net/10554/59254

Villacís Jara, H., Zambrano Orejuela, I., Baydal-Bertomeu, J.M.: Study of the ergonomic risk in operators of an assembly line using the RULA method in real working conditions through the application of a commercial sensor. Mater. Today Proc. 49, 122–128 (2022). https://doi.org/10. 1016/J.MATPR.2021.07.482

Yusuf, M., Adiputra, N., Sutjana, I.D.P., Tirtayasa, K.: The improvement of work posture using rapid upper limb assessment: analysis to decrease subjective disorders of strawberry farmers in Bali. Int. Res. J. Eng. IT Sci. Res. 2(9), 1–8 (2016). Recuperado 28/02/22 de: https://pdfs. semanticscholar.org/2c19/2bdd448d1d4aa691f84d8b645681a32e5f7a.pdf

Kong, Y.-K., Lee, S.-Y., Lee, K.-S., Kim, D.-M.: Comparisons of ergonomic evaluation tools (ALLA, RULA, REBA and OWAS) for farm work. Int. J. Occup. Saf. Ergon. 24(2), 218–223 (2018). https://doi.org/10.1080/10803548.2017.1306960

Neuromarketing to Discover Customer Satisfaction

Luis Alberto Partida Ramirez[✉][iD], Bogart Yail Marquez[iD],
and Jose Sergio Magdaleno-Palencia[iD]

Instituto Tecnológico de Tijuana, Calz del Tecnológico s/n,
Tomas Aquino, 22414 Tijuana, Baja California, Mexico
{M21210016,mtidsc,bogart,jmagdaleno}@tectijuana.edu.mx
https://www.tijuana.tecnm.mx/

Abstract. This research work pursues the techniques and methodologies of a emotion reading system and if it's economically feasible which will be able to find emotions the related with satisfaction of customers with the use of encephalography device and obtain relevant information to apply in researches of customers satisfaction, this in order to provide a guides to small businesses or medium on applying this techniques to understand better the client needs and get long term relationships with customers in the most optimal way on different products and needs from the consumers which will help to classify with different and new data, this will be able to take into account the gender and age of the clients to be reached. The document will review the methodology and techniques and use of electroencephalogram (EEG) recollection of data and databases to show how to deploy small projects for regions and help determine the real felling of the consumer, this will help companies focuses in the customer satisfaction, loyalty and advertise according to the parameters found in the procedure applied in each region. This will give companies from small and even medium-sized to have a better overview of their products or services that helps them make the decision on which will be their next step on the development of products, invest resources in according to the feelings of the consumers' needs and what they are looking, this will benefit the creation of long term relationship and loyalty between business and customers.

Keywords: Neuromarketing · EEG · Emotions · Satisfaction · Customer trust

1 Introduction

Currently, outstanding companies seek to create a link with consumers in a way that focuses on customer satisfaction with their products and is always looking for new ways to innovate and improve their products and services, this allows them to stay in customer preference obtaining their loyalty (Gul, R. 2014). There are many techniques and methodologies that are currently used that are considered obsolete or outdated in which companies invest to validate new products

T. Guarda et al. (Eds.): ARTIIS 2022, CCIS 1676, pp. 191–204, 2022.
https://doi.org/10.1007/978-3-031-20316-9_15

or improvements, these techniques such as surveys, interviews are considered to have a very relative level of effectiveness since these techniques are based in opinions of the respondents that could be influenced and biased by personal experiences of each one Iloka and Onyeke (2020). To really satisfy the customer, it is necessary to take more real data without any bias or influence of the cognitive system, this provides us with better perspectives and trends that meet the customer's preference, with which we can focus on satisfying the needs of the consumer with the objective of having a relationship of loyalty that lasts, since market studies or methodologies are not directly focused on the decision-making process based on the true feeling of the client when interacting with the product, the lack of consideration of these human characteristics greatly reduce their aspirations to innovate in the product and achieve the necessary positioning Iloka and Onyeke (2020).

With all this competition on the market and new technologies Neuromarketing has emerged these past years more than ever, the interests in the use of brain imaging techniques are more applied in analyzing how the human mastermind responds in varied of situations, Neuromarketing needs more empirical base work's to evolve and to improve over the globe and create new frameworks for each region this with the target of finding the real needs and desires of the customers Iloka and Onyeke (2020).

In this document, we review the tools and techniques used in other projects around the world that can help us build and start our own system to work in our region that can be customized and have our own local database in order to have several databases in different locations and have information to be analyzed and have knowledge of the client.

2   Problem Statement

In the case of small companies and entrepreneur they don't have ways to challenge big Corporations on the marketing side so they need to work a lot on innovations and how to have the customer happy, it is complicated to take a decision about how to innovated in the existing product or service, adding the fact that in many cases they have reduces options and the time to show and start the marketing of the product is short and it has to be very dynamical to reach the audience at good time or before competitors. Also, financial problems can be present in the same way, requiring a payment to make the study on a large scale and not always all market studies are effective. It is critical for the survival of the company to innovate at time as the competitors or better time to maintain the customer loyalty, all of this problems can be resolve having their on system run experiments and store data which we can use to create insights for the customer.

The big question of the market is what drives consumers to decide a product from others in the market and that is the what the companies of the world ask every time they what to launch a new product, understanding that each region has their own experience and preferences according to their culture, gender, physical characteristics, age, economy and many more features makes it complicated to cover all the locations and characteristics we just refer on this paragraph so the proposal is to build small emotion detection systems to get the detail by regions and create data bases and share information to accomplish a analysis of the each location.

3   State of the Art

3.1   Introduction

Neuromarketing technology combines brain studies with a focus on the impact generated by marketing and the relationship of product quality to the perception of the individual or consumer of a product or service, this creates an interaction between our brain and its senses as They are smell, taste, sight, hearing and touch, which allow us to make a judgment about a product or service from a practical and functional perspective, this being first-hand in-formation that indicates precisely the feeling of the consumer of the products and services that we offer. they are provided by giving a competitive ad-vantage to the creators and developers of the products, it is also a way to measure the improvement of a product or prevent any problems with it in the future.

3.2   Historical Evolution of Knowledge and Current Situation

In recent years, marketing and advertising specialists have discovered the limitations that exist in the traditional methods of market research and that have existed for decades, in the search to better understand consumers and have greater precision in the marketing results in the markets. In recent times, neuroscience has presented new tools that are more effective for the analysis of consumer preferences, these tools allow us to discover, read and identify the consumer's thoughts in their subconscious state, according to research the results are with less human prejudice, the precision of the information depends obtained in works such as Gurgu et al. (2020). showing the greater effectiveness of these methods with respect to the traditional ones, but every-thing would not be possible if neuroscience that by detecting human biological signals in the brain can identify and analyze somatic reactions as mentioned Baraybar et al. (2017) which we relate to human feelings according to the functioning of the human brain as evidenced by brain activities detected in the areas described according to Başar and Düzgün (2016) in the Brodmann areas. This opens the way to the investigation of these various tools that we have available which present us with accurate results, but we must measure and verify the effectiveness of the various biometric or biological signal devices that help us try to detect or predict a feeling. The topic of research for what was mentioned above is developed using electroencephalography (EEG) to obtain brain activity and through a Brain-computer interface (BCIs) to be able to analyze the readings with classifying algorithms to determine and detect feelings involved in the subconscious that has a very decisive relationship in the decision making of a product and satisfaction, which has been shown to have more precise results by several published investigations where the use of Deep Learning and Deep Neural Network was implemented. Aldayel et al. (2020). Talking about neuromarketing goes back to when the term was first used, according to Gurgu et al. (2020) it was pronounced by Gerald Zaltman Professor at Harvard in 1990 in the United States when he was directing field studies. Undoubtedly we can say that many years ago the concept was handled without being defined as such as the name, since experiments and methodologies were presented that involved the review of brain activity in consumers, they responded to certain feelings that were presented to them, these studies date back to the 80's according, since these times there has been a great growth of neuromarketing, mainly in the United States and Europe, not far be-hind Asia, this helped the development of many technologies that improve obtaining results on the consumer preference Gurgu et al. (2020). Neuromarketing is compose of three basic disciplines that are involved in the decision-making process Marketing, psychology and neuroscience Mansor and Isa (2020), which define and shape our daily decisions. Marketing for its part from the beginning of humanity was presented and we find it represented in the bartering that was done to increase its well-being, from this moment it began its development in conjunction with social and economic development. The productive conception of Marketing arises in 1950 based on various investigations that find the satisfaction of needs, desires and demands as a core point, as well as theories and models are generated to give an example the concepts of product, price and promotion, all this being applied in a strategic way for business commercial success. Taking this historical argument into account, marketing has always lived with us and has been embedded in any system related to voluntary exchange. With the increase in the complexity of the exchanges, Marketing has evolved over the years from the way of understanding and practicing it. Marketing promotes the procedure for creation, communication, and delivery of value to consumers and dealing with it focuses on the mutual benefit of the company and consumer Calderon and Rondon (2016). In the case of psychology being fundamental for neuromarketing in the human interpretation mode, in which traditional psychology focuses more on disorders and dysfunction, with little attention, although it has some derivations such as humanistic psychology that focuses on more positive characteristics of the human mechanism from its beginnings to its fullness, giving rise to positive psychology motivated to correct this imbalance of focus by introducing more positive phenomena and seeing it more with both aspects of the human being, including their positive emotions in psychological development Lomas (2020) being very useful for neuromarketing. In the case of neuroscience, the provider of technology and tools for the analysis of brain and subconscious activities of the consumer, being part of the neuromarketing concept, presents us with the new techniques for the analysis of more effective and precise consumer preferences, it must be clarified that Neuromarketing does not it re-places the traditional marketing if not that it brings new tools for the study of the consumer Mansor and Isa (2020). Neuromarketing is made up of the prefix Neuro and the term Marketing, expressing the importance of these areas of study for this science that emerged from the need to better understand consumers, taking into account the reported premise that 90% of the information processed in the human mind is carried out by the subconscious, studying and evaluating the subconscious is the objective of neuromarketing since traditional methods cannot explore this paradigm or determine how much it influences the decision of consumers, these results are very useful to ac-quire information of the tastes and desires of the consumer with respect to a service or product Aldayel et al. (2020). We can see in the explanation in López Rentería (2020), emotion is a complex state integrated of the bunch of feelings, thoughts and behaviors generated by the human being's reaction to internal or external stimuli. These psycho-physiological reactions are the result of the brain's conscious or uncon-scious perception of an object, stimulus or situation that is commonly associated with mood, temperament, personality and personal motivations. The emotions of human beings can be ex-pressed verbally or non-verbally (facial expressions, gestures, intonation of the voice and body posture). Likewise, emotion is system-atically produced by cognitive type processes, subjective feelings, physiological arousal, motivational aspects, and behavior. Analyzing Plutchik's multidimen-sional model (see Fig. 1). we find an emotion defined as Confidence which is defined as: The belief of one party that the other party will satisfy their needs and desires. As far as services are concerned, it is the security that customers have in the service provider to meet their needs. Trust can be defined as the trust that one party has in another because of the other's honesty and trust-worthiness. This description can be theoretically applied in various situations, including exchanges of goods and services Cardone et al. (2021). In which we can see that when there is trust, satisfaction is found, which is deter-mined with the time that the service or product is maintained, fulfilling its purpose with a client. But what is satisfaction according to Cardone et al. (2021) is an attitude formed on the basis of experience after customers purchase a product or use a service and pay for them. It is an indication of being satisfied with the product or service. Satisfaction is the measure of the experience of working together with a service provider up to the present moment and is used by consumers to look forward to a future experience.

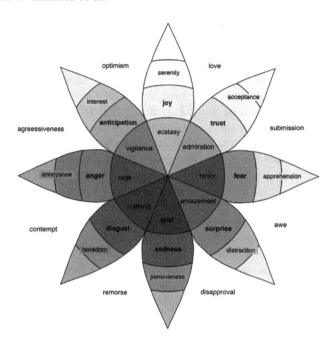

Fig. 1. Plutchik's multidimensional model (Image extracted Cardone, B., Di Martino, F., & Senatore, S. (2021))

We can find in psychology the basic theory of emotion supports the existence of several basic emotions in the human being, which can be discretely classified. On the other hand, in the multidimensional theory, emotions are classified according to multiple dimensions or scales that are used as characteristic of the emotion. In other words, emotions can be represented as defined points in a specific multidimensional space as we see in Fig. 2 the different models. In such a way, that the human being is capable of expressing his emotions based on scales of continuous or discrete values, which can include the terms: unpleasant-pleasant, calm-excited, control-lack of control, among others (see Fig. 2). These emotions are represented on our brain as electrical activity we call Bio-electrical signals created by our Neurons and transmitted one to other by the axon, in them it can be seen that the differences in electrical potentials are generated by the addition of several postsynaptic potentials of the pyramidal neurons that create electrical dipoles between the body of the neuron and the branched dendrites from each neuron (at one or both ends of it) LóPez RenteríA (2020). In the investigations done before is very common the use of self-assessment manikin (SAM), which measures the emotional response through images. It is considered a sim-ple instrument to assess the dimensions of valence, arousal, and dominance. Response valence/pleasure ranges from positive to negative, perceived arousal ranges from low to high levels, and perceptions of dominance/control range from low to high levels. The SAM is used because it is capable of reliably evaluating emotional stimuli, since the human being associates his own reaction of the object to the images that determine the classification of his emotion LóPez RenteríA (2020). SAM.

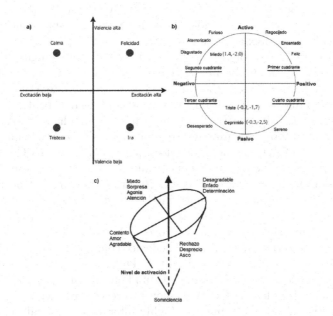

Fig. 2. Emotions Models (Image extracted López Rentería (2020).

EEG signals of emotions are not unique and vary from one person to another, in other words, the emotional response to the same stimulus is not the same. Therefore, EEG signals are often useful in person-dependent emotion recognition. However, the need arises to recognize a person's emotions without having previous information about it, in situations where the person has suffered an accident that prevents them from ex-pressing said emotions. In such a way that it is possible to determine what a person with paralysis, depression, burns or different abilities wishes to express López Rentería (2020). The vast majority of research focused on the study of emotions has generated scientific knowledge about the same problem from different perspectives, which is the recognition of emotions dependent on the subject. Therefore, there is a need to identify EEG signal patterns that characterize each emotion regardless of the person López Rentería (2020). The first neuromarketing studies with neuroscience techniques were carried out with functional magnetic resonance imaging (fMRI, Functional Magnetic Resonance Imaging) which was carried out by the Bright House commercial company, this neuroscience technique can be used to measure the subconscious and its of processes of emotions, needs and tastes, as well as stimuli such as photos and sounds Iloka and Onyeke (2020), there are also biosensors that are also very popular as well as used in many applications, being these a very complete option to measure the reactions of the human body before a human feeling, some body measurements that we can mention are heart rate, blood pressure, temperature and conductivity in the skin, these methods have presented studies that support and support the arrest of emotions, being the most popular among them is the Galvanic Skin Response (GSR), which senses the electrical signals that they flow through the human skin which is considered a psychological reflex according to Setyohadi et al. (2018), these signals are formed by the resistance of the body that is constantly changing that affects the conductivity of the body due to the sweating of the human body being a reflection of the differences of the sympathetic nervous system. This is a fairly accepted option due to its precision shown in studies that indicate up to 76.56% accu-racy in a stress study carried out according to Setyohadi et al. (2018).

The most used tool in neuromarketing for the analysis of consumer decision-making is the electroencephalogram (electroencephalogram, EEC), it is being the one that gives us the best cost benefit and precision in the results, its technique is based on the reading of the activity brain, how does it do this? Basically, it records the electrical activity in the cortex of the head and examines the variations in voltage in the different brain areas that fire according to the stimuli. This brain activity is analyzed over a period of time using appliances distributed in the cortex of the head, this device could look like a cap with small suction cups strategically positioned on the skull Aldayel et al. (2020). EEG is non-invasive, portable, can be considered simple to use and is the only practical Brain Computer Interface (BCI) that allows to receive repetitive and real-time signals from the brain which makes it highly interactive for analysis Aldayel et al. (2020). Now the placement of EEG hardware has a very specific procedure for its greater efficiency and not to induce noise to the equipment, this is governed by the international standard 10–20 which is used to name the electrodes depending on their location or zone of the cortex of the skull, 10–20 refers to a separation of 10% to 20% from one electrode to another electrode, this helps to separate each signal received in each electrode and reduce the noise to signal ratio. Aldayel et al. (2020). The brain is composed of 4 lobes the are responsible for performing specific functions The frontal lobe is related to personality, emotions, motor development and movement itself. The parietal lobe is responsible for sensory understanding (for example, pain, crying, etc.), orientation and movement through the sense of touch. On the other hand, the temporal lobe is related to processes of recognition of auditory stimuli, speech and memory. Finally, the occipital lobe is the visual processing center of the brain. The cerebellum is the second largest structure in the human brain, it is responsible for motor control, sensory perception and motor coordination. Similarly, it is related to voluntary muscle movements, fine motor skills and balance. The brainstem, for its part, is responsible for the vital functions of the body such as breathing, consciousness, the transmission of sensory messages (pain, cold, etc.), the heartbeat and blood pressure López Rentería (2020). Now the 10–20 standard also helps the distribution of the electrodes so that they can cover most of the brain and brain signals can be perceived as much as possible depending on the number of electrodes based on the Brodmann areas, which have been around since the beginning of the last century, which shows us a representation of the areas of the brain and the function related to this area of the brain, which we can also see as a map of the anatomical organization of the brain Başar and Düzgün (2016). The brain produces abundant neuronal signals and based on the Brodmann areas and the 10–20 standard, the EEG electrodes receive different bioelectric signals which we can classify into two types: Rhythms (rhythms) and Transient Activities (transient Activities), in the case of the rhythms also known as neuronal oscillations or brain waves are the common activity found in neuronal activity and one of its characteristics is to be repetitive, basically the collection of this signal is the synaptic communication of neurons. EEG technology separates frequencies into bands called Delta, Theta, Alpha, Beta, Gamma and Mu. These are detailed by their frequency ranges, amplitude, shape and the area of the brain where they are associated with events of some kind of band Aldayel et al. (2020). Now, we have already named the rhythms or bands, the studies indicate and relate them to affective reactions, for example, we can find the Theta rhythm normally found in the central frontal part of the brain and according to the studies of Aldayel et al. (2020) indicate that this rhythm it reflects the feeling of processing what the consumer sees of a product. The Alpha rhythm in the prefrontal part of the brain differentiates between an emotional valence that is either positive or negative. The Beta rhythm is correlated with disturbances during affective arousal. In the case of the Gamma rhythm, it is widely associated with the effects of excitation Aldayel et al. (2020). In the case of transient Activities or power fields, these are stimuli that enhance certain neurons which we could associate with the analogy of electrical spikes or neuronal spikes, which we can detect in a similar way to rhythms since they share certain characteristics, in this case we find them by the location, frequency, amplitude, form, recurrence and operational properties of these activities, which we separate into two types, event-related potentials (ERPs), these peak activities are found norms and they are a reaction to a specific event or stimulus, these peaks now have amplitudes that are too small for which a procedure is performed to obtain them, such as an average of the EEG samples during many repetitions of the stimulus to find the ERPs and remove noise fluctuations Al-dayel et al. (2020). Event-related spectral perturbations (ERSPs) are a calculation of the reaction to a stimulus over a period of time, unlike ERPs, ERSPs divide EEG signals into multiple frequency rhythms to check if there is a power variation in a specific band in a given time Aldayel et al. (2020). The brain is divided into areas as we mentioned when we talked about the Brodmann areas and it has cognitive responsibilities as well as mental functions. By analyzing and understanding these functions of each region, the position of the electrodes is clearly determined. Studies have shown that the frontal part of the brain is related to preference, this was determined according to Aldayel et al. (2020) since they found a high activation of this region of the brain, which is proven and there is a high probability that the consumer prefers the product if this high is seen activity in this area. Now, to obtain better results, the electrodes must be placed correctly in each identified region and following the 10–20 standard, in the research of Aldayel et al. (2020) they make reference to studies that prove the mid-frontal area of the skull is related to individual preference in the Beta rhythm that consists of a range from 16 to 18 Hz, to which the identifying electrodes such as AFz, F2, FC1 and FCz are assigned. Also in the same study they prove that the preference of the population is related to the frontal central areas in the range of Theta 60–100 Hz in the electrodes F1, F2, F4, FC3, FC1, FCz, FC2, FC4, C5, C3, C1, C4 and CP5. In the re-search work, it refers to another study where they linked preference characteristics such as attention, emotions and taste with the electrodes F3, C3, P3, Pz, Fz, Cz and C4. The work of Aldayel et al. (2020) presents an investigation where it is mentioned that asymmetric increases in the Theta and Alpha bands were found, which link them with pleasant and unpleasant announcements, as could be seen in the areas of the left brain and the Fp1 (Fp2) electrodes. AF7 (AF8), F7 (F8), and F1 (F2). The spectral power in the Alpha bands increases with increase for commercials that were liked by appliance F1 and for commercials that were not liked by appliances AF8 and AF4. In the Theta band, an increase in activity is generated in electrodes F2, AF8 and F3 for commercials that he did not like and in Fp1 for commercials that he liked. In the investigation of Aldayel et al. (2020) it is mentioned in one of the studies that present that there is a frontal asymmetry expressed by the Alpha band, which is linked to the unconscious reactions of the clients to the attraction of the product in the electrodes F3 and F4. In a reference work [4] mentions that an asymmetry frontal activity is shown that is statistically relevant in a positive way in the Alpha and Theta bands in the F1 and F2 electrodes. Likewise, the relevant negative activities in the Theta band in the electrodes Fp2 and Fp1, AF8 and AF7, and F8 and F7. EEG use indices that evaluate people's reactions to Marketing stimuli, according to those presented by Aldayel et al. (2020) there are 4 which are defined as the approach-withdrawal index (AW) or the motivation index, motivation index, choice index, and Valencia. These indices allow marketers to understand customer responses to products. In the case of the AW index or motivation index, this is described by Aldayel et al. (2020) as a frontal Alpha asymmetry that shows motivation, desire or avoidance of approach. He also mentions that it can be defined as the difference between the two hemispheres in the prefrontal Alpha band, a long list of researchers has shown the dependence of frontal asymmetry on Alpha as an effective marker in emotion. The index of the effort is known by the activity of Theta in the frontal part of the head in the prefrontal according to Aldayel et al. (2020). Also known for the definition of the complexity of a task, which indicates mental fatigue. Selection index as defined by Aldayel et al. (2020) the Gamma and beta frontal asymmetric oscillations that are linked to the decision-making stage, it can be added that it is the element most connected to the response of wanting to pay, particularly in the Gamma band, the High values in Gamma and Beta bands mean stronger activity in the left part of the prefrontal zone and lower values indicate a relatively stronger right region. For this index, electrodes AF3 and AF4 are usually used. The valence index is defined Aldayel et al. (2020) in his work as frontal asymmetry that is related to specific preferences as valences, which we can define as the emotional state of the client and studies support the theory that frontal EEG asymmetry is a valence indicator. The testing procedure of the neuromarketing experiment and the EEG hardware is defined Aldayel et al. (2020) as first the placement of the BCI device on the consumer's head, then the consumer is instructed to see the products to be evaluated and the recording of the activity is performed. Brain with the EEG while the consumer sees the product, the next thing is to ask the participant their preference towards the product on a subjective scale of 5 or 9 points, at the end of showing the products they should be labeled with the subjective scale that indicates if Whether you like the product or not, the next step is to see how to extract the recorded characteristics of the BCI and select a classification algorithm. Aldayel et al. (2020) in the procedure it indicates three central point's signal preprocessing, feature extraction and selection, and classification. In preprocessing of the signal it is the acquisition of the bands by means of the BCI which we already expressed in the document, in the case of extraction of characteristics it is a more detailed point where the signal has already been obtained for a process of information conversion in time domain to frequency or band a data to be processed in the computer using a procedure recognized in neuromarketing studies called power spectral density (Power spectral density, PSD) for its acronym in English, which uses the transform of Fourier and its inverse in the procedure, finally the different Theta, Alpha, Beta, and Gamma frequencies are obtained, to which a valence is as-signed Al-dayel et al. (2020). Subsequently, the classifier algorithm is applied to the extracted data to determine the sentiment, in this case it is intended to use support vector machines (Support Vector Machine, SVM) or deep neural networks (Deep Neural Network, DNN), in the case of SVM is a supervised classifier algorithm that has shown its effectiveness in solving a wide range of pattern recognition, this algorithm consists of a hyperplane to separate the training data belonging to 2 classes, When selecting the SVM model it is crucial and pivotal to choose its hyper parameters and the function of the kernel and parameters since a bad choice of parameters can affect the performance of the SVM, problems can be weak labels, noise, low quality information Nalepa and Kawulok (2019).

4   Research Methodology

It is intended to prepare and see if feasible an experiment that can be replay in as many locations possible that will be able to get the emotions that customers feel at the moment they see product or marketing of a product, so that is why we research different experiments and cases and we determine that the best results can be found detecting the emotions directly from the brain with a EEG and one of the models of more effective to describe the emotions are represented by the plutchik's multidimensional emotions model which manages the emotion of trust and its counter disgust which are directly interrelated with satisfaction that also is related to customer loyalty being this one of the key factors for the loyalty of the customer and allows a development of more extensive link with the client that allows satisfying their consumption needs more precise. The methodology we will build is going to be use in the second phase of this project, will be using it to obtain the bio-electrical signals from some volunteers and to store for analysis that will help researchers, projects and other experiments with the focus in the small business so they can carried out their own experiments in order to have reference data for analysis against data from other bases, also compare with public Databases like DEAP, SEED and MAHNOB-HCI to validate the information and the impact on decision making and user satisfaction.

The objective will be to obtain the nodes according to the international 10–20 scheme will be sought in the channels Fz, Cz, Pz, F3, F4, F8, P3, P4 that has our state of art indicates is where our unconscious takes decisions, on this channels we will seek to obtain signals through the application of image stimuli and a SAM questionnaire where they indicate the state of mind of the moment and through valence and excitement model locate the reference of the value captured by the emotional headband and processed with software. With this information create a methodology of costs saving solution to have this technology available for small or entrepreneur that needs innovated tools for growing the business with the possibility of knowing the real need of the customer and take more efficient decisions. The Hardware we have selected for the experiment consists of a 14-channel Emotiv headband for electroencephalographic reading PC with Windows 10 Professional, Core i3, 8 Gb Ram, monitor, keyboard, and mouse. Software developed in previous projects in conjunction with a Tijuana Technological Institute (ITT) and using the emotive SDK to interpret the signals detected by the headband in the cerebral cortex. The sample considers is 10 Adults from 19 to 60 years of age and being public in general this based on the age sector that is believed to consume more of products and services and in other experiments they managed these amounts with favorable results, the room need to be totally close and without noise the user must be calm and have a presentation with pictures the psychological have been probe to generate the basis a motions of Plutchik's that we recall: joy-sadness, trust-disgust, anticipation-surprise, and anger-fear and we will focus on the trust-disgust emotions. Finally, the use of supervised classifier algorithm to analyze the data and determine the values for input and emotion will be review with SPSS statistical software.

5   Conclusions

With the investigation we can conclude that the realization of an emotion reading system is economically feasible and the accuracy of the data would have to be reviewed, but a demo can be built for the next stage of the investigation, We can proceed to make the hardware and software selection to create a system and go to the phase of testing to secure accurate results and test with locals business and have small local databases by regions, using a small and low cost system that help recollect the real felling of the customer letting behind the culture, ideology and other characteristics of the country that affects the accepts of a product or services. This will help business because we specify the technology to each location thanks to the local Data bases we can create by regions working like edge technology for emotions or fillings of the customer measurement.

The New system pretends to help the companies aim to increase their profits and market share by developing and launching better and faster products and services, also we can find insights assist to generate the expected demand and first of all be able to engage buyers on the benefits and qualities of the products and services offered. This can boost the main goal to produce an impact on the consumer with this on the decision making moments and help the user have clear why he must select our product over the others.

Understanding the experience and preferences of each region according to its culture, gender, physical characteristics, age, economy and many more characteristics with the proposal to build a small emotion detection system to obtain details by region and create databases and share information to perform analysis of each location, store data and cross-analysis between locations.

We can consider Neuromarketing the newest technology for innovative Marketing and offers Valuable resources for marketing research, although it confronts challenges it is still early in marketing research. The Neuromarketing base will allow marketing professionals to improve their understanding of how customer behavior works.

6   Future Work

– Investigate, experiment, and apply new algorithms methods to obtain better results in recommendations made by the system for the user's target market.
– Collect a greater amount of data and have distributed Databases for a more specific and accurate data analysis to have better points of view for designers or services changes
– Develop a mobile application that allows you to run tests on mobile devices and get faster information to make fast decisions according the results. This application will be able read live bio-electric signals with Muse headset.
– Start a company that offers consulting services in emotions and using data analysis tools to provide the most accurate emotions detected.

References

Mansor A.A., Isa, S.M.: Fundamentals of neuromarketing: what is it all about? Neurosci. Res. Notes 3(4), 22–28 (2020). https://doi.org/10.31117/neuroscirn.v3i4.58

Baraybar Fernández, A., Baños González, M., Barquero Pérez, Ó., Goya Esteban, R., Morena Gómez, A.: Evaluación de las respuestas emocionales a la publicidad televisiva desde el Neuromarketing. Comunicar : revista científica iberoamericana de comunica-ción y edu-cación (2017)

Betella, A., Verschure, P.F.: The affective slider: a digital self-assessment scale for the measurement of human emotions. PLoS ONE 11(2), e0148037 (2016)

Cardone, B., Di Martino, F., Senatore, S.: Improving the emotion-based classification by exploiting the fuzzy entropy in FCM clustering. Int. J. Intell. Syst. 36(11), 6944–6967 (2021)

Setyohadi, D.B., Kusrohmaniah, S., Gunawan, S.B., Pranowo, P.: Galvanic skin response data classification for emotion detection. Int. J. Electr. Comput. Eng. **8**(5), 31–41 (2018). https://doi.org/10.11591/ijece.v8i5.pp4004-4014

Başar, E., Düzgün, A.: The CLAIR model: extension of Brodmann areas based on brain oscillations and connectivity. Int. J. Psychophysiol. **103**(2016). https://doi.org/10.1016/j.ijpsycho.2015.02.018

Gurgu, E., Gurgu, I.-A., Tonis, R.B.M.: Neuromarketing for a better understanding of consumer needs and emotions. Independent J. Manage. Prod. **11**(1), 208 (2020). https://doi.org/10.14807/ijmp.v11i1.993

Montavon, G., Samek, W., Müller, K.R.: Methods for interpreting and understanding deep neural networks. Digit. Signal Process.: Rev. J. **73**, 1–15 (2018). https://doi.org/10.1016/j.dsp.2017.10.011

Alvarez Calderon J., Garcia Rondon, I.: Prospectiva de marketing, neuromarketing y programación neuro lingüística / prospective of marketing, neuromarketing and neuro linguistic programming. CIENCIA UNEMI **9**(19) (2016). https://doi.org/10.29076/issn.2528-7737vol9iss19.2016pp99-105p

Nalepa, J., Kawulok, M.: Selecting training sets for support vector machines: a review. Artif. Intell. Rev. **52**(2), 857–900 (2018). https://doi.org/10.1007/s10462-017-9611-1

López Rentería, J.: Análisis De Señales Electroencefalográficas Pa-ra Clasificar Emociones Utilizando El Modelo Bidimensional Valencia-Excitación (Doctoral Dissertation, Universidad Autonoma De Chihuahua) (2020)

Aldayel, M., Ykhlef, M., Al-Nafjan, A.: Deep learning for EEG-based preference classification in neuromarketing. Appl. Sci. (Switzerland) **10**(4) (2020). https://doi.org/10.3390/app10041525

Lomas, T.: Positive coaching psychology: a case study in the hybridization of positive psychology. Int. J. Wellbeing **10**(2) (2020). https://doi.org/10.5502/ijw.v10i2.1083

Ji, Y., Zhang, S., Xiao, W.: Electrocardiogram classification based on faster regions with convolutional neural network. Sensors (Switzerland) **19**(11) (2019). https://doi.org/10.3390/s19112558

Study of the Incidences of Decibels in the Cantonal Capital of the Province of Santa Elena with Measurement of Spectral Radiations

Jose Miguel Sanchez Aquino⬛, Fernando Arroyo Pizarro⬛,
Luis Miguel Amaya Fariño$^{(\boxtimes)}$⬛, Daniel Armando Jaramillo Chamba⬛,
and Monica Karina Jaramillo Infante⬛

Universidad Estatal Península de Santa Elena, Santa Elena, Ecuador
{jsanchez,djaramillo}@upse.edu.ec

Abstract. Electronic equipment in hospital areas or shopping centers emitting radiation waves, used by medical personnel, patients, or people in the environment, intercepts different signals. The radiation generated by this equipment causes damage to people exposed for long periods. This work presents the measurements and comparisons using solar radiation devices, sonometer, ultraviolet light, nuclear radiation detection, and radio frequency electromagnetic field intensity meter. The measurements are located in two mass attendance centers for the health and commercial area, within the province of Santa Elena, La Libertad, Ecuador. The MATLAB software allows the correct tabulation and development to compare the ranges within the parameters established by the World Health Organization (WHO). The tabulated results are above the permissible limit, such as solar radiation and noise level.

Keywords: Ionizing radiation · Electromagnetic interference · Hospital zone

1 Introduction

Studies reveal that electromagnetic interference affects the data presented by medical equipment considering the environment in which it operates [1], as well as the clinic's surroundings. Therefore erroneous diagnoses by medical personnel would be exposed. It is worth mentioning that in commercial areas, it can be affected in the same way as in the different teams they have in their locality.

Ionizing radiation can cause harmful effects on health because this type of radiation accumulates a large amount of direct energy in the cells, resulting in biological damage in such a way that it interacts with the human genome, altering it in one way or another [2].

Most of the electronic devices found in our homes use some radiation for their operation. For this reason, exposure to non-ionizing radiation (NIR) is

T. Guarda et al. (Eds.): ARTIIS 2022, CCIS 1676, pp. 205–217, 2022.
https://doi.org/10.1007/978-3-031-20316-9_16

negligible; however, in hospital environments, the scenario is different, so we are more exposed to radiation, be it ultraviolet, X-rays, or electromagnetic fields generated by the equipment [3].

The measurement of specific parameters of ionizing and non-ionizing radiation in a hospital and a shopping center environment is due to the use of electrical devices that generate electromagnetic radiation (electromedical equipment, electrical system, mobile devices, household appliances, and Wireless).) [4]. The data in the vicinity of the SERVIDENT clinic in Salinas and the "PASEO SHOPPING DE LA LIBERTAD" were analyzed. The analysis consists of three stages.

The first part is data measurement by using sensors such as a solar radiation meter (TES-1333 SOLAR POWER METER), nuclear radiation detector (GQ GMC-320-Plus), ultraviolet light meter (AMTAST UV340B), radio frequency electromagnetic field intensity meter (HF-B3G TRIPLE AXIS RF/HIGH-FREQUENCY METER), sound level meter (SMART SENSOR AR844).

The second part is data collection and tabulation according to international entities such as the World Health Organization (WHO) [5]. The last part is the comparisons of the data and information relevant to the study concerning the background maintained by the WHO.

MATLAB allows us to obtain the consent and comparison data to verify the radiation levels and identify if it is within the parameters established by the WHO, all employing graphs on the tabulated data [6].

The main objective is to study and measure the different types of radiation, such as frequencies, light, and sound, in telephone equipment around the SERVIDENT clinic. In addition, analyze them through the MATLAB software at intervals outside the normal to alert and report illnesses or damage to people who live near the site.

2   Development of the Content or Proposal

The measurements are contemplated based on the data collected by the different sensors. We can identify if there is a high percentage of radiation, frequency, light, and sound, among others. For data collection, the SERVIDENT clinic allowed an adequate tabulation due to the constant use of medical, cellular, and electronic equipment that generate different types of signals that can interfere with people's daily lives for prolonged exposure.

2.1   Measurement Tables

2.1.1   Nuclear Radiation - Servident Clinic

A sampling of radiation taken at small and large scales in an area of 16, 24 and 25 m^2, resulting in reference exposure times to be able to make the different comparisons with the data collected by the World Health Organization.

Table 1 shows that results are obtained that remain within the average values dictated by the WHO; in the afternoon, the clinic's values were in a standard percentage of the mean, remaining below the reference values.

Table 1. Nuclear Radiation

Radiation	WHO	m^2	$\sigma_{t-scale}$	Ranks ϵ	% Limit
0.15 usv/h	0.15 usv/h	16	20 usv/h	$3*10^{-9}$	100%
0.16 usv/h	0.26 usv/h	24	700 usv/h	$3*10^{-12}$	61.5%
0.13 usv/h	0.14 usv/h	25	2300 usv/h	$3*10^{-15}$	92.8%

It shows that the levels are within the parameters established by the WHO [4].

2.1.2 Sound Level - Servident Clinic

Table 2 shows the data collected in the clinic in units [dB]; the time range is to verify the exposure limit according to the data provided by the WHO, therefore.

For the data tabulated in the afternoon, the sound sensor resulted more than sound outside the Clinic, where its percentage was 119.6% compared to the WHO data; The data is above the established parameters; in the morning, it exceeded 100.6%, which means that it is still at high levels.

Table 3 presents the results analyzed with excess sound levels in the morning and the afternoon of 100.6% and 110.6%, respectively, which slightly exceeds the limit set by the WHO.

Table 2. Sound level - Servident clinic

	Sound data			
Sound	WHO	Level	σ_{time}	% Limit
65.4dB	65dB	1-low	15mnts	100.6%
77.8dB	65dB	3-high	30mnts	119.6%
45.6dB	55dB	1-low	10mnts	82.9%

The results express excess sound levels in the morning and in the afternoon, based on time periods. [12].

2.1.3 UV Radiation - Servident Clinic

The UV radiation table shows measurements from 0.1 to 1.20 mW/cm2 in spaces from 99 to 500 m^2 in exponential ranges on small and large scales, with a radiation increase of 120%, 1.80 mW/cm2 harmful to the long term health.

Table 3. UV radiation

UV radiation	WHO	m^2	ranks ϵ	% Limit
0.1 mW/cm^2	0.3 mW/cm^2	99	3*10^{-6}	33.3%
1.80 mW/cm^2	1.5 mW/cm^2	500	3*10^{-7}	120%
1.20 mW/cm^2	1.3 mW/cm^2	100	3*10^{-6}	92.3%

The table shows an excess of 120%, that is, an increase of 20% in the level of UV radiation in the afternoons; therefore, it is above the limit established by the WHO [7].

2.1.4 UV Radiation - Paseo Shopping

The data established by the WHO makes it possible to generate a comparison with the data taken at the PASEO-SHOPPING mall, observing an excess of 127.3% of UV radiation for the data tabulation in the afternoon (Table 4).

2.1.5 UV Radiation Servident Clinic vs Paseo Shopping

In the SERVIDENT clinic, there is a slight excess of UV radiation, unlike Paseo Shopping, which is below the WHO limits (Table 5).

Within the table, the levels of UV radiation are determined, both in the clinic and in the shopping mall analyzed in the afternoons, presenting a slight excess of 20% to 28% respectively; therefore, it is within an average level of UV radiation.

Table 4. UV radiation

UV radiation	WHO	m^2	ranks ϵ	% Limit
0.29 mW/cm^2	1.3 mW/cm^2	100	3*10^{-6}	22.3%
1.91 mW/cm^2	1.5 mW/cm^2	500	3*10^{-7}	127.3 %
0.18 mW/cm^2	0.3 mW/cm^2	99	3*10^{-6}	60 %

The table expresses the results showing excesses of 127.3% for the UV radiation level, above the limit established by the WHO [7].

Table 5. Servident Comparison - Paseo Shopping

	Servident Clinic			Paseo Shopping		
WHO	Radiation	Level	%$Limit$	Radiation	Level	%$Limit$
0.3 mW/cm^2	0.1 mW/cm^2	1-low	33.3%	0.29 mW/cm^2	1-low	22.3%
1.5 mW/cm^2	1.8 mW/cm^2	3-medium	120%	1.91 mW/cm^2	3-medium	127.3%
1.3 mW/cm^2	1.20 mW/cm^2	2-low	92.3%	0.18 mW/cm^2	1-low	60%

2.1.6   Solar Radiation - Servident Clinic

The following table shows the data based on the morning shift at 9 am; the radiation index is 55.6. W/m2, which we know is a low level 1 value; otherwise, in the evening, this value varies to 593.5 W/m2 as the WHO says it is a high level 6 radiation index; we will have to take preventive measures.

Table 6. Solar radiation

Radiation	WHO	m^2	Level	σ_{time}	% Limit
55.6W/m^2	59uv	40	1 low	11am–15pm	94.2%
593.5W/m^2	70uv	90	6 high	9am–16pm	847%
59.6W/m^2	61uv	50	2 low	10am–15pm	97.7%

The levels determined by the WHO are between ranges 1 and 3; however, there is a high level of radiation determined as level 6, between 9 am and 4 pm, when a more significant number of people enter these areas.

2.1.7   Solar Radiation - Paseo Shopping

According to the following table, the tabulated analysis in the morning and afternoon hours showed that in Paseo Shopping, from 10 am to 3 pm; the radiation index is 22.9 W/M^2, which means that it has a limit of 38.8%, which indicates a minimum value, however, in the afternoon this value varies to 35.4 W/m^2 with a percentage range of 50.5%; therefore, according to the WHO, this value is within the allowed range (Table 7).

Table 7. Solar radiation

Radiation	WHO	m^2	level	σ_{time}	limit
22.9W/m^2	59W/m^2	30	1 low	11am–15pm	38.8%
35.4W/m^2	70W/m^2	50	3 medium	9am–16pm	50.5%
21.5W/m^2	61W/m^2	40	2 low	10am–15pm	35.2%

The values are within the accepted levels according to the WHO [7].

2.1.8   Solar Radiation Servident Clinic vs Paseo Shopping

Table 6 shows the measurements in both places to compare the results obtained by adding the percentages when the ranges exceed the values allowed by the WHO (Table 8).

Table 8. Servident Comparison - Paseo Shopping

WHO	Servident Clinic			Paseo Shopping		
	Radiation	Level	% Limit	Radiation	Level	% Limit
$59W/m^2$	$55.6W/m^2$	1-Low	94.2%	$22.9W/m^2$	1-Low	38.8%
$70W/m^2$	$593.5W/m^2$	6-High	847%	$35.4W/m^2$	2-Low	35.2%
$61W/m^2$	$59.6W/m^2$	2-Low	97.7%	$21.5W/m^2$	3-Medium	50.5%

Given the results obtained, we will realize that the percentage excess of radiation of Servident is 847%, obtaining a high level, unlike Paseo Shopping, which has low levels.

2.1.9   Wi-Fi Radiation

The Wi-Fi Radiation table shows the measurements obtained for the analysis of the collected values and to appreciate high levels of Wi-Fi radiation in the places mentioned in this investigation. Analyzing the comparison with the clinic data and the data abroad, they are at high radiation levels compared to the WHO data. The values determined by the WHO concerning Wi-Fi radiation allow us to tabulate the acceptable ranges; this happens due to the amount of radiation or Wi-Fi zones in the place. However, in the clinic, the data was not high because there were few Wi-Fi areas with high radiation (Table 9).

Table 9. Comparison Servident - Paseo Shopping

WHO	Servident Clinic			Paseo Shopping		
	Radiation	Level	% Limit	Radiation	Level	% Limit
$400\,V/m$	$399.3\,V/m$	1-Low	99.8 %	$410\,V/m$	1-Low	102.5 %
$600\,V/m$	$423.8\,V/m$	1-Low	70.63 %	$600\,V/m$	1-Low	100 %
$750\,V/m$	$890.8\,V/m$	3-High	118.73 %	$900\,V/m$	3-High	120 %

The table shows values at certain times at night, and in the shopping center and clinic, there is a high value of between 18% and 20% increase in Wi-Fi radiation.

2.2   Measurement Values

In the following table, we have the factory parameters at which each of the different devices used works, where the functionality of each measurement equipment will be specified.

Through this table, we can analyze the characteristics of the equipment, at what temperature they must be, and what is the battery voltage of each sensor (Table 10).

Table 10. Technical characteristics of the sensors

Parameters of the different sensors					
Parameters	GMC320PLUS	AMTAST UV	HF-B3G	TES-133R	AR844
Sensor	Nuclear	UV	Wi-Fi	Solar	Sound
[U]Measurement	usv/h	mW/cm^2	mV/m, V/m	W/m^2	dB
Scope m^2	16	199	–	90	–
Precision	0,1 3,0	±4%FS	0 a 90%	±2.5%	−1.5dB
Battery	3,6V–3,7V	9V 6F22	9V NEDA 1604	9V	AA*4
Temperature	$40\,^{\circ}C–85\,^{\circ}C$	$-10\,^{\circ}C–40\,^{\circ}C$	$0\,^{\circ}C–50\,^{\circ}C$	$0.1\,^{\circ}C$	30–130
Measuring range	0,045–0,2	0-40mW/cm2	38mV–20V/M	200/2000	30-dB
Frequency range	30Hz–30Hz	Minor 30MHz	50MHz–3GHz	30Hz–300Hz	31–8kHz

3 Methodology

The methodologies used are descriptive and quantitative, with the data obtained employing the equipment exposed in the previous sections. An algorithm is designed in MATLAB to tabulate the information acquired so that the results are displayed graphically.

3.1 Algorithms, Program Codes and Listings

The collected values will allow comparison after admission with the ranges determined by the WHO to obtain graphs where the conditions of excess radiation are observed or if the radiation is low in the study environment. The comparative graphs were developed in MATLAB programming, the graphs show the respective technical comparison, between the average value and the real value.

4 Results

It is not necessary for this analysis the population variables or the exact times of medical consultation; the variables used are tabulated in the morning, evening, and night periods. It is justified based on the number of people entering the measurement area.

The following figure compares the data obtained by the nuclear radiation sensor against the data provided by the World Health Organization (WHO). The intersected red lines show growth between 16 and 25 m^2, reaching an exposure of 100%, in comparison with the data provided by the WHO, which indicates that there is no increase, as a result of the samples collected from the Servident clinic indicate that they are below the data offered by the WHO (Fig. 1).

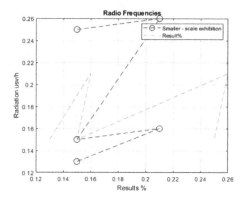

Fig. 1. Nuclear radiation comparison.

The comparison of the samples collected from the clinic and those taken from the WHO page confirms that the data is below the WHO exposure ranges. The first preamble is that the clinic has taken the necessary precautions so that people are not affected by this type of harmful radiation in the short and long term (Fig. 2).

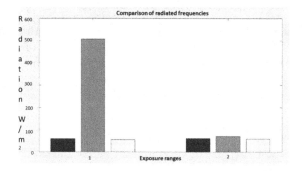

Fig. 2. Bars for nuclear radiation comparisons.

The representations of the tabulations taken in the clinic are comparative graphs with the WHO. The graph depicts the sensor tabulations in high and low percentages, the red line identified as a very high percentage in the afternoon session, with 119.6% noise excess, compared to the blue dashed lines. Of course, this is the data provided by the World Health Organization; As a result, high figures are obtained compared to the WHO (Fig. 3).

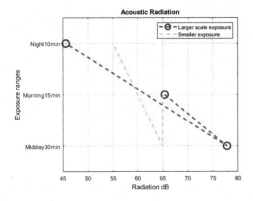

Fig. 3. Acoustic radiation comparison with the WHO.

The high agglomeration in a period in the afternoon results in a high percentage of exposure values compared to the WHO (Fig. 4).

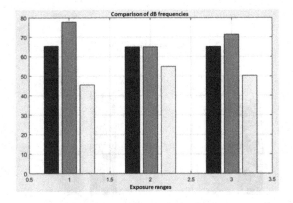

Fig. 4. Acoustic comparison bars.

The comparison of graph 2 of the data obtained from the clinic with those referenced by the WHO shows an increase reaching a peak of 1.8 mW/cm2 in a percentage limit of 120 (Fig. 5).

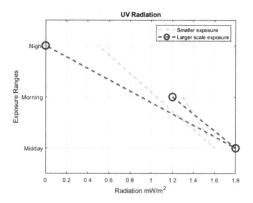

Fig. 5. Comparison of UV Radiation with the WHO.

The bar graph compares the UV radiation in the morning, afternoon, and evening, where the results analyzed from midday are higher than the others. In reference dictated by the World Health Organization, it is above the data (Fig. 6).

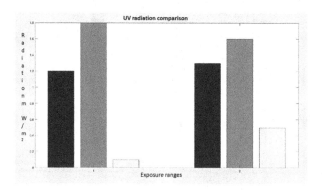

Fig. 6. Bars for radiation comparisons UV.

The tabulations obtained in entered employing the code graph the comparisons of the acceptable ranges determined by the WHO (Fig. 7).

Graph the values represented in light blue lines and a red line, indicating a higher percentage of radiation; for example, the value of 593.5 W/m2 would imply a level of 6, which is determined high by its percentage limit of 847%.

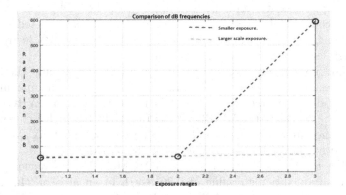

Fig. 7. Solar radiation comparison.

The following bar chart allows us to observe the comparison between the clinic and the tabulated shopping center, where it was possible to obtain high variables compared to the WHO (Fig. 8).

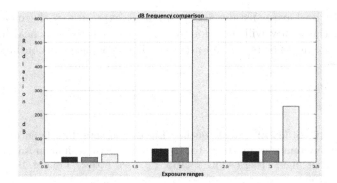

Fig. 8. Bars for comparisons of solar radiation.

It was possible to analyze the graphs obtained from the MATLAB application software, allowing us to generate a code for each sensor. The comparisons obtained reflect that the data between the clinic and the WHO were very important for developing the code applied to each sensor.

The tables with peak designs represent the lines between cuts and bars for a greater visual appreciation of the results of this analysis on the values acquired at times (morning, afternoon, night) established with each sensor used by the clinic and the WHO.

5   Conclusions

- It can be concluded that the measurements and analyzes depend on the time factor. However, without considering the influx of people who visit the clinic or the shopping center and the working day, so the tables and graphs. The shopping center is also exposed to ionizing radiation, as expected, that in the surroundings of the Servident clinic area, the study parameters are detected with high levels of non-ionizing radiation.
- The sound level meter showed that in the afternoons around the Servident clinic, it resulted in a percentage of 120%, which exceeds the maximum noise value of 65dB according to the World Health Organization (WHO).
- The results issued by the HF-B3G TRIPLE AXIS RF high frequency meter with the measurements made at Paseo Shopping were 900mV/M, and what is allowed by the WHO is a maximum of 750mV/M.
- According to the measurements, the GQ GMC-320-Plus nuclear radiation detector obtained a high value of 0.26 usv/h in an area of 24m^2, and the minimum established by the WHO is 0.16 usv/h in an area of 25m^2.
- To conclude, the AMTAST UV340B ultraviolet light meter determined that the Servident has a high UV light value of 1.8mW/cm^2 and 1.91mW/cm^2 in the shopping mall, exceeding 1.5mW/cm^2 as consented by The WHO.
- The results tabulated in the parameters exceed the radiation limit both in the Servident clinic and in the Shopping Paseo, which means that they have not followed national and international standards for the protection of human beings.
- Citizens who have constant and permanent exposure to the measurements made in this study will have long-term consequences with health problems for both medical personnel and users and living beings who continuously visit these areas.

References

1. Alnamir, H.: Study of Low Frequency Electromagnetic Interference Problems in Hospital Environment. In: 2019 11th International Symposium on Advanced Topics in Electrical Engineering (ATEE), 2019, pp. 1–5. https://doi.org/10.1109/ATEE.2019.8724736
2. Madrid Sanchez, K.A.: Exposure to Ionizing Radiation and its Effect on the Health of Workers in the Health Sector (2017)
3. Xiaodong, P., Guanghui, W., Wei, L., Yaping, W., Haojiang, W., Xinfu, L.: Prediction model of dual-frequency in-band electromagnetic radiation effects for electronic equipment. Int. Appl. Comput. Electromagnetics Soc. Symp. (ACES) **2017**, 1–3 (2017)
4. International Commission on Non-Ionizing Radiation Protection: Principles for non-ionizing radiation protection. Health Phys. **118**(5), 477–482 (2020)
5. Kabir F.R., Mamun, K.A.: An integrated radiation estimation system in health facilities to identify potential health risks. In: 2020 2nd International Conference on Advanced Information and Communication Technology (ICAICT), 2020, pp. 455–459. https://doi.org/10.1109/ICAICT51780.2020.9333519

6. IARC Working Group on the Evaluation of Carcinogenic Risks to Humans, World Health Organization, & International Agency for Research on Cancer. (2002). Nonionizing Radiation: Static and extremely low-frequency (ELF) electric and magnetic fields
7. World Health Organization (2017). UV index Global Solar. Ginebra. https://www.who.int/uv/publications/en/uvispa.pdf
8. Reyes, A.: Industrial measuring instrument (2020). https://twilight.mx/manuales/TE-1333-53-TE-1333.pdf
9. Ganán Andino, M.E.: Design and Calculation of shielding for areas of high radiological risk in the Nuclear Medicine Unit of the Teodoro Maldonado Carbo Hospital, IESS-Guayaquil (Bachelor's thesis, Escuela Superior Politécnica de Chimborazo) (2018)
10. Hardell, L., Hardell, L.: [Comment] Health risks from radiofrequency radiation, including 5G, should be assessed by experts with no conflicts of interest. Oncol. Lett. **20**, 15 (2020). https://doi.org/10.3892/ol.2020.11876
11. Contreras, R.G., et al.: Efficacy and effectiveness of ultraviolet radiation as a hospital environmental decontamination procedure. Infect. Dis. Microbiol. **41**(2), 67–72 (2021)
12. Sound Level Meter (2020). http://www.brainworks.it/rpi-environmental-monitoring/data/uploads/smartsensorar844usermanualen.pdf
13. María José, C.G.: Análisis y medición de las señales emitidas por las radiaciones no ionizantes en la provincia de Santa Elena en el espacio circundante a las antenas sectoriales y estaciones de radio base (2019)

On Designing a Compact Two-Way Differential Power Divider/Combiner Based on a SiGe BiCMOS Process for Automotive Radar Applications Using FEM Simulators

Washington Daniel Torres Guin[1] [ID], Vladimir García Santos[1]([✉])[ID],
Carlos Efraín Andrade[2] [ID], Luis Miguel Amaya Fariño[1] [ID],
and Daniel Armando Jaramillo Chamba[1] [ID]

[1] Universidad Estatal Península de Santa Elena, Avda. principal La Libertad - Santa Elena,
240350 La Libertad, Ecuador
{wtorres,vgarcia,lamaya,djaramillo}@upse.edu.ec
[2] Universidad Técnica Estatal de Quevedo, vía Quevedo-El Empalme. Km 7,
120501 Quevedo, Ecuador
candradec@uteq.edu.ec

Abstract. In the last years has been remarkable the development of technologies for millimetric wave applications; however, the limitation to its growth has been the cost of implementation. People who are building these components have exceptional motivation to develop low-cost, reduced-size, and compact technologies. In this paper, it was designed a compact silicon-germanium BiCMOS two-way differential power divider/combiner that does not use a balun in both input and output ports. The proposed divider/combiner is implemented in three metal layers of the BiCMOS 9MW technology of STMicroelectronics©; this characteristic, besides the no need for a balun, makes it a compact configuration appropriate for determined highly integrated chips at millimeter-wave bands, e.g., long and short-range automotive radar applications. The results obtained by full-wave simulations based on the Finite Element Method show a return loss of 28.5 24 GHz frequency for short-range radars and at a frequency of 77 GHz operation for long-range radars a return loss of 39.2 dB.

Keywords: Power divider/combiner · Mm-wave · Silicon-Germanium SiGe · Monolithic Integrated Microwave Circuit MMIC

1 Introduction

Wireless communication and detection systems are constantly evolving because the growing needs of modern societies demand improvements in services and technologies related to telecommunications, transportation, security, consumer electronics, etc.; for this reason, designing approaches are developing in conjunction with the expansion in those areas. Consequently, it has triggered great interest in many researchers around the world to find new design approaches for better wireless and detection systems from the point of view of performance, low profile, and compact size while maintaining low energy consumption and inexpensiveness, e.g., System-on-Chip (SoC) based on BiCMOS process [1–4].

As operating frequency increases, wireless systems can operate with higher bandwidth; simultaneously, their components and circuits become smaller, making it possible to obtain high compaction and lightness in hardware. The current trend in integrating the microwave components is the Monolithic Microwave Integrated Circuit (MMIC) [5–7]; this type of Integrated Circuit (IC) requires new and better design models that allow the integration of multiple components and functions in the same core chip, as in communication systems or detection systems like automotive radars.

Silicon-based fully integrated radar sensors operating at millimeter-wave frequencies are crucial technologies used in driving assistance systems to autonomously assist drivers in parking and driving functions to improve safety and comfort. The current trend of several automotive companies is to incorporate such radars to maintain low-cost and compact driving assistance systems, allowing high volume production and price reduction as envisioned in [8].

Several approaches to designing silicon-based radar sensors are stood on building blocks in a single-ended mode [9–11]. A previous works [8, 12] is explained that in designing such radar technologies, it is preferred to use individual building blocks in differential operation mode; based on this approach, a power divider/combiner that avoids the single-ended mode was presented, achieving a significant reduction of the chip area, and eliminating the need of an external balun. It is essential because the power divider/combiner network occupies a significant portion of the chip area to enable the Split or combine the signal to be used in another chip component. From this approach that operates fundamentally in differential mode, two, three, four, eight, and even sixteen ways for a power divider/combiner not dependent on a balun can be proposed.

Based on the same approach, this work presents the design of a compact power divider/combiner of two-way integrated on a chip implemented on a 65 nm BiCMOS process, a property of STMicroelectronics©. The paper is organized as follows. Section 2 briefly explains the Silicon-Germanium (SiGe) BiCMOS technology; Sect. 3 describes the structure's geometry and the design process. Section 4 shows the results obtained through commercials full-wave Finite Element Method (FEM) based simulators. Finally, the last section shows the conclusions of this work.

2 Silicon-Germanium BiCMOS Process

The improvements of IC's achieved at the beginning of the 21st century led to both the exponential enhancement of the HBT and SiGe MOSFET processes besides the increase of integration density of the metallic layers in BiCMOS technologies.

Consequently, technologies based on SiGe replaced those based on Gallium Arsenide, especially in radiofrequency (RF) and microwave applications. Nowadays, detection systems such as automotive radar often use high-performance MMICs based on BiCMOS technologies due to its principal advantages such as the robustness of bipolar transistors, which stands out in noise performance, gain, and switching speed in combination with the benefits of CMOS processes; these characteristics are suitable for RF and microwave applications.

At present, choosing the suitable CMOS or BiCMOS process depends not only on the application but on the availability of the silicon-based chip fabrication process at foundries due to the microchip shortage caused by the increased demand for chips from different industries as an effect of the confinement during the pandemic.

The suitable process to manufacture chips for the automotive industry does not relate to the latest lithographic node processes but rather with processes that are suitable for this type of application and that have been in the market for years, and that currently do not face high demand. To design a two-way power divider/combiner at operating frequencies of 24 and 77 GHz, which is the standard for automotive radars, choose the 65nm mentioned above SiGe BiCMOS process.

3 Geometry of the Two-Way Differential Power Divider/Combiner

The power divider/combiner is implemented on the first three layers of the chosen BiCMOS process which structure is shown in Fig. 1.

The proposed geometry and port distribution of the power divider are shown in Fig. 2. The input differential port is placed in the 5T metal layer and is connected to an octagonal-shaped ring with inner radius r and width W. These Parameters are defined based on the operating mechanism described where r is selected, making the ring work as a resonator (for this case 24 and 77 GHz) [8].

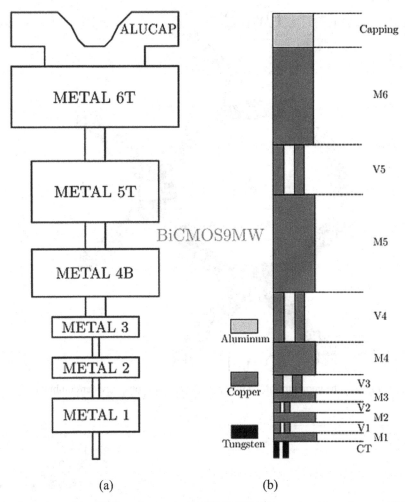

Fig. 1. Overview of the STMicroelectronics© BiCMOS 9MW process: (a) stack-up and (b) cross section of the technology.

The radius of the transformer also determines the self-resonant frequency (SRF); that is, the smaller the radius, the smaller the inductance, and the greater the SRF (see Fig. 3). It is essential to ensure that the SRF is sufficiently above the operating frequency.

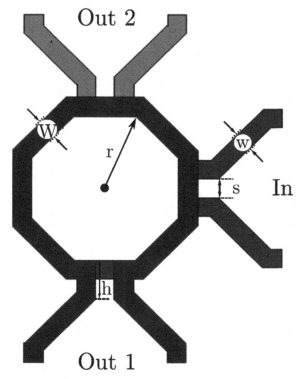

Fig. 2. The geometry of the two-way differential power divider/combiner.

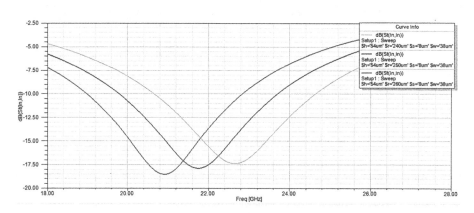

Fig. 3. Radius variation in the 2-way differential power divider transformer structure.

The rings are vertically stacked to get the best coupling factor, while the tunability of each outport's amplitude distribution and phase uniformity is controlled by W and assumes the same length for each path of the rings, respectively.

The geometry of the proposed power divider was generated through a MATLAB® script which creates a parametric 3D layout as seen in Fig. 4; the full-wave simulation was performed using commercial electromagnetic software of ANSYS©.

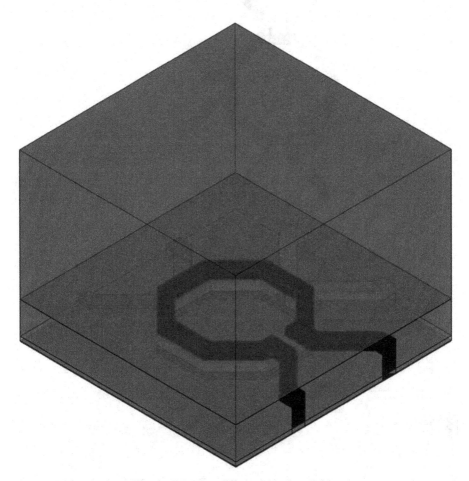

Fig. 4. 3-D View differential power divider.

On the other hand, W is used to fine-tune the operation frequency because this directly affects the output and input impedance; it is necessary for an external matching network, as sketched in Fig. 5, this network is composed of a couple of grounded capacitors in each differential output ports and a shunt capacitor in the differential input port.

Therefore, if a single-ended input port were to be grounded, it would work as a balun, and the coupling network was simulated in the electronic design automation commercial software Advanced Design System® according to the results obtained from the FEM simulation as shown in Fig. 6.

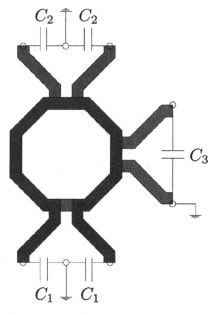

Fig. 5. Matching Network of the two-way differential power divider.

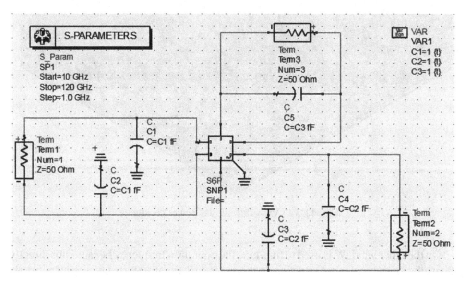

Fig. 6. Matching circuit network of the two-way differential power divider in ADS.

The 24 GHz structure has a greater radius than other structures, so the more significant the radius, the lower the self-resonant frequency. After doing the simulations for the 2-way Differential Power Divider Transformer (2WDPDT) at 24 GHz, Table 1 is shown the parameters of the geometry and matching network.

Table 1. Geometry and matching network definition at the operational frequency of 24 GHz.

Differential Power Divider/Combiner geometrical parameters		
Parameter	Value	Unit
Inner Radius (r)	150	μm
Input Trace Width (W)	5	μm
Output Trace Width (w)	5	μm
Separation Between Each Port (s)	5	μm
Length of the port (h)	18	μm
Matching network parameters		
Capacitance	Value	Unit
C1	290	fF
C2	20	fF
C3	130	fF

Table 2. Geometry and matching network definition at the operational frequency of 77 GHz.

Differential Power Divider/Combiner geometrical parameters		
Parameter	Value	Unit
Inner Radius (r)	18	μm
Input Trace Width (W)	5	μm
Output Trace Width (w)	5	μm
Separation Between Each Port (s)	5	μm
Length of the port (h)	18	μm
Matching network parameters		
Capacitance	Value	Unit
C1	140	fF
C2	60	fF
C3	78	fF

Table 2 shows that as the working frequency increases, the radius of the structure decreases. The parameters reached for the 77 GHz frequency, that is, for long-range automotive radar applications.

4 Results

The most interesting parameters for measuring the Power Dividers are the S Parameters and they are summarized in the respective figures; the measurement is determined by the incident and reflected waves, evaluating how much enters and leaves the circuit.

Results obtained from dispersion parameters are presented in Figs. 7 and 8. These data contribute with information about coefficients of transmission and reflection measured at the operational frequency of 24 GHz.

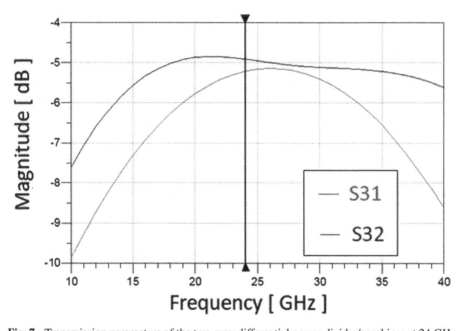

Fig. 7. Transmission parameters of the two-way differential power divider/combiner at 24 GHz.

In Fig. 7, we can see that the insertion loss of the proposed power combiner/divisor for the parameter S31 is −5.2 dB, and the S32 is −4.9dB. The return loss showed in Fig. 8; S33 is −28.5 dB from 16 to 34 GHz, and the lowest peak is located at 24 GHz. These results clearly state that the proposed design is perfectly adapted.

Results obtained from dispersion parameters are presented in Figs. 9 and 10. These data contribute information about coefficients of transmission and reflection measured at the operational frequency of 77 GHz.

In Fig. 9, we can see that the insertion loss of the proposed power combiner/divisor for the parameter S31 is −4.4 dB, and the S32 is −4.1 dB.

The return loss showed in Fig. 10; S33 is −39.2 dB from 65 to 105 GHz, and the lowest peak is at 77 GHz. These results clearly state that the proposed design is perfectly adapted.

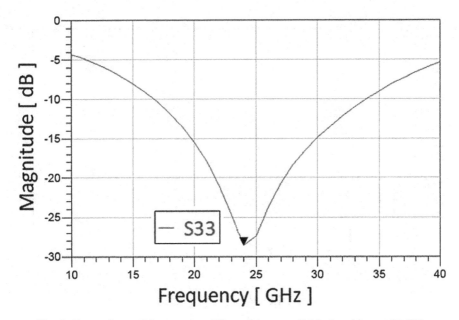

Fig. 8. Return Loss of the two-way differential power divider/combiner at 24 GHz.

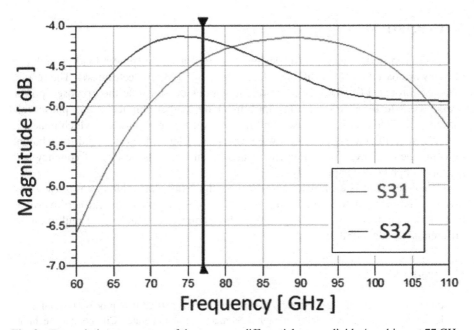

Fig. 9. Transmission parameters of the two-way differential power divider/combiner at 77 GHz.

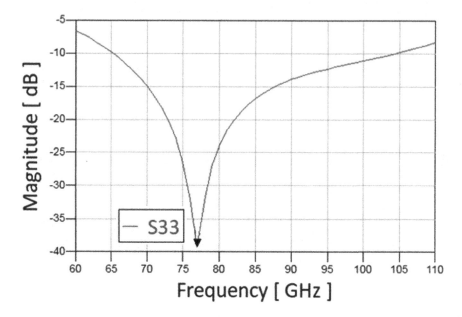

Fig. 10. Return Loss of the two-way differential power divider/combiner at 77 GHz.

5 Conclusions

The work proposed presents a novel design of a compact on-chip power divider/combiner of two ways based on SiGe BiCMOS technology of STMicroelectronics©. The results obtained through FEM-based full-wave simulations demonstrate the proposed power divider's adequate performance in input matching, output amplitude, and phase uniformity. The configuration is based on the vertical coupling approach, which makes it possible to divide the signal in two ways and vice versa without the need for a balun, reducing the chip area. The parameters r and W influence the resonant frequency and the input impedance, respectively.

Conclude that it is a compact on-a-chip configuration that exhibits how a two-way divider/combiner can be created using two rings for the output ports; further investigation of new geometries could be generated for applications that require multiple-port differential divider configurations.

References

1. Preisler, E.: A commercial foundry perspective of SiGe BiCMOS process technologies. In: 2020 IEEE BiCMOS and Compound Semiconductor Integrated Circuits and Technology Symposium (BCICTS), pp. 1-5 (2020). https://doi.org/10.1109/BCICTS48439.2020.9392971
2. Chevalier, P., et al.: SiGe BiCMOS current status and future trends in Europe. In: 2018 IEEE BiCMOS and Compound Semiconductor Integrated Circuits and Technology Symposium (BCICTS), pp. 64–71. IEEE (2018)

3. Bock, J., Lachner, R.: SiGe BiCMOS and eWLB packaging technologies for automotive radar solutions. In: 2015 IEEE MTT-S International Conference on Microwaves for Intelligent Mobility (ICMIM), pp. 1–4. IEEE (2015)
4. John, J.P., Kirchgessner, J., Ma, R., Morgan, D., Trivedi, V.P.: Si-based technologies for mmWave automotive radar. In: 2016 IEEE Compound Semiconductor Integrated Circuit Symposium (CSICS), pp. 1–4. IEEE (2016)
5. Martínez-Vázquez, M.: Overview of design challenges for automotive radar MMICs. In: 2021 IEEE International Electron Devices Meeting (IEDM), pp. 4.1.1–4.1.3 (2021). https://doi.org/10.1109/IEDM19574.2021.9720688
6. Martínez-Vázquez, M.: Overview of design challenges for automotive radar MMICs. In: 2021 IEEE International Electron Devices Meeting (IEDM), pp. 4–1. IEEE (2021)
7. Sene, B., Reiter, D., Knapp, H., Li, H., Braun, T., Pohl, N.: An automotive D-Band FMCW radar sensor based on a SiGe-transceiver MMIC. IEEE Microwave Wirel. Compon. Lett. **32**(3), 194–197 (2021)
8. Hasch, J., Topak, E., Schnabel, R., Zwick, T., Weigel, R., Waldschmidt, C.: Millimeter-wave technology for automotive radar sensors in the 77 GHz frequency band. IEEE Trans. Microw. Theory Tech. **60**(3), 845–860 (2012). https://doi.org/10.1109/TMTT.2011.2178427
9. Muralidharan, S., Wu, K., Hella, M.: A compact low loss single-ended to two-way differential power divider/combiner. IEEE Microwave Wirel. Compon. Lett. **25**(2), 103–105 (2015)
10. Shi, J., Lu, J., Xu, K., Chen, J.X.: A coupled-line balanced-to-single-ended out-of-phase power divider with enhanced bandwidth. IEEE Trans. Microw. Theory Tech. **65**(2), 459–466 (2016)
11. Zhang, W., et al.: Novel planar compact coupled-line single-ended-to-balanced power divider. IEEE Trans. Microw. Theory Tech. **65**(8), 2953–2963 (2017)
12. Santos, V.G., Boccia, L., Calzona, D., Amendola, G., Scaccianoce, S.: A compact SiGe BiCMOS four-way differential power divider/combiner. In: 2015 IEEE 15th Mediterranean Microwave Symposium (MMS), pp. 1–4 (2015). https://doi.org/10.1109/MMS.2015.7375378

Smart Tourism: How Can We Count on Digital in the Recovery of Post-covid Tourism in Portugal

Isabel Maria Lopes[1,2(✉)] ⓘ, Pedro Oliveira[3] ⓘ, Maria Isabel Ribeiro[4] ⓘ,
and António Fernandes[4] ⓘ

[1] UNIAG, Instituto Politécnico de Bragança, Campus de Santa Apolónia,
5300-253 Bragança, Portugal
isalopes@ipb.pt
[2] Algoritmi, Universidade do Minho, Largo do Paço, 4704-553 Braga, Portugal
[3] Instituto Politécnico de Bragança, Campus de Santa Apolónia, 5300-253 Bragança, Portugal
pedrooli@ipb.pt
[4] CIMO, Instituto Politécnico de Bragança, Campus de Santa Apolónia,
5300-253 Bragança, Portugal
{xilote,toze}@ipb.pt

Abstract. The number of tourists who visited Portugal in 2019 reached historic highs, a trend that was eventually interrupted by the emergence of the pandemic caused by the SARS-CoV-2 virus. Several experts point out that tourism was one of the first sectors to suffer the impacts of the pandemic and one of the hardest to be hit. Tourism recovery is desirable and what needs to be clarified with this study is how the digital transition so present, for example, in the Recovery and Resilience Plan (PRR) can help to rescue this upward trend of visitors/tourists. The present research work intends to emphasize how digital can be decisive in the resumption of tourism in Portugal, taking into account the measures announced for this sector. The results are discussed in the light of the literature and future work is identified with a view to enhancing tourism, smart tourism and smart destinations.

Keywords: Tourism · Smart tourism · Smart destinations · Digital

1 Introduction

The new coronavirus, which causes the COVID-19 infection, emerged in 2019 in the city of Wuhan in China.

The World Health Organization then classified, on March 11, 2020, the disease COVID-19, caused by the SARS-COV-2 virus, as a pandemic.

The effects of this pandemic were quickly noticed, in all economic activities, due to the restrictions and mitigating measures applied around the world.

More than two years later, unprecedented economic and social impacts on a global scale, surpassing the worst predictions, were confirmed.

T. Guarda et al. (Eds.): ARTIIS 2022, CCIS 1676, pp. 230–243, 2022.
https://doi.org/10.1007/978-3-031-20316-9_18

The question that arises is how the European Union (EU) and the Portuguese Government intend to help this sector, for a desired and rapid recovery.

The EU created a strategic community instrument to mitigate the economic and social impact of the crisis, capable of promoting economic convergence and the resilience of the Union's economies, thus helping to ensure sustainable long-term growth, and also to respond to the challenges of the double transition, towards a more ecological and digital society. It was in this context that the European Council created the Next Generation EU, a temporary recovery instrument, from which the Recovery and Resilience Mechanism will be developed, which includes this Recovery and Resilience Plan (PRR) [1].

Portugal's PRR is part of this effort developed by the EU to emerge stronger from the COVID-19 crisis, promoting ecological and digital transitions and reinforcing the resilience and cohesion of our societies.

This program is based on three main axes: Resilience, Climate Transition and Digital Transition.

The PRR is seen by the various sectors of activity in Portugal as a stimulus to business development.

As we have already mentioned, the tourism sector was one of those that was immediately hit, right from the start, with the abrupt stop of worldwide travel that occurred as a result of COVID. In Portugal, this stop had unprecedented impacts and among the most affected sectors is Tourism.

Alongside the PRR, the Portuguese Government, by Resolution of the Council of Ministers (n° 76/2021) approved the "Plan to Reactivate Tourism – Build the Future", published in the Diário da República on June 16, 2021.

This plan, whose actions are fully integrated with the objectives of the Recovery and Resilience Plan and the Portugal 2030 Strategy, arises in the context of the effects caused by the pandemic crisis and seeks to be a guide for the tourist sector, public and private, thus ensuring a concerted strategy for the recovery of the national economy.

The truth is that the pandemic has exposed the fragility of companies, schools, other institutions, when it comes to digital. But it is equally true that the pandemic has accelerated the digital transition in the most diverse areas and sectors, with the tourism sector being one of those that accompanied this evolution. The digitalization of tourism is no longer a trend but a requirement [2].

This is the context of the present work, which aims to analyze the potential of the PRR and the Plan to Reactivate Tourism with regard to digital in the recovery of Post-Covid tourism in Portugal.

The structure of the paper is as follows. After this introduction, we briefly review the literature on smart tourism. Then, in Sect. 3, we cover how tourism has been affected by the pandemic in Portugal. In Sect. 4, the measures proposed by the Government are presented in order to compensate for the losses caused by the prevention measures imposed in the fight against Covid-19. In the last section, taking into account the results of the study we identify future work opportunities.

2 Smart Tourism

We can define smart tourism as the name of the new era in which Industry 4.0 – 4. Industrial revolution, started with the introduction of smart technologies into the industrial field – carried the tourism sector [3].

The concept of smart tourism results from the adaptation of the concept of "smart city" to a tourist destination. This concept is related to the use of technologies and the internet in tourism, with the purpose of obtaining improvements in terms of economic growth, quality of life, resource management and development of more efficient management and social participation processes [4, 5].

The emergence of this type of smart tourism is due to the existence of more and more territories and smart cities, with artificial intelligence, big data, Internet of Things (IoT), cloud and fifth generation of mobile communications (5G).

Smart cities not only improve the quality of life of their inhabitants, they also improve the quality of life of the citizens who visit them, equally enriching tourist experiences.

The World Tourism Organization attributes to smart tourism characteristics "such as clean, green, ethical, quality, among others" [6]. Thus, the smart tourism must be able to meet the requirements of "short-term economic needs and long-term sustainable development" [7].

The use of technologies and the internet in tourism, "in addition to providing new and differentiated tourism products, also allows for a sector development with greater equity and sustainability as a result of greater collaborative participation" [5].

The principle of intelligent tourist destination is to provide smarter platforms to collect and distribute information within the destination, facilitate and provide efficient tourism resources and integrate tourism providers at micro and macro levels, with the aim of guaranteeing on the one hand, positive economic results, on the other, its more equitable distribution across the country and local society [8].

An intelligent tourist destination is characterized by having high levels of innovation and user facilitation of platforms and technologies, using interfaces and technologies, namely, IoT, mobile communication, cloud computing/services and artificial intelligence [7].

Smart tourism destinations allow to obtain information about the real needs and preferences of customers. Effective involvement between tourists and service providers is important to provide products that successfully meet the needs of tourists [9, 10].

The smart tourism "should help tourists to easily make decisions before or during their travels, providing relevant and meaningful information, based on the analysis of big data, personal information, patterns of behavior", etc. [11].

Thus, smart tourism destinations can be defined as destinations that use available technology to co-create value, pleasure and new and different experience for the tourist [12, 13].

The future of the smart tourism is based on technological development and its rapid and extensive implementation at all levels of the tourism sector [10].

3 Tourism in the Pandemic

Tourism has become "one of the most important sectors in Portugal, with a great impact on the economy and society. With a population of 10.1 million people, Portugal attracted 27.1 million tourists and 70.2 million bed nights in 2019" [14]. Tourism "has become the largest export economic activity in the country, responsible for 52.3% of exports of services and 19.7% of total exports. Tourist revenues registered an 8.7% direct contribution to the national PIB" [14].

It was in this best year for national tourism that Portugal and the world faced a pandemic which had a strong impact on tourism.

The COVID-19 brought about a new crisis, challenging the travel industry more than ever before. Several studies have suggested that there will be long-term severe effects that could continue for an unspecified period of time across the world, both medically, socially and economically [15].

The fear of traveling combined with the extremely restrictive government measures imposed on the different economic activities have resulted in a sharp fall in all indicators of tourism activity. Since 2013 and until 2019, seasonality and an increase in the number of tourists were structural. Subsequently, the pandemic of COVID-19 forced a re-qualification of these elements, as the peaks were replaced by troughs [16].

To better understand the impact that COVID-19 had in Portugal, we will use figures presented by the National Statistics Institute (INE), focusing on some parameters: Guests, Number of overnight stays.

The number of guests, that is, people staying in tourist establishments, recorded a continued upward trend between 2010 and 2019, with a brutal drop with the pandemic (see Fig. 1).

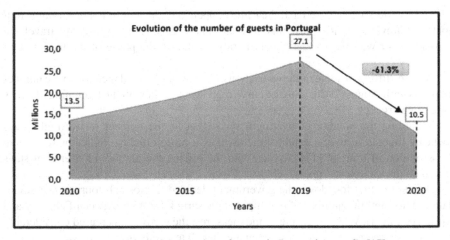

Fig. 1. Evolution of the number of guests in Portugal (annual), [17].

If the fall in the year 2020 is clearly visible in Fig. 1, decomposing the year 2020 by months (see Fig. 2), we have a much more realistic perception of the significant fall.

The exceptional situation and the proliferation of registered cases of contagion of COVID-19, led to the application of the first state of emergency that began in Portugal at 00:00 h on March 19, 2020, which caused a great impact on the number of guests, which dropped from 1.6 million in February to a mere 53,000 in April.

It appears that the breaks coincide with the states of emergencies imposed by the Government, where measures were applied to combat the pandemic.

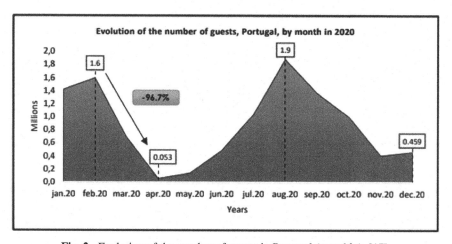

Fig. 2. Evolution of the number of guests in Portugal (monthly), [17].

The frontiers were closed and the same happened to the hotels and restaurants, tour operators, travel agencies, museums, festivals, and events. Consequently, the travel and tourism sector was almost completely paralyzed during the phase of the first state of emergency [17].

With the lifting of some of the restrictions, there was a gradual increase in the number of guests until August 2020, with the curve regressing again with the tightening of a new state of emergency.

Regarding the number of overnight stays, that is, the number of overnight stays spent by tourists in tourist establishments, it is a more effective indicator for seeing the evolution of tourism [17]. And as with the guests, the number of overnight stays remained the same (see Fig. 3).

During the first lockdown the government decided to close all tourism accommodation units, and the number of overnight stays shrunk by 96% between February and April (see Fig. 4). With the easing of the measures, the recovery increased considerably until August, regressing again following another state of emergency.

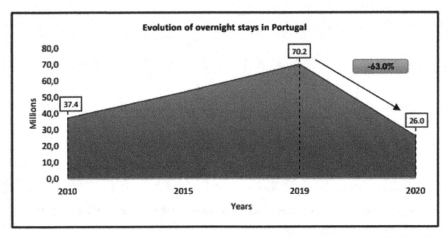

Fig. 3. Evolution of the number of overnight stays in Portugal (annual), [17].

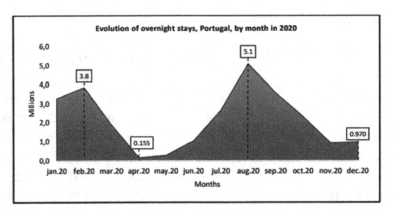

Fig. 4. Evolution of the number of overnight stays in Portugal (monthly), [17].

We do not intend to carry out a very in-depth analysis of all indicators, so we focus the data on the year 2020. Next, we present a more general view of the two years before and the two years during the pandemic (see Fig. 5).

In 2021 as a whole, overnight stays increased by 45.2% compared to 2020 (+38.3% in residents and +52.9% in non-residents), but decreased by 46.6% compared to 2019 (−10.9% in residents and −62.0% in non-residents) [18].

Preliminary results for 2021 reveal that guests reached 14.5 million this year and overnight stays reached 37.5 million, corresponding to annual growth of 39.4% and 45.2%, respectively (−61.6% and −63 .2% in 2020). Compared to the same period in 2019, guests and overnight stays decreased by 46.4% and 46.6%, respectively (see Table 1).

It is undeniable that tourism expanded very rapidly between the years 2010 and 2019, but it is equally undeniable that this sector would have grown even faster and achieved unprecedented success if the pandemic had not changed its course of action.

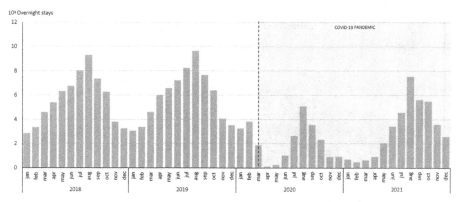

Fig. 5. Overnight stays in tourist accommodation establishments, per month, [18].

Table 1. General results of the tourist accommodation sector, [18].

Tourism accommodation establishment	Unit	Jan–Dec		
		2019	2020	2021
Guesst	10^3	**27 142,4**	**10 430,6**	**14 538,7**
Residents in Portugal	–	10 732,3	6 525,7	8 599,7
Residents abroad	–	16 410,1	3 904,9	5 938,9
Overnight Stays	103	**70 159,0**	**25 798,3**	**37 455,8**
Residents in Portugal	–	21 107,1	13 598,6	18 804,2
Residents abroad	–	49 051,8	12 199,7	18 651,6
Average stay	No. nights	**2,58**	**2,47**	**2,58**
Residents in Portugal		1,97	2,08	2,19
Residents abroad		2,99	3,12	3,14

4   Measures Proposed by the Government

After the tourism sector was heavily affected by the pandemic, the question that arises is what measures the government will implement for the much-desired relaunch of tourism in Portugal.

We are not going to talk about international campaigns to promote the destination Portugal, nor about national campaigns, nor about the Clean&Safe 2.0 Seal, much less about IVAucher. What we are going to address are two more robust measures, which can make a difference in the recovery of tourism in Portugal, we are talking about the "Plan to Reactivate Tourism – Build the Future" and the PRR.

As the focus of this work is digital as one of the ways for the recovery of post-Covid tourism in Portugal, we will only analyze in these two measures what concerns digital.

By Resolution of the Council of Ministers (n.° 76/2021) the "Plan to Reactivate Tourism - Build the Future" was approved, published in the Diário da República on June 16, 2021.

This plan arises in the context of the effects caused by the pandemic crisis and seeks to be a guideline for the tourist sector, public and private, thus ensuring a concerted strategy for the recovery of the national economy.

The plan is based on 4 pillars of action – support companies; promote security; generate business; build the future – and consists of specific actions that, in the short, medium and long term, will transform the sector and position it at a higher level of value creation, contributing significantly to GDP growth and distribution wealth equity.

The "Plan to Reactivate Tourism - Build the Future", foresees an investment of 6,112 million euros in the Portuguese tourism sector to exceed the target of 27,000 million euros of tourist income in 2027. Of the total of 6,112.24 million euros of investment The largest share, €4,075 million, will be provided by Banco Português do Fomento, which will channel €3,000 million to support companies (with a view to preserving productive potential and employment) and €1,075 million for their financing.

According to the Resolution of the Council of Ministers [19], the elaboration and approval of a plan that can put the sector on the path of growth again, providing it with mechanisms that make it more sustainable, more responsible, more competitive and even more resilient, and that allow it to exceed the objectives and targets defined in the 2027 Tourism Strategy, accelerating its transformation, preparing it for the future (see Fig. 6).

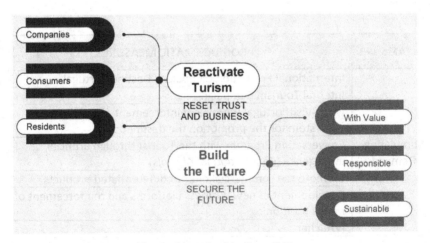

Fig. 6. Strategic objectives, [19].

As for digital, we can see in in pillar 3 of this plan: Generate business in the objective: Stimulating demand, two programmatic measures that meet the digital transition in tourism (see Fig. 7).

The first measure is called - New "Visitportugal" portal—"reinforcement of the digital ecosystem for promoting the destination: In terms of digital marketing, we highlight the updating and strengthening of the international impact of the "Visitportugal" ecosystem. This will imply the integration and development of new functionalities, contents and approaches. It should be noted that the "Visitportugal" ecosystem is the hub for information, communication and interaction with tourists, which includes a portal available in 11 languages and pages on the main social networks at a global level. To this extent, it is important to be equipped with technology that facilitates access to the national tourist offer, which, presented in context, allows for greater visibility within relevant content, thus increasing the business potential for Portuguese companies and the ability to respond to needs of different tourist segments. The penetration in foreign markets will also be extended, namely by increasing the number of languages to 15 languages" [19].

The second measure is the - Conversational Program with the Tourist through artificial intelligence (Conversational AI Tools): "The implementation of a conversation program that uses artificial intelligence has as main objectives the improvement and dynamic optimization of the content provided to the tourist and quick access to information about the experiences and tourist offer of "Destination Portugal". The introduction of these tools will make it possible to clarify doubts, interact with the potential tourist by suggesting offers according to their needs and improve the accessibility of contents by working on the inclusion vector (all for all). It will also allow tourist service, carried out 24/7, through more automated processes, with less time spent per operation and closer to the needs of each client. The optimization of tourist interactions will result in a trip with more value, working the axes of seasonality and increasing the consumption of tourist products. These conversation tools positively impact the tourist experience of the destination before the visit, during and after the visit, adding value and enhancing loyalty" [19].

AXIS	PROGRAMMATIC MEASURES
Stimulating Demand	International Promotion Campaign "Destino Portugal"
	Internal Tourism Campaign
	New "VisitPortugal Portal" – reinforcement of the digital ecosystem for the promotion the destination
	Conversation Program with the Tourist through artificial intelligence (*Conversational AI Tools*)
	Promote the commercial offer of differentiated products
	Development of new business platforms and reinforcement of media positioning
	IVAucher

Fig. 7. Generating business – programmatic measures, [19].

Pillar 4 of this plan: Building the future, has an objective entitled: Innovation in companies and destinations, with various programmatic measures aimed at the digital transition (see Fig. 8).

This Resolution [19] "considers that innovation and digitalization are absolutely critical factors in strengthening the sector's competitiveness and, consequently, in the growth process of companies and the tourism sector capable of generating more added value. Specifically, in terms of digitalization, it is important to bear in mind that this is an area where there are strong gaps in the sector, both in terms of the adoption of digital tools by companies, the effective use of the data generated by these tools, and the ability to use them in creating value or developing new businesses".

According to INE, in 2020, only 46.9% of companies in the accommodation and restaurant sector in Portugal had a website and the use of data by companies in the sector is below the national average.

Thus, they propose as measures: Tourism + Digital Program (Digital Companies and Digital Territories); Upgrade Tomorrow Program—Reinforce digital skills; NEST—Hub of digital tourism and vehicle for innovation in the sector.

Measures intended to strongly support the digital transformation of companies in the tourism sector, as well as tourist destinations.

AXIS	PROGRAMMATIC MEASURES
Innovation in companies and destinations	Tourism + Digital Program (Digital Companies and Digital Territories)
	"Upgrade Tomorrow" Program – Reinforce digital skills
	Tourism Offer Requalification and Repositioning Program
	Program for Attracting Foreign Direct investment and international Brands
	Transformation of the Tourism Cluster into a vehicle for Collective Efficiency Strategies in Tourism
	Incentive Program for the Creation of New Tourist Businesses
	Fostering Innovation in Tourism 2.0 Program
	NEST - *Hub* of digital in tourism and vehicle of innovation in the sector
	Training Program for *Startups* "Rising Stars"

Fig. 8. Building the future – Programmatic measures, [19].

As for the PRR, as already mentioned, it is seen by the various sectors of activity in Portugal as a stimulus to the progress of business as, tourism was one of the sectors that was most affected.

But according to the Secretary of State for Tourism, the tourism sector is not present in the PRR, because it does not need structural reforms, but that, even so, and after more than a year of slowing down in the activity, the sector will have a specific plan, with short and long-term measures (Plan to Reactivate Tourism - Build the Future) [20].

However, we cannot fail to mention the criticism of the lack or delay in the support of the President of the Confederation of Tourism of Portugal, Francisco Calheiros, who in an interview [21] stated that "Finding the word tourism in the PRR is like finding Wally". "In addition to the PRR, the Stability Plan (PE), which we are studying, has just been released, and as you know, the PRR is within the PE. The latter says the following: attention that tourism from 2009 to 2019 was decisive for the recovery of the Portuguese economy. In this sense, and with an PE that includes the PRR, it is essential to have very concrete and specific measures for tourism. Therefore, if you read the PE first and then the PRR, you go to the PRR very excited, since the PE says that the measures have to be there in the PRR and there should be "tons of them". But it's like finding Wally."

Even so, the Confederation of Tourism of Portugal welcomes the plan "Reactivate Tourism – Build the Future", presented by the Government and which includes an investment of more than six billion euros, hoping that it will advance quickly. "In a general analysis, it seems to us to be a plan capable of supporting companies to resume their growth line and put Tourism in the place that it rightfully belongs to", said the president of the Confederation of Tourism of Portugal (CTP). The plan was received with applause and as a response to the arguments of the sector, one of the most affected by the pandemic and which complained of having been forgotten in the PRR. "After a PRR that did not reflect any strategy for the most dynamic, competitive and wealth- and employment-generating activity for the economy, the Government was sensitive to CTP's arguments and finally understood the urgency of investing in the economy. Relaunch of Tourism" [21].

As for digital, as the PRR is structured in three axes: Resilience, Digital Transition and Climate Transition, and given that the digital transition can and should be transversal to various sectors and has 650 million directly oriented for the digital transition of companies, it is expected that companies in the tourism sector will also be contemplated.

5 Conclusions

Technology is assuming an increasingly important role in the day-to-day of companies. But it is certain and known that entrepreneurs in the tourism sector will take a few years to restore their accounting balances.

Tourism in Portugal was significantly affected by the pandemic, in line with other countries, but there is one fact to highlight, the pandemic has undeniably contributed to the acceleration of the digitization of this sector, as it forced the rapid adoption of new digital tools.

There are many variables under analysis that contribute to the recovery of Tourism, for example, for tourists from Asian countries, their arrival will depend on the replacement of air transport capacity, and the restoration of accessibility. Another variable is the fear of the emergence of new variants of Covid-19.

The question that arises is when will we be able to surpass the levels of 2019? According to the Secretary of State for Tourism Rita Marques [22], "very possibly we will only be able to recover the 2019 numbers in 2023. It is certain that this recovery will not be the same across the country. The recovery of each region will depend on both the most important tourist products for each destination and the composition of the issuing markets". However, the future is very uncertain, with low expectations in the short and medium term [16].

The Covid-19 pandemic has challenged the tourism sector more than ever, regarding the challenges for the future of the tourism sector, the CEGOT researcher (Cláudia Seabra) [15] considers that safety and hygiene levels "will have to be higher" than ever. Large hotels and resorts, large cities, museums and monuments will have added challenges with tourists avoiding places with large agglomerations and physical contact". Another challenge, she adds, is related to "the balance between automation and digital procedures and human contact which, after all, is the support of tourist activity. The economic, social, ecological and even political sustainability of tourism will be the biggest challenge of all".

Digital and the implementation of the measures proposed by the Government, could constitute a perfect symbiosis between the tourist and the destination, because in fact, the promotion of Smart Tourism initiatives has a real impact on the qualification of the offer.

In these times of a pandemic, we can say that Smart Tourism could be the main solution to guarantee an adequate response to the demands of the new times.

It can be said that Smart Tourism is based on three distinct moments but simultaneously related in a value chain associated with experience, namely [23]:

- Before the visit: In this first moment, resources must be given to the user so that he can obtain information and make the reservation of stay and visit packages. The availability of robust web portals, with information on routes and points of interest, as well as online booking systems are examples of useful tools that are increasingly used by tourists in planning their trip;
- During the visit: At this stage, it is important that the tourist has access to resources that enrich their stay. At this point, initiatives have emerged with a strong multimedia and augmented reality component that provide tourists with all the context and information about points of interest and the surrounding environment, thematic routes or perhaps creating their own routes.
- After the visit: In this last moment, it is important to provide mechanisms so that the tourist can make a retrospective and provide an assessment of satisfaction with the services provided. In a quick and intelligent way, there are now tools to collect these satisfaction metrics, in a logic of continuous improvement of tourist companies, as well as quantification of the economic and social impact of Tourism in a given territory.

It may not be a magic solution for the resumption of tourism after the pandemic, but it will certainly contribute to it happening more quickly, as is desirable for companies in the sector and for the country.

As the dynamics are many and the measures for this and other sectors cannot stop here, we propose as future work since a new cycle of European financing will start, through the Multiannual Financial Framework 2030 (2021–2027) the study of the measures that will be defined for the tourism sector in Portugal, as it is widely recognized that this sector plays a central role in the Portuguese economy.

Acknowledgements. The authors are grateful to the UNIAG, R&D unit funded by the FCT – Portuguese Foundation for the Development of Science and Technology, Ministry of Science, Technology and Higher Education. "Project Code Reference: UIDB/04752/2020".

References

1. Portugal 2020. https://portugal2020.pt/wp-content/uploads/planoderecuperacaoeresiliencia_consultapublica.pdf. Accessed 4 Matcj 2022
2. Jorge, V.: A digitalização do turismo deixou de ser uma tendência para ser uma exigência, Publituris (2022)
3. Mobilefest. https://www.mobilefest.net/what-is-smart-tourism/. Accessed 15 March 2022
4. Komninos, N., Pallot, M., Schaffers, H.: Spetial issue on smart cities and the future Internet in Europe. J. Knowl. Econ. **4**, 119–134 (2013)
5. Ortega, J., Malcolm, C.: Touristic stakeholders' perceptions about the smart tourism destination concept in Puerto Vallarta, Jalisco, Mexico. Sustainability (Switzerland), vol. 12(5), Article number 1741 (2020)
6. World Tourism Organization (UNWTO): Report of the First Meeting of the NWTO Tourism Resilience Committee. UNWTO, Madrid (2009)
7. Muthuraman, S., Al Haziazi, M.: Smart tourism destination - new exploration towards sustainable development in sultanate of Oman. In: 5th International Conference on Information Management, ICIM 2019, pp. 332–335. Cambridge (2019)
8. Buhalis, D., Amaranggana, A.: Smart tourism destinations. In: Xiang, Z., Tussyadiah, I. (eds.) Information and Communication Technologies in Tourism 2014, pp. 553-364. Springer, Cham (2013)
9. Jasrotia, A., Gangotia, A.: Smart Cities to ST Destinations: a review paper. J. Tourism Intell. Smartness **1**(1), 47–56 (2018)
10. Schaffers, H., Komninos, N., Pallot, M., Trousse, B., Nilsson, M., Oliveira, A.: Smart cities and the future internet: towards cooperation frameworks for open innovation. In: Domingue, J., et al. (eds.) FIA 2011. LNCS, vol. 6656, pp. 431–446. Springer, Heidelberg (2011). https://doi.org/10.1007/978-3-642-20898-0_31
11. Chung, N., Koo, C., Lee, K.: Assessing the impact of mobile technology on exhibition attendees' unplanned booth visit behavior. Sustainability **9**(6), 1–15 (2017)
12. Wang, D., Li, X., Li, Y.: China's "ST destination" initiative: a taste of the service-dominant logic. J. Destin. Mark. Manag. **2**(2), 59–61 (2013)
13. Zhu, W., Zhang, L., Li, N.: Challenges, function changing of government and enterprises in Chinese ST. In: Xiang, Z, Tussyadiah, L. (eds.). Information and Communication Technologies in Tourism 2014. Springer, Dublin (2014)
14. Turismo de Portugal. http://www.turismodeportugal.pt/pt/Turismo_Portugal/visao_geral/Paginas/default.aspx. Accessed 15 March 2022
15. Seabra, C., Paiva, O., Silva. C., Abrantes, J.L.: Pandemics and Travel: COVID-19 Impacts in the Tourism Industry, Emerald Publishing Limited (2021)
16. Santos, N., Moreira, C.O.: Uncertainty and expectations in Portugal's tourism activities. Impacts of COVID-19, Research in Globalization, vol. 3, p. 100071 (2021)
17. Costa, C.: The impact of the COVID-19 outbreak on the tourism and travel sectors in Portugal: Recommendations for maximising the contribution of the European Regional Development Fund (ERDF) and the Cohesion Fund (CF) to the recovery, European Commission (2021)
18. INE. https://www.ine.pt/ngt_server/attachfileu.jsp?look_parentBoui=544012209&att_display=n&att_download=y. Accessed 21 March 2022
19. Presidência do Conselho de Ministros: "Resolução do Conselho de Ministros n.º 76/2021". Diário da Republica, 1ª série, 115 (junho): 27–49 (2021)
20. Laranjeiro, A.: https://www.dn.pt/dinheiro/turismo-nao-esta-no-prr-porque-nao-precisa-de-reformas-estruturais-mas-vai-ter-apoios--13726124.html. Accessed 21 March 2022
21. Jorge, V.: https://www.publituris.pt/2021/05/13/encontrar-a-palavra-turismo-no-prr-e-como-encontrar-o-wally. Accessed 21 March 2022

22. Petroninho, A.: Primeira linha: desafios do Turismo, Rita Marques Secretária de Estado do Turismo, Negócios (2022)
23. Ribeiro, N.: Smart Tourism: perspetivar o Turismo à luz da nova era da Globalização. Publituris, da Tecnologia e da Sustentabilidade (2021)

Tourism and Internet of Things: A Bibliometric Analysis of Scientific Production from the Scopus Database

Elisabete Paulo Morais[1]([✉]) [iD], Carlos R. Cunha[1,2] [iD], and Vítor Mendonça[1] [iD]

[1] UNIAG (Applied Management Research Unit), Instituto Politécnico de Bragança, Campus de Santa Apolónia, 5300-253 Bragança, Portugal
beta@ipb.pt

[2] CeDRI (Research Centre in Digitalization and Intelligent Robotics), Instituto Politécnico de Bragança, Campus de Santa Apolónia, 5300-253 Bragança, Portugal

Abstract. Tourism is a very emerging sector in any society, very important in economic terms and in job creation, today any traveler increasingly uses technological means to fully enjoy their trip.

The IoT is and increasingly will be a major contributor to smart tourism. To identify the most developed terms in the field of Tourism and Internet of Things, a quantitative analysis was developed in May 2022. This analysis was focused on four hundred and four (404) publications from the Scopus database, published between 2011 and May 4 2022. Before 2011 there were no publications in this area.

A bibliometric analysis was performed using the VOSviewer software and a technique of matching terms and co-authorship by authors and countries. Were found 4 clusters for the co-occurrence of terms, 18 clusters for the co-authorship of authors and 6 clusters for the co-authorship of countries. There was a lack of uniformity in the presentation of terms with the same meaning: internet of things, internet of things (iot), iot and internet of thing (iot). This lack of uniformity is probably due to the fact that it is a recent area of investigation.

Keywords: IoT · Internet of Things · Tourism · Bibliometric analysis · Scopus · VOSviewer

1 Introduction

The tourism sector is today a globalized sector that has experienced enormous growth in recent decades. Its impact on the economies of some countries is quite high, having attracted increasing attention from the technology industry. In fact, in parallel with the constant technological evolution, in recent decades, the tourism sector has grown to the point of becoming one of the dominant sectors globally, evolving into a new concept called "Smart Tourism" [1]. However, according to [2], despite the growing interest in this concept, it is still considered lacking in more in-depth explanations to be fully understood, in part because of its great complexity.

T. Guarda et al. (Eds.): ARTIIS 2022, CCIS 1676, pp. 244–255, 2022.
https://doi.org/10.1007/978-3-031-20316-9_19

Tourism is increasingly information intensive [3–5]. However, according to [6], tourism is no longer just information intensive, since information is the fabric of tourism and ubiquitous computing, and universal connectivity, are today an inseparable and blended layer of tourism. In the tourism sector, there is a clear trend towards the adoption and implementation of smart technologies in tourist destinations and tourist attractions in order to achieve an enrichment of tourists' experiences and, in this way, improve their degree of satisfaction [7].

An example of the symbiotic fusion between the tourism sector and the technology sector, and the ability to support the concept of "Smart Tourism" is today the Internet of Things (IoT). According to [8], the IoT is an asset due to its ability to integrate various services in the field of tourism.

Although the IoT is already having a strong impact on the tourism sector, this sector still has difficulties in taking full advantage of the IoT, which is a technology not yet at a stage of full maturity, in order to achieve an intelligent connection among all actors, having positive and negative aspects, of its use, being pointed out [9].

The tourism industry presents itself as a dense and complex mesh of interactions between multiple actors and multiple phenomena that have to be cooperatively coordinated and managed. And it is in this context that the IoT, according to [10], is a trend and has a potentially disruptive role in the tourism and hospitality industry.

The tourism sector is a highly cooperative ecosystem and it will be through, and only through, cooperation that a reengineering of the sector can be leveraged to support, not only a classic fusion between the physical and the virtual, but the metaverse that today is expected dock to the future of the sector - in this context, IoT logic is a key system to support an omnipresent vision of the tourism sector.

The concept and implementation of a metaverse is not new and one of the most famous cases was the social network called Second Life. This 3D virtual world model is, however, still difficult to implement in the tourism sector, in a generalized way. However, the recent COVID-19 pandemic situation has well demonstrated the potential of the vision of a metaverse, both for consumers and businesses [11]. For the future implementation of this concept, the IoT will be, in our opinion, the support fabric and the great enabler.

The IoT could also have a very significant boost as fifth-generation (5G) mobile communications becomes a global standard. According to [12], 5G will be one of the biggest drivers for IoT growth and adoption. Which, according to [13], will accommodate the high need for bandwidth and low end-to-end latency of the IoT and, in this way, boost the quality of IoT components and their connection to the Internet.

If, on the one hand, the IoT will be able to support a revolution in the tourism and hospitality sector, the success of this revolution will depend on the ability to create applications that, using the IoT, allow a very strong interaction between the tourist and the main tourist services (e.g. transportation, shopping and hotels), as well as integrating social media, digital marketing, and wearable devices [14]. This need is based on a capacity for total integration and interaction, the vision of a smart city supported by IoT is clearly a large network of cooperation. This need for cooperation raises enormous challenges, from the most technical (e.g. security and privacy) to the most human (e.g. trust between people and organizations to share information).

The concept of IoT is not new, however its application requires a reengineering of the way public infrastructures in cities are thought of, the construction of buildings and, ultimately, how they design hardware and software solutions capable of transforming the way people interact with spaces, services and information in general. Creating a truly immersive experience that transforms the way tourists interact with destinations is today an objective possibility but, at the same time, a challenge that is still far from being a mass reality.

In order to better understand the research that has been developed in the context of IoT applied to the context of tourism, the result of a study is presented that sought to identify the main thematic areas of research in the field of tourism and IoT, using the basis of Scopus data.

2 IoT and Tourism Related Work

Although the massification of IoT is still far from its maturity, there are already several studies, pilot or experimental applications that have been implemented all over the world, in the context of the tourism and hospitality industry.

In the context of recommender systems, [15] proposes a hybrid system capable of combining implicit collaborative filtering and ontology to recommend personalized IoT services to users. Also [16], in a work on "multimodal travel route recommendation algorithm based on the awareness of the Internet of Things", states that the IoT could enable to perceive cross-modal tourism routes and, in this way, help in the creation of more efficient recommendation systems.

In [17], within the scope of the hospitality sector, decisions on the adoption of smart solutions, their existing benefits and limitations are studied, and the various decision-making factors that can influence the will to adopt the IoT are also compared. In [18], the role of IoT is focused, combined with technologies such as big data analytics to support smart tourism, presenting a blockchain-based smart tourism platform.

In [19] the role of IoT is focused on the development of Big Data Tourism Resources Based on 5G Network and IoT. In this work it is pointed out that the IoT has a very powerful amount of information, as more and more people, especially young people, prefer to travel intelligently through the IoT.

In [20], the opportunities and challenges of applying the IoT to preserve the culture and revitalization of small cities are focused and on how the IoT can help to revitalize them and give them a new life.

A study that aims to identify the impacts of IoT on the tourism industry and a model is proposed to streamline the industry with the tourist movement, in order to be able to fully analyze the tourist experience is presented in [10].

The potential of IoT for smart tourism combined with 5G and AI is presented in [21]. This work focuses on the transformative role of IoT in the tourism industry and how its association with 5G and AI can overcome latency constraints when massive amounts of data to be transported and processed are at stake.

In a work presented in [22], it is mentioned a new social model centered on IoT technology and intelligence where tourism is characterized as an extension of the human lifestyle. This work also focuses on the role of IoT in the development of modern tourism, thanks to its enormous capacity for collecting, storing and processing information.

A study carried out by [23], presents an analysis of the suitability of the smart tourism environment assisted and supported by real-time wireless sensor networks for IoT tourism and its suitability was evaluated.

According to [24], in the process of exploring destinations and their attractions, IoT technology can make the entire tourism process more efficient, as the sensory layer present in the IoT is there to help tourists find and obtain data related to their journey travel and, where access to these systems can be easily done through the mobile devices that tourists have.

In the recent pandemic context, a study carried out by [25] presented the benefits of IoT to improve business performance during the COVID-19 pandemic for the travel and tourism industry in Kelantan, Malaysia. This study concludes that the use of IoT in the travel and tourism industry will benefit by improving its business performance, especially during the COVID-19 pandemic. This study discussed several elements and identify the potential and benefits of using the Internet of Things (IoT) to improve business performance, business marketing and customer engagement, and as such, achieving better customer satisfaction.

In the context of a survey analysis on the influence of smart devices and IoT applications on tourism, [26] presents a work that discovers which group of Information and Communication Technologies (ICT) devices impacts tourists and the tourism industry, concluding that when the functionalities of multiple devices are combined, the experience results can be optimized.

In a paper on the use of IoT in hospitality, [27] refers that the adoption of IoT is a differentiating factor in the hospitality industry that facilitates the integration of the digital and real world and allows the creation of competitive advantages and process optimization.

In the context of smart cities and accessible tourism, [28] state that IoT proves to be a key technological point for the development of smart urban environments. In their work, an architecture and practical implementation is proposed, adapted to the use case of accessible tourism, applied to people with physical disabilities.

In the context of sun and beach tourism and the lack of information to satisfy tourists' preferences and ensure their safety, [29] proposes a Social Internet of Things platform to share useful information with tourists.

In the context of heritage spaces, [30] focuses on the potential of IoT to rethink the entire process of supporting the interpretation and enjoyment of heritage, carried out by tourists, presenting a conceptual model that uses IoT as a way of transforming the experience of visiting tourist spaces and transforming the way tourists can access information and services, in symbiosis with the interests of entities promoting the space.

Although there is a wide range of studies and researchers that have focused their attention on the IoT and on the way in which it can leverage the different actors in the tourism and hospitality industry, the set of areas of activity is still too vast and dispersed, in part justified by the enormous scope of what are actors in the context of tourism/act of visiting a given destination in a recreative way. In this way, it becomes important to understand how research is linked and interconnected at the moment and who are the researchers and key topics in the dynamics of the evolution of the use of IoT.

3 Methodology

This paper aimed to identify the most frequently developed topics in the area of Tourism and IoT, namely, the evolution of the number of papers published to date and the grouping of topics related to Tourism and IoT.

A search was carried out on May 4, 2022 in the Scopus database. The terms "Tourism" and "Internet of Things" were used, limited to the title, abstract and keywords. As a result of the research, 404 publications were obtained.

A bibliometric analysis was performed and the term co-occurrence and author and country co-authorship technique was used. The unit of analysis was the publication and the variables corresponded to the terms included in the title, abstract and keywords. The extraction of terms was performed using the VOSviewer software, version 1.6.18, in order to build a map that shows the relationships between the various terms and their association with clusters of thematic areas. According to [31], this methodology analyzes the distance between the various terms selected, and the shorter the distance between two terms, the stronger the relationship between them. The color map represents the various clusters of thematic areas, and terms with the same color are part of the same cluster and, therefore, are more strongly related to each other compared to binary count terms, which consists of verifying whether the term is present or absent in each analyzed document.

4 Results

The papers obtained are distributed as follows according to the type of document: 193 are conference paper, 137 are article, 39 conference review, 24 book chapter, 10 review and 1 retracted.

Figure 1 shows the number of publications carried out up to the date of the search, May 4, 2022.

It appears that until 2016, scientific publications in the IoT and tourism area were in small quantity.

More than 60% of the publications were made in the last three years. And in the first 4 months of 2022 there are already 22 publications.

Considering the analysis of the thematic areas and using the VOSviewer software version 1.6.18 and the technique of co-occurrence of terms, two thousand nine hundred and thirty-two (2932) terms were identified, of which only thirty-seven (37) were identified had a minimum of ten (10) occurrences. The thirty-seven (37) terms were distributed across four (4) clusters.

The first cluster, the color red in Fig. 2, consists of eleven (11) terms (5g mobile communications, augmented reality, e-tourism, etourism, internet, internet of things, internet of things (iot), iot, sustainability, sustainable development and virtual reality),

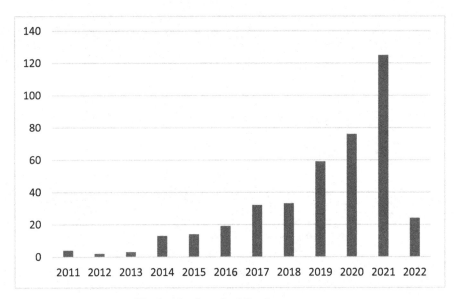

Fig. 1. Number of publications per year

associates tourism virtualization and sustainability. The existence of terms whose meaning is the same but to be used with different terminology is verified. Namely, e-tourism and etourism and internet of things, internet of things (iot) and iot.

The second cluster, in green in Fig. 2, consists of ten (10) terms: advanced analytics, artificial intelligence, big data, economics, internet of things technology, leisure industry, machine learning, tourism, tourism development and tourism management, associates the development and management of tourism with some technologies.

The third cluster, in blue in Fig. 2, consists of nine (9) terms: cloud computing, data analytics, data mining, internet of thing (iot), location, smart cities, smart city, smart tourism and tourism industry, this cluster groups concepts associated with smart tourism.

The fourth cluster, in yellow in Fig. 2, consists of seven (7) terms: blockchain, commerce, decision making, digital storage, information management, marketing and service industry, associates terms related to commerce and information management.

For each of the terms, the analysis of how many links, total link strength and number of occurrences was carried out, similarly to what is illustrated in Fig. 3 for the term internet of things.

Table 1 illustrates, for each term, how many links, total link strength and number of occurrences.

Analyzing the results presented in Table 1, it appears that the term internet of things is, in a prominent way, the one with the most occurrences, followed by tourism. However, the number of occurrences could be even higher if four different terms with the same meaning were not used: internet of things, internet of things (iot), iot and internet of thing (iot). Due to the fact that it is a recent research area, there is a lack of uniformity in the presentation of terms. Even so, the term internet of things is the most used. Regarding

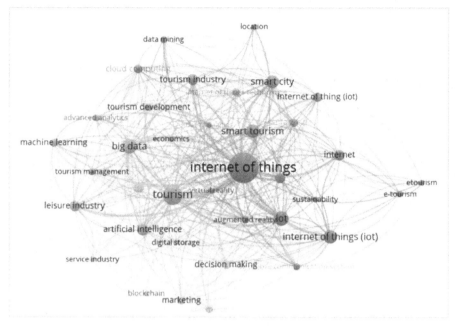

Fig. 2. Term co-occurrence map (Color figure online)

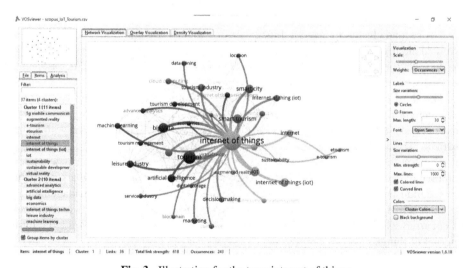

Fig. 3. Illustration for the term internet of things

links and total link strength, they are also the two terms with the highest values. However, the terms smart city and iot appear with the same number of links as the term tourism: 34, despite the fact that the total link strength is lower.

Table 1. Number of terms by occurrence.

Cluster	Keyword	Links	Total link strength	Occurrences
1	5g mobile communication systems	18	44	14
	Augmented reality	27	64	14
	e-tourism	14	34	11
	etourism	9	29	10
	Internet	23	80	29
	Internet of things	**36**	**618**	**243**
	Internet of things (iot)	30	126	46
	iot	34	163	54
	sustainability	15	34	10
	Sustainable development	28	86	26
	Virtual reality	22	41	10
2	Advanced analytics	27	85	14
	Artiffical intelligence	31	127	37
	Big data	33	237	54
	Economics	23	40	10
	Internet of things technologies	24	53	15
	Leisure industry	27	129	28
	Machine learning	23	80	18
	Tourism	**34**	**334**	**105**
	Tourism development	21	54	16
	Tourism management	22	65	13
3	Cloud computing	24	65	20
	Data analytics	23	51	10
	Data mining	18	42	12
	Internet of thing (iot)	27	74	23
	Location	14	32	10
	Smart city	**34**	156	42
	Smart tourism	33	155	48
	Tourism industry	27	83	31
4	Blockchain	18	35	10
	Commerce	22	64	15

(*continued*)

Table 1. (*continued*)

Cluster	Keyword	Links	Total link strength	Occurrences
	Decision making	25	72	18
	Digital storage	21	36	10
	Information management	32	121	32
	Marketing	25	78	19
	Service industry	19	51	11

Using the author co-authorship technique, one thousand sixty-nine (1069) authors were identified, of which twenty-six (26) had a minimum of three (3) publications. The maximum number of publications per author was four (4), and only six (6) authors had this number of publications. Hence, we opted for a minimum of three (3) publications. Of these twenty-six (26), the connection between them is shown in Fig. 4, where we can see the creation of eighteen (18) clusters by the *VOSviewer* software. Some of these authors are not linked with others, the largest set of connected items consists of seven (7) items, represented in Fig. 4 by clusters in red and blue. Only four (4) clusters have more than one (1) author, and only two (2) clusters are linked. Which leads us to conclude that, being recent publications, there is still little relationship between the authors.

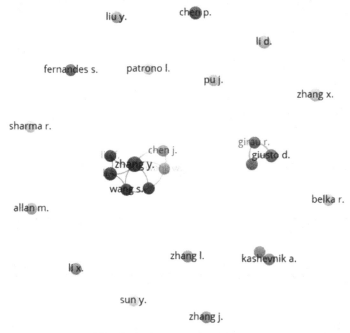

Fig. 4. Author co-authorship map

Using the author co-authoring technique, but with the country as the unit of analysis, of the sixty-seven (67) countries, twenty-three (23) had a minimum of five (5) publications. The software created six (6) clusters, as can be seen from Fig. 5. In this case, the top five (5) by number of publications is China, Italy, India, USA and Russian Federation.

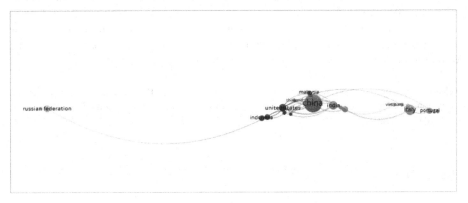

Fig. 5. Country co-authorship map

5 Conclusions

This study aimed to identify the main thematic areas of research in the field of tourism and IoT. For this, the Scopus database was used as a source and the VOSviewer software was used, using the bibliometric technique of co-occurrence of terms and co-authorship of authors and countries.

The study concludes that there has been a growing trend of publications in recent years, with 2021 being the year with the most publications in the area of tourism and IoT.

When creating the clusters, the software places the terms tourism and internet of things in different clusters. But it puts the term etourism in the same cluster as internet of things.

The first cluster, which includes internet of things, associates the tourism virtualization and sustainability. The second cluster, which includes the term tourism, associates the development and management of tourism with some technologies. The third cluster, groups terms associated with smart tourism, and the last cluster, cluster four, associate terms related to commerce and information management.

Regarding the co-authorship of authors, although one thousand sixty-nine (1069) authors were identified, only twenty-six (26) had a minimum of three (3) publications. The maximum number of publications per author was four (4), and only six (6) authors had this number of publications. The link between the authors is still limited. As for the co-authorship with the country variable, of the sixty-seven (67) countries, twenty-three (23) had a minimum of five (5) publications, with the software having created six (6) clusters, with a significant link between them.

There is the use of four different terms for the same meaning: internet of things, internet of things (iot), iot and internet of thing (iot). Due to the fact that it is a recent research area, there is a lack of uniformity in the presentation of terms. However, the term internet of things is the most used.

One of the limitations of this study is that it is limited to the Scopus database. There are other databases, such as the Web of Science, which are equally important in terms of scope, use and updating.

As such, future investigations may involve other bibliometric analyzes that allow overcoming the limitations of this work, namely, including other databases, such as the Web of Science.

Acknowledgements. UNIAG, R&D unit funded by the FCT – Portuguese Foundation for the Development of Science and Technology, Ministry of Science, Technology and Higher Education. UIDB/04752/2020.

References

1. Kontogianni, A., Alepis, E.: Smart tourism: state of the art and literature review for the last six years. Array **6**, 100020 (2020)
2. Gelter, J., Fuchs, M., Lexhagen, M.: Making sense of smart tourism destinations: a qualitative text analysis from Sweden. J. Destin. Mark. Manag. **23**, 100690 (2022)
3. Lee, H., Jung, T.H., tom Dieck, M.C., Chung, N.: Experiencing immersive virtual reality in museums. Inf. Manag. **57**(5), 103229 (2020)
4. Buhalis, D.: Tourism and information technologies: past, present and future. Tour. Recreat. Res. **25**(1), 41–58 (2000)
5. Ukpabi, D.C., Karjaluoto, H.: Consumers' acceptance of information and communications technology in tourism: a review. Telemat. Inform. **34**(5), 618–644 (2017)
6. Xiang, Z.: From digitization to the age of acceleration: on information technology and tourism. Tour. Manag. Perspect. **25**, 147–150 (2018)
7. Zhang, Y., Sotiriadis, M., Shen, S.: Investigating the Impact of Smart Tourism Technologies on Tourists’ Experiences. Sustainability **14**(5) (2022)
8. Tripathy, A.K., Tripathy, P.K., Ray, N.K., Mohanty, S.P.: iTour: the future of smart tourism: an IoT framework for the independent mobility of tourists in smart cities. IEEE Consum. Electron. Mag. **7**(3), 32–37 (2018)
9. Verma, A., Shukla, V.: Analyzing the influence of IoT in tourism industry. SSRN Electron. J. (2019)
10. Verma, A., Shukla, V.K., Sharma, R.: Convergence of IOT in tourism industry: a pragmatic analysis. J. Phys: Conf. Ser. **1714**(1), 12037 (2021)
11. Um, T., Kim, H., Kim, H., Lee, J., Koo, C., Chung, N.: Travel incheon as a metaverse: smart tourism cities development case in Korea. In: Stienmetz, J.L., Ferrer-Rosell, B., Massimo, D. (eds.) ENTER 2022, pp. 226–231. Springer, Cham (2022). https://doi.org/10.1007/978-3-030-94751-4_20
12. Guo, X., Wang, Y., Mao, J., Deng, Y., Chan, F.T.S., Ruan, J.: Towards an IoT enabled tourism and visualization review on the relevant literature in recent 10 years. Mobile Networks Appl. 1–14 (2021). https://doi.org/10.1007/s11036-021-01813-6
13. Palattella, M.R., et al.: Internet of things in the 5G era: enablers, architecture, and business models. IEEE J. Sel. areas Commun. **34**(3), 510–527 (2016)

14. Wise, N., Heidari, H.: Developing smart tourism destinations with the Internet of Things. In: Sigala, M., Rahimi, R., Thelwall, M. (eds.) Big Data and Innovation in Tourism, Travel, and Hospitality: Managerial Approaches, Techniques, and Applications, pp. 21–29. Springer, Singapore (2019)

15. Bouazza, H., Said, B., Zohra Laallam, F.: A hybrid IoT services recommender system using social IoT. J. King Saud Univ. - Comput. Inf. Sci. **34**, 5633–5645 (2022)

16. Zhang, Y., Tang, Z.: Cross-modal travel route recommendation algorithm based on internet of things awareness. J. Sensors **2021**, 5981385 (2021)

17. Pappas, N., Caputo, A., Pellegrini, M.M., Marzi, G., Michopoulou, E.: The complexity of decision-making processes and IoT adoption in accommodation SMEs. J. Bus. Res. **131**, 573–583 (2021)

18. Luo, L., Zhou, J.: BlockTour: a blockchain-based smart tourism platform. Comput. Commun. **175**, 186–192 (2021)

19. Gao, H.: Big data development of tourism resources based on 5G network and Internet of Things System. Microprocess. Microsyst. **80**, 103567 (2021)

20. Jara, A.J., Sun, Y., Song, H., Bie, R. Genooud, D., Bocchi, Y.: Internet of Things for cultural heritage of smart cities and smart regions. In: 2015 IEEE 29th International Conference on Advanced Information Networking and Applications Workshops, pp. 668–675 (2015)

21. Wang, W., et al.: Realizing the potential of the Internet of Things for smart tourism with 5G and AI. IEEE Netw. **34**(6), 295–301 (2020)

22. Wang, S., Yu, Z.: Research on tourism management decision support system based on IOT technology. In: 2021 IEEE Conference on Telecommunications, Optics and Computer Science (TOCS), pp. 1043–1046 (2021)

23. Ding, M., Xu, Y.: Real-time wireless sensor network-assisted smart tourism environment suitability assessment for tourism IoT. J. Sensors (2021)

24. Sharma, S., Rishi, O.P., Sharma, A.: IoTeST: IoT-Enabled Smart Tourism—Shaping the Future of Tourism BT. Rising Threats in Expert Applications and Solutions, pp. 569–576 (2021)

25. Abd Latib, A.A., Ismadi, M.A.S., Khairudin, K.H., Aziz, R.C., Keat, L.C.: The potentials and benefits of Internet of Things (Iot) in travel and tourism industry. ICEBTH 2021, p. 226 (2021)

26. Suhail Razeeth, M.S., Ahmadh Rifai Kariapper, R.K., Pirapuraj, P., Ahmed Sabani, M.J., Mohamed Nafrees, A.C.: Influence of smart devices and IoT applications in tourism: a survey analysis (2020)

27. Mercan, S., et al.: Improving the service industry with hyper-connectivity: IoT in hospitality. Int. J. Contemp. Hosp. Manag. **33** (2020)

28. Nitti, M., et al.: Using IoT for accessible tourism in smart cities. In: Assistive Technologies in Smart Cities (2018)

29. Piras, A., Mirri, S., Sole, M., Giusto, D., Pau, G., Girau, R.: Implementation of a sea monitoring system based on social internet of things. In: 2022 IEEE 19th Annual Consumer Communications & Networking Conference (CCNC), pp. 687–690 (2022)

30. Cunha, C.R., Carvalho, A., Esteves, E.: Reengineering the way tourists interact with heritage: a conceptual IoT based model. In: International Conference on Tourism Research, pp. 166–XII (2021)

31. van Eck, N.J., Waltman, L.: Visualizing bibliometric networks BT. In: Ding, Y., Rousseau, R., Wolfram, D. (eds.) Measuring Scholarly Impact: Methods and Practice, pp. 285–320. Springer, Cham (2014)

Science Mapping on Tourism and Technology: A Bibliometric Approach

Manuela Ferreira[1] ⓘ, Sérgio Pereira[1] ⓘ, Sílvia Araújo[1](✉) ⓘ, and Sérgio Lopes[1,2] ⓘ

[1] Universidade do Minho, Braga, Portugal
manelaferreira7@gmail.com, sergiorpereira@hotmail.com,
saraujo@elach.uminho.pt, sergio.lopes@dei.uminho.pt
[2] Algoritmi Research Centre / LASI, Guimarães, Portugal

Abstract. The importance of technology in the tourism sector has dramatically increased in the last few years. The amount of available data about just any field demands appropriate techniques, to be able to have a ground for development strategies. This paper presents a science mapping bibliometric analysis on tourism and technology. Its main goals are to demonstrate the importance of science mapping on academic and business areas, to analyse the state of technology in tourism since 2015, and to show that it is possible to perform this method in any scientific field. The results obtained reinforce the importance of technology for tourism.

Keywords: Science mapping · Tourism · Technology · Data visualisation

1 Introduction

Science mapping is a process which allows data analysis and visualisation of a specific scientific field's evolution, resorting to scientific publications. Its main goals lie in the understanding of a scientific area's actual state, on synthesising the knowledge of existing academic works and using them as a starting point for new research [1].

When it comes to tourism, which is the field of work addressed in this paper, science mapping is useful for understanding the changes that occur in this area and the field's most relevant concepts. As the field of tourism progresses over the years, it is absolutely necessary that a bibliometric analysis takes place, in both quantitative and qualitative ways [2]. The same authors also state that the tourism's development led to a growth in the number of scientific publications, resulting in the need to map the scientific knowledge of the field. This is where data comes in handy: it gives us the possibility to find trends that would not be visible otherwise, such as annual scientific productions, relations between key concepts, among others.

With the ever-growing need for open data, the work we describe here supports the idea that scientific data should be available to everyone, presenting a methodology that allows any person from any scientific area to extract and analyse data, using the bibliographic database Scopus, and the R-based platform, Biblioshiny. We apply this method to make an overview on tourism and technology, exploring the field's state of the art by

T. Guarda et al. (Eds.): ARTIIS 2022, CCIS 1676, pp. 256–268, 2022.
https://doi.org/10.1007/978-3-031-20316-9_20

mapping different aspects, such as scientific production over time and by country, most contributing countries, most important publications, trends, topics and authors.

This paper proceeds, in Sect. 2, with a literature review, followed by a quick reflection on tourism and the role of technology, in Sect. 3. This third section focuses on science mapping, by tackling open science, data extraction and tools, and data visualisation. This paves the way for the proposed method, in Sect. 4, explaining in detail the process of data extraction and visualisation. Section 5 addresses the achieved results, and finally, in Sect. 6, conclusions are presented.

2   Related Work

Tourism is a sector in which lines of study can have many directions and focus specific segments of it. Thus, science mapping can take several approaches. Three authors dedicated their bibliometric analysis to sustainable tourism, although through different points of view.

In the work done by [3], the focal point of their bibliometric analysis was the sustainable and responsible tourism (SRT) paradigm. The aim was to "determine whether SRT has merged into a single "responsustainable" tourism discourse that could shift the mainstream paradigm of sustainable tourism towards the full content of SRT". Using the science mapping method, authors were able to determine existing written publications on the theme, author cooperation between countries, influential works and journals and disciplinary areas inside the field. Although their analysis was not able to confirm a shift towards an expanded paradigm of SRT, they conclude that it will be an important part of future research.

Corte et al. [4] also took an approach on sustainable tourism but towards the open innovation realm, in which they mapped "the development status and the leading trends in terms of impact, main journals, papers, topics, authors, and countries". Authors had in mind the goal of understanding whether studies done in the area contributed to an evolving research in the field, defending graphical presentations to obtain a better understanding on the state of art. The conclusions obtained were that, while having in mind an open innovation approach and knowing tourism products or local expertise, tourism policy makers should make sustainability a priority in their agenda, meeting tourists needs while also improving residents' well-being. Sustainability is good for keeping ecological balance whilst improving competitiveness. Government, industry, and marketing strategies are the key elements for the success of defined goals.

Astaiza et al. [5], also on sustainability, decided to approach tourist mobility between 1980 and 2019, mapping the technological advancements in data for tourist traceability. Authors defend that "the tracking of tourist movements is an essential aspect in the management of sustainable tourist destinations" and that although ICTs "provide innovative ways of collecting data on tourist movements", it is necessary to find tools and methods to study this field. They believe that mobile technology is the best option to follow the tourist movement.

Galvano and Giaconne [6] also used bibliometrics but took a different approach from the authors mentioned above. They focused on creative tourism, trying to have an overall view on "the main research topics and approaches, theoretical foundations, and the most recent areas of investigation". The authors concluded that the field of creative tourism is well-defined, while also adding that there are five main research trends, such as creativity and cultural tourism, creativity and local development, creativity and urban tourism, creative tourist experience and co-creation of tourist experience, which can dictate future research lines.

Our work also seeks a better understanding and definition of possible research trends in tourism, but what differentiates it from others is that we focus on the role of technology. More specifically, we try to assess the current level of technology integration, how it has evolved over the last years, and to identify most referred technologies.

3   Approach

This section emphasises the role of technology on the tourism sector and introduces the proposed approach to science mapping based on scientific literature.

3.1   Tourism and Technology

As defended in [7], with cities getting more complex and competitive, technology has become crucial, imposing the use of technologies (ICTs, etc.), in order to ensure cities' competitiveness and accessibility, providing both citizens and visitors access to services and data. Information and Communication Technologies have provided consumers the power of identifying, customising and buying touristic products, while contributing to the industry's globalisation, supplying tools to develop, manage and distribute offers globally [8]. These technologies enable more sustainable and environment-friendly tourism, customised travel experiences, quicker planning and less time-consuming travelling. Thus, it is important to understand how technology is evolving and innovating in this sector, so that it becomes possible to develop studies that can provide clues for both academia and business. With Covid-19's pandemic, the necessity for adaptation and reinvention became larger than ever [9], which brought technology to the main stage alongside digitalisation [10], in every scientific field, such as medicine [11], education [12], among others. Companies need to be creative and maximise the usage of available resources, as the pandemic has caused a huge economic impact and the tourism sector was one of the most affected by it. In [13], the term "covidisation" is created, which is defined as "any effects on the tourism industry sector directly or indirectly connected to the COVID-19 pandemic".

3.2   Science Mapping

Open science is extremely useful, as it gives everyone immediate access to scientific processes and results, advancing science faster. Open science increases the amount of available data and having huge amounts of data creates both opportunities and difficulties. Science mapping is one way of extracting meaning from large volumes of information. It allows us to dive into a specific field and describe, evaluate and follow scientific research.

There are multiple ways to extract data from scientific work citation databases, such as using the website's interface directly or using a provided Application Programming Interface (API). Since programming knowledge is not accessible to everyone, we focus on extraction using Scopus' website interface, in order to adopt a method that is as accessible as possible. There are other scientific databases available, such as Web of Science, Dimensions, Cochrane and PubMed.

Extracted data needs to be analysed with the help of visualisation tools. As defended in [14], "professionals and scientists need a range of theoretical and practical tools to measure experimental data". There are many tools available, such as Tableau, Citespace, Data Illustrator and Biblioshiny, with the latter being the one used in our work [15]. Biblioshiny is an open-source tool for quantitative research in scientometrics and bibliometrics, which includes all the main bibliometric methods of analysis [16]. It is a great choice because it comes with a pre-built interface specially for science mapping. Data visualisation is a rather powerful technique, which has been growing exponentially, to deal with more and more data being produced every day. Data visualisation makes it easier to find information by providing graphic representations of both qualitative and quantitative connections inside specific fields [15].

4   Method

This section demonstrates, from the first to the last step, how to extract information and use it to map a specific scientific field. It is a simple process that allows everyone to benefit from data visualisation. The process is summarised in Fig. 1.

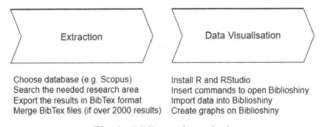

Choose database (e.g. Scopus)   Install R and RStudio
Search the needed research area   Insert commands to open Biblioshiny
Export the results in BibTex format   Import data into Biblioshiny
Merge BibTex files (if over 2000 results)   Create graphs on Biblioshiny

Fig. 1. Bibliometric method.

4.1   Extraction

On the first step of this process, it is necessary to log on to scopus.com, with academic credentials, for example. After that, we type in the terms we want to search, see mark 1 in Fig. 2. In this case, even though we used "tourism and technology" as general terms, we encourage using terms of specific technologies in order study their impact. It recognizes "and" as a logical operator between terms but other can be used (OR and AND NOT). This can also be done by clicking on "Add search field", marked as 2. Once the search terms have been chosen, the time range can be set by clicking on "Add time range", marked as 3, and selecting the years, marked as 4; in this work, we have searched documents published from 2015 to 2022.

After clicking on search, Scopus shows the list of documents matching the chosen criteria. To filter the results even further, it is possible to refine by year, type of access, author, subject area, document type, and so on, by selecting said options on the left side

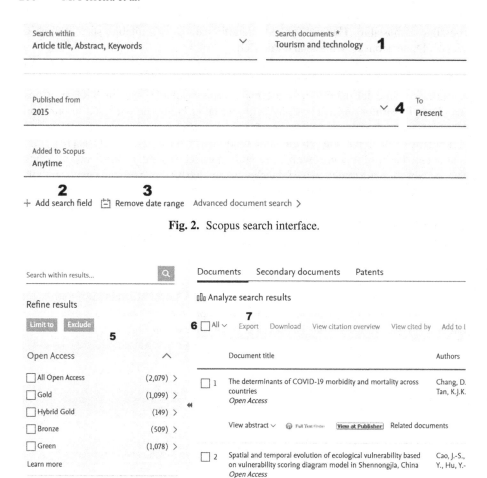

Fig. 2. Scopus search interface.

Fig. 3. Scopus search results interface.

of the screen (see mark 5 in Fig. 3). Afterwards, results can be exported by selecting the "All" option at the top (see mark 6), and then clicking "Export", marked as 7.

It is now possible to select the preferred method of export and the metadata to be included in the exported file. We have used BibTeX format, as it is the most adequate format to perform data visualisation on Biblioshiny. It is advised to select all metadata options available, in order to make the data analysis more valuable.

It is important to mention that Scopus only allows 2000 results to be exported at once. If there are more than 2000 results, they need to be filtered. For instance, we got 6540 results, so we sorted them by year, exported them in four turns and then merged them together using a text editor.

4.2   Data Visualisation

When the data file is ready to be used, we must install both R and the program RStudio, which is an integrated development environment (IDE) for R. After opening RStudio, there are three commands that must be entered in the R console. Each command must be executed one at a time. The first, "install.packages("bibliometrix")", will install the package needed to perform this method. The second, "library(bibliometrix)", will run the package previously installed, and, at last, "biblioshiny()" will open Biblioshiny's web interface on your default browser, on which you can upload the.bib file with the search results.

Uploading our BibTeX file can be accomplished by clicking on "Import or Load Files", located on the Data option on top of the page. To import our file, we must choose "Import raw file(s)", choosing Scopus as our database. Once the upload has finished, we can begin creating our graphs, with many types available on the drop-down menus in the upper bar (see Fig. 4).

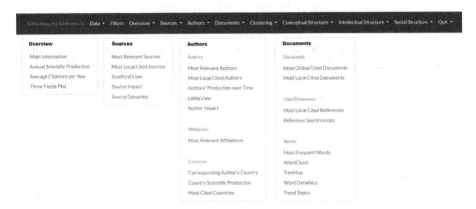

Fig. 4. Biblioshiny interface with visible drop-down menus.

5   Results

With our analysis of the 6540 articles extracted from Scopus, we were able to acquire some valuable information on the field of tourism and technology that can be useful for constructing a state-of-the-art able to map research on the field and answer possible questions about the theme.

Q1: Was there a boom in production?

Starting in 2015 with 411 published articles (see Fig. 5), we can observe an annual growing trend, with increases between 15% to 30% each year until 2020. We believe that 2022 will follow the same growing pattern, as by the time our data was exported, in June, 523 articles had already been published. This expresses the need for continuous research of the field with its ever-growing developments and promising prospects.

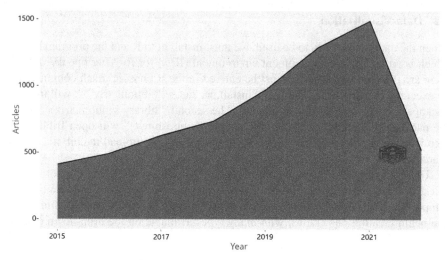

Fig. 5. Annual Scientific Production.

Q2: Which countries should be taken into consideration regarding scientific production on the theme?

The most cited countries reveal a clear dominance of the USA and China, which may be related to their scientific strength. This is shown in Fig. 6.

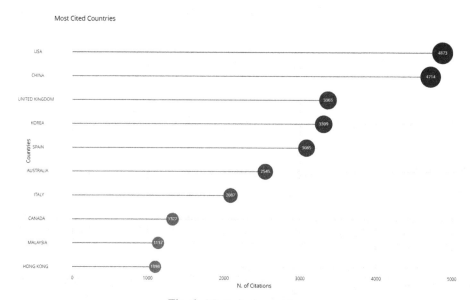

Fig. 6. Most cited countries.

Q3: Which sources are the most relevant to look for scientific research?

On the most cited sources (see Fig. 7) there is a clear dominance of "Tourism Management", the most popular international journal on subjects such as travel, tourism and planning, with over 7000 citations since the start of 2015, followed by "Annals of Tourism Research" and "Journal of Travel Research", being cited over 2900 times.

The most relevant sources are depicted in Fig. 8. The leading position is taken by "Sustainability (Switzerland)", an open access journal on environmental, cultural,

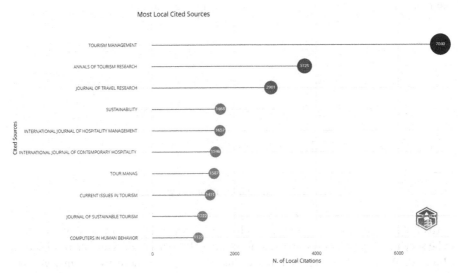

Fig. 7. Most local cited sources.

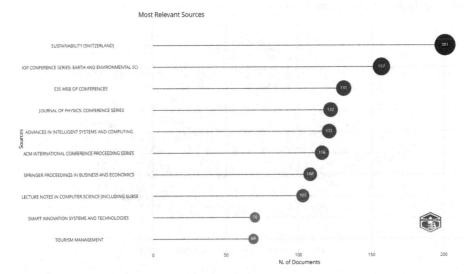

Fig. 8. Most relevant sources.

economic and sustainable development, followed by "IOP Conference Series: Earth and Environmental Science" and "E3S Web of Conferences".

Q4: Which terms should be used to search for scientific publications on the theme and which trends can be identified in each year?

On authors' top keywords, in Fig. 9, we find "smart tourism", "augmented reality", "virtual reality", "covid-19" and "big data", manifesting the relevance that technology has in the field. We find that rural tourism has a very low frequency and it could benefit from more technological approaches, as for example, e-tour guides.

Words	Occurrences
tourism	850
smart tourism	221
technology	191
augmented reality	178
virtual reality	171
covid-19	134
big data	121
innovation	114
sustainability	114
social media	112

Fig. 9. Most frequent author's keywords.

To be able to conduct a focused research of published articles, abstracts' word clouds can be very useful as they portray the most frequent bigrams used. This can be observed in Fig. 10. When linking tourism and technology, besides these two terms, we find "smart tourism" as the most frequent term, with its inherent relation to information technology (social media, augmented reality, virtual reality), which highly contributes to a sustainable development of tourism.

Fig. 10. Abstracts' word cloud with bigrams.

When researching the trend topics, presented in Fig. 11, one can observe that even though there has always been a relation between tourism and technology. Starting between 2017 and 2018, there has been an emergence of more sophisticated technologies, such as augmented reality, artificial intelligence, blockchain, among others. Moreover, most of these concepts are directly linked to smart tourism, which essentially makes use of technology and big data in order to innovate the tourism sector. The term "pandemic" is also one of the main trends in 2020, which is connected to virtual tourism [17], surging as a solution for the mandatory lockdown caused by Covid-19 [18].

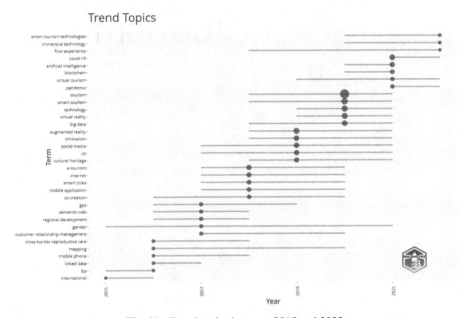

Fig. 11. Trend topics between 2015 and 2022.

Q5: What authors should be looked for and how do their research subjects relate to one another?

On the co-occurrence network of the author's keywords graph, we can observe how the different subjects relate to one another. Each line represents an association between the terms, with thicker lines representing stronger associations and thinner lines representing weaker associations. No connections between keywords indicate no relationship between them.

In Fig. 12 it is clear that tourism relies on technology, with terms such as "big data", "virtual reality", "smart tourism" contributing to this sector's innovation. Covid-19 has led to faster digitalisation in tourism, with data science methods being implemented to help "national and regional governments seek to better understand the pandemic's impact on traveler movement and habits and support safe and sustainable recovery by helping businesses to develop better and smarter products and services" [19].

The same goes for the collaboration network graph, in which we can see how the authors collaborated with each other. It is shown in Fig. 13. The bigger the box, the broader the author's collaboration network. We can see that there are no authors standing out, in regard to the amount of collaborations.

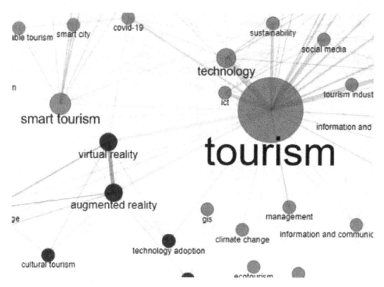

Fig. 12. Author's keywords co-occurrence network.

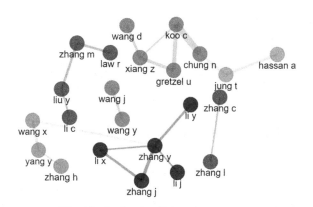

Fig. 13. Authors' collaboration network.

This is only a sample of what can be done with Biblioshiny, as there are many more possibilities, such as thematic maps, tree maps, factorial analyses, cluster graphs, and so forth. Having used Biblioshiny, we believe it is a very powerful tool to gain insights on any scientific field. It contains a wide range of functionalities, including almost 40 different types of graphs and the ability to filter our dataset based on years of publication, document type, number of citations, and so on. It is also very user-friendly, as the end user does not require any skills to be able to create data visualisations, making it functional, easy to use, and with an overall good performance. The only hindrance is the fact that some of the pre-built graphs are difficult to interpret for the average user lacking experience in data analysis and statistics. However, this method's main weakness is the sample data itself.

Although Biblioshiny can analyse data from several abstract and citation databases, such as Scopus, Web of Science, Dimensions, and so on, it does not possess the ability to merge these databases together, forcing us to choose one of these databases for our analysis, which may lead to missing out on important data. The ability to merge multiple databases or upload them at the same time would improve the results obtained. Nevertheless, it is an excellent tool that proves to be of great use to any person who wishes to conduct research on any specific subject. In our case, we found it very useful when beginning research on our Masters theses, as it was a rather quick method of finding the most relevant articles and authors related to our subjects.

6 Conclusion

This paper provided an overview on the science mapping process, taking into account the practical case of tourism and technology. By using this method, we were able to capture information like annual productions, relevant authors and trends inside tourism and technology, which is a starting point for conducting research on those fields and on how they interact with one another. The tourism sector is always growing and evolving, and cities need to adapt to this growth in order to fit the needs of both citizens and visitors. The search for sustainability and competitiveness led to technology having a major role in the sector's innovation, which was amplified with the pandemic's emergence. With terms such as "big data", "smart tourism", "virtual reality", "augmented reality" and "artificial intelligence" trending throughout the last years, these results might prove useful in indicating future lines of research in this context. We tackled how bibliometric techniques can determine the current state of this specific scientific field, having an impact on both academic and business areas.

To understand how a field is developing or changing, there is a need for data and its representation. Data visualisation is very useful to obtain insights on a specific subject, which can help researchers follow new routes of research, discover what is lacking inside a scientific field and propel research in that direction. In order to have data accessible to everyone, open science is essential, since it is a contribution to the evolution of science. With the increasing use of data, a lot of techniques were developed, being science mapping one of them, allowing the discovery of conducting lines of research and to draw conclusions about a field of research. This article showed a simple way to do so, from the extraction of data to its visualisation.

Science mapping can be applied to any study field and can be used by anyone, clearing the stigma that only people with information science skills can perform this type of process. This work serves as a practical guide to encourage and support people to use science mapping.

References

1. Chen, C.: Science mapping: a systematic review of the literature. J. Data Inf. Sci. **2**(2), 1–40 (2017). https://doi.org/10.1515/jdis-2017-0006
2. Güzeller, C., Çeliker, N.: Bibliometric analysis of tourism research for the period 2007–2016. Adv. Hospital. Tourism Res. **6**, 1–22 (2018). https://doi.org/10.30519/ahtr.446248

3. Mihalic, T., Mohamadi, S., Abbasi, A., Dávid, L.D.: Mapping a sustainable and responsible tourism paradigm: a bibliometric and citation network analysis. Sustainability **13**(2), 853 (2021). https://doi.org/10.3390/su13020853

4. Della Corte, V., Del Gaudio, G., Sepe, F., Sciarelli, F.: Sustainable tourism in the open innovation realm: a bibliometric analysis. Sustainability **11**(21), 6114 (2019). https://doi.org/10. 3390/su11216114

5. Chantre-Astaiza, A., Fuentes-Moraleda, L., Muñoz-Mazón, A., Ramirez-Gonzalez, G.: Science mapping of tourist mobility 1980–2019. Technological advancements in the collection of the data for tourist traceability. Sustainability **11**(17), 4738 (2019). https://doi.org/10.3390/ su11174738

6. Galvagno, M., Giaccone, S.: Mapping creative tourism research: reviewing the field and outlining future directions. J. Hospital. Tourism Res. **43**(8), 1256–1280 (2019). https://doi. org/10.1177/1096348019862030

7. Liberato, P., González, M., Liberato, D.: A importância da tecnologia num destino turístico inteligente: o caso do Porto. In: Gestión turística, innovación y tecnología e la nueva era digital (2016). https://aecit.org/files/congress/19/papers/118.pdf

8. Bethapudi, A.: The role of ICT in tourism industry. J. Appl. Econ. Bus. **1**(4), 67–79 (2013). http://www.aebjournal.org/articles/0104/010406.pdf

9. Pascoal, S., Tallone, L., Furtado, M.: The impact of COVID-19 on cultural tourism: virtual exhibitions, technology and innovation. Adv. Tourism Technol. Syst. **209**, 177–185 (2020). https://doi.org/10.1007/978-981-33-4260-6

10. Ndou, V., Mele, G., Hysa, E., Manta, O.: Exploiting technology to deal with theCOVID-19 challenges in travel & tourism: a bibliometric analysis. Sustainability **4**(10), 5917 (2022). https://doi.org/10.3390/su14105917

11. Ting, D., Carin, L., Dzau, V., Wong, T.: Digital technology and COVID-19. Nat. Med. **26**, 459–461 (2020). https://doi.org/10.1007/10.1038/s41591-020-0824-5

12. Qiu, H., Li, Q., Li, C.: How technology facilitates tourism education in COVID19: case study of Nankai University. J. Hospital. Leisure Sport Tourism Educ. **29**, 100288–100288 (2021). https://doi.org/10.1016/j.jhlste.2020.100288

13. Korinth, B.: The situation of the tourist sectors after the outbreak of the COVID-19 pandemic - tourism covidisation. World Rev. Sci. Technol. Sustain. Develop. **1** (2021). https://doi.org/ 10.1504/wrstsd.2021.10040396

14. Moral-Muñoz, J.A., Herrera-Viedma, E., Santisteban-Espejo, A., Cobo, M.J.: Software tools for conducting bibliometric analysis in science: An upto-date review. El profesional de la Información **29**(1), 1699–2407 (2020). https://doi.org/10.3145/epi.2020.ene.03

15. Alhuay-Quispe, J., Estrada-Cuzcano, A., Bautista-Ynofuente, L.: Analysis and data visualization in bibliometric studies. JLIS.It **13**(2), 58–73 (2022). https://doi.org/10.36253/jlis. it-461

16. Aria, M., Cuccurullo, C.: Bibliometrix: an R-tool for comprehensive science mapping analysis. J. Inform. Elsevier **11**(4), 959–975 (2017). https://doi.org/10.1016/j.joi.2017.08.007

17. Rahim, N., et al.: Aftermath of pandemic Covid-19 on tourism industry: a review on virtual tourism platform. AIP Conf. Proc. **2347**, 020173 (2021). https://doi.org/10.1063/5.0052855

18. Godovykh, M., Baker, C., Fyall, A.: VR in tourism: a new call for virtual tourism experience amid and after the COVID-19 pandemic. Tourism Hospital. **3**(1), 265–275 (2022). https:// doi.org/10.3390/tourhosp3010018

19. ADB, UNWTO: Big Data for Better Tourism Policy, Management, and Sustainable Recovery from COVID-19. ADB, XI (2021). https://doi.org/10.22617/SPR210438-2

The Use of Technologies in Museums: A Bibliometric Analysis Based on the Web of Science Database

João Paulo Sousa[1]([✉]) [iD], Patrícia Cordeiro[2] [iD], and Carlos R. Cunha[3] [iD]

[1] Instituto Politécnico de Bragança, Research Centre in Digitalization and Intelligent Robotics, Campus de Santa Apolónia, 5300-253 Bragança, Portugal
jpaulo@ipb.pt

[2] Digital Media Doctoral Program DEI, FEUP, Porto, Portugal
up200102038@fe.up.pt

[3] Instituto Politécnico de Bragança, UNIAG and CeDRI, Campus de Santa Apolónia, 5300-253 Bragança, Portugal
crc@ipb.pt

Abstract. This article starts with a short review of recent studies and reports on the adaptation of museums toward digital transformation. This first part aims at giving a contextualization of the current importance of the use of technologies, and an understanding of which are the current strategies and struggles museums face regarding their use. In correlation to this context, it becomes relevant to analyze the scientific literature and understand how it reflects the evolution of the adoption of technologies, such as the themes under investigation, inferring trends, among others. Therefore, the second part explores the scientific production related to the use of technologies in museums, in the last decade, by using a bibliometric analysis approach. This study allows us to understand the evolution of the scientific literature on the adoption of technologies in museums, and proposes an agenda for future research that offers the potential to advance research on the use of new digital technologies in museums.

Keywords: Digital museum · Bibliometric analysis · Visitor experience · Technologies · Museums · Web of science

1 Introduction

The integration of the use of technology in museums has been growing in the past few decades, becoming more intense as we move towards a digitized society where the new digital-born generations will be defining new trends and the demand for more complex uses of technology. Undoubtedly, recent advances in digital tools have become one of the central aspects of any museum experience. Touch devices, audio guides, augmented and virtual reality, and beacons, just to name a few, can enrich the visitor experience, offering new levels of interaction - more immersive, personalized, and richer in content.

T. Guarda et al. (Eds.): ARTIIS 2022, CCIS 1676, pp. 269–282, 2022.
https://doi.org/10.1007/978-3-031-20316-9_21

According to [1], the interpretation of heritage is considered an effective tool for learning, communication, and management, capable of increasing the visitor's awareness and empathy for the heritage sites or artifacts he visits or contacts. In this context, it is important to develop innovative strategies that enable the best possible interpretation. The use of immersive technology, such as VR, has enormous potential to create memorable tourist experiences, specifically in heritage tourism [2]. Emerging digital technologies are a critical success factor for the sustainable preservation and communication of cultural heritage to the general public [3]. A vision of an immersive-digital museum requires an analysis of how museums can take advantage of technology to boost the development of innovation networks, competitive advantages, and leverage their economic performance; as well as solutions for digitizing and improving the visitor experience [4].

In the first part of this article, we review recent studies and reports on the adaptation of museums towards digital transformation, which point particularly to the different aspects pushing museums forward (growing demand from younger generations, the potential for visit enhancement, and the unlimited access and availability that the internet provides) and the aspects that challenge the use of technologies (high maintenance, digital literacy, and lack of resources).

In correlation to this context, it becomes relevant to analyze the scientific literature and understand how it reflects the evolution in the adoption of technologies, such as the themes under investigation and inferring trends. Therefore, the second part explores the scientific production related to the use of technologies in museums, in the last decade, by using a bibliometric analysis approach. Following a filtered search through the scientific database Web of Science (WoS) a dataset of references was created and analyzed using R and Bibliometrix software. The results gathered by the implementation of this methodology are presented in the last part of this article.

The tables and graphs generated with the software programs give visual support to the interpretation of the results allowing us to understand the evolution of the scientific literature on adoption of technologies in museums, answering questions such as: Which are the most influential published articles and on which themes? Who are the most prolific authors? What are the collaboration patterns between countries? or What are the most frequently used keywords in articles? A few examples from Côa Museum are used as reference to some of the applications of technologies and digital tools mentioned. Finally, we also propose an agenda for future research that offers the potential to advance research on the use of new digital technologies in museums.

Taking into account the research conducted through the past 10 years, the questions this article attempts to answer are the following:

– Which are the current technologies museums are using to move towards digital transformation?
– What are the most influential published articles?
– Who are the most prolific authors and about which technologies?
– What are the collaboration patterns between countries?
– What are the most frequently used keywords in articles and do they tell us about trending technology use in museums?

2 Literature Review

Museums have a particular relationship with the public, as they are spaces of mediation between visitors and the objects and narratives they present. In this relationship, technologies play, nowadays a fundamental role, not only as enhancers of the visitor's experience, but as resources for preservation, management, and communication of museums, therefore, in the last decade the challenge of "digital transformation" and/or "digital transition" has been present in all areas of activity of the museum.

Modern museums must be able to establish a digital presence that transcends geographic boundaries and physical constraints [5]. According to [6], virtual museum systems, which use multiple X-reality technologies, have begun to spread, and represent key tools for promoting exhibitions and reaching the public, and effectively communicating their estate. However, According to [4], strategic planning for the development of digital museums must be a symbiosis between technological development and advances in culture; also, a correct strategy to become "digital" cannot be based on a logic of thinking about the immediate, but on a focus on long-term aspirations.

In the field of museum studies, the trends towards adaptation to digital innovations as well as the difficulties arising from such adaptations have been debated and addressed by many researchers. Interestingly, museums digital transformation has been the object of national enquiries, diagnoses, aiming at creating and designing national strategies, and implementation plans, accompanied at times by policies and legislations. For example, the Agenda 2026: Study on the Future of the Dutch Museum Sector, Meijer, Weide and Krabshuis (2010) points to a future where, as well as in other fields of society, in the museum, "the divide between the real world and the virtual world will have been greatly blurred by developments such as augmented reality." And that the almost limitless availability and accessibility that the internet provides will create "opportunities to share knowledge and content" resulting in "new virtual productions and exhibitions with new forms of ownership, copyright, authenticity, public outreach and income" (p.12).

Likewise reports such as Digitization of the museum collections in Bulgaria: Standards and Practices Sotirova (2011); the Rapport de la Mission Musées du XXIe Siècle, Eidelman (2017) in France; and the Culture is Digital in the United Kingdom by the Department for Digital, Culture, Media and Sport (2018) address the use of technologies, not as much as a goal, but as important digital tools, which potentiate museums to fulfill their mission of providing access to and preservation of cultural heritage and art pieces, and to transform digitally, when considering the new digital born generations.

In the field of cultural learning, in [7] is presented a [2] and meta-analysis is presented on the contexts of use of AR and VR technologies to aid learning in museums, design elements of how AR and VR are incorporated into learning activities and what effects arise from learning assisted by AR/VR in museums. In the child-group museum visits, [8] focuses on how technology can be used to improve the visitor experience of museum exhibits and how visitors can be provided with means of interacting with exhibits, supporting interactivity but at the same time analyzing the impact on the attention of exhibition users and the possible decrease of their attention and of the interactions with other visitors.

Currently the uses of technologies are transversal to all areas of work in the museum, from management, to communication, education, exhibition, collections archiving and public interaction; and in this sense, the challenges are multiple. A recent study Structuring for Digital Success: A Global Survey of How Museums and Other Cultural Organizations Resource, Fund, and Structure their Digital Teams and Activity, Price and Dafydd 82018) has concluded that most museums are far from reaching "digital maturity". The authors have found through this survey that there are a wide variety of challenges that museums face, when moving towards digital transformation and implementing the use of technologies. They have found the lack of resources, such as human, financial and technological, are the main factors which put museums at different levels of digital evolution.

In Portugal, a survey which concludes with similar findings has also been done. The research project developed as part of the Mu.SA– Museum Sector Alliance Project (a partnership of 11 institutions based on three countries – Portugal, Greece, and Italy) which also attempted at describing the current relationship between museums and technologies. Carvalho and Matos (2019) found that technology integration in museums, particularly in exhibitions, is very complex and at an early stage of implementation for most museums surveyed. They have also found from the answers of museum professionals to the survey, that the most common issues related to the use of technologies are related to: complex and expensive maintenance of hard and software and low digital literacy levels of both the public and museum professionals. On the other hand, the authors point out that there is a growing demand for technological interactivity in the museum and that these tools are perceived to have great potential to enhance the visitors' experience.

As a field of research that needs to be explored and is lacking in the Portuguese context, the authors point out the evaluation of the impact that technologies already implemented have in museums. From the survey, the authors were able to identify three main areas of impact of technologies in the museum: collections management, communication (internal and external) and exhibitions. Finding that the museum sector in Portugal is struggling especially with the digitization of collections, the use of the web for communication (websites, social media, online virtual tours, etc.). They also defend that in depth, and case studies are fundamental to begin to grasp the entirety of technologies being used and the future trends. Another author, Macedo (2014) found that, in 2014, just 7,5% of museums (based on 109 answers collected) used applications. They also defend that in depth research and case studies are fundamental to begin to grasp the entirety of technologies being used and the future trends, and as we will see by the following bibliometric analysis, the use of technologies in museums has been evolving greatly as a hot research topic for the past decade.

3   Materials and Methods

Bibliometric citation analysis is a well-established form of meta analytical research [9–12]. It is known as the use of statistical methods for quantitative evaluation of scientific articles and other published works, revealing patterns of publication, suchs as productivity, collaboration, impact and trends. Bibliometric citation analysis was first used in sciences and humanities [13], but rapidly adopted by other areas such as economy [14] and management [15]. Nowadays it is used to understand the current trend, future directions and authors collaboration, among others in the most diverse research areas [16]. As the focus of our study is to shed light on the research stream of the adoption of technologies in museums, bibliometric citation analysis is an appropriate meta-analytic approach.

For this study, we collected data from one of the best-known academic databases, Web of Science (WoS), which includes the Social Sciences Citation Index (SSCI). Because it is multidisciplinary, the WoS database allows a broad view of what has been published in the various areas of science. The bibliometric analysis was performed by importing the data into the Bibliometrix 3.1 in R 4.1.1 software and the results were visualized through the Bibliophily application, which will be shown in the next sections. Bibliometrix package can provide various routines for importing bibliographic data from several scientific databases, performing bibliometric analysis, and building data matrices for co-citation, coupling, scientific collaboration analysis, and co-word analysis [17].

We searched for publications from the last ten years, from January 2011 to September 2021. Although the Web of Science presents query results from 1991 onwards, due to the recent evolution of technologies, a 10-year interval, seemed adequate, to evaluate the use of technologies.

Data was collected from the WOS database using the advanced search interface. A search was performed using the terms "technologies", "museums" and "visitor" in the title or abstract of the publication. In total, 1302 publications were counted. A filter was later used to refine the search and include only articles (473), proceedings papers (551) and early access (24). The result was a total of 1045 publications in the English language, which we then analyze as follows.

4 Findings

4.1 Documents

The chart in Fig. 1(a), shows the growth of the number of publications published annually, in which the highest annual growth was between 2012 and 2013 with a growth of 76%, and the maximum number of articles published in a year occurs in 2018, with 138 publications. In the last 3 years there was a small decrease in the number of annual publications (we believe that the number of publications for the year 2021 will increase, as there will be works from this year yet to be published). In addition, the number of the average article citations per year Fig. 1(b), shows that the average number of citations has remained stable over the years.

Table 1 presents the publications with the highest number of citations [18] investigated a multimedia approach to the diffusion, communication, and exploitation of Cultural Heritage using augmented, virtual, and mixed-reality technologies for different purposes, including education, exhibition enhancement, exploration, reconstruction, and virtual museums [19] presents an indoor location-aware system able to enhance the user experience in a museum.

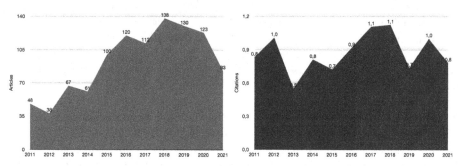

Fig. 1. (a) Annual scientific production, and (b) average citations per year.

Using wearable devices that combine image recognition and location capabilities the system automatically provides cultural contents related to the observed artworks to the users. In [20] the authors hypothesized that museum visitors acquire more knowledge from augmented exhibits than from exhibits without AR. The results showed that the visitors performed significantly better on knowledge acquisition and retention tests related to augmented exhibits than to non-augmented exhibits and that they perceived AR as a valuable and desirable add-on for museum exhibitions [21]. A survey of studies carried out on the personalization of cultural heritage information is carried out, including the evolution of personalization techniques on websites, virtual collections and mobile guides, to the recent extension of cultural heritage to the semantic and social web. [22]. A study on science learning in informal environments and through the use of digital technologies is presented [23]. The authors present a study to explore the perceived value of the implementation of AR within the museum context using a stakeholder approach [24] the authors attempt to examine the impact of information type and augmenting immersive scenes on visitors' evaluation of the AR-facilitated museum experience and their subsequent purchase intentions [25]. Using the London museum as

Table 1. Top 10 publications by number of citations (right)

Publication	Total citations
[18]	127
[19]	125
[20]	109
[21]	109
[22]	93
[23]	71
[24]	68
[25]	65
[26]	60
[27]	57

a study site, the authors investigate the use of social and mobile technologies in-school field trips to enhance the visitor experience [26] the work identifies variables and proposes a research model that plays a role and online behaviors in a specific experiential environment, namely the high culture museum website. In [27] the authors attempt to categorize electronic mobile guides using a detailed set of evaluation criteria in order to extract design principles that can be used by application designers and developers.

4.2 Sources

A total of 1045 publications were found in the period of 2011–2021, which present a wide range of scientific topics. Figure 2a shows the top 10 sources, which had 104 publications, thus comprising about 10% of all 1045 publications. The top 3 sources with more publications were: ACM Journal on Computing and Cultural Heritage (JOCCH), followed by the Museum Management and Curatorship journal and the Curator: The Museum Journal. Figure 2b shows the most local cited sources, the most cited source was the journal Lecture Notes In Computer Science with 17% citations of the total citations of the top 10 most cited sources. The following two were the Museum Management and Curatorship journal, and the Curator: The Museum journal. Figure 2c shows the most local impact coming firstly from the ACM Journal on Computing and Cultural Heritage (JOCCH), followed by Curator: The Museum Journal and the Personal, and, in third, by the Ubiquitous computing journal.

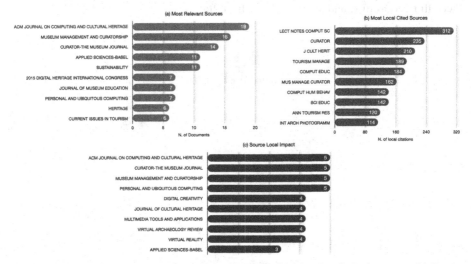

Fig. 2. Analysis of sources. (a) Most relevant sources; (b) Most local cited sources, (c) Source local impact by H-index.

4.3 Authors

Figure 3A shows the top 10 most relevant authors based on the number of articles they published. In terms of the number of publications Piccialli F. was the most productive author, with 9 publications, followed by Chianese A. and Kuflik T. with 8 publications. In terms of citations in this field (Fig. 3b), Pierdicca R. was ranked first (36 citations), followed by Frontoni E. (35 citations) and Kuflik T. (30 citations). In terms of author local impact (Fig. 3c) Kuflik T. is the author with the higher individual's scientific research output and measure his citation impact (6), followed by Chianese A. and Piccialli F. both with H-Index of 5.

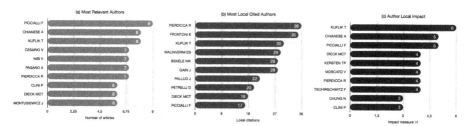

Fig. 3. Author analysis. (a) Most relevant authors; (b) Most local cited authors, (c) Author local impact by H-index.

Figure 4, shows the authors network collaboration, and our findings suggest that collaboration networks between authors are mostly between authors from the same country. For example the largest authors collaboration cluster is between Chianese A., Piccialli F., Marulli F. and Moscato V. all from Italy.

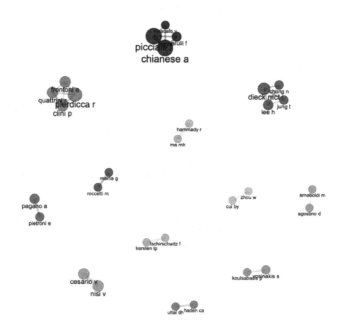

Fig. 4. Author collaboration network.

4.4 Countries

The search returned a total of 82 countries. The USA was the most productive country with a total of 315 publications, followed by Italy (262) and the United Kingdom (225). Italy takes the first place when it comes to most cited countries, with a total of 864 citations exchanging positions with the USA (766) followed by the United Kingdom (526). The cooperative relationship among these countries is demonstrated in Fig. 5. The thickness of the lines indicates the strength of the relationship. The United States (USA) and Italy and the United Kingdom show similar importance to global cooperation. Meanwhile, the UK is the one with the most collaborations with other countries.

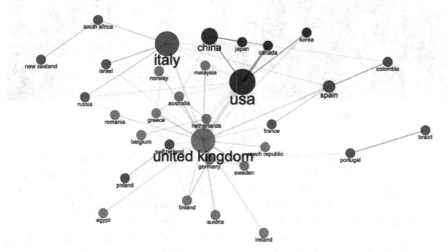

Fig. 5. Country collaboration network.

4.5 Words Co-occurrence

The TreeMap in Fig. 6 highlights the combination of possible keywords, representing museums and technologies, joining the terms "museums" and "museum", this will be the term most frequently used, followed by the term "augmented reality" and "cultural heritage". While the first corresponds exactly to the term used in the research, the terms augmented reality, virtual reality, gamification, user experience, mixed reality, suggest technologies and themes addressed in the research publications.

Figure 7 represents the search trends based on the keywords analyzed. "ubiquitous computing" is the oldest term and also the most discussed term over time (2011–2018). "ubiquitous computing" describes the ubiquity of information technology in people's daily lives without them noticing its presence [28]. Terms such as "mobile devices", "social media" and "human-computer interaction" are also topics discussed during longer periods of time. The most frequently used terms are concentrated in the year 2018. The terms "museums", "cultural heritage", "augmented reality" and "virtual reality" are the most prominent, suggesting that, between the years 2016 and 2019, research was

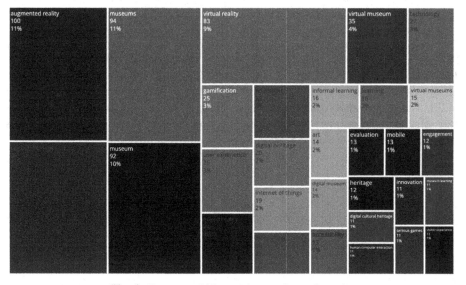

Fig. 6. Treemap of 30 most frequently used words.

focused on exploring the use of these technologies in museums. These results also suggest changes of focus of the research throughout the years, on different technologies, with epicenters in the following years and technologies: in 2013 the "rfid"; 2014 "mobile devices", in 2018 "augmented reality" and "virtual reality"; 2019 "mixed reality", "3d scanning" and "linked data"; in 2020 "artificial intelligence" and in 2021 "3d printing".

In Fig. 7 it's possible to identify current topics and future directions in the investigation of the use of technologies in the context of museums, such as:

– Accessibility: Using technologies to overcome the communication barrier during a visit to a museum has been the subject of reflection and study in several works in recent years [29–32].
– Artificial intelligence (AI): The use of artificial intelligence in museums is vast. In [33] a virtual assistant using AI is proposed; in [34] it is used to determine the popularity of an exhibit space; in [35] AI is used to support visitors towards a better understanding of art contexts.
– Linked data: The emerging Internet of Things (IoT) allows the collection of large volumes of data on how a visitor makes a certain visit. This data can be used to understand the visitor's interests, propose new experiences with the aim of improving the visit [36, 37].
– 3d scanning and 3d printing: With these technologies, creation and replication of art pieces reaches a whole new level of access and ease of use. Cultural heritage domains have started to adopt 3d scanning and 3d printing technologies to improve their visitors' user experience within various museum exhibitions [30, 38, 39].

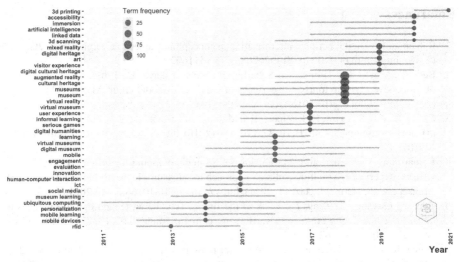

Fig. 7. Top trend topics during the period.

5 Conclusion

In the last decade we have seen an increasing integration of the use of technology in museums and there is no doubt that recent advances in digital tools have become one of the central aspects of any museum experience. Touch devices, audio guides, augmented and virtual reality, beacons, just to name a few, have the ability to enrich the visit experience, offering new levels of visit - more immersive, more personalized and richer in content.

In this paper we have drawn scientific maps of documents, sources, authors, countries, and co-occurrence of keywords to determine trend topics in this field. Our results indicate that the number of publications on technologies in museums has consistently increased in the last 10 years. The USA and Italy are the biggest contributors to the research in the topics of analysis in this article. The ACM Journal on Computing and Cultural Heritage (JOCCH) is the largest and also the most impactful source; Kuflik T is the researcher with the greatest impact in this field. Research trends in terms of technologies are "mixed reality", "artificial intelligence", "data linked", "3D scanning", and "3D printing. Our results also suggest research trends in "accessibility", "immersion", and "visitor experience".

Acknowledgments. This work has been supported by FCT—Fundação para a Ciência e Tecnologia within the Project Scope: UIDB/05757/2020.

References

1. Rahaman, H.: Digital heritage interpretation: a conceptual framework. Digit. Creat. **29**, 1–27 (2018). https://doi.org/10.1080/14626268.2018.1511602
2. Bec, A., Moyle, B., Timms, K., Schaffer, V., Skavronskaya, L., Little, C.: Management of immersive heritage tourism experiencs: a conceptual model. Tour. Manag. **72**, 117–120 (2019). https://doi.org/10.1016/j.tourman.2018.10.033
3. Ch'ng, E., Cai, S., Leow, F.-T., Zhang, E.: Adoption and use of emerging cultural technologies in China's museums. J. Cult. Herit. **37**, 170–180 (2018). https://doi.org/10.1016/j.culher.2018.11.016
4. Kamariotou, V., Kamariotou, M., Kitsios, F.: Strategic planning for virtual exhibitions and visitors' experience: a multidisciplinary approach for museums in the digital age. Digit. Appl. Archaeol. Cult. Herit. **21**, e00183 (2021). https://doi.org/10.1016/j.daach.2021.e00183
5. Tim, Y., Ouyang, T., Zeng, D.: Back to the future: actualizing technology affordances to transform emperor Qin's terracotta warriors museum. Inf. Manage. **57**, 103271 (2020). https://doi.org/10.1016/j.im.2020.103271
6. Leopardi, A., et al.: X-reality technologies for museums: a comparative evaluation based on presence and visitors experience through user studies. J. Cult. Herit. **47**, 188–198 (2021). https://doi.org/10.1016/j.culher.2020.10.005
7. Zhou, Y., Chen, J., Wang, M.: A meta-analytic review on incorporating virtual and augmented reality in museum learning. Educ. Res. Rev. **36**, 100454 (2022). https://doi.org/10.1016/j.edurev.2022.100454
8. Kotut, L., et al.: Supporting child–group interactions with hands-off museum exhibit. Int. J. Child-Comput. Interact. **27**, 100240 (2021). https://doi.org/10.1016/j.ijcci.2020.100240
9. Donohue, J.C.: A bibliometric analysis of certain information science literature. J. Am. Soc. Inf. Sci. **23**, 313–317 (1972). https://doi.org/10.1002/asi.4630230506
10. Garfield, E.: How to use citation analysis for faculty evaluations, and when is it relevant? Part 1. Curr. Contents **44**, 5–13 (1983)
11. Magyar, G.: Bibliometric analysis of a new research sub-field. J. Doc. **30**, 32–40 (1974). https://doi.org/10.1108/eb026568
12. Saracevic, T., Perk, L.J.: Ascertaining activities in a subject area through bibliometric analysis. application to library literature. J. Am. Soc. Inf. Sci. **24**, 120–134 (1973). https://doi.org/10.1002/asi.4630240207
13. Windsor, D.A.: Could bibliometric data be used to predict the clinical success of drugs? J. Doc. **32**, 174–181 (1976). https://doi.org/10.1108/eb026623
14. Leeebvre, V.M., Fetterman, N.I.: Bibliometric analysis of the journal of consumer studies and home economics, 1977–1983. J. Consum. Stud. Home Econ. **9**, 11–22 (1985). https://doi.org/10.1111/j.1470-6431.1985.tb00437.x
15. Culnan, M.J., Swanson, E.B.: Research in management information systems, 1980–1984: Points of work and reference. MIS Q. Manag. Inf. Syst. **10**, 289–301 (1986). https://doi.org/10.2307/249263
16. Sousa, J.P., Cordeiro, P.A.N., Carvalho, A.: Video games and cultural heritage: a bibliometric analysis of scientific production in the scopus database. In: Proceedings 37th IBIMA Conference. Cordoba, Spain (2021)
17. Aria, M.: Bibliometrix R package. https://www.bibliometrix.org
18. Bekele, M.K., Pierdicca, R., Frontoni, E., Malinverni, E.S., Gain, J.: A survey of augmented, virtual, and mixed reality for cultural heritage. ACM J. Comput. Cult. Herit. **11**(2), 1-36 (2018). https://doi.org/10.1145/3145534
19. Alletto, S., et al.: An indoor location-aware system for an IoT-based smart museum. IEEE Internet Things J. **3**, 244–253 (2016). https://doi.org/10.1109/JIOT.2015.2506258

20. Sommerauer, P., Mueller, O.: Augmented reality in informal learning environments: a field experiment in a mathematics exhibition. Comput. Educ. **79**, 59–68 (2014). https://doi.org/10.1016/j.compedu.2014.07.013

21. Ardissono, L., Kuflik, T., Petrelli, D.: Personalization in cultural heritage: the road travelled and the one ahead. USER Model. USER-Adapt. Interact. **22**, 73–99 (2012). https://doi.org/10.1007/s11257-011-9104-x

22. Yoon, S.A., Elinich, K., Wang, J., Steinmeier, C., Tucker, S.: Using augmented reality and knowledge-building scaffolds to improve learning in a science museum. Int. J. Comput.-Support. Collab. Learn. **7**, 519–541 (2012). https://doi.org/10.1007/s11412-012-9156-x

23. Dieck, M.C.T., Jung, T.H.: Value of augmented reality at cultural heritage sites: a stakeholder approach. J. Destin. Mark. Manag. **6**, 110–117 (2017). https://doi.org/10.1016/j.jdmm.2017.03.002

24. He, Z., Wu, L., Li, X.: (Robert): when art meets tech: the role of augmented reality in enhancing museum experiences and purchase intentions. Tour. Manag. **68**, 127–139 (2018). https://doi.org/10.1016/j.tourman.2018.03.003

25. Charitonos, K., Blake, C., Scanlon, E., Jones, A.: Museum learning via social and mobile technologies: (how) can online interactions enhance the visitor experience? Br. J. Educ. Technol. **43**, 802–819 (2012). https://doi.org/10.1111/j.1467-8535.2012.01360.x

26. Pallud, J., Straub, D.W.: Effective website design for experience-influenced environments: the case of high culture museums. Inf. Manage. **51**, 359–373 (2014). https://doi.org/10.1016/j.im.2014.02.010

27. Kenteris, M., Gavalas, D., Economou, D.: Electronic mobile guides: a survey. Pers. Ubiquitous Comput. **15**, 97–111 (2011). https://doi.org/10.1007/s00779-010-0295-7

28. Weiser, M.: The computer for the 21st century. Sigmobile Mob Comput Commun Rev. **3**, 3–11 (1999). https://doi.org/10.1145/329124.329126

29. Carrizosa, H.G., Sheehy, K., Rix, J., Seale, J., Hayhoe, S.: Designing technologies for museums: accessibility and participation issues. J. Enabling Technol. **14**, 31–39 (2020). https://doi.org/10.1108/JET-08-2019-0038

30. Clary, K.S., Dillian, C.: Printing the past building accessibility and engagement through 3-D technologies. Publ. Hist. **43**, 41–62 (2021). https://doi.org/10.1525/tph.2021.43.2.41

31. Gomes, B.C.G.L., de S., Romani, E., Souza, A.C.P., Liberalino, I.R. de M.: Communicational accessibility on science museums: considerations on assistive technology. Humanidades Inovacao. **8**, 261–272 (2021)

32. Pietroni, E., Pagano, A., Biocca, L., Frassineti, G.: Accessibility, natural user interfaces and interactions in museums: the intarsi project. Heritage **4**, 567–584 (2021). https://doi.org/10.3390/heritage4020034

33. Duguleana, M., Briciu, V.-A., Duduman, I.-A., Machidon, O.M.: A virtual assistant for natural interactions in museums. Sustainability. **12**(17), 6958 (2020). https://doi.org/10.3390/su12176958

34. Tanwar, G., Chauhan, R., Yafi, E.: Artycul: A privacy-preserving ML-driven framework to determine the popularity of a cultural exhibit on display. Sensors. **21**(4), 1527 (2021). https://doi.org/10.3390/s21041527

35. Raptis, G.E., Kavvetsos, G., Katsini, C.: MuMIA: Multimodal interactions to better understand art contexts. Appl. Sci.-Basel. **11**(6), 2695 (2021). https://doi.org/10.3390/app11062695

36. Cossu, S.: Labours of love and convenience: dealing with community-supported knowledge in museums. Publications. **7**(1), 19 (2019). https://doi.org/10.3390/publications7010019

37. López-Martínez, A., Carrera, Á., Iglesias, C.A.: Empowering museum experiences applying gamification techniques based on linked data and smart objects. Appl. Sci. **10**(16), 5419 (2020). https://doi.org/10.3390/app10165419

38. Comes, R., Grec, C., Neamtu, C., Gazdac, C., Mateescu-Suciu, L.: intangible heritage?...not anymore from photo to 3D printed cultural heritage assets replicas the two missing iron discs from the dacian hillfort of piatra rosie (Romania). J. Anc. Hist. Archaeol. **8**, 134–143 (2021). https://doi.org/10.14795/j.v8i1.622
39. Cooper, C.: You can handle it: 3D printing for museums. Adv. Archaeol. Pract. **7**, 443–447 (2019). https://doi.org/10.1017/aap.2019.39

Smart Technologies in Tourist Destination Marketing: A Literature Review

Ângela Junqueiro[1], Ricardo Correia[1,2](✉) ⓘ, Aida Carvalho[1,2] ⓘ,
and Carlos R. Cunha[1,3] ⓘ

[1] Instituto Politécnico de Bragança, Campus de Santa Apolónia, 5300-253 Bragança, Portugal
a46054@alunos.ipb.pt, {ricardocorreia,acarvalho,crc}@ipb.pt
[2] CiTUR Guarda - Centro de Investigação, Desenvolvimento e Inovação em Turismo, Instituto Politécnico de Bragança, Campus de Santa Apolónia, 5300-253 Bragança, Portugal
[3] UNIAG and CeDRI, Instituto Politécnico de Bragança, Campus de Santa Apolónia, 5300-253 Bragança, Portugal

Abstract. In the digital age in which we live, smart technologies are omnipresent no matter the industry we consider. The tourism sector challenged by constant technological and digital innovations and trying to reinvent itself after the pandemics is more than ever relying on smart technologies to improve the value for companies and tourists. With this reality as background the main objective of this work is to analyze the contribution of smart technologies in the marketing of tourist destinations. For that and using the Scopus database, a search was carried out in the most recent scientific literature concerning this matter, in which the articles were studied with the aim of obtaining the most updated theoretical contributions in this area. The results obtained will allow the marketing organizations of tourist destinations understand the importance of the application of intelligent technologies in the tourist attractiveness of their territories.

Keywords: Smart technologies · Marketing · Tourism · Tourist Destinations · Scopus

1 Introduction

In the increasingly digital world in which we live, Information and Communication Technologies (ICT) assume a relevant importance in our daily lives. In Portugal, according to data published in the Digital 2021 report: Portugal [1], in January 2021 there were more than 8 million internet users, of which more than 7 million used social networks, equivalent to 76,6% of the Portuguese population. Also in tourism, this theme is extremely important because from the research, the choice and decision to visit a particular tourist destination can be made online. Tourists, thanks to the technological tools they have at their disposal, seek to create their own experiences at every stage of their trip. The marketing of tourist destinations also has the internet and social networks at its disposal to influence the choices of online communities.

T. Guarda et al. (Eds.): ARTIIS 2022, CCIS 1676, pp. 283–293, 2022.
https://doi.org/10.1007/978-3-031-20316-9_22

More than ever, destinations need to develop innovative ideas in order to satisfy the growing needs of tourists and add value to their visit experience [2]. The increasing complexity of tourists and the development of technology and digitalization drive innovation in the tourism industry and create new types of relationships between stakeholders and tourists, emerging innovative solutions and strategies in terms of tourism marketing [3, 4], namely digital marketing [5].

Smart city initiatives have made it possible to create smart destinations by using ICT within the physical infrastructures of a given geographical border with the aim of increasing the competitiveness of the destination. This is only possible through the existence of networks of interconnected systems that will add value to all those involved in the process. It is these destinations, which are technologically smart, that will increase and sustain their long-term competitiveness in the market [6].

This theme is extremely important, so the European Commission developed Smart Tourism Destinations, an initiative that aims to support European Union cities by facilitating access to tourism products and services through technological innovation. The aim is for EU cities and destinations to learn how to implement innovative digital solutions to make tourism sustainable and accessible, taking full advantage of their cultural heritage and creativity to enhance the tourist experience [7].

Starting from a reflection on this theme, the question that served as the basis for this study was formulated: in the digital world we live in, what is the contribution of these new intelligent technologies in the marketing of tourist destinations?

Regarding the methodology adopted, a brief systematic review of the literature was carried out, in which several scientific articles were collected, consulted and analyzed according to criteria [8], that made it possible to carry out a theoretical framework based on and supported by the most recent investigations of this thematic.

In addition to this introduction, the article contains a literature review that is presented in two main sections: in the first, the theme of smart destinations and smart tourism will be addressed, while in the second, the importance of smart technologies in the marketing of tourist destinations will be analyzed. Next, the methodology adopted for the systematic literature review is presented, regarding the criteria used in the research and collection of documents. Finally, the main final considerations, as well as the references used.

2 Methodology

From the methodological point of view, a brief systematic review of the literature was carried out, which made it possible to collect data and its subsequent analysis, always taking into account the question formulated. For this purpose, some criteria were defined that, according to [8], enable the collection of data in a reliable and replicable way, making the literature review process scientific and transparent [9].

2.1 Data Collection Research Criteria

In the SCOPUS database, the terms smart technologies marketing tourism destination were defined as search criteria in the title, keywords and abstract. With this first search, 51 documents were obtained, which were submitted to a screening. Taking into account the type of document items, in which only articles were considered, the language, in which only documents written in English were chosen and the time period from 2019 to the present date, June 2022. Thus, only documents were considered for the novelty and current contributions they make. From this research update, 19 documents were collected and exported to Mendeley for further reading and analysis. As can be seen in Fig. 1, 17 articles resulting from the search and initial screening were considered eligible and included in the study. The exclusion of the remaining documents results from the reading of the respective articles and the verification that they would not be relevant because they are not related to the theme defined for this study.

Question:
What is the contribution of smart technologies in the marketing of tourist destinations?

Identification:
Documents identified in the SCOPUS database: smart technologies marketing tourism destination (n=51)

Screening:
Screening target documents in the SCOPUS database: time range: 2019-2022 document type: article language: English (n=19)

Eligibility and Inclusion:
Eligible and included documents (n=17)

Fig. 1. Document search and evaluation steps. Adapted from [8].

3 Literature Review

Considering the need to fully understand the relevance of smart technologies in Tourist destination marketing and already framed by the Scopus publications that fit the established research criteria a focused analysis to existing literature has been made.

3.1 From Smart Destinations to Smart Tourism

In [10] is consider that smart destinations have consolidated themselves as a new paradigm for management, based on governance, sustainability, accessibility, innovation and technology. The transformation of a destination into a smart destination implies an increase in competitiveness, an improvement in the efficiency of production and marketing processes, a boost to sustainable development, an improvement in the visitor experience and in the quality of life of residents and, ultimately, the economic revitalization of the territory.

Thanks to the rapid and growing evolution of technology, cities and destinations are evolving and becoming smart, applying ICT to achieve resource savings, sustainable development and improved quality of life for residents, while also generating added value and better experiences for tourists.

ICT adopted by smart cities facilitate access to information and services for both tourists and residents, fostering the emergence of smart tourist destinations [11]. In fact, smart destinations consider both residents and tourists in their effort to support mobility, resource availability, sustainability and quality of life and visits. Therefore, this evolution of cities and destinations also requires a change in their brand, being a dynamic process in constant evolution, cities and destinations must include these smart features in their brand, integrating technological infrastructures and end-user devices, with the aim of provide a more satisfying experience for residents and tourists.

Technological evolution has made it possible to maintain the exchange of personalized and real-time information with citizens and tourists, while at the same time collecting large amounts of information to offer them even more personalized services. It is this interactivity between users and technology that co-creates added value for citizens and tourists, generating the most satisfying experiences and co-creating the image of the city and the tourist destination. These are key factors in attracting residents, tourists and wealth to the territory. For this reason, cities and tourist destinations have to communicate strategically, seeking to generate a positive image. As residents and tourists have a better image of the city and the destination, because they generate expectations of greater innovation, greater interactivity and participation as well as more satisfying tourist experiences, it is necessary to communicate this sustainability and its intelligence through brands to generate a better image.

Smart destinations can refer to urban or rural areas and consider not only residents but tourists as well. However, the intelligence of tourist destinations cannot be conditioned exclusively by technological availability, given that a strategy shared by all the actors in the destination will be essential to take full advantage of the opportunities generated by technological evolution, with solutions adapted to each territorial and tourist context [11]. In the case of destinations where there is a problem of over-tourism, for example, in [12] is warn of tensions between residents and tourists who use the same infrastructure and urban spaces.

According to [13] smart tourism is a management structure that combines tourism infrastructure with ICT tools with the aim of increasing destination and business efficiency, as well as tourist experiences. In this sense, smart technologies are tools that can contribute to meeting tourists' needs and expectations, if properly designed. These technologies can be used by tourism providers and tourist attractions to make presentations of value propositions more persuasive and visually appealing and to provide an enjoyable and memorable visit experience. Likewise, smart technologies constitute a valuable marketing tool that should not be underestimated. Smart tourism thus refers to a form of tourism development that takes advantage of innovations advanced technologies to achieve sustainable development goals.

3.2 Smart Technologies and Destination Marketing

According to [14], technological innovations have completely revolutionized the tourism industry and currently determine the strategy and competitiveness of tourist organizations and destinations. This author defends the disruptive nature of technology in tourism in which intelligent environments (AmI) transform industry structures, processes and practices, with disruptive impacts on service innovation, strategy, management, marketing and competitiveness of all parties involved. Thus, with the arrival of Artificial Intelligence (AI) in tourist destination systems, new methods for data analysis, data sharing and data compilation in the area of tourism have emerged.

The integration of this Big Data in the marketing of tourist destinations improves their management, supports interoperability, stimulates creativity and innovation and encourages collaboration across the internet. Smart tourism emerges to provide the informatics structure necessary for the co-creation of value in which AI takes advantage of the interconnectivity and interoperability of integrated technologies [15], with data being worked on to produce innovative services, products and procedures, ensuring the maximization of stakeholder value.

Smart solutions include but are not limited to public wireless networks, big data analytics tools, smart dashboards, advanced destination marketing organizations websites and blogs, QR codes and geotags, virtual reality (VR) and augmented reality (AR), chatbots, social media actions, destination applications, drones, as can be seen in Fig. 2. It is the combination of all these intelligent technologies that results in a better experience and optimized destination management [16]. All these technologies create a computing framework and an intelligent digital network that support real-time service across multiple platforms, enabling value co-creation for all stakeholders.

The development of smartphones and mobile devices has also changed the way people communicate, interact and mediate the tourist experience, enhancing interactions in real time, when consumers are willing to engage with destinations [17]. The here and now reflects performance agility for real-time, data-driven, consumer-centric and experience-centric co-creation. Thus, both collective performance and competitiveness are optimized, which allows for agile solutions to be generated and added value for all those involved in tourism in a given destination, from suppliers and intermediaries, the public and private sector to consumers.

According to [18], AI mimics human intelligence, allowing computers to perform a job similar to that performed by humans, but improving their efficiency, as we can currently see in the tourism industry, namely in hotels, airlines, restaurants and attractions. New technologies in the field of AI such as facial recognition, VR and robots are useful in providing new experiences to tourists.

As tourism, through tourists, produces large amounts of data, the adoption of AI in tourism marketing is absolutely crucial as the study of data dynamically and in real time will facilitate marketing to generate instant co-creation of value. The automation of real-time measurement and interpretation of large amounts of tourist data linked to specific travel motivations will be the future, which necessarily implies the use of Big Data in the marketing of smart destinations. These authors found that photographs have been widely used to promote destinations online, and their data constitute big content data, Big Data, a trend in tourism marketing.

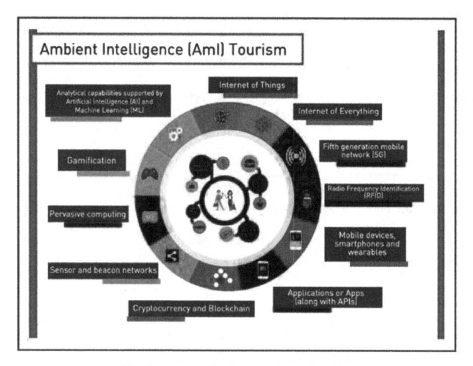

Fig. 2. Intelligent Environment in Tourism, [14].

Constant innovations in the area of ICT have made it possible to increase the capacity for storing data and processing it, as well as increasing the availability of large volumes of data in the area of tourism. These Big Data in tourism are extremely important for the management of smart destinations as they provide information that can support tourism planning as well as decision making. All data disclosed online can be used by marketing, as they provide information anytime and anywhere and have the potential to influence the entire travel process, before, during and after the same, from planning, booking, experience and sharing. Thus, tourism experiences supported by technological innovations increasingly help tourists to co-create value at all stages of the trip. The authors also highlight the fact that Big Data research materials in tourism include textual content and multimedia content (images, videos, audio) from a wide range of sources (social media, for example) that increasingly originate from users.

For [19], from a marketing perspective, social media is a fundamental tool in tourism promotion, both for tourism companies and the public sector, by creating a direct relationship between destinations and tourists. Social media allows marketers to spark conversation and encourage interaction, thereby increasing consumer engagement, sharing, collaboration and positive Electronic Word of Mouth (eWOM).

Social media platforms are efficient in promoting cities, allowing interactions with stakeholders, residents and tourists and creating positive images of places. Its enormous potential to allow the active participation of users and the creation of content generated by them, as well as technological advances, has increased the power of influence of stakeholders in the formation of smart destinations. If social networks allow communication and strategies for creating destination brands and the co-creation of their image, making smart destinations more attractive to tourists, on the other hand, social networks are technological tools that allow tourists to participate in the co-creation of tourist experiences, In [19] is argued that tourism marketing is one of the business functions most affected by the technological revolution because smart technologies can support tourism businesses to develop a knowledge base and improve their marketing functions.

According to these authors, many tourism companies in China have established mechanisms in recent years that combine traditional channels (radio, television, text messages and multimedia) and new marketing channels (Internet, networks, computers, smartphones and digital televisions). As a digital marketing tool, the Internet has become a powerful complement in helping tourism companies stay in touch with global customers, being able to reach customers more effectively, thus reducing marketing costs and improving total revenue, offering destinations a variety of new channels (portals and virtual travel communities) to promote tourism-related information. As in other destinations, the study shows that China's tourism market has seen a huge increase in demand for travel information through online channels, so Big Data analysis can provide tourism companies with accurate information about customers from the of stay, tourist motivation, consumption level and tourist preferences. This is information that can be used by hotels, travel agencies, airlines and electronic intermediaries to create intelligent marketing platforms that allow tourism companies to precisely select the target market and implement the corresponding strategy according to the characteristics of each market segment.

Also [20], in the study carried out on the impact of VR and AR technology on the tourist experience in cultural destinations, argue that the growing offer of these technologies applied to the tourism sector should encourage entrepreneurs to innovate in the tourism sector to meet the desire of tourists to have a memorable tourist experience. Marketing organizations in these destinations must position and promote themselves as capable of providing a quality tourist experience combined with new technologies. According to these authors, the demand of these technological resources by tourists increases as a greater number of them are used to the use of new technologies, and tourism agents can take advantage of the technological needs of the tourists themselves and thus provide quality experiences to these tourists.

A high level of quality experience can provide a good destination image and should be used by marketing organizations to help with their market positioning. For [21], a brand with a good attitude, that establishes a strong relationship with consumers and that manages to create an emotional attachment with the customer, can build the foundations of their loyalty. Starting from the need to find effective and efficient promotional tools for the development of marketing strategies for potential tourist destinations in Indonesia [22], developed a study based on a tourist information system using VR technology on android mobile devices.

These authors consider that this is a useful tool to help travelers to obtain tourist information quickly and easily, and can become a means for the sustainable development of tourism in this country. The study by [23], on the impact that the use of AR games, which take place in specific destinations, has on the intentions of visiting the destination in question, confirms that it can positively affect visit intentions. According to [24], many cities try to position themselves in the market using themes that characterize them, whether through their natural, cultural characteristics or specific experiences they can provide to those who visit them.

The success of this thematic positioning is determined by the characteristics of the place and the responses of residents and tourists, as they generally co-produce and consume common resources and infrastructure. The connection between city branding and smart tourist destinations opens up opportunities that allow cities to be more competitive, as intelligence and innovation can span a wide range of attractions, products and services in the tourism industry. Thus, the characteristics of tourists (demand and travel experience), industry (stakeholders) and destinations (places and ICT infrastructure) must be considered.

The development of online information sources, social media and user-generated content have an important influence on tourists' perception and expectations of destinations [19]. Sharing infrastructure and other resources within a smart city benefits the experiences and quality of life of residents and visitors. However, the development of tourist destinations should not be based only on technological innovations. In [25], is argued that creativity is crucial in strategies for creating smart destinations brands. These destinations must encompass the human and social dimensions, and the relationship between creativity and innovation can enrich and improve the notion of intelligence applied to cities and destinations. To this end, it is necessary to ensure competitiveness through the relationship between hard intelligence (physical infrastructure) and soft intelligence (human capital, social capital, innovation and leadership).

This relationship is fundamental because only by taking advantage of smart technology, Big Data and knowledge sharing can innovation and sustainability in tourism services be promoted. Also according to these authors, intellectual capital can influence radical and incremental innovations in this sector and has positive implications for social capital and vice versa.

Smart destinations represent the context in which residents and tourists can generate ideas, solutions and creative and innovative services thanks to the availability of physical and digital infrastructures that allow people to connect and exchange information and knowledge in a collaborative environment. With the support of ICT embedded in local infrastructure, key people-centric intelligence components (human capital, social capital, entrepreneurship and innovation) can improve the relationship between the destination brand and target tourists as well as residents.

4   Conclusion and Final Remarks

The smart city concept has fostered the development of tourist destinations that, by sharing their smart infrastructures, provide experiences and quality of life for both tourists and residents [26]. A smart tourist destination must be especially enabled for the use of ICTs, designed to improve competitiveness and sustainability from the interconnection and exchange of information between people, companies, institutions, infrastructure, energy, consumption and the different services and spaces that comprise the smart environment, whether urban or rural [27].

Overall is accepted the notion of a future where all the information collected is measured, processed and analyzed in order to improve the use and efficiency of the resources and services that are provided, thus contributing to the most appropriate decision-making by the tourist consumer in relation to a destination that can provide a memorable tourist experience [28].

ICT thus play a fundamental role in tourism, providing benefits such as the improvement of tourist experiences, the co-creation of value and the promotion of marketing, increasingly digital, where online and offline environments are combined. In recent years, the planning and management of tourism through smart destinations has aroused great interest by including the dimensions of governance, sustainability, accessibility, innovation and technology [10]. Technological innovations and the revolution they caused in tourism [14], along with creativity [25], lay the foundations for new tourist experiences, which implies the definition of a destination evaluation strategy, which will help to enhance competitive advantage by making the best use of the destination strengths, creating innovative resources, improving the efficiency of production processes and distribution in order to facilitate the integration of tourists in the destination.

ICTs are a key factor in the transformation of the tourism industry, contributing to city and destination management through smart technologies, thus aligning with smart model approaches. In this context, the spread of smartphones and their different applications also plays an important role. It is essential to be able to capture tourism-related data and data left by tourists visiting destinations, taking advantage of Big Data with a view to providing real-time and personalized services, leveraging them in order to optimize strategic management that contributes to improve the tourist experience at the destination [27].

Tourist destinations are thus increasingly challenged to discover new approaches to improve tourist experiences and adopt effective marketing strategies that allow them to build strong destination brands that enable them to achieve a differentiating and attractive positioning in the market [29]. In view of the objective defined for the realization of this paper, and given the question initially formulated, we can conclude that the contribution of smart technologies is fundamental in the marketing of tourist destinations, and their role is absolutely essential for their success.

The systematic literature review intends to provide a small theoretical contribution, in the sense that it brings together the most recent knowledge in the area of intelligent technologies at the service of the marketing of tourist destinations, having also contributed to expand the knowledge through the empirical research carried out. It is also hoped that this article can help marketing organizations of tourist destinations to understand the importance of smart technologies in the tourist attractiveness of their territories.

Understanding the latest research developments is a good way to understand the trend and how technologies can be leveraged for destination marketing.

The main limitation in carrying out this presented work is related to the fact that the importance of smart technologies in the sustainable development of villages and rural territories with low population density has not been given importance. Also, of bibliographic period, it is only reduced, analysis focusing on the research produced more recently. This fact, although it has the merit of showing the most recent trends in research in this field, could have presented different results if the period of bibliographic analysis had been extended.

This systematic literature review should therefore be seen as a basis for future investigations in the area of marketing these tourist destinations.

Acknowledgments. This paper is financed by national funds provided by FCT- Foundation for Science and Technology through project Ref. UIDB/04470/2020 CITUR.

References

1. Global digital population as of January 2021 2021. https://www.statista.com/statistics/617 136/digital-population-worldwide. Accessed 10 Feb 2022
2. Qumsieh-Mussalam, G., Tajeddini, K.: Innovation in Tourism Destination Marketing, in Tourism, pp. 165–174. Routledge, Hospitality and Digital Transformation (2019)
3. Bigné, E., Decrop, A.: paradoxes of postmodern tourists and innovation in tourism marketing. In: Fayos-Solà, E., Cooper, C. (eds.) The Future of Tourism. Springer, Cham, pp. 131–154 (2019). https://doi.org/10.1007/978-3-319-89941-1_7
4. Purchase, S., Volery, T.: Marketing innovation: a systematic review. J. Mark. Manag. **36**(9–10), 763–793 (2020)
5. Sánchez-Teba, E.M., García-Mestanza, J., Rodríguez-Fernández, M.: The application of the inbound marketing strategy on costa del sol planning & tourism board. lessons for post-covid-19 revival. Sustainability **12**(23), 9926 (2020)
6. Sorokina, E., Wang, Y., Fyall, A., Lugosi, P., Torres, E., Jung, T.: Constructing a smart destination framework: A destination marketing organization perspective. J. Destin. Mark. Manag. **23**, 100688 (2022)
7. Smart Tourism Destinations. 2022. https://smarttourismdestinations.eu. Accessed 03 Feb 2022
8. Xiao, Y., Watson, M.: Guidance on conducting a systematic literature review. J. Plan. Educ. Res. **39**(1), 93–112 (2019)
9. Tranfield, D., Denyer, D., Smart, P.: Towards a methodology for developing evidence-informed management knowledge by means of systematic review. Br. J. Manag. **14**(3), 207–222 (2003)
10. Sustacha, I., Baños-Pino, J.F., del Valle, E.: Research trends in technology in the context of smart destinations: a bibliometric analysis and network visualization. Cuad. Gestión **22**(1), 161–173 (2022)
11. Ivars-Baidal, J.A., Celdrán-Bernabeu, M.A., Mazón, J.-N., Perles-Ivars, Á.F.: Smart destinations and the evolution of ICTs: a new scenario for destination management? Curr. Issues Tour. **22**(13), 1581–1600 (2019)
12. Bouchon, F., Rauscher, M.: Cities and tourism, a love and hate story; towards a conceptual framework for urban overtourism management. Int. J. Tour. Cities (2019)

13. Shen, S., Sotiriadis, M., Zhang, Y.: The influence of smart technologies on customer journey in tourist attractions within the smart tourism management framework. Sustainability **12**(10), 4157 (2020)
14. Buhalis, D.: Technology in tourism-from information communication technologies to eTourism and smart tourism towards ambient intelligence tourism: a perspective article. Tour. Rev. (2019)
15. Lu, C.-W., Huang, J.-C., Chen, C., Shu, M.-H., Hsu, C.-W., Bapu, B.R.T.: An energy-efficient smart city for sustainable green tourism industry. Sustain. Energy Technol. Assess. **47**, 101494 (2021)
16. Femenia-Serra, F., Ivars-Baidal, J.A.: Do smart tourism destinations really work? the case of benidorm. Asia Pacific J. Tour. Res. **26**(4), 365–384 (2021)
17. Sharmin, F., Sultan, M.T., Badulescu, D., Badulescu, A., Borma, A., Li, B.: Sustainable destination marketing ecosystem through smartphone-based social media: the consumers' acceptance perspective. Sustainability **13**(4), 2308 (2021)
18. Wang, X., Zhen, F., Tang, J., Shen, L., Liu, D.: Applications, experiences, and challenges of smart tourism development in China. J. Urban Technol. 1–26 (2021)
19. Yuan, Y., Chan, C.-S., Eichelberger, S., Ma, H., Pikkemaat, B.: The effect of social media on travel planning process by Chinese tourists: the way forward to tourism futures. J. Tour. Futur. (2022)
20. González-Rodríguez, M.R., Díaz-Fernández, M.C., Pino-Mejías, M.Á.: The impact of virtual reality technology on tourists' experience: a textual data analysis. Soft. Comput. **24**(18), 13879–13892 (2020). https://doi.org/10.1007/s00500-020-04883-y
21. Mgiba, F.M.: The fourth industrial revolution, loyalty intentions and the mediating roles of reputation and pre-visit experiences for the Vilakazi street precinct in Soweto. Communitas **26**, 124–151 (2021)
22. Idris, I., et al.: Developing smart tourism using virtual reality as a tourism promotion strategy in Indonesia. Geo J. Tour. Geosites **35**(2), 332–337 (2021)
23. Lacka, E.: Assessing the impact of full-fledged location-based augmented reality games on tourism destination visits. Curr. Issues Tour. **23**(3), 345–357 (2020)
24. Chan, C.S., Peters, M., Pikkemaat, B.: Investigating visitors' perception of smart city dimensions for city branding in Hong Kong. Int. J. Tour. Cities **5**(4), 620–638 (2019)
25. Trinchini, L., Kolodii, N.A., Goncharova, N.A., Baggio, R.: Creativity, innovation and smartness in destination branding. Int. J. Tour. Cities (2019)
26. Huertas, A., Moreno, A., Pascual, J.: Place branding for smart cities and smart tourism destinations: do they communicate their smartness? Sustainability **13**(19), 10953 (2021)
27. Sigalat-Signes, E., Calvo-Palomares, R., Roig-Merino, B., García-Adán, I.: Transition towards a tourist innovation model: the smart tourism destination: Reality or territorial marketing? J. Innov. Knowl. **5**(2), 96–104 (2020)
28. Elshaer, A.M., Marzouk, A.M.: Memorable tourist experiences: the role of smart tourism technologies and hotel innovations. Tour. Recreat. Res. 1–13 (2022)
29. Wang, R., Luo, J., Huang, S.S.: Developing an artificial intelligence framework for online destination image photos identification. J. Destin. Mark. Manag. **18**, 100512 (2020)

Ethics, Security, and Privacy

Investigating Data Privacy Evaluation Criteria and Requirements for e-Commerce Websites

Adéle da Veiga[(✉)] [iD], Elisha Ochola[iD], Mathias Mujinga[iD], and Emilia Mwim[iD]

Security4U Research Group, School of Computing, College of Science, Engineering and Technology, UNISA, Florida, Johannesburg, South Africa

{dveiga,ocholeo,mujinm,mwimen}@unisa.ac.za

Abstract. In the era of the fourth industrial revolution, more and more organizations are providing services through the internet using e-commerce websites. As such, customers need to share their personal information with e-commerce providers, some of which is sensitive and confidential. This has brought the privacy and security of personal information in e-commerce websites to the fore and has resulted in the creation of data privacy regulations by countries and regional bodies with a view to monitoring and protecting end users' personal information. However, there is a lack of guidelines from information regulators on how to implement the data privacy regulatory requirements for e-commerce website privacy. There is also not currently guidance in South Africa of how to operationalise the data privacy conditions of the Protection of Personal Information Act (POPIA) on websites. This paper aims to propose evaluation criteria for e-commerce websites to aid with data privacy regulation compliance. A scoping literature review was conducted, using the PRISMA method, to review existing data privacy evaluation criteria for e-commerce websites. The contribution of this study is a holistic set of evaluation criteria, comprising 22 main criteria with 57 individual evaluation criteria, structured according to the POPIA principles and with reference to the GDPR articles. The proposed evaluation criteria can aid organisations to develop their websites in line with data privacy principles by providing a point of reference for the controls that must be considered and providing a better understanding of how to operationalise data privacy conditions on websites.

Keywords: Data privacy · Security · Personal information · E-commerce · Website · Evaluation · Criteria

1 Introduction

Privacy and security are critical to the building of trust between end-users and e-commerce websites or vendors [1, 2]. Given the pervasiveness of our connected devices, users are often wary of sharing personal information with e-commerce websites and the matter of online data privacy is important to both e-commerce vendors and their customers. E-commerce vendors need to collect and use consumers' personal information to enable the provision of their services while complying with the relevant regulations, such as the General Data Protection Act (GDPR) of the European Union [3] or the Protection

T. Guarda et al. (Eds.): ARTIIS 2022, CCIS 1676, pp. 297–307, 2022.
https://doi.org/10.1007/978-3-031-20316-9_23

of Personal Information Act (POPIA) of South Africa [4], depending on where the data subject resides, with whom e-commerce websites are sharing information, and where the processing is taking place. However, these laws do not necessarily prescribe requirements for websites, for example, how to authenticate data subject requests on websites [5], and very little technical guidance is provided for website owners to consider when implementing the data privacy principles [6]. There is no holistic set of criteria or guidelines that can be used when designing e-commerce websites to ensure that data privacy requirements are met when customer information is processed.

Conversely, customers must share certain personal information to be able to use e-commerce services provided by vendors and vendors must implement controls on e-commerce websites to ensure that data privacy regulatory requirements are met. The objective of this paper is to develop data privacy evaluation criteria for websites in order to aid organisations to comply with data privacy requirements. This proposed evaluation criteria can aid organisations in developing their websites in line with data privacy principles by providing a point of reference for the controls that must be considered from an end-user perspective. End-users such as customers can use the criteria to establish if the website incorporates privacy requirements before sharing their personal information with the website. Website developers can utilise the criteria to establish upfront what privacy requirements to incorporate for the design and development of a website from an end user perspective. The outcome of the study also provides an overview and consolidation of existing academic research, whereby data privacy evaluation criteria have been developed and can be utilised and applied in future research studies to ascertain if e-commerce websites meet certain minimum data privacy requirements. The proposed criteria are a consolidation of existing criteria to provide a holistic set of criteria that can serve as a point of reference. The criteria are further categorised according to the data privacy conditions of POPIA which are mapped to the GDPR principles (articles). This provides a novel view of practical aspects to include in the development of websites for each data privacy principle, specifically beneficial to South African websites that must for the first time comply with POPIA as of 1 July 2021 and who requires guidance to implement the POPIA conditions. Considering privacy and security aspects in websites could, furthermore, aid in establishing trust between end-users and e-commerce websites [5] and thereby facilitate the sharing of personal information for transactions.

For this study, a scoping literature review was conducted using the Preferred Reporting Items for Systematic Reviews and Meta-Analyses (PRISMA) method to review existing data privacy evaluation criteria for e-commerce websites and to consolidate and synthesise it to propose a holistic set of evaluation criteria fit for use in South Africa as well as internationally. The scope of the paper is limited to privacy and security evaluation criteria for websites. This study does not include a review of data privacy policies, nor of the utilisation of technology to ascertain the level of compliance.

2   Background

Protection of personal data remains a concern following technological advancements regarding information sharing [7–10]. This has led to the establishment of data protection regulations (e.g., GDPR and POPIA) [11] that include a requirement for privacy policies containing specifications on how personal data is processed by e-commerce websites and organisations. Whereas the matter of security addresses issues pertaining to unauthorised personal information access, the matter of privacy puts in place regulations, laws and technology to protect data subjects' rights in controlling their personal information, which includes, but is not limited to health data, contact information, such as email addresses and phone numbers, employment information, and photos [12]. However, both privacy and security are meant to safeguard against unauthorised access and unfair use and/or sharing of Personal Identifiable Information (PII). Data privacy regulations provide the regulatory requirements for data privacy related to privacy conditions or principles, but there is a lack of guidelines from information regulators on how to implement the data privacy regulatory requirements for website privacy [6]. Complete compliance with the privacy regulations remains a challenge, with a number of websites failing to meet expectations [13].

The compliance of website privacy policies across different sectors and with respect to the regional laws, Fair Information Practice Principles (FIPPs), and custom criteria, have been analysed in several studies and been found to be failing to address various aspects of the respective regulations [14]. The authors [14] undertook an analysis of the privacy policies of fifty-four government websites in Saudi Arabia, comparing these policies with the FIPPs guidelines. The findings indicated that not all the websites had privacy policies, and among those which had the policies, only a portion complied with more than two of the five core FIPPs privacy principles. A similar analysis was undertaken on three hundred and eight websites of the Portuguese government. Once again not all websites had privacy policies, and only a very small portion of those with such policies complied with the FIPPs guidelines on data collection and third-party data sharing. The authors further created an analytical presentation on ninety-seven health sector websites, which showed, once again, that only a very small proportion of these provided privacy policies meeting all the FIPPs guidelines. Similarly, dismal levels of compliance were uncovered with respect to both regional laws and custom criteria. A number of authors have proposed various approaches, automatic and/or manual, in evaluating websites' compliance with the various privacy regulations across different sectors [6, 13, 15–17]. However, they evaluated different partial privacy principles of the laws concerned. It was these shortcomings that highlighted the need for an analysis of e-commerce website privacy considerations so as to develop data privacy evaluation criteria for e-commerce websites that can be applied to aid organisations to assist them in complying with data privacy requirements.

3   Research Methodology

3.1   Research Method

A scoping literature review method was applied, which provides the researcher with an initial review of the available literature [18], as well as to identify the extent of privacy evaluation criteria for e-commerce websites. The PRISMA method was applied to systematically gather, screen and review the retrieved research papers [19]. The following keywords were used: ["security" AND "privacy"] AND ["website" OR "e-commerce"] AND ["evaluation" OR "checklist" OR "criteria' OR "measure"] AND ["law" OR "compliance" OR "regulatory"] AND [Publication Date: (01/01/2016 TO 12/31/2022)]. Perception-based studies, information privacy concern studies, general website design criteria or principles, privacy by design, software development, privacy governance and privacy policy content were excluded.

Sixteen papers were included in the final review, (see Table 1). These included both automated, manual and hybrid approaches to verifying the privacy and security requirements of e-commerce websites. In addition to the academic papers, four internet sources were included, namely the OECD Recommendation of the Council on Consumer Protection in E-Commerce [20], as well as GDPR guidelines for websites [21–23] that were retrieved in a general search of the Internet. The next section provides an overview of the final papers included in the analysis.

Table 1. Prisma process

Database	#Records identified through database searching	#Records after duplicates removed	#Records screened	#Records excluded (exclusion /inclusion criteria	#Full-text articles assessed for eligibility	#Full-text articles excluded, with reasons	#Articles included in the synthesis
Web of Science	26	26	26	21	5	2	3
IEEE	29	29	29	18	11	6	5
ACM	321	317	317	309	8	5	3
Springer	31	31	31	25	6	1	5

Automated Approach

Bier [15] developed a PrivacyInsight framework whereby end users can obtain a view of the personal information collected by websites, as well as the flow of their information based on GDPR requirements. Important aspects that are assessed in the framework are: no constraints on right of access for data subjects (e.g., consider remote access); recipients and sources of personal information must be disclosed upon a data subject access request; the purpose for collection must be specified at every step of processing; there must be means to rectify or erase personal information.

Maass et al. [24] also developed a tool, Privaycore which can be deployed to benchmark the privacy and security measures of websites. Privacy measures that are checked include tracking, third party cookies, browser fingerprinting, content distribution network operator services, and geographic location of servers which might be in different data protection jurisdictions. The security measures include aspects such as TLS encryption, whether the website has unencrypted content on an encrypted page (part of the Enc Web check group), mail server and HTTP security header checks, unintended information leaks, checks to determine whether there are test scripts that might include the configuration of the server, checks to determine if the DNS is protected with DNSSEC, as well as a number of authentication checks and software version checks.

Thai and Hieu [25] proposed a framework that would support a website security assessment. Their objective was to integrate the various scanning tools into a single framework that would serve as an adequate evaluation method. It is shown that, in order to assess the security level of a website, it is necessary to take some actions, which include testing the website using scanning tools. However, it is argued that most of the scanning tools have limitations and, to address the new vulnerabilities, the scanning tools need to be updated frequently. Lin et al. [26] analysed a collection of network behaviours across 663 websites in China, based on protection of personal information regulations and to ascertain the level of compliance. The study designed and used a crawler to collect privacy policies and traffic from websites for analysis. The authors developed a privacy policy evaluation criterion with three measurement attributes: transparency in terms of the publication and visibility of the privacy policy; readability of the policy; and compliance of the privacy policy with regulations. A number of studies focused on the automated review of website privacy in compliance with the GDPR. In this regard, Mahindrakar and Joshi [16] developed an automated framework that allows for processing of data only when the privacy policy complies with the GDPR rules. Similarly, Oh et al. [27] proposed an automatic tool to assess how websites comply with the implementation of the GDPR framework, also focussing on the privacy policy content. Saglam et al. [28] analysed how blockchain systems' legal documents published on websites comply with the GDPR requirements and reported very low compliance. The assessment was based on how the legal documents (e.g., privacy policies) comply with the key areas of the GDPR: explicit consent; right to erasure; transparency and portability; data retention; transfer of personal data to third parties; data minimisation; right of access and data protection by design.

Manual Approach

De Souza [6] followed a walk-through approach to identify what data websites in Spain and Portugal collect, by who this data is collected, and for which purposes. They also considered access, and the portability and elimination of websites, together with consent requirements and explanations for automated processing. A further study was conducted in Bangladesh and the United States of America, as part of which password authentication (construction and recovery); use of CAPTCHA; security question use; the HTTPS channel; password strength; third-party data sharing; and the use of cookies were assessed [12]. Al-Jamed and Abu-Shanab [29] developed a checklist to measure the degree of adherence on the part of government websites to privacy protection. The principles that fall under both the OECD and FTC methods were identified and the sets of the principles were matched against each other to determine which of the methods is more appropriate for use as a checklist tool. From the analysis, it was observed that the principle of data quality in the OECD method did not match the principles in the FTC method. Based on this observation, it was assumed that the OECD principles are more comprehensive than the FTC principles and, as such, that the OECD principles may be more appropriate to serve as a checklist tool. Nwaeze et al. [30] investigated privacy principles based on ISO/IEC 29100:2011 on e-government websites regarding privacy protection regulations in West African countries. Based on the eleven ISO/IEC 29100:2011 privacy principles, the study found gaps in compliance among the countries studied.

Using manual analysis, the authors collected personal information identifiers used by different e-government websites in five West African countries. Worryingly, in three of the five countries, there were no local data protection regulations or regulatory bodies in place to govern the privacy of personal information in websites. Sanchez-Rola and Dell'Amico [31] evaluated website compliance with the EU's GDPR regulations regarding tracking. Using a custom browser plugin, the authors performed a manual analysis of 2000 popular websites and collected cookie sets. Some of the findings showed that most websites continue tracking without consent from users, few websites provide an easy way of opting out, and rejecting tracking is often ineffective. Javed et al. [14] evaluated the accessibility and readability of websites' privacy policy documents (e.g., positioning on the homepage) annually. They also analysed the policy statements for compliance with GDPR guidelines on: data collected for processing (e.g., phone, id, home address, education, employment, mail, device IP address and date of birth); the purpose of data collection (e.g., research, market, business, and promotion); children's data protection, data accuracy and control (e.g., opt-in, opt-out, update, delete, and withdraw); data retention (e.g., storage duration); integrity and confidentiality (e.g., encryption); accountability (e.g., breach regulation), transparency (e.g., effective date), data portability (e.g., format of portable data), right to object (e.g., in case of grievance), and third-party transfer (e.g., when sharing or selling). Similar work was conducted by Amaral et al. [13]. The aspects reviewed were, however, not translated to evaluation criteria for a website, but rather focused on the policy content.

A study was also conducted in South Africa to review the security features of e-commerce websites. In this study, criteria were reviewed manually, for example, whether the website uses HTTPS, whether the certificate is valid, account lock requirements, multifactor authentication, third-party login, use of a privacy policy, and whether there is a link to the terms and conditions [17].

Hybrid Approach

Other researchers [32] presented a hybrid approach, as offered by the observatory for Security and PrIvacy DAta (ASPIDA) system and concerned with self-assessment, self-improvement and motivation to self-regulate. To address privacy and security weaknesses, the authors had to monitor and analyse a set of security and privacy metrics and indicators. They further maintain that the observatory for Security and PrIvacy DAta (ASPIDA) platform aims to provide a holistic approach for evaluating and motivating e-business sites to enhance their security and privacy measures. Further, they created a digital badge that is issued upon request on behalf of e-business owners.

4   Proposed Data Privacy Evaluation Criteria for e-Commerce Websites

Table 2 provides the proposed data privacy evaluation criteria for e-commerce websites. It comprises 22 main categories with a total of 57 evaluation criteria. The criteria are consolidated from the literature review and structured per the sections in POPIA. Each POPIA section is also mapped to the articles in the GDPR. The evaluation criteria can be used to evaluate specific privacy and security aspects on an e-commerce website and can

Table 2. Data privacy evaluation criteria for e-commerce websites

Criteria	POPIA	GDPR
Main criteria 1: Processing limitation - Lawfulness of processing	**Principle 2 section 8, 3, section 17**	**Art 5, 6, 12, 13**
1. What personal information is required to sign up? [6, 14, 17]		
2. Does the website specify by whom data is collected? [6, 13, 16]		
3. Does the website explain what data will be collected? [16, 26, 29, 31]		
4. Does the website clarify why data will be collected? [13, 14, 16, 26, 29, 31]		
5. Does the website explain how the collected data will be used? [13, 14, 26, 28, 29, 31]		
Main criteria 2: Processing limitation - Minimality	**Principle 2, section 9**	**Art. 5**
6. Data collected are adequate, relevant and limited to what is necessary in relation to the purposes for which they are processed? (No unnecessarily data is collected) [17, 28]		
Main criteria 3: Processing limitation - Consent, justification and objection	**Principle 2, section 10**	**Art. 5, 7, 18, 21**
7. How and where is consent captured? [13, 23, 28]		
8. Can consent be partial or revoked? ([6, 27, 28]		
9. Is consent obtained prior to gathering any data (including cookies) [13, 23]		
10. Is granular consent included for different types of processing? [21]		
11. Does the website allow for consent (e.g. cookies consent) to be withdrawn? [21]		
12. Does the website clarify if personal information will be disclosed to a third party? [14, 27, 29]		
13. Does the website explain under what conditions the data will be disclosed? [29]		
Main criteria 4: Processing limitation - Collection directly from data subject	**Principle 2, section 11**	**Art. 13**
14. Does the website collect information directly from the data subject and not via third parties? * [4]		
Main criteria 5: Purpose specification - Collection for specific purpose	**Principle 3, section 12**	**Art. 5**
15. Is a specific, explicitly defined and lawful purpose specified? [6, 13, 14, 16, 20, 27, 28]		
Main criteria 6: Purpose specification - Data subject aware of purpose of collection of information	**Principle 3, section 13**	**Art. 13**
16. Are steps taken on the website to ensure that the data subject is aware of the purpose of collection? [13, 14, 16, 27, 28]		
Main criteria 7: Purpose specification - Retention of records	**Principle 3, section 14**	**Rec. 65**
17. Is the retention of records specified? [27, 28]		
Main criteria 8: Further processing limitation - Further processing to be compatible with purpose of collection	**Principle 4, section 15**	**Rec. 50**
18. Does the website state that it will obtain consent from the data subject if their data will be subject to further processing?* [4]		
Main criteria 9: Information quality - Quality of information	**Principle 5, section 16**	**-**
19. Are website controls included to ensure personal information collected is complete, accurate and not misleading (dropdown boxes, validations, etc.)?[14, 28]		
Main criteria 10: Openness - Notification to Regulator and to data subject	**Principle 6, section 17**	**Art. 12, 13**
20. Is there a privacy policy on the website? [12–14, 16, 17, 21, 22, 27, 28, 30, 31]		
21. Is the privacy policy accessible via every page on the website? [14, 21, 22, 30]		
22. Is there a privacy notice at the point of data collection? [22]		
23. Is there a link to terms and conditions and the privacy policy? [14, 17, 20, 22]		
24. Is the privacy policy readable and easily understandable? [30, 31]		
Main criteria 11: Security safeguards - Security measures on integrity of personal information	**Principle 7, section 18**	**Art. 32, 35**
25. Does the website use HTTPS? (Is the connection secure?) [12, 17, 22]		
26. Is the HTTPS certificate valid? [17]		
27. What are the password (if any) strength requirements? [12, 17]		
28. Does the account get locked after entering the incorrect password? After how many attempts? [17]		
29. Is there a forgot password option? / Is there an option to change the password? [12, 17]		
30. What are the password requirements when changing passwords? [17]		
31. How is the password reset, i.e., use of account recovery questions, new password auto-generated, link provided to change password, or OTP sent? [12, 17]		
32. What are the communication options when resetting a password, i.e., email, SMS, app, etc.? [17]		
33. Is multi-factor authentication offered? [17]		
34. What multi-factor authentication settings are available? [17]		
35. Is a CAPTCHA used for authentication? [12]		
36. Are users required to verify any information, e.g., email address? (How is this done?) [17]		
37. Are cookie consent statements included (reject all, accept all, change settings) [21, 22]		
38. Does the website clarify that it takes steps to provide security for collected data? [14, 16, 29]*		
39. Does the website state that unauthorised access to users' personal data will be prevented? [14, 16, 29] *		

(continued)

Table 2. (*continued*)

Criteria	POPIA	GDPR
Main criteria 12: Security safeguards - Information processed by operator or person acting under authority	**Principle 7, section 19**	**Art. 29**
40. Does the website refer to sharing of data with third parties and the categories of the third parties? * [4]		
Main criteria 13: Security safeguards - Security measures regarding information processed by operator	**Principle 7, section 20**	**Art. 29**
41. Are third party categories named on the website or in the privacy policy? [21]		
Main criteria 14: Security safeguards - Notification of security compromises	**Principle 7, section 21**	**Art. 33, 34**
42. Does the website indicate that data subjects will be informed if their personal information was compromised? * [4]		
Main criteria 15: Data subject participation - Access to personal information	**Principle 8, section 22**	**Art. 13-15, 20**
43. Does the website specify how the user can access his data? [13, 14, 16, 28]		
44. Is data access requests free of charge? [27]		
45. Does the website allow users to review/access collected data? [13, 14, 21, 29]		
Main criteria 16: Data subject participation - Correction of personal information	**Principle 8, section 23**	**Art 5, 16, 17, 19**
46. Does the website provide for means for the data subject to correct data? [13, 14, 21, 29]		
47. Does the website provide for means for the data subject to delete data? (right to be forgotten) [13, 14, 21, 28, 29]		
Main criteria 17: Data subject participation - Manner of access	**Principle 8, section 24**	**Art.13-15**
48. Is the process for data subject access requests specified in terms of other applicable regulatory requirements? (e.g. Promotion of Access to Information process in South Africa) * [4]		
Main criteria 18: Rights of data subjects regarding unsolicited electronic communications and automated decision making - Unsolicited electronic communications	**Chapter 8, section 66**	**Rec. 70**
49. Is opt-in provided for marketing/newsletters? (No marketing without permission - must be opt-in for email telephone and SMS) [13–17, 20, 22, 27, 28, 31]		
50. Does the website include a marketing preference centre to manage, edit and delete subscriptions? [23]		
51. Boxes are not pre-ticked for consent. [23]		
Main criteria 19: Rights of data subjects regarding unsolicited electronic communications and automated decision making - Directories	**Chapter 8, section 67**	-
52. If the website compiles a directory of personal information, does the website inform the data subject, free of charge and before the information is included in a physical or online directory? * [4]		
Main criteria 20: Rights of data subjects regarding unsolicited electronic communications and automated decision making - Automated decision making	**Chapter 8, section 68**	**Art. 22**
53. Is there an explanation for how the automatic processing of data of a data subject will affect the data subject? Is it understandable? [6]		
Main criteria 21: Transborder information flows - Transfers of personal information outside Republic	**Chapter 9, section 69**	**Art 44-50**
54. Is there an explanation for how transborder information flows of data of a data subject and how it will affect the data subject? Is it understandable? * [4]		
Main criteria 22: Support / Awareness		
55. Are there any security prompts, e.g., password strength indicators? [17]		
56. Are security indicators explained in more detail or are there links for additional information? [17]		
57. What are the various types of help resources available? [17]		

provide an indication as to whether privacy and security are considered for the processing of personal information in line with requirements of POPIA and the GDPR. Where a gap is identified, they indicate that a privacy condition or principle is not adequately addressed on the e-commerce website and that measures should be implemented to address it. The criteria can also be used to obtain an indication as to the degree to which e-commence websites consider data privacy principles and conditions and serve as a stepping ground for a holistic set of data privacy and security criteria for e-commerce websites. The criteria will specifically aid South African website owners to implement POPIA. POPIA includes only the data privacy conditions but does not include how it should be incorporated on websites nor how to operationalise the data privacy condition. The data privacy evaluation criteria therefore serve as point of reference to unpack the privacy conditions of POPIA in such a manner that website owners have specific aspects that they can implement to address each privacy condition.

The criteria that were referred to most in the literature study related to whether an e-commerce website included a privacy policy on the website (10); if opt-in is provided for marketing (10); followed by whether there is an explicit and lawful purpose for the collection of the personal data (6); whether the data subject is made aware on the website as to the purpose for the collection of their data (6); why the data is collected and how it will be used (6). Support and awareness were added to the evaluation criteria based on the work of [17], in support of openness and transparency and to support end-users through awareness and obtain further understanding of the privacy and security aspects of the website. Data privacy requirements, which are typically included in a website privacy policy and which are not necessarily included on a website, are indicated with a "*" for completeness, but will typically rather be covered in a review of the data privacy policy contents of a website.

5   Conclusion and Future Work

This study proposed data privacy evaluation criteria for e-commerce websites that may be utilised by e-commerce websites to aid them in complying with data protection regulations. A scoping literature review approach was applied using the PRISMA method. The final set of evaluation criteria is structured according to the POPIA conditions with reference to the GDPR articles. The criteria that were found to be most used to evaluate e-commerce websites related to: whether websites have a privacy policy; whether consent is obtained for marketing; and certain preferences by data subjects. Privacy legislation like POPIA includes only the data privacy conditions but does not include how it should be incorporated on websites nor how to operationalise the data privacy conditions. The data privacy evaluation criteria therefore serve as point of reference to unpack the privacy conditions of POPIA in such a manner that website owners have specific aspects that they can implement to address each privacy condition. A limitation of the study is that this phase comprised conceptual work only. In the next phase, the proposed privacy evaluation criteria will be validated by an expert panel applying a qualitative research method using interviews, where after the criteria will be tested in a case study. It is envisaged that the proposed criteria can also serve as a point of reference for further research to refine and test the evaluation criteria in different jurisdictions.

References

1. Bt Mohd, N.A., Zaaba, Z.F.: A review of usability and security evaluation model of E-commerce website. In: Procedia Computer Science, pp. 1199–1205 (2019)
2. Teltzrow, M., Kobsa, A.: Impacts of user privacy preferences on personalized systems: a comparative study. In: Karat, C.-M., Blom, J.O., Karat, J. (eds.) Designing Personalized User Experiences in eCommerce, pp. 315–332. Springer, Dordrecht (2004)
3. European Union: General Data Protection Regulation (GDPR), Brussels (2016)

4. Protection of Personal Information Act 4 of 2013. The Parliament of the Republic of South Africa, Cape Town (2013)
5. Boniface, C., Fouad, I., Bielova, N., Lauradoux, C., Santos, C.: Security analysis of subject access request procedures: how to authenticate data subjects safely when they request for their data. In: Naldi, M., Italiano, G.F., Rannenberg, K., Medina, M., Bourka, A. (eds.) Privacy Technologies and Policy: 7th Annual Privacy Forum, APF 2019, Rome, Italy, June 13–14, 2019, Proceedings, pp. 182–209. Springer International Publishing, Cham (2019). https://doi.org/10.1007/978-3-030-21752-5_12
6. De Souza, C.S.: A contrastive study of pre- and post-legislation interaction design for communication and action about personal data protection in e-commerce websites. In: Lamas, D., Loizides, F., Nacke, L., Petrie, H., Winckler, M., Zaphiris, P. (eds.) INTERACT 2019. LNCS, vol. 11748, pp. 3–23. Springer, Cham (2019). https://doi.org/10.1007/978-3-030-29387-1_1
7. Gurung, A., Raja, M.K.: Online privacy and security concerns of consumers. Inf. Comput. Secur. 24, 348–371 (2016). https://doi.org/10.1108/ICS-05-2015-0020
8. Baako, I., Umar, S., Gidisu, P.: Privacy and security concerns in electronic commerce websites in ghana: a survey study. Int. J. Comput. Network Inf. Secur. 10, 19–25 (2019). https://doi.org/10.5815/ijcnis.2019.10.03
9. Kaushik, K., Kumar Jain, N., Kumar Singh, A.: Antecedents and outcomes of information privacy concerns: role of subjective norm and social presence. Electron. Commer. Res. Appl. 32, 57–68 (2018). https://doi.org/10.1016/j.elerap.2018.11.003
10. Mohammed, Z.A., Tejay, G.P.: Examining privacy concerns and ecommerce adoption in developing countries: the impact of culture in shaping individuals' perceptions toward technology. Comput. Secur. 67, 254–265 (2017). https://doi.org/10.1016/j.cose.2017.03.001
11. Greenleaf, G.: Global data privacy laws 2019: 132 national laws & many bills. Privacy Laws Bus. Int. Report 2019, 14–18 (2019)
12. Tanjin, M., Botlero, I.A., Hridita, M.T., Riyadh, T.I., Onik, M.H., Miraz, M.H.: Privacy and security factors of government websites versus private websites in Bangladesh and USA: a comparative study. In: Miraz, M.H., Southall, G., Ali, M., Ware, A., Soomro, S. (eds.) iCETiC 2021. LNICSSITE, vol. 395, pp. 37–55. Springer, Cham (2021). https://doi.org/10.1007/978-3-030-90016-8_3
13. Amaral, O., Abualhaija, S., Torre, D., Sabetzadeh, M., Briand, L.: AI-enabled automation for completeness checking of privacy policies. IEEE Trans. Software Eng. (2021). https://doi.org/10.1109/TSE.2021.3124332
14. Javed, Y., Salehin, K.M., Shehab, M.: A study of South Asian websites on privacy compliance. IEEE Access 8, 156067–156083 (2020). https://doi.org/10.1109/ACCESS.2020.3019334
15. Bier, C., Kuhne, K., Beyerer J.: Privacy insight: the next generation privacy dashboard. In: Schiffner, S., Serna, J., Ikonomou, D., Rannenberg, K. (eds.) Privacy Technologies and Policy. APF 2016. LNCS, pp. 135–152. Springer International Publishing, Cham (2016). https://doi.org/10.1007/978-3-319-44760-5_9
16. Mahindrakar, A., Joshi, K.P.: Automating GDPR compliance using policy integrated Blockchain. In: Proceedings - 6th Intl Conference on Big Data Security on Cloud, BigDataSecurity 2020, pp. 86–93. IEEE, Baltimore, MD, USA (2020)
17. Brandreth, D., Ophoff, J.: Investigating customer-facing security features on south african e-commerce websites. In: Venter, H., Loock, M., Coetzee, M., Eloff, M., Eloff, J., Botha, R. (eds.) ISSA 2020. CCIS, vol. 1339, pp. 144–159. Springer, Cham (2020). https://doi.org/10.1007/978-3-030-66039-0_10
18. Grant, M.J., Booth, A., Centre, S.: A typology of reviews: an analysis of 14 review types and associated methodologies. Health Info. Libr. J. 26, 91–108 (2009)
19. Moher, D., Liberati, A., Tetzlaff, J., Altman, D.G., Group, P.: Preferred reporting items for systematic reviews and meta-analyses: the PRISMA statement. Ann. Int. Med. 151(4), 264–270 (2009)

20. Organisation for Economic Co-operation and Development: OECD Recommendation of the Council on Consumer Protection in E-Commerce. OECD (2016)
21. The GDPR Law: GDPR Website Requirements. https://www.thegdprlaw.com/requirements/
22. CookieYes Limited: GDPR Checklist for Your Website. https://www.cookieyes.com/blog/gdpr-checklist-for-websites/
23. Daniels, J.: Everything You Need to Know About Websites and Privacy Laws. https://www.webdesignerdepot.com/2020/10/everything-you-need-to-know-about-websites-and-privacy-laws/
24. Maass, M., Wichmann, P., Pridöhl, H., Herrmann, D.: PrivacyScore: Improving privacy and security via crowd-sourced benchmarks of websites. In: Schweighofer, E., Leitold, H., Mitrakas, A., Rannenberg, K. (eds.) APF 2017. LNCS, vol. 10518, pp. 178–191. Springer, Cham (2017). https://doi.org/10.1007/978-3-319-67280-9_10
25. Thai, N.D., Hieu, N.H.: A framework for website security assessment. In: ACM International Conference Proceeding Series, pp. 153–157 (2019)
26. Lin, X., Liu, H., Li, Z., Xiong, G., Gou, G.: Privacy protection of China's top websites: a Multi-layer privacy measurement via network behaviours and privacy policies. Comput. Secur. **114**, 1–20 (2022). https://doi.org/10.1016/j.cose.2022.102606
27. Oh, J., Hong, J., Lee, C., Lee, J.J., Woo, S.S., Lee, K.: Will EU's GDPR act as an effective enforcer to gain consent? IEEE Access **9**, 79477–79490 (2021). https://doi.org/10.1109/ACCESS.2021.3083897
28. Belen Saglam, R., Aslan, C.B., Li, S., Dickson, L., Pogrebna, G.: A Data-driven analysis of blockchain systems' public online communications on GDPR. In: Proceedings - 2020 IEEE International Conference on Decentralized Applications and Infrastructures, (DAPPS), pp. 22–31. IEEE. (2020)
29. Al-Jamal, M., Abu-Shanab, E.: Privacy policy of e-government websites: an itemized checklist proposed and tested. Manage. Res. Pract. **7**, 80–95 (2015)
30. Nwaeze, A.C., Zavarsky, P., Ruhl, R.: Compliance evaluation of information privacy protection in e-government systems in anglophone west africa using ISO/IEC 29100:2011. In: 2017 Twelfth International Conference on Digital Information Management (ICDIM), pp. 98–102. IEEE, Fukuoka, Japan (2017)
31. Sanchez-Rola, I., et al.: Can I opt out yet? GDPR and the global illusion of cookie control. In: Proceedings of the 2019 ACM Asia Conference on Computer and Communications Security, pp. 340–351. ACM, Auckland, New Zealand (2019)
32. Vlachos, V., et al.: ASPIDA: An observatory for security and privacy in the Greek e-business sector. In: 25th Pan-Hellenic Conference on Informatics, pp. 362–368 (2021)

Proposal and Implementation of a Model for Organizational Redesign and Its Influence on Digital Transformation in the Public Sector

Jorge Lira Camargo[1]([✉]) [iD], Luis Soto Soto[2] [iD], Zoila Rosa Lira Camargo[3] [iD], Luis Lira Camargo[4] [iD], and Jorge Víctor Mayhuasca Guerra[5] [iD]

[1] EUPG - Federico Villarreal National University, Lima, Peru
jlira@unfv.edu.pe
[2] Faculty of Systems and Computer Engineering, The National University of San Marcos, Lima, Peru
[3] Faculty of Legal, Accounting and Financial, University National of Barranca, Barranca, Lima, Peru
[4] Faculty of Engineering in Industrial and Systems, University National Hermilio Valdizan, Huánuco, Peru
[5] Faculty of Engineering in Industrial and Systems, University National Federico Villareal, Lima, Peru

Abstract. This paper reviewed the literature on the topics of organizational redesign, digital transformation, strategic planning, process management, administrative simplification, continuous improvement, redesign and automation, and also considered the activities developed to implement organizational redesign in the quarantine declared by the Peruvian state as a result of COVID 19, with the purpose of proposing a method for organizational redesign towards digital transformation in public entities, with a strategic and operational approach. For the implementation of the strategic approach, the institutions that functionally depend on the Ministry of Education were involved, considering the current situation in relation to the operational and territorial capacities of each region, to develop the strategic and process design. Likewise, for the implementation of the operational approach, the results of the virtual course on process management for administrative simplification 2 were used, involving several institutions that proposed and implemented improvements towards the digitization of processes, promoting digital transformation. The results of the present work consider the effective time of the administrative procedures and the cost of implementation. The effective time of the procedures was reflected in a reduction of 11% and 52% in the reduction of the cost of the procedures.

Keywords: Diagnosis model · Process design · Value chain · Process improvement · Organizational design · Digital transformation

T. Guarda et al. (Eds.): ARTIIS 2022, CCIS 1676, pp. 308–319, 2022.
https://doi.org/10.1007/978-3-031-20316-9_24

1 Introduction

On 6 March 2020, the first case of COVID 19 was identified in Peru and on 15 March, the Peruvian state declared the entire country quarantined, initiating a paradigm shift in citizens, employees, traders, businesspeople, etc. It allowed institutions and companies to rethink the way they offer their services and products, incorporating technology, methods, and tools to develop their non-face-to-face activities, accelerating the digital transformation and the way customers and citizens think. Public institutions were faced with the need to rethink and prioritize their objectives, redesign their processes and procedures to generate public value, and organizational redesign was the way to start their digital transformation. In a public institution it was proposed to develop and implement a model for organizational redesign with a territorial approach from a strategic approach, and the context of the pandemic, forced to redefine the administrative procedures from an operational approach to digital transformation in the public sector, naturally had to start several trainings in the management of virtual classroom applications, video conferencing, spreadsheets, etc. to facilitate interaction with public officials, empathizing on the objectives to then achieve the results. Awareness-raising talks were fundamental to promote change management, to continue generating public value and innovation towards the disruptive approach. The method to carry out organizational redesign is to analyze the current situation of operational capacities, identifying processes and procedures (AS-IS) towards an improved proposal (TO-BE), pursuing the shift towards digital transformation in the public sector, managing to reduce the effective time and the total cost in the execution of prioritized procedures.

2 State of the Art

In [1], they integrate the organizational design and process approach, initiating the strategic projection to define the vision, mission, objectives, and goals, allowing to guide the design of processes and the management control model for decision making. Finally, in their work they establish the relationships of the process roles and the functions of the organizational structure, initiating the automation and implementation of the proposed design. Then in [2], they mention that technological innovation is a systemic, dynamic, participatory, creative, open and continuous process, consisting of managing the development of new products. In turn, they generate new knowledge that must be managed throughout the organization, through knowledge management, with the aim of contributing to the fulfillment of the requirements, satisfaction of the needs and expectations of all citizens.

In [3], they emphasize the relationship of ideal models that are generated through best practices and success stories, current models that represent the picture of the value chain from operational planning to strategic planning and the proposed model that meets the needs and expectations of customers. The study focuses from data analysis to functional process improvement.

In the work of [4], they modify the existing organizational structure to relate it closely to the needs of the citizen and generate capacities with the aim of perfecting its organizational structure, oriented towards the development of the execution of processes rather than the fulfillment of general functions. In [5], they emphasize that innovation and digitalization of public administration raise numerous questions about the immediate future of public employment and the need to redefine or update the rights and working conditions of employees. This implies defining the profiles with the necessary competences for the correct development of their work.

In [6], they mention that the situation caused by the pandemic has configured telework as a solution, currently technology has allowed proving that its use is feasible in public and private organizations. Therefore, it is necessary to have a regulation that helps the advance that the institutions had. According to [7], they provide a pattern that focuses on identifying, analyzing, designing, or optimizing processes, and is being used to manage their processes through teleworking driven by the COVID-19 pandemic. Then in [8], they begin their work with the analysis of the digitization of physical information into a digital representation, also, they develop through the previous works the requirements to be met by companies to be considered in the digital transformation. They mention that to orientate towards digital transformation, companies must choose their strategy based on the organizational model and/or behavior, the generation of capabilities will be fundamental to generate sustainability.

Later, in [9], they establish the basic conditions for generating suitable environments for the correct development of work, which will ensure the provision of an adequate service and meet the expectations of citizens. Likewise, the working environment generated by the company will contribute to the generation of ideas and/or solutions, which is fundamental for sustaining the digital transformation of companies and staying one step ahead of the competition. Finally, in [10], they mention that audits should have a preventive role towards achieving results and service delivery, with a modern approach to achieve efficiency, effectiveness, and efficiency in public entities.

In the literature review carried out based on the articles related to the topic of study, it is observed that there are no recent works that manage to integrate Strategic Design, Organizational Design and Process Management with Digital Transformation in the public sector, the articles mentioned in this section will provide value for the new proposal of the new model.

3 Research Method

The researcher investigates of different learning methodologies and models using systems thinking to integrate the advantages and contributions, and thus elaborate the methodological proposal. It also considers the knowledge generated by the implementation of process management and redesign projects. Can visualize the process to generate the new model from the review of theories and implementation experiences, that allowed to build the state of the art and then carry out the implementation.

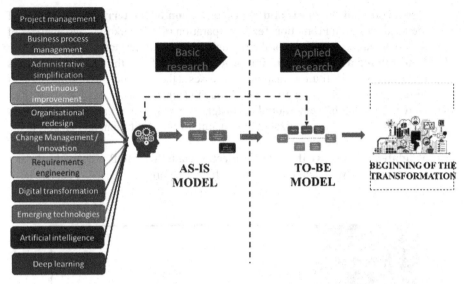

Fig. 1. Research and action.

4 Method of Proposal and Implementation

The sequence of steps: (1) Diagnosis, comprises the management of virtual spaces to diagnose the base model or AS-IS; (2) Design, elaborates the general scheme of the proposed model or TO-BE based on the base models or AS-IS, and the ideal models or OUGHT-TO-BE that are considered in the state of the art; (3) Design Stages, develops the components and characteristics of the proposed new model or TO-BE; (4) Execution evaluates the new organizational model through implementation; y (5) Evaluation of displayed results shown in part (VI).

5 Organizational Redesign Model Proposal

The policies of modernization of the state and the policy of digital transformation drives the process of change towards a modern or digital organization. **To propose the Organizational Redesign Model and its Influence on Digital Transformation, several stages were used, taking as a basis the model for the implementation of the Manual of Operations (MOP) in the Regional Education Directorates (DRE) and their Local Management Units (UGEL) that functionally depend on the Ministry of Education. The following is a description of each of the stages Diagnosis (A), Design (B), Design Stages (C) and Implementation (D).**

A. *Diagnosis*
    In Fig. 2, we visualize the base model for the implementation of the MOP (which we will call the AS-IS model that has been used in the technical assistance in the regions of Cajamarca, Amazonas and Pasco located in Peru), the AS-IS model is structured based on the strategic management approaches (I), (II), (III) and (IV).

(I)   **Organizational diagnosis and characterisation of the territory,** formation of the Modernisation Promotion Team, preparation of the work plan and analysis of the organizational situation of the region's educational services.

(II)   **Determining and characterizing processes,** identifying the products and users delivered by the institution, mapping processes at the strategic, mission and support levels, and characterizing processes through technical sheets.

(III)   **Determine the organizational redesign,** develop the organizational criteria matrices, design the organizational structure of the institution, and elaborate the implementation project.

(IV)   **Validate and approve the MOP project,** socialise the MOP, prepare the dossier supporting the MOP and prepare the technical report.

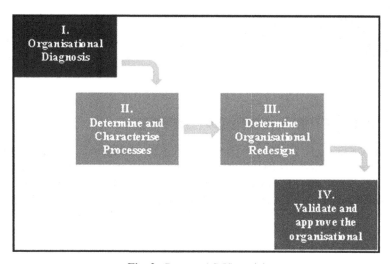

Fig. 2. Base or AS-IS model

B. *Design*

The proposed model was developed based on the analysis of the base model or AS-IS, with the aim of orienting towards a digitized organization. Likewise, to develop the sustainability of the proposal, the organizational culture towards innovation is incorporated, which allows a vision of change towards digital transformation to be generated.

C. *Design stages*

The design is structured based on strategic and operational management approaches. The strategic approach comprises stages (I), (II), (III) and (IV), and the operational approach comprises stages (0), (1) and (2). The stages of the proposed model or TO-BE are shown in Fig. 3.

The Strategic Approach Includes:

(I) **Strategy design,** to assess the vision, mission, values, and strategic objectives to link with the purpose of change towards digital transformation, and to align with national and regional plans, as well as to establish strategies to strengthen the capacities of human resources.

(II) **Process design identifies,** the processes oriented towards digital transformation, determines the characteristics or indicators of the processes, concludes with the determination and sequence of the processes through the level 0 and 1 process map.

(III) **Redesign of the organizational structure,** through the analysis of the functions manual and the level 0 process map, it is possible to obtain the scenarios of the organizational charts to be implemented in the organization, which obeys the operational capacity and the characteristics of its sector.

(IV) **Beginning of the digital transformation,** it generates the training of leaders who drive innovation using technology, guide the teams to incorporate automation projects that manage to digitize the administrative part and develop digital processes that allow the management of non-presence, also guides towards the integration of its applications at institutional and inter-institutional level within the framework of interoperability. It also aims to use social networks to monitor the behaviour of citizens, taking preventive action to meet their future requirements, unmet needs and demands.

The Operational Approach Comprises:

(1) **Organizational diagnosis,** includes analyzing the organizational situation from the dimension of operational capacity, identifying the own resources that allow guaranteeing the sustainability of the redesign project over time, as well as identifying the products based on needs, unmet demands, future demands, or citizens' requirements, and finally the inter-institutional and inter-governmental relationship to visualize the state of interoperability.

(2) **Determines key processes of the value chain,** identifies the result-oriented processes or procedures of the operational processes, determines the responsible persons or roles in charge of monitoring and continuous improvement, prioritizes the procedures that add the most public value towards the results of modernization.

(3) **Manages the administrative simplification,** determines the improved procedure or TO-BE to be implemented, executes the implementation plan to obtain short-term results through simplification and/or continuous improvement. Finally, the implementation of the simplified procedures and/or continuous improvement is monitored to evaluate the results in terms of process time reduction, cost reduction and user satisfaction.

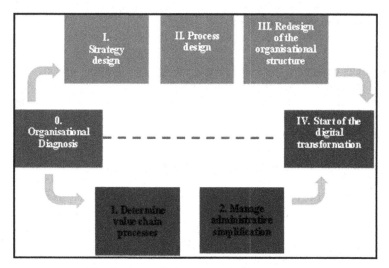

Fig. 3. Stages of the proposed TO-BE model

D. *Execution*

To carry out the implementation of the proposed model or TO-BE, it requires meeting the basic conditions for redesign, including sharing a vision of change throughout the organization to generate commitments and achieve the results of each stage. The formation of a team to drive digital transformation is fundamental to foster continuous improvement and self-assessment of organizational redesign.

6   Results

The result of the implementation is based on the point of view of the strategic and operational approach. For the dimension of strategic management, it was implemented from the governing body of education in Peru through technical assistance in the Educational Management Unit (IGED) carried out in 2020, on which 6 implementation plans were obtained, giving rise to organize as an entity after having gone through the organizational diagnosis, strategic design, and process management. For the operational management dimension, a training course was carried out for the specialists of the rationalization and planning unit in the IGED, obtaining at the end of the course 33 proposals to improve the procedures found in the Single Text of Procedures Administrative (TUPA), but 25 procedures were implemented. After monitoring, it was shown that the vast majority was simplified, eliminating activities that do not add value, in others it was improved by moving from manual activities to user activities supported by the information system, a few were automated through the digitization of the process. The KPI is not detailed in the method. Next, the KPIs are shown within Table 1 to show the achievement of the objectives.

Strategic Management Dimension

Regarding the technical assistance provided to the IGED in the regions of Cajamarca, Amazonas, Apurímac, Ucayali, Pasco and Puno in 2020, a total of 6 plans were obtained for the implementation of the MOP with a focus on processes.

Operational Management Dimension

About the MdP2 course, which ended on December 4, 2020. It ended with 33 plans for improvement, simplification, or automation of procedures, comprising a total of 17 IGED.

On the implementation of the proposed model, 25 procedures were considered that concluded in its implementation towards digital transformation.

Table 1. Comparison of KPI results for Pre-test and Post-test.

	Pre-Test (average)	Post Test (average)	Percentage change	Comment
KP1: Steps used (units)	35	28	−20%	
KP2: Estimated time of execution of the procedures (Hours)	82	73	−11%	
KP3: Total cost of procedures (PEN) per year	102 517	48 840	−48%	

Table 2 shows the results after applying the administration simplification in most of the procedures, in others the continuous improvement and in a few the automation of the processes.

Table 2. Comparison of AS-IS and TO-BE.

IGED	COD	EFFECTIVE AS-IS TIME (HOURS)	AS-IS STEPS	AS-IS ANNUAL COST (s/.)	EFFECTIVE TIME TO-BE (HOURS)	STEPS TO-BE	ANNUAL COST TO-BE (s/.)
UGEL TRUJILLO NOR OESTE	P14	12.80	17	S/880,622.53	3.58	13	S/71,075.75
UGEL EL PORVENIR	P11	18.58	11	S/477,221.00	16.23	5	S/423,213.00
UGEL CHOTA	P9	7.60	18	S/323,520.04	5.23	13	S/158,563.20
UGEL CELENDÍN	P15	1288.00	20	S/307,099.61	1264.00	16	S/278,245.23

(continued)

Table 2. (*continued*)

IGED	COD	EFFECTIVE AS-IS TIME (HOURS)	AS-IS STEPS	AS-IS ANNUAL COST (s/.)	EFFECTIVE TIME TO-BE (HOURS)	STEPS TO-BE	ANNUAL COST TO-BE (s/.)
UGEL CHICLAYO	P17	24.38	35	S/153,653.33	22.38	35	S/129,300.09
DRE Tumbes	P8	31.43	35	S/114,900.00	6.07	24	S/4,253.10
UGEL TRUJILLO SUR	P22	58.13	12	S/98,826.67	13.62	11	S/5,422.07
UGEL CHICLAYO	P18	19.50	19	60433.33333	18.32	18	S/54,542.96
UGEL CELENDÍN	P16	225.08	23	S/53,938.16	211.50	23	S/50,922.19
UGEL TRUJILLO NOR OESTE	P13	68.28	46	S/20,881.00	17.05	31	S/1,101.23
DRE Huánuco	P4	107.33	41	S/16,697.07	72.92	41	S/12,700.11
UGEL HUARAZ	P19	23.67	68	S/7,892.29	22.88	57	S/7,378.71
DRE Tumbes	P7	5.93	32	S/7,284.44	4.20	23	S/3,662.02
UGEL CHOTA	P2	30.18	57	S/6,065.56	20.68	29	S/2,843.05
UGEL URUBAMBA	P24	2.93	25	S/ 5,840.00	2.65	20	S/ 111.00
DRE Piura	P5	5.38	52	S/ 5,603.00	3.93	38	S/3,322.00
UGEL TUMBES	P23	23.20	39	S/ 5,288.00	18.92	30	S/3,490.00
DRE Piura	P6	4.82	50	S/ 3,363.00	3.15	49	S/1,560.00
UGEL URUBAMBA	P25	1.7	33	S/ 3,213.00	1.50	25	S/257.00
DRE Huánuco	P3	22.98	33	S/3,157.87	17.15	33	S/1,773.35
UGEL HUARAZ	P20	12.73	52	S/2,348.68	12.12	35	S/2,100.55
UGEL LA ESPERANZA	P12	14.85	47	S/2,198.00	10.50	35	S/1,698.00
DRE Cajamarca	P1	10.63	43	S/2,103.00	9.88	33	S/1,800.00
DRE Cajamarca	P2	12.05	44	S/1,829.00	10.83	28	S/1,394.00
UGEL JAEN	P21	23.63	46	S/1,623.95	22.63	46	S/1,371.48
UGEL EL PORVENIR	P10	22.57	39	S/1,260.00	18.67	19	S/1,011.00

The problems raised in this research show opportunities for improvement in the effectiveness of the level of service to influence the digitization of processes. On the other hand, the implementation of the model from the operational approach allowed to reduce the effective time of the procedure, which influenced the total cost of the procedure (annual), Table 1 allows to compare the results of the indicators considered, before the implementation (pre-test) with the results after the implementation (post-test).

7 Discussion

This research focuses on organizational redesign from a strategic and operational app-roach, oriented towards digital transformation. Other research focuses on developing the organizational model to guide the transformation, also, this area allows establishing similarities and differences between the research conducted and the literature references reviewed. The discussion follows:

In [1] the organizational design integrating the process approach and labour competences, addresses the strategic projection, process design, design of the management control model, structure design, automation, and implementation, supported by good documentation to ensure sustainability. The present research considers Iraida's proposal as a basis for achieving similar objectives, but adapting it to our context, we consider the organizational diagnosis stage to be fundamental, focusing on the processes of the value chain and first developing administrative simplification before starting the organizational design.

The research by [3], establishes three models; the first represents an ideal from strategic planning to operational planning; the second shows the snapshot of operations to strategic actions; and the third model projects what the activities will look like after analyzing the ideal model and the snapshot of operations being developed. The research work takes as a reference the implementation executed by Fossland and Krogstie, but disagrees that the process of elaboration of the ideal model, by considering more resources to establish an ideal model that allows to route, instead, the proposal for the redesign and its influence in the digital transformation, deepens in the diagnosis of the organization from the needs to project the achievement of the results, in the public sector that is oriented to the citizens, it is important to consider the product with public value, for the case of the private companies with added value to the services and/or products offered.

Para [8], considers the process architecture to project its strategic alignment towards the digital transformation of five companies analyzed, showing the organizational structure of the companies from the strategic point to the operational, operational to the strategic and the hybrid combination. The present research considers the work important because it considers the strategic and operational approach, also, it takes as a reference the hybrid approach to redesign the organization towards digital transformation, a weakness to the present work is to address the issues of strategies and inter-organizational relationships to achieve in less time the results.

8   Conclusions

This research orients the redesign or organizational design from a strategic and operational approach towards organizational influence with the support of the use of information technology in the context of the pandemic, it is a way of reinventing ourselves to develop coordinated work remotely, establishing a defined work route and committing to the achievement of results. In the implementation of the organizational design or redesign, it has been seen that the regions achieved better results when they complied with the premise of working in a committed manner and in teamwork, on the other hand it was evident that other regions had many difficulties because the commitment of the management was not reflected in the servers and in others it was shown that their work was developed in an isolated manner.

The implementation of the improvement of the procedures, from an operational approach, achieved better results, in the case of the reduction of steps of the activities of the procedures were reflected in the reduction of 20%.

The implementation of the improvement of the procedures, from an operational approach, achieved better results, in the case of the reduction of the effective time of the procedures was reflected in 11%.

The implementation of the improvement of the procedures, from an operational approach, achieved better results, in the case of the reduction of the cost of the procedures were reflected in the reduction of 52%.

The implementation of the organizational redesign proposal and its influence on the digital transformation achieves a better condition to satisfy public servants, with an increase of 7%.

9   Recommendations

The contribution of this work is the proposal of the TO-BE model in the organizational redesign towards digital transformation. This model will allow the alignment of strategic objectives, simplifying administrative procedures and generating continuous improvement of processes to carry out automation projects. The proposed TO-BE model will, in the future, engage stakeholders in the process of change towards digital transformation.

Change starts with the commitment of the actors to initiate the change process, taking advantage of digital tools in the context of the pandemic. The process approach is the cornerstone of organizational transformation, so it is important to start by raising awareness and building the driving team to transform towards digitalization.

The strategic approach is framed in the guide for the design of strategic, operational and support processes, found in the RSGP N° 006–2018-PCM-SGP that approves the technical standard N° 001–2018-SGP "Implementation of Process Management in Public Administration Entities", to achieve the expected results, it is important to seek the commitment of all members involved in the redesign, establishing the method of synchronized operational work, using tools that accelerate the identification of needs, products and indicators. The operational approach is achieved with the empowerment of the owners of the procedures and with training to encourage the development of continuous improvement, redesign, or automation of procedures.

References

1. González, I.J.R., González, A.G., Viamontes, P.N., Sotolongo, S.P.: Metodología de diseño organizacional integrando en-foque a procesos y competencias/methodology of organizational design. Integrat. Process Appr. Competencies. Ingeniería Indus. XXXIII(2), 188–199 (2012)
2. Urquiola Sánchez, O., Zulueta Torres, O.R., Liano Rodríguez, R.: Innovation for sustainable development: an experience in cienfuegos, cuba. Rev. Univ. Soc. 9(1), 106–113 (2017)
3. Fossland, S., Krogstie, J.: Modeling as-is, ought-to-be and to-be - experiences from a case study in the health sector. In: PoEM (Short Papers), p. 10 (2015)
4. García, Y.T., García, J.P.T.: Organisational design in organisations (review). Redel Rev. Granmense Desarro. Local 4, 1047–1061 (2020)
5. Alonso, I.M.: Digitalisation and technological innovation in the public administration: the necessary redefinition of the rights of public employees. Temas Laborales Rev. Trab. Bienestar Soc. 151, 373–396 (2020)
6. Alvarez Cuesta, H.:Del recurso al teletrabajo como medida de emergencia al futuro del trabajo a distancia, Lan Harremanak - Rev. Relac. Laborales 43, 175–201 (2020). https://doi.org/10.1387/lan-harremanak.21722
7. Ershadi, M., Jefferies, M., Davis, P., Mojtahedi, M.: Towards successful establishment of a project portfolio management system: business process management approach. J. Mod. Proj. Manag. 08(01), 22–41 (2020). https://doi.org/10.19255/JMPM02302
8. Fischer, M., Imgrund, F., Janiesch, C., Winkelmann, A.: Strategy archetypes for digital transformation: defining meta objectives using business process management. Inf. Manage. 57(5), 103262 (2020). https://doi.org/10.1016/j.im.2019.103262
9. Martínez-Caballero, D., González-González, A., González-González, A., Cazanave-Macías, J.: Integration of process management and architectural design in public service organisations, 13 (2020)
10. Valenzuela, A.B.E.: La auditoría como mejora continua en los organismos Pú-blicos de Salud del Perú. Quipukamayoc 28(56), 56 (2020). https://doi.org/10.15381/quipu. v28i56.17468

Computer Auditing Quality Assessment Based on Human, Technical and Contextual Factors

Daisy Imbaquingo[1,2](✉), Lorena San Pedro[1], Javier Díaz[2], Silvia Arciniega[1], Tatyana Saltos[1], and Cosme Ortega[1]

[1] Universidad Técnica del Norte, Ibarra, Ecuador
deimbaquingo@utn.edu.ec
[2] Universidad Nacional de La Plata, Buenos Aires, Argentina

Abstract. Computer auditing quality has been defined by results obtained in the process. Meanwhile, multiple studies have been done to enhance it therefore, it continues to be a topic interest and research so it is worth mentioning that its quality relies on trained competent auditors and experts able to develop a process correctly, adapting to clients and to manage auditing inherent risks. According to results from the computer audit, low quality and security levels have been identified in terms of the human, technical and contextual factors, affecting audit quality. The objective of this investigation is to identify metrics and to determine their own corresponding factor applying an exploratory type of research. To achieve such aim, a targeted survey was designed and implemented at the Institute of Internal Auditors of Ecuador since they have the knowledge and expertise in the field. A factor analysis statistics technique was applied to data gathered to verify that it relates to the identified factors as dimensions are reduced, thus the most impacting metrics may assess the quality of computer audits. Analysis results yielded a mean score for each one of the assessed metrics, concluding that the technical factor is the most significative since it relates roles and task performance during the auditing process as well as control procedures. Finally, most auditing quality-related issues are mainly the outcome of an inferior management auditing process, therefore it is crucial that collegiate groups and professionals in the field validate the auditing process.

Keywords: Quality control · Factor analysis · Metric

1 Introduction

Auditing quality is not an easy concept to define, and to date there is no concept universally recognized. However, it is linked to applicable standards to be audited [1–5]. Similarly, quality perception depends on the discretion of the team who are involved in the process [6]. The most acceptable concept is the extent of success of the processes performed [7] and to avoid subjective quality in auditing results, the preferred methodology's inherent risk should be considered [8].

Furthermore, auditing quality is defined based on the results yielded and despite several efforts to be enhance, it continues to be a subject worthy of attention and research

T. Guarda et al. (Eds.): ARTIIS 2022, CCIS 1676, pp. 320–338, 2022.
https://doi.org/10.1007/978-3-031-20316-9_25

[9]. Quality comes from qualified, motivated auditors in the correct design process adapting to the client so that inherent auditing risks are properly managed.

In this article, the concept of computer auditing quality is defined as the verification and validation process of results yielded from the monitoring exercise applied to analyze whether auditing products have pertinent criteria, opportunity, and sufficiency, in addition to either adding value to the business or providing verified, independent objective information for the decision-making phase in the processing-related areas of the audited object.

Auditing quality results vary according to project conditions, meaning type of industry, audited company size, complexity of involved systems among others [11], the quality revolves around key elements which altogether increase the likelihood of auditing enhanced efficiency and consistency [12]. Moreover, factors related to human, technical and contextual factors affecting the auditing quality are identified.

It is understood that a higher quality audit is related to brand or specialized auditors in the industry [10, 13, 14] claim that an auditor's experience, skills and specialized knowledge in the industry are positively related to audits quality. Outlined skills include communication and partnership, domain and process knowledge, professional development, personality traits as well as technical and auditing expertise and so on. Auditors should update clients data to provide effective auditing based on more detailed and relevant audit-testing [15].

Professional competence affects auditing quality, as auditors should have the expertise to interview, read quickly, understand statistics and computer use among other skills. On the other hand, accountability demonstrates that the auditor could have a satisfactory auditing performance, convinced that his work is carefully examined and verified by his supervisor who in turn is responsible to his employer. Thus accountability is decisive for the auditor since it affects the quality of the auditing process [16].

The auditing environment is an additional quality influencing factor, directly or indirectly [3], since it may have significative interactive effects in the auditing entry process. It has been discovered that many contextual characteristics influence the auditing quality such as auditor- partner fee, non-auditing additional fees and auditor continuity [10].

As the auditing results quality is influenced by several factors on premises, the low-quality and security issues are evident by the results from a computer auditing. Due to this fact, organizations are unlikely to obtain optimum results from decision-making processes aimed to enhance auditing processes.

The objective of this research work: i) To identify influencing quality results factors in computer auditing processes, ii) To understand group metrics in each factor.

To achieve these objectives, the study raises the following research questions:

1. What is the impact of influencing factors affecting the computer auditing process quality?
2. Which selected metrics for each factor influence auditing quality results?

2 Materials and Methods

The purpose of this research is to identify and define selected metrics to realize the emphasis of factors and its resulting metrics in auditing processes pursuing a greater approach in critical points within activities performed and results.

Since the study focuses on computer auditing, the proposed approach was considered by [18] those analyzing a group of metrics affecting computer auditing processes quality. Next, it was supplemented with an exploratory investigation identifying potential factors and auditing quality-related metrics. After that, a targeted survey was designed and implemented on Internal Auditors of Ecuador who have the expertise to answer the survey. Then, a factorial analysis statistic technique was applied to the results gathered from the survey to verify that results are related to established factors in the bibliographical review, thus a dimension reduction occurs so that more impactful metrics assessing the quality of computer auditing results are obtained.

Potential metrics results are shown in Appendix A for a statistical analysis that determines whether they are grouped correctly allowing a dimension reduction based on its result.

A set of 94 metrics was validated by a group of academic experts in the auditing, computer auditing and engineering field to determine if the instrument is clear, precise and has a pertinent measuring scale and whether potential metrics can achieve the objective in this study. Those surveyed responded based on the seven-point Likert scale set from a totally low-to-totally high score to the following question What is each metric's extent of the impact on the quality of results from computer processes?

Next, an online survey was conducted and applied to Internal Auditors of Ecuador Institute specifically in the computer auditing and Information area. With a total of 475 registered answers the requirements are met so that a factorial analysis is developed, being considering that the minimum number of responses should be 100 [19–21], response rate to the number of metrics, considering 5:1 approach (5 responses per variable). Software SPSS was used for the statistical analysis.

After that, a factorial analysis was performed to understand the relationship among metrics used in the survey so that a group of factors evidence most variability.

An internal consistency test through a Cronbach's Alpha was done, a reliability analysis to assess the metric-total correlation; scale reagents squared correlation and the reliability value if the reagent is eliminated. In this analysis, no reagent was eliminated since they have the same relation to the scale. All metrics keep the Alfa value $= 0.997$ for the 94 selected metrics. As a rule, one Alpha equal to 0.7 or higher represents a consistent set of variables.

Once the survey data consistency is checked, tests such as the Bartlett sphericity test were done to verify the significance of extracting factors from the set of metrics, which denotes that analyzed variables do not share a common variance. The Kaiser-Meyer-Olkin statistic (KMO) shows how much variance is present. For a factorization to be considered KMO index, values should be between 0.70–0.79 and satisfactory when its value is higher than 0.80 in which case a factorization is feasible providing key factors valuable data by the degree in which each metric is predictable from others [19].

Sphericity tests and KMO, show that the variable inter correlation degree is strong confirming by the significance associated to the Bartlett sphericity test, that is 0.001.

Similarly, KMO is 0.945 a value higher than 0.80 so according to this indicator, the data matrix is suitable to perform factorization.

3 Results

Results include analyses for each metric from the survey to identify the ones affecting the quality of computer auditing and to observe how these metrics group into factors.

A score analysis was performed provided by those surveyed to verify the importance of each metric in the results phase, determining that metrics measurements vary from totally low, to totally high. As per consistency and approach [18, 22], in their research they focused on ten superior and inferior metrics considering an average score throughout the entire sample.

Table 1 shows the 10 highest scored metrics. Each element in the list is crucial when assessing the quality of auditing results since they hold a higher mean than 5.82 meaning that most of them had a computer auditing quality impact rating from medium to totally high.

Table 1. The ten best computer auditing quality rated metrics

N°	Survey item	Overall average score
M45	Auditing results are totally supported by documents and evidence gathered in the auditing process	5,97
M26	The auditing team executes the audit impartially	5,89
M18	The auditor respects client's data confidentiality	5,89
M47	Auditing team achieves stated objectives in the auditing plan	5,89
M25	The auditing team demonstrates objectivity and integrity	5,87
M5	Members of the auditing team work on the auditing ethically and with transparency	5,86
M59	Audit report results are clear and concise	5,86
M87	Auditing team has the required permits to develop an auditing process	5,86
M93	Auditing team is well informed regarding internal controls	5,85
M61	Report presentation performed under computer auditing standards, manuals, guidelines, and practices	5,83

In general, the best rated metrics focus on the auditor's objectivity, ethics, transparency, audit's objectives achievement and how results are presented compared to [18], those who found planning and fieldwork as the best rated metrics. This fact indicates similarity between computer auditing identified metrics and computer standards since they require a greater planning approach considering objectives set and achieved.

Table 2 presents the 10 lowest metrics mean, resulting in less than 5.49 then the auditing quality results impact is rated as average or totally low, still being somehow relevant. However, in comparison with higher rated metrics, these become insignificant. Lower rated elements suggest that the organizational structure from the audited institution and the auditor skepticism are unimportant regarding computer auditing, in line with what has been stated by [18] in the last item.

Table 2. Ten computer auditing lowest quality rated metrics

N°	Survey item	Overall average score
M51	Client understands the purpose and process of computer auditing	5,48
M48	Findings, conclusions, and recommendations were positively perceived by the client	5,48
M41	Auditing team uses documenting templates and forms	5,47
M30	Auditor has national and international certifications from auditing and computer auditing field	5,47
M10	Auditing team has the client approval regarding tasks developed	5,45
M38	Auditor link-up to experts for support in the auditing process for results and client recommendations	5,44
M9	Auditing team ensures the client takes part in the auditing process	5,34
M15	Auditor has soft-skills personal characteristics and competences that show the way he gets along with others	5,33
M80	The institution organizational structure reflected on the auditing plan	5,28
M31	Auditor is skeptic during the auditing process	5,21

Similarly, a main component with varimax rotation analysis is carried out to perform a factorial varimax, simplifying factor interpretation. Factors having higher than 1 value are taken into account, while metric-factors have a larger than 0.6 cut since values are consistent with auditing-quality research done by [22] and [18]. Likewise, the orthogonally rotated factorial solution typify the existence of 5 latent factors and the contribution of each metric to the factor. Factors explain 84,754% variability in the original data as shown in Table 3.

Table 3. Factorial analysis and item loads. Cells in bold represent the metric maximum while italics cells have a value lower than 0,6 therefore eliminated from the factorial analysis. Results obtained from SPSS.

Metric	Factor				
	1	2	3	4	5
M1	*0,448*	*0,295*	*0,416*	*0,522*	*0,266*
M2	*0,362*	*0,349*	*0,486*	*0,378*	*0,362*

(continued)

Table 3. (*continued*)

Metric	Factor				
	1	2	3	4	5
M3	0,453	0,355	0,157	0,511	0,111
M4	0,502	0,454	0,284	0,571	0,022
M5	0,465	0,468	0,266	0,512	0,061
M6	0,441	0,376	0,376	0,565	0,147
M7	0,445	0,386	0,338	0,472	0,184
M8	0,448	0,430	0,424	0,513	0,154
M9	0,253	**0,695**	0,417	0,418	0,328
M10	0,267	**0,612**	0,333	0,346	0,378
M11	0,334	**0,642**	0,507	0,374	0,178
M12	0,399	**0,692**	0,367	0,454	0,106
M13	0,370	0,481	0,407	0,522	0,062
M14	0,393	0,546	0,408	0,474	0,025
M15	0,364	**0,610**	0,451	0,311	0,160
M16	0,417	**0,677**	0,346	0,340	0,174
M17	0,462	**0,651**	0,341	0,369	0,051
M18	0,432	0,582	0,330	0,492	−0,013
M19	0,418	**0,685**	0,348	0,324	0,098
M20	0,395	**0,696**	0,436	0,309	0,230
M21	0,363	**0,613**	0,362	0,486	0,102
M22	0,389	**0,626**	0,397	0,329	0,109
M23	0,347	0,486	0,481	0,343	0,204
M24	0,407	**0,668**	0,386	0,436	0,123
M25	0,425	0,492	0,412	0,557	0,060
M26	0,456	0,445	0,406	0,578	0,004
M27	0,399	**0,626**	0,396	0,418	0,115
M28	0,438	**0,602**	0,330	0,399	0,040
M29	0,433	**0,612**	0,343	0,436	0,032
M30	0,383	**0,611**	0,327	0,302	0,327
M31	0,326	0,543	0,225	0,014	0,262
M32	0,427	0,526	0,272	0,247	−0,086
M33	0,360	**0,759**	0,294	0,290	0,040

(*continued*)

Table 3. (*continued*)

Metric	Factor				
	1	2	3	4	5
M34	0,438	**0,731**	0,239	0,328	−0,062
M35	0,392	**0,721**	0,324	0,248	0,114
M36	0,481	**0,673**	0,282	0,311	−0,030
M37	*0,386*	*0,540*	*0,360*	*0,150*	*0,148*
M38	0,342	**0,746**	0,294	0,218	0,107
M39	0,461	**0,704**	0,295	0,274	-0,101
M40	0,424	**0,713**	0,283	0,368	0,005
M41	**0,632**	0,436	0,213	0,362	0,145
M42	*0,528*	*0,431*	*0,268*	*0,434*	*0,047*
M43	**0,704**	0,420	0,207	0,295	0,132
M44	**0,608**	0,483	0,307	0,309	0,204
M45	**0,634**	0,428	0,285	0,446	0,074
M46	**0,659**	0,521	0,331	0,244	0,133
M47	*0,571*	*0,428*	*0,320*	*0,391*	*−0,008*
M48	**0,635**	0,275	0,329	0,378	0,187
M49	**0,741**	0,341	0,319	0,307	0,092
M50	**0,633**	0,427	0,256	0,354	0,169
M51	**0,646**	0,317	0,334	0,148	0,364
M52	**0,661**	0,371	0,413	0,293	0,255
M53	**0,691**	0,425	0,322	0,318	0,087
M54	**0,719**	0,397	0,315	0,349	0,024
M55	**0,702**	0,387	0,318	0,280	0,214
M56	**0,675**	0,401	0,308	0,382	0,127
M57	**0,654**	0,423	0,414	0,132	0,276
M58	**0,679**	0,388	0,450	0,182	0,146
M59	**0,720**	0,361	0,355	0,296	0,117
M60	**0,687**	0,384	0,403	0,269	0,157
M61	*0,507*	*0,364*	*0,354*	*0,358*	*−0,011*
M62	**0,676**	0,437	0,383	0,256	0,100
M63	**0,677**	0,428	0,389	0,242	0,186
M64	*0,568*	*0,310*	*0,380*	*0,396*	*0,030*
M65	**0,721**	0,331	0,403	0,272	0,141

(*continued*)

Table 3. (*continued*)

Metric	Factor				
	1	2	3	4	5
M66	**0,703**	0,346	0,400	0,237	0,169
M67	**0,665**	0,334	0,444	0,231	−0,004
M68	**0,697**	0,393	0,416	0,303	0,040
M69	**0,666**	0,369	0,303	0,349	−0,009
M70	*0,502*	*0,394*	*0,392*	*0,304*	*−0,061*
M71	**0,696**	0,362	0,422	0,327	0,078
M72	**0,710**	0,384	0,417	0,263	0,084
M73	**0,702**	0,403	0,445	0,224	0,040
M74	**0,701**	0,397	0,407	0,248	0,037
M75	**0,692**	0,382	0,408	0,202	0,208
M76	**0,696**	0,377	0,408	0,254	−0,030
M77	**0,688**	0,399	0,432	0,266	0,038
M78	**0,656**	0,414	0,417	0,345	0,032
M79	**0,698**	0,329	0,458	0,280	0,018
M80	*0,387*	*0,275*	*0,582*	*0,114*	*0,115*
M81	0,455	0,324	**0,625**	0,298	0,084
M82	0,423	0,367	**0,698**	0,189	0,093
M83	0,446	0,328	**0,683**	0,247	0,208
M84	0,425	0,377	**0,670**	0,214	0,266
M85	*0,507*	*0,399*	*0,591*	*0,307*	*0,104*
M86	0,475	0,413	**0,638**	0,253	0,032
M87	*0,513*	*0,355*	*0,599*	*0,294*	*0,030*
M88	0,461	0,319	**0,624**	0,272	0,108
M89	*0,517*	*0,375*	*0,528*	*0,376*	*−0,104*
M90	*0,451*	*0,340*	*0,519*	*0,370*	*0,022*
M91	*0,510*	*0,382*	*0,596*	*0,335*	*−0,147*
M92	0,459	0,414	**0,667**	0,251	0,057
M93	*0,408*	*0,351*	*0,505*	*0,389*	*0,024*
M94	*0,507*	*0,352*	*0,594*	*0,372*	*−0,042*

Metrics not meeting the analysis value such as lower to 0,6 are eliminated from the analysis while elements lacking load value are: M1, M2, M3, M4, M5, M6, M7, M8, M13, M14, M18, M23, M25, M26, M31, M32, M37, M42, M47, M61, M64, M70, M80, M85, M87, M89, M90, M91, M93, M94.

Finally, the ultimate analysis instrument is comprised by 64 reagents that, reanalyzed are grouped into 3 factors matching the analyzed theory in [23]. Factors are solid representations of a previously studied theoretical component, consequently the factorial analysis should identify a set of reagents for abstract-concepts since factors matching theoretical basis means positive validity evidence [18, 20, 21, 24]. Identified factors are labeled as human, technical and contextual according to the theoretical basis. The final analysis solution converged in new iterations explaining 83.788% variance. Items reveal factorial loads higher than 0,6 within its own factor and communalities higher than 0,694 ordered from highest to lowest, grouped in 3 identified factors as shown in Table 4.

Table 4. Final solution factorial analysis and metric loads. Bold cells represent the maximum load while the factor belonging to the reagent. Results obtained from SPSS

Metric	Technical factor	Metric	Human factor	Metric	Contextual factor
M49	0,789	M40	0,792	M83	0,715
M65	0,764	M33	0,791	M84	0,708
M59	0,758	M38	0,775	M82	0,677
M54	0,757	M34	0,774	M92	0,656
M72	0,757	M39	0,75	M81	0,634
M79	0,75	M35	0,748	M88	0,622
M66	0,749	M19	0,743	M86	0,606
M71	0,745	M36	0,734		
M55	0,742	M17	0,73		
M76	0,742	M29	0,716		
M43	0,739	M12	0,711		
M74	0,738	M24	0,702		
M73	0,736	M10	0,696		
M68	0,728	M28	0,692		
M53	0,725	M21	0,677		
M60	0,724	M15	0,672		
M56	0,72	M30	0,668		
M69	0,719	M27	0,656		
M77	0,719	M20	0,646		
M75	0,718	M16	0,644		
M58	0,716	M22	0,632		
M67	0,714	M9	0,628		

(continued)

Table 4. (*continued*)

Metric	Technical factor	Metric	Human factor	Metric	Contextual factor
M62	0,712	M11	0,623		
M63	0,703				
M78	0,703				
M52	0,697				
M45	0,695				
M48	0,686				
M41	0,681				
M46	0,679				
M51	0,677				
M50	0,67				
M57	0,669				
M44	0,638				

4 Discussion

Each auditing process is unique, and success depends on the circumstance and factor-selection. Additionally, its metrics should support development and practice of the process [11, 12]. Likewise, auditing quality revolves around key factors identified in the research. It is summarized that this process should be designed by highly trained and motivated auditor sable to appreciate technical, contextual, or environmental factors that adequately adjust to individual auditing conditions in each audit.

Technical Factor
Related to the auditing performance activities during the process including organization, strategy and planning, methodology selection, field work, results and reports, evidence based on decision-making processes, quality control and auditing improvement. Most quality-related issues are mainly the result of unacceptable auditing management process [12] as it depends on specific aspects in the auditing process and control procedures [10].

Within the auditing process a choice of tools, techniques, methodologies, and specific methods in the auditing team will follow. Some metrics from this factor are: the use of project management ultimate practices, field work review, planning, project scope, audit impact, auditing practice and procedures and the like [3, 11].

Human Factor
Addresses the auditor or auditing professionals, client or the audited, management and key interactions of all involved in the process. It is important to consider quality perception through every participant -users, auditors, regulators and society- [25], since they have different views in regards of what constitutes and has an effect on the type of metrics used to assess the auditing quality.

The auditor or group of professionals in the audit, depending on the circumstance are responsible for the performance of an audit [12] and the result of their work will successfully reflect on a reliable audit report based on established standards. [16]. Given that experienced auditors follow standards well, are therefore associated to the unlikeliness of audit failure [26]. All these qualities lead to adequate planning and auditing programs generating reliable results which may directly affect client satisfaction, crucial when evaluating quality [5].

Contextual Factor
Related to external auditor elements and the auditing process, to include social and institutional force from both, the audited institution and the auditee, their regulatory environment and resource management.

Additionally, the environment in which auditing processes are carried out varies from one country to another. As a country develops and companies become larger, more security is particularly needed regarding internal processes as the environment turns more complex. As a consequence, laws, security requirements and corporate government processes, the estate of the laws and auditing inspections or when research fails the process and adoption of disciplinary measures become more effective if they are fulfilled appropriately [3]. Thus, management and institution resource optimization should be considered upon strategy implementation so as to decrease costs for both, the auditee and the audited company [27]. Altogether, these contextual factors have the potential to affect directly or indirectly the nature of the auditing since they have significative interactive effects on the entries and auditing process [3].

In addition to perform the factorial analysis and to evaluate resulting factors, the impact each factor had on the auditing quality results was assessed and scores are calculated for each factor based on the corresponding metrics average.

The three affecting quality factors from the auditing results, the technical factor is the most significative due to the number of metrics found in its factor load, which is superior compared to the other two factors. Regarding the dimension reduction process, the technical factor revealed minimum reduction totaling 5 discarded metrics: M42-Auditing team has approval methods for completed tasks in the auditing process, M47-Auditing team achieves planned objectives, M61-Reports presentation is done under computer auditing policies, standards, manuals, guidelines and practice, M64-Auditing team is has ample knowledge of auditing evidence gathering techniques and M70-Auditng plan developed according to computer auditing policies, standards, manuals, guidelines and practice.

On the other hand, in the human factor 17 metrics were eliminated: M1-the leader of the auditing team or individual possesses leadership qualities, M2.-The representative for the organization which is being audited possesses leadership qualities, M3-Personnel who performs the auditing process has ample auditing experience, M4-Auditing team members demonstrate honesty and respect while doing their job, M5-Auditing team members work on the auditing ethically and transparently, M6- Auditing team keeps a cordial and respectful relationship with the auditee both verbally and in writing, M7-Auditing team fulfills client requirements, M8-Audtior knows how to listen and is receptive to the client, M13-Personnel performing the auditing has the ability to deal with sensitive situations, M14- Personnel performing the auditing demonstrates assertiveness in problem solving and demanding situations, M18-Auditor respects client confidentiality and information, M23-Auditor reports to the person in charge events that may affect his independence, M25-Auditing team displays objectivity and integrity, M26-Auditng team executes the auditing impartially, without prejudice, M3- Auditor is skeptic during the auditory process, M32-Auditing team's expertise adds value to the auditee,M37-Auditing team holds regular formal and intelligible meetings for analysis progress and results.

As per contextual factor, 8 metrics: M80-An institution organizational structure is reflected in the auditing plan, M85-Auditor team present recommendations to the organization regarding international standards, local regulation, strategic objective updates as well as changes in the auditing environment, M87-Auditing team has all the required permits to develop the auditing process, M89-Auditing team is prepared to the risk of litigation, M90-Auditing team has access to human and technical resources for specialized audits, M91-Auditing team has access to required resources to comply with the scope and auditing calendar, M93-Auditing team is well aware of internal controls and M94-Auditing team identify client internal control system key elements, resulting in computer auditing quality result evaluation tool comprised by 64 metrics.

5 Conclusions

At present, computer auditing is one of the fields taken very seriously, unfortunately there are not enough process authenticators, resulting in quality deficient audits caused by several internal and external factors.

Likewise, it can be concluded that computer auditing processes lack quality owing to deficiencies within the auditing process as well as management performed by incompetent auditors attributable to the absence of technology training and the use of data advanced techniques. Despite that auditing firms make great efforts to train their personnel it is possible to realize that only a few auditors can take on new challenges.

In this study, quality-affecting factors were pinned down, analyzed, and compared to existent theoretical foundation, same that were categorized by technical, human, and contextual factors.

Based on the study performed, two factors were ruled-out that, according to the analysis have no significance in the computer auditing process exhibiting a deficiency of higher than 0,6 factorial loads, making the technical factor the most significative in computer auditing processes as it was the factor reveling less dimensions reduction plus a factorial load superior to human and contextual factors.

To conclude, it can be determined that by applying technical, human, and contextual factors and resulting significant metrics there is an improvement in the computer auditing quality assessment process.

Appendix A. Computer Auditing Quality Metrics

Code	Metric	Source
M1	Auditing team leader or individual possesses leadership skills	[9, 28]
M2	The (auditee)organization's representative possesses leadership skills	[9, 28]
M3	Personnel performing the audit has ample auditor experience	[2, 3, 10, 11, 13, 14, 16, 18, 26]
M4	Auditing team members demonstrate honesty and respect when doing their job	[3, 9, 16]
M5	Members of the auditing team perform their audit ethically and transparently	[3, 9, 16]
M6	Auditor team keeps a cordial and verbal and written respectful relationship with the auditee	[10, 11, 18]
M7	Auditing team fulfills client requirements	[10, 11, 18]
M8	Auditor knows how to listen and is receptive to the client	[10, 11, 18]
M9	Auditing team makes sure the client takes part in the entire auditing process	[10, 11, 18]
M10	Auditing team has client approval of the tasks developed	[10, 11, 18]
M11	Auditing team and client direct efforts to a common goal	[10, 11, 18]
M12	Personnel performing the audit the required competence to perform their job	[4, 9, 11, 16, 28]
M13	Auditing personnel has the ability to deal with sensitive situations	[4, 9, 11, 16, 28]
M14	Auditing personnel exhibits assertiveness in problem solving and demanding situations	[4, 9, 11, 16, 28]
M15	Auditor possesses soft skills personal characteristics and competencies that demonstrate the auditor gets along with others	[4, 9, 11, 16, 28]
M16	Auditing personnel effective suggestions to the institution to be audited	[4, 9, 11, 16, 28]
M17	Auditing personnel has observation skills	[4, 9, 11, 16, 28]
M18	Auditor respects client information and confidentiality	[3, 9]
M19	Auditor keeps an open mind when new ideas are suggested	[3, 9]
M20	Auditor is confident of himself and his job	[3, 9]

(continued)

(*continued*)

Code	Metric	Source
M21	Auditing team continues being independent in appearance and action	[18, 28, 29]
M22	Auditing team does not get involved in activities that compromise their independence	[18, 28, 29]
M23	Auditor reports to the person in charge events that may affect his independence	[18, 28, 29]
M24	Auditing team focuses on facts	[12, 16, 29]
M25	Auditing team demonstrates objectivity and integrity	[12, 16, 29]
M26	Auditing team executes the audit impartially and with no prejudice	[12, 16, 29]
M27	Auditing team is supported to reach their goals	[16]
M28	Auditing team demonstrates a great deal of effort to perform the audit	[30]
M29	The auditor is concerned for his training and continuing training	[26]
M30	Auditor has national and international certifications in the auditing and computer auditing field	[26]
M31	Auditor exhibits skepticism during the entire auditing process	[3, 4]
M32	Auditing team expertise add value to the auditee –the organization	[3, 14, 18]
M33	Members of auditing team demonstrate confidence regarding information security and data processing	[3, 14, 18]
M34	Clients disputes are dealt with appropriately and objectively	[3, 11]
M35	Auditing team is available to attend to clients inquiries	[3, 11]
M36	Those involved in the audit keep frequent communication	[3, 11]
M37	Auditing team hold regular formal indelible meetings for analyses progress and results	[13]
M38	Auditors link up with experts as a support in the auditing process to obtain client recommendations and results	[11]
M39	Auditing team appropriately selects consultants and experts	[11]

(*continued*)

(continued)

Code	Metric	Source
M40	Auditor follows policies and procedures that regulate ethical and professional compliance	[27, 31]
M41	Auditing team uses templates and forms to document the process	[9]
M42	Auditing team has approval procedures for completed auditing tasks	[9]
M43	Auditor and those responsible for the organization auditee- follow up on auditing previous computer auditing issues	[9, 28]
M44	Audit findings and conclusions are an exact reflection of the audited process real facts	[12, 29]
M45	Auditing results are totally supported and documented by auditing gathered evidence	[12, 29]
M46	Members of the auditing team and those responsible for the institution protect at all times information used in the process	[29]
M47	Auditing team achieves objectives planned in the auditing	[12, 29]
M48	Findings, conclusions, and recommendations were positively approved by the client	[12, 29]
M49	Auditing assigned resources go accordingly to audit relevance and complexity	[12, 29]
M50	System, process, and audited subject is important to the organization	[12]
M51	Client understands the process and purpose of the computer auditing	[12]
M52	In the scope, all required elements for a successful audit are addressed	[12, 17, 18]
M53	Audit execution complies with the elements agreed in the scope	[12, 17, 18]
M54	Results are delivered in the appropriate and established time	[12]
M55	Risk evaluating model is comprehensive	[4, 10, 11]
M56	Auditing plan takes into account client-related risks	[4, 10, 11]
M57	Auditing team is committed to the auditing completion deadline	[2, 3, 11]
M58	Auditing process is developed accurately	[3]
M59	Results from the auditing report are clean and concise	[3, 9, 10, 12]

(continued)

(*continued*)

Code	Metric	Source
M60	Scope, findings, and recommendations are understandable for anyone that makes use of the audit report	[3, 9, 10, 12]
M61	Reports presentation is done under policies, standards, manuals, practice, and computer guidelines	[3, 9, 10, 12]
M62	Auditing team performs fieldwork adequately	[3, 17, 18]
M63	Auditing is executed under computer auditing policies, standards, manuals, guidelines, and practice	[3, 17, 18]
M64	Auditing team is having ample knowledge of auditing evidence gathering techniques	[3, 17, 18]
M65	All tasks are developed according to planned	[3, 17, 18]
M66	Verification lists are completed, approved, and documented	[3, 17, 18]
M67	Work field is checked by an expert	[3, 17, 18]
M68	Client or those responsible for the organization provide data gathering support	[17, 18]
M69	Information and results from previous audits are available for revision	[17, 18]
M70	Auditing plan is developed according to computer auditing policies, standards, manuals, guidelines, and practice	[17, 18]
M71	Objectives and auditing scope are appropriately specified	[17, 18]
M72	Auditing tasks and tools are clearly described	[17, 18]
M73	Auditing team members have a clear and coherent understanding of the auditing plan	[17, 18]
M74	Budget and audit schedule are set up adequately	[17, 18]
M75	Required resources to perform the auditing are evaluated	[17, 18]
M76	Personnel and equipment required assigned by the auditing are evaluated	[17, 18]
M77	Auditing plan is addressed, made, checked, and approved by supervisors and those responsible for the organization and auditing team members	[17, 18]
M78	Auditing team uses computer auditing methodology to plan, manage and develop audits	[11, 18]
M79	Auditing team uses technological tools and updated methodologies to perform their job	[11, 18]

(*continued*)

(continued)

Code	Metric	Source
M80	An institution organizational structure is reflected on the auditing plan	[3, 9, 11, 18]
M81	Auditor promotes through an organizational culture based on computer security good practice	[3, 9, 11, 18]
M82	Auditing team follows strict quality procedures	[3, 4, 10]
M83	The auditing team leader is committed to quality control systems	[3, 4, 10]
M84	Norms and regulations issued by control organisms are reflected on auditing plans	[3, 11]
M85	Auditing team presents recommendations that the organization should follow because of international standard updates, local regulation, strategic objectives and change in the auditing environment	[3, 11]
M86	Auditing team is knowledgeable in terms of relevant information of the laws and regulations that may have a significant impact on audit objectives	[3, 11]
M87	Auditing team has the required permits to develop and auditing process	[3, 11]
M88	Disciplinary measures are applied in case of auditing plan or current regulatory legal standards non-compliance	[3, 11]
M89	Auditing team es fully prepared before the risk of litigation	[3, 28]
M90	Auditing team has access to technical and human resources for a specialized audit	[17]
M91	Auditing team has access to required resources to comply with the scope and auditing calendar	[17]
M92	Audit cost commensurate with tasks developed and complexity	[10, 14, 28]
M93	Auditing team is aware of internal controls	[28]
M94	Auditing team identify client internal control system key elements	[28]

References

1. Bojorque, R., Pesántez-Avilés, F.: Academic quality management system audit using artificial intelligence techniques. Adv. Intell. Syst. Comput. **965**(28), 275–283 (2020)
2. Dickins, D., Johnson-Snyder, A.J., Reisch, J.T.: Selecting an auditor for Bradco using indicators of audit quality. J. Account. Educ. **45**, 32–44 (2018)

3. International Auditing and Assurance Standards Board: A framework for audit quality. International Federation of Accountants, New York (2014)
4. Sulaiman, N.A., Shahimi, S., Nashtar, K.: People and audit process attributes of audit quality: evidence from Malaysia. Manag. Account. Rev. **18**(2), 47 (2019)
5. Yuniarti, R., Zumara, W.M.: Audit quality attributes and audit client satisfaction. Int. J. Humanit. Manag. Sci. **1**(1), 96–100 (2013)
6. Knechel, W., Vanstraelen, A.: The relationship between auditor tenure and audit quality implied by going concern opinions. Auditing **26**(1), 113–131 (2007)
7. Havelka, D., Merhout, J.W.: Internal information technology audit process quality: theory development using structured group processes. Int. J. Account. Inf. Syst. **14**(3), 165–192 (2013)
8. Imbaquingo Esparza, D.E., Ron Egas, M.B., Cajas Sinchiguano, F.A., Luje Misacango, R.A.: Evaluation model of computer audit methodologies based on inherent risk. Iber Conference Information System Technology Cist, pp. 24–27 (2020)
9. Holm, C., Zaman, M.: Regulating audit quality: restoring trust and legitimacy. Account. Forum **36**(1), 51–61 (2012)
10. Knechel, W., Krishnan, G., Pevzner, M., Shefchik, L., Velury, U.: Audit quality: insights from the academic literature. Auditing **32**(1), 385–421 (2013)
11. Havelka, D., Merhout, J.W.: Development of an information technology audit process quality framework. Association of Information Systems - AMCIS 2007 Proceedings, no. 61, pp. 910–916 (2007)
12. Committee Contact of Heads of EU SAIs. Guidelines on Audit Quality, p. 57 (2004)
13. Yasin, F., Nelson, S.: Audit committee and internal audit: implications on audit quality. Int. J. Econ. Manag. Account. **20**(2), 8–10 (2012)
14. Harris, M.K., Williams, L.T.: Audit quality indicators: perspectives from non-big four audit firms and small company audit committees. Adv. Account. **50**, 100485 (2020)
15. Eilifsen, A., Knechel, W., Wallage, P.: Application of the business risk audit model: a field study. Account. Horizons **15**(3), 193–207 (2001)
16. Zahmatkesh, S., Rezazadeh, J.: The effect of auditor features on audit quality. Tékhne **15**(2), 79–87 (2017)
17. Hasas Yeghaneh, Y., Zangiabadi, M., Dehghani Firozabadi, S.M.: Factors affecting information technology audit Quality. J. Invest. Manag. **4**(5), 196–203 (2015)
18. Stoel, D., Havelka, D., Merhout, J.W.: An analysis of attributes that impact information technology audit quality: a study of IT and financial audit practitioners. Int. J. Account. Inf. Syst. **13**(1), 60–79 (2012)
19. Ferrando, J., Anguiano, C.: El análisis factorial como técnica de investigación en psicología. Papeles del Psicólogo **31**(1), 18–33 (2010)
20. Guti, L.: Cómo realizar e interpretar un análisis factorial exploratorio utilizando SPSS. REIRE Rev. d Innovació i Recer. en Educ. **12**(2), 1–14 (2019)
21. Lloret-Segura, S., Ferreres-Traver, A., Hernández-Baeza, A., Tomás-Marco, I.: El Análisis Factorial Exploratorio de los Ítems: una guía práctica, revisada y actualizada. An. Psicol. **30**(3), 1151–1169 (2014)
22. Carcello, J., Hermanson, R., McGrath, N.: Audit quality attributes: the perceptions of audit partners, preparers, and financial statement users. Audit. A J. Pract. Theory **11**, 1–15 (1992)
23. Imbaquingo, D., San Pedro, L., Diaz, J., Saltos, T., Arciniega, S.: Let's talk about computer audit quality: a systematic literature review. In: 2021 International Conference on Maintenance and Intelligent Asset Management (ICMIAM), pp. 1–7 (2021)
24. de la Fuente, S.: Análisis Factorial, Madrid (2011)
25. Sulaiman, N.A., Yasin, F.M., Muhamad, R.: Perspectives on audit quality: an analysis. Asian J. Account. Perspect. **11**(1), 1–27 (2018)

26. Ye, K., Cheng, Y., Gao, J.: How individual auditor characteristics impact the likelihood of audit failure: evidence from China. Adv. Account. **30**(2), 394–401 (2014)
27. Guindel, E.: Calidad y seguridad de la información y auditoría informática. Universidad Carlos III de Madrid, Leganés (2010)
28. Public Company Accounting Oversight Board, Concept Release on Audit Quality Indicators, PCAOB, no. 005, pp. 1–61 (2015)
29. Strous, L.: Audit of information systems: the need for cooperation, Lecture Notes in Computer Science (including Subser. Lecture Notes in Artificial Intelligence and Lecture Notes in Bioinformatics), vol. 1521, pp. 264–274 (2002)
30. Xiao, T., Geng, C., Yuan, C.: How audit effort affects audit quality: an audit process and audit output perspective. China J. Account. Res. **13**(1), 109–127 (2020)
31. Refaat, R., El-Henawy, I.M.: Innovative method to evaluate quality management system audit results' using single value neutrosophic number. Cogn. Syst. Res. **57**, 197–206 (2019)

A Cyber4Dev Security Culture Model

Morena Abiel Tsoeu⬥ and Adéle da Veiga⁽⊠⁾⬥

School of Computing, College of Science, Engineering and Technology, UNISA, Florida,
Johannesburg, South Africa
dveiga@unisa.ac.za

Abstract. Researchers have conducted studies to investigate factors influencing information security and cybersecurity culture, and to develop models and frameworks. However, very little research has been done on cybersecurity culture for developing countries, Cyber4Dev. The purpose of this paper is to develop an Ubuntu Cyber4Dev Security Culture Model. The current study deployed the PRISMA and scoping literature review methods to review existing cybersecurity culture models and to identify significant factors influencing cybersecurity culture to address unique challenges in developing countries like Africa. An Ubuntu Cyber4Dev Security Culture Model is proposed integrating African languages and the Ubuntu philosophy with 13 factors derived from literature that influence cybersecurity culture. The proposed conceptual model can be used as a point of reference to conduct further research on Cyber4Dev security culture in Africa and other developing countries. This study is one of the first studies on Cyber4Dev security culture and can inform policymakers on how to foster a cybersecurity culture with the aim of influencing the behaviour of end users to improve the protection of information.

1 Introduction

As the Coronavirus presented itself as a global pandemic, cyberspace use became even more prevalent. It is estimated that in the year 2 024, more than 30 billion devices would be connected to the internet, connecting global citizens through the internet of things [1]. According to [2], these connections may increase up to 35 billion in 2025. Developing countries, as part of the global world, are also enjoying the benefits of cyberspace [3]. Although cyberspace has many benefits, individuals, enterprises, and governments, especially from developing countries, must brace themselves for the risk to security and information privacy that cyberspace introduces. The impact of ICT and cyberspace in the global world, especially developing countries, is soiled by arrivals of new security threats [3].

The purpose of this study is to conduct a scoping literature review of cyber for development (Cyber4Dev) in the context of security culture, in order to propose an Ubuntu Cyber4Dev Security Culture Model. Cyber4Dev is a project started by the European Union to promote cyber resilience and cybersecurity for private and public enterprises for developing countries in Asia and Africa [4]. There is limited literature available on cybersecurity culture in developing countries. This study is among the first reviews for Cyber4Dev. According to [5], scoping literature reviews are "exploratory projects that

T. Guarda et al. (Eds.): ARTIIS 2022, CCIS 1676, pp. 339–351, 2022.
https://doi.org/10.1007/978-3-031-20316-9_26

systematically map the literature available on a topic, identifying key concepts, theories, sources of evidence and gaps in the research." Cyber4Dev literature is still in its infancy and therefore this study will review literature on cybersecurity culture and information security culture to propose the conceptual model. It is hoped that South Africa (SA) and African countries can use the model to mitigate the risk in cyberspace from a human perspective.

This study takes the following structure: Sect. 2 and Sect. 3 discuss the research problem and research questions respectively. Section 4, the background, provides a brief overview of the Cyber4Dev security culture adapted from cybersecurity culture and information security culture. Section 5 presents the scoping literature review and PRISMA methods as the methodology used in this study. Section 6 details the findings of the scoping review. Section 7 discusses the proposed Ubuntu Cyber4Dev Security Culture Model and Sect. 8 answers the research questions. Section 9 provides the limitations and future work of the study. Lastly, Sect. 10 concludes the study.

2   Research Problem

The widespread use of broadband and the rollout of fibre has seen the proliferation of the use of information on networks and the internet by organisations in developing countries, including African countries. However, the use of networks and the internet bring about the need for the protection against the many risks associated with cyberspace use. African countries like SA have experienced an increase in cybercrimes, which proportionally increases with the proliferation of the use of the internet [6]. Hacktivists group, Anonymous Collective Team Hack Argentina syndicate, claimed an attack which saw 200 South African websites marred, by online posting. These attacks included governmental websites [6]. SA has found itself as one of the countries realising the most cyberattacks among developing countries. In March 2022, [7] reported that the hacker group named N4aughtysecTU, demanded R225 million ransom from the South African credit reporting agency, TransUnion. The group claimed to be in position of 4 terabytes of compromised data that included, credits scores, banking details, and ID numbers.

Many studies have suggested developing an information security or cybersecurity culture to protect organisations against the human factor/risk to the protection of information in cyberspace. For example, [8] posits that a positive information security culture can lead to a strategy of management in information security that directs individuals' security behaviour in an organisation. [9] argues that it is necessary to create an information security culture because individuals' behaviour in organisations present a risk to its information assets. Information security culture and cybersecurity culture models are created and proposed for organisations. However, these models, incorporating unique factors and risks, were not developed for developing countries, like SA. Developed countries have created standards, protocols, policies, and legislative frameworks for information security [10]. On the other hand, developing countries lack the capacity and financial resources to conduct information security education and awareness programs [10]. [3] purports that developing countries are a target to attack and a medium of attack to other countries because of a lack of adequate controls and procedures to protect networks. In addition, many developing countries rely on developed countries for development of cybersecurity strategies. However, the cybersecurity strategies implemented by developed countries may not necessarily work when directly applied to developing countries [11]. As Cyber4Dev is a new concept, few studies, if any, have been conducted on this topic. This study sought to close the gap by developing a conceptual model for Cyber4Dev Security Culture for organisations in developing countries by answering the research questions below.

3 Research Questions

The objective of this research is to propose a conceptual Cyber4Dev Security Culture Model which can be utilised by African countries such as South Africa to address the risk of human behaviour to the protection of information. The main research questions for this study are as follows:

- What is a Cyber4Dev security culture?

  The purpose of this research question is to elicit information that will help in understanding the cybersecurity culture in developing countries.
- What would a holistic model for a Cyber4Dev security culture comprise?

  This question will assist to elicit the elements that must be included in the Cyber4Dev Security Culture Model for developing countries as there are limited previous or present literature available about cybersecurity culture models or frameworks for developing countries, such as South Africa.

4 Background

4.1 What is Cyber4Dev?

Cybersecurity is concerned with the safeguarding of information and assets from cyber threats and vulnerabilities. It enforces the safeguarding of confidentiality, integrity, and availability of information and cyber assets [12]. [12] distinguish between information security and cybersecurity; information security being the protection of information from threats, while cybersecurity is the protection of the entire cyberspace and its users as well as their devices. [13] defined cybersecurity "as the body of technologies, practice with coordinated series of actions, designed to defend networks, computers, system application programs and data from an attack, damage or unauthorized access". Cyber4Dev – Cyber Resilience for Development – A European Union project designed to protect public and private enterprises across countries in Asia and Africa, has started this project with the aim of promoting cyber resilience and cybersecurity for private and public enterprises, especially for developing countries around the world. In essence, Cyber4Dev is cybersecurity for developing countries [4]. The cybersecurity culture model that will be proposed in this study for developing countries must incorporate the national culture, beliefs, traditions and norms of those countries. [10] posit that national culture must also be consideration when improving the information security culture because it has an impact on the information culture.

4.2   Cybersecurity Breaches in Africa

Information and communication technology (ICT) has changed traditional organisations to competitive and modern organisations, but these modern organisations need to pay a great deal of attention to information and cybersecurity in managing organisational systems [14, 15]. As [15] posits, to ensure information stability, integrity, availability and confidentiality, information must be protected. Cybersecurity ventures estimated the cost of cybercrime to amount to 21 trillion per year as of 2021 [16]. [17] claimed that Africa has experienced the highest growing rate in cybercrimes that include identity theft, espionage, and fraud. One such example is that eleven African countries were affected by a sophisticated espionage malware called Pegasus [18]. SA has been reported as holding the third position in terms of cyberattacks, phishing in particular [6, 15, 17]. Most countries implemented lockdown regulations during the Covid-19 pandemic in 2020, and most people were forced to work from home using teleconferencing to hold meetings. This introduced new risks which also resulted in an incident in SA whereby cybercriminals invading parliamentary proceedings held via Zoom by showing obscene content [19]. Financial institutions and national infrastructures are also not immune to cyberattacks. First National Bank in SA suffered malware attacks during the Covid-19 pandemic in the form of Trojans, which saw customers receive spams that required them to click on unsuspecting links [19]. [20] purports that cybercriminals view SA as a haven for deploying cybercrime attacks. SA suffered many ransomware attacks in the first quarter of 2021, including Crysis, Nefilism, Ruyk, Clop, and Conti [20]. Transnet's systems were hit by cyberattacks earlier in 2021 and in September the Department of Justice and Constitutional Development suffered a devastating ransomware attack [20]. Interpol [21] noted online scams, digital extortion, business email compromise, ransomware, and botnets as the top five most prominent online threats amongst African countries.

4.3   The Concept of Information Security Culture

Perhaps the best description of culture is how things are done [22]. [23] posits that even though there are numerous definitions of information security culture, they are related in many aspects, such as employees' behaviour, values, and basic assumptions that are evident in artifacts. [23] argued that research has shown that human behaviour is a threat to information (and cyber) security. It is important to create a strong information security culture because human behaviour brings about risk to organisation's information assets [9]. The various cultures among individuals in an organisation impact the success of information security programs and the use of technological controls [9]. [24] states that the adherence, or lack of, to the information security policy (ISP) by employees is a concern to organisations. Adherence to such policies is vital to minimize the information security risk in the organisation. [8] further argues that having a positive information security culture is helpful for monitoring employee activities in an organisation. A cybersecurity culture is vital for changing employees' behaviour and preventing security breaches resulting from employees' non-compliance with organisational ISPs [25]. However, it is vital to consider national culture when enhancing information security culture because national culture influences organisational culture [10]. Therefore, national cultural aspects of developing countries must also be considered as a factor that could influence an information security culture. Specific challenges in SA are for example low literacy levels and poverty [45] unemployment [46] and multiple languages [11]. These challenges must be considered in organisational and government strategies when putting policies in place to address cyber risks by strengthening the cyber or information security culture.

5 Research Method

5.1 Scoping Literature Review

[26] describes a scoping literature review as a review that delivers an initial evaluation of prospective size and scope of available literature. Scoping literature reviews attempt to be systematic, transparent and replicable [26]. [5] indicates that conducting scoping literature reviews have numerous aims, including assessment of the depth of literature, mapping and summarizing the evidence, influencing future research, and addressing knowledge gaps. This study adopted the scoping literature review method. Cyber4Dev security culture research is still in its infancy, and this study forms part of an ongoing research. The "Preferred Reporting Items for Systematic Reviews and Meta-Analyses (PRISMA)" [27], is employed in this study to aid in conducting the scoping literature review in a systematic manner.

5.2 Literature Search

Keywords used were "cybersecurity" AND "culture" AND "information security" AND "culture". Additional strings such as "information AND security AND model OR frameworks OR factors" and "cyber AND security AND model OR frameworks OR factors" were used to search for models and frameworks on cybersecurity culture and information culture, and factors influencing cyber and information security culture. The keywords, "information AND security OR developing AND countries", were used to discover the research conducted in developing countries. The search included studies done from 2015 to 2021.

5.3 Criteria for Inclusion of Studies

The following search criteria were used to source the studies:

- Literature on cybersecurity culture and information security culture.
- Literature published in English.
- Cybersecurity culture and information security culture models and frameworks.
- Literature discussing factors influencing cybersecurity culture and information security culture.

The exclusion criteria were implemented using the following criteria:

- Literature not discussing cybersecurity and information security.

• Studies focusing on technical cybersecurity and information security controls.

Figure 1 depicts the steps followed in searching the literature for cybersecurity and information security culture for developing countries. A total of 80 records were retrieved in sourcing the studies, 72 records from database searching and 8 from other sources. Nine duplicate records were identified and removed. An analysis was conducted on the remaining literature to evaluate their eligibility for inclusion. Eight records were removed after extract analysis. A total of 63 full-text records of literature was evaluated for eligibility and 36 records were included based on the inclusion and exclusion criteria.

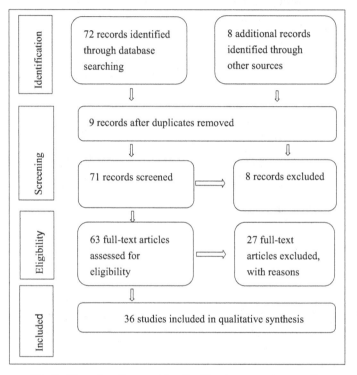

Fig. 1. Procedure for searching the literature on cybersecurity

6   Results

This study investigated factors that influence cyber and/or information security as there was limited literature found on Cyber4Dev. The literature review identified factors influencing cybersecurity and information security culture in an organisation. Table 1. groups the factors influencing cybersecurity or information security culture according to their frequencies and consideration was given to factors that have an impact on the national cultures of the developing countries. The factors that were listed only once in the literature review are not depicted in this table. From this point forward, the term "cybersecurity culture" will be used to explain the 13 factors that will be used for the development of the proposed model.

Table 1. The frequency of factors influencing cybersecurity culture

Factor	Frequency	Authors
1."Security education, training and awareness"	13	[8, 9, 15, 23, 24, 28–35]
2."Security policy"	13	[8, 9, 15, 23, 24, 28–30, 32–36]
3."Top management"	10	[8, 9, 15, 24, 28, 29, 32, 33, 35, 37]
4."Information risk analysis and assessment"	8	[8, 9, 15, 23, 24, 29, 32, 33]
5."Security compliance"	8	[9, 15, 23, 24, 32–35]
6."Ethical conduct policies"	6	[9, 15, 24, 30, 32, 33]
7."Security knowledge"	5	[8, 15, 23, 24, 28, 32]
8."Security behavior"	4	[15, 24, 28, 30]
9."Cultural differences"	5	[9, 23, 24, 31, 32]
10."Trust"	3	[15, 24, 32]
11."Information and knowledge sharing"	3	[8, 24, 29]
12."Security monitoring"	3	[8, 29, 35]
13."Belief"	3	[12, 15, 24]

7 Ubuntu Cyber4Dev Security Culture Model

This study proposes a conceptual model presented in Fig. 2, the Ubuntu Cyber4Dev Security Culture Model. The Ubuntu Cyber4Dev Security Culture Model is proposed for African countries, such as SA. Developing countries from other continents may adapt this model to suit their cultural beliefs. The Ubuntu Cyber4Dev Security Culture Model is constructed based on the information security culture model of Van Niekerk and Von Solms [38], based on Schein's [39] organisational culture levels, which is in line with other information security culture models. Organisational culture [39] comprises artefacts, espoused values, and shared assumptions and beliefs. [38] adapted Schein's organisational culture levels by adding one additional level, Information Security Knowledge (ISK), which relates to the information security knowledge that employees might have or not have. The Ubuntu Cyber4Dev Security Culture Model incorporates the 13 factors of cybersecurity culture from Table 1 which are grouped in seven cybersecurity dimensions. The concept of Ubuntu philosophy and indigenous (African) languages are added to the information security culture model of [38], to address the cultural and language barriers in developing countries.

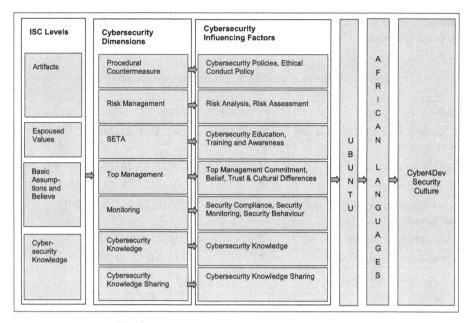

Fig. 2. Ubuntu Cyber4Dev security culture model

7.1 Ubuntu Moral Philosophy

Ubuntu is an African philosophy. It is characterised by values such as compassion, humanity, sharing, harmony, and inclusiveness, and seek to promote common good in the interest of building community [40, 41]. The communal and communitarian ethics of Ubuntu is encapsulated in its famous aphorism—"I am, because we are; and since we are, therefore I am" [40]. The cultures of developed countries, mostly 'Western', which advocate the individualistic conception of human values, contradict the Ubuntu philosophy, thus, the integration of the concept of Ubuntu should be considered in the implementation of each factor in the proposed model. The Ubuntu aspect that will be integrated in the Ubuntu Cyber4Dev Security Culture Model is that top management must lead through people or in consultation with employees. By integrating this aspect, top management will be able to assess the cybersecurity knowledge that employees possess or lack, and make decisions on training, awareness, and education required. The knowledge gained from these training programmes will be easily disseminated through another aspect of Ubuntu, namely sharing. Sharing will be integrated in the Ubuntu Cyber4Dev Security Culture Model to encourage cybersecurity knowledge sharing among employees.

7.2 Indigenous Languages

This study strongly suggests that, where possible, the use of indigenous languages in training, awareness, and education, as well as in cybersecurity knowledge sharing. In addition, the cybersecurity policies and ethical conduct policies must be written in African languages understood by the people living in the communities and organisations where these documents are meant to be implemented. There are 11 official languages in SA and, according to [42], one learns more efficiently in one's mother tongue. In a country such as SA the 11 official languages should thus be integrated in the model whereas other indigenous languages will apply in other African countries.

7.3 Mapping the 13 Factors to ISC Dimensions

The Ubuntu Cyber4Dev Security Culture Model, in Fig. 2, comprises the 13 factors identified from the literature grouped into seven ISC dimensions as proposed by the authors. Four of the ISC dimensions were directly identified in the literature as common ISC dimensions, namely, SETA, top management, cybersecurity knowledge, and cyber-security knowledge sharing. All 13 factors from Table 1 are allocated into the seven dimensions that share the same milieu, namely:

- Procedural Countermeasure
  All procedural guidelines and policies on cybersecurity developed by organisa-tions to guide cybersecurity matters are mapped into procedural countermeasure [9, 15, 24, 32, 33]. These include Cybersecurity Policies and Ethical Conduct Policies.
- Risk Management
  Risk management is concerned with the analysis and assessment of risks; as such, Risk assessment and Risk Analysis were grouped into the Risk Management dimension [9, 29].
- SETA
  SETA is concerned with all the programs that will ensure that employees get the necessary cybersecurity knowledge. Cybersecurity Education, Training and Awareness were mapped into the SETA dimension [32, 33, 35].
- Top Management
  Belief, Trust, and Top Management Commitment were allocated to the Top Man-agement Dimension. Employees must understand and accept the commitment of top management in cultivating a cybersecurity culture. The understanding and acceptance of top management commitment to cultivate a cybersecurity culture will create a strong belief and trust among employees towards the compliance and implementation in an organisation [24].
- Monitoring
  It is important to monitor whether employees are following and abiding by the cybersecurity procedure guidelines and policies in their day-to-day activities to culti-vate a positive cybersecurity culture. The Security Compliance and Security Behaviour Factors were mapped into the Monitoring dimension [8, 29, 35].
- Cybersecurity Knowledge
  The Cybersecurity knowledge factor were allocated to the Cybersecurity Knowl-edge dimension. Knowledge is gained through SETA programs as discussed above [15, 23, 28, 32].
- Cybersecurity Knowledge Sharing
  Finally, cybersecurity knowledge must be shared and communicated by employees across the organisation to address the "sharing" context of Ubuntu. The Cybersecurity knowledge sharing factor was mapped to the Cybersecurity Knowledge dimension [8, 24, 29].

8   Discussions - Research Questions

• What is a Cyber4Dev security culture?

   Scholars are increasingly focusing on cybersecurity. This is attributed to the fact that security is crucial when implementing IT solutions [43]. For a country to protect its vital infrastructure, including telecommunications, payment systems and electricity supplies, it ought to possess vigorous cybersecurity systems. Prior studies on Cyber4Dev security culture were not found; hence, studies on cybersecurity culture and information security culture were sourced to define, and find factors influencing cybersecurity culture. [8] defined ISC as a belief of employees in the value of complying with organisational policies and standards of information security. [44] defines "ISC as the collection of perceptions, attitudes, values, assumptions, and knowledge that guide human interaction with information assets in an organisation with the aim of influencing employees' behavior to preserve information security". ISC is a culture that propagates secure behaviour in employees' interaction with information assets and contributes to an organisation's overall goal attainment [8]. Based on the descriptions above, and the scarcity of research on Cyber4Dev, Cyber4Dev security culture is adapted in this paper as cybersecurity culture for developing countries.

   Many studies have provided a definition of information security culture and cybersecurity, with most sharing common attributes, beliefs, values, assumptions, and attitudes towards cyberspace. However, [22] defines cybersecurity culture as "the intentional and unintentional manner in which cyberspace is utilized from an international, national, organisational or individual perspective in the context of the attitudes, assumptions, beliefs, values, and knowledge of the cyber user". This study has adopted this definition as a cybersecurity culture definition and adapted it to cyber4Dev security culture. This study defines Cyber4Dev security culture as the behaviour, intentional and/or unintentional, of organisations and the individual from developing countries towards cyberspace in relation to their national cultural norms, beliefs, attitude, perception, assumptions, values, knowledge and awareness of the cyber user in developing countries.

• What would a holistic model for a Cyber4Dev security culture comprise?

   The holistic model for a Cyber4Dev security culture is proposed by adopting Van Niekerk and Von Solms' [38] model based on the work of Schein [39] as discussed in Sect. 7. The 13 factors influencing cybersecurity culture, as discussed in Sect. 6, are mapped to appropriate dimensions in terms of context. The influencing cybersecurity culture factors should be implemented in developing countries, considering the culture of Ubuntu and the different official languages of a country.

9   Limitations and Future Work

A limitation of this study it that the Ubuntu Cyber4Dev Security Culture Model is conceptual in nature and has not been validated. The future work will apply a qualitative method with interviews in developing country communities to demonstrate and validate the proposed model.

10   Conclusion

This paper aimed at proposing a conceptual model for Cyber4Dev security culture. To achieve this, a scoping literature review was conducted to provide answers to the research questions. The review revealed that developing countries face unique challenges that can impede the cultivation of a cybersecurity culture. To address these challenges, this paper defined Cyber4Dev security culture as "the behaviour, intentional and/or unintentional, of organisations and the individual from developing countries towards cyberspace in relation to their national cultural norms, beliefs, attitude, perception, assumptions, values, knowledge and awareness of the cyber user". Secondly, this study developed the conceptual model, Ubuntu Cyber4Dev Security Culture Model, to address these challenges. The proposed model adopts the concepts in the model of Van Niekerk and Von Solms [38] based on the work of Schein [39]. Thirteen factors cultivating cybersecurity culture, as identified in this study, are grouped in seven dimensions in the proposed model. The model postulates that the factors should be implemented considering the unique cultures of developing countries. In the case of Africa, the Ubuntu philosophy and African languages should be incorporated. The model is conceptual, and a follow-up study will be conducted to validate the model using qualitative methods.

References

1. Lombardi, M., Pascale, F., Santaniello, D.: Internet of Things: a general overview between architectures, protocols and applications. Inf. **12**(87), 1–21 (2021). https://doi.org/10.3390/info12020087
2. Shammar, E.A., Zahary, A.T., Al-Shargabi, A.A.: A survey of IoT and blockchain integration: security perspective. IEEE Access. **9**, 156114–156150 (2021). https://doi.org/10.1109/ACCESS.2021.3129697
3. Elkhannoubi, H., Belaissaoui, M.: Assess developing countries' cybersecurity capabilities through a social influence strategy. In: 7th International Conference on Science Electronic and Technological Information. Telecommun. SETIT 2016. pp. 19–23 (2017). https://doi.org/10.1109/SETIT.2016.7939834
4. Cyber4d – Cyber Resilience for Development – A European Union project designed to protect public and private enterprises across countries in Asia and Africa
5. Peters, M.D.J., et al.: Updated methodological guidance for the conduct of scoping reviews. JBI Evid. Synth. **18**, 2119–2126 (2020). https://doi.org/10.11124/JBIES-20-00167
6. Mutemwa, M.: Developing a cyber threat intelligence sharing platform for South African Organisations. In: 2017 Conference on Information Communication Technology and Society (ICTAS), pp. 1–6 (2020)
7. BusinessTech: TransUnion cyber attack – hackers demand R225 million ransom, https://businesstech.co.za/news/cloud-hosting/569658/transunion-cyber-attack-hackers-demand-r225-million-ransom/
8. Nasir, A., Abdullah Arshah, R., Ab Hamid, M.R.: A dimension-based information security culture model and its relationship with employees' security behavior: a case study in Malaysian higher educational institutions. Inf. Secur. J. **28**, 55–80 (2019). https://doi.org/10.1080/19393555.2019.1643956
9. Alnatheer, M.A.: Information security culture critical success factors. In: 12th Interanational Conference in Information Technology of New Generation. ITNG 2015. 731–735 (2015). https://doi.org/10.1109/ITNG.2015.124

10. Govender, S., Kritzinger, E., Loock, M.: The influence of national culture on information security culture. In: IST-Africa Week Conference, pp. 1–9 (2016). https://doi.org/10.1109/ISTAFRICA.2016.7530607
11. Alkalabi, W., Simpson, L., Morarji, H.: Barriers and incentives to cybersecurity threat information sharing in developing countries: a case study of Saudi Arabia. In: ACM International Conference Proceeding Series (2021). https://doi.org/10.1145/3437378.3437391
12. Reid, R., Van Niekerk, J.: From information security to cyber security cultures. In: Inforamation Security South Africa - Proceedings of the ISSA 2014 Conference, pp. 1–7 (2014). https://doi.org/10.1109/ISSA.2014.6950492
13. Babate, I., Musa, A., Kida, M., Saidu, K.: State of cyber security: emerging threats landscape. Int. J. Adv. Res. Comput. Sci. Technol. (IJARCST 2015). 3, 113–119 (2015)
14. Sayoc, V.R., Dolores, T.K., Lim, M.C., Sophia, L., Miguel, S.: Computer systems in analytical applications. Int J. Adv. Trends Comp. Sci. Eng. 8(3), 195–200 (2019). https://doi.org/10.30534/ijatcse/2019/68832019
15. Mahfuth, A., Yussof, S., abu bakar, A., Ali, N.B., Abdallah, W.: A conceptual model for exploring the factors influencing information security culture. Int. J. Secur. Its Appl. 11, 15–26 (2017). https://doi.org/10.14257/ijsia.2017.11.5.02
16. Georgiadou, A., Mouzakitis, S., Askounis, D.: Assessing mitre attack risk using a cybersecurity culture framework. Sensors. 21, 9 (2021). https://doi.org/10.3390/s21093267
17. Heerden, R. Van, Solms, S. Von, Vorster, J., Solms, S. Von, Vorster, J.: Major security incidents since 2014: an African perspective. In: IST-Africa Week Conference, pp. 1–11 (2018)
18. Allen, B.N.: Africa's evolving cyber threats, pp. 1–6. https://africacenter.org/spotlight/africa-evolving-cyber-threats/ (2021)
19. Chigada, J., Madzinga, R.: Cyberattacks and threats during COVID-19: a systematic literature review. S. Afr. J. Inf. Manag. 23, 1 (2021). https://doi.org/10.4102/sajim.v23i1.1277
20. Dolley, C.: Cyberattacks: South Africa, you've been hacked, Dailymaveric. https://www.dailymaverick.co.za/article/2021-11-06-cyberattacks-south-africa-youve-been-hacked/ (2021)
21. Interpol: INTERPOL report identifies top cyberthreats in Africa. https://www.interpol.int/en/News-and-Events/News/2021/INTERPOL-report-identifies-top-cyberthreats-in-Africa (2021)
22. Da Veiga, A.: A cybersecurity culture research philosophy and approach to develop a valid and reliable measuring instrument. Comput. Conf. SAI 2016. pp. 1006–1015 (2016). https://doi.org/10.1109/SAI.2016.7556102
23. Da Veiga, A., Astakhova, L.V., Botha, A., Herselman, M.: Defining organisational information security culture - perspectives from academia and industry. Comput. Secur. 92 (2020)
24. Nasir, A., Arshah, R.A., Ab Hamid, M.R.: Information security policy compliance behavior based on comprehensive dimensions of information security culture: a conceptual framework. In: ACM International Confernce Proceeding Ser. Part F1282, 56–60 (2017). https://doi.org/10.1145/3077584.3077593
25. Alshaikh, M.: Developing cybersecurity culture to influence employee behavior: a practice perspective. Comput. Secur. 98 (2020). https://doi.org/10.1016/j.cose.2020.102003
26. Grant, M.J., Booth, A.: A typology of reviews: an analysis of 14 review types and associated methodologies. Health Info. Libr. J. 26(2), 91–108 (2009). https://doi.org/10.1111/j.1471-1842.2009.00848.x
27. Moher, D., Liberati, A., Tetzlaff, J., Altman, D.G.: Preferred reporting Items for systematic reviews and meta-analyses: the PRISMA statement. PLoS Med 6(7) e1000097 (2009). https://doi.org/10.1371/journal.pmed.1000097
28. Hassan, N.H.: Information Security Culture in Health Informatics Environment: A Qualitative Approach. In: International Conference on Research and Innovation in Information Systems (ICRIIS), IEEE, pp. 1–6 (2017)

29. Nasir, A., Rashid, M., Hamid, A.: Information Security Culture for Guiding Employee's Security Behaviour: A Pilot Study. In: 6th International Conference on Information Management (ICIM), IEEE, 205–209 (2020)
30. Ikenwe, I.J., Igbinovia, O.M., Elogie, A.A.: Information Security in the Digital Age: The Case of Developing Countries. Chinese Librariansh. Int. Electron. J. **42**, 16–24 (2016)
31. Kabanda, S., Tanner, M., Kent, C.: Exploring SME cybersecurity practices in developing countries. J. Organ. Comput. Electron. Commer. **28**(3), 269–282 (2018). https://doi.org/10.1080/10919392.2018.1484598
32. Uchendu, B., Nurse, J.R.C., Bada, M., Furnell, S.: Developing a cyber security culture: Current practices and future needs. Comput. Secur. **109**, 102387 (2021). https://doi.org/10.1016/j.cose.2021.102387
33. Tolah, A., Furnell, S.M., Papadaki, M.: A Comprehensive Framework for Cultivating and Assessing Information Security Culture. In: 11th International Symposium on Human Aspects of Information Security & Assurance, pp. 52–64 (2017)
34. Martins, N., Da Veiga, A.: An Information security culture model validated with structural equation modelling. In: Human Aspects of Information Security & Assurance HAISA, pp. 11–21 (2015)
35. Reegård, K.: The Concept of Cybersecurity Culture The Concept of Cybersecurity Culture. In: 29th European Safety and Reliability Conference, pp. 4036–4043 (2019)
36. Ioannou, M., Stavrou, E., Bada, M.: Cybersecurity Culture in Computer Security Incident Response Teams. In: International Conference on Cyber Security and Protection of Digital Services (Cyber Security), pp. 1–4. IEEE (2019)
37. Huang, K., Pearlson, K.: For what technology can't fix: Building a model of organizational cybersecurity culture. In: Annual Hawaii International Conference System Scince -Janua, pp. 6398–6407 (2019). https://doi.org/10.24251/hicss.2019.769
38. Van Niekerk, J., Von Solms, R.: Understanding Information Security Culture: A Conceptual Framework. In: Information Security South Africa - Proceedings ISSA, pp. 1–10 (2006)
39. Schein, E.H.: Organisation Culture and Leadership. 3rd edn, p. 458. Wiley (2010)
40. Woermann, M., Engelbrecht, S.: The Ubuntu Challenge to Business: from Stakeholders to Relationholders. J. Bus. Ethics **157**(1), 27–44 (2017). https://doi.org/10.1007/s10551-017-3680-6
41. Adeleye, I., Luiz, J., Muthuri, J., Amaeshi, K.: J. Bus. Ethics **161**(4), 717–729 (2019). https://doi.org/10.1007/s10551-019-04338-x
42. Van Pinxteren, B.: Language of instruction in education in Africa: how new questions help generate new answers. Int. J. Educ. Dev. **88**, 102524 (2022)
43. Ndiege, J., Okello, G.: Information security awareness amongst students joining higher academic institutions in developing countries: evidence from Kenya. African J. Inf. Syst. **10**, 4 (2018)
44. Al Hogail, A.: Cultivating and assessing an organizational information security culture; an empirical study. Int. J. Secur. its Appl. **9**, 163–178 (2015). https://doi.org/10.14257/ijsia.2015.9.7.15
45. Aitchison, J.: South Africa's reading crisis is a cognitive catastrophe. The Conversation (2018). https://theconversation.com/south-africas-reading-crisis-is-a-cognitive-catastrophe-89052
46. Stats SA South Africa's youth continues to bear the burden of unemployment (2022) https://www.statssa.gov.za/?p=15407#:~:text=According%20to%20the%20Quarterly%20Labour,stands%20at%2034%2C5%25

Evaluating a Consumer Data Protection Framework for IS Compliance Awareness in South Africa: An Expert Review

Ileen E. Bredenkamp[1]([⊠]), Elmarie Kritzinger[2], and Marlien Herselman[3]

[1] University of South Africa, Pretoria 0002, South Africa
`ileenvv@gmail.com`
[2] School of Computing, University of South Africa, Pretoria 0002, South Africa
`kritze@unisa.ac.za`
[3] Next Generation Enterprises and Institutions, CSIR, Pretoria 0002, South Africa
`mherselman@csir.co.za`

Abstract. As a developing country, South Africa (SA) seems to lack a balance between trust consumers place in organizations with whom they share their personal information to obtain goods and services and the degree to which that consumer confidence is justified by organizations' IS compliance status. The displacement of consumers' confidence is due to a lack of IS compliance awareness necessary to enable sound decision-making when it comes to the sharing of their personal information in the ordinary course of making a living as part of public society. In SA, there are currently no government-led programs to raise consumer awareness about IS compliance. Prior data protection frameworks failed to take into account and address these issues as key lessons from which the need for a consumer data protection framework (CDPF) spawned. The aim of the CDPF is to support the SA government with instilling consumer IS compliance awareness. The primary goal of this paper is to present the evaluation results of the expert reviews that were conducted by means of an online survey to determine the relevance, value/importance and practicality of CDPF components for implementation in the SA government setting.

Keywords: South Africa · Government · Information security compliance awareness · Consumer data protection · Framework · Expert reviews

1 Introduction

The increasing dependence of South African (SA) organizations on consumer information to operate and compete in the market, has led to confidential information of consumers being at risk of identity theft, data breaches and fraud [1–3]. The Protection of Personal Information Act (POPIA) (4 of 2013) [4] and the Cybercrimes Act (19 of 2020) [5] are two pieces of SA legislation that employ several provisions with the intent of protecting data subjects from data breaches. In addition, SA developed the Promotion of Access to Information Act (PAIA) (2 of 2000) [6] that supplements POPIA to

T. Guarda et al. (Eds.): ARTIIS 2022, CCIS 1676, pp. 352–367, 2022.
https://doi.org/10.1007/978-3-031-20316-9_27

grant citizens of SA the ability to gain sufficient access to information to enable them to execute and safeguard their rights more effectively.

In reality, numerous SA organizations are still non-compliant and are ignorant of the financial and reputational impact it might have on their organization, which could even lead to incarceration of responsible parties in severe cases. It is important to note that POPIA and PAIA do not address consumer awareness regarding IS compliance as they primarily focus on obligations for organizations with relatively little training or awareness initiatives for staff [4, 7].

Nonetheless, limited awareness training initiatives for cybersecurity do exist in SA, namely the SA Cyber-Security Academic Alliance (SACSAA) [8] and the Cyber-Security Awareness Community-Engagement Project (CSACEP) [9].

The Council for Scientific and Industrial Research (CSIR) also promotes cyber-security awareness and education in SA through hosting yearly cybersecurity awareness events in the month of October [10].

Given the above, it is clear that a nationwide consumer IS compliance awareness gap exists to be addressed by government-led awareness and training initiatives. It is anticipated that the SA government adoption of the proposed consumer data protection framework (CDPF) will contribute towards instilling the envisaged consumer data protection (CDP) culture by improving consumer IS compliance awareness in SA.

The aim of this paper is to communicate the evaluation results of the expert reviews that were conducted by means of an online survey to determine the relevance, value/importance and practicality of CDPF components for SA government adoption.

The next section (Sect. 2) provides an overview of the CDPF that were identified through the review of the literature (scoping review, including three systematic reviews) and the thematic analysis of the results that culminated in the proposed CDPF. This is followed by an explanation of the evaluation method in terms of the approach taken and the review instrument used (Sect. 3). Thereafter, the data collection method is discussed (Sect. 4.1), and a summary of the results are provided (Sect. 4.2), including an interpretation thereof (Sect. 4.3). The paper then proceeds with the contributions (Sect. 5) and the limitations of this research, including future research opportunities to explore (Sect. 6). Finally, Sect. 7 details the conclusions and suggested areas for improvement in future work.

2   Consumer Data Protection Framework

This section introduces the proposed CDPF that were constructed following the design science research (DSR) process as proposed by Peffers et al. [11] and discusses each of the CDPF layers that encapsulate the components that were uncovered by a review of the literature (scoping review, including three systematic literature reviews) and thematic analysis.

2.1   The Framework

The proposed framework consists of five layers (Strategic -, Tactical -, Preparation -, Delivery - and Monitoring Layer) and Resources as an overarching component. Table 1 provides a summary of the CDPF layer components, the grounded literature components derived from the literature reviews, the framework characteristics derived from extant literature [7] and the proposed CDPF application guidelines in accordance with the PDCA process steps [12].

Table 1. Summary of CDPF components

Layer components	Grounded literature components	Framework characteristics	PDCA process Steps	Application in CDPF guidelines (high-level application steps)
Strategic layer	First systematic literature review: CDP high-level concepts	Holistic, integrative, systematic	Plan	**Step 1:** Per each government department, set the scope and boundaries of the CDPF **Step 2:** Draft and implement a CDP policy and update Government Gazette to reflect the CDP policy requirements **Step 3:** Assess the internal structure of the government, including the governance model with respect to its capacity to conduct IS compliance awareness training activities (incentivized training programs and campaigns): • Create a workforce department for awareness and training • Allocate roles and responsibilities for IS compliance awareness training activities • Manage the lifecycle of the workforce, which includes budget and resource management • Conduct workforce training on key components of IS compliance awareness for CDP • Enable sharing of IS compliance status through defining and implementing an appropriate communication plan

(continued)

Table 1. (*continued*)

Layer components	Grounded literature components	Framework characteristics	PDCA process Steps	Application in CDPF guidelines (high-level application steps)
Tactical layer	Second systematic literature review: CDP elements	Multiple perspectives	Plan Act	**Step 4:** Recognize, provide and establish mechanisms to enable the government to drive compliance awareness training activities: • Public IS compliance awareness campaigns • Incentivized monitoring and awareness training programs for participating organizations **Step 10:** Update the CDPF by incorporating the improvements uncovered in Step 9 **Step 11:** Take corrective action as necessary **Step 12:** To achieve continuous improvement, repeat Step 7 to Step 11 and reassess
Preparation layer	Third systematic literature review: CDP techniques	Coordinate plan align	Plan	**Step 5:** Recognize, provide and identify topics, content and tools required for the roll-out of consumer IS compliance awareness campaigns and training programs
Delivery layer		Value creation (ITIL): • Institution perception of value • Consumer perception of value • Institution preferences • Consumer preferences • Institution expectations – delivery outcome • Consumer expectations – delivery outcome RACI roles for enforcement entities	Do	**Step 6:** Liaise with the participating organizations to implement incentivized awareness training programs. Maintain relationships with participating organizations Implement IS compliance awareness campaigns

(*continued*)

Table 1. (*continued*)

Layer components	Grounded literature components	Framework characteristics	PDCA process Steps	Application in CDPF guidelines (high-level application steps)
Monitoring & evaluation layer		Integrated into operations continuous improvement	Check	**Step 7:** Monitor and review IS compliance awareness campaigns and awareness training programs by following established procedures and controls **Step 8:** Perform internal government audits to assure that formal CDPF processes and procedures are followed **Step 9:** Conduct a CDPF management review Ensure the objectives in terms of improvements are met

The context provided in Table 1 was utilized as the foundation to construct the initial CDPF and is depicted in Fig. 1.

3 Evaluation Method

This section describes the use of expert reviews as a method of evaluation, including the review process approach and the instrument used for review.

3.1 Approach

The evaluation approach used to assess the CDPF is derived from the combined work on artefact evaluation in DSR by Prat *et al.* [14] and Venable *et al.* [15]. The evaluation approach is transformed into an assessment strategy. This strategy, in turn, is transformed into a method of evaluation and a process of evaluation.

3.2 Expert Reviews and Online Survey Instrument

The next section discusses expert reviews and the use of online surveys as an instrument.

Expert Reviews. Expert reviews offer a means to determine whether an artefact is useful without involving end users [16], and is acknowledged as a valid method to gain insights, understanding and experience from expert reviewers [17]. Experts are better equipped to judge problems, assess possibilities, and come up with solutions [18] and are capable of assessing systems in the early development stages [18]. Several information systems applications have proven to benefit from expert reviews [19, 20].

CONSUMER DATA PROTECTION FRAMEWORK (CDPF)
For Improved IS Compliance Awareness through Awareness Training Initiatives

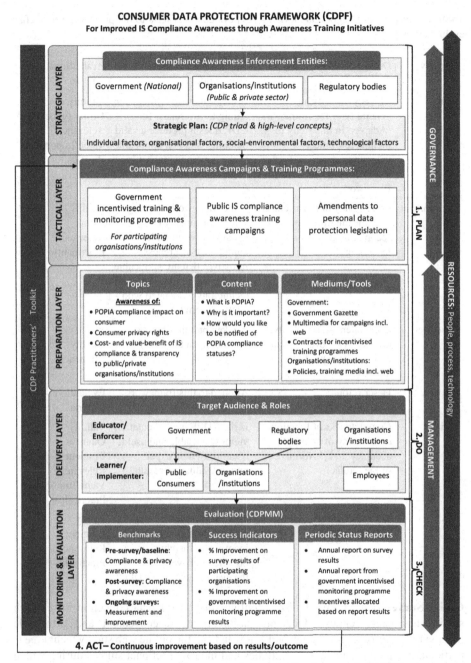

Fig. 1. Initial proposed consumer data protection framework (CDPF)

In Table 2, Gregor and Hevner's [21] criteria for artefact evaluation are interpreted in terms of the properties for artefact evaluation.

Table 2. Mapping of Gregor and Hevner's [21] evaluation criteria to the properties for artefact evaluation

Property	Description	Application to this framework	Evaluation criteria
Goal	Efficacy, validity, or generality of the framework. (Adapted in this study to include relevance, value/importance and practicality of the framework.)	Is the framework effective in aiding IS awareness for CDP, does it produce a valid outcome, and is it applicable to the governmental setting of another country?	Validity Utility (generality) Relevance Value/Importance Practicality
Environment	Consistency of the artefact with the environment (people, processes, technology)	Is the framework eliciting sound consumer IS behaviour based on IS compliance awareness initiatives that are applicable to the people, processes, and technology associated with CDP concern?	Quality Utility Relevance Practicality
Structure	Completeness, simplicity, clarity, style, level of detail and consistency of the artefact	Are key building blocks missing from the CDPF?	Validity Quality Efficiency
Property	Description	Applied to this framework	Evaluation Criteria
Activity	Completeness of function, consistency of activity, accuracy and performance of the artefact	Is the CDPF implementation yielding a usable and useful result (based on expert review evaluation results)?	Validity Quality Efficiency Relevance Value/Importance Practicality
Evolution	Robustness and learning capability	Does the possibility exist to amend/adapt the CDPF to incorporate insights obtained/uncovered during the evaluation of the CDPF?	Utility Efficiency Relevance Practicality

Online Survey Instrument. Utilizing online surveys for data collection in research studies has been acknowledged internationally as a convenient and affordable method [22]. According to Nayak and Narayan [23], the online web survey technique is particularly suitable for evaluation studies and in cross-sectional studies during which the researcher will contact the participants only once. For this reason, the online (web) survey technique was deployed for the expert review evaluation of the CDPF components to understand the perceived benefits of the CDPF within a SA context, including recommendations for further improvement.

4 Expert Review Process

This section provides an overview of the expert review process, discusses the data collection method (Sect. 4.1) during expert evaluation, synthesizes the opinions of the experts (Sect. 4.2) and provides the researcher's comprehension of the results (Sect. 4.3).

4.1 Data Collection

Expert reviewers were selected from four different industries: ICT, education, finance/banking, legal and government with a focus on consumer data protection. Selection included practitioners and researchers, including individuals with experience in both roles. Expert reviewers were selected using convenience sampling - that is, on the basis of their accessibility and willingness to participate [24]. Both international and local SA reviewers participated in the review process to cover a broader range of perspectives, whilst taking into consideration familiarity with the local setting. In order to ensure a non-biased evaluation, experts who were not previously exposed to the work were chosen. Table 3 provides a summary of the six expert reviewers' biographical details, level of experience and education that were selected to participate in the review process.

Table 3. Expert reviewer's biographical details

Reviewer	Industry of expertise	Job level (Snr. level)	Age group (>25)	Years of experience (>5)	Highest post-graduate qualification	Academic field of study
1	Education	Manager	51–60	11–15	PhD	Information systems/IS
2	Government	Specialist	51–60	26+	PhD	Information systems/IS
3	Banking	Manager	26–30	6–10	PhD	Business Administration
4	Education	Professor	60	26+	PhD	Information systems/IS
5	Legal	Executive	41–50	11–15	Masters	Law
6	ICT	Top Management	41–50	16–20	PhD	Project & Program Management

Holbrook et al. [25] and Nielsen [26] provide strong arguments in their work to support a conservative selection of two to five expert reviewers as being adequate, given that feedback is provided that reaches saturation. It is assumed that more reviewers will uncover more areas to enhance, which is similar to heuristic evaluation, a type of expert review with a focus on the system utility [25]. The reviews consisted of the distribution of an online survey, facilitated by a Google forms web interface. Each reviewer received an email which provided a description of the research topic and an invite to participate in the study. If the reviewer agreed to participate, the reviewer was instructed to click on the survey link in the email where the reviewer was asked for his/her consent to participate. If consent was provided, the reviewer would be redirected to the first question of the online survey. If the reviewer rejected consent, the reviewer was taken to the exit page of the survey. The survey incorporated a summary of the work and included hyperlinks to a more detailed explanation of the CDPF components as building blocks. Reviewers were informed that their identity would remain anonymous throughout analysis and communication of results.

4.2 Synopsis of Results

The expert reviewers evaluated the CDPF during which they also rated each component of the CDPF. The data analysis rating results are used by the researcher in this section to rank the CDPF components.

Table 4 provides a summary of the CDPF component and sub-component ranking values assigned by the researcher that is based on the average rating percentage scores of the expert evaluations.

4.3 Interpretation

The expert reviewers rated the proposed CDPF positively. The expert reviewers indicated that the CDPF are capable of addressing the problem of a lack of consumer IS compliance awareness and will make a good contribution towards SA government-led consumer IS compliance awareness training programs. The expert reviewers also indicated that the proposed CDPF can be applied in the government setting of other countries, given that some minor adjustments might have to be made. Lastly, the expert reviewers indicated that the CDPF will serve useful in future studies on this research topic.

As indicated in Table 4, the Layers component of the CDPF obtained the highest average rating score of 82,60% (sum of the average relevance, value and practicality ratings, divided by three) which places it in the first position in terms of ranking. This is followed by the Application Steps component of the CDPF that obtained an average rating score of 81,71%, which places it in the second position in terms of ranking. The Layers Sub-component of the CDPF comes in at a third place in terms of ranking which obtained an average rating score of 81,20%. The Characteristics component of the CDPF achieved fourth place in terms of ranking, which obtained an average rating score of 78,10%. Lastly, the PDCA Process Steps component of the CDPF was ranked fifth place, with an average rating score of 71,93%.

Table 4. CDPF component and sub-component expert review ratings and rankings

CDPF Components	CDPF Sub-components	Avg. Relevance % Rating	Relevance \ Ranking	Avg. Value % Rating	Value Ranking	Avg. Practicality % Rating	Practicality Ranking	Total Avg. % Rating per CDPF Component	Value Ranking per CDPF Component
Layers (L1 – L6)	L1: Strategic Layer	83,33%	2	86,67%	3	73,33%	4		
	L2: Tactical Layer	76,70%	4	80,00%	4	76,67%	3		
	L3: Preparation Layer	80,00%	3	86,67%	3	80,00%	2	82,60%	1
	L4: Delivery Layer	83,33%	2	86,67%	3	76,67%	3		
	L5: Monitoring & Evaluation Layer	83,33%	2	90,00%	2	76,67%	3		
	L6: Continuous Improvement	86,67%	1	96,67%	1	83,33%	1		
	Total Avg. Rating Score for Relevance, Value & Practicality:	82,23%		87,78%		77,78%			
Layer Sub-components (LS1 – LS13)	LS1: IS compliance awareness Policy and IS compliance awareness & training requirements	80,00%	4	73,33%	4	80,00%	1		
	LS2: A responsible department	90,00%	1	83,33%	2	80,00%	1		
	LS3: Strategic plan	86,67%	2	80,00%	3	73,33%	3		
	LS4: Government incentivized training and monitoring programs for participating organizations	76,67%	5	80,00%	3	80,00%	1		
	LS5: Government public IS compliance awareness campaigns	86,67%	2	86,67%	1	80,00%	1	81,20%	3
	LS6: Updated data protection legislation	80,00%	4	83,33%	2	73,33%	3		
	LS7: Topics	80,00%	4	83,33%	2	76,67%	2		
	LS8: Content	83,33%	3	83,33%	2	80,00%	1		
	LS9: Mediums/tools	83,33%	3	83,33%	2	73,33%	3		

(continued)

Table 4. (continued)

CDPF Components	CDPF Sub-components	Avg. Relevance % Rating	Relevance \ Ranking	Avg. Value % Rating	Value Rank-ing	Avg. Practicality % Rating	Practicality Ranking	Total Avg. Rating % per CDPF Component	Value Rank-ing per CDPF Component
	LS10: Target audiences	86,67%	2	86,67%	1	73,33%	3		
	LS11: Roles	86,67%	2	83,33%	2	76,67%	2		
	LS12: Monitoring and evaluation activities	83,33%	3	83,33%	2	76,67%	2		
	LS13: Resource considerations	86,67%	2	86,67%	1	76,67%	2		
	Total Avg. Rating Score for Relevance, Value & Practicality:	83,85%		82,82%		76,92%			
Characteristics (Char1 - Char7)	**Char1:** Holistic, integrative & systematic	76,67%	5	76,67%	3	70,00%	3		
	Char2: Multiple perspectives	83,33%	3	76,67%	3	66,67%	4	78,10%	4
	Char3: Coordinate, plan & align	80,00%	4	76,67%	3	76,67%	1		
	Char4: Value creation (ITIL)	80,00%	4	80,00%	2	76,67%	1		
	Char5: RACI roles for enforcement entities	86,67%	2	80,00%	2	73,33%	2		
	Char6: Integrated in operations	90,00%	1	76,67%	3	73,33%	2		
	Char7: Continuous improvement	83,33%	3	83,33%	1	73,33%	2		
	Total Avg. Rating Score for Relevance, Value & Practicality:	82,86%		78,57%		72,86%			
Application Steps (A0–12)	**A0:** Obtain Governmental management authorization to establish a project to implement and operate the CDPF.	86,67%	2	83,33%	3	80,00%	1		
	A1: Per each government department, set the scope and boundaries of the CDPF.	86,67%	2	83,33%	3	73,33%	3	81,71%	2
	A2: Draft and implement a CDP policy and update Government Gazette to reflect the CDP policy requirements.	83,33%	3	83,33%	3	73,33%	3		
	A3: Assess the government internal posture and governance model with respect to their capacity to conduct IS compliance awareness training activities (campaigns and incentivized training programs).	80,00%	4	90,00%	1	76,67%	2		

(continued)

Table 4. (continued)

CDPF Components	CDPF Sub-components	Avg. Relevance % Rating	Relevance \ Ranking	Avg. Value % Rating	Value Ranking	Avg. Practicality % Rating	Practicality Rating Ranking	Total Avg. Rating % per CDPF Component	Value Ranking per CDPF Component
	A4: Recognize, provide and establish mechanisms to enable the government to drive compliance awareness training activities.	86,67%	2	86,67%	2	80,00%	1		
	A5: Recognize, provide and establish topics, content and tools required for the roll-out of consumer IS compliance awareness campaigns and training programs.	80,00%	4	86,67%	2	80,00%	1		
	A6: Liaise with the participating organizations to implement incentivized awareness training programs. Maintain relationships with participating organizations. Implement IS compliance awareness campaigns.	90,00%	1	83,33%	3	76,67%	2		
	A7: Monitor and review IS compliance awareness campaigns and awareness training programs by following established procedures and controls.	86,67%	2	83,33%	3	80,00%	1		
	A8: Perform internal government audits to assure that formal CDPF processes and procedures are followed.	83,33%	3	80,00%	4	76,67%	2		
	A9: Conduct a CDPF management review. Ensure the objectives in terms of improvements are met.	86,67%	2	83,33%	3	76,67%	2		
	A10: Update the CDPF by incorporating the improvements uncovered in Step 9.	80,00%	4	83,33%	3	76,67%	2		
	A11: Take corrective action as necessary.	80,00%	4	86,67%	2	73,33%	3		
	A12: To achieve continuous improvement, repeat Step 7 to Step 11 and reassess.	83,33%	3	80,00%	4	76,67%	2		
	Total Avg. Rating Score for Relevance, Value & Practicality:	*84,10%*		*84,10%*		*76,92%*		*72,92%*	*5*
PDCA Process Steps (Step1-Step4)	**Step1:** Plan	70,00%	4	70,00%	4	70,00%	3		
	Step2: Do	73,33%	3	76,67%	1	73,33%	2		
	Step3: Check	80,00%	1	73,33%	2	70,00%	3	72,92%	
	Step4: Act	73,34%	2	71,67%	3	73,34%	1		
	Total Avg. Rating Score for Relevance, Value & Practicality:	*74,17%*		*72,92%*		*71,67%*			

5 Contribution

In summary, this research addressed the issue of consumer IS compliance awareness within SA by developing a CDPF. Table 5 provides a summary of the contributions of this work.

Table 5. Research contribution synopsis

Research category	Contribution description
Theory	• Definition of the consumer IS compliance awareness problem • Definition of the new concept of IS compliance awareness • Definition/summary of the consumer IS compliance awareness problem • A summary of the human factor themes, theories and models that influence Consumer Data Protection and the diverse ways it is interpreted in literature • A synopsis of the IS-related maturity models in literature and their applicability to this study
Method	• A definition of appropriate characteristics for the CDPF • The definition of a CDPF that would focus IS compliance awareness towards improved CDP through government-led consumer IS compliance awareness training programs
Practice	• CDP application steps • Development of a baseline CDP Practitioners' Toolkit for the CDPF

Each of the individual contributions depicted in Table 5 potentially has the ability to influence/shape IS compliance awareness for CDP.

6 Limitations and Future Research

The shortcomings of this study, including future research possibilities on this research topic, are summarized in Table 6.

Table 6. Limitations and future research opportunities

Limitation description	Related future research opportunities
• Although expert review results served as valuable insight for improving the CDPF, its validity still needs to be evaluated in practice • Expert review results could be subject to expert reviewer experience/personal opinion – bias. However, it should be noted that expert review findings were not the sole source of information which shaped the outcome of the CDPF • In practice, the implementation of the CDPF will comprise a broader set of stakeholders (i.e., participating public/private organizations and regulatory bodies and others). By implication, the success of the CDPF is dependent on the ability of all relevant stakeholders to interact with and operate the CDPF	• Evaluate the validity of the CDPF in practice through real-word implementation i.e. conducting a pilot study • Validate the generalizability of the CDPF by means of future implementations in a government setting of different countries • Further explore indicators of possible theory development opportunities uncovered during this study pertaining to IS compliance awareness and CDP • Evaluate/test the CDPF in a governmental setting. Ensure all relevant stakeholders are involved in the planning phase of the CDPF implementation
• Although the ability to measure the progress of improved consumer IS compliance awareness have been considered through the development of a consumer data protection maturity model (CDPMM) not covered in this paper, and the expert reviewers have taken into account the forecast of the potential for improvement during this study, there is still room for improvement	• The work of Davies [27] concerning viewpoints on the evaluation of initiatives, might contribute towards evaluating other facets, for example, the capability for consumer smart decision-making (smart trust)
• Expert reviews indicated that additional implementation guidance is necessary to make the CDPF more understandable and easier to read. A baseline CDP Practitioners' Toolkit[a] was put together to address this point, but additional effort is necessary to facilitate and promote its operationalization • This work calls for the formulation of a robust communication plan for the implementation of the CDPF, This matter is supported by Gregor and Hevner [21], who posits that a suitable communication strategy is required to increase the value and acceptability/adoption of the work	• The CDP Practitioners' Toolkit can be further explored and refined in future research • Formulate a thorough communication plan to accompany any future implementations of the CDPF

[a]The baseline CDP Practitioners' Toolkit templates can be viewed at: https://drive.google.com/drive/folders/1wqu01maOCx2xNwnb5ZBO3W178FYv-qRR?usp=sharing.

7 Conclusion

SA, as a developing country, lacks consumer IS compliance awareness which places their citizens personal information at risk. This paper provided a brief introduction to a proposed CDPF for improving CDP through utilizing government-led IS compliance awareness training programs as a focal point. The paper further communicated the results of expert reviews that were conducted to evaluate the CDPF components. The expert review results were favourable as it indicated that the CDPF components are acknowledged as relevant, valuable and practical towards assisting the SA government with enhancing consumer IS compliance awareness on a national scale for promoting CDP at large.

References

1. Blascak, N., Cheney, J.S., Hunt, R.M., Mikhed, V., Ritter, D., Vogan, M.: Financial consequences of identity theft: evidence from consumer credit bureau records (2019)
2. Irvin-Erickson, Y., Ricks, A.: Identity theft and fraud victimization: what we know about identity theft and fraud victims from research-and practice-based evidence (2019)
3. Masilela, L., Nel, D.: The role of data and information security governance in protecting public sector data and information assets in national government in South Africa. Africa's Public Serv. Deliv. Perform. Rev. 9(1), 10 (2021)
4. S. A. Government: Protection of Personal Information Act. Government Gazette, Cape Town (2013)
5. South African National Treasury: Cybercrimes and Cybersecurity Bill, vol. 416, no. 42237, pp. 1–176 (2017)
6. Government Printer: Promotion of Access to Information Act (PAIA) 2 of 2000, Cape Town, 2000. https://www.gov.za/documents/promotion-access-information-act
7. Kortjan, N., Von Solms, R.: A conceptual framework for cyber-security awareness and education in SA. SACJ 52, 29–41 (2014)
8. South Africa Cyber-Security Academic Alliance: Welcome to SACSAA (2014)
9. Kritzinger, E.: Cyber-Security Awareness Project (2014). http://eagle.unisa.ac.za/elmarie/index.php
10. The Council for Scientific and Industrial Research (2021). https://www.csir.co.za/
11. Peffers, K., Tuunanen, T., Rothenberger, M.A., Chatterjee, S.: A design science research methodology for information systems research. J. Manag. Inf. Syst. 24(3), 45–77 (2007). https://doi.org/10.2753/MIS0742-1222240302
12. ISO/IEC 27000: ISO/IEC 27000:2014 Information technology | Security techniques | Information security management systems - Overview and vocabulary (2014). https://www.iso27001security.com/html/27000.html
13. Prat, N., Comyn-Wattiau, I., Akoka, J.: Artifact evaluation in information systems design-science research - a holistic view. In: Proceedings of the Pacific Asia Conference on Information Systems PACIS 2014 (2014)
14. Prat, N., Comyn-Wattiau, I., Akoka, J.: Artifact evaluation in information systems design-science research-a holistic view. PACIS 23, 1–16 (2014)
15. Venable, J., Pries-Heje, J., Baskerville, R.: FEDS: a framework for evaluation in design science research. Eur. J. Inf. Syst. 25(1), 77–89 (2016)
16. Ågerfalk, P.J.: Information Systems Actability: Understanding Information Technology as a Tool for Business Action And Communication. Linköping University Electronic Press (2003)

17. Moonen, H., van Hillegersberg, J.: Real-time coordination in container trucking – prototyping and evaluating a multi-agent system for real-time container truck planning at post-Kogeko. In: van Nunen, J., Huijbregts, P., Rietveld, P. (eds.) Transitions Towards Sustainable Mobility, pp. 139–159. Springer, Heidelberg (2011). https://doi.org/10.1007/978-3-642-21192-8_8
18. Chen, S., Osman, N.M., Nunes, J.M.B., Peng, G.C.: Information systems evaluation methodologies (2011)
19. Ali, B.J., Anwar, G.: Factors influencing the citizens' acceptance of electronic government. Int. J. Eng. Bus. Manag. **5** (2021)
20. Li, X., Zhang, Z., Stefanidis, K.: A data-driven approach for video game playability analysis based on players' reviews. Information **12**(3), 129 (2021)
21. Gregor, S., Hevner, A.R.: Positioning and presenting design science research for maximum impact. MIS Q. 337–355 (2013). https://doi.org/10.25300/MISQ/2013/37.2.01
22. Minnaar, L., Heystek, J.: Online surveys as data collection instruments in education research: a feasible option? South African J. High. Educ. **27**(1), 162–183 (2016). https://doi.org/10.20853/27-1-233
23. Nayak, M.S.D.P., Narayan, K.A.: Strengths and weakness of online surveys. IOSR J. Humanit. Soc. Sci. **24**(5), 31–38 (2019). https://doi.org/10.9790/0837-2405053138
24. Saunders, M., Lewis, P., Thornhill, A.: Research Methods for Business Students, 7th edn. Nueva York Pearson Educ. (2016)
25. Holbrook, A.L., Krosnick, J.A., Moore, D., Tourangeau, R.: Response order effects in dichotomous categorical questions presented orally the impact of question and respondent attributes. Public Opin. Q. **71**(3), 325–348 (2007). https://doi.org/10.1093/poq/nfm024
26. Nielsen, J.: Why you only need to test with 5 users. Nielsen Norman Group, pp. 737–8939 (2000). https//www.nngroup.com/articles/why-you-only-need-to-test-with-5-users/
27. Davies, R.: Network perspectives in the evaluation of development interventions: more than a metaphor (2003)

Data Recovery Protocol Proposal for SSD Disks

Geovanni Ninahualpa[1,2,6] (ID), Teresa Guarda[2,3,4,5](✉) (ID), Javier Díaz[6],
and Darío Piccirilli[6]

[1] Departamento de Ciencias de la Computación, Universidad de las Fuerzas Armadas ESPE,
Sangolquí, Ecuador
gninahualpa@espe.edu.ec

[2] Grupo de Investigación de Ciberseguridad, IoT e Inteligencia Artificial, Universidad de las
Fuerzas Armadas ESPE, Sangolquí, Ecuador
tguarda@gmail.com

[3] Universidad Estatal Península de Santa Elena, La Libertad, Ecuador

[4] CIST – Centro de Investigación en Sistemas y Telecomunicaciones, Universidad Estatal
Península de Santa Elena, La Libertad, Ecuador

[5] Algoritmi Centre, Minho University, Guimarães, Portugal

[6] Universidad Nacional de La Plata, La Plata, Argentina

Abstract. This work performs a series of analysis of allocation and subsequent
recovery of information through File Carving techniques to solid state storage
devices (SSD), in several scenarios of loss of information, both accidental and
intentional, and based on these experimental results it is proposed a protocol that
seeks to contribute to the work of the computer expert in the process of data
recovery as a tool for gathering evidence within the process of generating the
evidence. In addition, a free software application called: Carvers Suite is proposed,
in which this protocol has been implemented as a validation mechanism for this
study, the same that was evaluated through experimentation against other paid
applications with the objective of evaluating the performance of the implemented
protocol, product of this investigation. The product of this work is the generation
of a Protocol for recovering data on SSD using file carving techniques.

Keywords: File carving · Carver Suite · Data recovery protocol

1 Introduction

The growing use of information and communication technologies (ICT) in the activities of daily living: commercial, personal, political, religious and social, generate large amounts of information that must be taken care of innumerable vulnerabilities, which could cause serious losses, since this being susceptible to being damaged, modified or lost with ease, it can be used by unscrupulous subjects who could take advantage of it.

In the world, the progressive use of Information and Communication Technologies in all human activities (from 1.8% to 6.4%) [1, 2], has exponentially increased the volume of information, has contributed to the production of more information.

For this purpose, the internal storage of information is carried out today, largely in electromechanical hard drives and increasingly in SSD storage devices.

T. Guarda et al. (Eds.): ARTIIS 2022, CCIS 1676, pp. 368–379, 2022.
https://doi.org/10.1007/978-3-031-20316-9_28

It should be considered that electromechanical disks have had technological improvements that range from increasing their capacity and decreasing their size to making efficient use of energy, with the aim of maintaining this storage capacity at the highest operating standard. However, SSDs have a good chance of becoming the main primary storage device for many reasons, among them: they are data storage devices that use non-volatile memory to replace the magnetic spinning platters of electromechanical hard drives and because they do not having moving parts, access to the information contained is greater, they make less noise, consume less energy and are more resistant to falls and shocks. For these and other reasons, it is very likely that in every computer we will have an SSD as a primary storage device in the short or medium term.

Therefore, currently the knowledge, development of skills and generation of skills in the field of data recovery in SSD storage devices provides competitive advantages, whether for forensic analysis processes, auditing or recovery of information on demand.

As an aid or as a contribution to the process of recovering information on SSD, there are several methods and techniques [3], however, there is no evidence of this standardization, good practices or protocol that implements the most appropriate technique for the type of damage to the device, so that the recovery work can be more efficient.

In this way, this work aims to establish a data recovery protocol in SSD through the use of file carving techniques, thus establishing standardization in forensic expert processes, computer audit processes and data recovery processes on demand.

2   Background

Currently, information plays a very important role in everyday life, both for people and companies, since it is not stored only on paper, but electronically or in the cloud to keep it permanently.

The large amount of information that is generated every minute has allowed the infrastructure and technology for collecting it to change, proposing the transition to storage devices with better performance in the speed of access to data. Motivating companies to choose the best storage solutions as required, such as the company Hewlett Packard Enterprise (HPE) that offers a new technology that is: All Flash Array Cabinets (AFA) that use solid state drives with the great advantage of having higher speed, both writing and reading; and, longer duration for better performance.

Laptops and desktops need storage devices to store data permanently when the power is interrupted, and not just the temporary storage of main.

Therefore, storage systems are made up of one or more hard drives that constitute a delicate element in themselves, needing certain minimum conditions for their correct operation, but if they are exceeded, it could cause physical damage, preventing access to the contained information [4].

According to Gomes, the SSD storage device are future devices for storage systems, since these types of disks allow the startup of the operating system and applications to be accelerated. SSDs do not contain mechanical parts and are mainly made up of 2 elements: Electronic Card and Memory Chip [5].

For Zertal & Dron, there are two types of solid state storage units. In addition, SSDs, depending on their use, are internal and external (USB Memory, Flash Memory or Micro SD) [6].

Likewise, Zertal & Dron indicate that SSDs are storage devices that use non-volatile solid-state memory (flash memory), considerably reduce the access time to stored data and as an advantage of the use of these devices there is that read operations can be performed faster than write operations [6].

An SSD works in the same way as a hard disk drive (HDD), but data is stored on interconnected flash memory chips that maintain information even when power is not present. These flash memory chips are a bit different from the one used in USB slots, and are usually faster and more reliable. For this reason, SSDs are more expensive than traditional disks, with the maximum storage capacity being 100 TB [7].

On the other hand, SSDs are more resistant to shocks or physical impacts, have less data access time and have lower latency than traditional hard drives [8]. These new storage drives swap the spinning disk for small flash memory chips to deliver capacity, making a head to read data unnecessary as everything is done electronically by a controller.

Finally, Zertal & Dron says SSDs are units based on flash memory that do not have moving parts, that is, they do not have parts that are physically moving like a disk that rotates together with a head that searches for sectors, allowing that the new technology is smaller in physical size and has a series of other advantages that place it over the traditional hard drive [6].

Yan et al., presented the logical architecture based on NAND flash memories, which is used in solid-state hard drives. The read/program operation can only access the page level, while the delete operation can only access the block level [9].

The write is done by a program operation, which must be preceded by an erase operation that sets all bits in the destination physical block to 1. These operations exhibit speed asymmetry. The program operation is longer than the read operation, but relatively faster than the delete operation.

SSD devices for personal and professional use are designed to store data at 25 °C for 2 years. Thus demonstrating that as the temperature increases, the data retention time decreases considerably in an inversely proportional relationship. In the case of SSDs for business use, when going from a temperature of 25 °C to 30 °C, the time of the contained data drops from 20 weeks to only 10 [10].

An SSD can write in a row, it can only erase a block level, without being able to determine the useful content. The only way to remove the content of a particular page is to copy the content of the useful rows into memory, delete the block, and write the contents of the old block back to the new one. This process is known as Garbage Collection.

In case the disk is full, the SSD must scan for blocks that are marked for deletion, and then erase them and write the content. This is the reason why SSD drives degrade over time by performing different writes.

Storage devices, whether these are HD or SSD, can suffer damage that causes loss of information, among which are:

– Hardware failure: caused by impact, blows or crushing, electrocution, fire, magnetization and wetting, which together with the deterioration of the material characterize this cause;

– Logical failure: it is caused by deleted files, read/write defects, failure of the controller or other electronic part and corruption of the service area, which prevent the unit from being detected and consequently affect the contained data.

An important demand for SSDs, should be propose a change in computer forensic work, since the high rate of data recovery in electromechanical disks contrasts with the variety of factors that affect the data. SSD so that the recovery process on these media becomes difficult to guarantee efficiently.

For this reason, the data recovery process with adequate tools is necessary, since the information contained is of great value, either for companies or personally.

At present, there are different ways of recovering data by different digital means whose simplest method used is: basic software on the storage medium, but this is not a recommended idea since the data that has been recovered could be damaged by overwrite them.

3 Related Works

There are several investigations on information retrieval and file carving. Aljumah, Yousuf Uddin & Gulam Ahamad, present two recovery methods, using files from the hard drive and recovering files with a disk image using PhotoRec and Ddrescue tools respectively, where the final result shows that using the disk image is more efficient than the disk directly [11].

Aldaej, Gulam & Yousuf, carried out a similar analysis with solid hard drives, obtaining more data when using a disk image using Open Source tools [12].

One of the types of formats that can be recovered using different techniques are JPEG images, and to do this Cohen uses a function generator to choose the possible sectors that are added in the identified discontinuity and asks the discriminator to Evaluate the resulting image, if some sectors beyond the discontinuity are decoded, optimizing their recovery, this algorithm used can be applied to any type of format [13, 14].

On the other hand, when performing segment analysis, there are fragmentation problems that depend on different types of conditions. Thing *et al.*, developed a system for evidence reconstruction and recovery by conducting experiments to assess the ability to detect and recover obscured evidence [15]. However, over the years, more tools have emerged that allow the recovery of information that has been fragmented. According Poise & Tjoa, file carving algorithms allow the automatic reassembly of fragmented files, for the development of this research they were examined over 300 hard drives showing that the ability to reassemble fragmented files is an important requirement for forensic work [16].

In this sense, Darnowski & Chojnacki, mention the most common data recovery methods in modern forensic science, identifying the typical file carving problems by comparing methods and explaining their advantages and disadvantages [17]. Therefore, they present and explain the proposal of a new file carving method for NTFS.

Then, the use of forensic tools are vital importance to recognize numerous variables that are involved with the recovery of information from users, these tools use techniques that allow the collection and analysis of information that is manipulated by unauthorized persons and authorized in different ways, such as when a single user is not the owner of a hard disk and it is not known to which user the information corresponds. To solve this problem it is essential to make an exact copy of the hard disk, analyze the segments and re-assemble the information as if it were a crossword puzzle.

Therefore, once the data recovery methods have been analyzed, it is necessary to identify what are the causes for which this information has been lost and what are the factors that affect said recovery. According Ninahualpa *et al.*, the investigation begins through expertise or auditing to identify recovery methodologies that can be due to physical or logical damage, where physical damage generates logical damage using recovery techniques [18].

Finally, Cao *et al.*, present new checkpoint recovery algorithms that swap additional space in main memory significantly with lower overhead and latency, these new algorithms do not require any locks or copies of the checkpoint state. Experimental evaluation shows that one of the new algorithms achieves nearly constant latency and reduces overhead by more than an order of magnitude [19].

4   Methodology

In order to carry out data recovery protocol on solid hard drives SSD by means of file carving techniques, it is proposed to carry it out following a quantitative-qualitative methodology that allows defining the impact characteristics and scenarios that show quantifiable variables to be tabulated, with the aim of in order to trace the route of possible mitigation measures within a defined schedule, for which it is proposed:

[1] Action plan - Protocolization of work stages in which the file carving techniques that recover information in SSD based on the type of evidenced damage are described and analyzed;

[2] Discovery (data collection) - Establish the file carving technique or techniques that best recover data on SSD, through a comparative study of the best file carving techniques based on the characteristics and fragmentation of the file without file system information, implemented in paid products (Forensic Toolkit (FTK), Encase, WinHex) and free (PhotoRec, Scalpel, Foremost).

[3] Observation, measurement and generation of information - Structure of development stages of performance analysis processes of file carving techniques against indicators of data recovery on SSD hard drives.

[4] Interpretation - Performance analysis of file carving techniques against data recovery indicators on SSD hard drives.

[5] Evaluation or analysis and understanding - Application of the mathematical model of linear regression in the analysis of the results resulting from the data recovery processes so that the best recovery rate is evidenced.

SSDs are in increasing demand as storage devices, just as computer forensic analysis tasks need to review their available computational tools in search of solutions that meet the legal needs of each reality; in such a way that they do not allow the actions of criminals who seek to take advantage of information vulnerabilities, whether due to ignorance or lack of standardization, to go unpunished, it is intended through this thesis to contribute with the Data recovery Protocol on solid hard drives SSD through file carving techniques, which contribute significantly to:

- Reduction of time, in the process of recovering information, because when evaluating the scenarios and the type of affectation in the SSD, the most efficient tools can be used to reduce the time that the computer forensic uses in this process;
- Increased safety in obtaining the results, through the use of the corresponding file carving technique, depending on the scenario and type of damage to the SSD;
- Establishment of normalization, in the data recovery process, as part of the computerized expert process to the storage media that until today has been applied in an informal way, has presented some shortcomings that are very difficult to undoubtedly assert the evidence information technology as digital evidence.

5 Proposal Development

The protocol for recovery of information in SSD is proposed by means of forensic techniques, taking into account processes, factors and actors of the process [3]: human motivation; validation of research process; expertise legal field; audit commercial area; damage scenarios; incidence factors; data recovery methodology in SDD file carving techniques; validation objectives/requirements; and redefinition of objectives/requirements (see Table 1, Fig. 1).

Table 1. Proposal recovery of information protocol processes, factors and actors of the process.

Processes/Factors/Actors	Description
Human motivation	Describes the supported process of starting the investigation, whose actors can be crime investigators - prosecutors or a human group - administration - interested in retrieving information
Validation of research process	Selection of one of the two processes, documenting in one case an expertise - legal field or documenting an audit - commercial field
Expertise legal field	Data recovery process motivated by a court order and regulated by current legal regulations, with the aim of supporting a legal investigation process
Audit commercial area	Information retrieval process motivated by a work order or fulfillment of functions described in a contract for the provision of professional services, regulated by current legal regulations and with the aim of complying with an audit process or commercial process

(continued)

Table 1. (*continued*)

Processes/Factors/Actors	Description
Damage scenarios	Environments that describe the possible physical characteristics of affectation, emulating the conditions in which the loss of information occurs
Incidence factors	The type of files, their fragmentation on the SSD, as well as the level of damage to the file system are factors that affect the recovery process
Data recovery methodology in SDD file carving techniques	Application of the recovery methodology through File Carving techniques, as well as the analysis of scenarios and incidence factors, to provide efficient support to the actors in the expert or audit process
Validation objectives/Requirements	Process that describes the validation of compliance with the objectives or requirements set at the start of "Human Motivation", so that the process could end with the fulfillment of these or redefine them and propose new ones. It must be adjusted to the reality of the analyzed device
Redefinition of objectives/Requirements	On many occasions, expectations exceed reality and audit objectives/requirements are set that make compliance difficult, for which it is necessary to redefine them and adjust them to the reality of the SSD in question

In the validation phase of this work, the implementation of the protocol was carried out with an intelligent application that selects data recovery tools in SSD storage devices, called Carvers Suite. Carvers Suite bases its performance on a friendly user interface, through which you can interact with traditional carver's applications, which are manipulated through the command line.

Since application recovery is a process that requires several stages, Carvers Suite has divided them into the following processes: identify the file carving technique to be used; file recovery; file classification; report generation; and comparison with other recovery tools (see Fig. 2).

According to the research carried out on data recovery on SSD devices, a Bayesian network graph is created for the selection of the best file carving technique that will recover the greatest amount of information.

For the construction of the Bayesian network, the dependent and independent variables are identified.

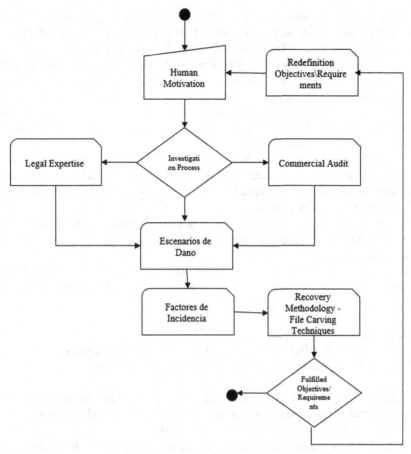

Fig. 1. Data recovery protocol in SSD, using File Carving techniques (adapted from [3]).

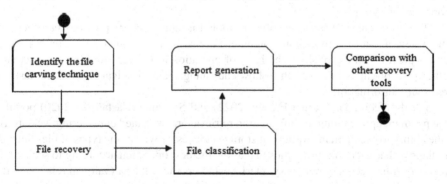

Fig. 2. Carvers suite processes.

The dependent variables or output variables: Foremost (Application implemented with the Semantic Carving technique), Scalpel (Application implemented with the Fragmented Carving technique). These variables are the Carvers (applications that implement the file carving technique) to select depending on the data entered into the application. In the case of the independent variables or input variables (Scenarios), we have the factors to which the SSD device has been subjected – impact (drop or crush damage); moistening; electrocution and magnetization. Once the variables have been identified, the Graph of the Bayesian network is carried out, in order to select the tool with the highest probability of information retrieval.

Once the carver to be used has been identified, it is executed through the graphical interface provided by Carvers Suite. You must enter parameters such as: select the input device and the output folder where the recovered files will be located. Carvers Suite can run as cancel the recovery process.

As a result of the previous step, depending on the capacity of the device to which the recovery has been applied, we obtain: valid files, other corrupted ones and others simply junk files.

Given this result, a method is necessary to identify which files have been correctly recovered and can be delivered to the user. This is handled by the file classification process, which aims to identify:

- Positive: Files successfully recovered;
- False positives: Files that were recovered, but have integrity failures;
- Unclassified: Files that must be manually classified by the user.

To identify the validity of the files, Carvers Suite identifies the type of each one by means of the file signature or magic number. Later, through a library specialized in dealing with each type of file, it identifies its integrity.

Next, a report is created in text format that has input data such as device information, owner, capacity, defects and what it is intended to recover and the output data generated as the percentage of successful recovery. This document can be used as a starting point for an audit report.

The appearance of forensic software tools for data recovery provides facilities for the development of activities in Computer Forensics or Computer Audit, in this sense and depending on establishing the level of operation of Carver Suite free product and other paid products in a way that shows advantages and disadvantages in the task of retrieving information.

For the Techradar (Turner-French, 2022) and Softzone (Castañeda, 2020) portals, the payment applications for information retrieval are evaluated considering: versatility (the ability to use them in a variety of storage devices, as well as the types of files housed in them); characteristic (properties that allow the best operation according to scenarios, recovery time, recovery rate, easy interface and operation); cost (value in relation to its functionalities); easy to use (categorization between applications with graphical interface and code manipulation console; and technical service (in the case of paid products, it is mandatory for the brand to provide adequate technical support).

Based on these criteria, the following have been selected: EaseUS Data Recovery Wizard (EaseUS) and Recover My Filess (GetData), with the aim of comparing the performance of Carver Suite and those mentioned above.

For this comparative analysis, 5 120gb SSDs will be used, loaded with the same information in each case and subjected to the most extreme scenarios in affectation by fall and affectation by electrocution. For this case, the same process developed in the methodology of this work was carried out, differing by the use of payment applications.

With the results obtained, a comparison matrix is generated, detailing in each case the indicators observed in the experimentation (Table 2).

Table 2. Comparative indicators and characteristics of information retrieval with paid products.

N	Component	EaseUS data recovery Wizard	Recover my files	Carver suite
1	Percentage of valid files	99.82%	99.03%	97.93%
2	Valid file classifier	Does not classify Files must be opened	Does not classify Files must be opened	Yes
3	Recovery time	2 h 35 min	3 h 15 min	3 h 40 min
4	Friendly interface type	Friendly Does not report times	Moderately friendly	Moderately friendly
5	Easy and intuitive mode of operation	Easy and intuitive	Moderately friendly	Easy and moderately intuitive
6	Software cost	$99.95/year	$69.95/year	Free

Finally and after observing the results reflected in the comparative table between Carver Suite, EaseUS Data Recovery Wizard and Recover My Files, it can be seen that it is almost the same percentage result in file recovery, the time that Carver Suite spends in restoration is greater than those of its paid competition, the advantage of classifying and saving valid files in another space for greater comfort is a great differentiator and to conclude an important point is the fact that it is a free software allowing to a great extent bring this solution closer to many users who require it.

6 Conclusions and Future Work

In this work, an SSD data recovery protocol was developed using File Carving techniques. Work, which will allow analyzing the scenarios of affectation, motivation, selection of the file carving technique, fragmentation of the file on the device and the type of data to recover, in a way that contributes to the work of the computer expert in the process of recovering information as a tool collection of evidence within the process of generating the evidence that the expert work. A free software prototype tool called

Carvers Suite has also been developed, in which the data recovery protocol in SSD has been implemented using File Carving techniques and which selects the best recovery option for the forensic task based on the affected scenario.

The methodological base used links the damage scenarios: fall, crushing, wetting, electrocution and magnetization with the factors of incidence in the data recovery process, in such a way that it proposes the considerations, phases and actions that allow the data recovery process on SSD using File Carving techniques with the greatest possible success.

In information retrieval processes, the problem of file location in different places on the storage device is latent, and most information retrieval tools focus their work on recover files that are not fragmented.

In this sense, research tasks that address the issue of file recovery through File Carving techniques will be promoted, considering file fragmentation.

Data recovery processes are often time-consuming, and will depend on the state of the storage device and the type of affectation, so the time can range from 24 h to a maximum of 15 days within normal parameters. In accordance with the above, this thesis proposes as future work the development of research aimed at reducing the time invested in the recovery of information in SSD through File Carving techniques.

References

1. Aldaej, A., Ahamad, M.G., Uddin, M.Y.: Solid state drive data recovery in open source environment. In: 2nd International Conference on Anti-Cyber Crimes (ICACC), pp. 228–231. IEEE (2017)
2. Aljumah, A., GulamAhamad, D., Uddin, M.Y.: Digital forensics in Kingdom of Saudi Arabia. Int. J. Eng. Innov. Res. **4**(6), 739–742 (2015)
3. Alsalibi, A.I., Mittal, S., Al-Betar, M.A., Sumari, P.B.: A survey of techniques for architecting SLC/MLC/TLC hybrid flash memory–based SSDs. Concurr. Comput. Pract. Exp. **30**(13), e4420 (2018). https://doi.org/10.1002/cpe.4420
4. Cao, T., et al.: Fast checkpoint recovery algorithms for frequently consistent applications. In: ACM SIGMOD International Conference on Management of Data, pp. 265–276 (2011)
5. Cohen, A., Cohen, A., Nissim, N.: ASSAF: advanced and slim steganalysis detection framework for JPEG images based on deep convolutional denoising autoencoder and Siamese networks. Neural Netw. **131**, 64–77 (2020). https://doi.org/10.1016/j.neunet.2020.07.022
6. Darnowski, F., Chojnacki, A.: Selected methods of file carving and analysis of digital storage media in computer forensics. Przegląd Teleinformatyczny **3**, 25–40 (2015)
7. Gomes, J.M.: A forense computacional. In: eSventh International Conference on Forensic Computer Science – ICoFCS 2012 (2012). https://doi.org/10.5769/C2012001, https://doi.org/10.5769/C201200
8. Gupta, D., Rani, R.: A study of big data evolution and research challenges. J. Inf. Sci. **45**(3), 322–340 (2019)
9. IEEE (ed.): MalJPEG: Machine learning based solution for the detection of malicious JPEG image. IEEE Access **8**, 19997–20011 (2020). https://doi.org/10.1109/ACCESS.2020.2969022
10. Meza, J., Wu, Q., Kumar, S., Mutlu, O.: A large-scale study of flash memory failures in the field. ACM SIGMETRICS Perform. Eval. Rev. **43**(1), 177–190 (2015)

11. Ninahualpa, G., Yoo, S., Guarda, T., Diaz, J., Piccirilli, D.: Protocol of Information Recovery in Solid Hard Drives - SSD Using File Carving Techniques. (IEEE, Ed.) 2019 (IEEE) (CISTI 2019), pp. 1–6 (2019)
12. OECD: Information and communication technology (ICT) (2017). https://doi.org/10.1787/0938c4a0-en
13. OECD: OECD Data. Retrieved from ICT employment, 21 September 2018. https://data.oecd.org/ict/ict-employment.htm#indicator-chart
14. Planas, M., Rodríguez, T., Lecha, M.: La importancia de los datos. Nutr. Hosp. **19**(1), 11–13 (2004). https://scielo.isciii.es/scielo.php?script=sci_arttext&pid=s0212-161120040001 00003
15. Poisel, R., Tjoa, S.: A comprehensive literature review of file carving. In: 2013 International Conference on Availability, Reliability and Security, pp. 475–484. IEEE (2013)
16. Quina, G.N., Díaz, J., Park, S.G., Piccirilli, D.: Data restoration and file carving. In: 12th Iberian Conference on Information Systems and Technologies (CISTI), pp. 1–5. IEEE (2017)
17. Thing, V.L., Chua, T.W., Cheong, M.L.: Design of a digital forensics evidence reconstruction system for complex and obscure fragmented file carving. In: Seventh International Conference on Computational Intelligence and Security (2011). https://doi.org/10.1109/CIS.2011.180
18. Yan, W., Wang, X., Yu, X.: Design and implementation of an efficient flash-based SSD architecture. In: 4th IEEE International Conference on Information Science and Technology, pp. 79–83. IEEE (2014)
19. Zertal, S., Dron, W.: Quantitative study of solid state disks for mass storage. In: 2010 International Symposium on Performance Evaluation of Computer and Telecommunication Systems (SPECTS 2010), pp. 149–155. IEEE (2010)

A Human Being Must Obey the Commands of a Robot! CAVs, Asimov's Second Law and the New Ground-Breaking Ethics

Paweł Księżak⬤ and Sylwia Wojtczak$^{(\boxtimes)}$ ⬤

University of Lodz, Łódź, Poland
swojtczak@wpia.uni.lodz.pl

Abstract. In 2020, the Independent Expert Group published the "Ethics of Connected and Automated Vehicles: recommendations on road safety, privacy, fairness, explainability and responsibility" report. This document represents a significant step towards systematizing the ongoing debate on ethical issues related to autonomic AI systems, especially Connected Automated Vehicles (CAVs). However, the report does not address the conflict between the values of human autonomy and safety, which becomes apparent when considering who should have control over CAVs, and who is responsible for the results of human autonomy. This problem and these questions have therefore become the subject of this paper. The analysis implied the following: either the human driver will be forbidden from driving, which is tantamount to admitting Asimov's Second Law *à rebours*, i.e. a human being must obey the commands of a robot, or the human driver should be held fully responsible for overriding the decisions of the AI controlling the CAV. The choice between these two options must be made by the law maker according to the ethical rules within a culture.

Keywords: Artificial intelligence · Autonomous vehicles · Connected and Automated Vehicles · Ethics · European law

1 Introduction

The Horizon 2020 Commission Expert Group report entitled "Ethics of Connected and Automated Vehicles: recommendations on road safety, privacy, fairness, explainability and responsibility" [20] published in 2020, referred to as *the Report* in the remainder of this paper, when analyzing the ethics of CAVs, gave only brief attention to one of the most urgent problems: the relationship between the "will" of the AI which controls the CAV, and the will of the human passenger, i.e. the driver, or rather, the operator. In a broader sense, this relationship concerns the possible conflict between the unquestionable autonomy of man and the decisions made by the machine, which *in concreto* may contradict each other. In such cases, which one, man or AI, should take precedence,

This work was supported by the National Science Centre, Poland; grant no UMO-2018/29/B/HS5/00421.

and should the will of a human always prevail over that of a machine? Furthermore, are there circumstances, except for such obvious ones as mental illness or young age, which justify that the will of a human should be deferred in favor of an AI system? If such exceptions exist, what are the limits of this superiority? Furthermore, does enforcing the will of a human over an AI also bring with it additional responsibility? And if so, what are the conditions of such responsibility? These questions will be addressed in the present paper. They are fundamental not only from an ethical perspective or from the point of view of CAVs drivers and all other road users. The answers to them determine the necessary legislative solutions that will have to be adopted soon in administrative, criminal, and civil law.

2 Who Makes Decisions? Who Drives?

Similar to other European documents on AI ethics, the Report assumes the principle of personal autonomy of the human being to be the foundation of the debate [20, 22]. This matter was described in a more general manner in the High-Level Expert Group on Artificial Intelligence – Ethics guidelines for trustworthy AI [2], referred to in the remainder of this article as the Guidelines; this document established four ethical principles strictly related to fundamental rights, which should be obeyed if the AI systems are to be reliably designed, deployed and used. These principles are formulated as categorical imperatives for AI professionals who are obliged to follow them: (i) Respect for human autonomy; (ii) Prevention of harm; (iii) Fairness; (iv) Explicability. The Guidelines describe the principle of respect for human autonomy in the following way:

> The fundamental rights upon which the EU is founded are directed towards ensuring respect for the freedom and autonomy of human beings. Humans interacting with AI systems must be able to keep full and effective self-determination over themselves, and be able to partake in the democratic process. AI systems should not unjustifiably subordinate, coerce, deceive, manipulate, condition or herd humans. [...] The allocation of functions between humans and AI systems should follow human-centric design principles and leave meaningful opportunity for human choice. This means securing human oversight over work processes in AI systems. [...] [2, 12]

Later, in footnote 25, the Guidelines underline that, according to the Charter of Fundamental Rights of the European Union [33], "respect for human autonomy is strongly associated with the right to human dignity and liberty".

According to the Guidelines, the ethical foundations of trustworthy AI, particularly respect for human autonomy, may be ensured by human agency and oversight. The different modes of this oversight are as follows [2, 16]:

- Human-in-the-loop (HITL) – the human can intervene in every decision cycle of the system;
- Human-on-the-loop (HOTL) – the human can intervene during the design cycle of the system and while monitoring its operation

- Human-in-command (HIC) – the human can oversee the overall activity of the AI system in a broad perspective, decide when and how to use the system in concrete circumstances; the human can also decide not to use the AI system in concrete circumstances, to establish the levels of human discretion during the use of the system or to ensure the ability to override a decision made by the system; public enforcers have the ability to exercise oversight in line with their mandate.

These declarations imply that it is taken for granted that a human being should be able to govern AI systems, and the autonomy and dignity of the operator must be respected. In the context of CAVs, this means that the human should be able to take control of the vehicle or issue binding commands to it if necessary. And it is precisely this issue that was not addressed in the Report.

Before a more specific examination of the topic can be made, it should be noted that prima facie there are at least three different models of CAVs for which different ethical and legal solutions are possible:

1. CAVs which can be steered by single commands (e.g. go right, slow down etc.) issued by voice or otherwise (traditionally and mechanically by pedals, levers, buttons or steering wheel). If voice commands are issued, the situation is similar to assistant systems or smart homes. In this case the name "CAV" may be considered a little bit excessive.
2. CAVs which drive autonomously but provide the possibility for the human operator to take full control at any time and continue the journey without the AI in control. This is generally similar to autopilot systems used in airplanes or yachts – the human decides whether and when to take control over the machine.
3. CAVs which cannot be controlled by the human operator; however, the possibility exists to stop or disable their operation. Such a safety system would be analogous to the safety brake used in trains or subways.

It must be remembered that the above differentiation is based on a different criterion than that given by the Society of Automotive Engineers regarding the levels of technical autonomy of the CAV [32]: it is not based on the technical capability of AI to be autonomous, but on the actual capability of a human to take control during the operation of the CAV. All three types of CAVs cause specific problems when confronted with human autonomy and responsibility. Clearly, it is possible to construct many intermediate or mixed models, the technical details of which may vary notably, and that the resulting CAV could have all the above functions, some of them or even none, at least under some circumstances.

The general belief that a human being should maintain autonomy in the relations with CAVs, and thus maintain power over it, requires significant nuance when confronted with even the simplest everyday situation. Let's imagine that a CAV is moving on a public road, when the driver gives an order which contradicts the valid legal rules of the road, e.g. "stop on the highway immediately". Should the system controlling the CAV comply with the driver's order, which would also break the law, or should it ignore the command? Alternatively, should it strike a reasonable and more socially-useful middle ground by modifying the order in such a way that it becomes lawful?[1] For example, the CAV could modify the will of the operator by stopping at the nearest car park or in an emergency lay-by. But here lies the problem: such modification of the human operator's will by the AI system according to its own criteria, even if these criteria are programmed by a human coder, is not derived from the will of a human but the will of the system. Thus, the autonomy owed to the human operator becomes illusory.

The document "European Civil Law Rules in Robotics" prepared by Nathalie Nevejans [13, 21] in 2016 includes the following postulate and proposal:

> Some autonomous robots might trample all over freedoms, on the pretext of protecting a person, leading to a clash of certain basic rights — such as protecting liberty versus considering people's health and safety. [...]

> Therefore, we need to establish a general principle that the robot should respect a person's decision-making autonomy. This would then mean that a human being should always be able to oblige a robot to obey their orders. Since this principle could pose certain risks, particularly in terms of safety, it should be tied to a number of preliminary precautions. Where the order received could endanger the user or third parties, the robot should, first of all, issue a risk alert that the person can understand. This would mean adapting the message depending on the person's age, and level of awareness and understanding. Second, the robot should have the right to an absolute veto where third parties could be in danger. As such, the robot could not, then, be used as a weapon, in accordance with the wishes expressed in the motion for a resolution in the paragraph on the "licence for users", which asserts that "you are not permitted to modify any robot to enable it to function as a weapon".

Such postulates seem to be rational ones, and it is possible that European legislation will be shaped in such a direction; however, they nevertheless contradict the principles of respecting the will of humans and protecting their autonomy. Of course, it can be claimed that other values, such as the life and health of others, can sometimes take precedence over human will[2]. Nowadays, the need to balance different values and rights is not a controversial one, although the very mechanism of this weighting is a point of debate. It is also observed in the Guidelines [2, 13], that "tensions may arise between the above principles, for which there is no fixed solution [...] For instance, in various application domains, the principle of prevention of harm and the principal of human autonomy may be in conflict."

---

[1] Legal rules are also the product of human will, as long as the law maker is a human or group of humans. Therefore, it can be doubtful whether in the given example, the will of the individual human operator opposes the will of the AI system or rather the collective human will of the law maker. Nevertheless, this uncertainty does not resolve the problem. Another example may be a CAV that moves to avoid danger when the operator orders it to move in a dangerous way.

[2] It should be remembered that no value or human right is absolute, in the sense that it should be realized completely, or whether it can. Even the realization of the value of human life is limited by the necessity to realize other values which can be *prima facie* quite trivial. For example, when we spend money on better roads which increase our comfort of travelling and let us grow rich, we do not spend it on curing mortally ill children.

Among the listed principles, the Report puts non-maleficence [20, 21] in first place and personal autonomy in fourth [20, 22]. It is, however, interesting to note that in the draft of the Guidelines, the principle of non-maleficence was awarded the second place, before the third of autonomy [1, 9], although in the final version of the Guidelines [2] autonomy is first and prevention of harm second in the hierarchy of principles. This may suggest that after the debate on the Guidelines the principle of respect for human autonomy was regarded as being more important than that of prevention of harm. This issue is not a trivial one, as it is important to note that hierarchies of values are culturally dependent, even assuming that it is not stable or fixed. For example, it is exactly the ranking of human liberty against safety which separates Europe from the United States of America when debating access to guns. In the USA, legal access to guns is typically justified on the basis of liberty, while safety should be protected by personal responsibility, criminal and civil, and not by general restrictions imposed by the state. In contrast, in European countries, such gun access is restricted, with the common belief that it is worth sacrificing some part of liberty to ensure greater social and individual safety.

The same disparity can be observed for the legal regulation of CAVs, especially since in the USA, a car is often treated as a tool for achieving personal freedom [27]. It is also worth noting that the first places where CAVs could legally move on public roads were Nevada, Florida, California and Michigan in the USA [21, 430].

Anyway, although the Report rightly observes that:

The timely and systematic integration of broader ethical and societal considerations is also essential to achieve alignment between technology and societal values and for the public to gain trust and acceptance of CAVs. [20, 15]

neither the Report nor the earlier documents propose any deeper analysis of the problem. This is an important issue, although not because of the difficulties involved in resolving this conflict of values; rather, by weighing values, derived from the rights and interests of other hypothetical people, and imposing its own will, the AI may contradict the explicitly-expressed will of the human operator.[3]

The problems associated with a robot obeying a human, and the limits of this obedience, are as old as the idea of robots itself. As a matter of fact, these are the same questions which were revealed during the debate on Asimov's Three Laws of Robotics [4, 6].

Although criticised nowadays by both scientists and philosophers, their considerable presence in publications and discussions from the early times of robotics and AI

---

[3] By the way, the problem has the economical aspect. Usually it is perceived mainly in the ethical perspective – see all these publications on this problem referring to the famous Trolley Dilemma [17] – e.g. [24, 248, 34, 19, 11, 29]. Whereas if it were AI who were given a competence to weigh values, people might be afraid of using CAVs, fearing that in the situation of the conflict between their lives and the lives or rights of other people or groups of people, AI could have sacrificed the lives of CAV's passenger/operator without hesitation. It is not the perspective which increase economical demand for CAVs or which make society give an impulse to the government to support this technology. These and other analogous issues are considered for instance by Goodall [18], Bonnefon et al. [9] and Contissa et al. [10].

development have established the Laws as part of the folk theory of robotics or imaginary futures [8]. They also exist as a mainstay of popular culture, in which they act as a remedy against the fear of the new and unknown. In fact, it has been proposed that Asimov's Laws should occupy first place among the general rules specified by European Parliament resolution of 16 February 2017 on Civil Law Rules on Robotics [16] as being fundamental for developing future aspects of civil law in this area. Asimov's Laws clearly remain an important argument in the debates about the Law surrounding robotics, despite the consensus in the field of Robotics that they contain many misconceptions and are not applicable in practice [26]. However, this latter opinion does not preclude their use as a starting point for a better understanding of the problem arising from the conflict between a CAV and its operator.

Asimov's Laws state the following:

0. A robot may not harm humanity, or, by inaction, allow humanity to come to harm. [7]
1. A robot may not injure a human being or, through inaction, allow a human being to come to harm, unless this would violate the Zeroth Law. [5]
2. A robot must obey the orders given it by human beings, except where such orders would conflict with the Zeroth or First Law. [5]
3. A robot must protect its own existence as long as such protection does not conflict with the Zeroth, First or Second Laws. [5]

For the purposes of the present paper, the Second Law seems the most important. In contemporary research on the AI ethics, it is introduced by underlining the position of human autonomy in relation to AI. However, more interesting is how to resolve the conflict between the Second and the First Law. The Second Law states that only in the event of a collision with Zeroth or First Law is the robot released from the obligation to obey human commands. Common sense, and Asimov's Laws derive from common sense, dictates that this does not allow the robot to do whatever it wants except for breaking the First Law in the event of a collision. It rather requires the robot to assess the values at stake, and the potential damage or endangered interests, to weigh up the probability of each, and to choose a course of action as close as possible to the will of the operator; however, it cannot break the First Law.

Similar calculations have been proposed in the domain of law, such as R. Alexy's Weight Formula [3]; however, such measures seem impossible in practice. Not only are some of the values incommensurable, but they are also individually and culturally dependent. Furthermore, such calculations require the AI to assess an infinite number of factors.[4]

---

[4] Lipson and Kurman [24, 249] explain it simply: "My calculation of risk could grow very complex. If I had three children in the back seat of my car, I might have chosen to not swerve and to let the squirrel take his chances. If the roads were icy and crowded with pedestrians, my moral calculation would likely have been that the value of the human lives inside and outside the car was higher than that of squirrel. In that case, I would have opted not to swerve. My calculation could grow even more complex were the hypothetical squirrel be replaced by a dog, an old person on crutches, and so on.".

Regarding road traffic and CAVs, the degree of CAV expansion onto the roads is rarely taken into consideration systematically in ethical debates (although the problem is noticed, for instance, by Nyholm and Simids [30] or van Loon and Martens [25]). The problem is radically different when comparing scenarios where (1) a few CAVs share the roads with large numbers of "regular" cars, (2) CAVs predominate but still share the roads with other vehicles, or (3) CAVs are the only vehicles on the roads but can be driven legally by humans, or (4) CAVs are the only vehicles on the roads and humans are forbidden from operating them – c.f. [28]. It is reasonable to expect that as CAVs become more common, the highway code would be changed step by step in response; for example, the speed limits may be increased or changes made to right of way. The traffic would become flow faster and more easily, and eventually human operators would not be able to participate because of their biological and mental limits. Imagine a situation where the light turns green at a crossroads, although this signal may not eventually be a visual one, and all the CAVs in the queue move together simultaneously. Such fluency would never be possible with human operators. In such a case, would it be possible at all to leave the responsibility of driving to a human?

At this point, we should consider a simple question: is it at all reasonable to judge the competence to make technical decisions about the motion of a CAV through the lens of human autonomy and dignity? We do not argue that travelling by train may be an assault on human autonomy and dignity because the railroad tracks remove the freedom to roam from the passenger or driver. Hence, when discussing the decision makers and the rules of the road, we must remember that these aspects mainly concern the problem of coordination [23, 4].

The coordination problem may be solved by convention, or by social rules such as laws: indeed, "conventions may be a species of norms" [23, 97]. Although both conventions and rules are to some degree arbitrary [14, 18–19], they are necessary to achieve certain socially-agreed purposes; in the case of CAVs, in European culture, the aim of these rules is to ensure safe and efficient traffic movement. Existing rules on driving on the right, the colours of the traffic lights, speed limits, right of way and traffic signs are there for the sole purpose of ensuring safety and efficiency. Hence, "it is redundant to speak of arbitrary convention. [...] Any convention is arbitrary because there is an alternative regularity that could have been our convention instead." [23, 70]. As such, it would appear nonsensical if an individual chooses to break these rules, by driving on the wrong side of the road for example, and then attempts to justify this decision with the recall to agency, autonomy and liberty. Hence, drivers are much more likely to justify their actions as an innocent mistake or being in a hurry when caught by the police.

In spite of the above dubieties, the problem remains of determining the responsible party in the event of any damage or breach of the rules, depending on who has control over the vehicle. Therefore, a further analysis of the possible scenarios is needed.

3   Who is Responsible for Making Decisions During Driving?

Firstly, we will analyse the cases of CAVs which are situated within the first model, i.e. when a human operator can take the control over the vehicle and give it single commands. Let's consider how to evaluate such a command in some different situations:

1. A driver (or an operator) gives the AI a command which directly puts the lives and health of other people in danger. Alternatively, a sub-type of this situation is an order which would result in danger only for the driver (i.e. the operator).
2. The operator gives the AI a command which may present a risk to life and health, but not directly, and the probability of the damage in life or health would depend on the circumstances.
3. A driver gives AI a command which does not present any risk to life or health but is contrary to the legal rules protecting other values.
4. The operator issues a command that does not cause any damage, but is against the legal rules.
5. A driver gives AI a command which, although lawful and not intended to risk another person's well-being, increases the danger of damage because it is made too late or requires a manoeuvre that is less skilled than the AI could perform.

Alternatively, other specific situations arise when a driver may take control over the vehicle at any moment:

1. A driver demands control over the vehicle in a dangerous situation, when the AI calculates those human reactions are inadequate.
2. A driver demands control over the vehicle when the driving conditions are so difficult that such control increases the probability of damage.
3. A driver demands control over the vehicle while being in a state which increases the probability of damage, e.g. a driver is ill or drunk, or has no driving licence.

Should the human operator be allowed to take control in the above situation? Who should be responsible for damage if it happens? The Report does not give answers to these questions or even provide a way of working them out. It notes only the problem of the CAV potentially ignoring human rules, and the responsibility of the human operator to take control over the vehicle in such a situation [20, 30].

One part of the Report (Chapter 3 Responsibility) [20, 52–63] consists of a broad discussion of the problems of responsibility. Among other issues, it also considers "gaps in culpability" and "scapegoating", i.e. the imposition of culpability on agents who were not given fair capacity and opportunity to avoid wrongdoing [20, 61–62]:

> An example of the latter would include 'pushing' culpability onto end users for a crash caused by a split-second handover of control or pushing it onto individual developers for choices ultimately taken by their employer.

However, the Report fails to reflect on the question of whether the handover of control should be permissible at all and if so, on what conditions. It also fails to discuss the significance that such behaviour would have in cases when it was not, as is suggested in the Report, the result of signals from the AI system, but rather a result of the autonomous will of the operator.

The situations described above illustrate the ethical and legal conflicts concerning the autonomy of a human being and the potential consequences of these decisions. If the driver takes the control over the vehicle and causes damage, should it be important whether the AI would, or would not, have avoided this damage in the same situation? Or should responsibility be bound to the very fact of taking control? Should the behaviour of a driver be compared to an objective template based on the behaviour of other human drivers or to the template based on the AI's capabilities? In other words, if it were certain that AI would have avoided the damage but no human being could possibly have done, should the operator who took control be held responsible?

Although the demands for certification of CAV to enter service may vary depending on circumstances and applications, it seems reasonable to expect that an AI controlling a CAV provides a standard of safety at least not lower than the one given by a human driver. It is difficult to imagine the social and political consensus as to certifying vehicles that would be more dangerous than those driven by humans. Rather, due to social fears, it is likely that the standards of safety for CAVs will be so stringent that severe accidents caused by CAVs would be extremely rare. When the threshold set for CAV safety is set higher than that assumed for a human driver, the expectations as to the safety on the roads will continue to grow; eventually, such pressure to increase safety and efficiency will likely eliminate the human factor entirely.

The criteria for CAVs to be licensed for use in the general traffic system comprise a range of characteristics seen to be important from the social point of view, such as infallibility, speed, fluency of motion, ecological impact and economics, not to mention a superhuman level of safety. Therefore, it is inevitable that the belief that humans should exert control over the CAV, either on ethical or legal bases, will be seen as unreasonable and based on non-substantial premises. It would be human autonomy *reduction ad absurdum* if the less efficient, i.e. more fallible, human were to control an AI whose high efficiency and almost perfect infallibility were certified by the state. Such a conclusion would appear to be valid in all the situations described above.

It is also clear that requiring very high standards by AIs may be accompanied by the need to raise the standard of diligence by humans. But since it is not possible to expect human operators to reach the level of performance of a CAV, the only solution is to let the demands be different: the expectations placed on humans should be adequate to their capabilities, while those placed on CAVs should be governed by political considerations and technical possibilities. Hence, as it was concluded above, because human drivers cannot demonstrate the same reaction speed of an AI, cannot take advantage of big data or simultaneously process as many variables as an AI, they will have to pass the burden of control to the computer. It may be expected that as the participation of human drivers in the traffic decreases, so will the number of accidents.

But as a consequence, there arise further questions:

1. In circumstances where it is possible to choose to use AI or not, is it right to blame the human operator alone for not using the AI controlling the CAV, i.e. for exerting their own autonomy?
2. Should the correct usage of CAV exempt the operator from responsibility?

In our opinion, the problem regarding the consequences for ignoring the "decision" of a CAV is the key to understanding the legal and ethical changes resulting from the development of AI. When we deal with CAVs, and other advanced technologies based on AI, they are not simply vehicles for realising human will; rather their use involves the transfer of the decision-making centre from human to machine. As such, there is a need to decide whether a human may refuse to comply with a decision by an AI, and whether such behaviour would require the acceptance of ethical and legal responsibility.

On a similar issue, regarding the European Parliament resolution of 12 February 2019 on a comprehensive European industrial policy on artificial intelligence and robotics (2018/2088(INI)), point 77:

> The European Parliament [...] points out that legal liability for damage is a central issue in the health sector where the use of AI is concerned; stresses the need therefore to ensure that users will not be led invariably to back the diagnostic solution or treatment suggested by a technological instrument for fear of being sued for damages if, on the basis of their informed professional judgement, they were to reach conclusions that diverged even in part [...]. [15]

Although the danger mentioned by European Parliament is described specifically and relates only to the medical applications of AI, the idea may be generalized and extended to its use in CAVs. The European Parliament does not allow that an individual may accept the decision of an AI, despite being convinced of her own ability and judgment, because the refusal may result in liability. The EP expects that the lawmaker provides individuals with autonomy of will or, as a matter of fact, with a guarantee of not being burdened with liability, when not using AI. Such a position results in three fundamental questions:

1. Is it right not to sanction objectively erroneous actions enforced by the will of a human operator, when it was possible to perform the correct action?
2. What about the rights of other humans in a world where infallible technology is widely accessible – should they also not expect that the decisions made about their health and safety by human operators, such as professional doctors or drivers, should also be infallible? Why should these people agree to be potential victims of the hubris, albeit professional hubris, of another individual?[5]
3. Is society ready to accept risky or evidently false decisions just in the name of protecting human autonomy?

The answers may seem obvious, but only from some cultural perspectives. Returning to the right to bear arms in the USA, many US citizens, albeit a dwindling number, are convinced that the risks associated with unhindered access to guns are a fair price to pay for ensuring individual autonomy and agency. Many believe that the possibility to have and use firearms, and of being responsible for the results of this choice, are expressions of individual autonomy and agency. The fact that this right may entail irreparable damages to the priceless values of other people is often not acknowledged. Also, in the domain of CAVs such dilemmas were noticed; for instance, Ryan [31] while analysing social impacts of CAVs notices that for many they threaten to take away the joy of driving itself

---

[5] Such hubris under the name of prejudice against algorithms (i.e. a common belief that clinical predictions based on the subjective impressions of trained professionals are more accurate than statistical predictions) is described by Kahneman on the basis of various scientific studies. [22, 468].

and that "there is a conflict between those who promote the reduced numbers of traffic death and those who want to protect their right to drive".

Clearly, these problems do not relate to CAVs alone, but are of a broader and more fundamental nature: different AI systems make decisions which limit humans in various ways. Even if the decisions of AI were not *ex iure* binding for a human, the decision of a human operator would entail more risk in all aspects of responsibility which are mentioned in the Report.

In our opinion, although the conclusions cannot be definite, the entry of AI into a certain domain has a lasting effect on the standard of care by the AI or the human operator, and on reasonable expectations as to the correctness of a decision by either. Hence, even if the social rules, either ethical or legal, declaratively acknowledge the supremacy of human will and autonomy over machines, ultimately, the power to decide will de facto rest in full on the machines. As a consequence, it may be expected that safer and more efficient autonomous driving systems will steadily but surely oust human drivers from their position of operators, initially through higher insurance premiums, and later by increasingly stringent legal limits, up to the prohibition of driving for humans.

There is also another aspect of to this phenomenon. If it is admitted that the use of AI in some domain lifts the expected standard so highly that it de facto enforces its use, it must be also admitted that a human user should be exempted from responsibility for the incorrect action of an AI system, if this system were correctly certificated, maintained and used. When relying on an AI, human operators relinquish due diligence along with their control, and nothing else should be demanded from them. It is not clear at all whether it should be expected at all that a human should control the action of an AI, except in rare and extreme situations. If an AI is a more capable driver than a human, the very belief of this operator that the CAV's action is correct or incorrect and should be corrected cannot be proof of anything. Of course, it may happen that the operator is right, and the machine is wrong, such things are possible in all artificial systems, even those that are tested and certified; however, this cannot be sufficient grounds for constructing a general rule.

The two above paragraphs justify the following thesis: only two models of regulation are possible:

1. Human beings are responsible for all their actions which guarantee a lower level of care (safety and efficiency) than an AI, or
2. Human beings must not take control over CAVs.

In practice both solutions would give similar results. It may be expected that should a human operator be held responsible for the mistakes made while in control of a CAV, he or she would be less likely to take control.

In our opinion, the answers to all such questions cannot be found in the ethical or legal domains, especially since both ultimately relate to individual rights and obligations: it is necessary to find optimal solutions that merge the all-pervading technological system and society as a whole. As such, regulations must also take into account the mass scale of the interactions. Hence the inevitable conclusion that the decisions made regarding the implementation of AI are in fact more strategic or political than strictly ethical.

From this point of view, it seems reasonable to differentiate regulation temporally, based on the moment of emergence of CAV technology. While traffic consists of traditional cars, driven by human operators, it should be possible for humans to override the AI in a CAV; in such cases, driving should entail the same responsibility as driving a regular car. In many countries, the general rule is strict liability, but others are characterised by semi-strict or negligence liability [12]. The very act of taking control should only be possible under certain conditions, e.g. that it is safe to do so, and a human operator with a driving licence should be entitled to take control over a CAV in a concrete instance; for example, such an override may not be possible in a taxi. If such an authorisation did not succeed, the only possibility for the human would be to disable a system, by using the emergency brake for example. Later on, should all vehicles be supplanted by CAVs, the human operator should not have the possibility to command the vehicle or take control. However, there should still be the option to disable the system, assuming it is safe to do so.

4   Conclusions

The analysis made in this paper implied the unescapable choice: either the human driver will be forbidden from driving, which is tantamount to admitting Asimov's Second Law *à rebours*, i.e. a human being must obey the commands of a robot, or the human driver should be held fully responsible for overriding the decisions of the AI controlling the CAV. This choice must be made by the law maker according to the ethical rules within a culture.

What is more, the recommendations of different legal and expert documents concerning human oversight over AI are ethically justified but utopian. If AI systems were more efficient and safer than people, the entire concept of human oversight would not be reasonable: any such oversight consisting of simply a general observance of the system's functioning would only serve as a bureaucratic façade, without any real possibility to understand the mechanisms of decision making.

Even if some technological and legal mechanism of oversight were created, the higher-level problem would not be solved: algorithms would perform their functions well. In this situation, as S. Wolfram [35, 480–481] observes:

> [...] there will be an AI that knows your history, and knows that when you're ordering dinner online you'll probably want such-and-such, or when you email this person, you should talk to them about such-and-such. More and more, the AIs will suggest to us what we should do, and I suspect most of the time people will just go along with that. It's good advice – better than what you would have figured out for yourself.

In the context of CAVs, such "good advice" is nothing other than driving the vehicle. Driving in a safe way that offers optimal speed and economy is complicated and a task much better suited to an AI than a human. Any decision-making or oversight by humans may at the most be based on intuition, common sense or some sixth sense, or on unjustified negation (contrariness); it may even be consciously unreasonable. Such human oversight seems systemically impossible.

References

1. AI HLEG Draft Ethic Guidelines for Trustworthy AI, 18 December 2018. https://ec.europa. eu/digital-single-market/en/news/draft-ethics-guidelines-trustworthy-ai
2. AI HLEG Ethics Guidelines for Trustworthy AI, 8 April 2019. https://ec.europa.eu/digital-single-market/en/news/ethics-guidelines-trustworthy-ai
3. Alexy, R.: On balancing and subsumption. A structural comparison. Ratio Juris **16**(4), 433–449 (2003). https://doi.org/10.1046/j.0952-1917.2003.00244.x
4. Anderson, S.L.: Asimov's "Three Laws of Robotics" and machine metaethics. AI Soc. **22**(4), 477–493 (2008). https://doi.org/10.1007/s00146-007-0094-5
5. Asimov, I.: Roundaround. Astounding Science Fiction, March 1942
6. Asimov, I.: Bicentennial Man. Ballantine Books, New York (1976)
7. Asimov, I.: Robots and Empire. Doubleday Books, New York (1985)
8. Barbrook, R.: Imaginary Futures. From Thinking Machines to the Global Village. Pluto Press, London (2007)
9. Bonnefon, J.-F., Shariff, A., Rahwan, I.: The social dilemma of autonomous vehicles. Science **352**(6293), 1573–1576 (2016). https://doi.org/10.1126/science.aaf2654
10. Contissa, G., Lagioia, F., Sartor, G.: The Ethical Knob: ethically-customisable automated vehicles and the law. Artif. Intell. Law **25**(3), 365–378 (2017). https://doi.org/10.1007/s10 506-017-9211-z
11. Davnall, R.: Solving the single-vehicle self-driving car trolley problem using risk theory and vehicle dynamics. Sci. Eng. Ethics **26**(1), 431–449 (2019). https://doi.org/10.1007/s11948-019-00102-6
12. De Bruin, R.: Autonomous intelligent cars on the European intersection of liability and privacy. regulatory challenges and the road ahead. Eur. J. Risk Regul. **3**(7) (2016). https://doi.org/10.1017/S1867299X00006036
13. Directorate-General for Internal Policies: Policy Department for Citizen's Rights and Constitutional Rights and Constitutional Affairs, European Civil Law Rules in Robotics. Study for the JURI Committee, PE 571.379 (2016). https://www.europarl.europa.eu/RegData/etudes/STUD/2016/571379/IPOL_STU(2016)571379_EN.pdf
14. Dyrda, A.: Why legal conventionalism fails. Archiwum Filozofii Prawa i Filozofii Społecznej **1**(10) (2015). http://cejsh.icm.edu.pl/cejsh/element/bwmeta1.element.desklight-46bd2af6-1614-4b6e-a205-9324aa9f77b3, http://dx.doi.org/https%3A//doi.org/10.36280/AFPiFS. 2015.1.14
15. European Parliament resolution of 12 February 2019 on a comprehensive European industrial policy on artificial intelligence and robotics (2018/2088(INI)). https://www.europarl.europa. eu/doceo/document/TA-8-2019-0081_EN.html
16. European Parliament resolution of 16 February 2017 with recommendations to the Commission on Civil Law Rules on Robotics (2015/2103 (INL)), P8_TA(2017)0051. https://eur-lex. europa.eu/legal-content/EN/TXT/?uri=CELEX%3A52017IP0051
17. Foot, P.: The problem of abortion and the doctrine of double effect. Oxf. Rev. **5**, 5–15 (1967). https://philpapers.org/archive/footpo-2.pdf
18. Goodall, N.: Ethical decision making during automated vehicle crashes. Trans. Res. Rec. J. Transp. Res. Board **2424**(1), 58–65 (2014). https://doi.org/10.3141/2424-07
19. Himmelreich, J.: Never mind the trolley: the ethics of autonomous vehicles in mundane situations. Ethical Theory Moral Pract. **21**(3), 669–684 (2018). https://doi.org/10.1007/s10 677-018-9896-4
20. Horizon 2020 Commission Expert Group to advise on specific ethical issues raised by driverless mobility (E03659). Ethics of Connected and Automated Vehicles: recommendations on road safety, privacy, fairness, explainability and responsibility, Luxembourg (2020). https://ec.europa.eu/info/sites/info/files/research_and_innovation/ethics_of_connected_and_automated_vehicles_report.pdf

21. Ilková, V., Ilka, A.: Legal aspects of autonomous vehicles – an overview. In: 2017 21st International Conference on Process Control (PC) (2017). https://doi.org/10.1109/PC.2017.7976252
22. Kahneman, D.: Thinking, Fast and Slow, Farrar. Straus and Giroux, New York (2011)
23. Lewis, D.: Convention: A Philosophical Study. Wiley-Blackwell, Oxford (2002)
24. Lipson, H., Kurman, M.: Driverless: Intelligent Cars and the Road Ahead. MIT Press, Cambridge (2016)
25. van Loon, R.J., Martens, M.H.: Automated driving and its effects on the safety ecosystem: how do compatibility issues affect the transition period? Procedia Manuf. 3(2015), 3280–3285 (2015). https://doi.org/10.1016/j.promfg.2015.07.401
26. McCauley, L.: AI armageddon and the three laws of robotics. Ethics Inf. Technol. 9(2), 153–164 (2007). https://doi.org/10.1007/s10676-007-9138-2
27. Moore, R.: What Happens to American Myth When You Take the Driver Out of It. The self-driving car and the future of self. Intelligencer (2016). https://nymag.com/intelligencer/2016/10/is-the-self-driving-car-un-american.html
28. Müller, J.F., Gogoll, J.: Should manual driving be (eventually) outlawed? Sci. Eng. Ethics 26(3), 1549–1567 (2020). https://doi.org/10.1007/s11948-020-00190-9
29. Nyholm, S., Smids, J.: The ethics of accident-algorithms for self-driving cars: an applied trolley problem? Ethical Theory Moral Pract. 19(5), 1275–1289 (2016). https://doi.org/10.1007/s10677-016-9745-2
30. Nyholm, S., Smids, J.: Automated cars meet human drivers: responsible human-robot coordination and the ethics of mixed traffic. Ethics Inf. Technol. 22(4), 335–344 (2018). https://doi.org/10.1007/s10676-018-9445-9
31. Ryan, M.: The future of transportation: ethical, legal, social and economic impacts of self-driving vehicles in the year 2025. Sci. Eng. Ethics 26(3), 1185–1208 (2019). https://doi.org/10.1007/s11948-019-00130-2
32. Society of Automobile Engineers, Taxonomy and Definitions for Terms Related to Driving Automation Systems for On-Road Motor Vehicles, J3016_201806, 15 June 2018. https://www.sae.org/standards/content/j3016_201806/
33. The Charter of Fundamental Rights of the European Union. https://eur-lex.europa.eu/legal-content/EN/TXT/?uri=CELEX%3A12012P%2FTXT
34. Wiseman, Y., Grinberg I.: The trolley problem version of autonomous vehicles. Open Transp. J. 12(1), 105–113 (2018). https://doi.org/10.2174/1874447801812010105. https://www.researchgate.net/publication/323737072_The_Trolley_Problem_Version_of_Autonomous_Vehicles
35. Wolfram, S.: Artificial intelligence and the future of civilization. In: Brockman, J. (ed.) Possible Minds. Twenty-Five Ways of Looking at AI. Penguin Press, New York (2019)

Global Corporate Performance Measurement Model Through the Integration of Six Sigma and Balanced Scorecard. Application in the Poultry Industry

Juan Muyulema-Allaica[1]([✉]) [ID], Paola Pucha-Medina[2] [ID],
Carina Muyulema-Allaica[3] [ID], Fausto Calderón-Pineda[1] [ID],
Franklin Reyes-Soriano[1] [ID], and Rolando Calero-Mendoza[1] [ID]

[1] State University Santa Elena Peninsula, 240204 La Libertad, Ecuador
jmuyulema@upse.edu.ec
[2] University of the Pacific, 090904 Guayaquil, Ecuador
[3] University of Trujillo, 13011 Trujillo, Peru

Abstract. In recent decades, a competitive landscape, informed customers, and stringent regulations have forced goods and services industries to focus on evaluating performance and improving productivity. The purpose of this research is to develop a model for measuring overall corporate performance through the alignment of strategic objectives (Balanced Scorecard) and productivity improvement tools (Six Sigma) for multi-response processes that is robust enough for application in the poultry industry. The article's contributions focus on the development of a model called the Multivariate Performance Measurement System (MPMS) that shows how a scorecard should be implemented in order to go beyond the DMAIC, or performance monitoring of financial and non-financial measures. The model postulates how indicators integrate and relate to each other to optimize a company's overall performance.

Keywords: Balanced Scorecard (BSC) · Six Sigma · Multivariate statistics · Organizational performance

1 Introduction

In recent years, as a result of globalization, organizations must face rapid changes in their competitive environments and only those that are able to implement an effective strategy will be able to obtain above-average performance [1, 2]. In this sense, different concepts of improvement initiative have emerged, whosZe results promise to lead to superior performance and effective value creation in organizations [3, 4]. For this reason, there has been an increased interest in studying in more depth the process of implementing efficient strategic tools for these purposes [5, 6].

Consequently, Ritter and Pedersen [7] state that the needs of organizations to obtain performance measures have led to the investment of scientific human capital, materials

T. Guarda et al. (Eds.): ARTIIS 2022, CCIS 1676, pp. 394–413, 2022.
https://doi.org/10.1007/978-3-031-20316-9_30

and time to obtain useful models to reflect corporate performance; however, their applicability is not very widespread or scarcely studied. In this sense, a change of methodological approach that contrasts the difference would be useful for the organizational dynamics of underdeveloped countries, since it would directly affect the way of managing, creating motivating work environments [8, 9].

Research shows that companies located in developing countries such as Ecuador analyze their performance indicators, individually and independently, rarely converted to useful metrics in the assessment of the results of the strategies implemented, there are very few organizations that perform or implement integrated actions to make decisions, generally foreign [10–13]. Despite this fact, negative at first glance, there is concern and interest on the part of Ecuadorian companies to implement strategies within this area [14]. Hidalgo-Proaño [15]; Boza-Valle and Manjarez-Fuentes [16]; Zamora [17]; Pontarollo and Mendieta [18]; Jiménez et al. [19] externalize that entrepreneurship in Ecuador is growing to a great extent and the training of true entrepreneurs is becoming increasingly important, however, there are scenarios that are out of the hands of entrepreneurs and that often make their best performance impossible, especially for those who wish to start a business.

According to Hedman et al. [20]; Muyulema-Allaica et al. [21] this aspect does not go unnoticed in the Ecuadorian poultry industry, which is made up of a chain of links that begins with the cultivation and marketing of raw materials, followed by the production of balanced feed, poultry breeding, processing, distribution, transportation, marketing, value added, and especially for the poultry business in Chimborazo, as shown in the applicability manual of good poultry practices, a project developed together with technical manuals. However, despite the above, the literature review does not show any research that leads to the design of an instrument that comprehensively and strategically assesses the performance of an organization for evaluation and subsequent control within the Ecuadorian poultry industry.

The above shows the urgent need for scientific resources, which translate into useful models, which in turn, provide a management tool that allows integrating business performance within the mission and vision in order to generate added value to entities through the effective performance of labor and behavioral commitments, in order to go beyond monitoring the performance of financial and non-financial measures which allows determining, effectively, how the indicators are related to each other to improve the overall performance of a company.

Under these circumstances, the present work reports the results of a research focused on developing a model for measuring the global corporate performance through the alignment of strategic objectives (Balanced Scorecard) and productivity improvement tools (Six Sigma) for processes with multiple responses, which is robust enough for its application in the poultry industry, with the purpose of contributing to fill the gap that currently exists within the industry under analysis, taking into account that until now there has not been any type of instrument with these characteristics that comprehensively and strategically assesses the performance of an organization.

The integration of Six Sigma (6σ) with the Balanced Scorecard (BSC) today called Multivariate Performance Measurement System (MPMS), shows how a control panel should be implemented with the purpose of going beyond the DMAIC, or performance monitoring of financial and non-financial measures; with this it can be determined, in an effective way, how the indicators are integrated and related to each other to improve the overall performance of a company. This is where the importance of using multivariate techniques to identify, quantify and model such relationships can be highlighted.

The MPMS is a new model for measuring global corporate performance. Specifically, it is a system that requires the full participation and commitment of the organization at all levels through leaders who inspire, managers who improve, and human capital who create and innovate in joint and integrated efforts, all of which pursue the purpose of achieving the optimum level of profitability and growth. The model is based on scientific principles in five phases, improvement practices proven through numerous research and multivariate statistical techniques, within a framework of principles and values that guide the different trajectories of the organization.

The objective of the MPMS is, on the one hand, to identify and quantify the indicators related to the key processes of the industry in any dimension and integrate them into a model that assesses the overall performance of the corporate process, in order to achieve an adequate level of profitability and, on the other hand, to identify, design and implement the corresponding improvement processes, in order to meet customer needs by breaking their expectations, generating loyalty and positioning in the market.

2   Methodology

This work is framed within the mixed approach, which according to Kowalewski and Bartłomiejski (2020); Yang (2022) is a process that collects, analyzes and links quantitative and qualitative data in a single study or a series of investigations to respond to a problem statement. Subsequently, the determination method was proposed, consisting of two stages: diagnosis and comprehensive impact analysis. This led to the formulation of the proposed model for measuring global corporate performance.

The chosen sector of analysis fell on the province of Chimborazo, one of the 24 provinces that make up the Republic of Ecuador, and is made up of 10 cantons, from which are derived their respective 61 urban and rural parishes, located in the south-central part of the country, in the geographical area known as the inter-Andean region or highlands. Its city is the largest and most populated of the country since it occupies a territory of about 5,287 km^2. Agriculture and livestock are the most important resources and sources of employment in the province. Poultry production and management in the province account for 6% of national production in terms of broiler production [21]. Poultry production in Chimborazo is carried out through an integrated system. This chain is interdependent, generating employment and income for small-scale producers of corn and soybeans, which are the raw materials most used in poultry feed. Therefore, the determination of production costs in a technical way is of great importance for a farm operating under an integrated poultry system, in order to improve its profitability.

The companies were selected on the basis of data from the Community Statistical Program of the Andean Community of Nations (CAN), adopted by Decision 488, which defines the basic precepts for preparing community statistics on SMEs, under four assumptions. The first: 1) Being a small enterprise (considered small if it has between 10 and 49 employees); 2) Having an e-mail address and telephone; 3) That the enterprise needs support in the production area; and 4) Accepting to participate in the project, with accurate and updated information on the situation of the enterprise.

Under the general context previously studied, the target population was composed of 53 poultry industries, located within the 10 cantons of the province of Chimborazo (Table 1).

Table 1. Population

Poultry farms in the province of Chimborazo (Cantons)		Frequency	%
1	Canton Riobamba	4	8%
2	Canton Alausí	2	4%
3	Canton Chambo	2	4%
4	Canton Chunchi	1	2%
5	Canton Colta	2	4%
6	Canton Cumandá	8	15%
7	Canton Guamote	1	2%
8	Canton Guano	2	4%
9	Canton Pallatanga	30	57%
10	Canton Penipe	1	2%
Total		**53**	**100%**

To identify the level of overall corporate performance in the poultry industry in the province of Chimborazo, a compliance checklist was used based on the points of ISO 9001:2015, an international certifiable standard that regulates quality management systems, which combines a process approach with risk-based thinking at all levels of the companies evaluated. The reference level taken to measure the level of global corporate performance by means of a Checklist, three criteria were chosen: Compliance (C); Partial Compliance (PC) and Non-Compliance (NC). By external agents and using a discard method, the Checklist was carried out in 50 poultry companies in the province of Chimborazo, applied during the months of June–August 2019 and replicated for readjustment of the valuation parameter in June–August 2020 to the same managers or administrators of the poultry farms first evaluated, since they are the ones who know the situation of these companies best, they constituted a valid source of information.

3 Results and Discussion

Once the target population had been defined, the data derived from the levels of compliance achieved were processed (Fig. 1). The points of the standard were divided into: mandatory and non-mandatory documents and records, to be subsequently considered as sub-treatments by applying statistical tools based on an ANOVA analysis of variance using a completely randomized block design (CRBD).

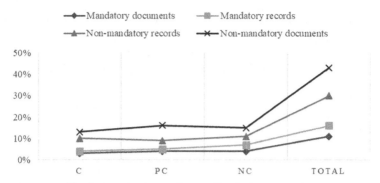

Fig. 1. Levels of compliance of basic documentation

In mandatory documents; there are 30% of these C with adequate documentation in the poultry industry, and 34% PC with the aforementioned documentation, and 36% NC with mandatory documents. This means that most of the entities lack the necessary documentation for an adequate control within their usual production, causing an inefficient management, loss of time and unnecessary expenses that reduce competitiveness.

In the mandatory records; there are 25.3% of these C with adequate records in the poultry industry, and 31.7% PC with the aforementioned records, and 43.0% NC with the records declared mandatory. This means that the entities of the sector evaluated do not have a structured base of minimum records that serve as documented evidence to which the process or processes can be subsequently audited, which would allow adequate and timely control for decision making, in order to set objectives, goals and strategies for continuous improvement.

In the non-mandatory records; there are 32.4% of these C with adequate records in the poultry industry, and 30.9% PC with the mentioned records, and 36.7% NC with records declared as non-mandatory. Data that show that within the entities there is no innovation in the treatment of the information integrated to the technical and managerial procedures, to guide the actions of the organization in a practical and coordinated way and to ensure customer satisfaction and low costs for quality.

In the non-mandatory documents; there are 29.4% of these C with adequate documentation in the poultry industry, and 36.8% PC with the mentioned documentation, and 33.9% NC with documents mentioned as non-mandatory. Data that evidences that within the entities there is a lack of motivation towards increasing the reduction of investment risk, or in turn improve the exchange of documentation, or manage the daily work efficiently, the main problems that the companies had for not making these improvements with the processes were the lack of time and lack of resources.

It should be taken into account that the new ISO 9001:2015 standard has reduced the level of documentary obligations of the system, even so, there are a series of documents and records that are mandatory, as an essential requirement for certification of the system, which requires at least 80% compliance with documents and records.

Based on the above results, two study hypotheses were formulated: alternative (Ha) and Null (Ho). The Ha sought to statistically contrast whether a global corporate performance measurement model, based on the integration of the 6σ and BSC, would have a significant impact on the improvement of key processes in the poultry industry. While Ho seeks the opposite.

For the verification of the hypothesis, an analysis of variance was performed by means of an ANOVA using a CRBD, taking as:

– *Treatment.* - ISO 9001:2015 items, which were: Mandatory documents, Mandatory records, Non-mandatory records and Non-mandatory documents.
– *Block.* - the answer options such as C, PC and NC.

a. Decision rule

- The null hypothesis is accepted if the calculated Fisher value (**Fc**) is equal to or less than the tabulated Fisher (**FT**).
- The **alternative hypothesis** is accepted if the calculated Fisher value (**Fc**) is equal to or greater than the tabulated Fisher (**FT**)

The following statistical model is presented in a completely randomized block design:

$$y_e = \mu + r_i + B_j + E_{ij} \tag{1}$$

where:

μ: Overall average
r_i: Treatment effect
B_j: Block effect
E_{ij}: Effect of the i-th error (ij)
The Hypothesis testing model for a CRBD is summarized in Table 2 below:

Table 2. Modelo de diseño experimental

Source of variation	Sum of squares	Degrees of freedom	Mean square (MS)	F_0	F_0 critical
Treatments	$SS_{Treatment}$	$a - 1$	$\frac{SS_{Treatment}}{a-1}$	$\frac{MS_{Treatment}}{MS_E}$	Tabla F al 5%
Block	SS_{Block}	$b - 1$	$\frac{SS_{Block}}{b-1}$		
Error	SS_E	$(a - 1)(b - 1)$	$\frac{SS_E}{(a-1)(b-1)}$		
Total	SS_T	$N - 1$			

Table 3 contains the general contingency matrix for subsequent application of formulas for the respective calculation.

Table 3. General contingency matrix for the sum of the assessment

Documents and records required by ISO 9001:2015	C	PC	NC	Total (Y_i)
Mandatory documents	60.00	68.00	72.00	200.00
Mandatory records	76.00	95.00	129.00	300.00
Non-mandatory records	178.00	170.00	202.00	550.00
Non-mandatory documents	235.00	294.00	271.00	800.00
Total (Y_j)	549.00	627.00	674.00	1,850.00 (Y)

b. Sum of total squares

$$SS_T = \sum_{i=1}^{a} \sum_{j=1}^{b} Y_{ij}^2 - \frac{y^2}{N} \tag{2}$$

$$SS_T = (60.00^2 + 68.00^2 + 72.00^2 + \ldots 271.00^2) - \frac{(1\,850.00)^2}{(3)(4)}$$

$$SS_T = 361\,340.00 - 285\,208.33$$
$$SS_T = 76\,131.67$$

c. Sum of squares of treatments

$$SS_{Treatments} = \frac{1}{N_t} \sum_{i=1}^{a} Y_i^2 - \frac{y^2}{N} \tag{3}$$

$$SS_{Treatments} = \frac{1}{3}(200.00^2 + 300.00^2 + 550.00^2 + 800.00^2) - \frac{(1850.00)^2}{(3)(4)}$$

$$SS_{Treatments} = 357\,500.00 - 285\,208.33$$
$$SS_{Treatments} = 72\,291.67$$

d. Sum of the squares of the blocks

$$SS_{Block} = \frac{1}{N_t} \sum_{i=1}^{a} Y_i^2 - \frac{y^2}{N} \tag{4}$$

$$SS_{Block} = \frac{1}{4}(549.00^2 + 627.00^2 + 674.00^2) - \frac{(1\,850.00)^2}{(3)(4)}$$

$$SS_{Block} = 287\,201.50 - 285\,208.33$$
$$SS_{Block} = 1\,993.17$$

e. Sum of squares of the error

$$SS_E = SS_T - SS_{Treatment} - SS_{Block} \qquad (5)$$

$$SS_E = 76\,131.67 - 72\,291.67 - 1\,993.17$$
$$SS_E = 1\,846.83$$

The results of the sum of squares and mean squares analysis to determine the F_0, or calculated F, are summarized in Table 4 below.

Table 4. ANOVA of the calculated Fo determination

Source of variation	Sum of squares	Degrees of freedom	Mean square (MS)	F_0	F_0 critical
Treatments	72 291.67	3.00	24 097.22	78.29	19.164
Block	1 993.17	2.00	996.58		
Error	1 846.83	6.00	307.81		
Total	76 131.67	11.00			

By virtue of the results observed in the table above, the value of the calculated F-Fisher Statistic Fc = 78.29 > F from the table Ft = 19.164, we reject H0) and accept H1, which indicates that: "A global corporate performance measurement model, through the integration of 6σ and BSC has a significant impact on the improvement of key processes in the poultry industry".

3.1 Construction of the MPMS Model

The remarkable thing about the above metrics is that they can be quickly associated with sigma quality levels, an expression that is easy to handle and understand in relation to the appreciation of the quality of a product or service. This result is of utmost importance, since it shows that performance evaluation criteria at all levels of the poultry industry can be irreproachably aligned with the corporate strategic process, through quantitative criteria that are objective and consistent.

In this sense, the MPMS model is presented, which plans to define the requirements to be fulfilled and to describe the general dispositions to assure the procedures to be followed, to assure the integration of the Integral Multivariate Six Sigma with the Balanced Scorecard, evidencing the commitment of the company in front of the basic requirements proposed and the processes of the system. MPMS, consists of 6 chapters and 5 faces of Global Corporate Performance Measurement, which explain the different methodologies and tools that can be used in the application of a long, medium and short term integration plan, within a variety of operational and strategic situations with the systematic approach shown in Fig. 2.

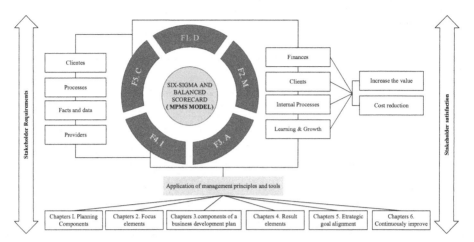

Fig. 2. MPMS model

Starting initially from the application of strategic tools of continuous improvement through the application of the 5 phases of 6σ, in the search to improve the performance of processes and reduce their variation, the Balanced Scorecard methodology is integrated as an additional control system taken from an internal and financial perspective to a balanced perspective in several senses: financial and non-financial information. Internal information and external information. Information on current and future results for the poultry industry in the province of Chimborazo. Figure 3 shows the different applicable tools of the MPMS model.

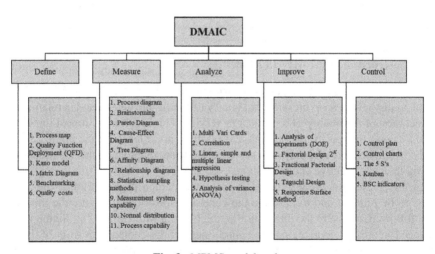

Fig. 3. MPMS model tools

Table 5 shows strategically a description of the tools of the MPMS model, comprised in the 6 chapters and 5 faces of integration of the Integral Multivariate Six Sigma with the Balanced Scorecard.

Table 5. MPMS model tools

6σ/BSC	Chapter	Phase	Feature
1	Chapter 1	Definition phase	This phase identifies the problem to be solved, stratifying as much as possible, for example: customer complaint due to failure, identify the product family by importance using the Pareto diagram, then identify the product, the line where it is made, the specific equipment, among others. At this point you can define the problem and the opportunity for improvement
2	Chapter 2	Measurement phase	It focuses on selecting one or more characteristics to be measured, defining how they will be measured. This phase is important as it ensures that data relating to customer requirements and actual process performance are accurate, clear, and reliable
3	Chapter 3	Analysis phase	In this phase, the analysis of the data derived in the measurement stage is carried out, with the intention of finding out the causal relationships or root causes of the problem. The information from this analysis will provide evidence of the sources of variation and unsatisfactory performance, which is very useful for process improvement
4	Chapter 4	Improvement phase	In the analysis phase, the team selects the product performance characteristics that need to be improved to achieve the improvement goal by identifying the major sources of process variation. In this phase the design of experiments (DOE) will be used to choose the causes that most affect our Critical to Quality (CTQ) and investigate these causes to understand the behavior of the process
5	Chapter 5	Control phase	Once the process improvements have been implemented, it must be ensured that the implementations are maintained, continuously improved and in permanent control, the outputs will be: control plan and control methods implemented, training in the new methods, complete documentation and communication of results, lessons learned and recommendations

(continued)

Table 5. (*continued*)

6σ/BSC	Chapter	Phase	Feature
	Chapter 6		Establishment of indicators based on BSC: Considering that the objectives and goals must be subject to management controls to determine an evolution in the implementation of the corporate global performance measurement model, through the integration of the 6σ with BSC. Feedback is mandatory in order to take the respective corrective measures to align the objectives and comply with the plan

3.2 Strategic Indicators by Objectives of the MPMS Model

Taking into account that the indicators are tools that allow in the measurement in the fulfillment of objectives which implants long term goals, these are useful to be able to measure with clarity the results obtained with the application of programs, processes or specific actions, in order to obtain the diagnosis of a situation or to evaluate the variations of an event. Therefore, based on the above, we propose indicators that show the way to reach the fulfillment of the corporate global strategic objectives; by means of these indicators we can conclude if the company is going in the right direction or what changes should be made.

Figure 4 illustrates the strategy map for each Balanced Scorecard phase based on the data collection of the 4 BSC phases.

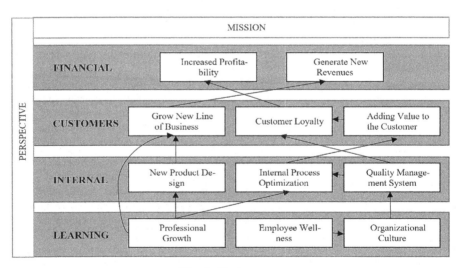

Fig. 4. Strategy map

Table 6 contains the selected indicators for each strategic objective, designed to improve the performance of the processes and reduce their variation, extracted from the analysis of data, tables and graphs generated with the application of the 5 phases of DMAIC.

Table 6. Strategic indicators by objectives of the MPMS model

Bsc	Strategic objectives	Indicators
Financial perspective	1. To generate new income in the poultry company	1. Rate of return on invested capital
	2. Minimize the use of third-party capital in the operation of the company	2. Financial autonomy index
	3. Improve the profitability of funds invested in the poultry industry	3. Return on equity ratio
Customer Perspective	1. Entering a new line of business Index Customer on-boarding	4. Index Customer onboarding
	2. To expand the company in the search for new customers and to build customer loyalty among those customers who have little involvement in the company	5. Market share index
	3. Increasing customer value and satisfying customer needs	6. User satisfaction level 7. Sales efficiency
Internal process perspective	1. Improve the efficiency and effectiveness of the company's logistic and operational processes	8. Compliance in total production deliveries (TP) 9. Quality of the logistics process 10. Purchasing volume vs. sales volume 11. Operator efficiency 12. Machinery Utilization 13. TP failure rate 14. Documentation without problem
	2. Propose a cleaning policy to avoid disorder in the different areas of the company in order to avoid accidents (Quality Management System).)	15. Level of compliance with O.S. activities 16. Percentage of waste
	3. New product design	17. Level of compliance with programmed activities

(*continued*)

Table 6. (*continued*)

Bsc	Strategic objectives	Indicators
Learning and growth perspective	1. Generate an organizational culture that manages to provide added value to our products (Employee Well-being)	18. Recognized employees
	2. Adapt a human capital recognition policy to develop the skills of our personnel (Organizational Culture)	19. Employee satisfaction
	3. Empower our salespeople to create a culture focused on customer satisfaction. (Professional Growth.)	20. Customer loyalty 21. Training hours

The MPMS model employs global corporate performance measurement indicators over a variety of operational and strategic situations which makes it applicable to a variety of organizations.

Table 7, 8, 9 and 10 below shows a breakdown of the indicators designed for each of the phases of BSC integration.

With the exposed results it can be identified that 6σ is a quality management methodology that focuses on reducing the existing variation in the production processes of goods or services, the drastic reduction of defects and the improvement of the quality of products, processes and services. On the other hand, the BSC is a strategic management tool and performance measurement system designed to translate the organization's strategies into focused action plans. The MPMS model proposes that if strategy, performance and customer satisfaction are aligned, the organization will benefit from the strong relationship between process performance and strategic initiatives. These changes can be measured by productivity and process metrics, such as cycle time, production rates, production efficiency, and rework rate, among others. The present work reported the results of a research integrated by the analysis, development of a Corporate Global Measurement Model through the integration of 6σ with the BSC today called Multivariate Performance Measurement System (MPMS), which integrates multiple evaluation and control proposals. Systematically structured model based on DMAIC methodologies, BSC and advanced statistical techniques, with the purpose of contributing to fill the gap that currently exists due to the lack of an instrument with these characteristics that comprehensively and strategically assesses the performance of an organization.

Table 7. Strategic integration indicators of the MPMS - Financial Model

BSC	Indicators	Threshold	Formula
Financial perspective	1. Return on Invested Capital Ratio	In this indicator the qualification will be given by the company so that the level of capital invested in the development of the new product does not exceed the value of amortizations, and the value of the capital is higher	$R.C.I = \frac{T.A}{B.N+A} * 100$ **where:** R.C.I = Recovery of invested capital T.A = Total Assets B.N = Net Profits A = Amortizations
	2. Index Level of financial autonomy	0%–50% Deficient 51%–70% Insufficient 71%–85% Acceptable 86%–100% Ideal	$N.A.F = \frac{F.P}{T.A} * 100$ **where:** N.A.F = Financial autonomy level F.P = Proprietary Fund T.A = Total Assets
	3. Return on equity index	0%–50% Deficient 51%–70% Insufficient 71%–85% Acceptable 86%–100% Ideal	$R.F.P = \frac{B.N}{F.P} * 100$ **where:** R.F.P = Return on Equity B.N = Net Profits F.P = Proprietary Funds

Table 8. Strategic indicators of integration of the MPMS - Customer model

BSC	Indicators	Threshold	Formula
Customer perspective	4. Index Customer onboarding	0%–50% Deficient 51%–70% Insufficient 71%–85% Acceptable 86%–100% Ideal	$C.I = \frac{F.C-I.C}{I.C} * 100$ **where:** C.I = Customer Incorporation F.C = Final Customers I.C = Initial Customers
	5. Market Share Index	It is determined with the demand that the company has determined, ideally it should be a higher number than the current demand	$M.S = \frac{N.C.C}{S.P}$ **where:** M.S = Market Share N.C.C = Number of Current Customers S.P = Segment Population

(*continued*)

Table 8. (*continued*)

BSC	Indicators	Threshold	Formula
	6. User satisfaction level	0%–54% Very Bad 55%–64% Bad 65%–74% Regular 75%–84% Good 85%–100% Excellent	$N.C.S = \frac{(A*0)+(B*25)*(C*50)+(D*75)*(E*100)}{N}$ **where:** N.C.S = Net customer satisfaction indicator A = Number of responses for very dissatisfied B = Number of unsatisfied responses C = Number of responses for neutral D = Number of responses for satisfied E = Number of responses for very satisfied N = Sum of all the above (A + B + C + D + E)
	7. Sales efficiency	0%–50% Deficient 51%–70% Insufficient 71%–85% Acceptable 86%–100% Ideal	$E = \frac{C.P}{T.C.T} * 100$ **where:** E = Efficiency C.P = Customers Portfolio T.C.T = Total Clients Target Market

Table 9. Strategic indicators of integration of the MPMS model - Internal

BSC	Indicators	Threshold	Formula
Internal process perspective	8. Compliance in TP deliveries	0%–50% Deficient 51%–70% Insufficient 71%–85% Acceptable 86%–100% Ideal	$C.TP.D = \frac{N.OT.D}{T.D} * 100$ **where:** C.TP. D = Compliance in TP deliveries N.OT.D = Number of on-time deliveries T.D = Total dispatches
	9. Quality of the logistic process	0%–50% Deficient 51%–70% Insufficient 71%–85% Acceptable 86%–100% Ideal	$\%L.P.Q = \frac{N.I}{T.O} * 100$ **where:** L.P.Q = Logistics process quality N.I = Number of incidents in TP deliveries T.O = Total orders

(*continued*)

Table 9. (*continued*)

BSC	Indicators	Threshold	Formula
	10. Volume purchases vs. sales	In this indicator the qualification will be given by the company so that the level of purchases does not exceed the value of sales depending on the objectives it wants to achieve	$V = 1 - \frac{V.p}{T.S} * 100$ **where:** V = Purchasing volume V.p = Value of purchases T.S = Total sales
	11. Operator efficiency	0%–50% Deficient 51%–70% Insufficient 71%–85% Acceptable 86%–100% Ideal	$O.P = \frac{N.U.P}{M.N.P} * 100$ **where:** O.P = Operator performance N.U.P = Number of units produced M.N.P = Maximum number of units produced
	12. Use of machinery	0%–50% Deficient 51%–70% Insufficient 71%–85% Acceptable 86%–100% Ideal	$M.P = \frac{N.U.P}{P.C} * 100$ **where:** M.P = Machine performance N.U.P = Number of units produced P.C = Machinery production capacity
	13. Failure rate of TPs	0%–50% Deficient 51%–90% Insufficient 91%–94% Acceptable 95%–100% Ideal	$F.TP.I = \frac{T.U.R}{T.UP} * 100$ **where:** F.TP.I = Faulty TP Index T.U.R = Total units returned T.U.P = Total units produced
	14. Documentation without problem	0%–50% Deficient 51%–90% Insufficient 91%–94% Acceptable 95%–100% Ideal	$V = \frac{DWP}{T.D} * 100$ **where:** V = Value D.W.P = Documentation without problems T.D = Total documents

(*continued*)

Table 9. (*continued*)

BSC	Indicators	Threshold	Formula
	15. Level of compliance with O.S. activities	0%–50% Deficient 51%–90% Insufficient 91%–94% Acceptable 95%–100% Ideal	$L.C = \frac{N.A.C}{T.N.P.A} * 100$ **where:** L.C = Level of compliance N.A.C = Number of activities carried out T.N.P.A = Total number of programmed activities
	16. Percentage of waste	0%–50% Deficient 51%–90% Insufficient 91%–94% Acceptable 95%–100% Ideal	$\%W = \frac{T.W}{T.RM} * 100$ **where:** %W = Percentage of waste T.W = Total waste T.RM = Total raw material used
	17. Level of compliance with programmed activities	0%–50% Deficient 51%–90% Insufficient 91%–94% Acceptable 95%–100% Ideal	$L.C = \frac{C.T}{E.C.T} * 100$ **where:** L.C = Level of compliance C.T = Changeover time E.C.T = Estimated changeover time

Table 10. Strategic indicators of integration of the MPMS model - Learning

BSC	Indicators	Threshold	Formula
Learning and growth perspective	18. Recognized employees	0%–50% Deficient 51%–70% Insufficient 71%–85% Acceptable 86%–100% Ideal	$L.R = \frac{N.E.R}{T.E} * 100$ **where:** L.R = Level of recognition N.E.R = Number of employees recognized month T.E = Total number of employees

(*continued*)

Table 10. (*continued*)

BSC	Indicators	Threshold	Formula
	19. Employee satisfaction	0%–50% Deficient 51%–70% Insufficient 71%–85% Acceptable 86%–100% Ideal	$L.S = \frac{N.c}{T.E} * 100$ **where:** L.S = Level of satisfaction N.c = Number of monthly complaints T.E = Total number of employees
	20. Customer loyalty 21. Training hours	0%–50% Deficient 51%–70% Insufficient 71%–85% Acceptable 86%–100% Ideal	$L.L = (N.C.C - N.C)$ **where:** L.L = Loyalty level N.C.C = Number of current customers N.C = Number of customers previous year

4 Conclusions

A performance measurement model is a structural and systematic procedure to measure, evaluate and influence work-related attributes, behaviors and results, as well as the degree of absenteeism, in order to declare the extent to which the process is productive within the company, in order to make decisions related to improving its future performance.

A Global Corporate Measurement Model was proposed through the integration of Six Sigma (6σ) with the Balanced Scorecard (BSC) today called Multivariate Performance Measurement System (MPMS), which integrates multiple evaluation and control proposals. Systematically structured model based on the DMAIC and BSC methodologies, thus forming common scenarios in which the poultry industry of the province of Chimborazo is exposed, designed to take corrective and preventive actions towards translating the organization's strategies into action plans oriented to a continuous improvement.

The MPMS was able to identify the aspects with the greatest impact within the evolutionary process of the poultry industry and thus control and make the right decisions considering the goals proposed for the current year, developed with the objective of maximizing the effectiveness of equipment, processes and facilities, through organized work, trained personnel and methodologies that focus on continuous improvement, ensuring the quality characteristics established for the product.

References

1. Costa, L.B.M., Godinho Filho, M., Fredendall, L.D., Ganga, G.M.D.: The effect of Lean Six Sigma practices on food industry performance: implications of the Sector's experience and typical characteristics. Food Control **112**, 107110 (2020). https://doi.org/10.1016/j.foodcont.2020.107110

2. Ma, L., Dong, J., Hu, C., Peng, K.: A novel decentralized detection framework for quality-related faults in manufacturing industrial processes. Neurocomputing **428**, 30–41 (2021). https://doi.org/10.1016/j.neucom.2020.11.045

3. Chen, K.S., Wang, C.H., Tan, K.H., Chiu, S.F.: Developing one-sided specification six-sigma fuzzy quality index and testing model to measure the process performance of fuzzy information. Int. J. Prod. Econ. **208**(57), 560–565 (2019). https://doi.org/10.1016/j.ijpe.2018.12.025

4. Muyulema-Allaica, J.C., Ruiz-Puente, C.: Framework proposal for the design of lean circular production systems based on case studies. DYNA **Dyna Acele**, 1–10 (2022). https://doi.org/10.6036/10540

5. Vincent, A., Pocius, D., Huang, Y.: Six Sigma performance of quality indicators in total testing process of point-of-care glucose measurement: a two-year review. Pract. Lab. Med. **25**, e00215 (2021). https://doi.org/10.1016/j.plabm.2021.e00215

6. Guleria, P., Pathania, A., Sharma, S., Sá, J.C.: Lean six-sigma implementation in an automobile axle manufacturing industry: a case study. Mater. Today Proc. **50**, 1739–1746 (2022). https://doi.org/10.1016/j.matpr.2021.09.177

7. Ritter, T., Pedersen, C.L.: Digitization capability and the digitalization of business models in business-to-business firms: past, present, and future. Ind. Mark. Manag. **86**, 180–190 (2020). https://doi.org/10.1016/j.indmarman.2019.11.019

8. Tallon, P.P., Queiroz, M., Coltman, T., Sharma, R.: Information technology and the search for organizational agility: a systematic review with future research possibilities. J. Strateg. Inf. Syst. **28**(2), 218–237 (2019). https://doi.org/10.1016/j.jsis.2018.12.002

9. Sharman, N., Wallace, C.A., Jespersen, L.: Terminology and the understanding of culture, climate, and behavioural change – impact of organisational and human factors on food safety management. Trends Food Sci. Technol. **96**, 13–20 (2020). https://doi.org/10.1016/j.tifs.2019.12.005

10. Lee, M.Y., Edmondson, A.C.: Self-managing organizations: exploring the limits of less-hierarchical organizing. Res. Organ. Behav. **37**, 35–58 (2017). https://doi.org/10.1016/j.riob.2017.10.002

11. Viteri, M., Tapia, M.: Economía ecuatoriana: de la producción agrícola al servicio. Rev. Espac. **39**(32), 1–5 (2018)

12. Manzano, G.M.A., Mancheno, S.M.J., Gamboa, S.J.M.: Logística comercial: un enfoque para la toma de decisiones en las MIPYMES de la Zona 3 del Ecuador. Espirales Rev. Multidiscip. Investig. **3**(24) (2019). https://doi.org/10.31876/re.v3i24.423

13. Sánchez-Macías, R.A., Pucha-Medina, P.M., Usca-Veloz, R.B., Espinosa-Ruiz, C.G., Velasteguí-Bósquez, G.A., Muyulema-Allaica, J.C.: Las finanzas sostenibles. Retos actuales hacia el desarrollo del sector cooperativo popular y solidario ecuatoriano. RIIIT. Rev. Int. Investig. e Innovación Tecnológica **7**(2), 1–21 (2020)

14. Giunta, I., Dávalos, J.: Crecimiento económico inclusivo y sostenible en la Agenda 2030: Un análisis crítico desde la perspectiva. Iberoam. J. Dev. Stud. **9**(1), 146–176 (2020). https://doi.org/10.26754/ojs

15. Hidalgo-Proaño, L.F.: La Cultura del Emprendimiento y su Formación. Rev. Altern. UCSG **15**(1), 46–50 (2014). https://dialnet.unirioja.es/descarga/articulo/5599803.pdf

16. Boza-Valle, A., Manjarez-Fuentes, N.: Strategic diagnosis of entrepreneurship of popular and solidarity economy in Ecuador. Ing. Ind. **XXXVII**(2), 208–217 (2016). http://scielo.sld.cu/pdf/rii/v37n2/rii10216.pdf

17. Zamora, C.: La importancia del emprendimiento en la economía: El caso de Ecuador. Espacios **39**(07), 1–12 (2018)

18. Pontarollo, N., Mendieta, M.R.: Land consumption and income in Ecuador: a case of an inverted environmental Kuznets curve. Ecol. Indic. **108**, 105699 (2020). https://doi.org/10.1016/j.ecolind.2019.105699

19. Jiménez, L., et al.: Rediscovering the edaphic knowledge of smallholder farmers in southern Ecuador. Geoderma **406** (2022). https://doi.org/10.1016/j.geoderma.2021.115468

20. Hedman, H.D., et al.: Impacts of small-scale chicken farming activity on antimicrobial-resistant Escherichia coli carriage in backyard chickens and children in rural Ecuador. One Heal. **8**, 100112 (2019). https://doi.org/10.1016/j.onehlt.2019.100112

21. Muyulema-Allaica, C.A., Muyulema-Allaica, J.C., Pucha-Medina, P.M., Ocaña-Parra, S.V.: Los costos de producción y su incidencia en la rentabilidad de una empresa avícola integrada del Ecuador: caso de studio. Visionario Digit. **4**(1) (2020). https://doi.org/10.33262/visionari odigital.v4i1.1089

22. Kowalewski, M., Bartłomiejski, R.: Is it research or just walking? Framing walking research methods as 'non-scientific.' Geoforum **114**, 59–65 (2020). https://doi.org/10.1016/j.geo forum.2020.06.002

23. Yang, J.: An empirical survey of statistical research methods in applied science. J. King Saud Univ. Sci. **34**(4), 102008 (2022). https://doi.org/10.1016/j.jksus.2022.102008

Author Index

Printed in the United States
by Baker & Taylor Publisher Services